NINTH EDITION

PUBLIC SPEAKING

AN AUDIENCE-CENTERED APPROACH

Steven A. Beebe
Texas State University

Susan J. Beebe
Texas State University

PEARSON

Boston   Columbus   Indianapolis   New York   San Francisco   Upper Saddle River
Amsterdam   Cape Town   Dubai   London   Madrid   Milan   Munich   Paris   Montreal   Toronto
Delhi   Mexico City   São Paulo   Sydney   Hong Kong   Seoul   Singapore   Taipei   Tokyo

Publisher, Communication: Karon Bowers
Editorial Assistant: Jennifer Nolan
Senior Marketing Manager: Blair Zoe Tuckman
Marketing Assistant: Karen Tanico
Marketing Coordinator: Theresa Rotondo
Director of Development: Sharon Geary
Senior Managing Editor: Linda Behrens
Procurement Manager: Mary Fischer
Senior Procurement Specialist: Mary Ann Gloriande
Program Manager: Anne Ricigliano
Creative Director: Blair Brown
Interior Designer: Cenveo® Publisher Services
Director of Digital Media: Brian Hyland
Digital Media Specialist: Sean Silver
Full-Service Project Management and Composition: Cenveo® Publisher Services
Printer/Binder: R.R. Donnelley/Harrisonburg
Cover Printer: R.R. Donnelley/Harrisonburg
Text Font: Minion Pro

Credits and acknowledgments for materials borrowed from other sources and reproduced, with permission, in this textbook appear on appropriate page within text or on pages 388–392.

Many of the designations by manufacturers and seller to distinguish their products are claimed as trademarks. Where those designations appear in this book, and the publisher was aware of a trademark claim, the designations have been printed in initial caps or all caps.

Library of Congress Cataloging-in-Publication Data
Beebe, Steven A., Date-
 Public speaking: an audience-centered approach / Steven A. Beebe, Texas State University, Susan J. Beebe, Texas State University. — Ninth Edition.
  pages cm
 ISBN-13: 978-0-205-91463-0
 ISBN-10: 0-205-91463-2
 1. Public speaking. 2. Oral communication. I. Beebe, Susan J. II. Title.
 PN4129.15.B43 2014
 808.5'1—dc23
                           2013042939

10 9 8 7 6 5 4 3

Student Edition:
ISBN 10: 0-205-91463-2
ISBN 13: 978-0-205-91463-0
A La Carte Edition:
ISBN 10: 0-205-89728-2
ISBN 13: 978-0-205-89728-5

PEARSON

www.pearsonhighered.com

Dedicated to our parents,
Russell and Muriel Beebe
and Herb and Jane Dye

And to our children,
Mark, Matthew, and Brittany Beebe

BRIEF CONTENTS

CONTENTS

3 SPEAKING FREELY AND ETHICALLY 40

4 LISTENING TO SPEECHES 53

5 ANALYZING YOUR AUDIENCE   77

6 DEVELOPING YOUR SPEECH   110

8 ORGANIZING AND OUTLINING YOUR SPEECH 153

9 INTRODUCING AND CONCLUDING YOUR SPEECH 178

10 USING WORDS WELL: SPEAKER LANGUAGE AND STYLE   194

11 DELIVERING YOUR SPEECH   210

12 USING PRESENTATION AIDS 239

13 SPEAKING TO INFORM 261

14 UNDERSTANDING PRINCIPLES OF PERSUASIVE SPEAKING   283

PREFACE

The ninth edition of *Public Speaking: An Audience-Centered Approach* is written to be the primary text in a course intended to help students become better public speakers. We are delighted that since the first edition of the book was published over two decades ago, educators and students of public speaking have found our book a distinctively useful resource to enhance public-speaking skills. We've worked to make our latest edition a preeminent resource for helping students enhance their speaking skills by adding new features and retaining the most successful elements of previous editions.

New to the Ninth Edition

We've refined and updated the book you are holding in your hands to create a powerful and contemporary resource for helping speakers connect to their audience. We've added several new features and revised features that both instructors and students have praised.

Support for First Speeches

In response to suggestions from instructors who use the book, we've created a new Chapter 2, Presenting Your First Speech. The chapter gives students a concise overview of the audience-centered speaking model as it offers them suggestions for effectively and confidently making an initial speech early in the term of their public-speaking class.

Integration with Online Material

Video of select speeches in the printed textbook is available at MyCommunicationLab, allowing students to observe and analyze the speakers' delivery, as well as their organization and word choices. We've also moved the Speech Workshop feature that appeared at the end of every chapter in the previous edition to the MyCommunicationLab, where students can interact with these helpful guides to applying chapter material. In addition, we've added margin icons to cue students to speeches or study materials from MyCommunicationLab that will enhance their understanding of the concepts presented in the printed textbook.

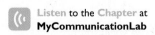 Listen to the Chapter at MyCommunicationLab

 Watch the Video at MyCommunicationLab

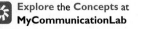 Explore the Concepts at MyCommunicationLab

Study and Review at MyCommunicationLab

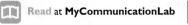 Read at MyCommunicationLab

 Study and Review the Flashcards at MyCommunicationLab

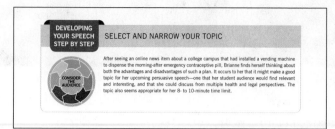

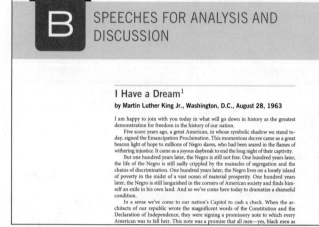

New and Updated Features

In the ninth edition, new *Learning Objectives* appear at the start of each chapter to provide students with strategies and key points for approaching the chapter. Objectives reappear at key points in the chapter to help students gauge their progress and monitor their learning. An updated and expanded *Study Guide* at the end of each chapter reviews the learning objectives and key terms, and guides students to think critically about chapter concepts and related ethical issues. We have also added more margin *Recap* boxes and tables to help students check their understanding, review for exams, and to reference key advice as they prepare their speeches. Finally, we have updated the extended example that appears in *Developing Your Speech Step by Step* boxes throughout the book.

New Speeches

We've added new annotated student speeches and speech examples throughout the book. In addition, nearly every speech in our revised Appendix B is new, selected to provide readers with a variety of positive models of effective speeches.

New Examples and Illustrations

New examples and illustrations integrated in every chapter provide both classic and contemporary models to help students master the art of public speaking. As in previous editions, we draw on both student speeches and speeches delivered by well-known people.

New Material in Every Chapter

In addition to these new and expanded features, each chapter has been revised with new examples, illustrations, and references to the latest research conclusions. Here's a summary of the changes and revisions we've made:

Chapter 1: Speaking with Confidence

- New comparison of public speaking with conversation helps build confidence by showing students that speechmaking builds on skills they have already mastered.
- The benefits of public speaking for improving employment opportunities and developing empowering critical thinking skills are reinforced.
- Expanded summary of the history of public speaking adds discussion of Roman orators and of today's communication technologies.
- Updated research reinforces advice for overcoming speaking anxiety and building confidence.

Chapter 2: Presenting Your First Speech

- This new chapter provides an overview of the audience-centered speaking process, jump-starting the speechmaking process for students who are assigned to present speeches early in the term.
- Advice is provided for effectively delivering speeches via videoconferencing and similar communication technology.
- New sample first speech helps students see how another student speaker successfully applied the concepts discussed in the chapter.

Chapter 3: Speaking Freely and Ethically

- A revised and updated discussion of free speech helps students understand the evolution of interpretation of the First Amendment.
- New discussion and figure emphasize the global nature of free speech in the era of social media.
- New examples throughout the chapter keep material current and relevant to readers.

Chapter 4: Listening to Speeches

- The chapter is streamlined by removing the discussion of receiver anxiety as a barrier to listening.
- Updated discussion of listening styles helps students use the strengths and overcome the challenges of their particular listening style.
- A new figure can be used by students as a guide or checklist when evaluating other speakers.
- Updated research throughout the chapter keeps material current and relevant to readers.

Chapter 5: Analyzing Your Audience

- An updated discussion of sex, gender, and sexual orientation emphasizes the importance of considering variations in listeners' gender and sexual identities.
- This chapter introduces the first of the updated *Developing Your Speech Step by Step* boxes, which provide students with an extended example of how to implement audience-centered speechmaking concepts.

Chapter 6: Developing Your Speech

- Updated lists of potential speech topics can spark students' own topic brainstorming.
- New examples throughout the chapter keep the material in this popular chapter current and relevant to readers.

Chapter 7: Gathering and Using Supporting Material

- An updated section on evaluating Internet resources adds new discussions of *Wikipedia* and page domains as it guides students to think critically about information they find on the Internet.
- New examples throughout the chapter model effective incorporation of the different types of supporting material discussed in the chapter.

Chapter 8: Organizing and Outlining Your Speech

- This chapter combines two previously separate but closely related chapters on organizing and outlining speeches.
- The combined chapter has been streamlined by removing the discussion of delivery outlines, as they are synonymous with speaking notes for many speakers.
- A revised discussion of signposting helps students understand how these organizational clues help communicate their message to listeners.
- The chapter offers information to help students evaluate technological options, such as using a tablet computer to hold speaking notes.
- A new *Sample Preparation Outline* gives students a complete model of the best practices in organization and outlining.

Chapter 9: Introducing and Concluding Your Speech

- New examples of effective introductions and conclusions from both student and seasoned speakers show students how to implement the techniques described in the chapter.

Chapter 10: Using Words Well: Speaker Language and Style

- New table reinforces students' understanding by providing a visual analysis of memorable word structures John F. Kennedy used in his inaugural address.
- New examples clarify discussions of metaphors, inversion, suspension, parallelism, antithesis, and alliteration.

Chapter 11: Delivering Your Speech

- This chapter provides additional guidance in effective use of eye contact, gestures, and facial expressions when delivering speeches using videoconferencing or similar technology.
- Discussions of using microphones and proper attire have been updated with advice on current trends.

Chapter 12: Using Presentation Aids

- Updated information on two-dimensional presentation aids discusses using photographs, drawings, maps, graphs, and charts the "old-fashioned way," as well as in computer-generated presentation aids.
- The discussion of computer-generated presentation aids has been extended beyond PowerPoint™ to include other popular presentation software.
- An updated discussion of using video aids and audio aids includes references to current technology, such as smartphones, that makes it easy for speakers to create their own video or audio aids, as well as an evaluation of cloud storage of presentation aids.

Chapter 13: Speaking to Inform

- New information on storytelling helps students understand the universal appeal of stories and their use in gaining and maintaining listeners' attention.
- New examples and updated research throughout the chapter keep material current and relevant to readers.

Chapter 14: Understanding Principles of Persuasive Speaking

- Expanded discussion and examples clarify and enhance students' understanding of cognitive dissonance theory.
- Clarifications and examples help students understand theories related to persuasion and how those theories are applied at every step of the audience-centered speaking model to their persuasive speeches.

Chapter 15: Using Persuasive Strategies

- New section on reasoning by sign expands the repertoire of reasoning techniques students can use in their persuasive speeches.
- Advice for adapting persuasive techniques to culturally diverse audiences has been enhanced by introducing each technique with a reminder of the central role of the audience in public speaking.
- A new *Sample Persuasive Speech* gives students a complete model of how to use the motivated sequence and other principles of persuasion.

Chapter 16: Speaking for Special Occasions and Purposes

- New chapter-opening examples reinforce the value of public speaking with dollars-and-cents evidence.
- New examples throughout the chapter demonstrate models of speeches for ceremonial occasions including commencement addresses, keynote addresses, and eulogies, as well as humorous speeches.

Successful Features Retained in This Edition

The goal of the ninth edition of *Public Speaking: An Audience-Centered Approach* remains the same as that of the previous eight editions: to be a practical and user-friendly guide to help speakers connect their hearts and minds with those of their listeners. While adding powerful new features and content to help students become skilled public speakers, we have also endeavored to keep what students and instructors liked best. Specifically, we retained five areas of focus that have proven successful in previous editions: our audience-centered approach; our focus on overcoming communication apprehension; our focus on ethics; our focus on diversity; and our focus on skill development. We also continue our partnership with instructors and students by offering a wide array of print and electronic supplements to support teaching and learning.

Our Audience-Centered Approach

The distinguishing focus of the book is our audience-centered approach. More than 2,300 years ago, Aristotle said, "For of the three elements in speechmaking—speaker, subject, and person addressed—it is the last one, the hearer, that determines the speaker's end and object." We think Aristotle was right. A good speech centers on the needs, values, and hopes of the audience, who should be foremost in the speaker's mind during every step of the speech development and delivery process. Thus, in a very real sense, the audience writes the speech. Effective and ethical public speaking does not simply tell listeners only what they want to hear—that would be a manipulative, speaker-centered approach. Rather, the audience-centered speaker is ethically responsive to audience interests without abandoning the speaker's end and object.

It is not unusual or distinctive for a public-speaking book to discuss audience analysis. What is unique about our audience-centered approach is that our discussion of audience analysis and adaptation is not confined to a single chapter; rather, we emphasize the importance of considering the audience throughout our entire discussion of the speech preparation and delivery process. From the overview early in the text of the public-speaking process until the final chapter, we illuminate the positive power of helping students relate to their audience by keeping their listeners foremost in mind.

Preparing and delivering a speech also involves a sequence of steps. Our audience-centered model integrates the step-by-step process of speech preparation and delivery with the ongoing process of considering the audience. Our audience-centered model of public speaking, shown here and introduced in Chapter 2, reappears throughout the text to remind students of the steps involved in speech preparation and delivery, while simultaneously emphasizing the importance of considering the audience. Viewing the model as a clock, the speaker begins the process at the 12 o'clock position with "Select and Narrow Topic" and moves around the model clockwise to "Deliver Speech." Each step of the speech preparation and delivery process touches the center portion of the model, labeled "Consider the Audience." Arrows connecting the center with each step of the process illustrate how the audience influences each of the steps involved in designing and presenting a speech. Arrows pointing in both directions around the central process of "Consider the Audience" represent how a speaker may sometimes revise a previous step because of further information or thought about the audience. A speaker may, for example, decide after having gathered supporting material for a speech that he or she needs to go back and revise the speech purpose. Visual learners will especially appreciate the illustration of the entire public-speaking process provided by the model. The colorful, easy-to-understand synopsis will also be appreciated by people who learn best by having an overview of the entire process before beginning the first step of speech preparation.

After introducing the model early in the book, we continue to emphasize the centrality of considering the audience by revisiting it at appropriate points throughout the book. A highlighted version of the model appears in several chapters, as a visual reminder of the place the chapter's topic occupies in the audience-centered speechmaking process. Similarly, highlighted versions appear in *Developing Your Speech Step by Step* boxes. Another visual reminder comes in the form of a miniature version of the model, the icon shown here in the margin. *When you see this icon, it will remind you that the material presented has special significance for considering your audience.*

Our Focus on Communication Apprehension

> **CONFIDENTLY CONNECTING WITH YOUR AUDIENCE**
>
> **Re-create the Speech Environment When You Rehearse**
>
> As you rehearse your speech, don't just sit at your desk and mentally review your message. Instead, stand up and imagine that you are in the very room in which you will deliver your speech while you rehearse your speech out loud. Or, if it is possible, rehearse your speech in the room in which you will present your speech. Just by imagining the exact room and audience you will have when presenting your speech, you are helping to manage your anxiety. When you do give your speech, you will have less anxiety because you've had experience imagining or presenting your speech in the environment in which you will speak.

One of the biggest barriers that keeps a speaker, especially a novice public speaker, from connecting to his or her audience is apprehension. Fear of failure, forgetting, or fumbling words is a major distraction. In this edition, we help students to overcome their apprehension of speaking to others by focusing on their listeners rather than on their fear. We've updated and expanded our discussion of communication apprehension in Chapter 1, adding the most contemporary research conclusions we can find to help students overcome the anxiety that many people experience when speaking publicly. To help students integrate confidence-boosting strategies through their study of public speaking, we offer students powerful pointers for managing anxiety in the *Confidently Connecting with Your Audience* features found in each chapter.

Our Focus on Ethics

Being audience-centered does not mean that a speaker tells an audience only what they want to hear; if you are not true to your own values, you will have become a manipulative, unethical communicator rather than an audience-centered one. Audience-centered speakers articulate truthful messages that give audience members free choice in responding to a message, while they also use effective means of ensuring message clarity and credibility.

From the first chapter onward, we link being an audience-centered speaker with being an ethical speaker. Our principles and strategies for being rhetorically skilled are anchored in ethical principles that assist speakers in articulating a message that connects with their audience. We not only devote an entire chapter (Chapter 3) to being an ethical speaker, but we also offer reminders, tips, and strategies for making ethical speaking and listening an integral part of human communication. As part of the *Study Guide* at the end of each chapter, students and instructors will find questions to spark discussion about and raise awareness of ethical issues in effective speechmaking.

Our Focus on Diversity

Just as the topic of audience analysis is covered in most public-speaking textbooks, so is diversity. Sometimes diversity is discussed in a separate chapter; sometimes it is presented in "diversity boxes" sprinkled throughout a book. We choose to address diversity not as an add-on to the main discussion but rather as an integral part of being an audience-centered speaker. To be audience-centered is to acknowledge the various ethnic and cultural backgrounds, attitudes, beliefs, values, and other differences present when people assemble to hear a speech. We suggest that inherent in the process of being audience-centered is a focus on the diverse nature of listeners in contemporary audiences. The topic of adapting to diverse audiences is therefore not a boxed afterthought but is integrated into every step of our audience-centered approach.

Our Focus on Skill Development

We are grateful for our ongoing collaboration with public-speaking teachers, many of whom have used our audience-centered approach for more than two decades. We have retained those skill development features of previous editions that both teachers and students have applauded. What instructors tell us most often is "You write like I teach" or "Your book echoes the same kind of advice and skill development suggestions that I give my students." We are gratified by the continued popularity of *Public Speaking: An Audience-Centered Approach*.

Clear and Interesting Writing Style   Readers have especially valued our polished prose, concise style, and engaging, lively voice. Students tell us that reading our book is like having a conversation with their instructor.

Outstanding Examples   Students need to be not only *told* how to speak effectively, but also *shown* how to speak well. Our powerful and interesting examples, both classic and contemporary and drawn from both student speakers and famous orators, continue to resonate with student speakers.

Built-in Learning Resources   We've retained the following built-in pedagogical features of previous editions:

- Chapter outlines
- Learning objectives
- Crisply written narrative summaries

In the ninth edition, we have expanded many of our popular *Recap* boxes and tables to summarize the content of nearly every major section in each chapter. We've also provided a revised, expanded *Study Guide* at the end of each chapter.

Instructor and Student Resources

Public-speaking students rarely learn how to be articulate speakers only from reading a book. Students learn best in partnership with an experienced instructor who can guide them through the process of being an audience-centered speaker. And experienced instructors rely on support from textbook publishers. To support instructors and students who use *Public Speaking: An Audience-Centered Approach*, Pearson provides an array of supplementary materials for students and instructors. Key instructor resources include an Instructor's Manual (ISBN 0-205-91463-2), Test Bank (ISBN 0-205-91463-2), and PowerPoint™ Presentation Package (ISBN 0-205-91463-2). These supplements are available at www.pearsonhighered.com/irc (instructor login required). MyTest online test-generating software (ISBN 0-205-91463-2) is available at www.pearsonmytest.com (instructor login required). For a complete list of the instructor and student resources available with the text, please visit the Pearson Communication catalog, at www.pearsonhighered.com/communication.

MyCommunicationLab®

www.mycommunicationlab.com

MyCommunicationLab is an online homework, tutorial, and assessment program that truly engages students in learning. It helps students better prepare for class, quizzes, and exams—resulting in better performance in the course. It provides educators a dynamic set of tools for gauging individual and class performance. And **MyCommunicationLab** comes from Pearson, your partner in providing the best digital learning experiences.

- **Assessment** tied to videos, applications, and chapter content enables both instructors and students to track progress and get immediate feedback—and helps instructors find the best resources with which to help students.

- The **Pearson eText** lets students access their textbook anytime, anywhere, and any way they want—including listening online or accessing on a smartphone or tablet device.

- **Videos and Video Quizzes:** Sample student and professional speeches offer students models of the types of speeches they are learning to design and deliver. Many interactive videos include short, assignable quizzes that report to the instructor's gradebook.

- **PersonalityProfile:** Pearson's online library for self-assessment and analysis provides students with opportunities to evaluate their own and others' communication styles. Instructors can use these tools to show learning and growth over the duration of the course.

- **MediaShare:** A comprehensive file upload tool that allows students to post speeches, outlines, visual aids, video assignments, role plays, group projects, and more in a variety of formats including video, Word, PowerPoint, and Excel. Structured much like a social networking site, MediaShare helps promote a sense of community among students. Uploaded files are available for viewing, commenting, and grading by instructors and class members in face-to-face and online course settings. Integrated video capture functionality allows students to record video directly from a webcam to their assignments, and allows instructors to record videos via webcam, in class or in a lab, and attach them directly to a specific student and/or assignment. In addition, instructors can upload files as assignments for students to view and respond to directly in MediaShare. Grades can be imported into most learning management systems, and robust privacy settings ensure a secure learning environment for instructors and students. Upload videos, comment on submissions, and grade directly from our new MediaShare app, available free from the iTunes store; search for Pearson MediaShare.

- **Class Preparation Tool:** Finding, organizing, and presenting your instructor resources is fast and easy with Pearson's class preparation tool. This fully searchable database contains hundreds of resources such as lecture launchers, discussion topics, activities, assignments, and video clips. Instructors can search or browse by topic and sort the results by type. You can create personalized folders to organize and store what you like or download resources as well as upload your own content.

- **Pearson's Writing Space:** The best way to develop and assess concept mastery and critical thinking through writing. Writing Space provides a single place within MyCommunicationLab to create, track, and grade writing assignments, access writing resources, and exchange meaningful, personalized feedback quickly and easily. Plus, Writing Space will have integrated access to Turnitin, the global leader in plagiarism prevention.

Acknowledgments

Writing a book is a partnership not only with each other as co-authors but also with many people who have offered us the benefit of their experience and advice about how to make this the best possible teaching and learning resource. We appreciate all of the authors and speakers we have quoted or referenced; their words and wisdom have added resonance to our knowledge and richness to our advice. We are grateful for our students, colleagues, adopters, friends, and the skilled editorial team at Pearson.

Many talented reviewers have helped us shape the content and features of this edition. These talented public-speaking teachers have supplemented our experience to help us make decisions about how to present and organize the content of this book. We express our sincere appreciation to the following reviewers who have shared their advice, wisdom, and expertise:

Reviewers of the ninth edition:
Cynthia Brown El, Macomb Community College; Deborah Burns, Merrimack College; Brady Carey, Mt. Hood Community College; Laurence Covington, University of the District of Columbia; Kamesha Khan, Chicago State University; Jeff Kurtz, Denison University; Marjorie Nadler, Miami University; and Valerie Smith, California State University, East Bay

Reviewers of previous editions:
Melanie Anson, Citrus College; Richard Armstrong, Wichita State University; Nancy Arnett, Brevard Community College; David E. Axon, Johnson County Community College; Ernest W. Bartow, Bucks County Community College; John Bee, University of Akron; Jaima L. Bennett, Golden West College; Donald S. Birns, SUNY—Albany; Tim Borchers, Moorhead State University; Barry Brummett, University of Wisconsin, Milwaukee; John Buckley, University of Tennessee; Thomas R. Burkholder, University of Nevada—Las Vegas; Judy H. Carter, Amarillo College; Mark Chase, Slippery Rock University; Marilyn J. Cristiano, Paradise Valley Community College; Dan B. Curtis, Central Missouri State University; Ann L. Darling, University of Illinois, Urbana—Champaign; Conrad E. Davidson, Minot State University; Terrence Doyle, Northern Virginia Community College; Gary W. Eckles, Thomas Nelson Community College; Thomas G. Endres, University of St. Thomas; Richard I. Falvo, El Paso Community College; John S. France, Owens State Community College; Kristina Galyen, University of Cincinnati; Darla Germeroth, University of Scranton; Donna Goodwin, Tulsa Community College; Myra G. Gutin, Rider University; Larry Haapanen, Lewis-Clark State College; Dayle C. Hardy-Short, Northern Arizona University; Carla J. Harrell, Old Dominion University; Tina Harris, University of Georgia; Phyllis Heberling, Tidewater Community College; James L. Heflin, Cameron University; Susan A. Hellweg, San Diego State University; Wayne E. Hensley, Virginia Polytechnic Institute and State University; Patricia S. Hill, University of Akron; Judith S. Hoeffler, Ohio State University; Stephen K. Hunt, Illinois State University; Paul A. Hutchins, Cooke County College; Ann Marie Jablonowski, Owens Community College; Elaine B. Jenks, West Chester University; Nanette Johnson-Curiskis, Gustavus Adolphus College; Kherstin Khan-Brockbank, Fresno City College; Cecil V. Kramer, Jr., Liberty University; Michael W. Kramer, University of Missouri; Linda Kurz, University of Missouri, Kansas City; Ed Lamoureux, Bradley University; David Lawless, Tulsa Junior College; Robert S. Littlefield, North Dakota State University; Jeré W. Littlejohn, Mississippi State University; Harold L. Make, Millersville University of Pennsylvania; Jim Mancuso, Mesa Community College; Deborah F. Meltsner, Old Dominion University; Rebecca Mikesell, University of Scranton; Maxine Minson, Tulsa Junior College; Christine Mixan, University of Nebraska at Omaha; Barbara Monaghan, Berkeley College; Jay R. Moorman, Missouri Southern State University; Marjorie Keeshan Nadler, Miami University; Karen O'Donnell, Finger Lakes Community College; Rhonda Parker, University of San Francisco; Roxanne Parrott, University of Georgia; Richard L. Quianthy, Broward Community College; Carol L. Radetsky, Metropolitan State College; Renton Rathbun, Owens Community College; Mary Helen Richer, University of North Dakota; K. David Roach,

Texas Tech University; Kellie W. Roberts, University of Florida; Rebecca Roberts, University of Wyoming; Val Safron, Washington University; Kristi Schaller, University of Hawaii at Manoa; Cara Schollenberger, Bucks County Community College; Shane Simon, Central Texas College; Cheri J. Simonds, Illinois State University; Glenn D. Smith, University of Central Arkansas; David R. Sprague, Liberty University; Jessica Stowell, Tulsa Junior College; Edward J. Streb, Rowan College; Aileen Sundstrom, Henry Ford Community College; Susan L. Sutton, Cloud County Community College; Tasha Van Horn, Citrus College; Jim Vickrey, Troy State University; Denise Vrchota, Iowa State University; Beth M. Waggenspack, Virginia Polytechnic Institute and State University; David E. Walker, Middle Tennessee State University; Jamille Watkins-Barnes, Chicago State University; Lynn Wells, Saddleback College; Nancy R. Wern, Glenville State College; Charles N. Wise, El Paso Community College; Marcy Wong, Indian River State College; Argentina R. Wortham, Northeast Lakeview College; Merle Ziegler, Liberty University

Kosta Tovstiadi is a good friend and trusted researcher who assisted with research for this edition. We are grateful that Karon Bowers, Publisher, Communication, continued to be a strong source of support and encouragement to us as we worked on this edition, as she was on previous editions. Sheralee Connors, our development editor, has done an exceptional job of offering skilled advice and creative suggestions to make this a better book. She helped lighten our workload with her many helpful comments and suggestions.

We have enjoyed strong support and mentorship from a number of teachers, friends, and colleagues who have influenced our work over the years. Our colleagues at Texas State University continue to be supportive of our efforts. Tom Willett, retired professor from William Jewell College; Dan Curtis, emeritus professor at the University of Central Missouri; John Masterson, emeritus professor at Texas Lutheran University; and Thompson Biggers, professor at Mercer University, are longtime friends and exemplary teachers who continue to influence our work and our lives. Sue Hall, Department of Communication Studies senior administrative assistant at Texas State, again provided exceptional support and assistance to keep our work on schedule. Meredith Clayton, also an administrative assistant at Texas State, helped us in innumerable ways.

We view our work as authors of a textbook as primarily a teaching process. Both of us have been blessed with gifted teachers whose dedication and mentorship continue to inspire and encourage us. Mary Harper, former speech, English, and drama teacher at Steve's high school alma mater, Grain Valley High School, Grain Valley, Missouri; and Sue's speech teacher, the late Margaret Dent, who taught at Hannibal High School, Hannibal, Missouri, provided initial instruction in public speaking that remains with us today. We also value the life lessons and friendship we receive from Erma Doty, another former teacher at Grain Valley High, who continues to offer us encouragement and support not only with what she says but also by how she lives her life in service for others. We appreciate the patience and encouragement we received from Robert Brewer, our first debate coach at the University of Central Missouri, where we met each other more than forty years ago and where the ideas for this book were first discussed. We both served as student teachers under the unforgettable, energetic guidance of the late Louis Banker at Fort Osage High School, near Buckner, Missouri. Likewise, we have both benefited from the skilled instruction of Mary Jeanette Smythe, now retired from the University of Missouri—Columbia. We wish to express our appreciation to Loren Reid, emeritus professor from the University of Missouri—Columbia; to us, he remains the quintessential speech teacher.

Finally, we value the patience, encouragement, proud support, and love of our sons and daughter-in-law, Mark, Matthew, and Brittany Beebe. They offer many inspiring lessons in overcoming life challenges and infusing life with music. They continue to be our most important audience.

STEVEN A. BEEBE
SUSAN J. BEEBE

1 SPEAKING WITH CONFIDENCE

Magnus Zeller (1888-1972). *The Orator*, circa 1920. Museum Associates/LACMA/Art Resource, NY

OBJECTIVES

After studying this chapter you should be able to do the following:

1.1
Compare and contrast public speaking and conversation.

1.2
Explain why it is important to study public speaking.

1.3
Sketch and explain a model that illustrates the components and the process of communication.

1.4
Discuss in brief the history of public speaking.

1.5
Use several techniques to become a more confident speaker.

(((Listen to Chapter 1 at **MyCommunicationLab**

There are two kinds of speakers: those that are nervous and those that are liars.

—Mark Twain

1

Perhaps you think you have heard this speaker—or even taken a class from him: His eyes were buried in his script. His words in monotone emerged haltingly from behind his mustache, losing volume as they were sifted through hair. Audiences rushed to see and hear him, and after they had satisfied their eyes, they closed their ears. Ultimately, they turned to small talk among themselves while the great man droned on.[1]

The speaker described here in such an unflattering way is none other than Albert Einstein. Sadly, although the great physicist could attract an audience with his reputation, he could not sustain their attention and interest because he lacked public-speaking skills.

As you begin reading this book, chances are that you are also beginning a course in public speaking. You're in good company; nearly a half million college students each year take a public-speaking class.[2] If you haven't had much previous experience speaking in public, you're also in good company. Sixty-six percent of students beginning a public-speaking course reported having had little or no public-speaking experience.[3]

The good news is that this book and this course will provide you with the knowledge and experience needed to become what Einstein was not: a competent public speaker.

1.1 Compare and contrast public speaking and conversation.

What Is Public Speaking?

Public speaking is the process of presenting a message to an audience, small or large. You hear speeches almost every day. Each day when you attend class, an instructor lectures. When watching a newscast on TV or via the Internet, you get a "sound bite" of some politician delivering a speech. When you hear a comedian delivering a monologue on a late-night talk show or the Comedy Channel, you're hearing a speech designed to entertain you.

The skill of public speaking builds upon your normal, everyday interactions with others. In fact, as you begin to study and practice public speaking, you will discover that it has much in common with conversation, a form of communication in which you engage every day. Like conversation, public speaking requires you to focus and verbalize your thoughts.

When you have a conversation, you also have to make decisions "on your feet." If your friends look puzzled or interrupt with questions, you may need to explain your idea a second time. If they look bored, you insert a funny story or talk more animatedly. As a public speaker, you will learn to make similar adaptations based on your knowledge of your listeners, their expectations for your speech, and their reactions to what you are saying. In fact, because we believe that the ability to adapt to your audience is so vital, this book focuses on public speaking as an audience-centered activity.

But if public speaking were exactly like conversation, Albert Einstein's lectures would have been more riveting, there would be no reason to take a public-speaking class, and there would be no need for this book. Let's take a look at some of the ways in which public speaking differs from conversation.

public speaking
The process of presenting a message to an audience

- *Public speaking requires more preparation than conversation.* Although you may sometimes be asked to speak on the spur of the moment, you will usually know in advance whether you will be expected to give a talk on a specific occasion. A public speaker might spend hours or even days planning and practicing his or her speech.

- *Public speaking is more formal than conversation.* The slang or casual language we often use in conversation is usually not appropriate for most public speaking. Audiences expect speakers to use standard English grammar and vocabulary. The nonverbal communication of public speakers is also more formal than the nonverbal behavior of people engaged in ordinary conversation.

- *Public speaking involves more clearly defined roles for speaker and audience than conversation.* During a conversation, there is typically interaction between speaker and listener. But in public speaking, the roles of speaker and audience are more clearly defined and remain stable. Although in some cultures a call-and-response speaker–audience interaction occurs (such as saying "That's right" or "Amen" when responding to a preacher's sermon), in the majority of the United States, audience members rarely interrupt or talk back to speakers.

Learning the new skills of public speaking can be challenging and take time. What are the benefits to you of putting in the effort to become an effective speaker?

Public speakers take more time to prepare their remarks than conversationalists do. Public speaking is also more formal than conversation, with defined roles for speaker and audience.

Photo: val lawless/Shutterstock

Why Study Public Speaking?

1.2   Explain why it is important to study public speaking.

Although you've heard countless speeches during your lifetime, you may still have questions about why it's important for *you* to study public speaking. Here are two reasons: By studying public speaking you will gain long-term advantages related to *empowerment* and *employment*.

Empowerment

You will undoubtedly be called on to speak in public at various times in your life: as a student participating in a seminar class; as a businessperson convincing your boss to let you undertake a new project; as a concerned citizen addressing the city council's zoning board. In each of these situations, the ability to speak with competence and confidence will provide **empowerment**. To be empowered is to have the resources, information, and attitudes that allow you to take action to achieve a desired goal. Being a skilled public speaker will give you an edge that less skilled communicators lack—even those who may have superior ideas, training, or experience. It will position you for greater things. Former presidential speechwriter James Humes, who labels public speaking "the language of leadership," says, "Every time you have to speak—whether it's in an auditorium, in a company conference room, or even at your own desk—you are auditioning for leadership."[4]

One of the empowering resources that you develop by studying public speaking is **critical thinking**. To think critically is to be able to listen and analyze information you hear so that you can judge its accuracy and relevance. While you are learning

empowerment

Having resources, information, and attitudes that lead to action to achieve a desired goal

critical thinking

Analyzing information to judge its accuracy and relevance

RECAP

WHY STUDY PUBLIC SPEAKING?

- Empowerment: You will gain confidence and skill in communicating with others.
- Employment: You will enhance your career and leadership opportunities.

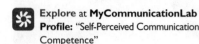

Explore at **MyCommunicationLab** **Profile:** "Self-Perceived Communication Competence"

how to improve your speaking in this course, you are also learning the critical thinking skills to sort good ideas from bad ideas. Being a critical thinker and an effective communicator is a powerful and empowering combination.

Yet, if you're typical, you may experience fear and anxiety about speaking in public. As you start your journey of becoming an effective public speaker, you may have questions about how to bolster your confidence and manage your apprehension. Before you finish this chapter, you'll have read about more than a dozen strategies to help you feel both more empowered and more confident. Being both a confident and an empowered public speaker is within your grasp. And being an empowered speaker can open up leadership and career opportunities for you.

Employment

If you can speak well, you possess a skill that others value highly. In fact, industrialist Charles M. Schwab once said, "I'll pay more for a person's ability to speak and express himself than for any other quality he might possess."[5] Billionaire stock investor Warren Buffet agrees. In an interview with CNN reporter Christiane Amanpour, extolling the virtues of his public-speaking course, he said, "If you improve your communication skills I guarantee you that you will earn 50 percent more money over your lifetime."[6]

Whether you're currently employed as an entry-level employee or aspire to the highest rung of the corporate leadership ladder, being able to communicate effectively with others is key to success in any line of work. The skills you learn in a public-speaking course, such as how to ethically adapt information to listeners, organize your ideas, persuade others, and hold listeners' attention, are among the skills most sought after by any employer. In a nationwide survey, prospective employers of college graduates said they seek candidates with "public-speaking and presentation ability."[7] Other surveys of personnel managers, both in the United States and internationally, have confirmed that they consider communication skills the top factor in helping graduating college students obtain employment (see Table 1.1).[8]

TABLE 1.1   TOP SKILLS VALUED BY EMPLOYERS

RANK	RESULTS OF SURVEY OF PERSONNEL DIRECTORS[9]	RESULTS OF SURVEY OF A COLLEGE CAREER SERVICES DEPARTMENT[10]	RESULTS OF SURVEY OF PROSPECTIVE EMPLOYERS[11]	SURVEY RESULTS FROM SEVERAL RESEARCH STUDIES[12]
1	Spoken communication skills	Communication and interpersonal skills	Communication skills	Communication skills
2	Written communication skills	Intelligence	Honesty and integrity	Analytical/research skills
3	Listening ability	Enthusiasm	Teamwork	Technical skills
4	Enthusiasm	Flexibility	Interpersonal skills	Flexibility/adaptability
5	Technical competence	Leadership	Motivation/initiative	Interpersonal skills

Source: Copyrighted by Pearson Education, Upper Saddle River, NJ

The Communication Process

1.3 Sketch and explain a model that illustrates the components and the process of communication.

Even the earliest communication theorists recognized that communication is a process. The models they formulated were linear, suggesting a simple transfer of meaning from a sender to a receiver, as shown in Figure 1.1. More recently, theorists have created models that better demonstrate the complexity of the communication process. Let's explore what some of those models can teach us about what happens when we communicate.

Communication as Action

Although they were simplistic, the earliest linear models of communication as action identified most of the elements of the communication process. We will explain each element as it relates to public speaking.

Source A public speaker is a **source** of information and ideas for an audience. The job of the source or speaker is to **encode**, or translate, the ideas and images in his or her mind into verbal or nonverbal symbols (a **code**) that an audience can recognize. The speaker may encode into words (for example, "The fabric should be 2 inches square") or into gestures (showing the size with his or her hands).

Message The **message** in public speaking is the speech itself—both what is said and how it is said. If a speaker has trouble finding words to convey his or her ideas or sends contradictory nonverbal symbols, listeners may not be able to **decode** the speaker's verbal and nonverbal symbols back into a message.

Channels A message is usually transmitted from sender to receiver via two **channels**: *visual* and *auditory*. Audience members see the speaker and decode his or her nonverbal symbols—eye contact (or lack of it), facial expressions, posture, gestures, and dress. If the speaker uses any visual aids, such as graphs or models, these too are transmitted along the visual channel. The auditory channel opens as the speaker speaks. Then the audience members hear words and such vocal cues as inflection, rate, and voice quality.

Receiver The **receiver** of the message is the individual audience member, whose decoding of the message will depend on his or her own particular blend of past

source
The public speaker

encode
To translate ideas and images into verbal or nonverbal symbols

code
A verbal or nonverbal symbol for an idea or image

message
The content of a speech and the mode of its delivery

decode
To translate verbal or nonverbal symbols into ideas and images

channels
The visual and auditory means by which a message is transmitted from sender to receiver

receiver
A listener or an audience member

FIGURE 1.1 The earliest models viewed communication as the action of transferring meaning from source to receiver.

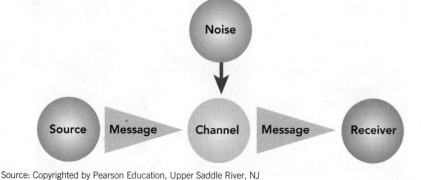

Source: Copyrighted by Pearson Education, Upper Saddle River, NJ

experiences, attitudes, beliefs, and values. As already emphasized, an effective public speaker should be receiver- or audience-centered.

Noise Anything that interferes with the communication of a message is called *noise*. Noise may be physical and external. If your 8 A.M. public-speaking class is frequently interrupted by the roar of a lawn mower running back and forth under the window, it may be difficult to concentrate on what your instructor is saying. A noisy air conditioner, a crying baby, or incessant coughing is an example of **external noise** that may make it difficult for audience members to hear or concentrate on a speech.

Noise may also be internal. **Internal noise** may stem from either *physiological* or *psychological* causes and may directly affect either the source or the receiver. A bad cold (physiological noise) may cloud a speaker's memory or subdue his or her delivery. An audience member worrying about an upcoming exam (psychological noise) is unlikely to remember much of what the speaker says. Regardless of whether it is internal or external, physiological or psychological, or whether it originates in the sender or the receiver, noise interferes with the transmission of a message.

Communication as Interaction

Realizing that linear models were overly simplistic, later communication theorists designed models that depicted communication as a more complex process (see Figure 1.2). These models were circular, or interactive, and added two important new elements: feedback and context.

Feedback As we've noted, one way in which public speaking differs from casual conversation is that the public speaker does most or all of the talking. But public speaking is still interactive. Without an audience to hear and provide **feedback**, public speaking serves little purpose. Skillful public speakers are audience-centered. They depend on the nods, facial expressions, and murmurs of the audience to adjust their rate of speaking, volume, vocabulary, type and amount of supporting material, and other variables to communicate their message successfully.

Context The **context** of a public-speaking experience is the environment or situation in which the speech occurs. It includes such elements as the time, the place, and

external noise
Physical sounds that interfere with communication

internal noise
Physiological or psychological interference with communication

feedback
Verbal and nonverbal responses provided by an audience to a speaker

context
The environment or situation in which a speech occurs

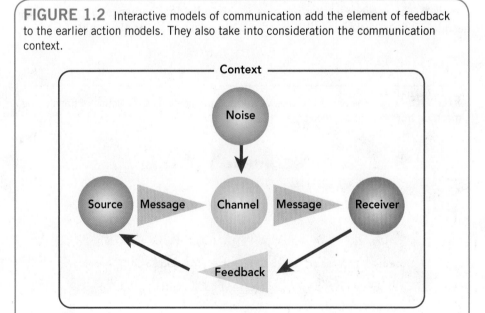

FIGURE 1.2 Interactive models of communication add the element of feedback to the earlier action models. They also take into consideration the communication context.

Source: Copyrighted by Pearson Education, Upper Saddle River, NJ

the speaker's and audience's cultural traditions and expectations. To rephrase John Donne, no *speech* is an island. No speech occurs in a vacuum. Rather, each speech is a blend of circumstances that can never be replicated exactly.

The person whose job it is to deliver an identical message to a number of different audiences at different times and in different places can attest to the uniqueness of each speaking context. If the room is hot, crowded, or poorly lit, these conditions affect both speaker and audience. The audience that hears a speaker at 10 A.M. is likely to be fresher and more receptive than a 4:30 P.M. audience. A speaker who fought rush-hour traffic for 90 minutes to arrive at his or her destination may find it difficult to muster much enthusiasm for delivering the speech.

Many of the skills that you will learn from this book relate not only to the preparation of effective speeches (messages) but also to the elements of feedback and context in the communication process. Our audience-centered approach focuses on "reading" your listeners' responses and adjusting to them as you speak.

FIGURE 1.3 A transactive model of communication focuses on the simultaneous exchanges that happen between source and receiver.

Source: Copyrighted by Pearson Education, Upper Saddle River, NJ

Communication as Transaction

The most recent communication models do not label individual components. Transactive models focus instead on communication as a simultaneous process. As the model in Figure 1.3 suggests, we send and receive messages concurrently. In a two-person communication transaction, both individuals are sending and receiving at the same time. When you are listening, you are simultaneously expressing your thoughts and feelings nonverbally.

An effective public speaker should not only be focused on the message he or she is expressing but also should be tuned in to how the audience is responding to the message. A good public speaker shouldn't wait until the speech is over to gauge the effectiveness of a speech. Instead, because of the transactive nature of communication, a speaker should be scanning the audience during the speech for nonverbal clues to assess the audience's reaction, just as you do when you have a conversation with someone.

Although communication models have been developed only recently, the elements of these models have long been recognized as the keys to successful public speaking. As you study public speaking, you will continue a tradition that goes back to the very beginnings of Western civilization.

> **RECAP**
>
> ### THE COMMUNICATION PROCESS
>
> Audience and speaker send messages simultaneously. Elements of the process include:
>
> - Source: The originator of the message
> - Message: The content of what is expressed both verbally and nonverbally
> - Channel: The means by which a message is expressed from sender to receiver
> - Receiver: The listener or audience member who sees and hears the message
> - Feedback: Responses provided by an audience to a speaker
> - Context: The situation and environment in which the speech occurs

The Rich Heritage of Public Speaking

1.4 Discuss in brief the history of public speaking.

Long before many people could read, they listened to public speakers. **Rhetoric** can be described as the use of words and symbols to achieve a goal. Although rhetoric is often defined as the art of speaking or writing aimed at persuading others (changing or reinforcing attitudes, beliefs, values, or behavior), whether you're informing, persuading, or even entertaining listeners, you are using rhetoric because you are trying to achieve a goal.

rhetoric

The use of words and symbols to achieve a goal

The Golden Age of Public Speaking

The fourth century B.C.E. is called the golden age of rhetoric in the Greek Republic because it was during this time that the philosopher Aristotle formulated guidelines for speakers that we still follow today. In later chapters in this book you will be learning principles and practices of public speaking that were first summarized by Aristotle in his classic book *The Art of Rhetoric,* written in 333 B.C.E.

Roman orators continued the Greek rhetorical tradition. The Roman orator Cicero was known not only for being an excellent public speaker but also for what he wrote about how to be an effective speaker. Marcus Fabius Quintilianus, born in what is today Spain and known as Quintilian, also sought to teach others how to be an effective speaker. As politicians and poets attracted large followings in ancient Rome, Cicero and Quintilian sought to define the qualities of the "true" orator. Quintilian famously wrote that the ideal orator should be "a good person speaking well." On a lighter note, it is said that Roman orators invented the necktie. Fearing laryngitis, they wore "chin cloths" to protect their throats.[13]

Centuries later, in medieval Europe, the clergy were the most polished public speakers. People gathered eagerly to hear Martin Luther expound his Articles of Faith. In the eighteenth century, British subjects in the colonies listened to the town criers and impassioned patriots of what would one day become the United States.

 Read at **MyCommunicationLab**
Learning From Great Speakers:
Martin Luther King Jr.

Nineteenth- and Twentieth-Century Age of Political Oratory

Vast nineteenth-century audiences heard speakers such as Henry Clay and Daniel Webster debate states' rights; they listened to Frederick Douglass, Angelina Grimke, and Sojourner Truth argue for the abolition of slavery and to Lucretia Mott plead for women's suffrage; they gathered for an evening's entertainment to hear Mark Twain as he traveled the lecture circuits of the frontier.

declamation
The delivery of an already famous speech

elocution
The expression of emotion through posture, movement, gesture, facial expression, and voice

Students of nineteenth-century public speaking spent very little time developing their own speeches. Instead, they practiced the art of **declamation**—the delivery of an already famous address. Favorite subjects for declamation included speeches by such Americans as Patrick Henry and William Jennings Bryan and by the British orator Edmund Burke. Collections of speeches, such as Bryan's own ten-volume set of *The World's Famous Orations,* published in 1906, were extremely popular.

Hand in hand with declamation went the study and practice of **elocution**, the expression of emotion through posture, movement, gesture, facial expression, and voice. From the mid-nineteenth century to the early twentieth century, elocution manuals—providing elaborate and specific prescriptions for effective delivery—were standard references not only in schools but also in nearly every middle-class home in the United States.[14]

The Technological Age of Public Speaking

In the first half of the twentieth century, radio made it possible for people around the world to hear Franklin Delano Roosevelt decry December 7, 1941, as "a date which will live in infamy" following the attack on Pearl Harbor in Hawaii. In the last half of the century, television provided the medium through which audiences saw and heard the most stirring speeches:

Civil rights leader and human rights activist Dr. Martin Luther King Jr. delivered one of the great speeches of history as the keynote of the August 1963 civil rights march on Washington, D.C. Turn to Appendix B to study Dr. King's famous speech.

Photo: AP Images

- Martin Luther King Jr. proclaiming his dream of equality
- Ronald Reagan beseeching Mikhail Gorbachev to "tear down this wall"
- Holocaust survivor Elie Wiesel looking beyond the end of one millennium toward the next with "profound fear and extraordinary hope"

With the twenty-first century dawned a new era of speechmaking. It was to be an era that would draw on age-old public-speaking traditions—an era in which U.S.

soldiers serving in Iraq and Afghanistan would watch their children's commencement addresses live via streaming video. And it was to be an era that would summon public speakers to meet some of the most difficult challenges in history—an era in which President Obama would empathize with the grief felt by the community of Newtown, Connecticut, after 20 young children and six adults were shot to death at Sandy Hook Elementary School. He assured his listeners that ". . . you're not alone in your grief; that our world too has been torn apart; that all across this land of ours, we have wept with you, we've pulled our children tight."[15] Speakers of the future will continue to draw on a long and rich heritage, in addition to forging new frontiers in public speaking.

You may be more likely to hear a speech today presented as a YouTube video or a podcast and delivered on your smartphone or other digital device than you are a live-and-in person presentation. In fact, you may be taking this course in an online format and may present your speeches to your classmates and instructor as video recordings. Although the electronic context of the message influences both how the message may be prepared and received, the primary process of developing and presenting your speech is the same as it has been for centuries. We will offer tips and strategies for delivering a speech via video in Chapter 11.

The ancient Romans identified five classical *canons,* or elements of preparing and presenting a speech:

- *Invention:* the creative process of developing your ideas
- *Arrangement:* how the speech is organized
- *Style:* your choice of words
- *Memory:* the extent to which you use notes or rely on your memory to share your ideas
- *Delivery:* the nonverbal expression of your message

Whether you are presenting your message in person or via video, you will find that these same five elements will shape how your audience responds to your message.

Another unchanging truth of public speaking is that the core of all you do in public speaking is a focus on your audience. Your audience will ultimately determine if your message has achieved your objective. For this reason, we suggest that you keep your audience foremost in your mind from the first moments of thinking about your speech topic to the time when you utter the concluding sentence of your speech. In the next chapter we present a step-by-step guide to preparing any speech that will connect speaker to audience regardless of the channel used.

RECAP

THE RICH HERITAGE OF PUBLIC SPEAKING

Period	Event
Fourth to first centuries B.C.E.	Greek rhetoric flourishes in the Age of Aristotle. Roman orators continue the tradition.
Fifteenth century	European clergy are the primary practitioners of public speaking.
Eighteenth century	American patriots make impassioned public pleas for independence.
Nineteenth century	Abolitionists and suffragists speak out for change; frontier lecture circuits flourish.
Twentieth century	Electronic media make possible vast audiences.
Twenty-first century	A new era of speechmaking uses rapidly evolving technology and media while drawing on a rich heritage of public speaking.

Improving Your Confidence as a Speaker

1.5 Use several techniques to become a more confident speaker.

Actor and celebrated emcee George Jessel once wryly observed, "The human brain starts working the moment you are born and never stops . . . until you stand up to speak in public." Perhaps public speaking is a required class for you, but, because of the anxiety you feel when you deliver a speech, you've put it off for as long as possible.

The first bit of comfort we offer is this: *It's normal* to *be nervous.* In a classic survey seeking to identify people's phobias, public speaking ranked as the most anxiety-producing experience most people face. Forty-one percent of all respondents reported public speaking as their most significant fear: Fear of death ranked only sixth![16] Based on these statistics, comedian Jerry Seinfeld suggests, "Given a choice, at a funeral most of us would rather be the one in the coffin than the one giving the eulogy." New research continues to confirm that most people are apprehensive about giving a speech.[17] Other studies have found that more than 80 percent of the population feels anxious when they speak to an audience.[18] Some people find that public speaking is quite frightening: Studies suggest that about 20 percent of all college students are highly apprehensive about speaking in front of others.[19]

Even if your anxiety is not overwhelming, you can benefit from learning some positive approaches that allow your nervousness to work *for you*.[20] First, we will help you understand why you become nervous. Then we will offer specific strategies to help you speak with greater comfort and less anxiety.

Understand Your Nervousness

Explore at MyCommunicationLab
Profile: "Situational Communication Apprehension Measure"

Watch at MyCommunicationLab
Video: "Fear of Public Speaking"

What makes you feel nervous about speaking in public? Why do your hands sometimes shake, your knees quiver, your stomach flutter, and your voice seem to go up an octave? What is happening to you?[21]

Researchers have found that public-speaking anxiety is both a *trait* (a characteristic or general tendency that you may have) and a *state* (anxiety triggered by the specific incidence of giving a speech to an audience).[22] A study by two communication researchers found that among the causes of public-speaking anxiety were fear of humiliation, concern about not being prepared, worry about one's looks, pressure to perform, personal insecurity, concern that the audience wouldn't be interested in oneself or the speech, lack of experience, fear of making mistakes, and an overall fear of failure.[23] Another study found that men are likely to experience more anxiety than women when speaking to people from a culture different from their own.[24] There is also evidence that being a perfectionist may be linked to increased apprehension when speaking to others.[25] As you read the list of possible speaking-anxiety causes, you'll probably find a reason that resonates with you because most people feel some nervousness when they speak before others. You're not alone if you are apprehensive about giving a speech.[26] Understanding why you and many others may experience apprehension can give you insights into how to better address your anxiety.[27]

Your Biology Affects Your Psychology Increasingly, researchers are concluding that communication apprehension may have a genetic or biological basis: Some people may inherit a tendency to feel anxious about speaking in public.[28] You may wonder, "So if I have a biological tendency to feel nervous, is there anything I can do to help manage my fear?" The answer is *yes*. Even if you are predisposed to feel nervous because of your genetic makeup, there are strategies you can use to help manage your apprehension.[29] Perhaps you've heard that the secret to serenity is to focus on the things you can change, rather than on the things you can't, and to have the wisdom to know the difference between what is changeable and what isn't. For increased serenity when speaking in public, we suggest you focus on behaviors that you can change, enhancing your speaking skills, rather than on your biologically based speaking apprehension, which is much more difficult to change. A better understanding of the biological reasons you feel apprehensive is a good starting point on the journey to speaking with greater confidence and serenity.[30]

Your Psychology Also Affects Your Biology Your view of the speaking assignment, your perception of your speaking skill, and your self-esteem interact to create anxiety.[31] You want to do well, but you're not sure that you can or will. Presented with this conflict, your brain signals your body to switch to its default fight-or-flight mode:

You can either fight to respond to the challenge or flee to avoid the cause of the anxiety. Your body responds by summoning more energy to deal with the conflict you are facing. Your breathing rate increases, more adrenaline pumps through you, and more blood rushes through your veins.[32] To put it more technically, you are experiencing physiological changes because of your psychological state, which explains why you may have a more rapid heartbeat, shaking knees and hands, a quivering voice, and increased perspiration.[33] You may also experience butterflies in your stomach because of changes in your digestive system. As a result of your physical discomfort, you may make less eye contact with your audience, use more vocalized pauses ("Um," "Ah," "You know"), and speak too rapidly. Although you see your physical responses as hindrances, your brain and body are simply trying to help you with the task at hand. Sometimes they offer more "help" than needed, and their assistance is not useful.

Your Apprehension Follows a Predictable Pattern When are you most likely to feel nervous about giving a speech in your communication class? Research suggests there are typical times when people feel nervous. As shown in Figure 1.4, many people feel most nervous right before they give their speech. That's when the uncertainty about what will happen next is very high.[34] If you're typical, you'll feel the second-highest level of anxiety when your instructor explains the speech assignment. You'll probably feel the *least* anxiety when you're preparing your speech.

One practical application of this research is that now you can understand when you'll need the most help managing your anxiety—right before you speak. It will also help to remember that as you begin to speak, anxiety begins to decrease—often dramatically. Another application of the research is to help you realize that you'll feel less anxious about your speech when you're doing something positive to prepare for it. Don't put off working on your speech; if you start preparing well in advance, you'll not only have a better speech, you'll also feel less anxious about presenting it.

To identify patterns in how people experience communication apprehension, one researcher measured speakers' heart rates when they were delivering speeches and asked them several questions about their fear of public speaking.[35]

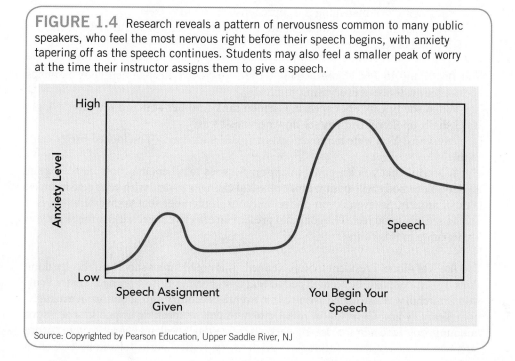

FIGURE 1.4 Research reveals a pattern of nervousness common to many public speakers, who feel the most nervous right before their speech begins, with anxiety tapering off as the speech continues. Students may also feel a smaller peak of worry at the time their instructor assigns them to give a speech.

After studying the results, he identified the following four styles of communication apprehension.

- **Average.** You have an *average style* of communication apprehension if you have a generally positive approach to communicating in public; your overall heart rate when speaking publicly is in the average range. Speakers with this style rated their own speaking performance the highest compared to those with other styles.

- **Insensitive.** The *insensitive style* is likely to be your style only if you have had previous experience in public speaking. Perhaps because of your experience, you tend to be less sensitive to apprehension when you speak; you have a lower heart rate when speaking and rate your performance as moderately successful.

- **Inflexible.** If you have an *inflexible style,* you have the highest heart rate when speaking publicly. Some people use this high and inflexible level of anxiety to enhance their performance: Their fear motivates them to prepare and be at their best. For others, the anxiety of the inflexible style creates so much tension that their speaking performance is diminished.

- **Confrontational.** You have a *confrontational style* if, like many people, you have a very high heart rate as you begin presenting a speech, and then your heart rate tapers off to more average levels. This style occurred in people who reported a strong emotional, or affective, response to speaking and was characteristic of more experienced speakers, or people with at least some public-speaking background.

What difference does it make which style of communication apprehension you have? First, it may help to know that you are not alone in how you experience apprehension and that others likely share your feelings. Although each person is unique, there are nonetheless general styles of apprehension. Second, having a general idea of your own style may give you greater insight into how to better manage your apprehension. For example, if you know that your apprehension tends to spike upward at the very beginning of speaking to an audience (the confrontational style), you will need to draw on strategies to help manage your anxiety at the beginning of your talk. Finally, the research on apprehension styles lends support to the theory that communication apprehension may be a genetic trait or tendency.[36] This means that, depending on your own tendencies, you may need more information to help *you* develop constructive ways of managing the apprehension you may feel.

What else can you do to understand and manage your fear and anxiety? Consider the following observations.

You Are Going to Feel More Nervous Than You Look Realize that your audience cannot see evidence of everything you feel.

When she finished her speech, Carmen sank into her seat and muttered, "Ugh, was I shaky up there! Did *you* see how nervous I was?"

"Nervous? You were nervous?" asked Kosta, surprised. "You looked pretty calm to me."

Worrying that you are going to appear nervous to others may only *increase* your anxiety. Your body will exhibit more physical changes to deal with your self-induced state of anxiety. So even if you do feel nervous, remember that your listeners aren't able to see what you feel. The goal is to present an effective speech using the skills you are learning in this course.[37]

You Are Not Alone President John F. Kennedy was noted for his superb public-speaking skills. When he spoke, he seemed perfectly at ease. Former British prime minister Winston Churchill was also hailed as one of the twentieth century's great orators. Amazingly, both Kennedy and Churchill were extremely fearful of speaking in public. The list of famous people who admit to feeling nervous before they speak may surprise you: Barbra Streisand, Al Roker, Andrea Bocelli, Mariah Carey, Katie Couric, Julia Roberts, Conan

O'Brien, Jay Leno, Carly Simon, and Oprah Winfrey have all reported feeling anxious and jittery before speaking in public.[38] Almost everyone experiences some anxiety when speaking. It is unrealistic to try to eliminate speech anxiety. Instead, your goal should be to manage your nervousness so that it does not create so much internal noise that it keeps you from speaking effectively.

You Can Use Your Anxiety Extra adrenaline, increased blood flow, pupil dilation, increased endorphins to block pain, increased heart rate, and other physical changes caused by anxiety improve your energy level and help you function better than you might otherwise. Your heightened state of readiness can actually help you speak better, especially if you view the public-speaking event positively instead of negatively. Speakers who label their increased feelings of physiological arousal as "nervousness" are more likely to feel anxious and fearful, but the same physiological feelings could also be labeled as "enthusiasm" or "excitement." You are more likely to gain the benefits of the extra help your brain is trying to give you if you think positively rather than negatively about speaking in public. Don't let your initial anxiety convince you that you cannot speak effectively.

How to Build Your Confidence

"Is there anything I can do to help manage my nervousness and anxiety when I give a speech?" you may wonder. Both contemporary research and centuries of experience from seasoned public speakers suggest some practical advice.[39] We summarize their suggestions in Table 1.2 below.

Know Your Audience Know to whom you will be speaking, and learn as much about your audience as you can. The more you can anticipate the kind of reaction your listeners will have to your speech, the more comfortable you will be in delivering your message.[40] As you are preparing your speech, periodically visualize your listeners'

Explore at **MyCommunicationLab**
Activity: "Overcoming Nervousness"

Explore at **MyCommunicationLab**
Profile: "Personal Report of Speaking Anxiety"

TABLE 1.2 TIPS FOR BUILDING CONFIDENCE

What to Do Before You Speak

- Don't procrastinate; give yourself plenty of time to work on your speech.
- Learn as much as possible about your audience.
- Select a topic you are interested in or know something about.
- Be prepared and well organized.
- Be familiar with how you will begin and end your speech.
- Rehearse aloud while standing, and try to re-create the speech environment.
- Use breathing techniques to help you relax.
- Channel nervous energy.
- Visualize being successful.
- Give yourself a mental pep talk.

What to Do as You Speak

- Focus on connecting your message to your audience rather than on your fear.
- Look for and respond to positive listener support for you and your message.

What to Do After You Speak

- Focus on your accomplishments and success rather than only on reviewing what you may have done wrong.
- Seek other speaking opportunities to gain experience and confidence.

response to your message. Consider their needs, goals, and hopes as you prepare your message. Be audience-centered rather than speaker-centered. Don't keep telling yourself how nervous you are going to be.[41] An audience-centered speaker focuses on connecting to listeners rather than focusing on fear. Chapter 4 provides a detailed approach to analyzing and adapting to your audience.

Don't Procrastinate　One research study confirmed what you probably already know: Speakers who are more apprehensive about speaking put off working on their speeches, in contrast to speakers who are less anxious about public speaking.[42] The lack of thorough preparation often results in a poor speech performance, reinforcing the speaker's perception that public speaking is difficult. Realize that if you fear that you'll be nervous when speaking, you'll tend to put off working on your speech. Take charge by tackling the speech assignment early, giving yourself every chance to be successful. Don't let your fear freeze you into inaction. Prepare early.

Select an Appropriate Topic　You will feel less nervous if you talk about something that is familiar to you or with which you have had some personal experience. Your comfort with the subject of your speech will be reflected in your delivery.

Judy Shepard, whose son Matthew Shepard was brutally murdered in 1998 for being gay, is a frequent conference speaker and ardent proponent of gay rights. Always apprehensive about giving a speech during her college years, she said, "Speech class was my worst nightmare."[43] But today, because of her fervent belief in her cause, she gives hundreds of speeches. "This is my survival; this is how I deal with losing Matt," she explained to students at South Lakes High School in Reston, Virginia.[44] Talking about something you are passionate about can boost your motivation and help you manage your fear. In the chapters ahead, we offer more detailed guidance about how to select a topic.

Prepare　One formula applies to most speaking situations you are likely to experience: The better prepared you are, the less anxiety you will experience. Being prepared means that you have researched your topic and practiced your speech several times before you deliver it. One research study found clear evidence that rehearsing your speech reduces your apprehension.[45] Being prepared also means that you have developed a logically coherent outline rather than one that is disorganized and difficult to follow. Transitional phrases and summaries can help you present a well-structured, easy-to-understand message.

Be Organized　One of the key skills you'll learn in *Public Speaking: An Audience-Centered Approach* is the value of developing a well-organized message. For most North American listeners, speeches should have a beginning, middle, and end and should follow a logical outline pattern. Communication researcher Melanie Booth-Butterfield suggests that speakers can better manage their apprehension if they rely on the rules and structures of a speaking assignment, including following a clear outline pattern, when preparing and delivering a speech.[46] Her research showed that anxiety about a speech assignment decreased and confidence increased when speakers closely followed the directions and rules for developing a speech. So, to help manage your apprehension about speaking, listen carefully to what the specific assignment is, ask for additional information if you're unclear about the task, and develop a well-organized message.

Know Your Introduction and Your Conclusion　You are likely to feel the most anxious during the opening moments of your speech. Therefore, it is a good idea to have a clear plan for how you will start your speech. We aren't suggesting memorizing your introduction word for word, but you should have it well in mind. Being familiar with your introduction will help you feel more comfortable about the entire speech.

If you know how you will end your speech, you will have a safe harbor in case you lose your place. If you need to end your speech prematurely, a well-delivered conclusion can permit you to make a graceful exit.

Make Practice Real When you practice your speech, pretend that you are giving the speech to the audience you will actually address. Stand up. Imagine what the room looks like, or consider rehearsing in the room in which you will deliver your speech. What will you be wearing? Practice rising from your seat, walking to the front of the room, and beginning your speech. Practice aloud, rather than just saying the speech to yourself. A realistic rehearsal will increase your confidence when your moment to speak arrives.

Breathe One symptom of nervousness is a change in your breathing and heart rate. Nervous speakers tend to take short, shallow breaths. To help break the anxiety-induced breathing pattern, consider taking a few slow, deep breaths before you rise to speak. No one will detect that you are taking deep breaths if you just slowly inhale and exhale before beginning your speech. Besides breathing deeply, try to relax your entire body. Deep breathing and visualizing yourself as successful will help you relax.

Channel Your Nervous Energy One common symptom of being nervous is shaky hands and wobbly knees. As we noted earlier, what triggers this jiggling is the extra boost of adrenaline your body is giving you—and the resulting energy that has to go somewhere. Your muscles may move whether you intend them to or not. Take control by channeling that energy. One way to release tension is to take a leisurely walk before you arrive wherever you will be speaking. Taking a slow, relaxing walk can help calm you down and use up some of your excess energy. Once you are seated and waiting to speak, grab the edge of your chair (without calling attention to what you are doing) and gently squeeze the chair to release tension. No one needs to know you're doing this—just unobtrusively squeeze and relax, squeeze and relax. You can also purposely tense and then release your muscles in your legs and arms while you're seated. You don't need to look like you're going into convulsions; just impercepti-bly tense and relax your muscles to burn energy. One more tip: You may want to keep both feet on the floor and gently wiggle your toes rather than sit with your legs crossed. Crossing your legs can sometimes cause one leg or foot to go to sleep. Keep-ing your feet on the floor and slightly moving your toes can ensure that all of you will be wide awake and ready to go when it's your turn to speak.

As you wait to be introduced, focus on remaining calm. Act calm to feel calm. Give yourself a pep talk; tense and release your muscles to help you relax. Then, when your name is called, walk to the front of the room in a calm and collected manner. Before you present your opening, attention-catching sentence, take a moment to look for a friendly, supportive face. Think calm and act calm to feel calm.

Physical symptoms of nervousness are signs that your body is trying to help you meet the challenge of public speaking. Labeling your body's arousal as excitement can help build your confidence as you speak, as can the other tips described in this chapter.

Photo: Cultura Limited/SuperStock

CONFIDENTLY CONNECTING WITH YOUR AUDIENCE

Begin with the End in Mind

One of the habits cited by the late Stephen Covey in his influential book *The 7 Habits of Highly Successful People* is "Begin with the end in mind."[52] From the moment you begin thinking about preparing and presenting your speech, picture yourself being confident and successful. If you find your anxiety level rising at any point in the speech-preparation process, change your mental picture of yourself and imagine that you've completed your speech and the audience has given you a rousing round of applause. Begin imagining success rather than focusing on your fear. Using the principles, skills, and strategies we discuss in this book will help you develop the habit of speech success.

Visualize Your Success Studies suggest that one of the best ways to control anxiety is to imagine a scene in which you exhibit skill and comfort as a public speaker.[47] As you imagine giving your speech, picture yourself walking confidently to the front and delivering your well-prepared opening remarks. Visualize yourself giving the entire speech as a controlled, confident speaker. Imagine yourself calm and in command. Positive visualization is effective because it boosts your confidence by helping you see yourself as a more confident, accomplished speaker.[48]

Research has found that it's even helpful to look at a picture of someone confidently and calmly delivering a speech while visualizing yourself giving the speech; such positive visualization helps manage your apprehension.[49] You could even make a simple drawing of someone speaking confidently.[50] As you look at the image, imagine that it's you confidently giving the speech. It's helpful if the visual image you're looking at is a person you can identify with— someone who looks like you or someone you believe is more like you than not.[51]

Give Yourself a Mental Pep Talk You may think that people who talk to themselves are slightly loony. But silently giving yourself a pep talk can give you confidence and take your mind off your nervousness. There is some evidence that simply believing that a technique can reduce your apprehension may, in fact, help reduce your apprehension.[53] Giving yourself a positive message such as "I can do this" may be a productive way to manage your anxiety. Here's a sample mental speech you could deliver to yourself right before you speak: "I know this stuff better than anyone else. I've practiced it. My message is well organized. I know I can do it. I'll do a good job." Research provides evidence that people who entertain thoughts of worry and failure don't do themselves any favors.[54] When you feel yourself getting nervous, use positive messages to replace negative thoughts that may creep into your consciousness. Examples include the following:

Negative Thought	Positive Self-Talk
I'm going to forget what I'm supposed to say.	I've practiced this speech many times. I've got notes to prompt me. If I lose my place, no one will know I'm not following my outline.
So many people are looking at me.	I can do this! My listeners want me to do a good job. I'll seek out friendly faces when I feel nervous.
People think I'm dull and boring.	I've got some good examples. I can talk to people one-on-one, and people seem to like me.
I just can't go through with this.	I have talked to people all my life. I've given presentations in classes for years. I can get through this because I've rehearsed and I'm prepared.

Focus on Your Message, Not on Your Fear The more you think about being anxious about speaking, the more you will increase your level of anxiety. Instead, think about what you are going to say. In the few minutes before you address your listeners, mentally review your major ideas, your introduction, and your conclusion. Focus on your ideas rather than on your fear.

Look for Positive Support Evidence suggests that if you think you see audience members looking critical of you or your message, you may feel more apprehensive and nervous when you speak.[55] Stated more positively, when you are aware of positive audience support, you will feel more confident and less nervous. To reiterate our previous advice: It is important to be audience-centered. Although you may face some audience members who won't respond positively to you or your message, the overwhelming majority of listeners will be positive. Looking for positive, reinforcing feedback and finding it can help you feel more confident as a speaker. One study found that speakers experienced less apprehension if they had a support group or a small "learning community" that provided positive feedback and reinforcement.[56] This research finding has implications for you as a speaker and listener. When you have a speaking assignment, work with others to provide support both as you prepare and when you present your speech. When you're listening to speakers in your communication class, help them by being a positive, supportive listener: Provide eye contact and offer additional positive nonverbal support, such as nodding in agreement and maintaining a positive but sincere facial expression. You can help your fellow students feel more comfortable as speakers, and they can do the same for you; watch for their support. One study found that nonnative speakers may feel anxious and nervous because English is not their native language; so providing positive and supportive feedback is especially important when you know a speaker is quite nervous.[57]

Seek Speaking Opportunities The more experience you gain as a public speaker, the less nervous you will feel.[58] As you develop a track record of successfully delivering speeches, you will have more confidence.[59] This course in public speaking will give you opportunities to enhance both your confidence and your skill through frequent practice. Researchers have found that those speakers who were the most nervous at the beginning of a public-speaking class experienced the greatest decreases in nervousness by the end of the class.[60] Another research study found that students who took a basic public-speaking course later reported having less apprehension and more satisfaction about speaking than students who had not had such a course.[61] To add to the practice you will get in this class, consider joining organizations and clubs such as Toastmasters, an organization dedicated to improving public-speaking skills by providing a supportive group of people to help you polish your speaking and overcome your anxiety.

Focus on What You Have Accomplished, Not on Your Fear When you conclude your speech, you may be tempted to fixate on your fear. You might amplify in your own mind the nervousness you felt and think everyone could see how nervous you looked. Resist that temptation. When you finish your speech, tell yourself something positive to celebrate your accomplishment. Say to yourself, "I did it! I spoke and people listened." Don't replay your mental image of yourself as nervous and fearful. Instead, mentally replay your success in communicating with your listeners. There is evidence that as you continue to gain experience presenting speeches you will gain confidence and have a greater willingness to communicate. So when you finish your speech, congratulate yourself on having achieved your goal knowing that your success is likely to result in more success in the future.[62]

Because managing communication apprehension is such an important skill for most public speakers, in each chapter of this book we'll remind you of tips to help you enhance your confidence. Look for techniques of *confidently connecting with your audience* in the margins.

RECAP

BUILD CONFIDENCE

- Label your physical arousal as *excitement*.
- Understand and plan for your anxiety style.
- Focus on your audience and message.
- Don't wait; prepare early.
- Follow guidelines for speech assignments carefully.
- Make practice as real as possible.
- Breathe and exercise to channel nervous energy.
- Visualize success and use mental pep talks.
- Look for support from listeners.
- Form a "support community" of classmates.
- Congratulate yourself after you speak.

STUDY GUIDE
REVIEW, APPLY, AND ASSESS

WHAT IS PUBLIC SPEAKING?

1.1 Compare and contrast public speaking and conversation.

Public speaking—presenting a message to an audience—builds upon other communication skills. Public speaking is similar to conversation in that it requires focus, expression, and adapting to an audience. However, public speaking is more planned, more formal, and has more defined roles for speakers than conversation.

WHY STUDY PUBLIC SPEAKING?

1.2 Explain why it is important to study public speaking.

Key Term

Since you are likely to be called on to speak in public at various times throughout your life, skill in public speaking can empower you. It can also help you secure employment or advance your career.

Key Terms

Thinking Critically

How do you think this course in public speaking can help you with your career goals? With your personal life?

Assessing Your Audience-Centered Speaking Skill

Review Table 1.1 on page 4. Rate yourself, using a scale of 1 to 5 (1 = poor; 5 = excellent), on the skills listed in the table. How does your assessment of your spoken communication skills compare with other skills listed in the table?

THE COMMUNICATION PROCESS

1.3 Sketch and explain a model that illustrates the components and the process of communication.

Like other forms of communication, public speaking is a process. Different theorists have explained the communication process as (1) an action, by which a source transmits a message through a channel to a receiver; (2) an interaction, in which the receiver's feedback and the context of the communication add to the action; and (3) a transaction, in which source and receiver simultaneously send messages to build a shared meaning.

Key Terms

Thinking Critically

Reflect on the most recent public-speaking situation in which you were an audience member. Identify the specific elements in the communication model presented on page 5. If the speaker was effective, what elements of the model explain the effectiveness (for example, the message was interesting and there was little noise)? Or if the speaker was ineffective, which elements in the model explain why the speaker was ineffective?

Assessing Your Audience-Centered Speaking Skill

Give an example of internal noise that is affecting you as you read this question. What could a public speaker do or say that would help you focus on the speaker instead of the internal noise that may distract you from the speaker's message?

THE RICH HERITAGE OF PUBLIC SPEAKING

1.4 Discuss in brief the history of public speaking.

The study of public speaking goes back more than 2,000 years. As you develop your own public-speaking skills, your study will be guided by experience and knowledge gained over centuries of making and studying speeches. Today you are likely to hear speeches presented on TV, YouTube, Skype, or by other video means.

Key Terms

Thinking Ethically

Declamation is defined in this chapter as "the delivery of an already famous address." Is it ethical to deliver a speech written and/or delivered by someone else? Explain your answer.

Assessing Your Audience-Centered Speaking Skill

Identify a famous public speaker, perhaps someone in politics, community service, or a religious leader, who you believe is an excellent public speaker. What factors make this person an effective speaker? Which of those qualities would you like to develop to enhance your own speaking skill?

IMPROVING YOUR CONFIDENCE AS A SPEAKER

1.5   Use several techniques to become a more confident speaker.

Some beginning public speakers feel nervous at even the thought of giving a speech. Don't be surprised if you feel more nervous than you look to others. Remember that almost every speaker experiences some nervousness and that some anxiety can be useful. Specific suggestions to help you manage your apprehension include being prepared and knowing your audience, imagining the speech environment when you rehearse, and using relaxation techniques such as visualization, deep breathing, and focusing thoughts away from your fears.

Thinking Critically

Mike Roberts, president of his fraternity, is preparing to address the university academic council in an effort to persuade council members to support establishment of a Greek housing zone on campus. This is his first major task as president, and he is understandably nervous about his responsibility. What advice would you give to help him manage his nervousness?

Assessing Your Audience-Centered Speaking Skill

Take a quiz, available at www.jamescmccroskey.com/measures/prca24.htm, to assess your level of communication apprehension. At the end of the course, reassess your level of communication apprehension to see if the course has had an effect on your overall level of communication apprehension.

Explore at **MyCommunicationLab**
Speaker's Workshop: Improving Your Confidence as a Public Speaker

2 PRESENTING YOUR FIRST SPEECH

Arthur Segal (1875–1944), *The Speaker*, 1912. Collection of Henri Nannen, Emden, Germany. Photo: Erich Lessing/Art Resource, N.Y.

Listen to Chapter 2 at **MyCommunicationLab**

If all my talents and powers were to be taken from me by some inscrutable Providence, and I had my choice of keeping but one, I would unhesitatingly ask to be allowed to keep the Power of Speaking, for through it, I would quickly recover all the rest.

—Daniel Webster

Unless you have some prior experience in higher mathematics, you may not have the foggiest notion of what calculus is when you first take a class in that subject. But when you tell people that you are taking a public-speaking class, most at least have some idea of what a public speaker does. A public speaker talks while others listen. You hear speeches almost every day. Increasingly many of the speeches you hear are presented via electronic media. Online, whether in a YouTube video, as a TED Talk, or even in a video on Facebook, you are likely to encounter speeches. Yet even with the ubiquitous presence of social media, you undoubtedly experience many presentations live and in person, in your classes or where you work. Although you have heard countless speeches, you may still have questions about how a speaker prepares and presents a speech.

In Chapter 1, we discussed the importance of learning to speak publicly and described the components of effective communication. We also presented tips and strategies for becoming a confident speaker. In this chapter, we will preview the preparation and presentation skills that you will learn in this course. Undoubtedly, you will be given a speech assignment early in your public-speaking course. Although it would be ideal to read *Public Speaking: An Audience-Centered Approach* from cover to cover before tackling your first speech, doing so would be impractical. To help you begin, we present this chapter, a step-by-step overview designed to serve as the scaffolding on which to build your skill in public speaking.

Consider Your Audience

2.1 Explain why it is important to be audience-centered during each step of the speechmaking process.

You've been speaking to others since you were 2 years old. Talking to people has seemed such a natural part of your life that you may never have stopped to analyze the process. But as you think about preparing your first speech for your speech class, you may wonder, "What do I do first?" Your assignment may be to introduce yourself to the class. Or your first assignment may be a brief informative talk—to describe something to your audience. Regardless of the specific assignment, however, you need some idea of how to begin.

As we noted earlier, you don't need to read this book cover to cover before you give your first speech. But it is useful to have an overview of the various steps and skills involved in giving a speech. To help you see this overview, Figure 2.1 on page 22 diagrams the various tasks involved in the speechmaking process, emphasizing the audience as the central concern at every step of the process. We'll refer to this audience-centered model of public speaking throughout the text. *To emphasize the importance of being audience-centered, we have placed a smaller version of this model in the margins throughout the text to draw your attention to information that discusses the importance of always being mindful of your audience.* (See the icon in the margin.) When you see the icon, it means we're discussing the central theme of this book: **Always make choices in designing and delivering your speech with your audience in mind.**

We will preview our discussion of the speechmaking process with the central element: considering your audience. We will then discuss each step of the process, starting with selecting and narrowing a topic, and moving clockwise around the model, examining each interrelated step.

Why should the central focus of public speaking be the audience? Why is it not topic selection, outlining, or research? The simple truth is that your audience

FIGURE 2.1 The reminder to consider the audience is at the center of this model of the speechmaking process because your audience influences your work on each task involved in designing and presenting a speech. As we discuss each task in depth throughout the book, we also use a smaller image of this model to flag information and advice that remind you to consider your audience.

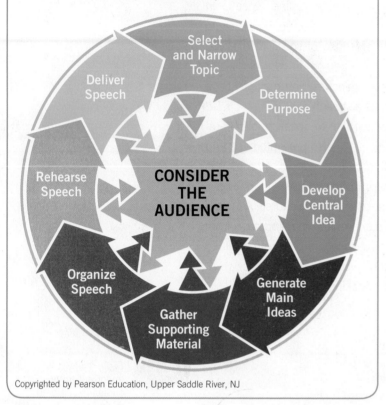

Copyrighted by Pearson Education, Upper Saddle River, NJ

influences the topic you choose and every later step of the speechmaking process. Your selection of topic, purpose, and even major ideas should be based on a thorough understanding of your listeners. In a very real sense, your audience "writes" the speech.[1] Think of this first step of speechmaking less as a "step"—something you do once and go on to the next step—and more as the beginning of a continuous process. Whether pondering what to speak about or delivering your concluding remarks, we suggest that you never stop thinking about the reason you are speaking—to communicate with your audience.

Gather and Analyze Information about Your Audience

To be audience-centered, you should first identify and then analyze information about your listeners. For example, just by looking at your audience in your speech class, you will be able to determine such basic information as approximately how old they are and the percentage of men and women in your audience; you also know that they are all students in a public-speaking class. To determine less obvious information, you may need to ask them questions or design a short questionnaire.

As we've noted, audience analysis is not something you do only at the beginning of preparing your speech. It is an ongoing activity. The characteristics of your audience influence the choices you make about your speech at every step of the speech-preparation process. That's why, in the audience-centered speech model, arrows connect the center of the diagram with each stage of designing and delivering your speech. At any point during the preparation and delivery of your message, you may need to revise your thinking or your material if you learn new information about your audience. So the model has arrows pointing both ways across the boundary between the central element and each step in the process. Chapter 5 includes a comprehensive discussion of the principles and strategies involved in analyzing your audience.

Being audience-centered involves making decisions about the content and delivery of your speech *before* you speak, based on knowledge of your audience's values, beliefs, and knowledge. It also means being aware of your audience's responses *during* the speech so that you can make appropriate adjustments.

When you speak to a live audience, you will be looking your listeners directly in the eye and you'll have the benefit of their immediate reactions, whether it be their rapt attention characterized by returned eye contact, a slight forward lean and no fidgeting, or the unfocused stares that signal their inattentiveness. Speaking in person permits you to modify your message on the spot so that you can achieve your goal. When you use video technology to deliver your speech, you often can't see your listeners, especially if you record the speech for listeners to see and hear later, so it's more challenging to reactively modify your talk during your presentation. For video or online presentations where you can't see or hear your audience, you must, instead, do your best to *anticipate* how listeners may respond. Selecting examples and illustrations that you think will gain and maintain their attention, organizing your message for maximum clarity, and delivering your message with eye contact, appropriate vocal variation, and meaningful gestures can help you connect to your virtual audience.

Consider the Culturally Diverse Backgrounds of Your Audience

You need not give speeches in foreign countries to recognize the importance of adapting to different cultural expectations of individual audience members. People in the United States are highly diverse in terms of their culture, age, ethnicity, and religious tradition. Consider the various cultural backgrounds of your classmates. How many different cultural and ethnic traditions do they represent? Several years ago, the typical college student was likely to be a recent high school graduate between the ages of 18 and 21. Today your classmates probably reflect a much wider range of ages, backgrounds, and experiences. You will want to adjust not only your delivery style but also your topic, pattern of organization, and the examples you use, according to who your audience members are and what topics they are interested in.

Different cultures have radically different expectations about public speaking. In Russia, for example, speakers have a "no frills" approach that emphasizes content over delivery. A presentation that seems perfectly sensible and acceptable to a U.S. businessperson who is accustomed to straightforward, problem-oriented logic may seem shockingly rude to a Chinese businessperson who expects more circuitous, less overtly purposeful rhetoric. And some African American audiences "come to participate in a speech event,"[2] expecting the speaker to generate audience response through rhythmic "call response formulas"[3] from the African American oral tradition. When one of this book's authors taught public speaking for several semesters in the Bahamas, however, he shocked students by suggesting that they should achieve a conversational, informal delivery style. Bahamian audiences, he quickly discovered, expect formal oratory from their speakers, very much as U.S. audiences in the nineteenth century preferred the grandiloquence of Stephen A. Douglas to the quieter, homespun style of Abraham Lincoln. So your author had to embellish his own style when he taught the Bahamian class.

Being sensitive to your audience and adapting your message accordingly will serve you well not only when addressing listeners with cultural backgrounds different from your own but also in all types of situations. If you learn to analyze your audience and adapt to their expectations, you can apply these skills in numerous settings: interviewing for a job via Skype, delivering a business presentation, or speaking to the city council—even while proposing marriage.

Watch at **MyCommunicationLab**
Video: "Intercultural Listening"

RECAP

CONSIDER YOUR AUDIENCE

- Keep your audience in mind at every step of preparing your speech.
- Gather and analyze as much information as you can.
- Be sensitive to the cultural diversity of your audience.

Select and Narrow Your Topic

2.2 Select and narrow an appropriate topic for a speech.

While keeping your audience foremost in mind, your next task is to determine what you will talk about and to limit your topic to fit the constraints of your speaking assignment. Pay special attention to the guidelines your instructor gives you for your assignment.

If your first speech assignment is to introduce yourself to the class, your **speech topic** has been selected for you—*you* are the topic. It is not uncommon to be asked to speak on a specific subject. Often, though, you will be asked to speak but not given a topic. The task of selecting and narrowing a topic will be yours. Choosing or finding a topic on which to speak can be frustrating. "What should I talk about?" can become a haunting question.

speech topic
The key focus of the content of a speech

Although there is no single answer to the question of what you should talk about, you may discover a topic by asking three standard questions:

- "Who is the audience?"
- "What are my interests, talents, and experiences?"
- "What is the occasion?"

It's a good idea to give yourself plenty of time to select and narrow your topic. Don't wait until the last minute to ponder what you might talk about. One of the most important things you can do to be an effective speaker is to start preparing your speech well in advance of your speaking date. One research study identified some very practical advice: *The amount of time you spend preparing for your speech is one of the best predictors of a good grade on your speech.*[4]

Who Is the Audience?

Read at **MyCommunicationLab**
Learning From Great Speakers:
Abraham Lincoln

Your topic may grow from basic knowledge of your audience. For example, if you know that your audience members are primarily between the ages of 25 and 40, this information should help you select a topic of interest to people who are probably working and either seeking partners or raising families. An older audience may lead you to other concerns or issues: "Will Social Security be there when I need it?" or "The advantages of belonging to the American Association of Retired Persons."

What Are My Interests, Talents, and Experiences?

Rather than racking your brain for exotic topics and outlandish ideas, examine your own background. Your choice of major in college, your hobbies, and your travels are sources for topic ideas. What issues do you feel strongly about? Reflect on jobs you've held, news stories that catch your interest when surfing the Internet, events in your hometown, your career goals, or interesting people you have met. Chapter 6 contains a discussion of specific strategies for finding topics.

Once you have chosen your topic, narrow it to fit the time limits for your talk. If you've been asked to deliver a ten-minute speech, the topic "how to find counseling help on campus" would be more manageable than the topic "how to make the most of your college experience." As our model suggests, your audience should be foremost in your mind when you work on your topic.

Your recent snowshoeing trip might provide the basis for a good speech topic.

Photo: ARochau/Fotolia

What Is the Occasion?

Besides your audience, you should consider the occasion for the speech when choosing a topic. A commencement address calls for a different topic, for example, than does a speech to a model rail-road club. Another aspect of the occasion you'll want to consider is the physical setting of your speech. Will you be speaking to people seated in chairs arranged in a circle, will your listeners be sitting around a table, watching you via a webcast or teleconference, or will you be standing in front of rows of people? The physical sur-roundings, including whether your speech is communicated via media, as well as the occasion affect the degree of formality your audience expects in your choice of topics.

Determine Your Purpose

You might think that once you have your topic, you are ready to start the research process. Before you do that, however, you need to decide on both a general and a specific purpose.

2.3 Differentiate between a general speech purpose and a specific speech purpose.

Determine Your General Purpose

Your **general purpose** is the overarching goal of your speech. There are three types of general purposes for speeches: to *inform*, to *persuade*, and to *entertain*.

When you inform, you teach, define, illustrate, clarify, or elaborate on a topic. The primary objective of class lectures, seminars, and workshops is to inform. Chapter 13 will show you how to construct an effective speech with an informative purpose.

A speech to persuade seeks to change or reinforce listeners' attitudes, beliefs, values, or behavior. Ads on TV, radio, and pop-up commercials on the Internet; ser-mons; political speeches and sales presentations are examples of messages designed to persuade. To be a skilled persuader, you need to be sensitive to your audience's attitudes (likes and dislikes) toward you and your topic. Chapters 14 and 15 will dis-cuss principles and strategies for preparing persuasive speeches.

To entertain listeners is the third general purpose of a speech. After-dinner speeches and comic monologues are mainly intended as entertainment. As Chapter 16 describes, often the key to an effective entertaining speech lies in your choice of stories, examples, and illustrations, as well as in your delivery. Appendix B includes examples of speeches designed to inform, persuade, and entertain.

Determine Your Specific Purpose

Your **specific purpose** is a concise statement indicating what you want your listeners to be able to do, remember, or feel when you finish your speech. A specific-purpose statement identifies the precise, measurable audience response you desire. Here again, we emphasize the importance of focusing on the audience as you develop your specific purpose. Perhaps you have had the experience of listening to a speaker and wondering, "What's the point? I know he's talking about education, but I'm not sure where he's going with this subject." You may have understood the speaker's general purpose, but the specific one wasn't clear. If you can't figure out what the specific purpose is, it is probably because the speaker does not know either.

general purpose
The overarching goal of a speech—to inform, persuade, or entertain

specific purpose
A concise statement of the desired audience response, indicating what you want your listeners to remember, feel, or do when you finish speaking

DETERMINE YOUR PURPOSE

Develop Your General Purpose

To inform	To share information by teaching, defining, illustrating, describing, or explaining
To persuade	To change or reinforce an attitude, belief, value, or behavior
To entertain	To amuse with humor, stories, or illustrations

Develop Your Specific Purpose

What do you want your audience to remember, do, or feel when you finish your speech?

General Purpose	*Specific Purpose*
To inform	At the end of my speech, the audience will be able to identify three counseling facilities on campus and describe the counseling services each facility offers to students.
To persuade	At the end of my speech, the audience will visit the counseling facilities on campus.
To entertain	At the end of my speech, the audience will be amused by the series of misunderstandings I created when I began making inquiries about career advisors on campus.

Deciding on a specific purpose is not difficult once you have narrowed your topic: "At the end of my speech, the class will be able to identify three counseling facilities on campus and describe the best way to get help at each one." Notice that this purpose is phrased in terms of what you would like the audience to be able to *do* by the end of the speech. Your specific purpose should be a fine-tuned, audience-centered goal. For an informative speech, you may simply want your audience to restate an idea, define new words, or identify, describe, or explain something. In a persuasive speech, you may try to rouse your listeners to take a class, buy something, change a bad habit, or vote for someone. A persuasive speech can also reinforce a behavior as well as an attitude, belief, or value.

Once you have formulated your specific purpose, write it down and keep it before you as you read and gather ideas for your talk. Your specific purpose should guide your research and help you choose supporting materials that are related to your audience. As you continue to work on your speech, you may even decide to modify your purpose. But if you have an objective in mind at all times as you move through the preparation stage, you will stay on track.

2.4 Develop a sentence that captures the central idea of a speech.

Develop Your Central Idea

You should now be able to write the **central idea** of your speech. Whereas your statement of a specific purpose indicates what you want your audience to do when you have finished your speech, your central idea identifies the essence of your message. Think of it as a one-sentence summary of your speech. Here's an example:

TOPIC:	The Wheat Belly diet
GENERAL PURPOSE:	To inform
SPECIFIC PURPOSE:	At the end of my speech, the audience will be able to identify the three key elements in the Wheat Belly diet.
CENTRAL IDEA:	The Wheat Belly diet is based on reducing the amount of processed foods that you eat, avoiding all processed flour, and increasing the amount of exercise you get.

Here's another way to think about how to develop your central idea sentence. Imagine that you have just finished presenting your speech and you get into an elevator. Someone who missed hearing your talk says, "Oh, I'm sorry I missed your speech. What did you say?" Between the second floor and the first, you have only 15 seconds to summarize your message. You might say, "I said there are two keys to parent and child communication: First, make time for communication, and second, listen effectively." That brief recap is your central idea sentence. To clarify the difference between your purpose and the central idea sentence: Your purpose sentence is what you want the audience to be able to *do*; the central idea sentence is your speech in a nutshell—your speech in one sentence.

central idea
A one-sentence summary of the speech content

Generate the Main Ideas

In the words of columnist H. V. Prochnow, "A good many people can make a speech, but saying something is more difficult." Effective speakers are good thinkers; they say something. They know how to play with words and thoughts to develop their **main ideas**. The ancient Romans called this skill **invention**—the ability to develop or discover ideas that result in new insights or new approaches to old problems. The Roman orator Cicero called this aspect of speaking the process of "finding out what [a speaker] should say."

Once you have an appropriate topic, a specific purpose, and a well-worded central idea down on paper, the next task is to identify the major divisions of your speech or key points that you wish to develop. To determine how to subdivide your central idea into key points, ask these three questions:

1. Does the central idea have logical divisions?
2. Can you think of several reasons the central idea is true?
3. Can you support the central idea with a series of steps?

Let's look at each of these questions along with examples of how to apply them.

Does the Central Idea Have Logical Divisions?

If the central idea is "There are three ways to interpret the stock market page of your local newspaper or financial website," your speech can be organized into three parts. You will simply identify the three ways to interpret stock market information and use each as a major point. A speech about the art of applying theatrical makeup could also be organized into three parts: eye makeup, face makeup, and hair coloring. Looking for logical divisions in your speech topic is the simplest way to determine key points.

Can You Think of Several Reasons the Central Idea Is True?

If your central idea is "New legislation is needed to ensure that U.S. citizens' privacy is protected," each major point of your speech could be a reason you think new privacy laws are needed. For example, new privacy laws are needed because (1) more retail stores are collecting information about the products we buy, (2) our Internet surfing habits may be traceable through the search engines we use, and (3) more companies and political parties have access to "Big Data" in order to develop specific persuasive messages tailored to individuals. If your central idea is a statement that something is good or bad, you should focus on the reasons your central idea is true. Use these reasons as the main ideas of the speech.

main ideas
The key points of a speech

invention
The development or discovery of ideas and insights

Can You Support the Central Idea with a Series of Steps?

Suppose your central idea is "Running for a campus office is easy to do." Your speech could be developed around a series of steps, telling your listeners what to do first, second, and third to get elected. Speeches describing a personal experience or explaining how to build or make something can usually be organized in a step-by-step progression.

Your time limit, topic, and the information gleaned from your research will determine how many major ideas will be in your speech. A three- to five-minute speech might have only two major ideas. In

---

RECAP

CENTRAL IDEA AND MAIN IDEAS

Develop Your Central Idea
Write a single sentence that summarizes your speech.

Use Your Central Idea to Develop Your Main Ideas
Ask yourself:
- Does my central idea have logical divisions?
- Are there several reasons my central idea is true?
- Can my central idea be divided into a series of steps?

If the central idea of your speech is, "You can conduct your own home energy audit," you might discuss energy audits of various rooms of a home or you might present a series of steps in conducting a home energy audit.

Photo: auremar/Fotolia

a very short speech, you may develop only one major idea with examples, illustrations, and other forms of support. Don't spend time trying to divide a topic that does not need to be divided. In Chapters 6 and 8, we will discuss how to generate major ideas and organize them.

2.6 Describe several types of supporting material that could be used to support speech ideas.

Gather Supporting Material

With your main idea or ideas in mind, your next job is to gather material to support them—facts, examples, definitions, and quotations from others that illustrate, amplify, clarify, provide evidence, or tell a story. Here, as always when preparing your speech, the importance of being an audience-centered speaker can't be overemphasized. There's an old saying that an ounce of illustration is worth a ton of talk. If a speech is boring, it is usually because the speaker has not chosen supporting material that is relevant or interesting to the audience. Don't just give people data; connect facts to their lives. As one sage quipped, "Data is not information any more than 50 tons of cement is a skyscraper."[5]

Gather Interesting Supporting Material

Supporting material should be personal and concrete, and it should appeal to your listeners' senses.

Don Hewitt, the founding and longtime producer of TV's popular and award-winning *60 Minutes*, was repeatedly asked by young journalists, "What's the secret of your success as a communicator?" Hewitt's answer: "Tell me a story." Everyone likes to hear a good story. As Hewitt noted, the Bible does more than describe the nature of good and evil; it masterfully tells stories about Job, Noah, David, and others.[6]

Tell stories based on your own experiences and provide vivid descriptions of things that are tangible so that your audience can visualize what you are talking about. Besides sight, supporting material can appeal to touch, hearing, smell, and taste.

The more senses you trigger with words, the more interesting your talk will be. Descriptions such as "the rough, splintery surface of weather-beaten wood" or "the sweet, cool, refreshing flavor of cherry Jell-O" evoke sensory images. In addition, relating abstract statistics to something tangible can help communicate your ideas more clearly. For example, if you say Frito-Lay sells 2.6 billion pounds of snack food each year, your listeners will have a hazy idea that 2.6 billion pounds is a lot of corn and potato chips, but if you add that 2.6 billion pounds is triple the weight of the Empire State Building, you've made your point more memorably.[7] Or, rather than simply saying that 4,000 teens die each year in car accidents, say this: "If 12 fully loaded jumbo jets crashed every year, something would be done about it. Every year, more than 4,000 teens die in car crashes—the equivalent of 12 large plane crashes." Relating statistics to something listeners can visualize makes the point more effectively.[8] We will discuss in Chapter 8 the variety of supporting material available to you.

How does a public speaker find interesting and relevant supporting material? By developing good research skills. President Woodrow Wilson once admitted, "I use not only all the brains I have, but all that I can borrow." Although it is important to have good ideas, it is equally important to know how to build on existing knowledge. You can probably think of a topic or two about which you consider yourself an expert. Chances are that if you gave a short speech about a sport that you had practiced for years or about a recent trip that you took, you would not need to gather much additional information. But sooner or later, you will need to do some research on a topic in order to speak on it intelligently to an audience. If your college classes up to this point have required only brief forays gathering information via the Internet or researching in the library, that experience is about to change! By the time you have given several speeches in this course, you will have learned to use a number of resources: your library's computerized card catalog, various electronic databases that your library subscribes to, the *Social Sciences Index*, an e-version of *Bartlett's Familiar Quotations*, both hard copy and online government documents, and a wide assortment of Internet indexes such as Google Scholar.

In addition to becoming a skilled user of online information and resources from your library, you will also learn to be on the lookout as you read, watch TV or YouTube, receive tweets, and surf the Internet for ideas, examples, illustrations, and quotations that could be used in a speech. Finally, you will learn how to gather information through interviews and written requests for information on various topics. Chapter 7 will explain more thoroughly how to use all these resources, with a special emphasis on using Internet and electronic research tools.

Gather Visual Supporting Material

For many people, seeing is believing. Besides searching for verbal forms of supporting material, you can also seek visual supporting material. Almost any presentation can be enhanced by reinforcing key ideas with presentation aids— something visual or, in some cases, auditory. Often the most effective presentation aids are the simplest: an object, a chart, a graph, a poster, a model, a map, or a person—perhaps you—to demonstrate a process or skill. Today there are many technologies for displaying presentation aids. The latest graphics packages for personal computers, such as PowerPoint, Prezi or Keynote, can help you generate colorful graphs, charts, signs, and banners. And with today's

Good research skills are essential to the speechmaking process.

Photo: CREATAS/JUPITER IMAGES/Alamy Images

RECAP

GATHER SUPPORTING MATERIAL

Use your own knowledge and research to find supporting materials that are:

- *Interesting.* Most audiences enjoy stories.
- *Relevant.* Help the audience understand and relate to statistics.
- *Memorable.* Visuals help the audience understand and remember.

technology you can project stunning video images with the proper equipment. Of course, using this high-tech equipment requires skill and additional extra rehearsal time.

In Chapter 12 we discuss some basic advice about using presentation aids: Make your visual images large enough to be seen and allow plenty of time to prepare them; use words sparingly rather than cramming too much your information on your visuals; look at your audience, not at your presentation aid; control your audience's attention by timing your visual displays; and keep your presentation aids simple. Always concentrate on communicating effectively with your audience, not on dazzling your listeners with glitzy presentation displays.

2.7 Develop a speech with three main organizational parts—an introduction, a body, and a conclusion.

Organize Your Speech

A wise person once said, "If effort is organized, accomplishment follows." A clearly and logically structured speech helps your audience remember what you say. A logical structure also helps you feel more in control of your speech, and greater control helps you feel more comfortable while delivering your message.

As we saw in Chapter 1, classical rhetoricians called the process of developing an orderly speech **disposition**. Speakers need to present ideas, information, examples, illustrations, stories, and statistics in an orderly sequence so that listeners can easily follow what they are saying.

Every well-prepared speech has three major divisions: the introduction, the body, and the conclusion. The introduction helps capture attention, serves as an overview of the speech, and provides your audience with reasons to listen to you. The body presents the main content of your speech. The conclusion summarizes your key

disposition

The organization and arrangement of ideas and illustrations

SAMPLE OUTLINE

TOPIC

How to invest money

Your instructor may assign a topic, or you may select it.

GENERAL PURPOSE

To inform

To inform, persuade, or entertain. Your instructor will probably specify your general purpose.

SPECIFIC PURPOSE

At the end of my speech, the audience should be able to identify two principles that will help them better invest their money.

A clear statement indicating what your audience should be able to do after hearing your speech

CENTRAL IDEA

Knowing the source of money, how to invest it, and how money grows can lead to increased income from wise investments.

A one-sentence summary of your talk

INTRODUCTION

Imagine for a moment that it is the year 2065. You are 65 years old. You've just picked up your mail and opened an envelope that contains a check for $300,000! No, you didn't win the lottery. You smile as you realize your own modest investment strategy over the last 40 years has paid off handsomely.

Attention-catching opening line

Today I'd like to answer three questions that can help you become a better money manager: First, where does money come from? Second, where do you invest it? And third, how does a little money grow into a lot of money?

Preview major ideas.

ideas. You may have heard this advice on how to organize a speech: "Tell them what you're going to tell them (the introduction), tell them (the body of the speech), and tell them what you told them (the conclusion)."

As a student of public speaking, you will study and learn to apply variations of this basic pattern of organization (chronological, topical, cause–effect, problem–solution) that will help your audience understand your meaning. You will learn about previewing and summarizing—information that will help your audience remember your ideas. In the outline of a sample speech, notice how the introduction catches the listener's attention, the body of the speech identifies the main ideas, and the conclusion summarizes the key ideas.

Because your introduction previews your speech and your conclusion summarizes it, most public-speaking teachers recommend that you prepare your introduction and conclusion *after* you have carefully organized the body of your talk. If you have already generated your major ideas by divisions, reasons, or steps, you are well on your way to developing an outline. Indicate your major ideas by Roman numerals. Use capital letters for your supporting points. Use Arabic numerals if you need to subdivide your ideas further. Do *not* write your speech word for word. If you do, you will sound stilted and unnatural. It may be useful, however, to use brief notes—written cues on note cards—instead of a complete manuscript. Increasingly speakers are using handheld computer tablets such as iPads to hold their speaking notes.

You may want to look in Chapter 8 for approaches to organizing a message and to see more sample outlines. Chapter 9 provides more detailed suggestions for beginning and ending your speech. Some public-speaking teachers may require a slightly different outline format. For example, your teacher may want you to outline your speech introduction using a Roman numeral I for the introduction, a II for the body, and a III for your conclusion. Make sure you follow the precise guidelines your instructor provides for outlining your speech. For your first speech, you may want to adapt the sample outline format shown here.[9] Your instructor may want you to add more detailed information about your supporting material in outlines you submit in class.

Knowing the answers to these three questions can pay big dividends for you. With only modest investments and a well-disciplined attitude, you could easily have an annual income of $300,000 or more.

Tell your audience why they should listen to you.

BODY

I. There are two sources of money.
  A. You already have some money.
  B. You will earn money in the future.
II. You can do three things with your money.
  A. You can spend it.
  B. You can lend it to others.
  C. You can invest it.
III. Two principles can help make you rich.
  A. The "magic" of compound interest can transform pennies into millions.
  B. Finding the best rate of return on your money can pay big dividends.

I. Major Idea
  A. Supporting idea
  B. Supporting idea
II. Major Idea
  A. Supporting idea
  B. Supporting idea
  C. Supporting idea
III. Major Idea
  A. Supporting idea
  B. Supporting idea

CONCLUSION

Today I've identified three key aspects of effective money management: (1) sources of money, (2) what you can do with money, and (3) money-management principles that can make you rich. Now, let's go "back to the future"! Remember the good feeling you had when you received your check for $300,000? Recall that feeling again when you are depositing your first paycheck. Remember this simple secret for accumulating wealth: Part of all you earn is yours to keep. It is within your power to "go for the gold."

Summarize main ideas and restate central idea.

FIGURE 2.2 Presentation graphic for the first major idea in your speech.

Sources: Figure: Shannon Kingston. Copyrighted by Pearson Education, Upper Saddle River, NJ. Photo: acekreations/Fotolia

FIGURE 2.3 Presentation graphic for the second major idea in your speech.

Sources: Figure: Shannon Kingston. Copyrighted by Pearson Education, Upper Saddle River, NJ. Photo: Edyta Pawlowska/Fotolia

FIGURE 2.4 Presentation graphic for the third major idea in your speech.

Sources: Figure: Shannon Kingston. Copyrighted by Pearson Education, Upper Saddle River, NJ. Photo: selensergen/Fotolia

In addition to developing a written outline to use as you speak, consider using presentation aids to add structure and clarity to your major ideas. Developing simple visual reinforcers of your key ideas can help your audience retain essential points.

In Chapter 12 we offer tips for designing computer graphics using software such as PowerPoint, Keynote, or Prezi. For example, the first major idea in the outline presented earlier could be summarized in a visual aid such as the one in Figure 2.2. The second major idea in our speech example could be emphasized with a visual like the one in Figure 2.3. The third major idea could be reinforced with a visual such as the one in Figure 2.4.

For all the steps we have discussed so far, your success as a speaker will ultimately be determined by your audience. That is why throughout the text we refer you to the audience-centered speechmaking model presented in this chapter.

Once you are comfortable with the structure of your talk and you have developed your visual aids, you are ready to rehearse.

| 2.8 | Identify successful strategies for rehearsing a speech. |

Rehearse Your Speech

Remember this joke? One man asks another, "How do you get to Carnegie Hall?" The answer: "Practice, practice, practice." The joke may be older than Carnegie Hall itself, but it is still good advice to all speakers, especially novice speakers. A speech is a performance. As with any stage performance, be it music, dance, or theater, you need to rehearse. Experienced carpenters know to "measure twice, saw once." Rehearsing your speech is a way to measure your message so that you get it right when you present it to your audience.

The best way to practice is to rehearse your speech aloud, standing just as you will when you deliver it to your audience. As you rehearse, try to find a comfortable way to phrase your ideas, but don't try to memorize your talk. In fact, if you have rehearsed your speech so many times that you are using exactly the same words every time, you have rehearsed long enough. Rehearse just enough so that you can discuss your ideas and supporting material without leaving out major parts of your speech. It is all right to use notes, but most public-speaking instructors limit the number of notes you may use.

As you rehearse, practice making eye contact with your imaginary audience as often as you can. Also, be certain to speak loudly enough for all in the room to hear. If you are not sure what to do with your hands when you rehearse, just keep them at your side. Focus on your message rather than worrying about how to gesture. Avoid jingling change with your hand in your pocket or using other gestures that could distract your audience. If you are delivering your speech via video (whether live or prerecorded), remember that the camera may make it appear to listeners that you are only a few feet away from them. For video, you need not use overly animated gestures or facial expressions. A natural, conversational quality will be valued whether you are speaking in front of a camera or speaking to a live audience.

If you practice your speech as if you were actually delivering it, you will be a more effective speaker when you talk to the audience. And there is evidence that, like preparing early for your speech, spending time rehearsing your delivery will enhance the overall quality of your speech.[10]

Besides rehearsing your physical delivery, you also will make decisions about the style of your speech. "Style," said novelist Jonathan Swift, "is proper words in proper places." The words you choose and your arrangement of those words make up the style of your speech. You can learn more about using words in Chapter 10. As we have said, some audiences respond to a style that is simple and informal. Others prefer a grand and highly poetic style. To be a good speaker, you must become familiar with the language your listeners are used to hearing and must know how to select the right word or phrase to communicate an idea. Work to develop an ear for how words will sound to your audience.

Explore at MyCommunicationLab Activity: "Build a Speech: Informative Speech"

CONSIDER THE AUDIENCE

Deliver Your Speech

The time has come, and you're ready to present your speech to your audience. Delivery is the final step in the preparation process. Before you walk to the front of the room, look at your listeners to see if the audience assembled is what you were expecting. Are the people of the age, race, and gender that you had predicted? Or do you need to make last-minute changes in your message to adjust to a different mix of audience members?

When you are introduced, walk calmly and confidently to the front of the room, establish eye contact with your audience, smile naturally, and deliver your attention-catching opening sentence. Concentrate on your message and your audience. Deliver your speech in a conversational style, and try to establish rapport with your listeners. Deliver your speech just as you rehearsed it before your imaginary audience: Maintain eye contact, speak loudly enough to be heard, and use some natural variation in pitch. Finally, remember the public-speaking advice of columnist Ann Landers: "Be sincere, be brief, and be seated."

Figure 2.5 summarizes this chapter's introduction to the audience-centered speaking process and refers you to other chapters for in-depth information about each step. For a model of many of the attributes of a well-crafted message that we have discussed, read the speech by student Grace Hildenbrand on page 35.[11]

2.9 Describe the essential elements of effective speech delivery.

CONFIDENTLY CONNECTING WITH YOUR AUDIENCE

Use Your Communication Apprehension to Enhance Your Performance

Recall that most speakers' nervousness peaks right before giving a speech. You can use this anxiety to help you enhance your performance. How? Exercise the skill of reframing to get yourself to think positively rather than negatively about speaking in public. Remember that anxiety is your body's way of trying to give you more energy to help you improve your performance. Don't dwell on the symptoms of anxiety; reframe them as signals that your brain is increasing your mental powers. Knowing that some apprehension can enhance your mental alertness can help you deliver a well-presented speech.

FIGURE 2.5 An overview of the public-speaking process

Audience-Centered Public Speaking

Consider the Audience
Chapter 5

- Analyzing the audience is central to the speechmaking process; consider your audience at every step of the way in preparing and presenting your speech.
- Gather information about your audience by asking questions or surveying them more formally.
- Summarize and analyze the information you have gathered.

Select and Narrow Your Topic
Chapter 6

- Consider the audience: Who are your listeners and what do they expect?
- Consider the occasion: What is the reason for the speech?
- Consider your own interests and skills: What are your strengths?

Deliver Your Speech
Chapters 11 and 12

- Look at individual listeners.
- Use movement and gestures that fit your natural style of speaking.

Rehearse Your Speech
Chapters 8, 10, 11, and 12

- Prepare speaking notes and practice using them well in advance of your speaking date.
- Rehearse your speech out loud, standing as you would stand while delivering your speech.
- Practice with well-chosen visual aids that are big, simple, and appropriate for your audience.

Determine Your Purpose
Chapters 6, 13, 14, 15, 16

- Decide whether your general speech purpose is to inform, to persuade, or to entertain, or a combination of these goals.
- Decide on your specific purpose: What do you want your listeners to be able to do after you finish your speech?
- Use your specific purpose to guide you in connecting your message to your audience.

Organize Your Speech
Chapters 8 and 9

- Remember the maxim: Tell us what you're going to tell us (introduction); tell us (body); and tell us what you told us (conclusion).
- Outline your main ideas by topic, chronologically, spatially, by cause and effect, or by problem and solution.
- Use signposts to clarify the overall structure of your message.

Develop Your Central Idea
Chapter 6

- State your central idea for your speech in one sentence.
- Your central idea should be a single idea presented in clear, specific language.
- Relate your central idea to your audience.

Gather Supporting Material
Chapter 7

- Remember that most of what you say consists of supporting material such as stories, descriptions, definitions, analogies, statistics, and opinions.
- The best supporting material both clarifies your major ideas and holds your listeners' attention.
- Supporting material that is personal, concrete, and appealing to the listeners' senses is often the most interesting.

Generate Main Ideas
Chapter 6

- Determine whether your central idea can be supported with logical divisions using a topical arrangement.
- Determine whether your central idea can be supported with reasons the idea is true.
- Determine whether your central idea can be supported with a series of steps.

CONSIDER THE AUDIENCE

Select and Narrow Topic · Determine Purpose · Develop Central Idea · Generate Main Ideas · Gather Supporting Material · Organize Speech · Rehearse Speech · Deliver Speech

CINDERELLA

Grace Hildenbrand

There are thought to be over five hundred different versions of *Cinderella*, making it one of the most popular fairy tales in the world. In the United States, most children have seen Disney's *Cinderella* and adults are either familiar with this movie or they know other versions of the *Cinderella* fairy tale. I know that I watched Disney's version of *Cinderella* many times as a kid. And then when I got to college, I took a German class and I learned about the Brothers Grimm version of *Cinderella*. I was surprised to find that it was actually quite different from Disney's version of *Cinderella*. In the Brothers Grimm there are two brothers, Jacob and Wilhelm Grimm, who compiled different fairy tales into books back in the 1800s and one of these fairy tales was *Cinderella*. Disney did change aspects of the Brothers Grimm version of *Cinderella* to make it more appropriate for children. These differences in these two versions are revealed in the characters, in the royal ball scene, and in the use of violence.

So to begin, I would like to discuss the differences in characters between the Disney and Brothers Grimm versions of *Cinderella*. Disney both added in and changed characters from the Brothers Grimm version of *Cinderella*. For example, the fairy godmother character did not exist in the Brothers Grimm version of *Cinderella*. It was actually a tree that Cinderella would go to for help and there were birds that lived in the tree that would help her out with whatever she needed. So, for example, when Cinderella was getting ready to go to the ball, she needed to make sure that she finished up her chores and she had a dress to wear. And so the birds that lived in the trees whenever she asked for help would help her finish her chores and also they gave her a dress to wear to the ball.

Another change that Disney made was to add in the other animal characters to *Cinderella*. So in the Brothers Grimm version, there are the birds that serve as the fairy godmother's role, but the Disney version not only had birds, but also they added in a dog, a cat, and a horse as well as mice to make it more appealing for kids. Neeley Tucker from the *Washington Post* discusses that most fairy tales were not originally for children but they were mostly written for adults. And so most fairy tales have actually been changed to be more appropriate for kids and this was definitely the case for *Cinderella*.

So now that I've discussed the differences in characters between the two versions, I would like to discuss the differences in the royal ball scene. If you recall from Disney, there's one royal ball scene where Cinderella meets her prince, but in the Brothers Grimm version there is a royal festival that includes three different royal balls in three days. At each royal ball, Cinderella dances with the prince, then she runs away and hides from him before the end of the night and she doesn't lose her slipper until the third night. According to Sharron McElmeel and her book on children's literature, there are a couple of other changes in this scene as well; one of them is that in the Brothers Grimm version, the shoe was golden and then in Disney, of course, it was a glass slipper. And then Disney also added the midnight curfew; so in the Brothers Grimm version, Cinderella did not need to be back by the stroke of midnight. She was simply trying to get away from the prince so that he wouldn't figure out that she was a housemaid. She was trying to hide her true identity. Also, the prince spreads pitch out along the steps of the castle on purpose on the third night, so that Cinderella will get stuck and he will be able to get her shoe and figure out who she is later on.

So now that we've talked a little bit about the differences in the characters between the two versions and the differences in the royal ball scene, I'd like to discuss the way that Disney omitted some violence from their version of *Cinderella* compared to the Brothers Grimm version.

The Brothers Grimm version of *Cinderella* is much gorier than Disney's version. For example, when the prince is trying to figure out who Cinderella is and he's having all these women trying to try on the slipper, he comes to Cinderella's stepsisters and both of them, their have feet that are too big. The first stepsister actually cuts off her toe to make the shoe fit, and the second stepsister actually cuts off her heel to make the shoe fit. So it's very bloody and it's actually kind of funny because the prince doesn't seem to realize that

The speaker has analyzed her audience and knows that most of them are from the United States.

This speaker's general purpose is to inform the audience about two of the most well-known versions of the Cinderella *story.*

After giving a verbal signal to mark the transition into the body of her speech, the speaker states her central idea.

This story helps keep the audience interested and supports the speaker's central idea.

The summary and preview help the audience follow the organization of the speech.

neither one of the stepsisters is Cinderella and, according to the *Greenwood Encyclopedia of Folktales and Fairytales,* the prince doesn't realize that neither of the stepsisters is Cinderella until the birds that serve the fairy godmother role tell him, "Hey, there's blood everywhere, neither one of these women is Cinderella!"

Another gory aspect of the Brothers Grimm version is that at Cinderella's wedding at the end of the story, as punishment for being wicked, the stepsisters actually get their eyes poked out by the birds and they are blinded. So with these changes, you can imagine that if Disney would have kept the fairy tale similar to the Brothers Grimm version, it likely would have changed the audience. You know, rather than having it geared toward children, it might be geared toward adults, and it definitely would have not become such a popular and important part of our childhood.

In conclusion, now you should better understand the differences between the Disney and Brothers Grimm versions of *Cinderella* and why Disney changed its version of *Cinderella*. Specifically these differences were that Disney added in and changed some of the characters; Disney also made changes to the royal ball scene and got rid of some of the violence from the Brothers Grimm version. So next time that you're watching Disney's *Cinderella* or any other version of *Cinderella*, I'd like you to imagine that if there was blood dripping from the eyes and feet of the stepsisters how this would change your reaction to this classic fairy tale.

Here the speaker gives an oral citation, mentioning the source of her supporting material.

The speaker directly addresses the audience members to engage their attention and involve them in the speech.

In her conclusion, the speaker summarizes the main points of her speech.

The speaker closes with a vivid image and a suggestion for action. Both will help the audience remember the content of this speech.

STUDY GUIDE REVIEW, APPLY, AND ASSESS

CONSIDER YOUR AUDIENCE

2.1 Explain why it is important to be audience-centered during each step of the speechmaking process.

Your audience influences your topic selection and every aspect of presenting a speech. The audience-centered model of public speaking introduced on page 22 suggests that you should consider the audience each step of the way when preparing and presenting a speech.

Key Term

Speech topic 23

Thinking Critically

Jonathan has just received his assignment for his first speech in his public-speaking class. What key pieces of information should Jonathan keep in mind as he begins to prepare his speech?

Assessing Your Audience-Centered Speaking Skill

What do you know about your public-speaking class as an audience, based only on observing them or hearing them introduce themselves to the class?

SELECT AND NARROW YOUR TOPIC

2.2 Select and narrow an appropriate topic for a speech.

Three questions can help you select and narrow your topic: Who is the audience? What are my interests, talents, and experiences? What is the occasion? Answers to these questions can help you select and narrow your speech topic.

Thinking Ethically

Your first assignment is to give a speech about something interesting that has happened to you. You have decided to talk about the joys and hassles of a train trip you took last year. Your sister recently returned from a cross-country train trip and had several interesting tales to tell. Would it be ethical to tell one of her experiences as if it had happened to you? Why or why not?

Assessing Your Audience-Centered Speaking Skill

Reflect on the information you already know about your pubic-speaking class as an audience. What are strategies for learning more about your audience that will help you select your speech topic?

DETERMINE YOUR PURPOSE

2.3 Differentiate between a general speech purpose and a specific speech purpose.

There are two categories of speech purposes: Your general purpose is the overarching goal of your speech (to inform, persuade, or entertain or some combination of two or all three of these purposes). Your specific purpose is a concise statement indicating what you want your listeners to be able to do when you finish your speech.

Key Terms

General purpose. 25
Specific purpose. 25

Thinking Critically

Amy's first speech is to introduce herself to her classmates. What is Amy's general purpose?

Assessing Your Audience-Centered Speaking Skill

Write possible specific-purpose sentences for three different speeches with the same topic—climate change—but with three different general purposes: to inform, to persuade, and to entertain.

DEVELOP YOUR CENTRAL IDEA

2.4 Develop a sentence that captures the central idea of a speech.

A central idea states the essence of your speech in a single sentence; think of it as a speech you could give if you were in an elevator going between the first and third floors.

Key Term

Thinking Critically

Barbara is planning to move to an independent living community for seniors and wants to tell other senior citizens the steps to follow when making a move. Write a possible central idea sentence for Barbara's speech.

Assessing Your Audience-Centered Speaking Skill

Select one of the speeches in Appendix B. Identify the central idea of the speech. Compare your answer to those of others in your class.

GENERATE THE MAIN IDEAS

> **2.5**   Identify three strategies for generating the main ideas for a speech.

Virtually any speech can be organized by answering the following three questions: Does the central idea have logical divisions? What are the reasons the central idea is true? Can you support the central idea with a series of steps?

Key Terms

Thinking Ethically

You read an article in *Reader's Digest* that could serve as the basis for a great speech about a possible new cure for AIDS. Would it be ethical to paraphrase the article, using most of the same examples and the overall outline as the basis for your speech, if you *tell* your listeners that your speech is based on the article?

Assessing Your Audience-Centered Speaking Skill

Your central idea is "Making your own wine from grapes in your garden is an easy and enjoyable hobby." Is the best way to generate main ideas from this central idea to use logical divisions, reasons, or steps?

GATHER SUPPORTING MATERIAL

> **2.6**   Describe several types of supporting material that could be used to support speech ideas.

Supporting material consists of the facts, examples, definitions, statistics, analogies, quotations, and stories that illustrate, amplify, and clarify your speech.

Thinking Ethically

One of your friends took a public-speaking course last year and still has a file of speech illustrations, stories, and statistics about crime on your campus. Since you plan to give a speech using the same topic, is it ethical to use the file of supporting material that you didn't prepare to support your message?

Assessing Your Audience-Centered Speaking Skill

You have found a statistic confirming that 350 active members of the military died by suicide last year. Rather than just stating that number in your speech, how can you illustrate the statistic so that it has greater meaning and impact on your audience?

ORGANIZE YOUR SPEECH

> **2.7**   Develop a speech with three main organizational parts—an introduction, a body, and a conclusion.

Think of your speech as having an introduction that provides an overview of your main points, the body of your speech that presents the key points, and a conclusion that summarizes what you have said.

Key Term

Thinking Critically

Shara is preparing to address the city council in an effort to tell them about the Food for Friendship program she has organized in her neighborhood. What steps should she follow to prepare and deliver an effective speech?

Assessing Your Audience-Centered Speaking Skill

During the next week, when you listen to a speech or class lecture, determine whether the speaker has an introduction, body, and conclusion. Note what effect a well-organized message has on you as you listen or when you later reflect on the message.

REHEARSE YOUR SPEECH

2.8 Identify successful strategies for rehearsing a speech.

Rehearsing your speech several times, in a way that recreates the actual speech presentation experience, will help improve your confidence and enhance your ability to deliver an effective presentation.

Thinking Critically

Amanda has prepared her speech outline and is ready to rehearse her speech. Give three suggestions Amanda can use as she rehearses to ensure a good final performance.

Assessing Your Audience-Centered Speaking Skill

Record a video of your rehearsal for your next speech. View the video to determine three things you are doing well and three ways in which you could enhance your performance.

DELIVER YOUR SPEECH

2.9 Describe the essential elements of effective speech delivery.

The essential aspects of effective delivery include good eye contact with your listeners, varied vocal expression, a volume that can be heard by all, and appropriate gestures and posture that seem natural for the speaker.

Thinking Ethically

Your teacher has asked that you deliver your speech extemporaneously, but because you are nervous, you think you can do a better job if you write out your speech and then memorize it word for word. Is it ethical to present a memorized speech when you have been asked to present an extemporaneous speech?

Assessing Your Audience-Centered Speaking Skill

After you deliver your first speech to your class, write a short self-analysis. Identify when during your speech you thought you were especially effective in connecting with your listeners. Also note times during your speech when you wondered if you were maintaining their interest. If you were to give the same speech to the same audience again, what would you do the same, and what would you do differently?

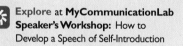

Explore at MyCommunicationLab
Speaker's Workshop: How to
Develop a Speech of Self-Introduction

3 SPEAKING FREELY AND ETHICALLY

OBJECTIVES

After studying this chapter you should be able to do the following:

3.1

Explain how free speech has been both challenged and defended throughout U.S. history.

3.2

List and explain five criteria for ethical public speaking.

3.3

Explain the relationship between ethics and credibility.

((•)) Listen to Chapter 3 at **MyCommunicationLab**

William H. Johnson (1901–1970), *Lift Up Thy Voice and Sing*. c. 1942–44. Oil on paperboard, 64.9 × 54.0 cm. Smithsonian American Art Museum, Washington, D.C./Art Resource, N.Y.

We're the free speech wing of the free speech party.

—Dick Costolo
(Twitter CEO)

In early 2013, Twitter complied with a French court order to block a flood of anti-Semitic tweets from being seen in France. A few months later, in response to a boycott against pages containing graphic images of violence against women, Facebook took down the offending pages and revised its content policies.

Once played out primarily in public gatherings or on radio or television, the balancing act between ethical speech and free speech has in the twenty-first century become most visible in social media. Jason Pontin, editor of the *MIT Technology Review*, explains the dilemma:

> . . . as the technologies created by [social media] have come to touch nearly everyone who lives, their peculiar understanding of free speech has collided with different notions of what forms of expression are legal or proper.[1]

In the United States and other countries in which **free speech** is protected by law, the right to speak freely must be balanced by the responsibility to speak ethically.

Ethics—the beliefs, values, and moral principles by which we determine what is right or wrong—serve as criteria for many of the decisions we make in our personal and professional lives and for our judgments of others' behavior. The student who refuses to cheat on a test, the employee who will not call in sick to gain an extra day of vacation, and the property owner who does not claim more storm damage than she actually suffered have all made choices based on ethics.

We read and hear about ethical issues every day in the media. Cloning, stem-cell research, and drug testing have engendered heated ethical debates among medical professionals. Advertising by some attorneys has incensed those who believe that an overall increase in frivolous litigation is tarnishing the profession. And in the political arena, debates about reforms of social programs, fiscal responsibility, and the collection of cell phone data by the federal government all hinge on ethical issues.

Although you are undoubtedly familiar with many of these ethical issues, you may have given less thought to ethics in public speaking. The National Communication Association's Credo for Communication Ethics emphasizes the fundamental nature and far-reaching impact of ethical communication:

> Ethical communication is fundamental to responsible thinking, decision making, and the development of relationships and communities within and across contexts, cultures, channels, and media. Moreover, ethical communication enhances human worth and dignity by fostering truthfulness, fairness, responsibility, personal integrity, and respect for self and others.[2]

Ethical considerations should guide you during every step of the public-speaking process. As you determine the goal of your speech, outline your arguments, and select your supporting material, think about the beliefs, values, and moral principles of your audience, as well as your own. Ethical public speaking is inherently audience-centered, always taking into account the needs and rights of the listeners.

In our discussion of speaking freely and ethically, we will turn first to free speech—both its protection and its restriction by law and public policy. Then we will discuss the ethical practice of free speech by speakers and listeners, providing guidelines to help you balance your right to free speech with your responsi-

free speech
Legally protected speech or speech acts

ethics
The beliefs, values, and moral principles by which people determine what is right or wrong

bilities as an audience-centered speaker. Within this framework, we will define and discuss plagiarism, one of the most troublesome violations of public-speaking ethics. And, finally, we will discuss the relationship between ethics and speaker credibility.

3.1	Explain how free speech has been both challenged and defended throughout U.S. history.

Speaking Freely

In May 2013, a heckler interrupted President Barack Obama three times while he was delivering a speech at the National Defense University in Washington, D.C. Obama responded by calmly reminding the woman that the right to free speech required not only that he listen to her but also that she listen to him. "You should let me finish my sentence," Obama admonished.[3] Even during a moment of confrontation—a moment in which one might question the heckler's *ethics*—the president defended the right of both parties to *free speech*. The history of free speech in the United States is summarized in Table 3.1, and we discuss it in more detail next.

First Amendment
The amendment to the U.S. Constitution that guarantees free speech; the first of the ten amendments to the U.S. Constitution known collectively as the Bill of Rights

Free Speech and the U.S. Constitution

In 1791, the **First Amendment** to the U.S. Constitution was written to guarantee that "Congress shall make no law . . . abridging the freedom of speech." In the more than 200 years since then, entities as varied as state legislatures, colleges and universities,

TABLE 3.1   HISTORY OF FREE SPEECH IN THE UNITED STATES

1791	First Amendment guarantees that "Congress shall make no law . . . abridging the freedom of speech"
1798	Sedition Act is passed (expired in 1801)
1919	Supreme Court suggests that speech presenting a "clear and present danger" may be restricted
1920	American Civil Liberties Union is formed
1940	Congress declares it illegal to urge the violent overthrow of the federal government
1964	Supreme Court restricts definition of slander; Berkeley Free Speech Movement is born
1989	Supreme Court defends the burning of the U.S. flag as a "speech act"
1997	Supreme Court strikes down Communications Decency Act of 1996, in defense of free speech on the Internet
1998	Oprah Winfrey successfully defends her right to speak freely on television
2001	September 11 terrorist attacks spark passage of the Patriot Act and new debate over the balance between national security and free speech
2006	State of Montana pardons those convicted under the Montana Sedition Act of 1918
2010	White House correspondent Helen Thomas retires amid controversy over what some saw as her exercise of free speech
2012	*FreeSpeechDebate.com* becomes a venue for global online discussion and debate about free speech

the American Civil Liberties Union, and the federal courts have sought to define through both law and public policy the phrase "freedom of speech."

Only a few years after the ratification of the First Amendment, Congress passed the Sedition Act, providing punishment for those who spoke out against the government. When both Thomas Jefferson and James Madison declared this act unconstitutional, however, it was allowed to lapse.

Free Speech in the Twentieth Century

During World War I, the U.S. Supreme Court ruled that it was lawful to restrict speech that presented "a clear and present danger" to the nation. This decision led to the founding, in 1920, of the American Civil Liberties Union, the first organization formed to protect free speech. In 1940, Congress declared it illegal to urge the violent overthrow of the federal government. However, even as they heard the hate speech employed by Hitler and the Nazis, U.S. courts and lawmakers argued that only by *protecting* free speech could the United States protect the rights of minorities and the disenfranchised. For most of the last half of the twentieth century, the Supreme Court continued to protect rather than to limit free speech, upholding it as "the core aspect of democracy."[4]

In 1964, the Supreme Court narrowed the definition of slander, false speech that harms someone. The Court ruled that before a public official can recover damages for slander, he or she must prove that the slanderous statement was made with "actual malice."[5] Another 1964 boost for free speech occurred not in the courts but on a university campus. In December of that year, more than 1,000 students at the University of California in Berkeley took over three floors of Sproul Hall to protest the recent arrest of outspoken student activists. The Berkeley Free Speech Movement that arose from the incident permanently changed the political climate of U.S. college campuses. In a statement on the 30-year anniversary of the protest, Berkeley's Vice Chancellor Carol Christ wrote, "Today it is difficult

Watch at **MyCommunicationLab**
Video: "Words That Wound"

Since the 1700s, court rulings and laws have been shaping our interpretation of the First Amendment. The amendment protects free speech, including the rights of protest speakers to speak out about controversial issues.

Photo: STAN HONDA/AFP/Getty Images/Newscom

to imagine life in a university where there are serious restrictions on the rights of political advocacy."[6]

Free speech gained protection in the last two decades of the twentieth century, when the Supreme Court found "virtually all attempts to restrain speech in advance . . . unconstitutional," regardless of how hateful or disgusting the speech may seem to some.[7] In 1989, the Supreme Court defended the burning of the U.S. flag as a "**speech act**" protected by the First Amendment. In 1997, the Court struck down the highly controversial federal Communications Decency Act of 1996, which had imposed penalties for creating, transmitting, or receiving obscene material on the Internet. The Court ruled that "the interest in encouraging freedom of expression in a democratic society outweighs any theoretical but unproven benefit of censorship."[8]

Perhaps no twentieth-century test of free speech received more publicity than the sensational 1998 lawsuit brought by four Texas cattlemen against popular talk-show host Oprah Winfrey. In a show on "mad cow disease," Winfrey had declared that she would never eat another hamburger. Charging that her statement caused cattle prices to plummet, the cattlemen sued for damages; however, Winfrey's attorneys successfully argued that the case was an important test of free speech. Emerging from the courtroom after the verdict in her favor, Winfrey shouted, "My reaction is that free speech not only lives, it rocks!"[9]

Free Speech in the Twenty-First Century

No sooner had the new century begun than the right to free speech in the United States experienced one of its most historically significant challenges. One month after the September 11, 2001, terrorist attacks on the United States, the pendulum again swung toward restriction of free speech with the passage of the Patriot Act, which broadened the investigative powers of government agencies. The Patriot Act was roundly criticized by various civil rights, free-speech, and publishing groups. One coalition of such groups described the Patriot Act as "the latest in a long line of abuses of rights in times of conflict."[10] It is ironic that even as Americans debated the restrictions imposed by the Patriot Act, they recognized and offered restitution for historical infringement on free speech. In May 2006, Montana Governor Brian Schweitzer formally pardoned 78 late citizens of Montana who had been imprisoned or fined under the Montana Sedition Act of 1918, convictions that "violated basic American rights of speech . . ."[11]

The pendulum swung back in June 2010, when the exercise of free speech created controversy for and hastened the retirement of veteran White House correspondent Helen Thomas. Asked by a rabbi to comment on Israel, Thomas responded that the Israelis should get out of Palestine. Although Thomas later both apologized and resigned from the White House Press Corps, her right to free speech was upheld by former CBS News foreign correspondent Terry Phillips, who noted wryly, "Apparently, journalists are now only willing to defend free speech when it is safe."[12]

In the twenty-first century, free speech has increasingly become an issue of global concern. In 2012, with the support of Wikipedia founder Jimmy Wales and Nobel Peace Prize winner Shirin Ebadi, an international team from Oxford University launched an international, multilingual Web site for the discussion of free speech. The site, *FreeSpeechDebate.com*, offers and invites discussion and debate about ten draft principles for global free speech, which you can read in Figure 3.1.

There can be little doubt that in the months and years to come, both the United States and the world will continue to debate the "unprecedented chances for free expression" that the digital age offers.[13]

speech act
A behavior, such as flag burning, that is viewed by law as nonverbal communication and is subject to the same protections and limitations as verbal speech

FIGURE 3.1 Ten Draft Principles for Global Free Speech

1 We – all human beings – must be free and able to express ourselves, and to seek, receive and impart information and ideas, regardless of frontiers.

2 We defend the internet and all other forms of communication against illegitimate encroachments by both public and private powers.

3 We require and create open, diverse media so we can make well-informed decisions and participate fully in political life.

4 We speak openly and with civility about all kinds of human difference.

5 We allow no taboos in the discussion and dissemination of knowledge.

6 We neither make threats of violence nor accept violent intimidation.

7 We respect the believer but not necessarily the content of the belief.

8 We are all entitled to a private life but should accept such scrutiny as is in the public interest.

9 We should be able to counter slurs on our reputations without stifling legitimate debate.

10 We must be free to challenge all limits to freedom of expression and information justified on such grounds as national security, public order, morality and the protection of intellectual property.

Published on Free Speech Debate (www.freespeechdebate.com). These principles were drafted as part of an Oxford University research project led by Timothy Garton Ash and published on Free Speech Debate www.freespeechdebate.com where they can also be debated online.

Speaking Ethically

As the boundaries of free speech expand, the importance of **ethical speech** increases. Although there is no definitive ethical creed for a public speaker, teachers and practitioners of public speaking generally agree that an ethical speaker is one who has a clear, responsible goal; uses sound evidence and reasoning; is sensitive to and tolerant of differences; is honest; and avoids plagiarism. In the discussion that follows, we offer suggestions for observing these ethical guidelines.

Have a Clear, Responsible Goal

The goal of a public speech should be clear to the audience. For example, if you are trying to convince the audience that your beliefs about gay marriage are more correct than those of others, you should say so at some point in your speech. If you keep your true agenda hidden, you violate your listeners' rights.

In addition to being clear, an ethical goal should be socially responsible. A socially responsible goal conveys respect and offers the listener choices, whereas an irresponsible, unethical goal is demeaning and/or psychologically coercive or oppressive. Adolf Hitler's speeches, which incited the German people to hatred and genocide, were demeaning and coercive, as were those of Chinese leader Deng Xiaoping, who tried to intimidate Chinese citizens into revealing the whereabouts of leaders of an unsuccessful 1989 student uprising in Tiananmen Square.

If your overall objective is to inform or persuade, it is probably ethical; if your goal is to demean, coerce, or manipulate, it is unethical. But lawyers and ethicists do not always agree on this distinction. As we have pointed out, although Congress and the Supreme Court have at times limited speech that incites sedition, violence, and riot, they have also protected free speech rights "for both the ideas that people cherish and the thoughts they hate."[14]

In a recent study of the relationship between people's perceptions of free speech and hate speech, researchers Daniel Downs and Gloria Cowan found that perceptions about the importance of the freedom of speech were negatively associated with

3.2 List and explain five criteria for ethical public speaking.

Explore at MyCommunicationLab Activity: "Ethical Speaking"

Read at MyCommunicationLab Learning From Great Speakers: Mohandas Gandhi

ethical speech
Speech that is responsible, honest, and tolerant

judgments of the harm of hate speech.[15] In other words, participants who considered freedom of speech to be more important considered hate speech to be less harmful. The investigators reason that, "Free-speech defenders may recognize the harm of hate speech but believe that freedom of speech is more essential than is censoring speech content."

Use Sound Evidence and Reasoning

Ethical speakers use critical thinking skills such as analysis and evaluation to formulate arguments and draw conclusions. Unethical speakers substitute false claims and manipulation of emotion for evidence and logical arguments.

In the early 1950s, Wisconsin senator Joseph McCarthy incited national panic by charging that Communists were infiltrating every avenue of American life. Never able to substantiate his claims, McCarthy nevertheless succeeded in his witch hunt by exaggerating and distorting the truth. One United Press reporter noted, "The man just talked in circles. Everything was by inference, allusion, never a concrete statement of fact. Most of it didn't make sense."[16] Although today we recognize the flimsiness of McCarthy's accusations, in his time he wielded incredible power. It may sometimes be tempting to resort to false claims to gain power over others, but it is always unethical to do so.

Some speakers bypass sound evidence and reasoning in order to make their conclusions more provocative. One contemporary rhetoric scholar offers this example of such short-circuited reasoning:

Let's say two people are observing who speaks in college classrooms and they come up with

1. Women are not as good at public speaking as men.
2. In college classes on coed campuses where most professors are male, women tend to talk less in class than men.[17]

The first conclusion, based on insufficient evidence, reinforces sexist stereotypes with an inflammatory overgeneralization. The second, more qualified conclusion is more ethical.

One last, but important, requirement for the ethical use of evidence and reasoning is to share with an audience all information that might help them reach a sound decision, including information that may be potentially damaging to your case. Even if you proceed to refute the opposing evidence and arguments, you have fulfilled your ethical responsibility by presenting the perspective of the other side. And you make your own arguments more convincing by anticipating and answering counterarguments and opposing evidence.

Be Sensitive to and Tolerant of Differences

The filmmaker who ate nothing but McDonald's meals for his Oscar-nominated movie *Super Size Me* apologized for a profanity-laced, politically incorrect speech at a suburban Philadelphia school.

Among other things, Morgan Spurlock joked about the intelligence of McDonald's employees and teachers smoking pot while he was speaking at Hatboro-Horsham High School. . . .

Like Hitler, Senator Joseph McCarthy knew how to manipulate emotions and fears to produce the results he wanted. McCarthy's false accusations of Communism cast suspicion over thousands of people, causing many of them to lose their jobs or their entire careers.

Photo: National Archives and Records Administration

Spurlock, 35, told *The Philadelphia Inquirer* in a telephone interview that he "didn't think of the audience" and could have chosen his words better.[18]

As we noted in Chapter 2, being audience-centered requires that you become as aware as possible of others' feelings, needs, interests, and backgrounds. Spurlock violated this ethical principle in his remarks.

Sometimes called **accommodation**, sensitivity to differences does not mean that speakers must abandon their own convictions for those of their audience members. It does mean that speakers should demonstrate a willingness to listen to opposing viewpoints and learn about different beliefs and values. Such willingness not only communicates respect; it can also help a speaker to select a topic, formulate a purpose, and design strategies to motivate an audience.

While involved in an informal educational exchange with a professor from the St. Petersburg Cultural Institute in Russia, your authors had a chance to visit the professor and her family in St. Petersburg. In talking with the professor's talented teenage daughter, we inquired about her plans after she finished her university education. Smiling at us in both amusement and amazement, she replied, "Americans are always planning what they are going to do several years in the future. In Russia, we do not plan beyond two or three weeks. Life is too uncertain here." Having gained this insight into Russian life, we know now that it would raise false hopes to attempt to motivate Russian audiences with promises of benefits far in the future.

Our new understanding not only helps us see that speaking of immediate, deliverable rewards is a more realistic and ethical approach to communication with our Russian friends, but it has broader implications as well. DePaul University Communication Professor Kathy Fitzpatrick notes,

> Our success in public diplomacy will turn on our ability to speak in ways that recognize and appreciate how [our audiences] will interpret our messages.[19]

A speaker who is sensitive to differences also avoids language that might be interpreted as being biased or offensive. Although it may seem fairly simple and a matter of common sense to avoid overtly abusive language, it is not so easy to avoid language that discriminates more subtly. In Chapter 10, we look at specific words and phrases that can be unintentionally offensive and that ethical speakers should avoid.

accommodation
Sensitivity to the feelings, needs, interests, and backgrounds of other people

Be Honest

In January 1998, President Bill Clinton's finger-wagging declaration that "I did not have sexual relations with that woman—Miss Lewinsky" was a serious breach of ethics that came back to haunt him. Many Americans were willing to forgive the inappropriate relationship; fewer could forgive the dishonesty.

In 2003, President George W. Bush and members of his staff accepted responsibility for having told the public that Iraq was getting nuclear fuel from Africa, even after intelligence reports several months earlier had discredited the claim.

And in 2012, Susan Rice, then U.S. ambassador to the United Nations, lost her chance to succeed Hillary Rodham Clinton as secretary of state when she provided erroneous information to the media and public about a terrorist attack on the U.S. consulate in Benghazi, Libya. Knowingly offering false or misleading information to an audience is an ethical violation with potentially serious consequences.

Remember That You Will Look More Confident Than You May Feel

As you listen to other people presenting speeches, you will note that most speakers don't appear to be nervous. They are not dishonestly trying to hide their apprehension; most people simply do not appear outwardly as nervous as they may feel. When you deliver your presentation, you may feel some apprehension, but it is ethical to keep such feelings to yourself. And unless you tell your audience that you're nervous, it's unlikely that they will notice it.

Watch at **MyCommunicationLab**
Video: "The Ethics of Deception"

A seeming exception to the directive to avoid false information is the use of hypothetical illustrations—illustrations that never actually occurred but that might happen. Many speakers rely on such illustrations to clarify or enhance their speeches. As long as a speaker makes clear to the audience that the illustration is indeed hypothetical—for example, prefacing the illustration with a phrase such as "Imagine that . . ."—such use is ethical.

Honesty also requires that speakers give credit for ideas and information that are not their own. The *Publication Manual of the American Psychological Association* states that "authors do not present the work of another as if it were their own work. This can extend to ideas as well as written words."[20] Presenting the words and ideas of others without crediting them is called *plagiarism*. This ethical violation is both serious enough and widespread enough to warrant a separate discussion.

Don't Plagiarize

Explore at **MyCommunicationLab**
Profile: "Avoiding Plagiarism"

Although some cultures may view unacknowledged borrowing from sources as a sign of respect and humility and an attempt to be audience-centered, in the United States and most other Western cultures, using the words, sentence structures, and/or ideas of another person without crediting the source is a serious breach of ethics. Yet even people who would never think of stealing money or shoplifting may feel justified in **plagiarizing**—stealing words and/or ideas. One student commencement speaker who plagiarized a speech by the writer Barbara Kingsolver explained his action as resulting from the "expectation to produce something amazing."[21]

Understand What Constitutes Plagiarism Even if you've never plagiarized anything as public as a commencement address, perhaps you can remember copying a grade-school report directly from an online or printed encyclopedia, or maybe you've even purchased or "borrowed" a paper to submit for an assignment in high school or college. These are obvious forms of plagiarism. Less obvious forms include **patchwriting**[22]—lacing a speech with compelling phrases you find in a source; failing to give credit to a source or adequate information in a citation; or relying too heavily on the vocabulary or sentence structure of a source.

Suppose your source says, "Based on historical data, it's clear that large areas of the west coast are overdue for a massive earthquake." You would be plagiarizing if you changed only a word or two to say, "Based on historical data, it's clear that many parts of the west coast are overdue for a huge earthquake." A better paraphrase would be, "For much of the west coast, historical trends show that 'the big one' should have already hit."

Understand That Plagiarism May Have Significant Consequences According to one source, 75 to 98 percent of college students admit to having cheated at least once.[23] At least one Web site claims to provide "non-plagiarized" custom term papers—ironic, because using any such paper is exactly what constitutes plagiarism![24] And communication researcher Todd Holm reports that more than half of the students he surveyed acknowledged cheating in some way in a public-speaking class.[25]

Despite the near-epidemic occurrence of plagiarism, most colleges impose stiff penalties on students who plagiarize. Plagiarists almost always fail the assignment in question, frequently fail the course, and are sometimes put on academic probation or even expelled. And the risk of being caught is much greater than you might suspect. Many colleges subscribe to a Web-based plagiarism detection company such as Turnitin; other professors routinely use free detection sites such as Grammarly or even Google.

A few years ago, one of your authors heard an excellent student speech on the importance of detecting cancer early. The only problem was that she heard the same speech again in the following class period! On finding the "speech"—actually a *Reader's Digest* article that was several years old—both students were certain that they had discovered a surefire shortcut to an A. Instead, they failed the assignment,

plagiarizing
Presenting someone else's words or ideas as though they were one's own

patchwriting
Failing to give credit for compelling phrases taken from another source

ruined their course grades, and lost your author's trust. The consequences of plagiarism in other arenas can be even more dire, including the loss of a job or the end of a promising career.

Do Your Own Work The <u>most flagrant cases of plagiarism result from not doing your own work</u>. For example, while you are idly surfing the Web for ideas for a speech assignment, you may discover a Web page that could easily be made into a speech. However tempting it may be to use this material, and however certain you are that no audience member could possibly have seen it, resist any urge to plagiarize. Not only is the risk of being detected great, but also you will be shortchanging yourself in the long run if you do not learn how to develop a speech step by step.

Another way speakers may attempt to shortcut the speech preparation task is to ask another person to edit a speech so extensively that it becomes more that other person's work than their own. This is another form of plagiarism and another way of cheating themselves out of the skills they need to develop.

Acknowledge Your Sources Our admonition to do your own work in no way suggests that you should not research your speeches and then share your findings with audience members. In fact, an ethical speaker is responsible for doing just that. Furthermore, some information is so widely known that you do not have to acknowledge a source for it. For example, you need not credit a source if you say that a person must be infected with the HIV virus in order to develop AIDS or that the Treaty of Versailles was signed in 1919. This information is widely available in a variety of reference sources. However, if you decide to use any of the following in your speech, you must give credit to the source:

- Direct quotations, even if they are only brief phrases
- Opinions, assertions, or ideas of others, even if you paraphrase rather than quote them verbatim
- Statistics
- Any nonoriginal visual materials, including graphs, tables, and pictures

To be able to acknowledge your sources, you must first practice careful and systematic note-taking. Indicate with quotation marks any phrases or sentences that you photocopy, copy by hand, or electronically cut and paste verbatim from a source, and be sure to record the author, title, publisher or Web site, publication date, and page numbers for all sources from which you take quotations, ideas, statistics, or visual materials. Additional suggestions for systematic note-taking are offered in Chapter 7. In addition to keeping careful records of your sources, you must also know how to cite sources for your audience, both orally and in writing.

Oral Citations Perhaps you have heard a speaker say "Quote" while holding up both hands with index and middle fingers curved to indicate quotation marks. This is an artificial and distracting way to cite a source; an **oral citation** can be integrated more smoothly into a speech.

For example, you might use the approach illustrated in the following sample oral citation. The publication date and author of a source are usually included in an oral citation. In the example, the speaker also mentions the type of resource (Web page) and its title ("Bed Bugs"). Follow your instructor's preferences for the level of detail to include in your oral citations. Note that when you include an oral citation in a speech, the beginning and end of the quoted passage are indicated by pauses. The sample preparation outline in Chapter 10 gives additional examples of oral citations.

Written Citations You can also provide a **written citation** for a source. In fact, your public-speaking instructor may ask you to provide a bibliography of sources along with the outline or other written materials required for each speech. Instructors who

oral citation
The spoken presentation of such information about a source as the author, title, and year of publication

written citation
The presentation in print of such information about a source as the author, title, and year of publication, usually formatted according to a conventional style guide

SAMPLE ORAL CITATION

On a 2013 Web page titled "Bed Bugs," the Centers for Disease Control and Prevention outlines three problems caused by bed bug infestations: "property loss, expense, and inconvenience."

- Provide the date.
- Specify the type of resource.
- Give the title.
- Provide the author or source.
- Pause briefly to signal that you are about to begin quoting.
- Quote the source.
- Pause again to indicate that you are ending the quoted passage.

require a bibliography will usually specify the format in which they want the citations; if they do not, you can use a style guide such as that published by the MLA (Modern Language Association) or the APA (American Psychological Association), both of which are available online as well as in traditional print format. Here is an example of a written citation in MLA format for the source quoted in the sample oral citation:

"Bed Bugs." Centers for Disease Control and Prevention, 13 January 2013. Web. 9 June 2013.

Notice that the citation provides two dates: the date the material was posted online and the date it was accessed by the researcher. If you are unable to find the date the material was posted—or any other single element of information—proceed directly to the next item in the citation. Additional information about citing sources and preparing a bibliography can be found in Chapter 7.

Perhaps now you are thinking, "What about those 'gray areas,' those times when I am not certain whether information or ideas I am presenting are common knowledge?" A good rule is this: When in doubt, document. You will never be guilty of plagiarism if you document something you didn't need to, but you could be committing plagiarism if you do not document something you should have documented.

> **RECAP**
>
> ### THE ETHICAL PUBLIC SPEAKER
>
> - Has a clear, responsible goal
> - Uses sound evidence and reasoning
> - Is sensitive to and tolerant of differences
> - Is honest
> - Doesn't plagiarize

3.3 Explain the relationship between ethics and credibility.

Speaking Credibly

Credibility is a speaker's believability. A credible speaker is one whom an audience perceives to be competent, knowledgeable, dynamic, and trustworthy. The last of those four factors—trustworthiness—is dependent in large part on the speaker's known consistent adherence to ethical principles.

You trust people whom you believe to be ethical. In fact, the Greek rhetorician Aristotle used the term *ethos*—the root word of *ethic* and *ethical*—to refer to a speaker's credibility. Quintilian, a Roman teacher of public speaking, believed that an effective public speaker also should be a person of good character, a "good person speaking well."

We examine credibility in more detail in Chapter 5, where we discuss analyzing your audience's attitudes toward you; in Chapter 10, where we discuss establishing your credibility in your speech introduction; and in Chapter 15, where we discuss the role of credibility in persuading an audience.

For now, keep in mind that speaking ethically is one key to being perceived by your audience as a credible speaker.

credibility

An audience's perception of a speaker as competent, knowledgeable, dynamic, and trustworthy

STUDY GUIDE
REVIEW, APPLY, AND ASSESS

SPEAKING FREELY

3.1 Explain how free speech has been both challenged and defended throughout U.S. history.

Although the U.S. Congress and courts have occasionally limited the constitutional right to free speech, more often they have protected and broadened its application. Freedom of speech has also been upheld by such organizations as the American Civil Liberties Union and by colleges and universities. Social media are a new context for twenty-first-century challenges to free speech.

Key Terms

Thinking Ethically

Social media sites such as Facebook, Twitter, and Flickr continue to review and revise their policies regarding the protection of free speech. Given their widely diverse audiences that include international users, commercial users, and political dissidents, how can social media best develop audience-centered policies regarding free speech?

Thinking Critically

Why do you think the U.S. Supreme Court has historically considered flag burning and pornography to be "free speech acts"?

SPEAKING ETHICALLY

3.2 List and explain five criteria for ethical public speaking.

Speakers who exercise their right to free speech are responsible for tempering what they say by applying ethics. Most people agree that an ethical public speaker should have a clear, responsible goal, use sound evidence and reasoning, be sensitive to and tolerant of differences, be honest, and take appropriate steps to avoid plagiarism in order to be ethical.

Accommodation, or sensitivity to differences, leads speakers to demonstrate a willingness to listen to opposing viewpoints and learn about different beliefs and values. A speaker who is sensitive to differences avoids language that might be interpreted as being in any way biased or offensive.

Plagiarism is one of the most common violations of speech ethics. You can usually avoid plagiarizing by understanding what it is, doing your own work, and acknowledging—orally, in writing, or both—the sources for any quotations, ideas, statistics, or visual materials you use in a speech.

Key Terms

Thinking Ethically

From at least the time of Franklin Delano Roosevelt, speechwriters have written many of the best speeches made by U.S. presidents. Is such use of speechwriters ethical? Is it ethical to give credit to the presidents for memorable lines from speeches written by professional speechwriters?

Assessing Your Audience-Centered Speaking Skill

The following passage comes from the book *Abraham Lincoln, Public Speaker*, by Waldo W. Braden:

> The Second Inaugural Address, sometimes called Lincoln's Sermon on the Mount, was a concise, tightly constructed composition that did not waste words on ceremonial niceties or superficial sentiment. The shortest Presidential inaugural address up to that time, it was only 700 words long, compared to 3,700 words for the First, and required from 5 to 7 minutes to deliver.[26]

Which of the following statements should be credited to Braden if you were to use them in a speech?

- "Lincoln's second inaugural address is sometimes called Lincoln's Sermon on the Mount."
- "Because he was elected and sworn in for two terms as president, Abraham Lincoln prepared and delivered two inaugural addresses."
- "Lincoln's second inaugural address was 700 words and 5 to 7 minutes long."

SPEAKING CREDIBLY

3.3   Explain the relationship between ethics and credibility.

Speaking ethically allows your audience to trust you. Being trustworthy is an important part of being credible, or believable.

Key Term

Thinking Ethically

An important requirement for the ethical use of evidence and reasoning is to share with an audience all information that might help them reach a sound decision, including information that may be potentially damaging to your case. Would you consider a speaker who shares such information more or less credible than one who does not?

Assessing Your Audience-Centered Speaking Skill

As you listen to classmates' speeches, try to identify specific ways in which they try to gain your trust.

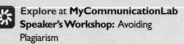
Explore at **MyCommunicationLab**
Speaker's Workshop: Avoiding Plagiarism

4 LISTENING TO SPEECHES

Sir Joshua Reynolds (1723–1792), *Self-Portrait as a Deaf Man*, 1775, Tate, London/Art Resource, NY

OBJECTIVES

After studying this chapter you should be able to do the following:

4.1
List and describe five barriers to effective listening.

4.2
Identify and implement strategies for becoming a better listener.

4.3
Identify and implement strategies for improving your critical listening and critical thinking skills.

4.4
Use criteria to effectively and appropriately evaluate speeches.

((●)) Listen to Chapter 4 at **MyCommunicationLab**

Learn how to listen and you will prosper—even from those who talk badly.

—Plutarch

A psychology professor had dedicated his life to teaching and worked hard to prepare interesting lectures, yet he found his students sitting through his talks with glassy-eyed expressions.[1] To find out what was on his students' minds if they were not focusing on psychology, he would, without warning, fire a blank from a gun and then ask his students to record their thoughts at the instant they heard the shot. Here is what he found:

20 percent were pursuing erotic thoughts or sexual fantasies.

20 percent were reminiscing about something (they weren't sure what they were thinking about).

20 percent were worrying about something or thinking about lunch.

8 percent were pursuing religious thoughts.

20 percent were reportedly listening.

12 percent were able to recall what the professor was talking about when the gun fired.

Like this professor, you would probably prefer that more than 12 percent of your audience could recall your messages. Understanding how listeners listen can help you improve your ability to connect with your audience. If you understand what holds listeners' attention, as well as how to navigate around the barriers to effective listening, you can make your messages stick like Velcro rather than slip off your listeners' minds like Teflon.

Considerable evidence also suggests that your own listening skills could be improved. Within 24 hours after listening to a lecture or speech, you will most likely recall only about 50 percent of the message. Forty-eight hours later, you are above average if you remember more than 25 percent of the message. Learning about listening can help you increase your listening skills so you can gain more benefits from the speeches you hear.

Listening is a complex process of selecting, attending to, understanding, remembering, and responding to verbal and nonverbal messages. Being able to describe these components of listening can help you retain more, and it can help you be a better speaker and a better listener.

- **Selecting.** To **select** a sound, the first stage of listening, is to single out a message from several competing messages. As a public speaker, your job is to develop a presentation that motivates your listeners to focus on your message.
- **Attending.** The sequel to selecting is attending. To **attend** to a sound is to focus on it. Most people's average attention span while listening to someone talk is about 8 seconds.[2] One of your key challenges as a public speaker is to capture and then hold the attention of your audience. Your choice of supporting material is often the key to gaining and maintaining attention.
- **Understanding.** Boiled down to its essence, communication is the process of *understanding*, or making sense of our experiences and sharing that sense with others.[3] We **understand** something when we create meaning out of what we experience. As a speaker, your job is to facilitate listener understanding by

**Explore at MyCommunicationLab
Activity:** "Steps in Listening"

listening
The process by which receivers select, attend to, understand, remember, and respond to senders' messages

select
To single out a message from several competing messages

attend
To focus on incoming information for further processing

understand
To assign meaning to the information to which you attend

making sure you clearly explain your ideas in terms and images to which your listeners can relate. Again, the challenge of being understood comes back to a focus on the audience.

- **Remembering.** The next stage in the listening process is *remembering*. To **remember** is to recall ideas and information. You hear more than one billion words each year, but how much information do you retain? It depends on how well you listen. Most listening experts believe that the main way to determine whether audience members have been listening is to determine what they remember. (That's the purpose of taking tests in school—to assess what you remember from what you've heard and read.)
- **Responding** The final stage in the listening process is to **respond**. When listeners respond, they react with their behavior to what they have heard. That's why it's useful for public speakers to develop specific behavioral goals for their talks. As a speaker, you should identify what you'd like listeners to be able to *do* after you speak. It could be that you want them simply to remember and restate your key ideas. Or you may want them to vote for someone, buy something, or enroll in a course.

Research confirms that good listening skills can improve the quality of both your life and your career.[4] In this chapter we discuss how people listen, and we identify barriers and pitfalls that keep both speakers and audiences from listening effectively. Our goal is not only to help you remember what speakers say but also to be a more thoughtful, ethical, and critical listener to the messages you hear. We'll offer tips to improve your ability to analyze and evaluate speeches, including your own.

Overcoming Barriers to Effective Listening

4.1 List and describe five barriers to effective listening.

Barriers are created when the listener doesn't select, attend, understand, remember, or respond to the message as planned by the speaker. The more you know about potential obstacles that keep your listeners from responding to your message the way you intend, the better able you will be to develop messages that hold their interest. We next discuss those barriers and how to deal with them.

Information Overload

We spend a large part of each day listening. That's both good news and bad news. The good news is that because we listen a lot, we have the potential to become very effective listeners. The bad news is that instead of getting better at it, we often tune out because we hear so much information that we get tired of listening. Listening researchers have developed what they call the **working memory theory of listening**, which explains why we sometimes just don't listen well. The theory suggests that when a listener's capacity is reached (when our working memory is full), then it's harder to concentrate and remember what we hear.[5]

Although this theory may make it appear that there's nothing you can do as either a speaker or a listener to manage this problem, listeners and speakers actually can use several strategies to overcome the limits of working memory.

remember
To recall ideas and information

respond
to react with a change in behavior to a speaker's message

working memory theory of listening
A theory that suggests that listeners find it difficult to concentrate and remember when their short-term working memories are full

What You Can Do as a Speaker You can keep your audience from tuning out by making sure your speech has a balance between new information and supporting material such as stories and examples. A speech that is too dense—chock-full of facts, new definitions, and undeveloped ideas—can make listening a tedious process. On the other hand, listeners don't want to listen to a bare-bones outline of ideas; they need ideas that are fleshed out with illustrations. Pace the flow of new ideas and information. Communication expert Frank E. X. Dance recommends a 30/70 ratio: 30 percent of your speaking time should be spent presenting new ideas and information, and 70 percent of your time should be spent supporting your ideas with vivid examples and interesting stories.[6]

Another way to combat information overload as a speaker is to build redundancy into your message. If listeners miss the idea the first time you present it, perhaps they will catch it during your concluding summary. Repeating key ideas can be part of that 70 percent of your message that extends the new information you present.

What You Can Do as a Listener If you find yourself tuning a speaker out because you're just tired of listening to someone talk, make a special effort to concentrate on the information you're hearing. The key to being a good listener is to recognize when you're not being a good listener and then to adjust how you are listening. Making sure that you are looking at the speaker, sitting up straight, and remaining focused on the message can help perk up your listening power.

Personal Concerns

You are sitting in your African history class on a Friday afternoon. It's a beautiful day. You slump into your seat, open your notebook, and prepare to take notes on the lecture. As the professor talks about an upcoming assignment, you begin to think about how you are going to spend your Saturday. One thought leads to another as you mentally plan your weekend. Suddenly you hear your professor say, "For Monday's test, you will be expected to know the principles I've just reviewed." What principles? What test? You were present in class, and you did *hear* the professor's lecture, but you're not sure what was said.

Your own thoughts are among the biggest competitors for your attention when you are a member of an audience. Most of us would rather listen to our own inner speech than to the message of a public speaker. As the psychology professor with the gun found, sex, lunch, worries, and daydreams are distractions for the majority of listeners.

What You Can Do as a Speaker To counteract the problem of listeners' focusing on their personal concerns instead of your message, consciously work to maintain your audience's attention by using occasional wake-up messages such as "Now listen carefully because this will affect your future grade (or family, or employment)." Delivering your message effectively by using good eye contact, speaking with appropriate volume and vocal variation, and using appropriate gestures for emphasis can also help keep listeners listening.

What You Can Do as a Listener To stay focused, it's important that you stop the mental conversation you're having with yourself about ideas unrelated to the speaker's message. Be aware of thoughts, worries, and daydreams that are competing for your attention. Then, once you are aware that you are off-task, return your attention to what the speaker is saying.

Outside Distractions

While sitting in class, you notice the person in front of you surfing the Internet on her tablet computer. Two classmates behind you are swapping stories about their favorite soap opera plots. You feel your phone vibrate in your pocket, which means someone just sent you a text. Out the window you see a varsity football hero struggling to break into his car to retrieve the keys he left in the ignition. As your history professor drones on about the Bay of Pigs invasion, you find it difficult to focus on his lecture. Most of us don't listen well when physical distractions compete with the speaker. And, with lives immersed in technology, the next distraction is only a text, phone call, or tweet away.

What You Can Do as a Speaker To minimize distractions, be aware of anything that might sidetrack your listeners' attention. For example, look at the way the room is arranged. Are the chairs arranged to allow listeners a clear view of you and any presentation aids you might use? Is there distracting or irrelevant information written on a chalkboard or whiteboard? Try to empathize with listeners by imagining what they will be looking at when you speak. Check out the room ahead of time, sit where your audience will be seated, and look for possible distractions. Then reduce or eliminate distractions (such as by closing windows or lowering shades to limit visual and auditory distractions or turning off blinking fluorescent lights, if you can). Also, tactfully discourage whispering in the audience.

What You Can Do as a Listener When listening, you too can help manage the speaking and listening environment by being on the lookout for distractions or potential distractions. If you must, move to another seat if people near you are talking or a rude cell phone user continues to text. If the speaker has failed to monitor the listening environment, you may need to close the blinds, turn up the heat, turn off the lights, close the door, or do whatever is necessary to minimize distractions.

Personal concerns and distractions such as texts are challenges to effective listening for many students. You can, however, learn to overcome these and other barriers and make yourself a better listener.
Photo: Monkey Business/Fotolia

Prejudice

Your buddy is a staunch Democrat. During the broadcast of a speech by the Republican governor of your state, he constantly argues against each of the governor's suggestions. The next day he is surprised to see new editorials praising the governor's speech. "Did those writers hear the same speech I did?" your friend wonders. Yes, they heard the same speech, but they listened differently. When you prejudge a message, your ability to understand it decreases.

Another way to prejudge a speech is to decide that the topic has little value for you before you even hear the message. Most of us at one time or another have not given our full attention to a speech because we decided beforehand that it was going to bore us.

Sometimes we make snap judgments about a speaker based on his or her appearance and then fail to listen because we have already dismissed the speaker's ideas as inconsequential or irrelevant. Female speakers often complain that males in the audience do not listen to them as attentively as they would to another male; members of ethnic and racial minorities may feel slighted in a similar way.

On the flip side, some people too readily accept what someone says just because they like the way the person looks, sounds, or dresses. For example, Tex believes that anyone with a Texas drawl must be an honest person. Such positive prejudices can also inhibit your ability to listen accurately to a message.

What You Can Do as a Speaker To keep your listeners from making snap judgments based on **prejudice**, do your best to get your audience's attention at the beginning of your message. Make sure you're not using examples, words, or phrases that could be misinterpreted. Keep your message focused on your listeners' interests, needs, hopes, and wishes.

prejudice
Preconceived opinions, attitudes, and beliefs about a person, place, thing, or message

When addressing an audience that may be critical of or hostile to your message, use detailed arguments and credible evidence rather than strong emotional appeals.

What You Can Do as a Listener One of the major problems with prejudice is being unaware of one's own preconceived notions. Guard against becoming so critical of a message that you don't listen to it or so impressed that you decide too quickly that the speaker is trustworthy without carefully examining the evidence the speaker offers. Keep your focus on the message rather than on the messenger.

Differences between Speech Rate and Thought Rate

Ralph Nichols, a pioneer in listening research and training, has identified a listening problem that centers on the way you process the words you hear.[7] Most people talk at a rate of 125 words a minute. But you have the ability to listen seven to ten times faster, to as many as 700 to 1,200 words a minute! The difference between your ability to process words and the speed at which a speaker can produce them gives you time to ignore a speaker periodically. Eventually, you stop listening; the extra time allows you to daydream and drift away from the message.

Nichols suggests that the different rates of speech and thought need not be a listening liability. Instead of drifting away from the speech, you can enhance your listening effectiveness by mentally summarizing from time to time what the speaker has said.

What You Can Do as a Speaker Avoid trying to speed up your speech. Even if you could speak 200 words a minute, your listeners would still want you to go about four times faster than that. Instead, develop a well-structured message. Build in message redundancy and internal summaries, use clear transitions, be well organized, and make your major ideas clear to help your listeners catch your message even when they've tuned out for a bit here and there.

What You Can Do as a Listener Because you have the ability to think much faster than people speak, you can use that dazzling mental power to stay focused on the message. Here's a powerful technique: Periodically making a mental summary of what a speaker has said can dramatically increase your ability to remember the information. The difference in speech rate and thought rate gives you time to sprinkle in several mental summaries while listening to a message.

RECAP

BARRIERS TO EFFECTIVE LISTENING

Barrier	Listener's Tasks	Speaker's Tasks
Information overload	• Concentrate harder. • Identify key points.	• Be clear. • Increase redundancy. • Use interesting stories and supporting material.
Personal concerns	• Focus on the message rather than your own thoughts.	• Use attention-maintaining strategies, such as startling information, statistics, or stories to "wake up" listeners.
Outside distractions	• Assertively control the listening environment.	• Adjust doors, curtains, windows, or other physical arrangements of the room.
Prejudice	• Focus on the message, not the messenger.	• Use strong opening statements that focus on listeners' interests.
Differences between speech rate and thought rate	• Mentally summarize the speaker's message while you listen.	• Build in redundancy. • Be well organized. • Use attention-maintaining strategies.

How to Become a Better Listener

4.2 Identify and implement strategies for becoming a better listener.

Now that we have examined barriers to effective listening and suggested a few strategies to overcome those barriers and be both a better speaker and a better listener, we offer a basketful of additional strategies for improving your listening skills. Specifically, we'll help you listen with your eyes. We'll help you be a mindful listener. And, finally, we will note specific behaviors that can help you listen skillfully.

 Explore at MyCommunicationLab
Activity: "Effective Listening"

Listen with Your Eyes as Well as Your Ears

To listen with your eyes is to be attuned to the unspoken cues of a speaker. Nonverbal cues play a major role in communicating a message. One expert has estimated that as much as 93 percent of the emotional content of a speech is conveyed by nonverbal cues.[8] Even though this statistic does not apply in every situation, emotion is primarily communicated by unspoken messages. To listen with your eyes, you need to accurately interpret what you see while ensuring that you don't allow yourself to be distracted by it, even when a speaker has poor delivery.

Accurately Interpret Nonverbal Messages Because the nonverbal message plays such a powerful role in affecting how you respond to a speaker, it's important to accurately interpret what a speaker is expressing nonverbally. A speaker's facial expressions will help you identify the emotions being communicated; a speaker's posture and gestures often reinforce the intensity of the specific emotion expressed.[9] If you have trouble understanding a speaker because he or she speaks too softly or speaks in an unfamiliar dialect, get close enough so that you can see the speaker's mouth. A good view can increase your level of attention and improve your understanding.

Watch at MyCommunicationLab
Video: "Listening and Nonverbal Communication"

To increase your skill in accurately interpreting nonverbal messages, consider the following suggestions:

- *Consider nonverbal cues in context.* When interpreting an unspoken message, don't just focus on one nonverbal cue; consider the situation you and the speaker are in.

- *Look for clusters of cues.* Instead of focusing on just one bit of behavior, look for several nonverbal cues to increase the accuracy of your interpretation of a speaker's message.

- *Look for cues that communicate liking, power, and responsiveness.* A nonverbal cue (eye contact, facial expression, body orientation) can often express whether someone likes us. We note people's degree of power or influence over us by the way they dress, how much space they have around them, or whether they are relaxed or tense. People who perceive themselves as having more power than those around them are usually more relaxed. Or we can observe whether someone is interested or focused on us by eye contact, head nods, facial expressions, and tone of voice.

Adapt to the Speaker's Delivery Good listeners focus on a speaker's message, not on his or her delivery style. To be a good listener, you must adapt to the particular idiosyncrasies some speakers have. You may have to ignore or overlook a speaker's tendency to mumble, speak in a monotone, or fail to make eye contact. Perhaps more difficult still, you may even have to forgive a speaker's lack of clarity or coherence. Rather than mentally criticizing an unpolished speaker, you may need to be sympathetic and try harder to concentrate on the message. Good listeners focus on the message, not the messenger.

> **RECAP**
>
> ## LISTEN WITH YOUR EYES AS WELL AS YOUR EARS
>
> Accurately interpret nonverbal messages:
> - Consider context.
> - Look for clusters.
> - Look for cues of liking.
> - Adapt your listening to the speaker's delivery.

Poor speakers are not the only challenge to good listening. You also need to guard against glib, well-polished speakers. An attractive style of delivery does not necessarily mean that a speaker's message is credible. Don't let a smooth-talking salesperson convince you to buy something without carefully considering the content of his or her message.

Listen Mindfully

Read at **MyCommunicationLab**
Learning From Great Speakers:
César Chávez

Mindful listeners are mentally focused on the listening task. Two listening researchers found that good listeners do the following:[10]

- Put their own thoughts aside
- Are present mentally as well as physically
- Make a conscious, mindful effort to listen
- Invest time in listening, patiently letting the speaker make his or her point
- Are open-minded

Bad listeners do just the opposite; they are distracted by their own thoughts, are mentally absent, are impatient, and are less open to what they hear. To be a mindful listener is to be aware of what you are doing when listening to others. How do you do that? Here are specific strategies to help you be a mindful listener.

Be Aware of Whether You Are Listening or Not Listening boils down to this: You are either on-task or off-task. If you are not either selecting or attending to a message, then you are not mentally engaged with what you are hearing. What's vital, yet simple, is that you be *aware* of whether you are on- or off-task when listening to someone. Unmindful listeners are not conscious of whether they are paying attention or daydreaming. As you are listening, occasionally take a moment to think about your own thoughts. Pretend you are in that class when the professor fires the gun. At the moment, are you thinking about the message, or have you allowed your thoughts to stray off-task?

If you become aware that you're not listening, research has found that you can increase your motivation to stay on-task by reminding yourself why listening is important.[11] Periodically engage in "self-talk" to tell yourself why the message you're hearing can be helpful or useful to you.

Monitor Your Emotional Reaction to a Message Heightened emotions can affect your ability to understand a message. If you become angry at a word or phrase a speaker uses, your listening comprehension decreases. Depending on their cultural backgrounds, religious convictions, and political views, listeners may become emotionally aroused by certain words. For most listeners, words that connote negative opinions about their ethnic origin, nationality, or religious views can trigger strong emotions. Cursing and obscene language are red flags for other listeners.

Yin Ping is an Asian American who has distinguished himself as a champion debater on the college debate team. One sly member of an opposing team sought to distract him by quoting a bigoted statement that disparaged Asian Americans for "taking over the country." It was tempting for Yin Ping to respond emotionally to the insult, but he kept his wits, refuted the argument, and went on to win the debate. When someone uses a word or phrase you find offensive, it's important to overcome your repugnance and continue to listen. Don't let a speaker's language close down your mind.

How can you keep your emotions in check when you hear something that sets you off? First, recognize when your emotional state is affecting your rational thought. Second, use the skill of self-talk to calm yourself

Good listeners are mentally fully present and invest effort in listening rather than allowing themselves to be distracted.

Photo: Kzenon/Fotolia

down. Say to yourself, "I'm not going to let this anger get in the way of listening and understanding." You can also focus for a moment on your breathing to calm down.

Be a Selfish Listener Although it may sound crass, being a selfish listener can help you maintain your powers of concentration. If you find your attention waning, ask yourself questions such as "What's in it for me?" and "How can I use information from this talk?" Granted, you will find more useful information in some presentations than in others—but be alert to the possibility in all speeches. Find ways to benefit from the information you are receiving, and try to connect it with your own experiences and needs.

Listen Skillfully

Besides being aware of nonverbal messages and being mindful listeners, good listeners exercise several skills that help them stay focused and remember what they've heard. They identify their listening goal, listen for major ideas, practice good listening methods, adapt their listening style as necessary, and are active listeners.

 Watch at **MyCommunicationLab** **Video:** "Guidelines and Suggestions for Improving Listening Skills"

Identify Your Listening Goal As Figure 4.1 shows, you invest a lot of your communication time in listening. If you are a typical student, you spend over 80 percent of your day involved in communication-related activities.[12] You listen a lot; research suggests you spend more than half of your communication time listening.[13] Your challenge is to stay on course and keep your listening focused.

One way to stay focused is to determine your listening purpose. There are at least four major listening goals: for pleasure, to empathize, to evaluate, and to gain information. Being conscious of your listening goal can help you listen more effectively. If, for example, your listening goal is simply to enjoy what you hear, you need not listen with the same intensity as when you want to remember what you hear.

Listening for Pleasure You listen to some things just for the fun of it. You might watch TV, listen to music, go to a movie, or chat with a friend. You won't be tested on Tumblr videos. Nor will you be asked to remember every joke in David Letterman's monologue. So, when listening for pleasure, just enjoy what you hear. You can, however, observe how effective speakers or entertainers gain and maintain your attention and keep you interested in their messages.

 **Explore** at **MyCommunicationLab** **Activity:** "Listening with Empathy"

Listening to Empathize To have empathy means to feel what the speaker is feeling. Usually, empathic listening occurs in one-on-one listening situations between friends. Sometimes, in your job, you may need to listen empathically to a client, customer, or coworker. Listening with empathy requires these essential steps:

1. **Stop.** Stop what you are doing and give your complete attention to the speaker.
2. **Look.** Make eye contact and pay attention to nonverbal cues that reveal emotions.
3. **Listen.** Pay attention to both the details and the major ideas of the message.
4. **Imagine.** Visualize how you would feel if you had experienced what the speaker has experienced.
5. **Check.** Check your understanding of the message by asking questions to clarify what you heard and by summarizing what you think you heard.

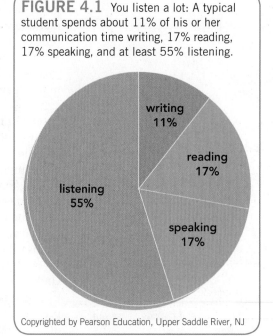

FIGURE 4.1 You listen a lot: A typical student spends about 11% of his or her communication time writing, 17% reading, 17% speaking, and at least 55% listening.

writing 11%

reading 17%

listening 55%

speaking 17%

Copyrighted by Pearson Education, Upper Saddle River, NJ

Listening to Evaluate When you evaluate a message, you are making a judgment about its content. You are interested in whether the information is reliable, true, or useful. When evaluating what you hear, the challenge is not to become so critical of the message that you miss a key point the speaker is making. You have to work harder when you listen to evaluate than in other situations because you must juggle two difficult tasks: You must make judgments as well as understand and recall the information you are hearing. Your biases and judgments act as noise that can cause you to misunderstand the intended meaning of the message.

Listening for Information Since preschool, you have been in listening situations in which someone wanted you to learn something. Keys to listening for information are listening for the details of a message and making certain you link the details to major ideas. As we will describe, poor listeners either listen only for facts and pieces of a message or are interested only in the bottom line. By concentrating on both facts and major ideas, while at the same time mentally summarizing the information you hear, you can dramatically increase your ability to remember messages. Also, remember to compare unfamiliar information to ideas and concepts with which you are familiar.

Listen for Major Ideas In a classic study, Ralph Nichols asked both good and poor listeners what their listening strategies were.[14] The poor listeners indicated that they listened for facts, such as names and dates. The good listeners reported that they listened for major ideas and principles. Facts are useful only when you can connect them to a principle or concept. In speeches, facts as well as examples are used primarily to support major ideas. Try to summarize in your mind the major ideas that the specific facts support.

If you heard President Barack Obama deliver his Second Inaugural Address in Washington, D.C., on the sunny morning of January 22, 2013, you heard him introduce his key idea about two minutes into his speech by repeating these three words: "We the people. . . ." A good listener would recognize that these words reveal a core idea of the speech—that it takes a collaborative effort to do good things.

How can you tell what the major ideas in a speech are? A speaker who is well organized or familiar with good speaking techniques will offer a preview of the major ideas early in the speech. If no preview is provided, listen for the speaker to enumerate major points: "My first point is that the history of Jackson County is evident in its various styles of architecture." Transitional phrases and a speaker's internal summaries are other clues that can help you identify the major points. If your speaker provides few overt indicators, you may have to discover them on your own. In that event, mentally summarize the ideas that are most useful to you. Be a selfish listener: Treat a disorganized speech as a river with gold in the sands, and take your mental mining pan and search for the nuggets of meaning.

Practice Listening Because you spend at least 55 percent of your day listening, you may wonder why we suggest that you practice listening. The reason is that listening skills do not develop automatically. You learn to swim by getting proper instruction; you're unlikely to develop good aquatic skills just by jumping in the water and flailing around. Similarly, you will learn to listen by practicing the methods we recommend. Researchers believe that poor listeners avoid challenge. For example, they listen to and watch TV situation comedies rather than documentaries or other informative programs. Your listening skill develops as you listen to speeches, music, and programs with demanding content.

Understand Your Listening Style New research suggests that not everyone listens to information in the same way. There are at least four different **listening styles**— preferred ways of making sense out of spoken messages. Listening researchers have discovered that many listeners have one of the following listening styles: relational,

listening styles
Preferred ways of making sense out of spoken messages

analytical, critical, or task-oriented.[15] Understanding your listening style can help you become a better and more flexible listener.[16]

About 40 percent of listeners have one primary listening style; another 40 percent use more than one style; and about 20 percent don't have a listening style preference. As you read the descriptions of the four listening styles, see if you can determine to which of these segments of the listening population you belong.[17] The best listeners are flexible listeners who can adapt their style to fit the occasion and the person speaking.[18]

Relational-Oriented Listeners You're a **relational-oriented listener** if you are comfortable listening to people express feelings and emotions. It's likely that you are highly empathic and that you seek common ground with the person you are listening to. You are easily moved by poignant illustrations and anecdotes. You enjoy hearing stories about people and personal relationships. Relational-oriented listeners are generally less apprehensive than other types when speaking with others in interpersonal and group situations.[19]

Task-Oriented Listeners Task-oriented listeners want to know what to do with the information that they hear. They listen for the verbs—the action words that indicate what task should be completed after listening to the information. The **task-oriented listener** wants people to get to the point and listens for actions that need to be taken. To a task-oriented listener, a long story or a lengthy personal example without some direction is less satisfying than is a call for action. Task-oriented listeners also seem to be more skeptical than people with other listening styles. They prefer to be given evidence to support the recommendations for action.

Analytical Listeners Analytical listeners prefer to listen to complex information that is laced with facts and details. They often withhold judgment before reaching a specific conclusion. You're an **analytical listener** if you reject messages because they don't have adequate evidence to support the conclusions. In addition, analytical listeners don't like rambling stories that don't seem to have a point; they want to know what the key facts are rather than listen to a long narrative. Analytical listeners make good judges or lawyers because they enjoy listening to debates and hearing arguments for and against ideas.[20]

Critical Listeners You're a **critical listener** if you spend time evaluating the messages you hear. Critical listeners are comfortable listening to detailed, complex information yet can focus on contradictions and inconsistencies in the information presented. Critical listeners are also likely to catch errors in the overall reasoning and evidence that are used to reach a conclusion.

Knowing your listening style can help you better adapt to a speaker whose style is not your style. For example, if you are an analytical listener and a speaker is telling long stories and meandering through the material, you'll have to tell yourself to concentrate harder on the message. If you are a relational-oriented listener and you're listening to a message that's primarily facts, principles, and ideas, you will be a better listener if you understand why the message may not be holding your attention and work to focus on the message. We've emphasized the importance of being an audience-centered speaker, but the opposite is true as well: As a listener you can increase your concentration if you adjust and adapt your listening style to the speaking styles of the

relational-oriented listener
Someone who is comfortable listening to others express feelings and emotions

task-oriented listener
Someone who prefers information that is well organized, brief, and precise

analytical listener
Someone who prefers messages that are supported with facts and details

critical listener
Someone who prefers to evaluate messages

RECAP

LISTENING STYLES

Relational-oriented listening	Listeners prefer to attend to feelings and emotions and to search for common areas of interest when listening to others.
Task-oriented listening	Listeners are focused on accomplishing something; they like efficient, clear, and brief messages. They listen for verbs to determine what action needs to be taken.
Analytical listening	Listeners prefer to withhold judgment, listen to all sides of an issue, and wait until they hear the facts before reaching a conclusion.
Critical listening	Listeners are likely to listen for the facts and evidence to support key ideas and an underlying logic; they also listen for errors, inconsistencies, and discrepancies.

speakers you hear. As we note in Chapter 3, the key, whether you are a speaker or a listener, is to ethically adapt and adjust to enhance the quality of communication.

Explore at **MyCommunicationLab**
Activity: "Active Listening"

Become an Active Listener An active listener is one who remains alert and mentally re-sorts, rephrases, and repeats key information while listening to a speech. Because you can listen to words much faster than a speaker can say them, it's natural for your mind to wander. But you can use the extra time to focus on interpreting what the speaker says.

1. **Re-sort.** Use your listening time to re-sort disorganized or disjointed ideas. If the speaker is rambling, seek ways to rearrange his or her ideas into a new, more logical pattern. For example, re-sort the ideas into a chronological pattern: What happened first, second, and so on? If the speaker hasn't chunked the ideas into a logical framework, see if you can find a structure to help you reorganize the information. Yes, it would be useful if the speaker had done that. But when the speaker isn't organized, you'll benefit if you can turn a jumbled mass of information into a structure that makes sense to you. For example, a speaker says, "There are three key dates to remember: 1776, 1492, and 1861." You re-sort: 1492, 1776, 1861.

2. **Rephrase.** Mentally summarize the key points or information that you want to remember. Listen for the main ideas and then paraphrase them in your own words. You are more likely to remember your mental paraphrase of the information than the exact words of the speaker. If you can, try to summarize what the speaker is saying in a phrase that might fit on a bumper sticker. Listening for "information handles" provided by the speaker in the form of previews, transitions, signposts, and summary statements can also help you remain actively involved as a listener. A speaker says, "If we don't stop the destructive overspending of the defense budget, our nation will very quickly find itself much deeper in debt and unable to meet the many needs of its citizens." You rephrase: "We should spend less on defense, or we will have more problems."

3. **Repeat.** Finally, do more than just rephrase the information as you listen to it. Periodically *repeat* key points you want to remember. Go back to essential ideas and restate them to yourself every five minutes or so. If you follow these steps for active listening, you will find yourself feeling stimulated and engaged instead of tired and bored as you listen to even the dullest of speakers.

RECAP

ACTIVE LISTENING

STEPS	DEFINITION	EXAMPLE
Re-sort	Reorganize jumbled or disorganized information.	What the speaker said: "There are several key dates to remember in America's history: 1776, 1492, 1861." You re-sort: 1492, 1776, 1861
Rephrase	Paraphrase to simplify the speaker's ideas rather than trying to remember his or her exact words.	What the speaker said: "If we don't stop the destructive over-spending of the defense budget, our nation will very quickly find itself much deeper in debt and unable to meet the many needs of its citizens." You rephrase: "We should spend less on defense, or we will have more problems."
Repeat	Periodically, mentally restate the key ideas you want to remember.	Repeat your paraphrase five minutes further into the speech.

Listen Ethically

An effective listener does more than just gain an accurate understanding of a speaker's message; effective listeners are also ethical listeners. An ethical listener participates in a communication event by honestly communicating his or her expectations, providing helpful feedback, and being sensitive to and tolerating differences when listening to others. In the fourth century B.C.E., Aristotle warned, "Let men be on their guard against those who flatter and mislead the multitude." And contemporary rhetorician Harold Barrett has said that the audience is the "necessary source of correction" for the behavior of a speaker.[21] The following guidelines for ethical listening incorporate what Barrett calls "attributes of the good audience."

Communicate Your Expectations and Feedback As an audience member, you have the right—even the responsibility—to enter a communication situation with expectations about the message and how the speaker will deliver it. Know what information and ideas you want to get out of the communication transaction. Expect a coherent, organized, and competently delivered presentation. Communicate your objectives and react to the speaker's message and delivery through appropriate nonverbal and verbal feedback. For example, maintain eye contact with the speaker. Nod in agreement when you support something the speaker says. There is evidence that by being a supportive listener (by having eye contact with the speaker, signaling agreement, and being attentive) you help the speaker feel more comfortable and less nervous.[22] We are not suggesting, however, that you fake your support for a speaker. If you show, with an honest quizzical look, that you do not understand a speaker's point, you can help an attentive, audience-centered speaker rephrase the message for better listener comprehension. Turn your head to one side and tilt it slightly forward to communicate that you are having trouble hearing. If a question-and-answer period follows the speech, ask questions you may still have about the speaker's topic or point of view.

Be Sensitive to and Tolerant of Differences As an ethical listener, remember that your preferred approach to speaking and listening may differ from the approach a speaker is using. But your preference doesn't make the speaker's approach a wrong one. For example, suppose you were to attend a high school baccalaureate ceremony at which the speaker was a dynamic African American minister who used a duet-style, call-and-response type of speaking, in which the audience periodically responds verbally to the speaker. If you were to disregard the minister's delivery for being too flamboyant, you might miss out on a powerful message. Different cultures have different styles of speaking.

Diverse cultural norms can sometimes pose a complex ethical-listening challenge. For example, political leader and civil rights advocate Jesse Jackson has been accused of making dishonest claims in some speeches about his background and behavior. He has said that he left the University of Illinois because racism on the football team caused him to be passed over for starting quarterback—yet former teammates insist that he did not become starting quarterback simply because he was not the strongest player. Jackson has also overstated the poverty he experienced as a child, when in fact he grew up in a fairly comfortable middle-class home. Although many have criticized exaggeration of this kind, at least one communication researcher has defended Jackson, arguing that although his "tall tales" are not necessarily "the truth" in a strictly objective sense, they are part of a valid African American oral tradition that focuses on the "symbolic import of the story" and in which speakers traditionally exaggerate to enhance the impact of their illustrations.[23] When you consider the cultural expectations and backgrounds of both the speaker and the listeners, you will be in a better position to interpret what is being expressed.

Be attentive and courteous. Consider cultural norms and audience expectations as part of the context within which you listen to and evaluate a speaker. Making

TABLE 4.1 HOW TO ENHANCE YOUR LISTENING SKILLS

	THE GOOD LISTENER . . .	THE POOR LISTENER . . .
Listen with Your Eyes as Well as Your Ears	• Looks for nonverbal cues to enhance understanding • Adapts to the speaker's delivery	• Focuses only on the words • Is easily distracted by the delivery of the speech
Listen Mindfully	• Is aware of whether or not he or she is listening • Controls emotions • Mentally asks, "What's in it for me?"	• Is not aware of whether he or she is on-task or off-task • Erupts emotionally when listening • Does not attempt to relate to the information personally
Listen Skillfully	• Identifies the listening goal • Listens for major ideas • Seeks opportunities to practice listening skills • Understands and adapts his or her listening style to the speaker • Listens actively by re-sorting, rephrasing, and repeating what is heard	• Does not have a listening goal in mind • Listens for isolated facts • Avoids listening to difficult information • Is not aware of how to capitalize on his or her listening style • Listens passively, making no effort to engage with the information heard
Listen Ethically	• Clearly communicates listening expectations • Is sensitive to and tolerant of differences	• Makes no effort to respond appropriately to a speaker's message • Expects others to have the same beliefs, values, and cultural expectations he or she has

RECAP

LISTEN ETHICALLY

• Communicate your expectations and feedback.
• Be sensitive to and tolerant of cultural and individual differences.

an effort to understand the needs, goals, and interests of both the speaker and other audience members can help you judge how to react appropriately and ethically as a listener.

Table 4.1 summarizes all of the skills of better listening that we have discussed.

4.3 Identify and implement strategies for improving your critical listening and critical thinking skills.

Improving Listening and Critical Thinking Skills

Effective listening requires the ability to listen critically. Listening critically and thinking critically both involve a variety of skills we reexamine throughout this text. **Critical listening** is the process of listening to evaluate the quality, appropriateness, value, or importance of the information you hear. Related to being a critical listener is being a critical thinker. **Critical thinking** is the process of making judgments about the conclusions presented in what you see, hear, and read. The goal of a critical listener or a critical thinker is to evaluate information in order to make a choice. Whether you are listening to a political candidate giving a persuasive presentation to get your vote, a radio announcer extolling the virtues of a new herbal weight-loss pill, or someone asking you to invest in a new technology company, your goal as a critical listener is to assess the quality of the information and the validity of the conclusions presented.

critical listening
Evaluating the quality of information, ideas, and arguments presented by a speaker

critical thinking
Making judgments about the conclusions presented in what you see, hear, and read

We should emphasize that being a critical listener does not mean you're looking only for what the speaker says that is wrong; we're not suggesting that you listen to a speaker just to pounce on the message and the messenger at the conclusion of the speech. Listen to identify what the speaker does that is effective as well as to identify what conclusions don't hold up. The educator John Dewey penned a lasting description of criticism:

> Criticism . . . is not fault-finding. It is not pointing out evils to be reformed. It is judgment engaged in discriminating among values. It is talking through as to what is better and worse . . . with some consciousness of why the worse is worse.[24]

How does a critical listener do all of this? Consider the following skills.

Separate Facts from Inferences

The ability to separate facts from inferences is a basic critical thinking and listening skill. **Facts** are information that has been proven to be true by direct observation. For example, it has been directly observed that water boils at 212 degrees Fahrenheit and that the direction of the magnetic north pole can be found by consulting a compass. An **inference** is a conclusion based on partial information or an evaluation that has not been directly observed. You infer that your favorite sports team will win the championship or that it will rain tomorrow. You can also infer, if more Republicans than Democrats are elected to Congress, that the next president might be a Republican. But you can only know this for a *fact* after the presidential election. Facts are in the realm of certainty; inferences are in the realm of probability and opinion—where most arguments advanced by public speakers reside. A critical listener knows that when a politician running for office claims, "It's a fact that my opponent is not qualified to be elected," this statement is *not* a fact but an inference.

Evaluate the Quality of Evidence

Evidence consists of the facts, examples, opinions, and statistics that a speaker uses to support a conclusion. Researchers have documented that the key element in swaying a jury is the quality and quantity of the evidence presented to support a case.[25] Without credible supporting evidence, it would not be wise to agree with a speaker's conclusion.

What should you listen for when trying to decide whether evidence is credible? When, for example, a radio announcer says "it is a fact that this herbal weight-loss pill helps people lose weight," your job as a listener is to determine whether that statement is, in fact, credible. Has it been proven by direct observation to be true? The speaker has an obligation to provide evidence to support the statement asserted.

Some speakers will support a conclusion with examples. But if the examples aren't typical, or only one or two examples are offered, or other examples are known to differ from the one the speaker is using, then you should question the conclusion.

Another form of evidence a speaker might use to convince you is an opinion. Simply stated, an opinion is a quoted comment from someone. The best opinions come from reliable, credible sources. What makes a source credible? A credible source is someone who has the credentials, experience, and skill to make an observation about the topic at hand. Listen for whom a speaker cites when quoting an expert on a subject.

A fourth kind of evidence often used, especially with skeptical listeners, is statistics. A statistic is a number that summarizes a collection of examples. Some of the same questions that should be asked about other

facts
Information that has been proven to be true by direct observation

inference
A conclusion based on partial information, or an evaluation that has not been directly observed

evidence
The facts, examples, opinions, and statistics that a speaker uses to support a conclusion

Critical listeners must pay close attention and keep an open mind in order to separate facts from inferences and to evaluate the quality of evidence, logic, reasoning, and the use of rhetorical strategies.

Photo: Rob/Fotolia

forms of evidence should be asked about statistics: Are the statistics reliable, unbiased, recent, representative, and valid?

Here we've introduced you to the importance of *listening for* good evidence. Because evidence is an important element of public speaking, we'll provide more information about how to *use* evidence when we discuss using supporting material, in Chapter 7, and using evidence to persuade, in Chapter 15.

Evaluate the Underlying Logic and Reasoning

An effective critical listener listens not only for evidence but also for the overall structure of the logic, or argument, the speaker uses to reach a conclusion. **Logic** is a formal system of rules applied to reach a conclusion. A speaker is logical when he or she offers appropriate evidence to reach a valid, well-reasoned conclusion. For example, Angela tried to convince her listeners to take Slimlean as a weight-loss herb by pointing out that many stores sell this diet product, but that is not a logical framework for her conclusion. Just because Slimlean is readily available does not mean that it's effective and safe.

Reasoning is the process of drawing a conclusion from evidence within the logical framework of an argument. Can we reasonably conclude that anyone can lose weight by taking Slimlean simply because it's available in many stores? That kind of evidence does not support this conclusion. When a speaker seeks to change your behavior, listen carefully to the logic or structure of the arguments presented. Is the speaker trying to convince you to do something by offering one or two specific examples? Is the speaker reaching a conclusion based on a fundamental principle such as "All herbal diet supplements will cause you to lose weight"? The critical listener appropriately reviews the logic and reasoning used to reach a conclusion. When we discuss reasoning fallacies in Chapter 15, we will elaborate on the types of reasoning and we'll identify the ways speakers misuse logic, reasoning, and evidence.

You might reasonably suspect that a primary goal of a public-speaking class would be to enhance your speaking skill, and you'd be right. But in addition to becoming a better speaker, a study of communication principles and skills should help you to become a better *consumer* of messages. Becoming a critical listener and thinker is an important benefit of learning how messages are constructed. Researchers have found that a student who has completed any communication course—debate, argumentation, or public speaking—is likely to show improved critical thinking ability. This introduction to critical listening and thinking skills is reinforced throughout the rest of the book by discussions of how to become an audience-centered public speaker.

---

logic
A formal system of rules used to reach a conclusion

reasoning
The process of drawing a conclusion from evidence

rhetorical criticism
The process of using a method or standards to evaluate the effectiveness and appropriateness of messages

---

RECAP

IMPROVING LISTENING AND CRITICAL THINKING SKILLS

Separate facts from inferences:
- Are the facts really facts—something that has been proven to occur or exist?
- Is the conclusion an inference—something that is based on partial or unobserved evidence?

Evaluate evidence:
- Facts: Are the facts from credible sources?
- Examples: Are there enough examples to prove the point?
- Opinions: Are the opinions from knowledgeable experts?
- Statistics: Is the source of the statistic reliable and unbiased?

Evaluate the logic and reasoning of conclusions:
- Is there credible evidence to support the conclusion?
- Is there enough evidence to support the conclusion?

4.4 | Use criteria to effectively and appropriately evaluate speeches.

Watch at MyCommunicationLab
Video: "Speech Critique"

Analyzing and Evaluating Speeches

Your critical thinking and listening skills will help you evaluate not only the speeches of others but your own speeches as well. When you evaluate something, you judge its worth and appropriateness. To make a judgment about the value of something, it's important to use relevant criteria. **Rhetorical criticism** is the process of using a method or standards to evaluate the effectiveness and appropriateness of messages.

To better understand the concept of rhetorical criticism, it's important to understand the meaning of the words *rhetoric* and *criticism*. The term *rhetoric* is both classical and contemporary.[26] The ancient Greek scholar Aristotle defined rhetoric as the faculty of discovering in any given case the available means of persuasion.[27] Another ancient Greek scholar, Isocrates, believed that effective rhetoric should have the "qualities of fitness for the occasion, propriety of style and originality of treatment."[28] A more contemporary rhetorical scholar, Kenneth Burke, said that rhetoric is a "symbolic means of inducing cooperation."[29] In summary, **rhetoric** is the process of using symbols to create meaning to achieve a goal. As a public speaker, you are a rhetorician in that you're using **symbols**—words, images, nonverbal cues—to create meaning in the minds of your listeners in order to achieve a goal (to inform, to persuade, to entertain). To be a rhetorical critic is to evaluate the effectiveness and appropriateness of the message and the delivery of a presentation as well as to *illuminate* or make better sense of the message.[30]

One important goal of studying public speaking is to be a better rhetorical critic of the many messages you hear every day. In our discussion of how to analyze and evaluate speeches, we'll suggest criteria for evaluating messages and then offer specific strategies for sharing your evaluations with others.

Understanding Criteria for Evaluating Speeches

What makes a speech good? For more than two thousand years, rhetorical scholars have been debating this question. Our purpose here is not to take you through the centuries of dialogue and debate about this issue but to offer practical ways to evaluate your own messages as well as the messages of others.

Your public-speaking teacher will probably have you use an evaluation form that lists the precise criteria for evaluating your speeches. Figure 4.2 lists the key questions to use in evaluating any speech. The questions reflect the audience-centered model of public speaking that we presented in Chapter 2.

Underlying any list of what a good speaker should do are two fundamental goals: *Any speech should be both effective and ethical.* The mission of the National Communication Association mirrors the same two goals—to promote effective and ethical communication. These two requirements can translate into general criteria for evaluating speeches you give as well as those you hear.

The Message Should Be Effective To be effective, the message of a speech should be understandable to listeners and should achieve its intended purpose.[31] Public speaking is sometimes called *public communication*. A goal of any communication effort is to create a common understanding of the message on the part of both the sender and the receiver. The words *common* and *communication* resemble each other. When listeners fail to comprehend the speaker's ideas, the speech fails. Even more difficult than saying something is saying something a listener will understand. In this course, you'll learn an array of principles and strategies to help you develop a common understanding between you and your audience. The process of communicating is anchored first and foremost in considering the needs of your listeners. As you listen to speeches, a fundamental criterion for determining whether the message is a good one or not is whether you understand the message.

Another way to evaluate the effectiveness of a message is to assess whether it achieved its intended goal. The challenge in using this criterion to evaluate speeches is that you may not always know the speaker's true intent. You might be able to discern whether the *general purpose* is to inform, persuade, or entertain, but decoding the *specific purpose* may be tricky unless the speaker explicitly states it. The best you can do is to be a careful listener.

The Message Should Be Ethical A good speaker is an ethical speaker. Ethics are the beliefs, values, and moral principles by which people determine what is right

rhetoric
The use of symbols to create meaning to achieve a goal

symbols
Words, images, and behaviors that create meaning

FIGURE 4.2 Audience-Centered Speaking Evaluation Questions

Audience Orientation
☐ Did the speaker make a specific effort to adapt to the audience?

Select and Narrow Topic
☐ Was the topic appropriate for the audience, the occasion, and the speaker?
☐ Was the speech narrowed to fit the time limits?

Determine Purpose
☐ Was the general purpose (to inform, to persuade, to entertain) clear?
☐ Was the specific purpose appropriate for the audience?

Develop Central Idea
☐ Was the central idea clear enough to be summarized in one sentence?

Generate Main Ideas
☐ Were the main ideas clearly identified in the introduction of the speech, developed in the body of the speech, and summarized in the conclusion of the speech?

Gather Supporting Material
☐ Did the speaker use varied and interesting supporting material?
☐ Did the speaker use effective and appropriate evidence to support conclusions?
☐ Did the speaker use credible supporting material?

Organize Speech
☐ Did the speech have a clear introduction that caught attention, provided a preview of the speech, and established the speaker's credibility?
☐ Did the speaker organize the body of the speech in a logical way?
☐ Did the speaker use transitions, summaries, and signposts to clarify the organization?
☐ Did the speaker appropriately summarize the major ideas and provide closure to the speech during the conclusion?

Rehearse the Speech
☐ Did the speech sound as though it was well rehearsed?
☐ Did the speaker seem familiar with the speech content?

Deliver Speech
☐ Did the speaker make appropriate eye contact with the audience?
☐ Did the speaker use appropriate volume and vocal variation?
☐ Did the speaker use gestures and posture appropriately?
☐ Did the speaker use presentation aids that were easy to see and of high quality?
☐ Did the speaker handle presentation aids effectively?

or wrong. An ethical public speaker tells the truth, gives credit for ideas and words where credit is due, and doesn't plagiarize. If a speaker's message is clearly understood by the audience and gets the reaction the speaker desired, but the speaker has used unethical means to achieve the goal, the message may be an *effective* message, but it is not an *appropriate* message.

You will probably speak to audiences that have a wide array of cultural backgrounds. Regardless of their cultural tradition, your listeners hold an underlying ethical code. As we noted in Chapter 3, although not every culture has the same application of ethical rules, many cultures adhere to precepts that in essence state the value of being audience-centered by considering how others would like to be treated. An ethical public speaker focuses not only on achieving the goal of the message but also on being sensitive and responsive to listeners.

Identifying and Analyzing Rhetorical Strategies

Rhetorical strategies are the methods and techniques that speakers employ to achieve their speaking goals. Recall that rhetoric is the use of symbols to achieve goals. Symbols can be words, images (a flag, a cross, a six-pointed star), or behaviors that create meaning for others. Whether you use them in an interview to convince an employer to hire you or you hear them in a pop-up Internet commercial to persuade you to buy something, words and images that symbolically inform and persuade are all around you. Public speakers are rhetoricians who use symbols to achieve their goals.

One way to enhance your listening skill and become more mindful of how messages influence your behavior is to analyze the rhetorical strategies a speaker is using. It's especially important to be aware of how some speakers may use unethical strategies—such as misusing evidence, relying too heavily on emotion, or fabricating information—to deceive or manipulate you.

Rhetorician Robert Rowland offers a simple but comprehensive framework for describing and analyzing rhetorical messages: Be conscious of the goal of the message, its organization, the speaker's role, the overall tone of the message, the intended audience, and the techniques the speaker uses to achieve the goal.[32] Whether it's a speaker in your public-speaking class, the president delivering a State of the Union address, a member of the clergy delivering a sermon, or a parent addressing the school board, each speaker uses rhetorical strategies to achieve a goal. The more clearly you can identify and analyze the speaker's methods, the more effectively you can assess whether the message and the messenger are worthy of your support—and you become a more discerning rhetorical critic.

Giving Feedback to Others

As you enhance your skills of listening to messages and identifying rhetorical strategies, you may be asked to evaluate the speeches of others and provide feedback to them. The speech evaluation questions in Figure 4.2 can serve you well as you evaluate others' messages. Your instructor may also provide you with a speech evaluation form that will help you focus on the essential elements of public speechmaking.

When you're invited to critique your classmates, your feedback will be more effective if you keep the following general principles in mind. Because the word *criticism* means "to judge or discuss," to criticize a speech is to discuss the speech—identifying both its strengths and those aspects that could be improved. Effective criticism stems from developing a genuine interest in the speaker, not from seeking to find fault.

1. **Be Descriptive.** In a neutral way, describe what you saw the speaker doing. Act as a mirror for the speaker to help him or her become aware of gestures and other nonverbal signals of which he or she may not be aware. (If you and the speaker are watching a videotape of the speech together, you can point out

rhetorical strategies
Methods and techniques that speakers use to achieve their speaking goals

behaviors.) Avoid providing only a list of your likes and dislikes; describe what you observe.

Effective: Stan, I noticed that about 50 percent of the time you had direct eye contact with your listeners.

Less Effective: Your eye contact was lousy.

2. **Be Specific.** When you describe what you see a speaker doing, make sure your descriptions are precise enough to give the speaker a clear image of your perceptions. Saying that a speaker had "poor delivery" doesn't give him or her much information—it's only a general evaluative comment. Be as specific and thoughtful as you can.

Effective: Dawn, your use of color on your PowerPoint slide helped to keep my attention.

Less Effective: I liked your visuals.

3. **Be Positive.** Begin and end your feedback with positive comments. Beginning with a negative comment immediately puts the speaker on the defensive and can create so much internal noise that he or she stops listening. Starting and ending with positive comments engenders less defensiveness. Some teachers call this approach the feedback sandwich. First, tell the speaker something he or she did well. This will let the speaker know you're not an enemy who's trying to shoot holes in his or her performance. Then share a suggestion or two that may help the speaker improve the presentation. End your evaluation with another positive comment or restate what you liked best about the presentation.

Effective: Gabe, I thought your opening statistic was very effective in catching my attention. You also maintained direct eye contact when you delivered it. Your overall organizational pattern would have been clearer to me if you had used more signposts and transition statements. Or perhaps you could use a visual aid to summarize the main points. You did a good job of summarizing your three points in your conclusion. I also liked the way you ended your speech by making a reference to your opening statistics.

Less Effective: I got lost in the body of your speech. I couldn't figure out what your major ideas were. I also didn't know when you made the transition between the introduction and the body of your speech. Your intro and conclusion were good, but the organization of the speech was weak.

4. **Be Constructive.** Give the speaker suggestions or alternatives for improvement. It's not especially helpful to rattle off a list of things you don't like without offering some ideas for improvement. As a student of public speaking, your comments should reflect your growing skill and sophistication in the speechmaking process.

Effective: Jerry, I thought your speech had several good statistics and examples that suggest you spent a lot of time in the library researching your topic. I think you could add credibility to your message if you shared your sources with the listener. Your vocal quality was effective, and you had considerable variation in your pitch and tone, but at times the speech rate was a little fast for me. A slower rate would help me catch some of the details of your message.

Less Effective: You spoke too fast. I had no idea whom you were quoting.

5. **Be Sensitive.** "Own" your feedback by using I-statements rather than you-statements. An *I-statement* is a way of phrasing your feedback so that it is clear that your comments reflect your personal point of view. "I found my attention drifting during the body of your speech" is an example of an I-statement. A *you-statement* is a less sensitive way of describing someone's behavior by implying that the other person did something wrong. "You didn't summarize very well in your conclusion" is an example of a you-statement. A better way to make the same point is to say, "I wasn't sure I understood the key ideas you mentioned in your conclusion." Here's another example:

Effective: Mark, I found myself so distracted by your gestures that I had trouble focusing on the well-organized message.

Less Effective: Your gestures were distracting and awkward.

6. **Be Realistic.** Provide usable information. Offer feedback about aspects of the presentation that the speaker can improve rather than about those things he or she cannot control. Maybe you have heard this advice: "Never try to teach a pig to sing. It wastes your time. It doesn't sound pretty. And it annoys the pig." Saying "You're too short to be seen over the lectern," "Your lisp doesn't lend itself to public speaking," or "You looked nervous" is not constructive. Comments of this kind will only annoy or frustrate the speaker because they refer to things the speaker can't do much to change. Concentrate on behaviors over which the speaker has some control.

Effective: Taka, I thought your closing quote was effective in summarizing your key ideas, but it didn't end your speech on an uplifting note. Another quote from Khalil Gibran that I'll share with you after class would also summarize your key points and provide a positive affirmation of your message. You may want to try it if you give this speech again.

Less Effective: Your voice isn't well suited to public speaking.

As you provide feedback, whether in your public-speaking class or to a friend who asks you for a reaction to his or her speech, remember that the goal of feedback is to offer descriptive and specific information that will help a speaker build confidence and skill.

Giving Feedback to Yourself

While you are collecting feedback from your instructor, classmates, family, and friends, keep in mind that *you* are the most important critic of your speeches. The goal of public-speaking instruction is to learn principles and skills that enable *you* to be your own best critic. As you rehearse your speech, use self-talk to comment about the choices you make as a speaker. After your speech, take time to reflect on both the speech's virtues and the areas for improvement in your speechmaking skill. As an audience-centered speaker, you must learn to recognize when to make changes on your feet, in the middle of a speech. For example, if you find that your audience just isn't interested in the facts and statistics you are sharing, you may decide to support your points with a couple of stories instead. We encourage you to consider the following principles to enhance your own self-critiquing skills.

Look for and Reinforce Your Skills and Speaking Abilities Try to recognize your strengths and skills as a public speaker. Note how your audience analysis, organization, and delivery were effective in achieving your objectives. Such positive reflection can reinforce the many skills you learn in this course. Resist the temptation to be too harsh or overly critical of your speaking skill.

Evaluate Your Effectiveness Based on a Specific Speaking Situation and Audience Throughout the book we offer many suggestions and tips for improving your speaking skill. We also stress that these prescriptions should be considered in light of your specific audience. Don't be a slave to rules. If you are giving a pep talk to the Little League team you are coaching, you might not have to construct an attention-getting opening statement. Be flexible. Public speaking is an art as well as a science. Give yourself permission to adapt principles and practices to specific speech situations.

Identify One or Two Areas for Improvement After each speaking opportunity, identify what you did right and then give yourself a suggestion or two for ways to improve. You may be tempted to overwhelm yourself with a long list of things you need to do as a speaker. Rather than try to work on a dozen goals, concentrate on two or three, or maybe even just one key skill you would like to develop. To help you decide which skill to focus on, keep in mind the audience-centered model of public speaking we introduced in Chapter 2.

Ultimately, the goal of this course is to teach you how to listen to your own commentary and become expert in shaping and polishing your speaking style.

RECAP

ANALYZING AND EVALUATING SPEECHES

Use standards to judge whether a message is effective and ethical:

- Understandable to listeners
- Achieves its purpose (inform, persuade, entertain)
- Appropriate, sensitive, and responsive to listeners

Identify and analyze rhetorical strategies:

- Speech goal
- Speech organization
- Speaker role
- Speaker tone
- Speaker techniques
- Audience

Give feedback that is:

- Descriptive
- Specific
- Positive
- Constructive
- Sensitive
- Realistic

STUDY GUIDE REVIEW, APPLY, AND ASSESS

OVERCOMING BARRIERS TO EFFECTIVE LISTENING

4.1 List and describe five barriers to effective listening.

Listening is a process that involves selecting, attending to, understanding, and remembering. Some of the barriers that keep people from listening at peak efficiency include information overload, personal concerns, outside distractions, prejudice, and differences between speech rate ad thought rate.

Key Terms

Thinking Critically

For some reason, when Alberto hears the president speak, he just tunes out. What are some of the barriers that may keep Alberto from focusing on the message he is hearing?

Thinking Ethically

Colter was planning to attend a charity event at which a congressional candidate would be speaking. Colter decided he would bring a book to read during the speech because the speaker was from a different political party than Colter's. Was Colter being fair to the speaker?

Assessing Your Audience-Centered Speaking Skill

The cultural background of your audience will affect how they listen to your message. What strategies can you use to adapt your message so that listeners with a cultural background different from your own will be more likely to remain attentive to your message?

HOW TO BECOME A BETTER LISTENER

4.2 Identify and implement strategies for becoming a better listener.

Overcome barriers to effective listening by practicing listening and working to become an active listener. "Listen" with your eyes as well as your ears to accurately interpret nonverbal messages and adapt to the speaker's delivery. Understand your listening style. Listen mindfully, monitoring your emotional reactions to messages, and avoid jumping to conclusions. Identify your listening goal and listen for major ideas. Re-sort, restate, or repeat key messages. Be an ethical listener who communicates expectations and feedback. Remain sensitive to and tolerant of differences between you and the speaker.

Key Terms

Thinking Critically

One of your professors does nothing during lectures but read in a monotone from old notes. What strategies can you use to increase your listening effectiveness in this challenging situation?

Thinking Ethically

Margo bought a classmate's notes from the previous semester of her world history course. The notes allowed Margo to pass the exams without attending class. Is this kind of "listening" behavior ethical? Why or why not?

Assessing Your Audience-Centered Speaking Skill

Two Web sites offer many classic and contemporary speeches on which you can practice the listening and analysis skills we've emphasized in this chapter. Use the questions from Figure 4.2 on page 70 to help you describe and analyze what you hear.

To hear the speeches on these Web sites, you will need software such as RealAudio, which can be downloaded from www.real.com/.

- Famous Speeches in History Archives www.history.com/speeches
- American Rhetoric www.americanrhetoric.com

IMPROVING LISTENING AND CRITICAL THINKING SKILLS

4.3 Identify and implement strategies for improving your critical listening and critical thinking skills.

Evaluate the speaker's use of facts, examples, opinions, and statistics as evidence. Listen critically to separate facts, which can be proven, from inferences, which are conclusions based on partial or unobserved evidence. Examine the logic and reasoning leading to the speaker's conclusions. As a speaker, when speaking to an audience that may be hostile to or critical of your message, take care to use credible arguments and evidence rather than rely on emotional appeals.

Key Terms

Thinking Critically

Harper is in the audience of a speaker who is trying to convince listeners that global warming is not occurring and that the concept of climate change was invented only to increase research expenditures. What kinds of evidence should Harper listen for to support or disagree with the speaker's conclusion?

Assessing Your Audience-Centered Speaking Skill

When listening to your classmates' speeches, practice the skill of distinguishing between facts and inferences. While listening to a speech, make two lists, one list of the facts that you hear and one list of inferences. Later, review your lists, noting your reasons for identifying facts as facts and inferences as inferences.

ANALYZING AND EVALUATING SPEECHES

4.4 Use criteria to effectively and appropriately evaluate speeches.

An effective speech should be understood by the audience and should achieve the intended goal. A good speech is also ethical. When offering feedback, be descriptive, specific, positive, constructive, sensitive, and realistic. Feedback you give to a speaker should provide information and suggestions the speaker can use. Use feedback to learn your own speaking strengths, evaluate the effectiveness of specific speeches, and identify areas for improvement.

Key Terms

Thinking Ethically

Janice was assigned the task of critiquing one of her classmate's speeches. Although she thought the speech was pretty good, she gave the speaker low marks because she strongly disagreed with what the speaker was saying. Was this an appropriate evaluation? Why or why not?

Assessing Your Audience-Centered Speaking Skill

When providing an analysis of your classmates' speeches, take time to evaluate your own feedback. Is your assessment descriptive, specific, positive, constructive, sensitive, and realistic? Which of these criteria were most difficult for you to meet? How can you improve your feedback?

Explore at MyCommunicationLab
Speaker's Workshop: Evaluating a Speaker's Rhetorical Effectiveness

Master of Tolentino (14th CE), Listening to an Augustinian Preach. Detail of a fresco in the Cappellone of San Nicola, Tolentino, Italy. Photo: © DeA Picture Library/Art Resource, N.Y.

For of the three elements in speechmaking—speaker, subject, and person addressed—it is the last one, the hearer, that determines the speech's end and object.

—Aristotle

I t seemed harmless enough. Charles Williams was asked to speak to the Cub Scout pack about his experiences as a young cowboy in Texas. The boys were learning to tie knots, and Williams, a retired rancher, could tell them how to make a lariat and how to tie and use other knots.

His speech started out well. He seemed to be adapting to his young audience. However, for some reason Williams thought the boys might also enjoy learning how to exterminate the screwworm, a pesky parasite of cattle. In the middle of his talk about roping cattle, he launched into a description of the techniques for sterilizing male screwworms. The parents in the audience fidgeted in their seats. The 7- and 8-year-olds didn't have the foggiest idea what a screwworm was, what sterilization was, or how male and female screwworms mate.

It got worse; his audience analysis skills deteriorated even further as Williams next talked about castrating cattle. Twenty-five minutes later, he finally finished the screwworm–castration speech. The parents were relieved. Fortunately, the boys hadn't understood it.

Williams's downfall resulted from his failure to analyze his audience. He may have had a clear objective in mind, but he hadn't considered the background or knowledge of his listeners. Audience analysis is essential for the success of any speech.

Chapter 1 identified the key elements in communication: source, receiver, message, and channel. All four elements are important, but perhaps the most important is the receiver. In public speaking, the receiver is the audience, and the audience is the reason for a speech. We also presented a model that provides an overview of the entire process of speech preparation and delivery; the model is shown again in Figure 5.1. We stressed in Chapter 1 and reemphasize here the concept of public speaking as an audience-centered activity.

The audience-analysis skills and techniques that we present in this chapter will help you at each stage of the public-speaking process. Consciousness of your audience will be important as you select a topic, determine the purpose of your speech, develop your central idea, generate main ideas, gather supporting material, firm up your organization, and rehearse and deliver your speech.

When you think of your audience, don't imagine some undifferentiated mass of people waiting to hear your message. Instead, think of a group of individuals, each with a unique point of view. Your challenge as an audience-centered public speaker is to find out as much as you can about these individuals. From your knowledge of the individuals, you can then develop a general profile of your listeners. If you are presenting your speech online or via video and you can't literally see your listeners, consider visualizing who your listeners are both before and during your message preparation and presentation.

FIGURE 5.1 Audience analysis is central to the speechmaking process.

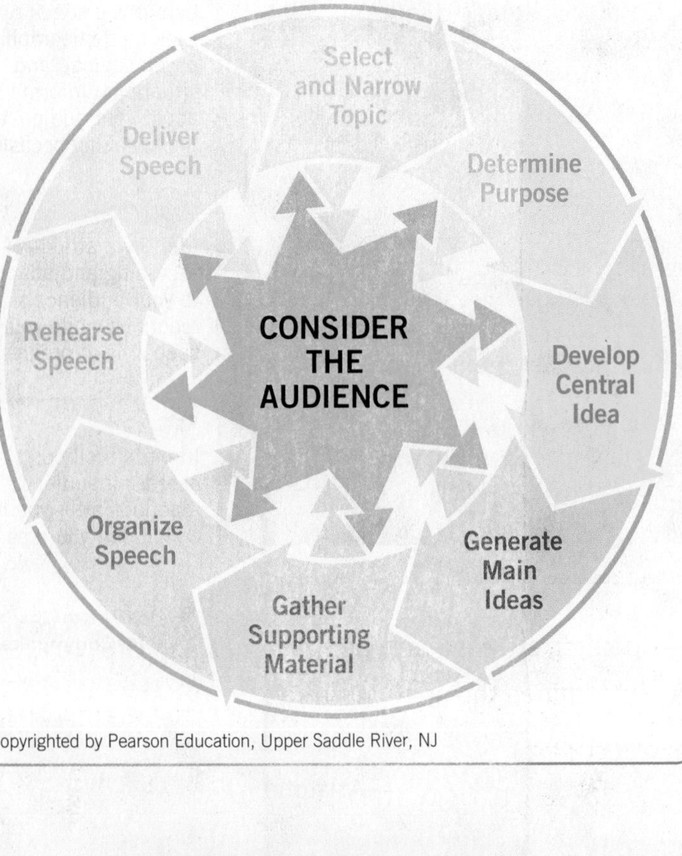

Select and Narrow Topic

Deliver Speech

Determine Purpose

CONSIDER THE AUDIENCE

Develop Central Idea

Rehearse Speech

Organize Speech

Generate Main Ideas

Gather Supporting Material

How do you become an audience-centered speaker? There are three steps:

1. **Step One: Gather Information about Your Audience**. Begin by gathering information about your audience. You can gather information informally just by observing your listeners or asking general questions about them. Or you can take a more formal approach and administer a survey to obtain specific information about them.

2. **Step Two: Analyze Information about Your Audience**. Once you have identified information about your listeners, you analyze it—you look for patterns to help you in formulating what you will say and how you will say it. Find patterns by categorizing and evaluating audience information to determine your listeners' psychological profile, as well as to consider the occasion at which you are speaking.

3. **Step Three: Ethically Adapt to Your Audience**. After you have gathered and analyzed information about your audience, use the information to adapt ethically to your listeners.

In this chapter, we'll talk about these three steps and discuss the process of analyzing your audience before, during, and after your speech.

Gathering Information about Your Audience

5.1 Describe informal and formal methods of gathering information about your audience.

As an audience-centered speaker, you should try to find out as much as you can about your audience before planning your speech. You may wonder, "How do I go about gathering information about my audience?" There are two approaches you can take: an informal one and a formal one.

Gathering Information Informally The simplest way to gather information about your audience informally is to observe them and ask questions before you speak. Informal observations can be especially important in helping you assess obvious demographic characteristics. **Demographics** are statistical information on population characteristics such as age, race, gender, sexual orientation, educational level, and ideological or religious views. For example, you can observe how many members of your audience are male or female, and you can make inferences from their appearance about their ethnic or cultural traits and approximate age.

If, for example, you were planning to address your local PTA about a new store you were opening to help students and parents develop science projects, you could attend a meeting before your speaking date. You might note the general percentage of men and women in the audience and the ages of the parents who attended. You could also ask whether most parents who show up for PTA meetings are parents of elementary, middle-school, or high-school students. Knowing these key pieces of information would help you tailor your speech to address your listeners' interests.

You could also talk with people who know something about the audience you will be addressing. If you are invited to speak to a group you have not spoken to before, ask the person who invited you about the audience members: What is their average age? What are their political affiliations? What are their religious beliefs? What are their attitudes toward your topic? Try to get as much information as possible about your audience before you give your speech.

demographics
Statistical information about the age, race, gender, sexual orientation, educational level, and religious views of an audience

Gathering Information Formally Rather than rely only on inferences drawn from casual observation and conversations with others, you may, if time and resources permit, want to conduct a more formal survey of your listeners. A survey allows you to gather both demographic information and information about what audience members like or dislike, believe to be true or false, or think is good or bad about the topic or issues you will discuss. To gather information formally requires that you develop a carefully written survey or questionnaire.

How do you develop a formal survey? First, decide what you want to know about your audience that you don't already know. Let your topic and the speaking occasion help you determine the kinds of questions you should pose. Once you have an idea of what you would like to know, you can ask your potential audience straightforward questions about such demographic information as age, sex, occupation, and their membership in professional organizations. Figure 5.2 shows a sample questionnaire.

You can modify the questionnaire in Figure 5.2 according to your audience and topic. If your topic is the best approach to finding a rental apartment and you are speaking in a suburban area, find out how many members of your audience own a home and how many are presently living in an apartment. You may also want to ask how they found their current apartment, how many are now searching for an apartment, and how many anticipate looking for one. Answers to these questions can give you useful information about your audience and may provide you with examples to use in your presentation.

Although knowing your audience's demographics can be helpful, you should be aware that inferences based on demographic information may lead you to make faulty conclusions. For example, it might seem reasonable to infer that if your audience consists mainly of 18- to 22-year-olds, they will not be deeply interested in retirement programs. But unless you have talked to them about this topic, your inference may be incorrect. Whenever possible, ask specific questions about audience members' attitudes.

To gather useful information about audience members' attitudes, beliefs, and values, you can ask two types of questions. **Open-ended questions** allow for unrestricted answers without limitation to choices or alternatives. Essay questions, for example, are open-ended. Use open-ended questions when you want detailed information from your audience. **Closed-ended questions** offer alternatives from which to choose.

open-ended questions
Questions that allow for unrestricted answers by not limiting answers to choices or alternatives

closed-ended questions
Questions that offer alternatives from which to choose, such as true/false, agree/disagree, or multiple-choice questions

FIGURE 5.2 You can use a questionnaire like this to gather demographic information about the people in your audience.

Demographic Audience-Analysis Questionnaire

1. Name (optional): _____
2. Sex: Male ☐   Female ☐
3. Occupation: _____
4. Religious affiliation: _____
5. Marital status: Married ☐   Single ☐   Divorced ☐
6. Years of schooling beyond high school: _____
7. Major in college: _____
8. Annual income: _____
9. Age: _____
10. Ethnic background: _____
11. Hometown and state: _____
12. Political affiliation: Republican ☐   Democrat ☐   Other ☐   None ☐
13. Membership in professional or fraternal organizations: _____

Multiple-choice, true/false, and agree/disagree questions are examples of closed-ended questions.

After you develop the questions, it is wise to test them on a small group of people to make sure they are clear and will encourage meaningful answers. Suppose you plan to address an audience about in-school health clinics that dispense birth-control pills to high-school students. The sample questions in Figure 5.3 are open-ended and closed-ended questions that might yield useful audience information on this subject.

Instead of, or in addition to, distributing a paper-and-pencil survey, you have the option of distributing your survey to your audience by means of technology. You could use email, send text messages, or invite audience members to click on a Web site or a Facebook page that you've designed to identify audience-member demographics and assess their attitudes and opinions. Several companies, such as Poll Daddy or Survey Monkey, offer free online survey capabilities.

> **RECAP**
>
> ## GATHERING INFORMATION TO ADAPT YOUR MESSAGE TO YOUR AUDIENCE
>
> **Gather demographic information informally.**
>
> **Formally survey demographics and attitudes:**
> - Closed-ended questions
> - Open-ended questions
>
> **Ethically adapt your message:**
> - Topic
> - Objectives
> - Content
> - Delivery

FIGURE 5.3 Samples of open-ended and closed-ended questions.

Open-Ended Questions

1. What are your feelings about having high-school health clinics dispense birth-control pills?
2. What are your reactions to the current rate of teenage pregnancy?
3. What would you do if you discovered your daughter was receiving birth-control pills from her high-school health clinic?

Closed-Ended Questions

1. Are you in favor of school-based health clinics dispensing birth-control pills to high-school students?
    Yes ☐   No ☐
2. Birth-control pills should be given to high-school students who ask for them in school-based health clinics. (Circle the statement that best describes your feeling.)
    Agree strongly   Agree   Undecided   Disagree   Disagree strongly
3. Check the statement that most closely reflects your feelings about school-based health clinics and birth-control pills.
    - ☐ Students should receive birth-control pills in school-based health clinics whenever they want them, without their parents' knowledge.
    - ☐ Students should receive birth-control pills in school-based health clinics whenever they want them, as long as they have their parents' permission.
    - ☐ I am not certain whether students should receive birth-control pills in school-based health clinics.
    - ☐ Students should not receive birth-control pills in school-based health clinics.
4. Rank the following statements from most desirable (1) to least desirable (5).
    - ____ Birth-control pills should be available to all high-school students in school-based health clinics, whenever students want them, and even if their parents are not aware that their daughters are taking the pills.
    - ____ Birth-control pills should be available to all high-school students in school-based health clinics, but only if their parents have given their permission.
    - ____ Birth-control pills should be available to high-school students without their parents' knowledge, but not in school-based health clinics.
    - ____ Birth-control pills should be available to high-school students, but not in school-based health clinics, and only with their parents' permission.
    - ____ Birth-control pills should not be available to high-school students.

Analyzing Information about Your Audience

Audience analysis is the process of examining information about the listeners who will hear your speech. That analysis helps you adapt your message so that your listeners will respond as you wish. You analyze audiences every day as you speak to others or join in group conversations. For example, most of us do not deliberately make offensive comments to family members or friends. Rather, we analyze our audience (often very quickly) and then adapt our messages to the individuals with whom we are speaking. Public speaking involves the same sort of process.

Precisely what do you look for when analyzing the information that you have gathered about your audience? Ask yourself the following questions:

1. How are audience members similar to one another?

2. How are audience members different from one another?

3. Based on audience members' similarities and differences, how can I establish common ground with the audience?

Look for Audience Member Similarities

Knowing what several members of your audience have in common can help you craft a message that resonates with them. For example, if your audience members are approximately the same age, you will have some basis for selecting examples and illustrations that your listeners will understand.

When looking for similarities, consider the following questions: What ethnic and cultural characteristics do audience members have in common? Are they all from the same geographic region? Do they (or did they) attend the same college or university? Do they have similar levels of education? Do they all like the same kinds of things? Answering these and other questions will help you develop your own ideas and relate your message to your listeners.

Look for Audience Member Differences

Besides noting similarities, you should note differences among your audience members. It is unlikely that audience members for the speeches you give in class will have similar backgrounds. The range of cultural backgrounds, ethnicities, and religious traditions among students at most colleges and universities is rapidly expanding. You can also note the range of differences in age and gender, as well as the variations in perspectives about your topic.

Establish Common Ground with Your Audience

When you know what your audience members have in common as well as how they differ, both in terms of demographic characteristics (such as age or education level) and in terms of attitudes and beliefs they may have about you or your topic, then you can seek to establish common ground with your audience. To establish **common ground** with your audience is to identify ways in which you and your listeners are alike. The more your listeners identify with you and the goals of your message, the more likely they are to respond positively. Keep in mind that although each audience member is unique, with his or her own characteristics and preferences, when you analyze your audience, you are looking for general ways in which they are alike or different. Sometimes the only common ground you may find is that both you and your listeners believe that the issue you are addressing is a serious problem; you may have different views about the best solution. If, for example, you were addressing a group

audience analysis
The process of examining information about those who are expected to listen to a speech

common ground
Similarities between a speaker and audience members in attitudes, values, beliefs, or behaviors

What are some possible areas of common ground this speaker might find with his audience?

Photo: Jamie Wilson/Shutterstock

of people who were mostly against increasing taxes to pay teachers higher salaries, but you were in favor of a tax increase, you could establish common ground by noting that both you and your listeners value education and want high-quality teachers in the classroom.

When you meet someone for the first time, you may spend time identifying people whom you both know or places you've both visited; in this way you begin to establish a relationship. A **relationship** is an ongoing connection you have with another person. A public speaker seeks to establish a relationship with audience members by identifying common ground with them. Use the information from your audience analysis to establish a relationship with your listeners; build bridges between you and your audience.

> **RECAP**
>
> ## ANALYZING INFORMATION ABOUT YOUR AUDIENCE
>
> Look for:
> - Similarities among listeners
> - Differences among listeners
> - Common ground with listeners

Adapting to Your Audience

Audience adaptation is the process of ethically using information you've gathered when analyzing your audience to help your audience clearly understand your message and to achieve your speaking objective. To adapt is to modify your message to enhance its clarity and to increase the likelihood that you will ethically achieve your goal. When adapting to your listeners, the goal is not merely to appease them but also to ensure that your listeners remain listeners. You don't want audience members to prematurely dismiss your ideas before they understand them. If you analyze your audience but don't use the information to customize your message, the information you've gathered will be of little value. Using your skill both to learn about your listeners and to adapt to them can help you maintain your listeners' attention and make them more receptive to your ideas.

Here's an example of how analyzing and adapting to others works: Imagine you live in an apartment complex that doesn't allow pets without the landlord's approval. You see an adorable cocker spaniel puppy that you'd like to buy. In fact, you've already named him Martin. Before you bring Martin home, however, you need not only your landlord's approval but also your roommate's blessing.

5.3 Identify and use strategies for adapting to your audience.

 Read at **MyCommunicationLab Learning From Great Speakers:** Winston Churchill

relationship

An ongoing connection you have with another person

audience adaptation

The process of ethically using information about an audience in order to adapt one's message so that it is clear and achieves the speaking objective

When trying to convince your landlord you say, "I've always paid the rent on time and never caused a problem. I will also pay an extra $300 security deposit if I can have a dog in my apartment." Your message to your roommate is, "No worries about you getting stuck with taking care of Martin if I go out of town. My friend Chris, who also lives in our apartment complex, has agreed to step in for me if I'm out of town." You had the same goal for each audience—approval for having a dog in your apartment—but you customized your message, tailoring your appeal to each listener based on your listener's interests and concerns. You adapted to your audience.

When you speak in public, you should follow the same process. The principle is simple yet powerful: An effective public speaker is audience-centered. The key questions in Table 5.1 can help you formulate an effective approach to your audience.

Being audience-centered does not mean you should tell your listeners only what they want to hear or that you should fabricate information simply to please your audience or achieve your communication goal. If you adapt to your audience by abandoning your own values and sense of truth, then you will become an unethical speaker rather than an audience-centered one. It was President Truman who pondered, "I wonder how far Moses would have gone if he'd taken a poll in Egypt?"[1] The audience-centered speaker ethically adapts his or her topic, purpose, central idea, main ideas, supporting material, organization, and even delivery so as to encourage the audience to listen to his or her ideas. An ethical speaker doesn't make up information just to get what he or she wants. The goal is to make the audience come away from the speaking situation, if not persuaded, then at least feeling thoughtful rather than offended or hostile.

In our overview of how to become an audience-centered speaker, we've pointed out the importance of gathering information, analyzing it to establish common ground, and then using the information to ethically adapt to your listeners. Now we'll discuss these ideas in more detail. You'll want to gather and analyze information and use it to adapt to your listeners at three stages of the speechmaking process: before you speak, as you speak, and after you speak.

TABLE 5.1   AUDIENCE-CENTERED ADAPTATION

Consider Your Audience

- To whom am I speaking?
- What topic would be most suitable for my audience?

Consider Your Speech Goal

- What is my general objective (to inform, persuade, or entertain)?
- What is my specific objective (precisely what do I want the audience to do)?

Consider Your Speech Content

- What kind of information should I share with my audience?
- How should I present the information to them?
- How can I gain and hold their attention?
- What kind of examples would work best?
- What method of organizing information will be most effective?

Consider Your Delivery

- What language differences and expectations do audience members have?
- What style of delivery will my audience members expect?

Analyzing Your Audience before You Speak

5.4   Develop methods of analyzing your audience before you speak by seeking demographic, psychological, and situational information about your audience and the speaking occasion.

Learning about your audience members' backgrounds and attitudes can help you select a topic, define a purpose, develop an outline, and carry out virtually all other speech-related activities. You can gather and analyze three primary types of information:

1. Demographic
2. Psychological
3. Situational

Explore at **MyCommunicationLab**
Activity: "Audience Analysis"

Demographic Audience Analysis

As we noted earlier, *demographics* are statistics about such audience characteristics as age, gender, sexual orientation, race and culture, group membership, and socioeconomic status. Some demographic audience characteristics can be inferred about your listeners by observing them (such as age), but not all demographic characteristics are easily determined by just looking at an audience (such as sexual orientation, cultural background, and group membership). If you are presenting your speech online or via video where you can't see your listeners, it's especially important to do some pre-speech analysis to make sure your inferences about the demographic characteristics of your audience are accurate. Now let's consider how examining demographic information, or **demographic audience analysis**, can help you better understand and adapt to your audience.

Age   Although you must use caution in generalizing from only one factor, information about the age of audience members can suggest the kinds of examples, humor, illustrations, and other types of supporting material to use in your speech. Many students in your public-speaking class will probably be in their late teens or early twenties; some may be older. The younger students may know the latest hip-hop performers or musicians, for example, but the older ones may not be familiar with Wiz Khalifa, Lil Wayne, Drake, or Nicki Minaj. If you are going to give a talk on music, you will have to explain who the performers are and describe or demonstrate their style if you want all the members of your class to understand what you are talking about.

For centuries, adults have lamented that younger generations don't seem to share the values of the older generation. The ancient Greek philosopher Socrates is reported to have complained, over two thousand years ago, "The children now love luxury; they show disrespect for elders and love chatter in place of exercise. . . . They contradict their parents, chatter before company, gobble up dainties at the table, cross their legs, and tyrannize over their teachers."[2] Two researchers who have studied generational differences have found that different generations do have distinctive values and hold differing assumptions about work, duty, and certain values. Table 5.2 on page 86 summarizes the values and generational characteristics of four generations—matures, baby boomers, generation X, and millennials.[3]

What do these generational differences have to do with public speaking? Aristotle noted that a good speaker knows how to adapt to audiences of different age levels. Your credibility as a speaker—how positively you are perceived by your audience—is dependent on your sensitivity to the values and assumptions of your listeners. Of course, the broad generalizations that we've summarized here don't apply across the board, but it's wise to consider how generational differences may affect how your message is interpreted.

demographic audience analysis
Examining demographic information about an audience so as to develop a clear and effective message

TABLE 5.2 SUMMARY OF GENERATIONAL CHARACTERISTICS		
GENERATION NAME	**BIRTH YEARS**	**TYPICAL VALUES AND CHARACTERISTICS**
Matures	1925–1942	• Duty • Sacrifice • A sense of what is right • Work hard • Work fast
Baby Boomers	1943–1960	• Personal fulfillment and optimism • Crusading causes • Buy now/pay later • Everybody's rights • Work efficiently
Generation X	1961–1981	• Live with uncertainty • Balance is important • Enjoy today • Every job is a contract • Save to prepare for uncertainty
Millennials	1982–2002	• Close to parents • Feel "special" • Goal-oriented • Team-oriented • Focus on achievement

Gender and Sexual Orientations Josh began his speech by thanking his predominantly female audience for taking time from their busy schedules to attend his presentation on managing personal finances. Not a bad way to begin a talk. He continued, however, by noting that their job of raising children, keeping their homes clean, and feeding their families was among the most important of jobs. Josh thought he was paying his audience a compliment. He did not consider that most women today work outside the home as well as in it. Many of his listeners were insulted. Many of his listeners stopped listening.

A key question to ask when considering your audience is "What are the gender roles and gender identifications of my audience?" **Gender** is the culturally constructed and psychologically based perception of one's self as feminine or masculine. One's gender-role identity, which falls somewhere on the continuum from masculine to feminine, is learned or socially reinforced by others as well as by one's own personality and life experiences; genetics also plays a part in shaping gender-role identity.

Try to ensure that your remarks reflect sensitivity to the diversity in your listeners' points of view and gender identities. No matter what the mix, you don't want to make judgments based on gender stereotypes, as Josh did.

Just knowing the sex of your audience members—the number of males and females—doesn't tell you the whole story about your listeners. Many of the men in Josh's audience were the ones who took a prime role in caring for their children. A person's **sex** is determined by biology, as reflected in his or her anatomy and reproductive system; someone is born either male or female. Drawing conclusions about

gender
The culturally constructed and psychologically based perception of one's self as feminine or masculine

sex
A person's biological status as male or female, as reflected in his or her anatomy and reproductive system

your audience based only on the biological sex profile of your listeners could lead you to adapt to your listeners inappropriately.

An audience-centered speaker is sensitive to issues and attitudes not only about gender but also about sexual orientation and gender identification in contemporary society. Sexual and gender orientations are not easily sorted into exclusive either-or categories. The audience-centered speaker's goal is to enhance understanding rather than create noise that may distract an audience from listening. Stories, illustrations, and humor whose point or punch line rely on ridiculing a person because of his or her sexual or gender orientation as lesbian, gay, bisexual, transgender/transsexual, questioning, intersex, or asexual (LGBTQIA) may lower perceptions of your credibility not only among LGBTQIA members of your audience but also among audience members who disdain bias.

Avoid sexist language or remarks. A sexist perspective stereotypes or prejudges how someone will react based on his or her biological sex or gender orientation. Remember, it's your audience, not you, who determines whether a comment is sexist or not. Take time to educate yourself about what words, phrases, or perspectives are likely to offend or create psychological noise for your listeners. Think carefully about the implications of words and phrases you take for granted. For example, many people still use the words *ladies* and *matrons* without thinking about their connotations in U.S. culture. Be especially wary about jokes; many are derogatory to people who identify as a particular sex, gender, or sexual orientation. Avoid stereotypes in your stories and examples as well.

In addition, make your language and your message as inclusive as possible. If you are speaking to a mixed sex and gender audience (as many audiences are), be sure your speech relates to all your listeners, not just to one sex or gender. If, for example, you decide to discuss breast cancer, you could note that men, too, are victims of breast cancer and that the lives of husbands, fathers, and brothers of female victims are also affected by the disease.

Finally, be cautious about assuming that male and female people will respond differently to your message. Early social science research found some evidence that females were more susceptible to efforts to persuade them than were males.[4] For many years, textbooks and communication teachers presented this conclusion to students. More contemporary research, however, suggests there is no major difference between men and women in their susceptibility to persuasive messages.[5]

Moreover, although some research suggests that women are socialized to be more emotional and empathic than men, other evidence suggests that men can be equally sensitive.[6] It is clear there are learned sex and gender differences in language usage and nonverbal behavior, but we caution against making sweeping gender- or sex-based assumptions about your audience.

People assess your credibility not by your intentions but by what you do and say. Sometimes we unintentionally offend someone by our subtle misuse of language. For example, gay men and lesbian women typically prefer to be referred to as "gay" or "lesbian" rather than as "homosexual." Further, it is not appropriate to single out separate categories of people who are assumed to hold political, ideological, or religious views consistently different from those of straight people. Monitor your language choice and use of illustrations and humor so you don't alienate members of your audience.[7]

Culture, Ethnicity, and Race **Culture** is a learned system of knowledge, behavior, attitudes, beliefs, values, and norms shared by a group of people. **Ethnicity** is that portion of a person's cultural background that includes such factors as nationality, religion, language, and ancestral heritage, which are shared by a group of people who also share a common geographic origin. A person's **race** is his

culture
A learned system of knowledge, behavior, attitudes, beliefs, values, and norms that is shared by a group of people

ethnicity
The portion of a person's cultural background that includes such factors as nationality, religion, language, and ancestral heritage, which are shared by a group of people who also share a common geographic origin

race
A person's biological heritage

CONFIDENTLY CONNECTING WITH YOUR AUDIENCE

Learn as Much as You Can about Your Audience

By learning about your audience's interests, attitudes, and beliefs as well as their demographic details, you'll be better able to customize a message for your listeners. The more you tailor your message directly to your audience, the more you'll be able to confidently connect to them. Because you have customized your message, they will want to hear it, and you'll be speaking directly to their interests and needs. Also, by focusing on your audience instead of on your nervousness about speaking, you will enhance your confidence. Because you're not dwelling on your own anxieties, you'll be focused on communicating your audience-centered message.

or her biological heritage—for example, Caucasian or Hispanic. One geneticist, however, has concluded that there is much more genetic variation *within* any given racial category than *between* one race and another.[8] There really aren't vast genetic differences among people who have been assigned to different racial categories. So the term *race* is less accurate in attempting to describe a group of people than the term *ethnicity*, which, as we noted, is based on more factors than biological heritage or genetics alone. The cultural, ethnic, or racial background of your audience influences the way they perceive your message. An effective speaker adapts to differences in culture, race, and ethnicity.

As you approach any public-speaking situation, avoid an ethnocentric mindset. **Ethnocentrism** is the assumption that your own cultural approaches are superior to those of other cultures. The audience-centered speaker is sensitive to cultural differences and avoids saying anything that would disparage the cultural background of the audience.

You need not have international students in your class to have a culturally diverse audience. Different ethnic and cultural traditions thrive among people who have lived in the United States all their lives. Students from a Polish family in Chicago, a German family in Texas, or a Haitian family in Brooklyn may all be native U.S. citizens and all have cultural traditions different from your own. Effective public speakers learn as much as possible about the cultural values and knowledge of their audience so that they can understand the best way to deliver their message.

Researchers classify or describe cultural value differences along several lines.[9] We summarize ten categories of differences in Table 5.3 and discuss them below. Understanding these value classifications may provide clues to help you adapt your message when you speak before diverse audiences.

- **Individualistic and collectivistic cultures.** Some cultures place a greater value on individual achievement; others place more value on group or collective achievement. Among the countries that tend to value individual accomplishment are Australia, Great Britain, the United States, Canada, Belgium, and Denmark. By contrast, Japan, Thailand, Colombia, Taiwan, and Venezuela are among countries that have more collectivistic cultures.

How to adapt to listeners from individualistic and collectivistic cultures. Audience members from individualistic cultures, such as the majority of people in the United States, value and respond positively to appeals that encourage personal accomplishment and recognize individual achievement. People from individualistic cultures are expected to speak up to champion individual rights.

Audience members from collectivistic cultures, such as many people who were raised in an Asian culture, may be more likely to value group or team recognition. They may not like to be singled out for individual accomplishments. Community is an important value for those from collectivistic cultures. And they value making sure that others are perceived in a positive way; it's important for them and others to be seen as valued persons. When speaking to a predominantly collectivistic audience, you might want to emphasize areas of consensus or community agreement on issues, use examples of community involvement, or ethically highlight the importance of shared effort and achievement in your proposals or appeals.

- **High-context and low-context cultures.** The terms *high-context* and *low-context cultures* refer to the importance of unspoken or nonverbal messages. In high-context cultures, people place considerable importance on such contextual factors as tone of voice, gestures, facial expression, movement, and other nonverbal aspects of communication. People from low-context traditions place greater emphasis on the words themselves; the surrounding context has a relatively low impact on the meaning of the message. The Arab culture is a high-context culture, as are the cultures of Japan, Asia, and southern Europe. Low-context cultures, which place a higher value on words, include those of Switzerland, Germany, the United States, and Australia.

Watch at **MyCommunicationLab**
Video: "Successful Japanese-U. S. Business Communication"

ethnocentrism
The assumption that one's own cultural perspectives and methods are superior to those of other cultures

TABLE 5.3 DESCRIBING AND ADAPTING TO CULTURAL DIFFERENCES

CULTURAL VALUE	CULTURAL CHARACTERISTIC	HOW TO ADAPT TO CULTURAL CHARACTERISTICS
Individualistic Culture	Individual achievement is emphasized more than group achievement.	• Stress the importance of individual rewards and recognition. • Identify how audience members will benefit from your ideas or proposal.
Collectivistic Culture	Group or team achievement is emphasized more than individual achievement.	• Stress the importance of community values. • Help audience members save face and be perceived in a positive way.
High-Context Culture	The context of a message—including nonverbal cues, tone of voice, posture, and facial expression—is often valued more than the words.	• Don't boast about your specific accomplishments. • Use a more subtle, less dramatic delivery style.
Low-Context Culture	The words in a message are valued more than the surrounding context.	• Be sure to make your ideas and recommendations explicit. • Although delivery cues are important, listeners will expect your message to be clear.
Tolerance for Uncertainty	People can accept ambiguity and are not bothered when they do not know all the details.	• It is not so important to develop a specific solution to a problem you may present in your speech. • The purpose of the speech need not be clearly explicated.
Need for Certainty	People want specifics and dislike ambiguity.	• Provide an explicit overview of what you will present in your speech. • Create a logical and clear organizational pattern for your speech.
High-Power Culture	Status and power differences are emphasized; roles and chains of command are clearly defined.	• Remember that listeners perceive people in leadership positions as powerful and credible. • Develop messages that acknowledge differences in status among people.
Low-Power Culture	Status and power differences receive less emphasis; people strive for equality rather than exalting those in positions of leadership.	• Discuss shared approaches to governance and leadership. • Develop solutions that involve others in reaching consensus.
Long-Term Time Orientation	Time is abundant, and accomplishing goals may take considerable time.	• Appeal to listeners' persistence, patience, and delayed gratification. • Emphasize how ideas and suggestions will benefit future generations.
Short-Term Time Orientation	Time is an important resource.	• Identify how the ideas and proposals you discuss will have an immediate impact on listeners. • Note how actions will have a direct impact on achieving results.

How to adapt to listeners from high-context and low-context cultures. Listeners from low-context cultures will need and expect more detailed and explicit information from you as a speaker. Subtle and indirect messages are less likely to be effective.

People from high-context cultures will pay particular attention to your delivery and to the communication environment when they try to interpret your meaning. These people will be less impressed by a speaker who boasts about his or her own accomplishments; such an audience will expect and value more indirect ways of establishing credibility. A listener from a high-context culture will also expect a less dramatic and dynamic style of delivery.

- **Tolerance of uncertainty and need for certainty.** Some cultures are more comfortable with ambiguity and uncertainty than others. Those cultures in which people need to have details nailed down tend to develop very specific regulations and rules. People from cultures with a greater tolerance of uncertainty are more comfortable with vagueness and are not upset when all the details aren't spelled out. Cultures with a high need for certainty include those of Russia, Japan, France, and Costa Rica. Cultures that have a higher tolerance for uncertainty include those of Great Britain and Indonesia.

How to adapt to listeners from cultures that tolerate or avoid uncertainty. If you are speaking to an audience of people who have a high need for certainty, make sure you provide concrete details when you present your message; they will also want and expect to know what action steps they can take. People who value certainty will respond well if you provide a clear and explicit preview of your message in your introduction; they also seem to prefer a clear, logical, and linear step-by-step organizational pattern.

People from cultures that are more comfortable with uncertainty do not necessarily need to have the explicit purpose of the message spelled out for them. In addition, they are generally less likely to need specific prescriptions to solve problems, compared to listeners who want to avoid uncertainty. Telling a story in which the point of the story is implied rather than explicitly identified may be an effective approach when communicating with listeners who have a high tolerance for uncertainty.

- **High-power and low-power cultures.** Power is the ability to influence or control others. Some cultures prefer clearly defined lines of authority and responsibility; these are said to be high-power cultures. People in low-power cultures are more comfortable with blurred lines of authority and less formal titles. Austria, Israel, Denmark, Norway, Switzerland, and Great Britain typically have an equitable approach to power distribution. Cultures that are high on the power dimension include those of the Philippines, Mexico, Venezuela, India, Brazil, and France.

How to adapt to listeners from high-power and low-power cultures. People from high-power cultures are more likely to perceive people in leadership roles—including speakers—as credible. They will also be more comfortable with proposals or solutions that identify or acknowledge differences in social class.

Those from low-power cultures often favor more shared approaches to leadership and governance. When speaking to people from low-power cultures, you may want to emphasize democratic collaborative approaches to solving problems or areas of consensus on an issue.

- **Long-term and short-term orientation to time.** Some cultures take the view that it may take a long time to accomplish certain goals. People from Asian cultures, for example, and from some South American cultures such as that of Brazil often value patience, persistence, and deferred gratification more than do people from cultures with a short-term orientation to time. People with a short-term time orientation, which is often a characteristic of industrialized Western cultures such as those of Canada and the United States, are very attuned to time and time management. Short-term cultures also value quick responses to problems.

How to adapt to listeners from cultures with long-term and short-term time orientations. When speaking to people who take a long-term orientation to time, you should to stress how issues and problems affect not only the present but also the future, especially future generations. It's not that people with a long-term orientation don't value efficiency and effectiveness; they simply accept that things don't always happen quickly.

People with a short-term orientation to time will want to learn about immediate action steps that can solve a problem. They are also results-oriented and expect that individual or group effort should result in a specific positive outcome. When possible, provide statistics or other evidence that documents results.

Group Membership It's said we are all members of a gang—it's just that some gangs are more socially acceptable than others. We are social creatures; we congregate in groups to gain an identity, to help accomplish projects we support, and to have fun. So it's reasonable to assume that many of your listeners belong to groups, clubs, or organizations. One way to gather information about a specific group you are going to speak to is to see if the group or organization has a Web site or Facebook or other social media presence. Knowing something about the history, purpose, values, and accomplishments of a group can help you customize your message.

- **Religious groups.** As a follower of Scientology, Marsha believes that the philosophy outlined in *Dianetics* (the book that is the basis of Scientology) is as important as the religious precepts in the Bible. Planning to speak before a Bible-belt college audience, many of whose members view Scientology as a cult, Marsha would be wise to consider how her listeners will respond to her message. This is not to suggest that she should refuse the speaking invitation. She should, however, be aware of her audience's religious beliefs as she prepares and presents her speech.

When touching on religious beliefs or an audience's values, use great care in what you say and how you say it. Remind yourself that some members of your audience will undoubtedly not share your beliefs, and that few beliefs are held as intensely as religious ones. If you do not wish to offend your listeners, plan and deliver your speech with much thought and sensitivity.

- **Political groups.** Are members of your audience active in politics? Knowing whether your listeners are active in such groups as Young Republicans, Young Democrats, or Young Libertarians can help you address political topics. Members of environmental groups may also hold strong ecological opinions on issues and political candidates.

- **Work groups.** Most professions give rise to professional organizations or associations to which people can belong. If you are speaking to an audience of professionals, it's important to be aware of professional organizations they may belong to (there may be several) and to know, for example, whether those organizations have taken formal stands that may influence audience members' views on certain issues. Work groups may also have abbreviations or acronyms that may be useful to know. Your communication instructor, for example, may be a member of the National Communication Association (NCA) and may belong to a specific division of the NCA, such as the IDD (Instructional Development Division).

- **Social groups.** Some groups exist just so that people can get together and enjoy a common activity. Book clubs, film clubs, cycling clubs, cooking groups, dancing groups, and bowling teams exist to bring people with similar ideas of fun together to enjoy the activity. Knowing whether members of your audience belong to such groups may help you adapt your topic to them or, if you are involved in similar groups, to establish common ground with them.

- **Service groups.** Many people are actively involved in groups that emphasize community service as their primary mission. If you are speaking to a service group such as the Lions Club or the Kiwanis Club, you can reasonably assume that your listeners value community service and will be interested in how to make their community a better place.

Socioeconomic Status Socioeconomic status is a person's perceived importance and influence based on such factors as income, occupation, and education level. In Europe, Asia, the Middle East, and other parts of the world, centuries-old traditions of acknowledging status differences still exist today. Status differences in the United States and Canada are often more subtle. A general estimate of your audience members' incomes, occupations, and education levels can be helpful as you develop a message that connects with listeners.

- **Income.** Having some general idea of the income level of your listeners can be of great value to you as a speaker. For example, if you know that most audience members are struggling to meet weekly expenses, it will be unwise to talk about how to see the cultural riches of Europe by traveling first class. But talking about how to get paid to travel to Europe by serving as a courier may hold considerable interest.
- **Occupation.** Knowing what people do for a living can give you useful information about how to adapt your message to them. Speaking to teachers, you will want to use different examples and illustrations than if you were speaking to lawyers, ministers, or automobile assembly-line workers. Many college-age students may hold jobs but not yet the jobs they aspire to after they graduate. Knowing their future career plans can help you adjust your topic and supporting material to your listeners' professional goals.
- **Education.** About 30 percent of American adults obtain a college degree. Slightly more than 10 percent of the population earns graduate degrees.[10] The educational background of your listeners is yet another component of socioeconomic status that can help you plan your message. For example, you have a good idea that your classmates in your college-level public-speaking class value education because they are striving, often at great sacrifice, to advance their education. Knowing the educational background of your audience can help you make decisions about your choice of vocabulary, your language style, and your use of examples and illustrations.

Watch at **MyCommunicationLab**
Video: "Same Holiday, Different Customs"

Adapting to Diverse Listeners The most recent U.S. Census figures document what you already know from your own life experiences: We all live in an age of diversity. For example:

- Two-thirds of emigrants worldwide come to the United States.[11]
- It is estimated that more than 40 million U.S. residents speak something other than English as their first language, including 18 million people whose first language is Spanish.[12]
- One in seven marriages occurs between spouses of different races or ethnicities.[13]
- If the current trend continues, by 2050 the percentage of U.S. population that is White will decrease to 53 percent, down from a current 79 percent. Asians will increase to 16 percent, up from 1.6 percent; Hispanics will more than triple their numbers to over 25 percent, up from just over 7.5 percent, and African Americans will increase their proportion slightly from the current 12 percent.[14]
- During the past decade in the United States, the combined population of African Americans, Native Americans, Asians, Pacific Islanders, and Hispanics grew 13 times faster than the non-Hispanic White population.[15]

Virtually every state in the United States has experienced a dramatic increase in foreign-born residents. If trends continue as they have during the past quarter-century, cultural and ethnic diversity will continue to grow during your lifetime. The U.S. Census predicts that in about three decades, the U.S. will become a "majority-minority" nation, with no single ethnic group making up a majority of the population.[16] This swell of immigrants translates to increased diversity in all aspects of society, including in most audiences you'll face—whether in business, at school-board meetings, or in your college classes.

socioeconomic status
A person's perceived importance and influence based on income, occupation, and education level

If a graduation speaker focuses on the target audience of graduating students, how can the speaker address the interests of graduates' families and friends, too?

Photo: Mat Hayward/Fotolia

Audience diversity, however, involves factors beyond ethnic and cultural differences. Central to our point about considering your audience is examining the full spectrum of audience diversity, not just cultural differences. Each topic we've reviewed when discussing demographic and psychological aspects of an audience contributes to overall audience diversity. Diversity simply means differences. Audience members are diverse. The question and challenge for a public speaker is, "How do I ethically adapt to listeners with such different backgrounds and experiences?" We offer several general strategies. You could decide to focus on a target audience, consciously use a variety of methods of adapting to listeners, seek common ground, or consider using powerful visual images to present your key points.

- **Focus on a target audience.** A **target audience** is a specific segment of your audience that you most want to address or influence. You've undoubtedly been a target of skilled communicators and may not have been aware that messages had been tailored just for you. For example, most colleges and universities spend a considerable amount of time and money encouraging students to apply for admission. You probably received recruitment literature in the mail during your high-school years. But not every student in the United States receives brochures from the same college. Colleges and universities targeted you based on your test scores, your interests, where you live, and your involvement in school-sponsored or extracurricular activities. Likewise, as a public speaker, you may want to think about the portion of your audience you most hope will understand your message or will be convinced.

The challenge when consciously focusing on a target audience is not to lose or alienate the rest of your listeners—to keep the entire audience in mind while simultaneously making a specific attempt to hit your target segment. For example, Sasha was trying to convince his listeners to invest in the stock market instead of relying only on Social Security. He wisely decided to focus on the younger listeners; those approaching retirement age have already made their major investment decisions. Although he focused on the younger members of his audience, however, Sasha didn't forget the mature listeners. He suggested that older listeners encourage their children or grandchildren to consider his proposal. He focused on a target audience, but he didn't ignore others.

- **Use diverse strategies for a diverse audience.** Another approach you can adopt, either separately or in combination with a target audience focus, is to use a variety of strategies to reflect the diversity of your audience. Based on your efforts

target audience
A specific segment of an audience that you most want to influence

to gather information about your audience, you should know the various constituencies that will likely be present for your talk. Consider using several methods of reaching the different listeners in your audience. For example, review the following strategies:

- Use a variety of supporting materials, including illustrations, examples, statistics, and opinions. Learn more about supporting materials in Chapter 7.

- Remember the power of stories. People from most cultures appreciate a good story. And some people, such as those from Asian and Middle Eastern cultures, prefer hearing stories and parables used to make a point or support an argument rather than facts and statistics.

- If you're very uncertain about cultural preferences, use a balance of both logical support (statistics, facts, specific examples) and emotional support (stories and illustrations).

- Consider showing the audience a brief outline to provide an overview of your key ideas, using PowerPoint™ or Prezi™. If there is a language barrier between you and your audience, being able to read portions of your speech as they hear you speaking may improve audience members' comprehension. If an interpreter is translating your message, an outline can also help ensure that your interpreter will communicate your message accurately.

- **Identify common values.** People have long debated whether there are universal human values. Several scholars have made strong arguments that common human values do exist. Communication researcher David Kale suggests that all people can identify with the individual struggle to enhance one's own dignity and worth, although different cultures express that struggle in different ways.[17] A second common value is the search for a world at peace. Underlying that quest is a fundamental desire for equilibrium, balance, and stability. Although there may always be a small but corrosive minority of people whose actions do not support the universal value of peace, the prevailing human values in most cultures ultimately do support peace.

Cultural anthropologists specialize in the study of behavior that is common to all humans. Cultural anthropologist Donald Brown has compiled a list of hundreds of "surface" universals of beliefs, emotions, or behavior.[18] According to Brown, people in all cultures

- Have beliefs about death
- Have a childhood fear of strangers
- Have a division of labor by sex
- Experience certain emotions and feelings, such as envy, pain, jealousy, shame, and pride
- Use facial expressions to express emotions
- Have rules for etiquette
- Experience empathy
- Value some degree of collaboration or cooperation
- Experience conflict and seek to manage or mediate conflict

Of course, not all cultures have the same beliefs about death or the same way of dividing up labor—but people in all cultures address these issues.

Intercultural communication scholars Larry Samovar and Richard Porter suggest other commonalities that people from all cultures share. They propose that all humans seek physical pleasure as well as emotional and psychological pleasure and confirmation and seek to avoid personal harm.[19] Although each culture defines what constitutes pleasure and pain, it may be useful to interpret human behavior with these general assumptions in mind. People also realize that their biological lives will end, that to some degree each person is isolated from all other human beings, that we each make choices, and that each person seeks to give life meaning. These similarities offer some basis for developing common messages with universal meaning.

Identifying common cultural issues and similarities can help you establish common ground with your audience, a goal we introduced earlier in this chapter. If you are speaking about an issue on which you and your audience have widely different views, identifying a larger common value that is relevant to your topic (such as the importance of peace, prosperity, or family) can help you find a foothold so that your listeners will at least listen to your ideas.

- **Rely on visual materials that transcend language differences.** Pictures and other images can communicate universal messages—especially emotional ones. Although there is no universal language, most listeners, regardless of culture and language, can comprehend visible expressions of pain, joy, sorrow, and happiness. An image of a mother holding the frail, malnourished body of her dying child communicates the ravages of famine without elaborate verbal explanations. The more varied your listeners' cultural experiences, the more effective it can be to use visual materials to illustrate your ideas.

Psychological Audience Analysis

Demographic information lets you make useful inferences about your audience and predict likely responses. A **psychological audience analysis** explores an audience's attitudes toward a topic, purpose, and speaker while probing the underlying beliefs and values that might affect these attitudes. Learning how the members of your audience feel about your topic and purpose may provide specific clues to help you anticipate their reactions to your presentation.

It is important for a speaker to distinguish among *attitudes*, *beliefs*, and *values*. The attitudes, beliefs, and values of an audience may greatly influence a speaker's selection of a topic and specific purpose, as well as other aspects of speech preparation and delivery.

psychological audience analysis
Examining the attitudes, beliefs, values, and other psychological information about an audience in order to develop a clear and effective message

---

DEVELOPING YOUR SPEECH STEP BY STEP

CONSIDER YOUR AUDIENCE

CONSIDER THE AUDIENCE

A Chinese proverb says that a journey of a thousand miles begins with a single step. Developing and delivering a speech may seem like a daunting journey. But we believe that if you take it one step at a time and keep your focus on your audience, you'll be rewarded with a well-crafted and well-delivered message.

To help you see how the audience-centered public speaking process unfolds step by step, we will explore each step of the speechmaking process by showing how one student prepared and delivered a successful speech. Brianne, an undergraduate student at Texas State University, developed the informative presentation entitled "Access Is Not Enough: Requiring Counsel with University Sale of the Morning-After Pill" that is outlined in Chapter 8.[21] In the chapters ahead, we will walk you through the process Brianne followed to develop her speech.

Brianne thought about her audience even before selecting her topic. Realizing that her listeners would be student peers, she knew she had to find a topic of interest and relevance to them. And she knew that she could discuss complex issues, using a fairly advanced vocabulary.

The *Developing Your Speech Step by Step* feature in the chapters ahead will provide a window through which you can watch Brianne at work on each step of the audience-centered public speaking process.

An **attitude** reflects likes or dislikes. Do you like health food? Are you for or against capital punishment? Should movies be censored? What are your views on gun control? Your answers to these widely varied questions reflect your attitudes.

A **belief** is what you hold to be true or false. If you think the sun will rise in the east in the morning, you hold a belief about the sun based on what you perceive to be true or false.

A **value** is an enduring concept of good and bad, right and wrong. More deeply ingrained than either attitudes or beliefs, values are therefore more resistant to change. Values support both attitudes and beliefs. For example, you like health food because you believe that natural products are more healthful. And you *value* good health. You are against capital punishment because you believe that it is wrong to kill people. You *value* human life. As with beliefs, a speaker who has some understanding of an audience's values is better able to adapt a speech to them.

Analyzing Attitudes toward the Topic It is useful to know how members of an audience feel about your topic. Are they interested or apathetic? How much do they already know about the topic? If the topic is controversial, are they for or against it? Knowing the answers to these questions from the outset lets you adjust your message accordingly. For example, if you plan to talk about increasing taxes to improve education in your state, you probably want to know how your listeners feel about taxes and education.

When you are analyzing your audience, it may help to categorize the group along three dimensions: interested–uninterested, favorable–unfavorable, and captive–voluntary. These dimensions are summarized in Table 5.4.

With an *interested* audience, your task is simply to hold and amplify their interest throughout the speech. If your audience is *uninterested*, you need to find ways to hook the members. In Chapter 14, we describe ways to motivate an audience by addressing issues related to their needs and interests. Given our visually oriented culture, consider using visual aids to gain and maintain the attention of apathetic listeners.

You may also want to gauge how *favorable* or *unfavorable* your audience may feel toward you and your message before you begin to speak. Some audiences, of course, are neutral, apathetic, or simply uninformed about what you plan to say. We provide explicit suggestions for approaching favorable, neutral, and unfavorable audiences in Chapter 15 when we discuss persuasive speaking. But even if your objective is simply to inform, it is useful to know whether your audience is predisposed to respond positively or negatively toward you or your message. Giving an informative talk about classical music would be quite challenging, for example, if you were addressing an audience of die-hard punk-rock fans. You might decide to show the connections between classical music and punk in order to arouse their interest.

Your Speech Class as Audience You may think that your public-speaking class is not a typical audience because class members are required to attend: Your speech class is a *captive* audience rather than a *voluntary* one. A captive audience has externally imposed reasons for being there (such as a requirement to attend class). Because class members must show up to earn credit for class, you need not worry that they will get up and leave during your speech. However, your classroom speeches are still *real* speeches. Your class members are certainly real people with likes, dislikes, beliefs, and values.

Your classroom speeches should connect with your listeners so that they forget they are required to be your audience. Class members will listen if your message gives them new, useful information; touches them emotionally; or persuades them to change their opinion or behavior in support of your position.

You will undoubtedly give other speeches to other captive audiences. Audiences at work or at professional meetings are often captive in the sense that they may be required to attend lectures or presentations to receive continuing-education credit or

attitude
An individual's likes or dislikes

belief
An individual's perception of what is true or false

value
Enduring concept of good and bad, right and wrong

TABLE 5.4 ADAPTING YOUR MESSAGE TO DIFFERENT TYPES OF AUDIENCES

TYPE OF AUDIENCE	EXAMPLE	HOW TO BE AUDIENCE-CENTERED
Interested	Mayors who attend a talk by the governor about increasing security and reducing the threat of terrorism	Acknowledge audience interest early in your speech; use the interest they have in you and your topic to gain and maintain their attention.
Uninterested	Junior-high students attending a lecture about retirement benefits	Make it a high priority to tell your listeners why your message should be of interest to them. Remind your listeners throughout your speech how your message relates to their lives.
Favorable	A religious group that meets to hear a group leader talk about the importance of their beliefs	Use audience interest to move them closer to your speaking goal; you may be more explicit in telling them in your speech conclusion what you would like them to do.
Unfavorable	Students who attend a lecture by the university president explaining why tuition and fees will increase 15 percent next year	Be realistic in what you expect to accomplish; acknowledge listeners' opposing point of view; consider using facts to refute misperceptions they may hold.
Voluntary	Parents attending a lecture by the new principal at their children's school	Anticipate why listeners are coming to hear you, and speak about the issues they want you to address.
Captive	Students in a public-speaking class	Find out who will be in your audience and use this knowledge to adapt your message to them.

as part of their job duties. Your goal with a captive audience is the same as with other types of audiences. You should make your speech just as interesting and effective as one designed for a voluntary audience. You still have an obligation to address your listeners' needs and interests and to keep them engaged in what you have to say.

Analyzing Attitudes toward You, the Speaker The attitude of audience members toward you in your role as speaker is another factor that can influence their reaction to your speech. Regardless of how they feel about your topic or purpose, if members of an audience regard you as credible, they will be much more likely to be interested in, and supportive of, what you have to say.

Your credibility—others' perception of you as trustworthy, knowledgeable, and interesting—is one of the main factors that will shape your audience's attitude toward you. If you establish your credibility before you begin to discuss your topic, your listeners will be more likely to believe what you say and to think that you are knowledgeable, interesting, and dynamic.

For example, when a high-school health teacher asks a former drug addict to speak to a class about the dangers of cocaine addiction, the teacher recognizes that the speaker's experiences make him credible and that his message will be far more convincing than a teacher's lecture on the perils of cocaine use.

An audience's positive attitude toward a speaker can overcome negative or apathetic attitudes they may have toward the speaker's topic or purpose. If your analysis reveals that your audience does not recognize you as an authority on your subject, you will need to build your credibility into the speech. If you have had personal experience with your topic, be sure to let the audience know. You will gain credibility instantly. We will provide additional strategies for enhancing your credibility in Chapters 9 and 15.

Situational Audience Analysis

So far we have concentrated on the people who will be your listeners, as the primary focus of being an audience-centered speaker. You should also consider your speaking situation. **Situational audience analysis** includes an examination of the time and place of your speech, the size of your audience, and the speaking occasion. Although these elements are not technically characteristics of the *audience*, they can have a major effect on how your listeners respond to you.

Time   You may have no control over when you will be speaking, but when designing and delivering a talk, a skilled public speaker considers the time of day as well as audience expectations about the speech length. If you are speaking to a group of exhausted parents during a midweek evening meeting of the band-boosters club, you can bet they will appreciate a direct, to-the-point presentation more than a long oration. If you are on a program with other speakers, speaking first or last on the program carries a slight edge because people tend to remember what comes first or last. Speaking early in the morning when people may not be quite awake, after lunch when they may feel a bit drowsy, or late in the afternoon when they are tired may mean you'll have to strive consciously for a more energetic delivery to keep your listeners' attention.

Be mindful of your time limits. If your audience expects you to speak for 20 minutes, it is usually better to end either right at 20 minutes or a little earlier; most North Americans don't appreciate being kept overtime for a speech. In your public-speaking class you will be given time limits, and you may wonder whether such strict time-limit expectations occur outside public-speaking class. The answer is a most definite yes. Whether it's a business presentation or a speech to the city council or school board, time limits are often strictly enforced.

Size of Audience   The size of your audience directly affects speaking style and audience expectations about delivery. As a general rule, the larger the audience, the more likely they are to expect a more formal style. With an audience of ten or fewer, you can punctuate a very conversational style by taking questions from your listeners. If you and your listeners are so few that you can be seated around a table, they may expect you to stay seated for your presentation. Many business "speeches" are given around a conference table.

A group of 20 to 30 people—the size of most public-speaking classes—will expect more formality than the audience of a dozen or fewer. Your speaking style can still be conversational in character, but your speech should be appropriately structured and well organized; your delivery may include more expansive gestures than you would display during a one-on-one chat with a friend or colleague.

Audiences that fill a lecture hall will still appreciate a direct, conversational style, but your gestures may increase in size, and you will be expected to speak with enough volume and intensity so that people in the last row will hear you. You may need to amplify your voice with a microphone.

Location   In your speech class, you have the advantage of knowing what the room looks like, but in a new speaking situation, you may not have that advantage. If at all possible, visit the place where you will speak to examine the physical setting and find out, for example, how far the audience will be from the lectern. Physical conditions such as room temperature and lighting can affect your performance, the audience response, and the overall success of the speech.

Room arrangement and decor may affect the way an audience responds. Be aware of the arrangement and appearance of the room in which you will speak. If your speaking environment is less than ideal, you may need to work especially hard to hold your audience's attention. Although you probably won't be able to make major changes in the speaking environment, it is ultimately up to you to obtain the best

situational audience analysis
Examination of the time and place of a speech, the audience size, and the speaking occasion in order to develop a clear and effective message

speaking environment you can. The arrangement of chairs, placement of audiovisual materials, and opening or closing of drapes should all be in your control.

Occasion Another important way to gain clues about your listeners is to consider the reason why they are here. What occasion brings this audience together? The mindset of people gathered for a funeral will obviously be different from that of people who've asked you to say a few words after a banquet. Knowing the occasion helps you predict both the demographic characteristics of the audience and the members' state of mind.

If you're presenting a speech at an annual or monthly meeting, you have the advantage of being able to ask those who've attended previous presentations what kind of audience typically gathers for the occasion. Your best source of information may be either the person who invited you to speak or someone who has attended similar events. Knowing when you will speak on the program or whether a meal will be served before or after you talk will help you gauge what your audience expects from you.

Advance preparation will help you avoid last-minute surprises about the speaking environment and the physical arrangements for your speech. Table 5.5 on page 100 provides a list of essential questions you should ask when preparing for a speaking assignment, as well as several suggestions for adapting to your speaking situation. A well-prepared speaker adapts his or her message not only to the audience but also to the speaking environment.

Also keep in mind that when you arrive to give your speech, you can make changes in the previous speaker's room arrangements. For example, the purpose of the speaker immediately before Yue Hong was to generate interest in a memorial for Asian Americans who fought in Vietnam. Because that speaker wanted to make sure the audience felt free to ask questions, the chairs were arranged in a semicircle and the lights were turned on. But Yue Hong was giving a more formal presentation on the future of the Vietnamese population, which included a brief slide show. So when the preceding speaker had finished, Yue Hong rearranged the chairs and darkened the room.

RECAP

ELEMENTS OF AUDIENCE ANALYSIS

Demographic Characteristics
- Age
- Gender
- Sexual orientation
- Cultural, ethnic, or racial background
- Group membership
- Socioeconomic status

Psychological Characteristics
- Attitudes: Likes and dislikes
- Beliefs: What is perceived to be true or false
- Values: What is perceived to be good or bad

Situational Characteristics
- Time
- Audience size
- Location
- Occasion

 Watch at **MyCommunicationLab**
Video: "Truman's Decision to Drop the Bomb"

How can a speaker analyze and adapt to a videoconference speaking situation?

Photo: Blend Images/John Fedele/Vetta/Getty Images

TABLE 5.5　ANALYZING AND ADAPTING TO THE SPEAKING SITUATION

QUESTIONS TO ASK	ADAPTATION STRATEGIES
Time	
What time of the day will I be speaking?	If your audience may be tired or not yet fully awake, consider increasing the energy level of your delivery.
Where will I appear on the program?	Audiences are more likely to get the strongest impressions from those who speak first or last. If you are in the middle of the lineup, you will need to be very dynamic in your delivery and build repetition into your speech, to aid your audience's memory.
What are the time limits for the speech?	Most listeners do not appreciate speakers who exceed their time limit. Unless you are a spellbinding speaker, don't speak longer than your listeners expect you to speak.
Size	
How many people will be in the audience?	Smaller audiences usually expect a more conversational, informal delivery; larger audiences usually expect a more formal presentation.
Will the audience be so large I'll need a microphone?	Make sure you understand the mechanics of the microphone system before you rise to speak.
Location	
How will the room be arranged?	If you want a more informal speaking atmosphere, consider arranging the chairs in a circle. In a large room, consider inviting people in the back of the room to move closer to the front if necessary.
What is the room lighting like?	If an audience is in the dark, it's more difficult to gauge their nonverbal responses. If you need to use presentation aids, make sure the room lighting is easy to adjust to a level that lets listeners see your images but still lets you see your listeners.
Will there be noise or distractions outside the room?	Before the speech begins, consider strategies to minimize outside noise, such as closing windows and doors, adjusting window blinds or shades, or politely asking that people in nearby rooms be mindful of your presentation.
Occasion	
What occasion brings the audience together?	Make sure you understand what your listeners expect, and strive to meet those expectations.
Is the speech an annual or monthly event? Has a similar speaking occasion occurred with this audience before?	Learn how other speakers have adapted to the audience. Ask for examples of what successful speakers have done to succeed with this audience. Or ask whether certain issues or topics may offend your audience.

5.5　Identify methods of assessing and adapting to your audience's reactions while your speech is in progress.

Adapting to Your Audience as You Speak

So far, we have focused on discovering as much as possible about an audience before the speaking event. Prespeech analyses help with each step of the public-speaking process: selecting a topic, formulating a specific purpose, gathering supporting material, identifying major ideas, organizing the speech, and planning its delivery. Each of these components depends on your understanding your audience. But audience analysis and adaptation do not end when you have crafted your speech. They continue as you deliver your speech.

Watch at **MyCommunicationLab**
Video: "The Process of Developing a Speech: Audience Analysis"

Generally, a public speaker does not have an exchange with the audience unless the speech is part of a question-and-answer or discussion format. Once the speech is in progress, the speaker must rely on nonverbal cues from the audience to judge how people are responding to the message.

Identifying Nonverbal Audience Cues

Once, when speaking in India, Mark Twain was denied eye contact with his listeners by a curtain separating him from his audience. Mark Twain's daughter, Clara, recalled this experience:

> One of Father's first lectures was before a Purdah audience; in other words, the women all sat behind a curtain through which they could peek at Mark Twain without being seen by him . . . a deadly affair for the poor humorist, who had not even the pleasure of scanning the faces of his mute audience.[20]

Mark Twain missed learning how well his speech was being received as he was speaking. You could experience the same disadvantage if you fail to look at your listeners while you speak.

Many beginning public speakers may find it challenging at first not only to have the responsibility of presenting a speech they have rehearsed, but also to have to change or modify that speech on the spot. We assure you that with experience you can develop the sensitivity to adapt to your listeners, much as a jazz or jam-band musician adapts to the other musicians in the ensemble. But it will take practice. Although it's not possible to read your listeners' minds, it is important to analyze and adapt to cues that can enhance the effectiveness of your message. The first step in developing this skill is to be aware of the often unspoken cues that let you know whether your audience either is hanging on every word or is bored. After learning to "read" your audience, you then need to develop a repertoire of behaviors to help you better connect with your listeners.

What do the nonverbal cues of this audience indicate about their level of interest in the speaker? How should the speaker respond?

Photo: Robert Kneschke/Shutterstock

Eye Contact   Perhaps the best way to determine whether your listeners are maintaining interest in your speech is to note the amount of eye contact they have with you. The more contact they have, the more likely it is that they are listening to your message. If you find them repeatedly looking at their phones, checking email, tapping out a text message, looking down at the program (or, worse yet, closing their eyes), you can reasonably guess that they have lost interest in what you're talking about.

Facial Expression   Another clue to whether an audience is with you is facial expression. Members of an attentive audience not only make direct eye contact but also have attentive facial expressions. Beware of a frozen, unresponsive face; we call this sort of expression the "listener-stupor" look. The classic listener-stupor expression consists of a slightly tilted head, a faint, frozen smile, and often a hand holding up the chin. This expression may give the appearance of interest, but more often it means that the person is daydreaming or thinking of something other than your topic.

Movement   An attentive audience doesn't move much. An early sign of inattentiveness is fidgeting fingers, which may escalate to pencil wagging, leg jiggling, and arm wiggling. Seat squirming, feet shuffling, and general body movement often indicate that members of the audience have lost interest in your message.

Nonverbal Responsiveness   Interested audience members respond verbally and nonverbally when encouraged or invited to do so by the speaker. When you ask for a show of hands and audience members sheepishly look at one another and eventually raise a finger or two, you can reasonably infer lack of interest and enthusiasm. Frequent applause and nods of agreement with your message are indicators of interest and support.

Verbal Responsiveness   Not only will audiences indicate agreement nonverbally, but some will also indicate their interests verbally. Audience members may shout out a response or more quietly express agreement or disagreement to people seated next to them. A sensitive public speaker is constantly listening for verbal reinforcement or disagreement.

Responding to Nonverbal Cues

Explore at **MyCommunicationLab**
Activity: "Nonverbal Communication"

The value in recognizing nonverbal cues from your listeners is that you can respond to them appropriately. If your audience seems interested, supportive, and attentive, your prespeech analysis has clearly guided you to make proper choices in preparing and delivering your speech.

When your audience becomes inattentive, however, you may need to make some changes while delivering your message. If you think audience members are drifting off into their own thoughts or disagreeing with what you say, or if you suspect that they don't understand what you are saying, then a few spontaneous adjustments may help. It takes experience and skill to make on-the-spot changes in your speech. Consider the tips from seasoned public speakers for adapting to your listeners listed in Table 5.6.[22]

Remember, it is not enough to note your listeners' characteristics and attitudes. You must also *respond* to the information you gather by adapting your speech to retain their interest and attention. Moreover, you have a responsibility to ensure that your audience understands your message. If your approach to the content of your speech is not working, alter it and note whether your audience's

---

RECAP

READING AUDIENCE CUES

Identify and respond to nonverbal cues that your audience is bored, doesn't understand, or disagrees:
- Lack of eye contact
- "Listener-stupor" expression
- Physical restlessness
- Sending or receiving email or text messages
- No response to humor or speaker invitations
- Talking to other listeners

TABLE 5.6 RESPONDING TO NONVERBAL CUES

If your audience seems inattentive or bored . . .	• Tell a story. • Use an example to which the audience can relate. • Use a personal example. • Remind your listeners why your message should be of interest to them. • Eliminate some abstract facts and statistics. • Use appropriate humor. If listeners do not respond to your humor, use more stories or personal illustrations. • Consider making direct references to listeners, using audience members' names or mentioning something about them. • Ask the audience to participate by asking questions or asking them for an example. • Ask for a direct response, such as a show of hands, to see whether they agree or disagree with you. • Pick up the pace of your delivery. • Increase your speaking energy. • Pause for dramatic effect while providing eye contact to gain attention.
If your audience seems confused or doesn't seem to understand your point . . .	• Be more redundant. • Try phrasing your information in another way. • Use more concrete examples to illustrate your point. • Use a visual such as a chalkboard or flip chart to clarify your point. • If you have been speaking rapidly, slow your speaking rate. • Clarify the overall organization of your message to your listeners using transitions or internal summaries. • Ask audience members whether they understand your message. • Ask for feedback from an audience member to help you discover what is unclear. • Ask someone in the audience to summarize the key point you are making.
If your audience seems to be disagreeing with your message . . .	• Provide additional data and evidence to support your point. • Identify issues about which you agree with your listeners. • Remind your listeners of your credibility, credentials, or background. • Rely less on anecdotes and more on facts to present your case. • Write facts and data on a chalkboard, whiteboard, or flip chart if one is handy. • If you don't have the answers and data you need, tell listeners you will provide more information by mail, telephone, email, or social media (and make sure you get back in touch with them).

responses change. If all else fails, you may need to abandon a formal speaker–listener relationship with your audience and open up your topic for discussion. In your speech class your instructor may expect you to keep going to fulfill the requirements for your assignment. With other audiences, however, you may want to consider switching to a more interactive question-and-answer session to ensure that you are communicating clearly. Later chapters on supporting material, speech organization, and speech delivery will discuss other techniques for adjusting your style while delivering your message.

Strategies for Customizing Your Message to Your Audience

Many people value having something prepared especially for them. Perhaps you've bought a computer that you ordered to your exact specifications. In a restaurant you order food prepared to your specific taste. Audiences, too, prefer messages that are adapted just to them; they don't like hearing a canned message. As a speaker, you may have worked hard to adapt your message to your audience, but your audience won't give you credit for it unless you let them know that you've done so. What are some ways to communicate to your listeners that your message is designed specifically for them? Here are a few suggestions:

- **Appropriately use audience members' names.** Consider using audience members' names in your talk to relate specific information to individual people. Obviously, you don't want to embarrass people by using them in an example that would make them feel uncomfortable. But you can selectively mention people you know who are in the audience. It's become a standard technique in State of the Union speeches for the president to have someone sitting in the balcony who can be mentioned in his talk. That person becomes a living visual aid to provide focus on an idea or a point made in the address. If you are uncertain whether you should mention someone by name, before you speak, ask the person for permission to use his or her name in your talk.

- **Refer to the town, city, or community.** Make a specific reference to the place where you are speaking. If you are speaking to a college audience, relate your message and illustrations to the school where you are speaking. Many politicians use this technique: They have a standard stump speech to tout their credentials but adapt the opening part of their message to the specific city or community in which they are speaking.

- **Refer to a significant event that happened on the date of your speech.** An easy way to find out what happened on any given day in history is to go to www .history.com and click on the link called "This Day in History." Or just type "This Day in History" in most any search engine, and you'll find out what happened on the day of your speech. For example, on the day this paragraph was written, Julius Caesar was assassinated in 44 B.C.E. It's also known as the Ides of March—a day Caesar was warned about in Shakespeare's famous play. If you were giving a speech on this day, a reference to the Ides of March might be especially apropos if your goal was to encourage your audience to beware of whatever issue or topic you were discussing.

  Many newspapers keep records of local historical events and list what happened 10, 25, or 50 years ago on a certain date. Relating your talk to a historical event that occurred on the same date as your talk and took place in the immediate geographical area can give your message a feeling of immediacy. It tells your audience that you have thought about this specific speaking event.

- **Refer to a recent news event.** Always read the local paper to see whether there is a news story that you can connect to the central idea of your talk. Or perhaps you can use a headline from your university newspaper or a recent story that appeared on your university Web site. If there is a newspaper headline that connects with your talk, consider holding up the paper as you refer to it—not so that people will be able to read the headline, but to emphasize the immediacy of your message.

- **Refer to a group or organization.** If you're speaking to an audience of service, religious, political, or work group members, by all means make specific positive references to the group. But be honest—don't offer false praise; audiences can sniff out phony flattery. A sincere compliment about the group will be appreciated, especially if you can link the goals of the group to the goal of your talk.

- **Relate information directly to your listeners.** Find ways to apply facts, statistics, and examples to the people in your audience. If, for example, you know that four out of ten women are likely to experience gender discrimination, customize that statistic by saying, "Forty percent of women listening to me now are likely to experience gender discrimination. That means that of the twenty women in this audience, eight of you are likely to be discriminated against." Or, if you live in a city of 50,000 people, you can cite the statistic that 50,000 people on our nation's highways become victims of drunk driving each year—and then point out that that number is equivalent to killing every man, woman, and child in your city. Relating abstract statistics and examples to your listeners communicates that you have them in mind as you develop your message.

Analyzing Your Audience after You Speak

5.6   Identify methods of assessing audience reactions after you have concluded your speech.

After you have given your speech, you're not finished analyzing your audience. It is important to evaluate your audience's positive or negative response to your message. Why? Because this evaluation can help you prepare your next speech. Postspeech analysis helps you polish your speaking skill, regardless of whether you will face the same audience again. From that analysis you can learn whether your examples were clear and your message was accepted by your listeners. Let's look at specific methods for assessing your audience's response to your speech.

Nonverbal Responses

The most obvious nonverbal response is applause. Is the audience simply clapping politely, or is the applause robust and enthusiastic, indicating pleasure and acceptance? Responsive facial expressions, smiles, and nods are other nonverbal signs that the speech has been well received.

Realize, however, that audience members from different cultures respond to speeches in different ways. Japanese audience members, for example, are likely to be restrained in their response to a speech and to show little expression. Some Eastern European listeners may not maintain eye contact with you; they may look down at the floor when listening. In some contexts, African American listeners may enthusiastically voice their agreement or disagreement with something you say during your presentation.[23]

Nonverbal responses at the end of the speech may convey some general feeling of the audience, but they are not much help in identifying which strategies were the most effective. Also consider what the members of the audience say, both to you and to others, after your speech.

Verbal Responses

What might members of the audience say to you about your speech? General comments, such as "I enjoyed your talk" and "Great speech," are good for the ego—which is important—but are not of much analytic help. Specific comments can indicate where you succeeded and where you failed. If you have the chance, ask audience members how they responded to the speech in general as well as to points you are particularly interested in.

Survey Responses

You are already aware of the value of conducting audience surveys before speaking publicly. You may also want to survey your audience after you speak. You can then assess how well you accomplished your objective. Use the same survey techniques discussed earlier. Develop survey questions that will help you determine the general reactions to you and your speech, as well as specific responses to your ideas and supporting materials. Professional speakers and public officials often conduct such surveys. Postspeech surveys are especially useful when you are trying to persuade an audience. Comparing prespeech and postspeech attitudes can give you a clear idea of your effectiveness. A significant portion of most political campaign budgets goes toward evaluating how a candidate is received by his or her constituents. Politicians want to know what portions of their messages are acceptable to their audiences so they can use this information in the future.

If your objective was to teach your audience about some new idea, a posttest can assess whether you expressed your ideas clearly. In fact, classroom exams are post-tests that determine whether your instructor presented information clearly.

Behavioral Responses

If the purpose of your speech was to persuade your listeners to do something, you will want to learn whether they ultimately behave as you intended. If you wanted them to vote in an upcoming election, you might survey your listeners to find out how many did vote. If you wanted to win support for a particular cause or organization, you might ask them to sign a petition after your speech. The number of signatures would be a clear measure of your speech's success. Some religious speakers judge the success of their ministry by the amount of contributions they receive. Your listeners' actions are the best indicators of your speaking success.

RECAP

WAYS TO ANALYZE YOUR AUDIENCE AFTER SPEAKING

- Quality and volume of applause and other nonverbal responses
- Content and tone of specific verbal responses
- Formal survey or posttest responses
- Behavioral responses: Did they do what you asked them to do?

STUDY GUIDE REVIEW, APPLY, AND ASSESS

GATHERING INFORMATION ABOUT YOUR AUDIENCE

5.1 Describe informal and formal methods of gathering information about your audience.

You can gather information about your audience by informally observing their demographics. Formal surveys, with either open-ended or closed-ended questions, can add more specific information about their opinions.

Key Terms

Thinking Ethically

Tynisha wants to convince her audience to ban alcohol in all city parks. Her survey results suggest that 85 percent of her audience wants to continue the current policy of permitting alcohol in city parks. Should she change her purpose to fit the existing attitudes of her audience?

Assessing Your Audience-Centered Speaking Skill

Phil Owens is running for a seat on the school board. He has agreed to speak to the chamber of commerce about his views, but he wants to know what his audience believes about a number of issues. How can he gather this information?

ANALYZING INFORMATION ABOUT YOUR AUDIENCE

5.2 Explain how to analyze information about your audience.

Your audience analysis involves looking at the information you've gathered to find (1) similarities among audience members, (2) differences among audience members, and (3) ways to establish a relationship, or common ground, with listeners.

Key Terms

Thinking Ethically

Do most politicians place too much emphasis on the results of political-opinion polls to shape their stands on political issues? Explain your position.

Assessing Your Audience-Centered Speaking Skill

Brendon wants to convince his audience of homeowners that the zoning laws should be changed so that he and his company can build a new apartment complex next to their quiet, residential neighborhood. What strategies could Brendon use to establish common ground with his listeners?

ADAPTING TO YOUR AUDIENCE

5.3 Identify and use strategies for adapting to your audience.

Ethical speakers use their audience analysis to adapt their message so that audience members will listen. They first consider their audience; then they adapt their speech goal, speech content, and speech delivery to connect to the audience.

Key Term

Thinking Ethically

On page 84, President Harry Truman was quoted as saying, "I wonder how far Moses would have gone it he'd taken a poll in Egypt?" What are the implications of President Truman's quotation for an ethical, audience-centered speaker?

Assessing Your Audience-Centered Public Speaking Skill

Answer the questions on page 100 about a speech you have already presented. Describe how your knowledge of your audience influenced the choices you made in designing your speech.

ANALYZING YOUR AUDIENCE BEFORE YOU SPEAK

5.4 Develop methods of analyzing your audience before you speak by seeking demographic, psychological, and situational information about your audience and the speaking occasion.

Before your speech, you can perform three kinds of analysis: demographic, psychological, and situational. Demographic analysis assesses audience diversity. Psychological audience analysis helps you gauge the interests, attitudes, beliefs, and values of listeners. Situational audience analysis includes examining the time and place of your speech, the size of your audience, and the speaking occasion.

Strategies for adapting to a diverse audience include (1) focusing on a target audience, (2) using diverse strategies, (3) using common audience perspectives, and (4) relying on visual materials that transcend language differences.

Key Terms

Thinking Ethically

Maria strongly believes the drinking age in her state should be increased to 22. Yet when she surveyed her classmates, the overwhelming majority thought the drinking age should be lowered to 18. Should Maria change her speech topic and her purpose to avoid facing a hostile audience? Why or why not?

Dan knows that most of the women in his audience will be startled and probably offended if he begins his speech by saying, "Most of you broads are too sensitive about sexist language." But this is how Dan really feels. Should he alter his language just to appease his audience? Explain.

Assessing Your Audience-Centered Speaking Skill

Dr. Ruiz thought the audience for her speech on birth control would be women of child-bearing age. After writing her speech, however, she found out that all the women to whom she will be speaking are at least 20 years older than she expected. What changes, if any, should she make?

ANALYZING YOUR AUDIENCE AS YOU SPEAK

5.5 Identify methods of assessing and adapting to your audience's reactions while your speech is in progress.

While speaking, you should look for feedback from your listeners. Audience eye contact, facial expression, movement, and general verbal and nonverbal responsiveness provide clues to how well you are doing. Listeners' nonverbal reactions may indicate that you need to change or adjust your message to maintain interest and achieve your speaking objective.

Thinking Ethically

Kale realized that his listeners were not responding favorably to his message about the hazards of texting while driving. He recalled reading an article online that included statistics that would help support his point, but he couldn't remember the precise statistics or the source of the article. Would it be ethical for Kale to use approximate versions of the statistics to convince his audience, knowing that the numbers are not quite accurate?

Assessing Your Audience-Centered Speaking Skill

How would you adapt your message if, while you were speaking, you realized that you were not holding your listeners' attention?

ANALYZING YOUR AUDIENCE AFTER YOU SPEAK

5.6 Identify methods of assessing audience reactions after you have concluded your speech.

Evaluate audience reaction after your speech. Again, nonverbal cues as well as verbal ones will help you judge your speaking skill. The best indicator of your speaking success is whether your audience is able or willing to follow your advice or remembers what you have told them.

Thinking Critically

Adeline's speaking goal was to convince listeners to support spaying or neutering all pets who live in the community. She asked them to take three actions: to visit her Web site and sign a petition, to write their city council members, and to tell their neighbors to support her proposition. How can Adeline assess whether her speech achieved her goal?

Assessing Your Audience-Centered Speaking Skill

After your next speech, describe the extent to which you accomplished your speaking goal based on assessment techniques described on pages 105–106.

 Explore at **MyCommunicationLab**
Speaker's Workshop: Developing Communication Strategies to Adapt to Your Audience

6 DEVELOPING YOUR SPEECH

((•)) **Listen** to **Chapter 6** at **MyCommunicationLab**

Jacob Lawrence (1917–2000), *Builders in the City,* 1993. Gouache on paper, 19 × 28 1/2". Courtesy of SBC Communications, Inc. Private Collection.
Photo: the Jacob and Gwendolyn Lawrence Foundation/Art Resource, N.Y.

> In all matters, before beginning, a
> diligent preparation should be made.
>
> —Cicero

Ed Garcia has arranged the books and papers on his desk into neat, even piles. He has sharpened his pencils and laid them out parallel to one another. He has even dusted his desktop and cleaned the computer monitor's screen. Ed can think of no other way to delay writing his speech. He opens a new word-processing document, carefully centers the words "Informative Speech" at the top of the first page, and then slouches in his chair, staring glumly at the blank expanse that threatens his well-being. Finally, he types the words "College Football" under the words "Informative Speech." Another long pause. Hesitantly, he begins his first sentence: "Today I want to talk to you about college football." Rereading his first ten words, Ed decides that they sound moronic. He deletes the sentence and tries again. This time the screen looks even blanker than before. He writes—deletes—writes—deletes. Half an hour later, Ed is exhausted and still mocked by a blank screen. And he is frantic—this speech *has* to be ready by 9 in the morning.

Getting from a blank screen or sheet of paper to a speech outline may be the biggest hurdle you will face as a public speaker. Fortunately, however, it is one that you can learn to clear. If your earlier efforts at speech writing have been like Ed Garcia's, take heart. Just as you learned to read, drive a car, or register for your college classes, so too can you learn to prepare a speech.

The first steps in preparing a speech are as follows:

1. Select and narrow your topic.
2. Determine your purpose.
3. Develop your central idea.
4. Generate your main ideas.

At the end of step 4, you will have a plan for the speech, and you will be ready to develop and polish your main ideas further. For most brief classroom speeches (under 10 minutes), you should allow at least one week between selecting a topic and delivering your speech. A week gives you enough time to develop and research your speech. Many habitual procrastinators like Ed Garcia, who grudgingly decide to begin an assignment a week in advance, learn to their surprise that the whole process is far easier than it would be if they put off working until the night before they are supposed to deliver their speech.

As we observed in Chapter 5, audience-centered speakers consider the needs, interests, and expectations of their audience during the entire speech-preparation process—needs, interests, and expectations that will be as diverse as the audiences themselves. As you move from topic selection to speech plan, remember that you are preparing a message for your listeners. Always keep the audience as your central focus.

Select and Narrow Your Topic

6.1 Select and narrow a topic for a speech that is appropriate to the audience, the occasion, the time limits, and yourself.

Your first task, as illustrated in Figure 6.1 on page 112, is to choose a topic on which to speak. You will then need to narrow this topic to fit your time limits. Sometimes you can eliminate one or both of these steps because the topic has been chosen and properly defined for you. For example, knowing that you visited England's Lake

FIGURE 6.1 Selecting and narrowing the topic and determining the general and specific purposes of the speech are early speech-making tasks.

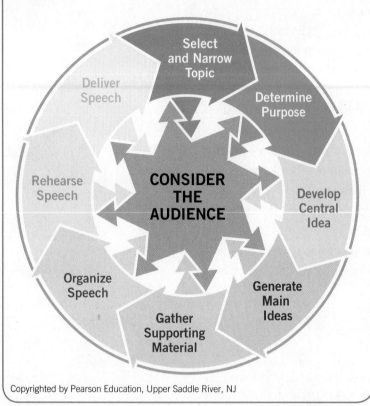

Watch at **MyCommunicationLab**
Video: "Tips on Developing a Topic for a Speech"

Watch at **MyCommunicationLab**
Video: "Emergency Preparedness"

District on your tour of Great Britain last summer, your English literature teacher asks you to speak about the mountains and lakes of that region before your class studies the poetry of Wordsworth and Coleridge. Or, knowing that you chair the local drug-abuse task force, the Lions Club asks you to speak at its weekly meeting about the work of your group. In both instances, your topic and its scope have been decided for you.

At other times, the choice of topic may be left entirely to you. In your public-speaking class, your instructor may specify a time limit and the type of speech (informative, persuasive, or entertaining) but allow you to choose your topic. In this event, you should realize that the success of your speech may rest on your decision. But how do you go about choosing an appropriate, interesting topic?

Guidelines for Selecting a Topic

In May 2012, CNN and *Time* journalist Fareed Zakaria delivered much the same speech to the graduating class of Harvard as he had delivered to Duke graduates less than two weeks earlier. After beginning both speeches with the same anecdote about missing his own college graduation, Zakaria went on to use similar, sometimes identical, language and content in the second speech. Afterward, a communication consultant noted that it was unusual for a speaker to deliver the same speech at two graduations within a few days of each other:

> One reason for that is Google, because you can just plug in the text from one school and—holy cow!—find it at the other.[1]

Consider the Audience More significant than having the duplication show up in a Google search is Zakaria's failure to tailor each speech to the specific audience. In Chapter 5 we discussed the reasons and methods for finding out about your audience. "What interests and needs do the members of this audience have in common?" and "Why did they ask me to speak?" are important questions to ask yourself as you search for potential speech topics. Keep in mind each audience's interests and expectations. For example, a university president invited to speak to a civic organization should talk about some new university program or recent accomplishment; a police officer speaking to an elementary school's PTA should address the audience's concern for the safety of young children. In contrast to Fareed Zakaria, autism activist and animal behaviorist Temple Grandin notes that when she is invited to deliver a commencement address, she makes it a point to find out about "each campus, the place, and the people," and to adapt her speech accordingly.[2]

Not only should a speaker's choice of topic be relevant to the *interests* and *expectations* of his or her listeners, it should also take into account the *knowledge* listeners already have about the subject. For example, the need for a campus-wide office for disability services would not be a good topic to discuss in a speech to a group of students with disabilities, who would already be well aware of such a need. The speech would offer them no new information.

Finally, speakers should choose topics that are *important*—topics that matter to their listeners as well as to themselves. Student speaker Roger Fringer explains the stakes for students in a public-speaking class:

> We work hard for our tuition, so we should spend it wisely. Spending it wisely means . . . we don't waste our classmates' time who have to listen to our speeches.[3]

Several years ago communication scholar and then-president of the National Communication Association Bruce Gronbeck reminded an audience of communication instructors that students should be giving "the important kinds of . . . speeches that show . . . people how to confront the issues that divide them. . . ."[4] Table 6.1 below offers examples of topics appropriate for the interests, expectations, knowledge, and concerns of given audiences.

Consider the Occasion   In December 1877, Mark Twain was invited to be one of the after-dinner speakers at American poet John Greenleaf Whittier's seventieth-birthday celebration.[5] The guest list included Henry Wadsworth Longfellow, Ralph Waldo Emerson, and Oliver Wendell Holmes.

When it was Twain's turn to speak, he began with a humorous sketch featuring Longfellow, Emerson, and Holmes as drunken card-playing travelers in Nevada. Used to laughter and applause from his audiences, Twain was stunned by the silence.

What had gone wrong? Was Mark Twain's topic of *interest* to his listeners? Undoubtedly. Did they *expect* to hear someone talk about the distinguished guests? Yes. Could Twain *add to their knowledge* of the subject? Probably. Was his topic *appropriate to the occasion*? Definitely not!

Although after-dinner speeches are usually humorous, Twain's irreverence was inappropriate to the dignity of the birthday observance. Even though he had considered his audience, he had not considered carefully enough the demands of the occasion. Twain's irreverent talk aroused quite a commotion at the time and is said to have embarrassed him for years afterward. To be successful, a topic must be appropriate to both audience and occasion.

Consider Yourself   What do you talk about with your friends? You probably discuss school, mutual friends, political or social issues, hobbies or leisure activities, or whatever other topics are of interest and importance to you. As with most people, your liveliest, most animated conversations revolve around topics of personal concern that arouse your deepest convictions.

 Watch at **MyCommunicationLab** Video: "Tall Girls"

 Read at **MyCommunicationLab Learning From Great Speakers:** Frederick Douglass

TABLE 6.1   SAMPLE AUDIENCE-CENTERED TOPICS

AUDIENCE	TOPIC
Retirees	Prescription drug benefits
Civic organization	The Special Olympics
Church members	Starting a community food bank
First graders	What to do in case of a fire at home
Teachers	Building children's self-esteem
College fraternity	Campus service opportunities

As you search for a topic, think about your own experiences.

Photo: mangostock/Fotolia

The best public-speaking topics are also those that reflect your personal experience or especially interest you. Where have you lived? Where have you traveled? Describe your family or your ancestors. Have you held a part-time job? Describe your first days at college. What are your favorite classes? What are your hobbies or interests? What is your favorite sport? What social issues especially concern you? Here is one list of topics that was generated by such questions:

Blues music

"Yankee, go home": the American tourist in France

Why most diets fail

Behind the counter at McDonald's

My first day at college

Maintaining family ties while living a long distance from home

Getting involved in political campaigns

An alternative to selecting a topic with which you are already familiar is to select one you would like to know more about. Your interest will motivate both your research and your delivery of the speech.

Strategies for Selecting a Topic

All successful topics reflect audience, occasion, and speaker. But just contemplating those guidelines does not automatically yield a good topic. Sooner or later, we all find ourselves unable to think of a good speech topic, whether for the first speech of the semester, for that all-important final speech, or for a speaking engagement long after our school years are over. Nothing is so frustrating to a public speaker as floundering for something to talk about! In such an instance, you may want to turn to one of the following strategies to help generate a speech topic.

Explore at MyCommunicationLab
Activity: "Visual Brainstorming"

brainstorming
A creative problem-solving technique used to generate many ideas

Brainstorming A problem-solving technique widely used in such diverse fields as business, advertising, writing, and science, **brainstorming** can easily be used to generate ideas for speech topics as well.[6] To brainstorm a list of potential topics, get a sheet of paper and a pencil or pen, or open a new document on your computer. Set a minimum time limit of, say, 3 to 5 minutes. Write down the first topic that comes to mind. Do not allow yourself to evaluate it. Just write it down in a word or a phrase, whether it's a vague idea or a well-focused one. Now jot down a second idea—again, anything that comes to mind. The first topic may remind you of a second possibility. Such "piggybacking" of ideas is perfectly okay. Continue without any restraints until your time is up. At this stage, anything goes. Your goal is quantity—as long a list as you can think up in the time you have.

The following list of 20 possible topics came from a brainstorming session of about 3 minutes:

Music	Censorship of music
Reggae	Movie themes
Bob Marley	Oscar-winning movies of the 1950s
Sound-recording technology	Great epic movies
Retro music	*Titanic* (the movie)
Buddy Holly	Salvaging the *Titanic* (the ship)
The Beatles	Treasure hunting
John Lennon	Key West, Florida
Alternative music	Ernest Hemingway
iTunes	Polydactyl cats

CONFIDENTLY CONNECTING WITH YOUR AUDIENCE

Selecting an Interesting Topic

The more confident you are about the topic you have selected, the more confident you will be in speaking to your listeners. Your own interest in and passion about a topic can replace some of the anxiety you may feel about speaking to others. Instead of focusing on your fear, you will more naturally express your interest to your audience, who in turn will find your topic more interesting because you do. Selecting an interesting topic will help you speak with confidence.

If your brainstorming yields several good topics, so much the better. Set aside a page or two in your class notebook for topic ideas, and list the topics you don't end up choosing. You can reconsider them when you get your next assignment.

Listening and Reading for Topic Ideas Very often something you see, hear, or read triggers an idea for a speech. A story on the evening news or at your favorite online news site may suggest a topic. The following list of topics was brought to mind by recent headline stories in a large daily news source:

Cyber-espionage

Recovery in the housing market

Issues for same-sex married couples

The rising cost of flood insurance

Mexican drug wars

Optimal advance warning time for tornadoes

In addition to discovering topics in news stories, you might find them in an interesting segment of *20/20, Dateline,* or even a daytime talk show. Chances are that a topic covered in one medium has been covered in another as well, allowing extended research on the topic. For example, Dr. Oz's report on the germiest places in your home may be paralleled by *Time*'s article on the dangers posed by the overuse of antibacterial cleaning products.

You may also find speech topics in one of your other classes. A lecture in an economics or political science class may arouse your interest and provide a good topic for your next speech. The instructor of that class could probably suggest additional references on the subject.

Sometimes even a subject you discuss casually with friends can be developed into a good speech topic. You have probably talked with classmates about such campus issues as dormitory regulations, inadequate parking, or your frustration with registration and advisers. Campuswide concerns would be relevant to the student audience in your speech class, as would such matters as how to find a good summer job and the pros and cons of living on or off campus.

Just as you jotted down possible topics generated by brainstorming sessions, remember to write down topic ideas you get from what's trending among your Facebook friends or on your Twitter feed, other media, class lectures, or informal conversations. If you rely on memory alone, what seems like a great topic today may be only a frustrating blank tomorrow.

Scanning Web Directories By now you probably have a list of topics from which to choose. But if all your efforts have failed to produce an idea that satisfies you, try the following strategy.

Access a Web directory, such as Yahoo! Directory (dir.yahoo.com), and select a category at random. Click on it, and look through the subcategories that come up. Click on one of them. Continue to follow the chain of categories until you see a topic that piques your interest—or until you reach a dead end, in which case you can return to the Yahoo! Directory homepage and try again.

A recent random directory search yielded the following categories, listed from general to specific:

Society and culture

Environment and nature

Ecotourism

Eco volunteer

RECAP

HOW TO BRAINSTORM FOR A TOPIC

- Start with a blank sheet of paper or computer screen.
- Set a time limit for brainstorming.
- Begin writing as many possible topics for a speech as you can.
- Do not stop to evaluate your topics; just write them down.
- Let one idea lead to another—free-associate; piggyback off your own ideas.
- Keep writing until your time is up.

RECAP

SELECTING A TOPIC

Strategies	Guidelines
Brainstorm.	Consider the audience.
Listen and read.	Consider the occasion.
Scan Web directories.	Consider yourself.

This search took only a few minutes (as will yours, as long as you resist the temptation to begin surfing the Web) and yielded at least one possible topic: becoming an Eco volunteer. An additional advantage of this strategy is that you begin to develop your preliminary bibliography while you are searching for a topic.

Narrowing the Topic

After brainstorming, reading the newspaper, surfing the Web, and talking to friends, you have come up with a topic. For some students, the toughest part of the assignment is over at this point. But others soon experience additional frustration because their topic is so broad that they find themselves overwhelmed with information. How can you cover all aspects of a topic as large as "television" in 3 to 5 minutes? Even if you trained yourself to speak as rapidly as an auctioneer, it would take days to get it all in!

The solution is to narrow your topic so that it fits within the time limits set by your assignment. The challenge lies in *how* to do this. If you have a broad, unmanageable topic, you might first try narrowing it by constructing categories similar to those created by Web directories. Write your general topic at the top of a list, and make each succeeding word in the list a more specific or concrete topic. Megan uses categories to help her narrow her general topic, music. She writes "Music" at the top of a sheet of paper and constructs a categorical hierarchy:

> Music
>
> Folk music
>
> Irish folk music
>
> The popularity of Irish folk music in the
>   United States

Megan soon discovers that her topic is still too broad. She simply cannot cover all the forms of Irish folk music popular in the United States in a talk of no more than 5 minutes. So she chooses one form of music—dance—and decides to talk about the kind of Irish hard-shoe dance music featured in *Riverdance*.

Be careful not to narrow your topic so much that you cannot find enough information for even a 3-minute talk. But if you do, just go back a step. In our example, Megan could return to the broader topic of the popularity of Irish folk music in the United States.

DEVELOPING YOUR SPEECH STEP BY STEP

SELECT AND NARROW YOUR TOPIC

CONSIDER THE AUDIENCE

After seeing an online news item about a college campus that had installed a vending machine to dispense the morning-after emergency contraceptive pill, Brianne finds herself thinking about both the advantages and disadvantages of such a plan. It occurs to her that it might make a good topic for her upcoming persuasive speech—one that her student audience would find relevant and interesting, and that she could discuss from multiple health and legal perspectives. The topic also seems appropriate for her 8- to 10-minute time limit.

Determine Your Purpose

6.2 Write an audience-centered specific-purpose statement for a speech.

 Watch at **MyCommunicationLab** **Video:** "Tips on Developing a Purpose of a Speech"

Now that you have selected and narrowed your topic, you need to decide on a purpose (the next step in Figure 6.1). If you do not know what you want your speech to achieve, chances are your audience won't either. Ask yourself "What is really important for the audience to hear?" and "How do I want the audience to respond?" Clarifying your objectives at this stage will ensure a more interesting speech and a more successful outcome.

General Purpose

The **general purpose** of any speech is to inform, to persuade, or to entertain. The speeches you give in class will generally be either informative or persuasive. It is important that you fully understand what constitutes each type of speech so you do not confuse them and fail to fulfill an assignment. You certainly do not want to deliver a first-rate persuasive speech when an informative one was assigned! Although Chapters 13 through 16 discuss the three general purposes at length, we summarize them here so that you can understand the basic principles of each.

Speaking to Inform   An informative speaker is a teacher. Informative speakers give listeners information. They define, describe, or explain a thing, person, place, concept, process, or function. In this excerpt from a student's informative speech on anorexia nervosa, the student describes the disorder for her audience:

> Anorexia nervosa is an eating disorder that affects 1 out of every 200 American women. It is a self-induced starvation that can waste its victims to the point that they resemble victims of Nazi concentration camps.
>
> Who gets anorexia nervosa? Ninety-five percent of its victims are females between the ages of 12 and 18. Men are only rarely afflicted with the disease. Anorexia nervosa patients are usually profiled as "good" or "model" children who have not caused their parents any undue concern or grief over other behavior problems. Anorexia nervosa is perhaps a desperate bid for attention by these young women.[7]

Most lectures you hear in college are informative. The university president's annual "state of the university" speech is also informative, as is the colonial Williamsburg tour guide's talk. Such speakers are all trying to increase the knowledge of their listeners. Although they may use an occasional bit of humor in their presentations, their main objective is not to entertain. And although they may provoke an audience's interest in the topic, their main objective is not to persuade. Chapter 13 provides specific suggestions for preparing an informative speech.

Speaking to Persuade   Persuasive speakers may offer information, but they use the information to try to change or reinforce an audience's convictions and often to urge some sort of action. For example, Brian offered compelling statistics to help persuade his audience to take steps to prevent and alleviate chronic pain:

> A hundred million Americans, nearly a third of the population, [suffer] from chronic pain due to everything from accidents to the simple daily stresses on our bodies.[8]

The representative from Mothers Against Drunk Driving (MADD) who spoke at your high-school assembly urged you not to drink and drive and urged you to help others realize the inherent dangers of the practice. The fraternity president talking to your group of rushees tried to convince you to join his fraternity. Appearing

general purpose
The broad reason for a speech: to inform, to persuade, or to entertain an audience

RECAP

**GENERAL PURPOSES
FOR SPEECHES**

To inform	To share information with listeners by defining, describing, or explaining a thing, person, place, concept, process, or function
To persuade	To change or reinforce a listener's attitude, belief, value, or behavior
To entertain	To help listeners have a good time by getting them to relax, smile, and laugh

on television during the last election, the candidates for president of the United States asked for your vote. All these speakers gave you information, but they used that information to try to get you to believe or do something. Chapters 14 and 15 focus on persuasive speaking.

Speaking to Entertain The entertaining speaker tries to get the members of an audience to relax, smile, perhaps laugh, and generally enjoy themselves. Storyteller Garrison Keillor spins tales of the town and residents of Lake Wobegon, Minnesota, to amuse his listeners. Comedian Louis C.K. delivers comic patter to make his audience laugh. As we describe in Chapter 16, most after-dinner speakers talk to entertain the banquet guests. Like persuasive speakers, entertaining speakers may inform their listeners, but providing knowledge is not their main goal. Rather, their objective is to produce at least a smile and at best a belly laugh.

Early on, you need to decide which of the three general purposes your speech is to have. This decision keeps you on track throughout the development of your speech. The way you organize, support, and deliver your speech depends, in part, on your general purpose.

Specific Purpose

Now that you have a topic and you know generally whether your speech should inform, persuade, or entertain, it is time you decided on its **specific purpose**. Unlike the general purpose, which can be assigned by your instructor, you alone must decide on the specific purpose of your speech because it depends directly on the topic you choose.

To arrive at a specific purpose for your speech, think in precise terms of what you want your audience to be able to *do* at the end of your speech. This kind of goal or purpose is called a **behavioral objective** because you specify the behavior you seek from the audience.

For an informative speech on how television comedy represents the modern family, you might write, "At the end of my speech, the audience will be able to explain how comedy portrays American family life today." The specific-purpose statement for a how-to speech using visual aids might read, "At the end of my speech,

specific purpose
A statement of what listeners should be able to do by the end of the speech

behavioral objective
Wording of a specific purpose in terms of desired audience behavior

The specific purpose of a speaker whose general purpose is to entertain is often simply to help the audience laugh and smile about the topic of the speech. The late entertainer Mississippi Slim (Walter Horn) also hoped these students would be able to recall and use information about the blues tradition in music.

Photo: Delta Democrat Times/Bill Johnson/AP Images

the audience will be able to use the principles of feng shui to select wall colors." Your specific-purpose statement for a persuasive speech could say, "At the end of my speech, the audience will be able to explain why the United States should ban texting while driving." A speech to entertain has a specific purpose, too. A stand-up comic may have a simple specific purpose: "At the end of my speech, the audience will laugh and applaud." An after-dinner speaker whose entertaining message has more informative value than that of the stand-up comic may say, "At the end of my speech, the audience will list four characteristics that distinguish journalists from the rest of the human species."

Formulating the Specific Purpose Note that almost all of the specific-purpose statements in the preceding paragraph begin with the same nine words: "At the end of my speech, the audience will. . . ." The next word should be a verb that names an observable, measurable action that the audience should perform or be able to perform by the end of the speech. Use verbs such as *list*, *explain*, *describe*, or *write*. Do not use words such as *know*, *understand*, or *believe*. You can discover what your listeners know, understand, or believe only by having them show their increased capability in some measurable way.

A statement of purpose does not tell what you, the *speaker*, will do. To say, "In my speech, I will talk about the benefits of studying classical dance" emphasizes your performance as a speaker. The goal of the speech is centered on you rather than on the audience. Other than restating your topic, this statement of purpose provides little direction for the speech. But to say, "At the end of my speech, the audience will be able to list three ways in which studying classical dance can benefit them" places the audience and their behavior at the center of your concern. This latter statement provides a tangible goal that can guide your preparation and by which you can measure the success of your speech.

The following guidelines will help you prepare your statement of purpose.

- **Use words that refer to observable or measurable behavior.**

  Not Observable: At the end of my speech, the audience will know some things about Hannibal, Missouri.

  Observable: At the end of my speech, the audience will be able to list five points of interest in the town of Hannibal, Missouri.

- **Limit the specific purpose to a single idea.** If your statement of purpose has more than one idea, you will have trouble covering the extra ideas in your speech. You will also run the risk of having your speech come apart at the seams. Your speech is likely to lack unity of ideas and coherence of expression.

  Two Ideas: At the end of my speech, the audience will be able to write a simple computer program in Just BASIC and play the video game Bioshock Infinite.

  One Idea: At the end of my speech, the audience will be able to write a simple computer program in Just BASIC.

- **Make sure your specific purpose reflects the interests, expectations, and knowledge level of your audience.** Also be sure that your specific purpose is important. Earlier in this chapter we discussed these criteria as guidelines for selecting a speech topic. Consider them again as you word your specific-purpose statement.

Behavioral statements of purpose help remind you that the aim of public speaking is to win a response from the audience. In addition, using a specific purpose to guide the development of your speech helps you focus on the audience during the entire preparation process.

DETERMINE YOUR PURPOSE

CONSIDER THE AUDIENCE

Because Brianne's assignment is a persuasive speech, she knows that her general purpose is to persuade. She will have to try to change or reinforce her listeners' attitudes and beliefs about providing access to and information about emergency contraception and perhaps also get them to take some sort of action.

Brianne also knows that her specific purpose must begin with the phrase, "At the end of my speech, the audience will. . . ." So she jots down,

> At the end of my speech, the audience will agree that counseling should be provided with emergency contraception.

As Brianne thinks about this draft specific purpose, she sees problems with it. How can she determine whether or not her audience "will agree" with her argument? She edits her purpose statement to read,

> At the end of my speech, the audience will explain why counseling should be provided with access to emergency contraception.

This version is more observable, but "explain" seems more appropriate for an informative speech than a persuasive one. She wants her audience to demonstrate their agreement by taking action. Maybe a better persuasive purpose statement would be:

> At the end of my speech, the audience will sign a petition advocating that the Food and Drug Administration require colleges and universities to provide counseling along with access to emergency contraception.

Brianne is pleased with this third version. It reflects a persuasive general purpose and includes an observable behavioral objective. She is ready to move on to the next step of the process.

RECAP

SPECIFIC PURPOSES FOR SPEECHES

Your specific purpose should . . .

Use words that refer to observable or measurable behavior

Be limited to a single idea

Reflect the needs, interests, expectations, and level of knowledge of your audience

Using the Specific Purpose Everything you do while preparing and delivering the speech should contribute to your specific purpose. The specific purpose can help you assess the information you are gathering for your speech. For example, you may find that an interesting statistic, although related to your topic, does not help achieve your specific purpose. In that case, you should not use it. Instead, find material that directly advances your purpose.

As soon as you have decided on it, write the specific purpose on a 3-by-5-inch note card. That way you can refer to it as often as necessary while developing your speech.

6.3 State a single audience-centered central idea with direct, specific language in a complete declarative sentence.

Develop Your Central Idea

Having stated the specific purpose of your speech, you are ready to develop your **central idea**, the first step highlighted in Figure 6.2 on page 121. The central idea (sometimes called the *thesis*) states in one sentence what the speech is *about*. You can use your purpose statement to help you as you write your central idea. However, as Table 6.2 on page 122 summarizes, a central idea differs from a purpose statement in both focus and application. A purpose statement focuses on audience behavior; the central idea focuses on the content of the speech. A purpose statement guides your

central idea

A one-sentence statement of what a speech is *about*

FIGURE 6.2 State your central idea as a one-sentence summary of your speech, and then generate main ideas by looking for natural divisions, reasons, or steps to support your central idea.

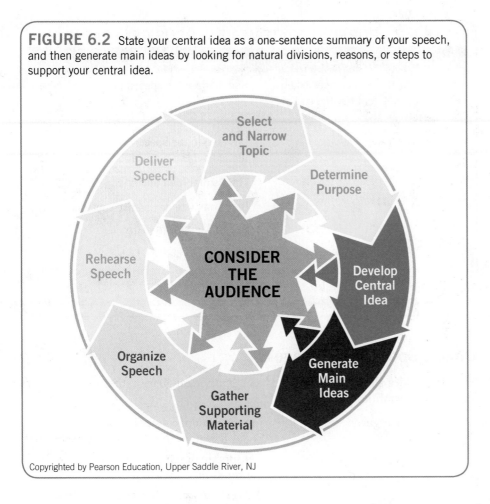

Copyrighted by Pearson Education, Upper Saddle River, NJ

decisions and choices as you prepare your speech; the central idea becomes part of your final speech.

Professional speech coach Judith Humphrey explains the importance of a central idea:

> Ask yourself before writing a speech . . . "What's my point?" Be able to state that message in a single clear sentence. Everything else you say will support that single argument.[9]

The following guidelines can help you put your central idea into words.

A Complete Declarative Sentence

The central idea should be a complete **declarative sentence**—not a phrase or clause, and not a question, but a grammatically complete sentence.

Phrase:	Car maintenance
Question:	Is regular car maintenance important?
Complete Declarative Sentence:	Maintaining your car regularly can ensure that it provides reliable transportation.

The phrase "car maintenance" is really a topic, not a central idea. It does not say anything about car maintenance. The question "Is regular car maintenance important?" is more complete but does not reveal whether the speaker is going to support the affirmative or the negative answer. By the time you word your central idea, you should be ready to summarize your stand on your topic in a complete declarative sentence.

declarative sentence
A grammatically complete sentence, rather than a clause, phrase, or question

TABLE 6.2 PURPOSE STATEMENT VERSUS CENTRAL IDEA

THE PURPOSE STATEMENT	THE CENTRAL IDEA
Indicates what the audience should know or be able to do by the end of the speech	Summarizes the speech in one sentence
Guides the speaker's decisions	Is stated in the speech and choices throughout the preparation of the speech
	The Central Idea Should . . .
	Be a complete declarative sentence
	Use direct, specific language
	Be a single idea
	Be an audience-centered idea

Copyrighted by Pearson Education, Upper Saddle River, NJ

Direct, Specific Language

The central idea should be stated in direct, specific language rather than qualifiers and vague generalities.

Qualified Language:	In my opinion, censorship of school textbooks threatens the rights of schoolchildren.
Direct Language:	Censorship of school textbooks threatens the rights of schoolchildren.
Vague:	A 2012 hurricane affected the northeastern United States.
Specific:	When Superstorm Sandy struck the coast of the northeastern United States in October 2012, it killed hundreds of people, caused billions of dollars in property damage, and closed the New York Stock Exchange for two days.

A Single Idea

The central idea should be a single idea.

Two Ideas:	Deforestation by lumber interests and toxic-waste dumping are major environmental problems in the United States today.
One Idea:	Toxic-waste dumping is a major environmental problem in the United States today.

Having more than one central idea, like more than one idea in a purpose statement, only leads to confusion and lack of coherence in a speech.

An Audience-Centered Idea

The central idea should reflect consideration of the audience. You considered your audience when selecting and narrowing your topic and when composing your purpose statement. In the same way, you should consider your audience's needs, interests, expectations, and knowledge when stating your central idea. If you do

DEVELOP YOUR CENTRAL IDEA

CONSIDER
THE
AUDIENCE

Brianne knows from having read this chapter that her central idea should be a complete declarative statement of a single audience-centered idea. She knows, too, that sometimes you can extract your central idea from your specific-purpose statement. She writes,

The Food and Drug Administration should require colleges and universities to provide counseling along with access to emergency contraception.

not consider your listeners, you run the risk of losing their attention before you even begin developing the speech. Only one of the following central ideas would be appropriate for an audience consisting mainly of college juniors and seniors.

Explore at **MyCommunicationLab**
Activity: "Topic"

Inappropriate: Scholarships from a variety of sources are readily available to first-year college students.

Appropriate: Although you may think of scholarships as a source of money for freshmen, a number of scholarships are available only to students who have completed their first year of college.

Generate and Preview Your Main Ideas

6.4 Apply three ways of generating main ideas from a central idea.

Next to selecting a topic, probably the most common stumbling block in developing speeches is coming up with a speech plan. Trying to decide how to subdivide your central idea into two, three, or four **main ideas**—detailed points of focus that help you develop your central idea—can make you chew your pencil, scratch your head, and end up as you began, with a blank sheet of paper. The task will be much easier if you use the following strategy.

Generating Your Main Ideas

Write the central idea at the top of a clean sheet of paper or computer screen. Then ask these three questions:

- Does the central idea have *logical divisions*? (They may be indicated by such phrases as "three types" or "four means.")
- Can you think of several *reasons* the central idea is true?
- Can you support your central idea with a series of *steps* or a chronological progression?

You should be able to answer yes to one or more of these questions. With your answer in mind, write down the divisions, reasons, or steps you thought of. Let's see this technique at work with several central idea statements.

Finding Logical Divisions Suppose your central idea is "A liberal arts education benefits the student in two ways." You now turn to the three questions. But for this

main ideas
Detailed points of focus for developing your central idea

example, you needn't go beyond the first one. Does the central idea have logical divisions? The phrase "two ways" indicates that it does. You can logically divide your speech into ways in which the student benefits:

1. Appreciation of culture
2. Concern for humankind

A brief brainstorming session at this point could help you come up with more specific examples of ways in which a liberal arts education might benefit students. At this stage, you needn't worry about Roman numerals, parallel form, or even the order in which the main ideas are listed. We will discuss these and the other features of outlining in Chapter 8. Your goal now is simply to generate ideas. Moreover, just because you write them down, don't think that the ideas you come up with now are engraved in stone. They can—and probably will—change. After all, this is a *preliminary* plan. It may undergo many revisions before you actually deliver your speech. For example, you might have four points, but four points may well prove to be too many to develop in the brief time allowed for most classroom speeches. But because it is much easier to eliminate ideas than to invent them, list them all for now.

Establishing Reasons Suppose your central idea is "Upholstered-furniture fires are a life-threatening hazard."[10] Asking yourself whether this idea has logical divisions is no help at all. There are no key phrases indicating logical divisions—no "ways," "means," "types," or "methods" appear in the wording. The second question, however, is more productive: Having done some initial reading on the topic, you can think of *reasons* this central idea is true. Asking yourself "Why?" after the statement yields three answers:

1. Standards to reduce fires caused by smoldering cigarettes have lulled furniture makers into a false sense of security.

A student can use logical divisions to divide the contents of her closet into three main categories: bedding, clothing, and towels. You might also be able to use logical divisions to divide your central idea into main ideas.

Photo: Kekyalyaynen/Shutterstock

2. Government officials refuse to force the furniture industry to reexamine its standards.

3. Consumers are largely ignorant of the risks.

Notice that these main ideas are expressed in complete sentences, whereas the ones in the preceding example were in phrases. At this stage, it doesn't matter. What does matter is getting your ideas down on paper; you can rewrite and reorganize them later.

Tracing Specific Steps "NASA's space shuttle program resulted in both great achievement and tragic failure." You stare glumly at the central idea you so carefully formulated yesterday. Now what? You know a lot about the subject; your aerospace science professor has covered it thoroughly this semester. But how can you organize all the information you have? Again, you turn to the three-question method.

Does the main idea have logical divisions? You scan the sentence hopefully, but you can find no key phrases suggesting logical divisions.

Can you think of several reasons why the central idea is true? You read the central idea again and ask "Why?" Answering that question may indeed produce a plan for a speech, one in which you would talk about the reasons for the achievements and failures. But your purpose statement reads, "At the end of my speech, the audience will be able to trace the history of the space shuttle." Giving reasons for the space shuttle program's achievements and failures would not directly contribute to your purpose. So you turn to the third question.

Can you support your central idea with a series of steps? You can generate main ideas for a speech about almost any historical topic, or any topic requiring a chronological progression (for example, topics of how-to speeches), by answering the third question. You therefore decide that your main ideas will be a chronology of important space shuttle flights:[11]

1. April 1981: Test flight of the space shuttle.
2. January 1986: Shuttle *Challenger* explodes on launch.
3. April 1990: Hubble space telescope deployed.
4. May–June 1999: Shuttle *Discovery* docks with the International Space Station.
5. February 2003: Shuttle *Columbia* disintegrates on re-entry.
6. July 2011: Shuttle *Atlantis* makes the program's final flight.

You know that you can add to, eliminate, or reorganize these ideas later. But you have a start.

Notice that for this last example, you consulted your purpose statement as you generated your main ideas. If these main ideas do not help achieve your purpose, you need to rethink your speech. You may finally change either your purpose or your main ideas; but whichever you do, you need to synchronize them. Remember, it is much easier to make changes at this point than after you have done your research and produced a detailed outline.

DEVELOPING YOUR SPEECH STEP BY STEP

GENERATE YOUR MAIN IDEAS

CONSIDER THE AUDIENCE

With her central idea in hand, Brianne knows that she next needs to generate her main ideas. She asks herself three questions:

- Does my central idea have *logical divisions*?
- Can I establish several *reasons* my central idea is true?
- Can I support my central idea by tracing specific *steps*?

Brianne's central idea does not seem to have logical divisions, but she can certainly think of reasons it is true. She jots down her central idea and writes *because* at the end of it:

The Food and Drug Administration should require colleges and universities to provide counseling along with access to emergency contraception *because* . . .

And she quickly adds,

1. Ease of access to emergency contraception has resulted in its increased use among college students.
2. Ease of access without required counseling has resulted in many students guessing on their own how to use the morning-after pill, or simply not knowing enough to use it effectively.

Brianne has two possible main ideas—a good start. But she looks back at her specific-purpose statement and remembers that she also wants her listeners to take steps to solve the problem. So she adds a third main idea:

3. To help solve these two problems, audience members should sign a petition calling for the FDA to mandate counseling for over-the-counter purchase of the morning-after pill on all college campuses.

Now Brianne has main ideas that both support her central idea and fulfill her specific purpose.

Previewing Your Main Ideas

Once you have generated your main ideas, you can add a preview of those main ideas to your central idea to produce a **blueprint** for your speech. Preview the ideas in the same order you plan to discuss them in the speech. In Chapter 8, we discuss how to organize your speech.

Some speakers, like Nicole, integrate their central idea and preview into one blueprint sentence:

> Obsolete computers are straining landfills because they contain hazardous materials and take a distinctively long time to decay.[12]

In this example, Nicole started with a central idea: "Obsolete computers are straining landfills." Asking herself "Why?" yielded two reasons, which became her two main points: "They contain hazardous materials" and "They take a distinctively long time to decay." Combining these reasons with her central idea produced a blueprint.

Other speakers, like Patrick in his speech on problems associated with mining oil by hydraulic fracturing, state their blueprint in several sentences:

> In order to understand the fundamental threat fracturing poses, we must first understand the dangers at each step of the process. Second, expose the corrupt legal maneuvering which protects it. And, finally, champion the simple solution that will save American lives.[13]

Patrick also started with a central idea: Fracturing poses a fundamental threat. Like Nicole, he generated reasons for his central idea, which in this case were "dangers at each step of the process" and "corrupt legal maneuvering which protects it." He decided at this early point in the speech simply to mention that there is a "simple solution that will save American lives." Thinking that a single sentence might become unwieldy, Patrick decided to use three shorter sentences for his blueprint.

Meanwhile, Back at the Computer . . .

It's been a while since we abandoned Ed Garcia, the student in the opening paragraphs of this chapter who was struggling to write a speech on college football. Even though he has procrastinated, if he follows the steps we have discussed, he should still be able to plan a successful informative speech.

Ed has already chosen his topic. His audience is likely to be interested in his subject. Because Ed is a varsity defensive tackle, the audience will probably expect him to talk about college football. And he himself is passionately interested in and knowledgeable about the subject. It meets all the requirements of a successful topic.

But "college football" is too broad a subject for a 3- to 5-minute talk. Ed needs to narrow his topic to a manageable size. He goes online to Yahoo! Directory and clicks on the category Recreation and Sports, then on Sports. He is just about to select College and University when another category catches his eye: Medicine. Sports medicine? Hmmmm. . . . Ed has suffered several injuries and feels qualified to talk about this aspect of football. Ed doesn't need to go further. He has his topic: "injuries in college football."

Now that he has narrowed the topic, Ed needs a purpose statement. He decides that his audience may know something about how players are injured, but they probably do not know how these injuries are treated. He types, "The audience will be able to explain how the three most common injuries suffered by college football players are treated."

blueprint
The central idea of a speech plus a preview of the main ideas

A few minutes later, Ed derives his central idea from his purpose: "Sports medicine specialists have developed specific courses of treatment for the three most common kinds of injuries suffered by college football players."

Generating main ideas is also fairly easy now. Because his central idea mentions three kinds of injuries, he can plan his speech around those three ideas (logical divisions). Under the central idea, Ed lists three injuries:

1. Bruises
2. Broken bones
3. Ligament and cartilage damage

Now Ed has a plan and is well on his way to developing a successful 3- to 5-minute informative speech.

STUDY GUIDE
REVIEW, APPLY, AND ASSESS

SELECT AND NARROW YOUR TOPIC

6.1 Select and narrow a topic for a speech that is appropriate to the audience, the occasion, the time limits, and yourself.

As a speaker, you may be asked to address a specific topic or given only broad guidelines, such as a time limit and an idea of the occasion. Being aware of several boundaries can help you select an appropriate speech topic. Keep in mind the interests, expectations, and knowledge levels of the audience. Choose an important topic. Consider the special demands of the occasion. Be sure to take into account your own interests, abilities, and experiences. If you are still undecided, brainstorming strategies, such as consulting the media or scanning Web directories for potential topics, may give you topic ideas. After choosing a broad topic area, narrow the topic so that it fits within the time limits that have been set.

Key Term

Brainstorming 114

Thinking Ethically

Some speakers prepare a stock speech and deliver it to a variety of audiences and on a variety of occasions. Is this practice ethical? Explain your answer.

Thinking Critically

A candidate for the state legislature visits your public-speaking class and talks for 30 minutes on the topic "Why the state should increase funding of public transportation." Analyze the candidate's choice of topic according to the guidelines presented in this chapter.

Assessing Your Audience-Centered Speaking Skill

Turn back to Table 6.1 on page 113. For each of the audiences listed in the left-hand column, generate at least one additional audience-centered topic.

DETERMINE YOUR PURPOSE

6.2 Write an audience-centered specific-purpose statement for a speech.

After choosing a topic, decide on, first, your general purpose and then your specific purpose. Your general purpose for speaking will be to inform, to persuade, or to entertain

your listeners. Your specific purpose should state what your audience will *do* at the end of the speech. Specifying target behaviors in your specific-purpose statement provides a yardstick for you to measure the relevance of your ideas and supporting materials as you develop your speech.

Key Terms

General purpose. 117
Specific purpose. 118
Behavioral objective 118

Thinking Ethically

In Chapter 3, we define ethical speech as speech that offers the listener choices. Do specific-purpose statements preclude listeners' right to choose?

Thinking Critically

Consider the following specific-purpose statements. Analyze each according to the criteria presented in this chapter. Rewrite the statements to correct any problems.

- At the end of my speech, the audience will know more about the Mexican Free-Tailed Bat.
- I will explain some differences in nonverbal communication between Asian and Western cultures.
- At the end of my speech, the audience will be able to list some reasons for xeriscaping one's yard.
- To describe the reasons I enjoy spelunking as a hobby.

Assessing Your Audience-Centered Speaking Skill

As you develop your specific purpose for your next speech, ask yourself the key question, "How will I be able to observe or measure my audience's response?"

DEVELOP YOUR CENTRAL IDEA

6.3 State a single audience-centered central idea with direct, specific language in a complete declarative sentence.

Specific-purpose statements indicate what speakers hope to accomplish; they tell what the speaker wants the *audience* to be able to do. Your central idea, in contrast, summarizes what *you*, the speaker, will say. The central idea should be a single idea, stated in a complete declarative sentence. Be direct and specific without using qualifiers.

Key Terms

Central idea 120
Declarative sentence 121

Thinking Critically

Below are the topic, general purpose, and specific purpose Marylin has chosen for her persuasive speech.

- Topic: America's crumbling roads and bridges
- General Purpose: To persuade
- Specific Purpose: At the end of my speech, the audience will be able to list and explain three reasons America should invest in its roads and bridges.

Write an appropriate central idea for Marylin's speech.

GENERATE AND PREVIEW YOUR MAIN IDEAS

6.4 Apply three ways of generating main ideas from a central idea.

After formulating your central idea, use it to generate main ideas. Determine whether the central idea (1) has logical divisions, (2) can be supported by several reasons, or (3) can be traced through a series of steps. These divisions,

reasons, or steps become the blueprint, or plan, of your speech. You will preview them in your introduction and summarize them in your conclusion.

Key Terms

Main ideas. 123
Blueprint 126

Thinking Critically

You have already written a central idea (above) for Marylin's persuasive speech on America's crumbling roads and bridges. Now use your central idea to generate main ideas for this speech. Be prepared to explain *how* you derived the main ideas from the central idea.

Assessing Your Audience-Centered Speaking Skill

Check the main ideas you drafted for the previous Thinking Critically activity against Marylin's specific-purpose statement. If any main idea does not contribute to what she wants the audience to do at the end of her speech, make appropriate revisions to either the specific purpose or the main idea(s).

Explore at MyCommunicationLab
Speaker's Workshop: Strategies for Selecting a Speech Topic

GATHERING AND USING SUPPORTING MATERIAL

After studying this chapter you should be able to do the following:

7.1

List five potential sources of supporting material for a speech.

7.2

Explain five strategies for a methodical research process.

7.3

List and describe six types of supporting material.

7.4

List and explain six criteria for determining the best supporting material to use in a speech.

Listen to Chapter 7 at **MyCommunicationLab**

Milton Avery (1893-1965), Homework, 1946. Oil on canvas, 91.4 x 61 cm. Museo Thyssen-Bornemisza, Madrid, Spain. Photo: Art Resource, N.Y.

Learn, compare, collect the facts! . . . always have the courage to say to yourself— I am ignorant.

—Ivan Petrovich Pavlov

Apple pie is your specialty. Your family and friends relish your flaky crust, spicy filling, and crunchy crumb topping. Fortunately, not only do you have a never-fail recipe and technique, but you also know where to go for the best ingredients. Fette's Orchard has the tangiest pie apples in town. For your crust, you use only Premier shortening, which you buy at Meyer's Specialty Market. Your crumb topping requires both stone-ground whole-wheat flour and fresh creamery butter, available on Tuesdays at the farmer's market on the courthouse square.

Just as making your apple pie requires that you know where to find specific ingredients, creating a successful speech requires a knowledge of the sources, research strategies, and types of supporting material that speechmakers typically use. This chapter covers the speech-development step highlighted in Figure 7.1: Gather Supporting Material.

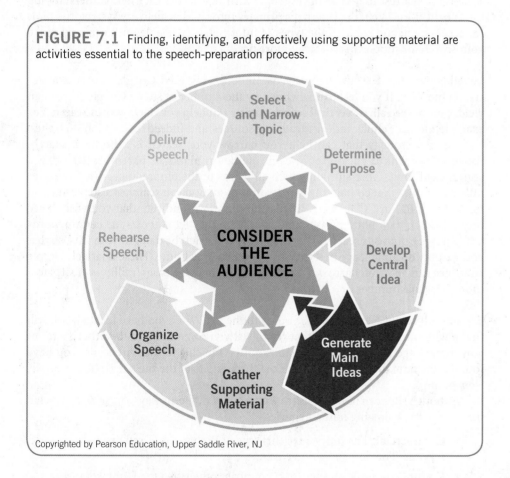

FIGURE 7.1 Finding, identifying, and effectively using supporting material are activities essential to the speech-preparation process.

Copyrighted by Pearson Education, Upper Saddle River, NJ

Sources of Supporting Material

Supporting material for your speech can come from a variety of sources, including personal knowledge and experience, the Internet, online databases, traditional library holdings, and interviews.

Personal Knowledge and Experience

Because you will probably give speeches on topics you are particularly interested in, you may find that *you* are your own best source. Your speech may be on a skill or

7.1 List five potential sources of supporting material for a speech.

 Explore at MyCommunicationLab Activity: "Research"

 Read at MyCommunicationLab Learning From Great Speakers: Eleanor Roosevelt

activity in which you are expert, such as keeping tropical fish, stenciling, or stamp collecting. Or you may talk on a subject with which you have had some personal experience, such as buying a used car, joining a service organization, or seeking assisted living for an elderly relative. It is true that most well-researched speeches include some objective material gathered from outside sources. But you may also be able to provide an effective illustration, explanation, definition, or other type of support from your own knowledge and experience. As an audience-centered speaker, you should realize, too, that personal knowledge often has the additional advantage of heightening your credibility in the minds of your listeners. They will accord you more respect as an authority when they realize that you have firsthand knowledge of a topic.

The Internet

When facing a research task, most people turn first to the Internet. Understanding the **World Wide Web**, the Internet's primary information-delivery system; the tools for accessing it; and some of the types of information available on it can help make your search for supporting material more productive.

Locating Internet Resources You have undoubtedly used Google to access material on the Web. If you feel overwhelmed by the number of sites a Google search can yield, a more specialized **vertical search engine** can help you narrow your search. For example, Google Scholar indexes academic sources, and Indeed indexes job Web sites.

Another strategy that can help you narrow your search is a **Boolean search**, which allows you to enclose phrases in quotation marks or parentheses so that a search yields only those sites on which all words of the phrase appear in that order rather than sites that contain the words at random. Boolean searches also permit you to insert "AND" or "+" between words and phrases to indicate that you wish to see results that contain both phrases, and, similarly, they let you exclude certain words and phrases from your search. They also let you restrict the dates of your hits, so that you see only documents posted within a specified time frame. These relatively simple strategies can help you narrow a list of hits from, in some cases, millions of sites to a more workable number.

Exploring Internet Resources As you go to the Web sites you have located, you will find a wide variety—from sites that try to sell you something, to the official sites of government agencies and news organizations. One clue to the type of site you have found is the **domain**, indicated by the last three letters of the site's URL (for example, *.com* or *.org*).

Although sites can be classified in a number of different ways, most Web sites fall into one of the following nine categories.[1]

- **Commercial.** The purpose of this type of Web site is to sell products or services. The domain is often *.com*.
- **Country codes.** Web sites from countries other than the United States include a country code. For example, Great Britain is *.uk* and Canada is *.ca*.
- **Educational.** This type of site provides information about an educational entity. The domain is usually *.edu*.
- **Entertainment.** Internet addresses ending with *.com* may indicate entertainment Web sites.
- **Government.** The purpose of this type of Web site is to provide information produced by government agencies, offices, and departments. The domain is usually *.gov*.
- **Military.** Information about or from the military is usually indicated by Internet addresses that end in *.mil*.

World Wide Web
The primary information-delivery system of the Internet

vertical search engine
A Web site that indexes World Wide Web information in a specific field

Boolean search
An advanced Web-searching technique that allows a user to narrow a subject or key word search by adding various requirements

domain
Category in which a Web site is located on the Internet, indicated by the last three letters of the site's URL

- **News.** Web sites that provide information about current events usually have the domain *.com*.
- **Organizational.** The purpose of this type of Web site is to advocate a group's point of view. The domain is usually *.org*.
- **Personal.** Information about or from an individual may be indicated by a variety of Internet addresses.

Evaluating Internet Resources Although the Web was founded on the principle of free speech, the lack of legal, financial, or editorial restriction on what is published on the Web presents both a logistical and an ethical challenge to researchers.

As you begin to explore the sites you discover, you will need to evaluate them according to a consistent standard. The six criteria in Table 7.1 on page 134 can serve as such a standard.[2] The first four of the criteria can serve as guides to evaluating any resource, regardless of whether it is a Web site, a print document, or even information you obtain in an interview.

No discussion of evaluating Internet resources would be complete without mentioning *Wikipedia*, the resource that often appears as the first hit from a Web search. *Wikipedia* can be useful, especially for general information about current events and new technology that may not find its way into print resources for years. But users need to keep in mind that anyone, regardless of expertise, can add to or change the content of any entry, thereby limiting *Wikipedia*'s reliability and its appropriateness for academic use.

Later in this chapter we provide additional criteria to help you make your final selection of supporting material from both electronic and print resources.

Watch at **MyCommunicationLab**
Video: "Credibility of Online Sources"

Watch at **MyCommunicationLab**
Video: "Wikipedia as a Primary Source of Information"

Online Databases

Online databases provide access to bibliographic information, abstracts, and full texts for a variety of resources, including periodicals, newspapers, government documents, and even books. Like Web sites, online databases are reached via a networked computer. Unlike Web sites, however, most databases are restricted to the patrons of libraries that subscribe to them.

Locating and Searching Databases To use a database to which your library subscribes, you will probably first have to go to your library's homepage and log in with your username and password. You can then find the names of the available databases, usually listed according to type and/or subjects, as well as alphabetically.

Searching a database is relatively simple. Each database opens with a search box, into which you type relevant information such as keywords and date ranges. Most also allow Boolean and other types of advanced searches.

In some cases you may be able to search more than one database at a time by searching providers that offer access to multiple databases. ProQuest, for example, provides databases of alternative newspapers, criminal justice periodicals, doctoral dissertations, and education journals as well as its popular *ABI/INFORM Global* database of business and finance publications.

Exploring Database Resources Many online databases that began as computerized indexes now provide access to full texts of the resources themselves. Your library may subscribe to several or all of the following popular full-text databases:

- **ABI/Inform Global.** This resource offers many full-text articles in business and trade publications from 1971 to the present.
- **Academic Search Complete.** This popular database offers many full-text articles from 1865 to the present, covering a wide variety of subjects.

online databases
Subscription-based electronic resources that may offer access to abstracts and/or the full texts of entries, as well as bibliographic data

TABLE 7.1 SIX CRITERIA FOR EVALUATING INTERNET RESOURCES

CRITERION	APPLYING THE CRITERION	DRAWING CONCLUSIONS
Accountability: Who is responsible for the site?	• The individual or organization responsible for the site may be clear from the title of the site and/or its URL. • See whether the site is signed. • Follow links or search the author's name to determine the author's expertise and authority. • If the site is unsigned, search for a sponsoring organization. Follow links, search the organization's name, or consider the domain to determine reputability.	• If you cannot identify or verify an author or sponsor, be wary of the site.
Accuracy: Is the information correct?	• Consider whether the author or sponsor is a credible authority. • Assess the care with which the site has been written. • Conduct additional research into the information on the site.	• If the author or sponsor is a credible authority, the information is more likely to be accurate. • A site should be relatively free of writing errors. • You may be able to verify or refute the information by consulting another resource.
Objectivity: Is the site free of bias?	• Consider the interests, philosophical or political biases, and source of financial support of the author and/or sponsor of the site. • Does the site include advertisements that might influence its content?	• The more objective the author and sponsor of the site are, the more credible their information may be.
Timeliness: Is the site current?	• Look at the bottom of the site for a statement telling when the site was posted and when it was last updated. • If you cannot find a date on the site, click on Page Info (from the View menu at the top of your browser screen) to find a "Last Modified" date. • Enter the title of the site in a search engine. The resulting information should include a date.	• In general, when you are concerned with factual data, the more recent it is, the better.
Usability: Do the layout and design of the site facilitate its use?	• Does the site load fairly quickly? • Is a fee required to gain access to any of the information on the site?	• Balance graphics and any fees against practical efficiency.
Diversity: Is the site inclusive?	• Do language and graphics reflect and respect differences in gender, ethnicity, race, and sexual preference? • Do interactive forums invite divergent perspectives? • Is the site friendly to people with disabilities (e.g., does it offer a large-print or video option)?	• A site should be free of bias, representative of diverse perspectives, and accessible by people with disabilities.

- **JSTOR.** This is a multisubject, full-text database of journal articles from the first volume to the present.
- **LexisNexis Academic.** Focusing on business and law, this database provides many full-text articles from newspapers, magazines, journals, newsletters, and wire services. Dates of coverage vary.
- **Newspaper Source.** This database offers many full-text articles from more than 40 U.S. and international newspapers; more than 330 full-text television and radio news transcripts from CBS News, CNN, CNN International, FOX News, NPR, and others; and selected full-text articles from more than 330 regional (U.S.) newspapers.

Traditional Library Holdings

Despite the rapid development of Internet and database resources, the more traditional holdings of libraries, both paper and electronic, remain rich sources of supporting material.

Locating Traditional Library Holdings Spend some time becoming familiar with your library's services and layout so that you know how to access and locate books and reference materials. Many encyclopedias, dictionaries, directories, atlases, almanacs, yearbooks, books of quotations, and biographical dictionaries are now available online. But if you are not able to find a specific reference resource online, you may be able to locate a print version by using your library's card catalog. You can access the computerized card catalog of most libraries from your own computer before you ever enter the library. As shown in the example in Figure 7.2, the catalog will supply each book's *call number*, which you will need in order to find the book.

FIGURE 7.2 A computerized card catalog entry for a book. The same entry will appear on the screen regardless of whether the work is accessed using title, author, or subject.

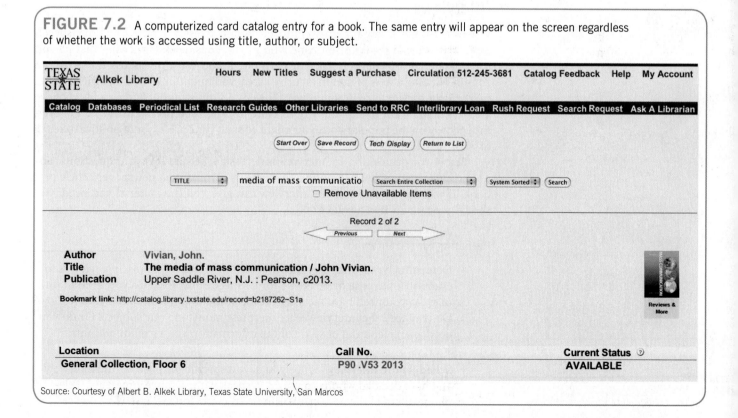

Source: Courtesy of Albert B. Alkek Library, Texas State University, San Marcos

CONFIDENTLY CONNECTING WITH YOUR AUDIENCE

Prepare Early

Gathering relevant and credible supporting material for your speech takes time. So it's a good idea to give yourself plenty of time to gather examples, stories, statistics, opinions, quotations, and other supporting material. By starting your speech preparation early, you'll get a bonus: Research suggests that people who prepare early rather than waiting until the last minute experience less apprehension about speaking in public.[3] So preparing early will give you time to find good supporting material *and* help you manage your anxiety.

RECAP

SUPPORTING MATERIAL AVAILABLE IN THE LIBRARY

Library resources may include . . .
- Books
- Periodicals
- Newspapers
- Reference resources

Exploring Traditional Library Holdings Once you have the call number, you are ready to venture into the library to obtain the item you want. It is a good idea to become familiar with your library's layout before you have to do research under the pressure of a deadline.

- **Books.** Libraries' collections of books are called the **stacks**. The stacks are organized by call numbers, which are available on card-catalog entries. Many libraries offer a location guide or map to guide you to the floor or section of the stacks that houses the books with the call numbers in which you are interested.

    Do not wait until the last minute to conduct library research for your speech. Increasing numbers of libraries are beginning to house some of their stacks off-site, meaning that you may have to fill out a request form and allow some wait time before a book becomes available to you.

- **Reference resources.** In a library's card catalog, the call numbers of print reference resources will have the prefix *ref*, indicating that they are housed in the reference section of the library. Print reference resources are usually available only for in-house research and cannot be checked out.

    Reference librarians are specialists in the field of information science. They are often able to suggest print or electronic resources that you might otherwise overlook. If you plan to use the reference section, visit the library during daytime working hours. A full-time reference librarian is more likely to be on hand and available to help you at that time than in the evenings or on weekends.

Interviews

When you don't know the answers to important questions raised by your speech topic, but you can think of someone who might, consider interviewing that person to get material for your speech. For example, if you want to discuss the pros and cons of building a new prison in an urban area, you might interview an official of the correctional service, a representative of the city administration, and a resident of the area. Or if you want to explain why Al Gore lost the 2000 presidential election even though he won the popular vote, you might consult your professor of political science or American history.

Before you decide that an interview is necessary, be sure that your questions cannot be answered easily by looking at a Web site or reading a newspaper article or a book. If you decide that only an interview can give you the material you need, you should prepare for it in advance.

Preparing for the Interview

- **Determine your purpose.** The first step in preparing for an interview is to establish a purpose or objective for it. Specifically, what do you need to find out? Do you need hard facts that you cannot obtain from other sources? Do you need the interviewee's expert testimony on your subject? Or do you need an explanation of some of the information you have found in print sources?

- **Schedule the interview.** Once you have a specific purpose for the interview and have decided whom you need to speak with, arrange a meeting. Telephone or email the person, explain briefly who you are and why you are

stacks
The collection of books in a library

calling, and ask for an appointment. Most people are flattered to have their authority and knowledge recognized and willingly grant interviews to serious students if their schedules permit.

If you are considering audio- or video-recording the interview, ask for the interviewee's okay during this initial contact. If the person does not grant permission, be prepared to gather your information without electronic assistance.

- **Plan your questions.** Before your interview, find out as much as you can about both your subject and the person you are interviewing. Prepare questions that take full advantage of the interviewee's specific knowledge of your subject. You can do this only if *you* already know a good deal about your subject.

    It is also helpful to think about how you should combine the two basic types of interview questions: closed-ended and open-ended. Open-ended questions often follow closed-ended questions: When the person you are interviewing answers a closed-ended question with a simple yes or no, you may wish to follow up by asking "Why?"

If both parties are comfortable recording the interview, doing so can free the interviewer and the interviewee from the need to concentrate on careful note-taking.
Photo: ArenaCreative/Fotolia.

Conducting the Interview

- **On your mark . . .** Dress appropriately for the interview. For most interviews, conservative, businesslike clothes show that you are serious about the interview and that you respect the norms of your interviewee's world.

    Take paper and pen or pencil for note-taking. Even if you are planning to record the interview, you may want to turn the recorder off at some point during the interview, so you'll need an alternative. Or Murphy's Law may disable your recording device. Ensure that the interview can continue despite any mishap.

- **Get set . . .** Arrive for the interview a few minutes ahead of schedule. Be prepared, however, to wait patiently if necessary.

    Once you are settled with the person you will interview, remind him or her of your purpose. If you are familiar with and admire the work the interviewee has done or published, don't hesitate to say so. Sincere flattery can help set a positive tone for the exchange. If you have decided to use a recorder, set it up. You may keep it out of sight once the interviewee has seen it, but never try to hide a recorder at the outset—such a ploy is unethical. If you are going to take written notes, get out your paper and pen. Now you are ready to begin asking your prepared questions.

- **Go!** As you conduct the interview, use the questions you have prepared as a guide but not a rigid schedule. If the person you are interviewing mentions an interesting angle you hadn't thought of, don't be afraid to pursue the point. Listen carefully to the person's answers. Television journalist Charles Osgood advises interviewers,

Don't just listen for the words and their cognitive, literal meanings, but listen for the connotations. You will learn something if you do that and the next question will come to you growing out of what you have just learned.[4]

And finally, ask for clarification of any ideas you don't understand.

Do not prolong the interview beyond the time limits of your appointment. The person you are interviewing is probably very busy and has been courteous enough to fit you into a tight schedule. Ending the interview on time is simply returning the courtesy. Thank your interviewee for his or her contribution, and leave.

Following Up the Interview As soon as possible after the interview, read through your notes carefully and revise any portion that may be illegible or unclear. If you recorded the interview, label the recording with the date and the interviewee's name.

7.2 Explain five strategies for a methodical research process.

Research Strategies

You have Internet access. You know the kinds of materials and services your library offers and how to use them. In short, you're ready to begin researching your speech. But unless you approach this phase of speech preparation systematically, you may find yourself wasting a good deal of time and energy retracing steps to find bits of information you remember seeing but forgot to bookmark, write down, or print out the first time.

Methodical research strategies will make your efforts easier and more efficient. You need to develop a preliminary bibliography, locate potential resources, evaluate their usefulness, take notes, and identify possible visual aids.

Develop a Preliminary Bibliography

Creating a **preliminary bibliography**, or list of promising resources, should be your first research goal. You will probably discover more resources than you actually look at or refer to in your speech; at this stage, the bibliography simply serves as a menu of possibilities. How many resources should you list in a preliminary bibliography for, say, a 10-minute speech? A reasonable number might be 10 or 12. If you have more than that, you may feel overwhelmed; if you have fewer, you may find too little information.

You will need to develop a system for keeping track of your resources. Web browsers let you bookmark pages for future reference and ready access; your bookmarks can serve as one part of your preliminary bibliography. If you are searching an online catalog or database, you can probably compile and then print out a record of the references you discover. Such files can be a second part of your preliminary bibliography.

Locate Resources

preliminary bibliography
A list of potential resources to be used in the preparation of a speech

You should have no trouble obtaining the actual texts of resources from the Web and online databases. For all the other items in your preliminary bibliography, you will need to locate the resources yourself. See the discussion earlier in this chapter on traditional library holdings.

Assess the Usefulness of Resources

It makes sense to gauge the potential usefulness of your resources before you begin to read closely and take notes. Think critically about how the various resources you have found are likely to help you achieve your purpose and about how effective they are likely to be with your audience. Glance over the tables of contents of books, and flip quickly through the texts to note any charts, graphs, or other visual materials that might be used as visual aids. Skim a key chapter or two. Skim articles and Web sites as well.

DEVELOPING YOUR SPEECH STEP BY STEP

GATHER SUPPORTING MATERIAL

With her purpose statement, central idea, and main ideas in hand, Brianne begins to research questions of access to and information about emergency contraception.

Seeking sources that meet the criteria of accountability, accuracy, timeliness, usability, and diversity, Brianne begins with the Web site of the Centers for Disease Control and Prevention. This search yields some useful information, and she bookmarks the site.

She turns next to her university library's general research databases. Newspaper Source and Academic Search Complete both provide some sources, as does Medline, a medical database.

With these sources in hand, Brianne begins to read and take notes. She is careful to copy verbatim material accurately and to put quotation marks around it.

Take Notes

Once you have located and assessed the usefulness of your resources, you are ready to begin careful reading and note-taking.

- Beginning with the resources that you think have the greatest potential, record any examples, statistics, opinions, or other supporting material that might be useful to your speech. Depending on the resources, you can photocopy them, cut and paste them or save them into a computer file, and/or print them out.

- If you copy a phrase, sentence, or paragraph verbatim from a source, be sure to put quotation marks around it. You may need to know later whether it is a direct quote or a paraphrase. (This information will be obvious, of course, on printouts or photocopies.)

- Record the source of the supporting material. In Chapter 3, we discuss the ethical importance of crediting all sources of ideas and information. If you consistently keep track of your sources as you take notes, you will avoid the possibility of committing unintentional plagiarism.

Identify Possible Presentation Aids

In addition to discovering verbal supporting material in your sources, you may also find charts, graphs, photographs, or other potentially valuable visual material.

You may think you will be able to remember what visuals were in which sources. But many speakers have experienced frustrating searches for that "perfect" presentation aid they remember seeing somewhere while they were taking notes for their speech. Even if you are not certain at this point that you will use presentation aids in your speech, it can't hurt to save, photocopy, and/or print out any good possibilities, recording those sources of information just as you did for your written materials. Then, when the time comes to consider whether and where presentation aids might enhance the speech, you will have some readily at hand. In Chapter 12 we discuss types of presentation aids and provide guidelines for their use.

RECAP

RESEARCH STRATEGIES

- Develop a preliminary bibliography.
- Locate sources.
- Assess the usefulness of sources.
- Take notes.
- Identify possible presentation aids.

7.3   List and describe six types of supporting material.

Types of Supporting Material

Once you have discovered likely sources, developed a preliminary bibliography of those sources, read them, assessed their usefulness, taken notes, and identified possible presentation aids, you are ready to make decisions about how to use your information to best advantage. You will need to look at your speech from your listeners' perspective and decide where an explanation might help them understand a point, where statistics might convince them of the significance of a problem, and where an illustration might stir their emotions. Next we will discuss these and other types of supporting material and present guidelines for using them effectively.

Illustrations

Novelist Michael Cunningham often reads to standing-room-only crowds. He explains the appeal of live readings in this way:

> It's very much about storytelling. . . . you're all gathered around the campfire—"I'm going to tell you about these people, and what happened then."[5]

Cunningham is right. A story or anecdote—an **illustration**—almost always guarantees audience interest by appealing to their emotions. "Stories get you out of your head and into your gut" is how one professional speech coach explains the universal appeal of illustrations.[6]

Let's look more closely at three kinds of illustrations and examine some guidelines for using them.

Brief Illustrations A **brief illustration** is often no longer than a sentence or two. In a speech to the United Nations, then-Secretary of State Hillary Rodham Clinton offered three brief illustrations of women making a difference:

> In South Africa, women living in shantytowns came together to build a housing development outside Cape Town all on their own, brick by brick. And today, their community has grown to more than 50,000 homes for low-income families, most of them female-headed.
>
> In Liberia, a group of church women began a prayer movement to stop their country's brutal civil war. It grew to include thousands of women who helped force the two sides to negotiate a peace agreement. And then, those women helped elect Ellen Johnson Sirleaf president, the first woman to lead an African nation.
>
> In the United States, a young woman had an idea for a Web site where anyone could help a small business on the other side of the world get off the ground. And today, the organization she co-founded, Kiva, has given more than $120 million in microloans to entrepreneurs in developing countries, 80 percent of them women.[7]

Why use multiple brief illustrations? Sometimes a series of brief illustrations can have more impact than either a single brief illustration or a more detailed, extended illustration. In addition, although an audience could dismiss a single illustration as an exception, two or more strongly suggest a trend or norm.

Extended Illustrations Longer and more detailed than the brief illustration, an **extended illustration** resembles a story. It is more vividly descriptive than a brief illustration, and it has a plot—an opening, complications, a climax, and a resolution.

Watch at **MyCommunicationLab**
Video: "Martha Margaret Clark Cherry Gaines"

illustration
A story or anecdote that provides an example of an idea, issue, or problem a speaker is discussing

brief illustration
An unelaborated example, often only a sentence or two long

extended illustration
A detailed example

Everybody loves a good story. Including appropriate illustrations and telling them well will help you keep the attention of your audience and help them remember your main ideas.

Photo: alersandr hunta/Shutterstock

Australian Prime Minister Kevin Rudd told this moving story of two British sisters who were forcibly taken to Australia under a Child Migrants Program in the 1950s:

> Judy remembers the day they were first taken to the home and her sister Robyn bolted from the gate and ran away.
>
> They later found her and dragged her back.
>
> Robyn and Judy remember that they kept waiting and waiting for just someone, someone to come and pick them up—but no-one, no-one ever came.
>
> They recall being hit with belt buckles and bamboo.
>
> They said the place they grew up in was utterly, utterly loveless.[8]

To use an extended illustration takes more time than to cite a brief example, but longer stories can be more dramatic and emotionally compelling. As we discuss in Chapter 9, extended illustrations can work well as speech introductions. And Chapter 13 considers the use of extended illustrations in informative speeches.

Hypothetical Illustrations A **hypothetical illustration** describes a situation or event that has not actually occurred. Rather, it is a scenario that *might* happen. Plausible hypothetical illustrations enable your listeners to imagine themselves or another person in a particular situation. The following hypothetical illustration comes from a speech on how cell phone technology can change communication in developing countries:

> Imagine someone in China or Africa who is gaining access to e-mail for the first time, how it will improve [his or her] efficiency and ability to connect with others.[9]

Notice the word *imagine* in this illustration. The purpose of a hypothetical illustration is not to trick your listeners into believing a bogus story. As Chapter 3 describes, ethical speakers make their listeners aware from the beginning that the illustration is hypothetical.

Using Illustrations Effectively Illustrations are almost guaranteed attention getters, as well as a way to support your statements. The following suggestions can help you use illustrations more effectively in your speeches.

- **Be certain that your illustrations are directly relevant to the idea or point they are supposed to support.**

- **Choose illustrations that represent a trend.** It is not ethical to find one or two isolated illustrations and use them as though they were typical. If your illustrations are rare instances, you owe it to your listeners to tell them so.

- **Make your illustrations vivid and specific.** Some years ago, a speech professor was fascinated to discover that one of his students had been on the last voyage of the ill-fated Italian ship *Andrea Doria*. Early in the semester, he urged the young man to relate his experience as part of an informative speech on how humans respond to danger. The professor expected a speech with great dramatic impact. Instead, much to his surprise, the student's narrative went something like this: "Well, there was a loud noise and then the sirens went off and we all got in lifeboats and the ship sank."[10] Hardly the stuff great drama is made of! If you have chosen to tell a poignant story, give it enough detail to make it come alive in the minds of your listeners.

- **Use illustrations with which your listeners can identify.** The best illustrations are those that your listeners can imagine experiencing themselves. Other compelling stories, like the sinking of the *Andrea Doria*, can illustrate such great human drama that everyone listening will be immediately interested and attentive.

hypothetical illustration
An example that might happen but that has not actually occurred

- **Remember that the best illustrations are personal ones.** Speakers gain conviction and credibility when they talk about their personal experiences. Near the close of her speech on decriminalizing drug addiction, student speaker Tunette gained additional respect from her audience with this revelation:

> Bruce Callis is 50 years old now. And he is still struggling with his addiction. While you all are sitting out there listening to this, I'm living it. Bruce Callis is my father, and for my entire life, I have watched our misguided system destroy him.[11]

If you have had personal experience with the subject on which you are speaking, be sure to describe that experience to the audience.

Descriptions and Explanations

Probably the most commonly used forms of support are descriptions and explanations. A **description** provides the details that allow audience members to develop mental pictures of what a speaker is talking about. An **explanation** is a statement that makes clear how something is done or why it exists in its present form or existed in its past form.

Describing

> Write for the eye, the ear, the nose, and all the senses. In other words, be as vivid as you possibly can.[12]

This advice from a professional speechwriter acknowledges that effective description creates images that make people, places, and events come alive for the audience. More specific instructions for constructing word pictures are given in Chapter 13.

Description may be used in a brief example, an extended illustration, a hypothetical instance, or by itself. British Prime Minister David Cameron vividly described World War II as

> A war which saw the streets of European cities strewn with rubble. The skies of London lit by flames night after night.[13]

Explaining How   In a speech about the dangers of lithium cell batteries, student speaker Alexandria explained how batteries can injure children who ingest them:

> When in contact with fluid-filled tissues such as a child's esophagus or stomach, the battery undergoes a chemical reaction [that] can cause anything from severe burns and internal bleeding to larger issues. . . .[14]

Speakers who discuss or demonstrate processes of any kind rely at least in part on explanations of how those processes work.

Explaining Why   Explaining why involves giving reasons for or the consequences of a policy, principle, or event. The president and founder of Study Abroad Alumni International explained to a Study Abroad conference *why* global awareness is important:

> Why is global awareness so important? . . . Every six seconds a child dies of hunger. I think we all need to be aware of this . . . and we need to do something about it.[15]

description
A word picture of something

explanation
A statement that makes clear how something is done or why it exists in its present form or existed in its past form

As a speaker, you can use words to paint pictures for your listeners. This speaker uses sensory descriptions of sight, sound, smell, taste, and touch to help her audience feel as though they are sharing her experiences as a war refugee.
Photo: Horizons WWP/Alamy

Using Descriptions and Explanations Effectively When large sections of a speech contain long, nonspecific explanations, audience eyelids are apt to fall. The following suggestions can help you use descriptions and explanations effectively in your speeches.

- **Keep your descriptions and explanations brief.** Too many unnecessary details may make your listeners say your speech was "everything I *never* wanted to know about the subject."

- **Use language that is as specific and concrete as possible.** Vivid and specific language helps you hold the audience's attention and paint in your listeners' minds the image you are trying to communicate. Chapter 10 provides more tips for making your language specific.

- **Avoid too much description and explanation.** You can hold your audience's attention more effectively if you alternate explanations and descriptions with other types of supporting material, such as brief examples or statistics.

Definitions

A **definition** has two justifiable uses in speeches. First, a speaker should be sure to define any and all specialized, technical, or little-known terms in his or her speech. Such definitions are usually achieved by *classification*, the kind of definition you would find in a dictionary. Alternatively, a speaker may define a term by showing how it works or how it is applied in a specific instance—what is known as an *operational definition*.

Definitions by Classification A **definition by classification** both places a term in the general class, group, or family to which it belongs and differentiates it from all the other members of that class. Student speaker Patrick defined the term *hydraulic fracturing* as "a drilling technique" (the general class to which it belongs) "which harnesses incredible amounts of natural gas, but at the cost of destroying our most precious resource: our drinking water" (differentiation of hydraulic fracturing from other drilling techniques).[16]

Operational Definitions Sometimes a word or phrase may be familiar to an audience, but as a speaker you may be applying it in a specific way that needs to be clarified. In

definition
A statement about what a term means or how it is applied in a specific instance

definition by classification
A "dictionary definition," constructed by both placing a term in the general class to which it belongs and differentiating it from all other members of that class

such cases you might provide an **operational definition**, explaining how something works or what it does.

In her speech on vitamin D deficiency, student speaker Nicole operationally defined *rickets* for her audience:

> Rickets leads to weakened bones that produce deformities such as bowed legs and curvature of the spine, making for consistent and sometimes life-long pain.[17]

Both Nicole and Patrick in the preceding examples provided oral citations of the sources of their definitions.

Using Definitions Effectively The following suggestions can help you use definitions more effectively in your speeches.

- **Use a definition only when needed.** Novice speakers too often use a definition as an easy introduction or a time-filler. Resist the temptation to provide a definition unless you are using a relatively obscure term or one with several definitions.

- **Be certain that your definition is understandable.** Give your listeners definitions that are immediately and easily understandable—or you will have wasted your time and perhaps even lost your audience.

- **Be certain that your definition and your use of a term are consistent throughout a speech.** Even seemingly simple words can create confusion if not defined and used consistently. For example, Roy opened his speech on the potential hazards of abusing nonprescription painkillers by defining *drugs* as nonprescription painkillers. A few minutes later, he confused his audience by using the word *drug* to refer to cocaine. Once he had defined the term, he should have used it only in that context throughout the speech.

Analogies

An **analogy** is a comparison. Like a definition, it increases understanding; unlike a definition, it deals with relationships and comparisons—between the new and the old, the unknown and the known, or any other pair of ideas or things. Analogies can help your listeners understand unfamiliar ideas, things, and situations by showing how these matters are similar to something they already know.

There are two types of analogies. A *literal* analogy compares things that are actually similar (two sports, two cities, two events). A *figurative* analogy may take the form of a simile or a metaphor.

Literal Analogies Student speaker James compared insects with ocean crustaceans when he advocated utilizing insects for food:

> Crustaceans are literally the insects of the sea: They're both arthropods. But where crustaceans feed on trash, insects feed on nature's salad bar.[18]

James's comparison is a **literal analogy**—a comparison between two similar things. If your listeners are from a culture or group other than your own or the one from which the speech derives, literal analogies that draw on the listeners' culture or group may help them understand more readily the less familiar places, things, and situations you are discussing. Literal analogies are often employed by people who want to influence public policy. For example, proponents of trade restrictions argue that because Japan maintains its trade balance through stringent import controls, so should the United States. The more similarities a policymaker can show between the policies or situations being compared, the better his or her chances are of being persuasive.

operational definition
A statement that shows how something works or what it does

analogy
A comparison

literal analogy
A comparison between two similar things

Figurative Analogies In his speech accepting the 2012 Nobel Peace Prize on behalf of the European Union, Nobel Committee Chair Throbjørn Jagland described two paintings that hang in the town hall in Siena, Italy:

> ["Allegory of the effects of good government"] shows a living medieval town, with the gates in the wall invitingly wide open to spirited people bringing the harvest in from fruitful fields. But Lorenzetti painted another picture, "Allegory of the effects of bad government." It shows Siena in chaos, closed and ravaged by the plague, destroyed by a struggle for power and war.[19]

A literal analogy might have compared pre–World War I Europe to twenty-first-century Europe. But Jagland went on to complete his **figurative analogy** by comparing the paintings to the present-day choice between harmony and conflict:

> The two pictures are meant to remind us that it is up to ourselves whether or not we are to live in well-ordered circumstances.

Because it relies not on facts or statistics but rather on imaginative insights, the figurative analogy is not considered hard evidence. But because it is creative, it is inherently interesting and should help grab an audience's attention. In a speech titled "Short-Term Demands vs. Long-Term Responsibilities," PepsiCo CEO Indra Nooyi used this figurative analogy:

> Like the characters in the Hindu epic, the Ramayana, capitalism has the ability to assume different forms for different times and different nations.[20]

Using Analogies Effectively These suggestions can help you to use literal and figurative analogies more effectively.

- **Be sure that the two things you compare in a literal analogy are very similar.** The more alike the two things being compared, the more likely it is that the analogy will stand up under attack.

- **Be sure that the essential similarity between the two objects of a figurative analogy is readily apparent.** When you use a figurative analogy, it is crucial to make clear the similarity on which the analogy is based. If you do not, your audience will end up wondering what in the world you are talking about.

Statistics

Many of us live in awe of numbers, or **statistics**. Perhaps nowhere is our respect for statistics so evident—and so exploited—as in advertising. If three out of four doctors surveyed recommend Pain Away aspirin, it must be the best. If Sudsy Soap is 99.9 percent pure (whatever that means), surely it will help our complexions. And if nine out of ten people like Sloppy Catsup in the taste test, we will certainly buy it for this weekend's barbecue. How can the statistics be wrong?

The truth about statistics lies somewhere between an unconditional faith in numbers and the wry observation that "There are three kinds of lies: lies, damned lies, and statistics."

Using Statistics as Support Statistics can be expressed as either counts or percentages. Verizon CEO Ivan Seidenberg used a count and a percentage in the same sentence in his speech to a communications conference:

> Using smart grids and mobile technologies to manage electric power could create 280,000 new jobs and cut carbon emissions by more than 20 percent by 2020.[21]

 Watch at MyCommunicationLab Video: "Mark Zuckerberg: Benefits of Advertising in Facebook"

figurative analogy
A comparison between two essentially dissimilar things that share some common feature on which the comparison depends

statistics
Numerical data that summarize facts or samples

Using Statistics Effectively The following guidelines can help you analyze and use statistics effectively and correctly.

- **Use reliable sources.** It has been said that figures don't lie but liars figure! And, indeed, statistics can be produced to support almost any conclusion desired. Your goal is to cite *authoritative* and *unbiased* sources.

- **Use authoritative sources.** The most authoritative source is the **primary source**—the original collector and interpreter of the data. If you find an interesting statistic in a newspaper or magazine article, look closely to see whether a source is cited. If it is, try to find that source and the original reporting of the statistic. Do not assume that the secondhand account, or **secondary source**, has reported the statistic accurately and fairly. As often as possible, go to the primary source.

- **Use unbiased sources.** As well as being authoritative, sources should be as unbiased as possible. We usually extend to government research and various independent sources of statistics the courtesy of thinking them unbiased. Because they are, for the most part, supposed to be unaffiliated with any special interest, their statistics are presumed to be less biased than those coming from such organizations as the American Tobacco Institute, the AFL-CIO, or Microsoft. All three organizations have some special interest at stake, and data they gather are more likely to reflect their biases.

  As you evaluate your sources, try to find out how the statistics were gathered. For example, if a statistic relies on a sample, how was the sample taken? A Thursday afternoon telephone poll of 20 registered voters in Brooklyn is not an adequate sample of New York City voters. The sample is too small and too geographically limited. In addition, it excludes anyone without a telephone or anyone unlikely to be at home when the survey was conducted. Sample sizes and survey methods do vary widely, but most legitimate polls involve samples of 500 to 2,000 people, selected at random from a larger population. Of course, finding out about the statistical methodology may be more difficult than discovering the source of the statistic, but if you can find it, the information will help you to analyze the value of the statistic.

- **Interpret statistics accurately.** People are often swayed by statistics that sound good but have in fact been wrongly calculated or misinterpreted. For example, a speaker might say that the number of children killed by guns in the United States has doubled every year since 1950, Joel Best, author of *Damned Lies and Statistics: Untangling Numbers from the Media, Politicians, and Activists*, points out that actually doing the math quickly demonstrates how wildly inaccurate this statistic is. If one child was killed in 1950, two in 1951, four in 1952, and so on, the annual number by now would far exceed the entire population of not just the U.S., but also of the entire Earth.[22]

  Both as a user of statistics in your own speeches and as a consumer of statistics in articles, books, and speeches, be constantly alert to what the statistics actually mean.

- **Make your statistics understandable and memorable.** You can make your statistics easier to understand and more memorable in several ways:

1. First, you can *dramatize* a statistic by strategically choosing the perspective from which you present it. Authors of a recent popular book about statistics offer this example of how dramatizing a statistic attracted the attention of the press:

   Researchers found that a genetic variant . . . present in 10 percent of the population *protected* them against high blood pressure. Although published

primary source
The original collector and interpreter of information or data

secondary source
An individual, organization, or publication that reports information or data gathered by another entity

in a top scientific journal, the story received negligible press coverage until a knowing press officer rewrote the press release to say that a genetic variant . . . had been discovered which *increased* the risk of high blood pressure in 90 percent of people.[23]

2. Second, you can *compact* a statistic, or express it in units that are more meaningful or more easily understandable to your audience. Student speaker Daniel made the staggering national consumer debt more comprehensible by compacting it in this way:

> . . . we have accumulated over 3.2 trillion dollars in unsecured consumer debt. With an estimated 237 million adult citizens, that averages out to $13,500 for every American adult.[24]

3. You might also make your statistics more memorable by *exploding* them. Exploded statistics are created by adding or multiplying related numbers— for example, cost per unit times number of units. Because it is larger, the exploded statistic seems more significant than the original figures from which it was derived. The CEO of AARP used the "exploding" strategy to emphasize the impact of lowering the growth rate of health care costs by just 1.5 percentage points per year:

> . . . lowering the growth rate of health care costs by 1.5 percentage points per year will increase the real income of middle-class families by $2,600 in 2020; $10,000 in 2030; and $24,300 by 2040. That's real relief for real people.[25]

4. Finally, you can *compare* your statistic with another that heightens its impact. Student speaker Andie compared the recommended level of water fluoridation to money:

> The [Centers for Disease Control and Prevention] recommends fluoridating water between 0.7 parts per million (PPM) and 1.7 PPM. . . . To put PPM into perspective, one PPM is like 1 cent in $10,000.[26]

- **Round off numbers.** It is much easier to grasp and remember "2 million" than 2,223,147. Percentages, too, are more easily remembered when they are rounded off. And most people seem to remember percentages even better when they are expressed as fractions.
- **Use visual aids to present your statistics.** Most audience members have difficulty remembering a barrage of numbers thrown at them during a speech. But if the numbers are displayed in a table or graph in front of listeners, they can more easily grasp the statistics. Figure 7.3 on page 148 illustrates how a speaker could lay out a table of statistics on how private health insurance coverage in the United States is distributed among various age groups. Using such a table, you would still need to explain what the numbers mean, but you wouldn't have to recite them. We discuss visual aids in Chapter 12.

Opinions

Three types of **opinions** may be used as supporting material in speeches: the testimony of an expert authority, the testimony of an ordinary (lay) person with firsthand or eyewitness experience, and a quotation from a literary work.

opinions
Statements expressing an individual's attitudes, beliefs, or values

FIGURE 7.3 Example of a table of statistics.

Percentage of Employed People without Health Insurance Coverage in the United States, by Age

Age	Percentage Uninsured
15–18 years	11%
19–25 years	31%
26–44 years	21%
45–64 years	13%
65 years and over	11%

Source: Data from U.S. Census Bureau, "Health Insurance Coverage Type by Age, Sex, and Labor Force Status: 2010." www.census.gov/prod/2013pubs/p70-134.pdf.

 **Watch at MyCommunicationLab**
Video: "Hillary Clinton: Immigration"

Expert Testimony Having already offered statistics on the number of cigars Americans consume annually, Dena emphasized the danger to both smokers and recipients of secondhand smoke by providing **expert testimony** from a National Cancer Institute adviser:

> James Repace, an adviser to the National Cancer Institute, states, "If you have to breathe secondhand smoke, cigar smoke is a lot worse than cigarette smoke."[27]

The testimony of a recognized authority can add a great deal of weight to your arguments. Or, if your topic requires that you make predictions—statements that can be supported in only a marginal way by statistics or examples—the statements of expert authorities may prove to be your most convincing support.

Lay Testimony You are watching the nightly news. Newscasters reporting on the forest fires that continue to rage in Colorado explain how these fires started. They provide statistics on how many thousands of acres have burned and how many hundreds of homes have been destroyed. They describe the intense heat and smoke at the scene of one of the fires, and they ask an expert—a veteran firefighter—to predict the likelihood that the fires will be brought under control soon. But the most poignant moment of this story is an interview with a woman who has just returned to her home and has found it in smoldering ashes. She is a layperson—not a firefighter or an expert on forest fires, but someone who has experienced the tragedy firsthand.

Like an illustration, **lay testimony** can stir an audience's emotions. And, although neither as authoritative nor as unbiased as expert testimony, lay testimony is often more memorable.

Literary Quotation Another way to make a point memorable is to include a **literary quotation** in your speech. Speaking on changes essential to the survival of the

expert testimony
An opinion offered by someone who is an authority on a subject

lay testimony
An opinion or description offered by a nonexpert who has firsthand experience

literary quotation
An opinion or description by a writer who speaks in a memorable and often poetic way

automotive industry, Chrysler Corporation CEO Sergio Marchionne drew on the words of philosopher Friedrich Nietzsche:

> The philosopher Friedrich Nietzsche once said that "what really arouses indignation against suffering is not suffering as such but the senselessness of suffering. . . ." And a crisis that does not result in enduring changes, in fundamental changes, will have been very senseless indeed.[28]

Note that the Nietzsche quotation is short. Brief, pointed quotations usually have greater audience impact than longer, more rambling ones. As Shakespeare said, "Brevity is the soul of wit" (*Hamlet*, II.2).

Literary quotations have the additional advantage of being easily accessible. You'll find any number of quotation dictionaries on the Web and in the reference sections of most libraries. Arranged alphabetically by subject, these compilations are easy to use.

Using Opinions Effectively Here are a few suggestions for using opinions effectively in your speeches.

- **Be certain that any authority you cite is an expert on the subject you are discussing.** Advertisers ignore this advice when they have well-known athletes endorse such items as flashlight batteries, breakfast cereals, and cars. Athletes may indeed be experts on athletic shoes, tennis rackets, or stopwatches, but they lack any specific qualifications to talk about most of the products they endorse.

- **Identify your sources.** If a student quotes the director of the Harry Ransom Humanities Research Center at the University of Texas but identifies that person only as Tom Staley, few listeners will recognize the name, let alone acknowledge his authority.

In Chapter 3, we discussed the importance of citing your sources orally. In the course of doing so, you can provide additional information about the qualifications of those sources. Note how the student speakers in the following examples use a variety of phrases and sentence structures to help them identify their sources for their audiences in a fluent way:

> . . . the September 29, 2012, *New York Times* warns that for the first time in history, today's children are projected to have shorter life spans than their parents. . . .[29]
>
> . . . as Professor Helen Norton of the University of Colorado explained in a February 16, 2011, press release from the Equal Employment Opportunity Commission, the rationale for jobless discrimination is that employers believe that those who've been out of work are not good employees and that their job skills are not up to par.[30]

- **Cite unbiased authorities.** Just as the most reliable sources of statistics are unbiased, so too are the most reliable sources of opinion. The chairman of General Motors may offer an expert opinion that the Chevy Cruze is the best compact car on the market today. His expertise is unquestionable, but his bias is obvious and makes him a less than trustworthy source of opinion on the subject. A better source would be the *Consumer Reports* analyses of the reliability and repair records of compact cars.

RECAP

TYPES OF SUPPORTING MATERIAL

Illustrations	Relevant stories
Explanations	Statements that make clear how something is done or why it exists in its present form or existed in a past form
Descriptions	Word pictures
Definitions	Concise explanations of a word or concept
Analogies	Comparisons between two things
Statistics	Numbers that summarize data or examples
Opinions	Testimony or quotations from someone else

Watch at **MyCommunicationLab**
Video: "In Defense of Lawyers"

- **Cite opinions that are representative of prevailing opinion.** Unless most of the experts in the field share an opinion, its value is limited. Citing such opinion only leaves your conclusions open to easy rebuttal.

- **Quote your sources accurately.** If you quote or paraphrase either an expert or a layperson, be certain that your quote or paraphrase is accurate and within the context in which the remarks were originally made.

- **Use literary quotations sparingly.** Be sure that you have a valid reason for citing a literary quotation, and then use only one or two at most in a speech.

 7.4   List and explain six criteria for determining the best supporting material to use in a speech.

Explore at **MyCommunicationLab**
Activity: "Testing for Relevance of Supporting Ideas"

The Best Supporting Material

In this chapter, we discussed six criteria for evaluating Web sites: accountability, accuracy, objectivity, timeliness, usability, and diversity. We also presented guidelines for using each of the six types of supporting material effectively. However, even after you have applied these criteria and guidelines, you may still have more supporting material than you can possibly use for a short speech. How do you decide what to use and what to eliminate? The following considerations can help you make that final cut.

- **Magnitude.** Bigger is better. The larger the numbers, the more convincing your statistics. The more experts who support your point of view, the more your expert testimony will command your audience's attention.

- **Proximity.** The best supporting material is whatever is the most relevant to your listeners, or the closest to home. If you can demonstrate how an incident could affect audience members themselves, that illustration will have far greater impact than a more remote one.

- **Concreteness.** If you need to discuss abstract ideas, explain them with concrete examples and specific statistics.

- **Variety.** A mix of illustrations, opinions, definitions, and statistics is much more interesting and convincing than the exclusive use of any one type of supporting material.

- **Humor.** Audiences usually appreciate a touch of humor in an example or opinion. Only if your audience is unlikely to understand the humor or if your speech is on a *very* somber and serious topic is humor not appropriate.

- **Suitability.** Your final decision about whether to use a certain piece of supporting material will depend on its suitability to you, your speech, the occasion, and—as we continue to stress throughout the book—your audience. For example, you would probably use more statistics in a speech to a group of scientists than in an after-luncheon talk to the local Rotary Club.

STUDY GUIDE — REVIEW, APPLY, AND ASSESS

SOURCES OF SUPPORTING MATERIAL

7.1 List five potential sources of supporting material for a speech.

Five sources of supporting material are personal knowledge and experience, the Internet, online databases, traditional library holdings, and interviews.

You may be able to draw on your own knowledge and experience for some supporting material for your speech.

Internet resources are accessible through Web searches, but you must evaluate who is accountable for the sources you find and whether the sources are accurate, objective, current, usable, and sensitive to diversity.

Online databases, accessed by library subscription via a networked computer, provide access to bibliographic information, abstracts, and full texts for a variety of resources, including periodicals, newspapers, government documents, and even books.

Traditional library holdings include books and other types of reference resources.

When conducting an interview, take written notes or audio- or video-record the interview.

Key Terms

Thinking Ethically

Electronic and print indexes and databases sometimes include abstracts of books and articles rather than full texts. If you have read only the abstract of a source, is it ethical to include that source in your preliminary bibliography?

Thinking Critically

Explain how you might use each of the five key sources of supporting material to help you develop an informative speech on how to choose a new computer.

RESEARCH STRATEGIES

7.2 Explain five strategies for a methodical research process.

A methodical research process includes the following strategies: Develop a preliminary bibliography, locate resources, assess the usefulness of resources, take notes, and identify possible presentation aids.

Key Term

Thinking Ethically

You neglected to record complete bibliographic information for one of your best information sources, a journal article you found on a database. You discover your omission as you are reviewing your outline just before you deliver your speech, and you have no way to look up the information now. How can you solve your problem in an ethical way?

TYPES OF SUPPORTING MATERIAL

7.3 List and describe six types of supporting material.

You can choose from various types of supporting material, including illustrations, descriptions and explanations, definitions, analogies, statistics, and opinions. A mix of supporting material is more interesting and convincing than the exclusive use of any one type.

Key Terms

Thinking Ethically

Is it ever ethical to invent supporting material if you have been unable to find what you need for your speech? Explain your answer.

Assessing Your Audience-Centered Speaking Skill

Review the guidelines for each type of supporting material. Which of these guidelines for the *effective* use of supporting material might also be considered a guideline for the *ethical* use of supporting material? Explain your choice(s).

THE BEST SUPPORTING MATERIAL

7.4 List and explain six criteria for determining the best supporting material to use in a speech.

Once you have gathered a variety of supporting material, look at your speech from your audience's perspective and decide where an explanation might help listeners understand a point, where statistics might convince them of the significance of a problem, and where an illustration might stir their emotions. Six criteria—magnitude, proximity, concreteness, variety, humor, and suitability—can help you choose the most effective support for your speech.

Assessing Your Audience-Centered Speaking Skill

The best supporting material is whatever is the most relevant to your listeners or "closest to home." Applying this criterion to the supporting material you gather for your next speech, determine which item or items are likely to be most effective.

 Explore at MyCommunicationLab
Speaker's Workshop: Identifying a Variety of Supporting Materials for Your Speech

8 ORGANIZING AND OUTLINING YOUR SPEECH

Luigi Russolo (1885–1947), © Copyright *Music*, 1911. Photo: M. E. Smith/DeA Picture Library/Art Resource, NY

Organized thought is the basis of organized action.

—Alfred North Whitehead

Maria went into the lecture hall feeling exhilarated. After all, Dr. Anderson was a Nobel laureate in literature. He would be teaching and lecturing on campus for at least a year. What an opportunity! Maria took a seat in the middle of the fourth row, where she had a clear view of the podium. She opened the notebook she had bought just for this lecture series, took out one of the three pens she had brought with her, and waited impatiently for Dr. Anderson's appearance. She didn't have to wait long. Dr. Anderson was greeted by thunderous applause when he walked onto the stage. Maria was aware of an almost electric sense of expectation among the audience members. Pen poised, she awaited his first words.

Five minutes later, Maria still had her pen poised. He had gotten off to a slow start. Ten minutes later, she laid her pen down and decided to concentrate just on listening. Twenty minutes later, she still had no idea what point Dr. Anderson was trying to make. And by the time the lecture was over, Maria was practically asleep. Disappointed, she gathered her pens and her notebook (which now contained one page of lazy doodles) and promised herself she would skip the remaining lectures in the series.

Dr. Anderson was not a dynamic speaker. But his motivated audience of young would-be authors and admirers might have forgiven that shortcoming. What they were unable to do was to unravel his seemingly pointless rambling—to get some sense of direction or some pattern of ideas from his talk. Dr. Anderson had simply failed to organize his thoughts.

The scenario described above actually happened. Dr. Anderson (not his real name) disappointed many who had looked forward to his lectures. His inability to organize his ideas made him an ineffectual speaker. You, too, may have had an experience with a teacher who possessed expertise in his or her field but could not organize his or her thoughts well enough to lecture effectively. No matter how knowledgeable speakers may be, they must organize their ideas in logical patterns to ensure that their audience can follow, understand, and remember what is said. Our model of audience-centered communication, shown in Figure 8.1, emphasizes that speeches are organized *for* audiences with decisions about organization being based in large part on an analysis of the audience.

In the first seven chapters of this book, you learned how to plan and research a speech based on audience needs, interests, and expectations. The planning and research process has taken you through five stages of speech preparation:

- Selecting and narrowing a topic
- Determining your purpose
- Developing your central idea
- Generating main ideas
- Gathering supporting material

As the arrows in the model in Figure 8.1 suggest, you may have moved *recursively*

FIGURE 8.1 Organize your speech to help your audience remember your key ideas and to give your speech clarity and structure.

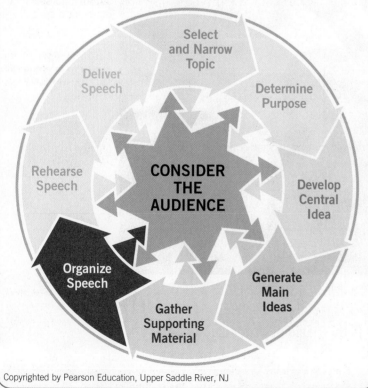
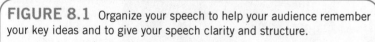

through these first five stages, returning at times to earlier stages to make changes and revisions based on your consideration of the audience. Now, with the results of your audience-centered planning and research in hand, it is time to move to the next stage in the audience-centered public-speaking process:

- Organizing your speech

In this chapter, we will discuss the patterns of organization commonly used to arrange the main ideas of a speech. Then we will explain how to integrate supporting materials into a speech. We will talk about previews, transitions, and summaries. And, finally, we will discuss and illustrate two types of speech outlines: the preparation outline and speaking notes. Chapter 9 discusses introductions and conclusions, the final component of the organizational stage of the preparation process.

Organizing Your Main Ideas

In Chapter 6, we discussed how to generate a preliminary plan for your speech by determining whether your central idea has logical divisions, could be supported by several reasons, or could be explained by identifying specific steps. These divisions, reasons, or steps become the main ideas of the body of your speech and the basis for the organization task highlighted in Figure 8.1 on page 160.

Now you are ready to decide which of your main ideas to discuss first, which one second, and so on. As summarized in Table 8.1 on page 160, you can choose from among five organizational patterns: (1) topical, (2) chronological, (3) spatial, (4) causal, and (5) problem-solution. Or you can combine several of these patterns. One additional variation of the problem-solution pattern is the motivated sequence. Because it is used almost exclusively in persuasive speeches, the motivated sequence is discussed in Chapter 15.

8.1 List and describe five patterns for organizing the main ideas of a speech.

 Explore at **MyCommunicationLab** Activity: "Organization"

 Explore at **MyCommunicationLab** Activity: "Scrambled Speech: Grant Proposal"

Organizing Ideas Topically

If your central idea has natural divisions, you can often organize your speech topically. Speeches on such diverse topics as factors to consider when selecting a mountain bike, types of infertility treatments, and the various classes of ham-radio licenses could all reflect **topical organization**.

Natural divisions are often essentially equal in importance. It may not matter which point you discuss first, second, or third. You can simply arrange your main ideas as a matter of personal preference. At other times, you may organize your main points based on one of three principles: primacy, recency, or complexity.

Primacy The principle of **primacy** suggests that you discuss your most important or convincing point *first* in your speech. The beginning of your speech can be the most important position if your listeners are either unfamiliar with your topic or hostile toward your central idea.

When your listeners are uninformed, your first point must introduce them to the topic and define unfamiliar terms integral to its discussion. What you say early in your speech will affect your listeners' understanding of the rest of your speech. If your listeners are likely to be hostile toward your central idea, putting your most important or convincing point first will lessen the possibility that you might lose or alienate them before you reach the end of your speech. In addition, your strongest idea may so influence your listeners' attitudes that they will be more receptive to your central idea.

 Watch at **MyCommunicationLab** Video: "Roommates"

topical organization
Arrangement of the natural divisions in a central idea according to recency, primacy, complexity, or the speaker's discretion

primacy
Arrangement of ideas from the most to the least important

Recognizing the controversial nature of stem-cell research, the speaker in the following example arranges the three main points of the speech according to primacy, advancing the most persuasive argument first.

PURPOSE STATEMENT:	At the end of my speech, the audience will be able to explain the applications of stem-cell research.
CENTRAL IDEA:	Stem-cell research has three important applications.
MAIN IDEAS:	I. At the most fundamental level, understanding stem cells can help us to understand better the process of human development.
	II. Stem-cell research can streamline the way we develop and test drugs.
	III. Stem-cell research can generate cells and tissue that could be used for "cell therapies."[2]

Recency According to the principle of **recency**, the point discussed *last* is the one audiences will remember best. If your audience is at least somewhat knowledgeable about and generally favorable toward your topic and central idea, you should probably organize your main points according to recency.

For example, if your speech is on the various living arrangements available to college students, and you want your audience of fellow students to consider living at home because of the savings involved, you would probably discuss that possibility as the fourth and last option. Your speech might have the following structure:

PURPOSE STATEMENT:	At the end of my speech, the audience will be able to discuss the pros and cons of four living arrangements for college students.
CENTRAL IDEA:	College students have at least four living arrangements available to them.
MAIN IDEAS:	I. Living in a dormitory
	II. Renting an apartment
	III. Joining a fraternity or sorority
	IV. Living at home

Complexity One other set of circumstances may dictate a particular order of the main ideas in your speech. If your main ideas range from simple to complicated, it makes sense to arrange them in order of **complexity**, progressing from the simple to the more complex. If, for example, you were to explain to your audience how to compile a family health profile and history, you might begin with the most easily accessible source and proceed to the more involved.

recency
Arrangement of ideas from the least to the most important

complexity
Arrangement of ideas from the simple to the more complex

PURPOSE STATEMENT:	At the end of my speech, the audience will be able to compile a family health profile and history.
CENTRAL IDEA:	Compiling a family health profile and history can be accomplished with the help of three sources.
MAIN IDEAS:	I. Elderly relatives
	II. Old hospital records and death certificates
	III. National health registries[3]

RECAP

PRIMACY, RECENCY, AND COMPLEXITY

- Primacy—most important point first
- Recency—most important point last
- Complexity—simplest point first, most complex point last

Teachers, from those in the very early elementary grades on up, use order of complexity to organize their courses and lessons. The kindergartner is taught to trace circles before learning to print a lowercase *a*. The young piano student practices scales and arpeggios before playing Beethoven sonatas. The college freshman practices writing 500-word essays before attempting a major research paper. You have learned most of your skills in order of complexity.

Ordering Ideas Chronologically

If you decide that your central idea could be explained best by a number of steps, you will probably organize those steps chronologically. **Chronological organization** is organization by time or sequence; that is, your steps are ordered according to when each step occurred or should occur. Historical speeches and how-to speeches are the two kinds of speeches usually organized chronologically.

Examples of topics for historical speeches might include the history of the women's movement in the United States, the sequence of events that led to the 1974 resignation of President Richard Nixon, or the development of the modern Olympic Games. You can choose to organize your main points either from earliest to most recent (forward in time) or from recent events back into history (backward in time). The progression you choose depends on your personal preference and on whether you want to emphasize the beginning or the end of the sequence. As we observed earlier, according to the principle of recency, audiences tend to remember best what they hear last.

In the following outline for a speech on the development of the Apple iPad, the speaker moves forward in time, making his last point the one that remains fresh in the minds of his audience at the end of his speech.

PURPOSE STATEMENT: At the end of my speech, the audience will be able to trace the major events in the development of the iPad.

CENTRAL IDEA: Drawing on the technology and market success of earlier devices, the Apple iPad quickly became a bestseller.

MAIN IDEAS:
I. 1993: Newton Message Pad marketed by Apple
II. 2001: iPod introduced
III. 2007: iPhone debuted
IV. 2010: iPad unveiled[4]

How-to explanations are also likely to follow a sequence or series of steps arranged from beginning to end, from the first step to the last—forward in time. A speech explaining how to clean up a broken compact fluorescent light bulb (CFL) might be organized as follows:

PURPOSE STATEMENT: At the end of my speech, the audience will be able to list the steps required to clean up a broken CFL.

CENTRAL IDEA: Cleaning up a broken CFL requires four steps.

MAIN IDEAS:
I. With the air conditioner turned off, allow the room to air out for 15 minutes.
II. Collect all the light bulb fragments with disposable gloves or a stiff piece of cardboard.
III. Wipe up any remaining debris with damp paper towels or sticky tape.
IV. Dispose of fragments and clean-up materials in a sealed container.[5]

In another chronologically organized speech, this one discussing the development of YouTube, the speaker wants to emphasize the inauspicious origins of the popular video site. Thus, she organizes the speech backward in time:

PURPOSE STATEMENT: At the end of my speech, the audience will be able to describe YouTube's rapid rise from humble beginnings.

CENTRAL IDEA: The popular video site YouTube grew rapidly from humble beginnings.

chronological organization
Organization by time or sequence

MAIN IDEAS:

    I. January 2012: YouTube exceeds 4 billion viewers a day.

    II. November 2006: YouTube acquired by Google

    III. December 2005: YouTube site publicly launched

    IV. February 2005: YouTube founded in a garage in Menlo Park, California[6]

Chronological organization, then, involves either forward or backward progression, depending on which end of a set of events the speaker intends to emphasize. The element common to both organization schemes is that dates and events are discussed in sequence rather than in random order.

Arranging Ideas Spatially

When you say, "As you enter the room, the table is to your right, the easy chair to your left, and the kitchen door straight ahead," you are using **spatial organization**: arranging ideas—usually natural divisions of the central idea—according to their location or direction. It does not usually matter whether you progress up or down, east or west, forward or back, as long as you follow a logical progression. If you skip up, down, over, and back, you will confuse your listeners rather than paint a distinct word picture.

Speeches on such diverse subjects as the National Museum of the American Indian, the travels of Robert Louis Stevenson, and the structure of an atom can all be organized spatially. Here is a sample outline for the first of those topics:

spatial organization
Organization based on location or direction

cause-and-effect organization
Organization that focuses on a situation and its causes or a situation and its effects

PURPOSE STATEMENT: At the end of my speech, the audience will be able to list and describe the four habitats recreated on the grounds of the National Museum of the American Indian in Washington, D.C.

CENTRAL IDEA: The grounds of the National Museum of the American Indian in Washington, D.C., are divided into four traditional American Indian habitats.

MAIN IDEAS:

    I. Upland hardwood forest

    II. Lowland freshwater wetlands

    III. Eastern meadowlands

    IV. Traditional croplands[7]

The organization of this outline is spatial, progressing through the grounds of the museum.

Organizing Ideas to Show Cause and Effect

If your central idea can be developed by discussing either steps or reasons, you might consider a **cause-and-effect organization** of your main ideas. A speech organized to show cause and effect may first identify a situation and then discuss the effects that result from it (cause→effect). Or the speech may present a situation and then seek its causes (effect→cause). As the recency principle would suggest, the cause-effect pattern emphasizes the effects; the effect-cause pattern emphasizes the causes.

In the following example, Vonda organizes her speech according to cause-effect, discussing the cause

A spatial organization may be right for a speech about the efforts of different nations to save endangered species, like this red panda. Or, if you wish to discuss the reasons species are endangered, you could use a cause-and-effect organizational pattern.
Photo: Ray Moller/Dorling Kindersley, Ltd.

(widespread adult illiteracy) as her first main idea, and its effects (poverty and social costs) as her second and third main ideas:

PURPOSE STATEMENT:	At the end of my speech, the audience will be able to identify two effects of adult illiteracy.
CENTRAL IDEA:	Adult illiteracy affects everyone.
MAIN IDEAS:	I. (*Cause*): Adult illiteracy is widespread in America today.
	II. (*Effect*): Adult illiterates often live in poverty.
	III. (*Effect*): Adult illiteracy is costly to society.[8]

In contrast, Joseph organizes his speech on for-profit universities according to an effect-cause pattern, discussing the effect (for-profit universities enrolling unqualified students) as his first main idea and its causes (misleading recruiters and false advertising) as his second and third main ideas:

PURPOSE STATEMENT:	At the end of my speech, the audience will be able to explain how for-profit universities are enrolling unqualified students.
CENTRAL IDEA:	For-profit universities are using two unethical tactics to enroll unqualified students.
MAIN IDEAS:	I. (*Effect*): For-profit universities are enrolling unqualified students who have struggled in more traditional college settings and who may not even have a high school diploma or GED.
	II. (*Cause*): Recruiters lie about or misrepresent their programs when recruiting students.
	III. (*Cause*): False Web and television advertising lures additional students.[9]

After presenting the cause or effect in the first main idea, you can use the principles of recency, primacy, or complexity to decide the order in which you will discuss your other main ideas.

Organizing Ideas by Problem-Solution

If you want to discuss why a problem exists or what its effects are, you will probably organize your speech according to cause and effect, as discussed in the previous section. However, if you want to emphasize how best to *solve* the problem, you will probably use a **problem-solution organization**. Because it is often appropriate for persuasive speeches, problem-solution organization is discussed further in Chapter 15.

Like causes and effects, problems and solutions can be discussed in either order. If you speak to an audience that is already fairly aware of a problem but uncertain how to solve it, you will probably discuss the problem first and then the solution(s). Speechwriter Cynthia Starks explains how Robert Kennedy utilized problem-solution organization to comfort and inspire a crowd in Indianapolis on April 4, 1968, immediately following the assassination of Martin Luther King Jr.:

With sensitivity and compassion, [Kennedy] told them of King's death (the devastating "problem"). He praised King's dedication to "love and to justice between fellow human beings," adding that, "he died in the cause of that effort."

Then he offered a solution—to put aside violence and to embrace love and understanding toward each other.[10]

problem-solution organization
Organization focused on a problem and its various solutions or on a solution and the problems it would solve

TABLE 8.1   ORGANIZING YOUR MAIN POINTS

PATTERN	DESCRIPTION
Topical	Organization according to primacy, recency, or complexity
Chronological	Organization by time or sequence
Spatial	Organization based on location or direction
Cause and effect	Organization that focuses on a situation and its causes or a situation and its effects
Problem-solution	Organization that focuses on a problem and then solutions to it or on a solution and then the problems it would solve

Starks concludes by offering evidence of the effectiveness of Kennedy's problem-solution speech:

> Many American cities burned after King's death, but there was no fire in Indianapolis, which heard the words of Robert Kennedy.

If your audience knows about an action or program that has been implemented but does not know the reasons for its implementation, you might select instead a solution-problem pattern of organization. In the following example, the speaker knows that her listeners are already aware of a new business-school partnership program in their community but believes that they may be unclear about why it has been established:

PURPOSE STATEMENT: At the end of my speech, the audience will be able to explain how business-school partnership programs can help solve two of the major problems facing our public schools today.

CENTRAL IDEA: Business-school partnership programs can help alleviate at least two of the problems faced by public schools today.

MAIN IDEAS:
I. (*Solution*): In a business-school partnership, local businesses provide volunteers, financial support, and in-kind contributions to public schools.
II. (*Problem*): Many public schools can no longer afford special programs and fine-arts programs.
III. (*Problem*): Many public schools have no resources to fund enrichment materials and opportunities.

Note that in both of the preceding examples, the main ideas are natural divisions of the central idea.

Acknowledging Cultural Differences in Organization

Although the five patterns just discussed are typical of the way speakers in the United States are expected to organize and process information, they are not necessarily

DEVELOPING YOUR SPEECH STEP BY STEP

ORGANIZE YOUR SPEECH

As she begins to organize her speech on emergency contraception, Brianne sees that her three main ideas represent two *problems* associated with emergency contraception, and a *solution* for those problems: requiring college health services to counsel women seeking morning-after pills. It is easy for Brianne to decide that a problem-solution organizational strategy will be ideal for her speech.

Next, she ponders a more difficult choice. Which of the two problems should she discuss first? Brianne applies the recency principle to help her decide. She will discuss the problem she most wants to emphasize—students' need for information—last, before she introduces her proposed solution. In her conclusion, Brianne plans to ask the audience to take a concrete step in support of the solution.

typical of all cultures.[11] In fact, each culture teaches its members patterns of thought and organization that are considered appropriate for various occasions and audiences. On the whole, U.S. speakers tend to be more linear and direct than speakers from Semitic, Asian, Romance, or Russian cultures. Semitic speakers support their main points by pursuing tangents that might seem "off topic" to many U.S. speakers. Asians may only allude to a main point through a circuitous route of illustration and parable. For example, audiences in China might be expected to determine the main ideas by analyzing the themes and messages of several stories the speaker shares. Unlike many American speakers, the Chinese speaker might never overtly state his or her main ideas. And speakers from Romance and Russian cultures tend to begin with a basic principle and then move to facts and illustrations that they only gradually connect to a main point. The models in Figure 8.2 illustrate these culturally diverse patterns of organization.

Of course, these are very broad generalizations. But as an audience member who recognizes the existence of cultural differences, you can better appreciate and understand the organization of a speaker from a culture other than your own. He or she may not be disorganized but simply using organizational strategies different from those presented in this chapter.

FIGURE 8.2 Organizational patterns of speaking will vary by culture.

| U.S. | Semitic | Asian | Romance | Russian |

Source: Lieberman, *Public Speaking in the Multicultural Environment*, "Organizational patterns by culture" © 1997. Reproduced by permission of Pearson Education, Inc.

Integrating Your Supporting Material

Once you have organized your main ideas, you are ready to organize the supporting material for each idea. You may realize that in support of your second main idea you have an illustration, two statistics, and an opinion. In what order should you present these items?

You can sometimes use one of the five standard organizational patterns to arrange your supporting material. Illustrations, for instance, may be organized chronologically. In the following example, the speaker uses a chronological sequence of several brief illustrations of cutting-edge technology:

> . . . miracle has followed upon miracle—from a television in every home in the 1950s, to the launching of the first communications satellite in the 1960s, to the introduction of cable TV in the 1970s, the rise of personal computers in the 1980s, the Internet in the 1990s, and social media in the 2000s.[12]

At other times, however, none of the five patterns may seem suited to the supporting materials you have. In those instances, you may need to turn to an organizational strategy more specifically adapted to your supporting materials. These strategies include (1) primacy or recency, (2) specificity, (3) complexity, and (4) "soft" to "hard" evidence.

Primacy or Recency We have already discussed how the principles of primacy and recency can determine whether you put a main idea at the beginning or the end of your speech. These patterns are used so frequently to arrange supporting materials that we mention them again here.

Suppose that you have several statistics to support a main point. All are relevant and significant, but one is especially gripping. American Cancer Society CEO John Seffrin showed images of and described the following brief examples of international tobacco advertising:

> The effort to build brand loyalty begins early. Here is an example of that in Africa— a young man wearing a hat with a cigarette brand logo. . . .
> Look at this innocent baby wearing a giant Marlboro logo on his shirt. . . .
> Notice how this ad links smoking to American values that are attractive to third-world kids—wealth, sophistication, and urbanity. It also shows African Americans living the American Dream. If you're a poor kid in Africa, this image can be very powerful.
> And finally, this one from Bucharest, Romania, which is my favorite. When the Berlin Wall came down, no one rushed into Eastern Europe faster than the tobacco industry. Here you can see the Camel logo etched in the street lights. In my opinion, this is one of the most disturbing examples of the public sector partnering with private industry to the detriment of its citizens.[13]

It is evident that Seffrin applied the principle of recency to his examples, as he identifies the final one as "my favorite" and "one of the most disturbing." The principle of primacy or recency can also be applied to groups of statistics, opinions, or any combination of supporting material.

Specificity Sometimes your supporting material will range from very specific examples to more general overviews of a situation. You may either offer your specific information first and end with your general statement, or make the general statement first and support it with specific evidence.

Another application of specificity might be to compact or explode statistics, as discussed in Chapter 7. Compacting moves statistics from general to specific. Exploding moves them in the other direction, from specific to general. In her speech on alternatives to imprisonment, Anastasia uses both tactics. She begins with a broad statistic and makes it more specific by compacting it. Then she moves back toward a general statement by exploding a related statistic:

> . . . there are more than 2.4 million U.S. residents who serve time in prison. That means that one in every 142 residents is in prison right now, or approximately 2.3 percent of the total population. While this number may seem reasonable, when you think about how many people went through prison at some point of their lives, that number rises to 25 percent of the total population.[14]

Complexity We have discussed organizing subtopics by moving from the simple to the complex. The same method of organization may also determine how you order your supporting material. In many situations, it makes sense to start with the materials that are easy to understand and work up to the more complex ones. In her speech on solar radiation, Nichole's supporting materials include explanations of two effects of solar storms. She presents the simpler explanation first—of electrical blackouts and disruptions in radio broadcasts—and then goes on to the more complex explanation of cosmic radiation:

> The sun produces storms on its surface in eleven-year cycles. During solar maximum, these storms will make their presence known to the land-bound public through electrical blackouts and disruptions in radio broadcasts. These storms cause the sun to throw off electrically charged ions that, combined with charged particles, enter the Earth's atmosphere from outer space. This is known collectively as cosmic radiation.[15]

From Soft to Hard Evidence Supporting material can also be arranged along a continuum from "soft" to "hard." **Soft evidence** rests on opinion or inference. Hypothetical illustrations, descriptions, explanations, definitions, analogies, and opinions are usually considered soft. **Hard evidence** includes factual examples and statistics.

Soft-to-hard organization of supporting material relies chiefly on the principle of recency—that the last statement is remembered best. Note how Beth moves from an illustration to expert testimony (both soft evidence) to a statistic (hard evidence) in her speech on the danger of sand holes on the beach:

RECAP

INTEGRATING YOUR SUPPORTING MATERIAL

Strategy	Description
Primacy	Most important material first
Recency	Most important material last
Specificity	From specific information to general overview or from general overview to specific information
Complexity	From simple to more complex material
Soft to hard	From opinion or hypothetical illustration to fact or statistic

---

soft evidence
Supporting material based mainly on opinion or inference; includes hypothetical illustrations, descriptions, explanations, definitions, and analogies

hard evidence
Factual examples and statistics

You can increase the impact of hard evidence by accompanying your presentation of statistics with a visual aid, such as a graph.

Photo: Monty Rakusen/Cultura/Getty Images

Illustration (soft evidence)	An article on the *Christian Science Monitor* Web site of August 24, 2012, describes how a South Korean exchange student suffocated in a Southern California beach sand pit that he had dug with fellow students and staff from the small California college he attended.
Expert testimony (soft evidence)	Father and son physicians Dr. Bradley Maron and Dr. Barry Maron explain that the unstable walls of a sand hole can unexpectedly collapse, leaving no evidence of a victim's location.
Statistic (hard evidence)	During the decade between 1997 and 2007, 52 documented accidents occurred in dry-sand holes dug for recreational purposes.[16]

The speaker has arranged her supporting material from soft to hard.

8.3 Use verbal and nonverbal signposts to organize a speech for the ears of others.

Explore at **MyCommunicationLab Activity:** "Annotated Outline: Helen Keller International"

signposts
Cues about the relationships between a speaker's ideas

preview
A statement of what is to come

initial preview
A statement in the introduction of a speech of what the main ideas of the speech will be

internal preview
A statement in the body of a speech that introduces and outlines ideas that will be developed as the speech progresses

Organizing Your Presentation for the Ears of Others: Signposting

You have a logically ordered, fairly complete plan for your speech. But if you delivered the speech at this point, your audience might become frustrated or confused as they tried to discern your organizational plan. So your next task is to develop **signposts**—organizational cues for your audience's ears. Signposts include previews, transitions, and summaries.

Previews

In Chapter 10, we discuss the differences between writing and speaking styles. One significant difference is that public speaking is more repetitive. Audience-centered speakers need to remember that the members of their audience, unlike readers, cannot go back to review a missed point. A **preview** "tells them what you're going to tell them," building audience anticipation of an important idea. Like transitions, previews also provide coherence.

Initial Previews An **initial preview** is a statement of what the main ideas of the speech will be. As discussed in Chapter 6, it is usually presented in conjunction with the central idea at or near the end of the introduction, as a *blueprint* for the speech.

Speaking on problems with the U.S. patent system, Robert offered the following blueprint at the end of his introduction:

> While patents are a good idea in principle, in practice they have turned into a disaster. First, I'll take you on a tour of our broken patent system. Then I'll walk you through the havoc it wreaks on us, our economy, and our future. Finally, we'll explore hope in potential solutions. . . .[17]

In this blueprint, Robert clearly previews his main ideas and introduces them in the order in which he will discuss them in the body of the speech.

Internal Previews In addition to using previews near the beginning of their speeches, speakers use them at various points throughout the speech. An **internal preview**

introduces and outlines ideas that will be developed as the speech progresses. Sometimes speakers couch internal previews in the form of questions they plan to answer. Note how the following question from a speech on hotel security provides an internal preview:

> . . . the question remains, what can we do, as potential travelers and potential victims, to protect ourselves?[18]

Just as anticipating an idea helps audience members remember it, so mentally answering a question helps them plant the answer firmly in their minds.

Transitions

A **transition** is a verbal or nonverbal signal that a speaker has finished discussing one idea and is moving to another.

Explore at **MyCommunicationLab**
Activity: "Better Transitions"

Explore at **MyCommunicationLab**
Activity: "Connecting to Key Ideas"

Verbal Transitions A speaker can sometimes make a **verbal transition** simply by repeating a key word from an earlier statement or by using a synonym or a pronoun that refers to an earlier key word or idea. This type of transition is often used to make one sentence flow smoothly into the next. (The previous sentence itself is an example: "This type of transition" refers to the sentence that precedes it.)

Other verbal transitions are words or phrases that show relationships between ideas. Note the italicized transitional phrases in the following examples:

- *In addition to* transitions, previews and summaries are also considered to be signposts.
- *Not only* does plastic packaging use up our scarce resources, it contaminates them *as well.*
- *In other words*, as women's roles have changed, they have *also* contributed to this effect.
- *In summary*, Fanny Brice was the best-known star of Ziegfeld's Follies.
- *Therefore*, I recommend that you sign the grievance petition.

Simple enumeration (*first, second, third*) can also point up relationships between ideas and provide transitions.

One type of transitional signpost that can occasionally backfire and do more harm than good is one that signals the end of a speech. *Finally* and *in conclusion* give the audience implicit permission to stop listening, and they often do. If the speech has been too long or has otherwise not gone well, the audience may even express their relief audibly. Better strategies for moving into a conclusion include repeating a key word or phrase, using a synonym or pronoun that refers to a previous idea, offering a final summary, or referring to the introduction of the speech. We discuss the final summary later in this chapter. Both of the last two strategies are also covered in Chapter 9.

As summarized in Table 8.2, repetition of key words or ideas, transitional words or phrases, and enumeration all provide verbal transitions from one idea to the next.

transition
A verbal or nonverbal signal that a speaker has finished discussing one idea and is moving to another

verbal transition
A word or phrase that indicates the relationship between two ideas

TABLE 8.2   VERBAL TRANSITIONS

STRATEGY	EXAMPLE
Repeating a key word, or using a synonym or pronoun that refers to a key word.	"*These problems* cannot be allowed to continue."
Using a transitional word or phrase	"*In addition* to the facts that I've mentioned, we need to consider one more problem."
Enumerating	"*Second*, there has been a rapid increase in the number of accidents reported."

Your nonverbal transition signals, as well as your verbal signposts, can help your audience follow the organization of your speech. One effective technique is to pause before moving to a new point, as this speaker is doing.

Photo: Kablonk!/Masterfile

You may need to experiment with several alternatives before you find the smooth transition you seek in a given instance. If none of these alternatives seems to work well, consider a nonverbal transition.

Nonverbal Transitions A **nonverbal transition** can occur in several ways, sometimes alone and sometimes in combination with a verbal transition. A change in facial expression, a pause, an altered vocal pitch or speaking rate, or a movement all may indicate a transition.

For example, a speaker talking about the value of cardiopulmonary resuscitation began his speech with a powerful anecdote about a man suffering a heart attack at a party. No one knew how to help, and the man died. The speaker then looked up from his notes and paused, while maintaining eye contact with his audience. His next words were "The real tragedy of Bill Jorgen's death was that it should not have happened." His pause, as well as the words that followed, indicated a transition into the body of the speech.

Like this speaker, most good speakers use a combination of verbal and nonverbal transitions to move from one point to another through their speeches. You will find more about nonverbal communication in Chapter 11.

Summaries

Like a preview, a **summary**, or recap of what has been said, provides additional exposure to a speaker's ideas and can help ensure that audience members will grasp and remember them. Most speakers use two types of summaries: the final summary and the internal summary.

Final Summaries A **final summary** restates the main ideas of a speech and gives an audience their *last* exposure to those ideas. It occurs just before the end of a speech, often doing double duty as a transition between the body and the conclusion.

Here is an example of a final summary from a speech on the U.S. Customs Service:

Today, we have focused on the failing U.S. Customs Service. We have asked several important questions, such as "Why is Customs having such a hard time

nonverbal transition
A facial expression, vocal cue, or physical movement that indicates that a speaker is moving from one idea to the next

summary
A recap of what has been said

final summary
A restatement of the main ideas of a speech, occurring near the end of the speech

doing its job?" and "What can we do to remedy this situation?" When the cause of a serious problem is unknown, the continuation of the dilemma is understandable. However, the cause for the failure of the U.S. Customs Service is known: a lack of personnel. Given that fact and our understanding that Customs is vital to America's interests, it would be foolish not to rectify this situation.[19]

This final summary leaves no doubt as to the important points of the speech. We discuss the use of final summaries in more detail in Chapter 9.

Internal Summaries   As the term suggests, an **internal summary** occurs within the body of a speech; it restates the ideas that have been developed up to that point.

Susan uses the following internal summary in her speech on the teacher shortage:

So let's review for just a moment. One, we are endeavoring to implement educational reforms; but two, we are in the first years of a dramatic increase in enrollment; and three, fewer quality students are opting for education; while four, many good teachers want out of teaching; plus five, large numbers will soon be retiring.[20]

Internal summaries are often used in combination with internal previews to form transitions between major points and ideas. Each of the following examples makes clear what has just been discussed in the speech as well as what will be discussed next:

Many are unaware of their own inadequate levels and uninformed about the importance of Vitamin D in their lives. And yet Vitamin D deficiency is a problem that can be so easily solved! The solutions are twofold and can be implemented on a universal and individual level.[21]

So now [that] we are aware of the severity of the disease and unique reasons for college students to be concerned, we will look at some steps we need to take to combat bacterial meningitis.[22]

It seems as though everyone is saying that something should be done about NutraSweet. It should be retested. Well, now that it is here on the market, what can we do to see that it does get investigated further?[23]

Presentation Aids

Transitions, previews, and summaries are the glue that holds a speech together. These signposts can help you achieve a coherent flow of ideas and help your audience remember those ideas. Unfortunately, however, you cannot guarantee that your audience will be attentive to your signposts. In Chapter 1, we discussed the concept of noise as it affects the public-speaking process. It is possible for your listeners to be so distracted by internal or external noise that they fail to hear or process even your most carefully planned verbal signposts.

One way you can increase the likelihood of your listeners' attending to your signposting is to prepare and use presentation aids to supplement your signposts. For example, you could display on a PowerPoint™ slide a bulleted or numbered outline of your main ideas as you initially preview them in your introduction, and again as you summarize them in your conclusion. Some speakers prefer to use one PowerPoint slide for each main point. Transitions between points are emphasized as the speaker moves to the next slide. In Chapter 12, we discuss guidelines for developing and using such presentation aids. Especially when your speech is long or its organization complex, you can help your audience remember your organization if you provide visual support for your signposts.

internal summary
A restatement in the body of a speech of the ideas that have been developed so far

RECAP

TYPES OF SIGNPOSTS

Initial previews

Internal previews

Verbal transitions

Nonverbal transitions

Final summaries

Internal summaries

8.4 | Develop a preparation outline and speaking notes for a speech.

Outlining Your Speech

Although few speeches are written in paragraph form, most speakers develop a **preparation outline**, a fairly detailed outline of the central idea, main ideas, and supporting material. Depending on your instructor's specific requirements, it may also include your specific purpose, discussed in Chapter 6; your introduction and conclusion, discussed in Chapter 9; and your references, discussed in Chapter 3. One CEO notes,

preparation outline
A detailed outline of a speech that includes the central idea, main ideas, and supporting material; and that may also include the specific purpose, introduction, conclusion, and references

speaking notes
A brief outline used when a speech is delivered

mapping
Using geometric shapes to sketch how all the main ideas, subpoints, and supporting material of a speech relate to the central idea and to one another

👁 **Watch** at **MyCommunicationLab**
Video: "Outline of the Informative Speech: Our Immigration Story"

> Unless you sit down and write out your thoughts and put them in a cogent order, you can't deliver a cogent speech. Maybe some people have mastered that art. But I have seen too many people give speeches that they really haven't thought out.[24]

From your detailed preparation outline, you will eventually develop **speaking notes**, a shorter outline that you will use when you deliver your speech. Let's look at the specific characteristics of both types of outlines.

Developing Your Preparation Outline

To begin your preparation outline, you might try a technique known as **mapping**, or clustering. Write on a sheet of paper all the main ideas, subpoints, and supporting material for the speech. Then use geometric shapes and arrows to indicate the logical relationships among them, as shown in Figure 8.3.

FIGURE 8.3 A map that shows the relationships among each of a speaker's three main ideas and their subpoints. Main ideas are enclosed by rectangles; subpoints, by ovals. Supporting material could be indicated by another shape and connected to the appropriate subpoints.

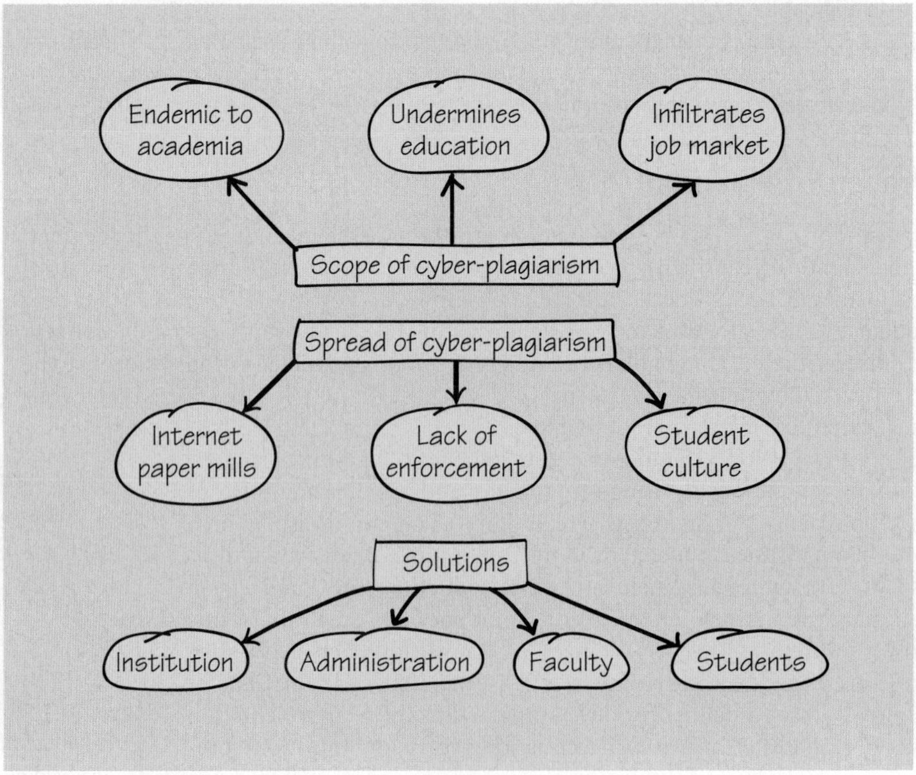

Nationwide Insurance speechwriter Charles Parnell describes another technique for beginning an outline:

> I often start by jotting down a few ideas on the [computer] screen, then move them around as necessary to build some sort of coherent pattern. I then fill in the details as they occur to me.
>
> What that means is that you can really start anywhere and eventually come up with an entire speech, just as you can start with any piece of a puzzle and eventually put it together.[25]

Whatever technique you choose to begin your outline, your ultimate goal is to produce a plan that helps you to judge the unity and coherence of your speech: to see how well the parts fit together and how smoothly the speech flows. The following suggestions will help you complete your preparation outline. However, keep in mind that different instructors may have different expectations for both outline content and outline format. Be sure to understand and follow your own instructor's guidelines.

Write Your Preparation Outline in Complete Sentences, Like Those You Will Use When Delivering Your Speech Unless you write complete sentences, you will have trouble judging the coherence of the speech. Moreover, complete sentences will help during your early rehearsals. If you write cryptic phrases, you may not remember what they mean.

Use Standard Outline Form Although you did not have to use standard outline form when you began to sketch out your ideas, you need to do so now. **Standard outline form** lets you see at a glance the exact relationships among various main ideas, subpoints, and supporting material in your speech. It is an important tool for evaluating your speech, as well as a requirement in many public-speaking courses. An instructor who requires speech outlines will generally expect standard outline form. To produce a correct outline, follow the instructions given here and summarized in Figure 8.4.

Explore at **MyCommunicationLab**
Activity: "Practicing with the Microsoft Outlining Tool"

Explore at **MyCommunicationLab**
Activity: "Using the Microsoft Outlining Tool"

standard outline form
Numbered and lettered headings and subheadings arranged hierarchically to indicate the relationships among parts of a speech

FIGURE 8.4 Use this summary as a reminder of the rules of proper outlining when you write your preparation outline.

CORRECT OUTLINE FORM

Rule	Example
1. Use standard outline numbers and letters.	I. A. 1. a. (1) (a)
2. Use at least two subpoints, if any, for each main idea.	I. A. B.
3. Properly indent main ideas, subpoints, and supporting material.	I. First main idea A. First subpoint of I 1. First subpoint of A 2. Second subpoint of A B. Second subpoint of I II. Second main idea

Use Standard Outline Numbering Logical and fairly easy to learn, outline numbering follows this sequence:

I. First main idea
  A. First subpoint of I
  B. Second subpoint of I
    1. First subpoint of B
    2. Second subpoint of B
      a. First subpoint of 2
      b. Second subpoint of 2
II. Second main idea

Although it is unlikely that you will subdivide beyond the level of lowercase letters (a, b, etc.) in most speech outlines, next would come numbers in parentheses and then lowercase letters in parentheses.

Use at Least Two Subdivisions, if Any, for Each Point Logic dictates that you cannot divide anything into one part. If, for example, you have only one piece of supporting material, incorporate it into the subpoint or main idea that it supports. If you have only one subpoint, incorporate it into the main idea above it. Although there is no firm limit to the number of subpoints you may have, if you have more than five, you may want to place some of them under another point. An audience will remember your ideas more easily if they are divided into blocks of no more than five.

Indent Main Ideas, Points, Subpoints, and Supporting Material Properly Main ideas, indicated by Roman numerals, are written closest to the left margin. Notice that the periods following the Roman numerals line up, so that the first words of the main ideas also line up.

I. First main idea
II. Second main idea
III. Third main idea

Letters or numbers of subpoints and supporting material begin directly underneath the first *word* of the point above.

I. First main idea
  A. First subpoint of I

If a main idea or subpoint takes up more than one line, the second line begins under the first *word* of the preceding line:

I. Every speech has three parts.
  A. The first part, both in our discussion and in the actual delivery, is the introduction.

The same rules of indentation apply at all levels of the outline. Note that if you are using a word-processing program, you may find it easier to format your outline with the AutoFormat feature turned off. The program's attempt to "help" you may be more frustrating than helpful; it may cause you to make more errors in your outline than you would if you formatted it yourself.

Write and Label Your Specific Purpose at the Top of Your Preparation Outline Unless your instructor directs you to do otherwise, do not work the specific purpose into the outline itself. Instead, label it and place it at the top of the outline. Your specific purpose can serve as a yardstick by which to measure the relevance of each main idea and piece of supporting material. Everything in the speech should contribute to your purpose.

Add the Blueprint, Key Signposts, and an Introduction and Conclusion to Your Outline Place the introduction after the specific purpose, the blueprint immediately following the introduction, the conclusion after the outline of the body of the speech, and other signposts within the outline. Follow your instructor's guidelines for incorporating these elements into your numbering system.

Once you have completed your preparation outline, you can use it to help analyze and possibly revise the speech. The following questions can help you in this critical thinking task.

- **Does the speech as outlined fulfill the purpose you have specified?** If not, you need to revise the specific purpose or change the direction and content of the speech itself.

- **Are the main ideas logical extensions (natural divisions, reasons, or steps) of the central idea?** If not, revise either the central idea or the main ideas. Like the first question, this one relates to the unity of the speech and is critical to making certain the speech fits together as a whole.

- **Do the signposts enhance the comfortable flow of each idea into the next?** If not, change or add previews, summaries, or transitions. If signposts are not adequate, the speech will lack coherence.

- **Does each subpoint provide support for the point under which it falls?** If not, then either move or delete the subpoint.

- **Is your outline form correct?** For a quick reference, check Figure 8.3 on page 168 and the Recap above.

The sample outline on pages 172–173 is for a ten-minute persuasive speech by student speaker Brianne, whose speech preparation process we have been following since Chapter 5.[26] Note that in this example, the purpose, introduction, blueprint, signposts, conclusion, and references are included but separated from the numbered points in the body of the speech.

Because Brianne kept good records during the preliminary bibliography stage of her research (see Chapter 7, pages 138–139), she can easily cite her references, as required by her instructor. As explained in Chapter 3, the two most common reference formats, or documentation styles, are those developed by the MLA (Modern Language Association) and the APA (American Psychological Association). MLA style is usually used in the humanities, APA style in the natural and social sciences. Check with your instructor about which format he or she prefers.

Developing Your Speaking Notes

As you rehearse your speech, you will find that you need your preparation outline less and less. Both the structure and the content of your speech will become set in your mind. At this point, you are ready to prepare a shorter outline to serve as your speaking notes.

Although your speaking notes should not be so detailed that you will be tempted to read rather than speak to your audience, this outline should provide clearly formatted detail sufficient to ensure that you can make your presentation as you have planned in your preparation outline. NASA blamed the loss of the space shuttle *Columbia* in part on the fact that an outline on possible wing damage was "so crammed with nested bullet points and irregular short forms that it was nearly impossible to untangle."[27]

Figure 8.5 on page 174 illustrates speaking notes for Brianne's presentation on emergency contraception. Here are a few specific suggestions for developing your own speaking notes.

Explore at **MyCommunicationLab**
Activity: "Creating a Speaking Outline"

Choose Your Technology Speaking notes can be either high tech or low tech. You may decide to display your outline on a laptop or electronic tablet—perhaps utilizing one of several apps available for speaking notes—or you may opt to use old-fashioned

SAMPLE PREPARATION OUTLINE

PURPOSE

At the end of my speech, the audience will take steps to ensure that colleges and universities provide counseling along with access to emergency contraception.

INTRODUCTION

Students at Shippensburg University in Pennsylvania can visit their student health center for emergency contraception without ever coming into any contact with any of the center's staff. A simple visit to a vending machine is enough. *Time* in 2012 explains that Shippensburg University is one institution that allows access to Plan B, known as an emergency contraceptive, without counseling. While this plan allows students to have liberation and independence regarding their sexual health, it does so at a very high cost. The Centers for Disease Control and Prevention in 2013 indicates that one-fourth of morning-after pill users fall between ages 20 and 24, meaning that many university students are both purchasing and using the medication. Because of the magnitude of the problem, and because I am concerned with my health as well as that of my peers, it is imperative that we consider the discussion regarding access to the morning-after pill and the effects that it has regarding our own health.

CENTRAL IDEA

The Food and Drug Administration should require that any over-the-counter purchase of the morning-after pill on a university campus be accompanied by a consultation.

PREVIEW

As we consider the discussion regarding access to the morning-after pill and the effects that it has on our health, we'll see that every student deserves both access and information.

BODY OUTLINE

I. First, let's consider several problems associated with this issue.

   A. The first problem is the ready accessibility of the morning-after pill.

      1. According to the Centers for Disease Control and Prevention in 2013, purchase of the morning-after pill has increased, especially among women ages 20 to 24.

      2. The Shippensburg University Web site in 2013 states that to meet the requirement for making emergency contraception readily available to students, it has provided the vending machine for the Plan B pill for more than three years.

      3. In January 2013, the *Boston Globe* reported that after visiting the Shippensburg campus, the Food and Drug Administration (FDA) concluded that although it is not technically "over the counter," the vending machine should stay.

   B. Ease of access without required consultation comes at a heavy cost: Many students guess on their own how to use the pill, or simply don't know enough to use it effectively. Drs. Chris Kahlenborn and Walter Severs explain, in the 2012 *Cleveland Clinic Journal of Medicine*, that misconceptions about the morning-after pill are perpetuated by the ease of access to the pill.

      1. One misconception is that the morning-after pill is equivalent to an abortion pill.

Placing the purpose statement at the top of the outline helps the speaker keep it in mind. But always follow your instructor's specific requirements for how to format your preparation outline.

Brianne catches her listeners' attention by opening her presentation with an illustration. Other strategies for effectively getting audience attention are discussed in Chapter 9.

Brianne writes out and labels her central idea and preview, which together form the blueprint of her speech. Again, follow your instructor's requirements for what to include in and how to label the various components of your outline.

The first main point of the speech, which explores problems associated with emergency contraception, is indicated by the Roman numeral I. The two specific problems are indicated by A and B.

Subpoints 1, 2, and 3 provide supporting material for A. Brianne plans oral citations of her supporting materials for these subpoints.

2. A second misconception is that the 72-hour window is a recommendation rather than a requirement.

Signpost. Because of students' misconceptions, and because they don't have access to ask questions or address these concerns, they are left in the dark. Fortunately, there is a solution that you and I can enact together to safeguard our own health as well as each other's.

II. The solution is for the FDA to mandate counseling for over-the-counter purchase of the morning-after pill on all college campuses. This is important for several reasons.

A. The first is that current students at Shippensburg University would no longer be missing out on the vital information that they deserve as consumers.

B. In addition, with the FDA deciding in January 2013 that the vending machine is an acceptable means for the purchase of the morning-after pill, many other campuses may decide to use this strategy. These students too deserve the necessary information.

C. Finally, this solution allows for an important channel of communication and conversation about sexual health, including that Plan B is an *emergency* contraceptive and should not replace other forms of birth control.

The signpost summarizes the problem explained in B and its effects, as well as previewing a solution.

CONCLUSION

In conclusion, it is easy to see problems with both ease of Plan B accessibility and risk. It is imperative that the FDA requires consultation with over-the-counter purchases of these medications. Thanks to our friends at Shippensburg University, we may never think of vending machines in the same way again—but it is important to understand that convenience can sometimes come at a cost. It is important that we keep ourselves and our campuses safe. Join me by signing my petition to ensure that our safety and health come first, because giving students' health a "college try" is just not safe enough.

In her conclusion, Brianne first summarizes her main ideas, then reaffirms her central idea. Finally, she encourages her audience to take a specific action.

REFERENCES

The American College of Obstetricians and Gynecologists (November 2012). Committee opinion: Access to emergency contraception. Retrieved from http://www.acog.org/Resources_And_Publications

Associated Press (2013, January 25). FDA won't regulate PA birth control machine. Retrieved from http://www.boston.com/news/nation/2013/01/25/fda-wont-regulate-birth-control-machine/As16xuqSxiCm6GOYGN1YTK/story.html

The Centers for Disease Control and Prevention (February 2013). Use of emergency contraception among women aged 15–44: United States, 2006–2010. Retrieved from http://www.cdc.gov/nchs/data/databriefs/db112.htm

Kahlenborn, C., & Severs, W. (2012). Emergency contraception. *Cleveland Clinic Journal of Medicine, 80* (3), 185.

Shippensburg University. Etter health center. Retrieved from http://www.ship.edu/Health_Center/

Springer, K. (2012, February 8). Pennsylvania college sells "morning after" pills in vending machine. *Time.* Retrieved from http://newsfeed.time.com/2012/02/08/pennsylvania-college-sells-morning-after-pills-in-vending-machine/

Following her instructor's requirements, Brianne includes in her preparation outline a list of her references, formatted in APA style.

note cards. Even if you plan to use an electronic option, you may want to have a backup outline on note cards in case of technical difficulty. Note cards don't rustle as paper does, and are small enough to hold in one hand. Write on one side only, and number your note cards in case they get out of order just before or during your speech. Regardless of which technology you select, make sure your letters and words are large enough to be read easily.

Use Standard Outline Form Standard outline form will help you find your exact place when you glance down at your speaking notes. You will know, for example, that your second main idea is indicated by "II." In addition, lay out your outline so that your introduction, each main idea, and your conclusion are distinct.

Include Your Introduction and Conclusion in Abbreviated Form Even if your instructor does not require you to include your introduction and conclusion on your preparation outline, include abbreviated versions of them in your speaking notes. You might even feel more comfortable delivering the presentation if you have your first and last sentences written out in front of you.

FIGURE 8.5 Your speaking notes can include delivery cues and reminders. Be sure to differentiate your cues from the content of your speech. One good way is to write speaking cues in a different color ink or font.

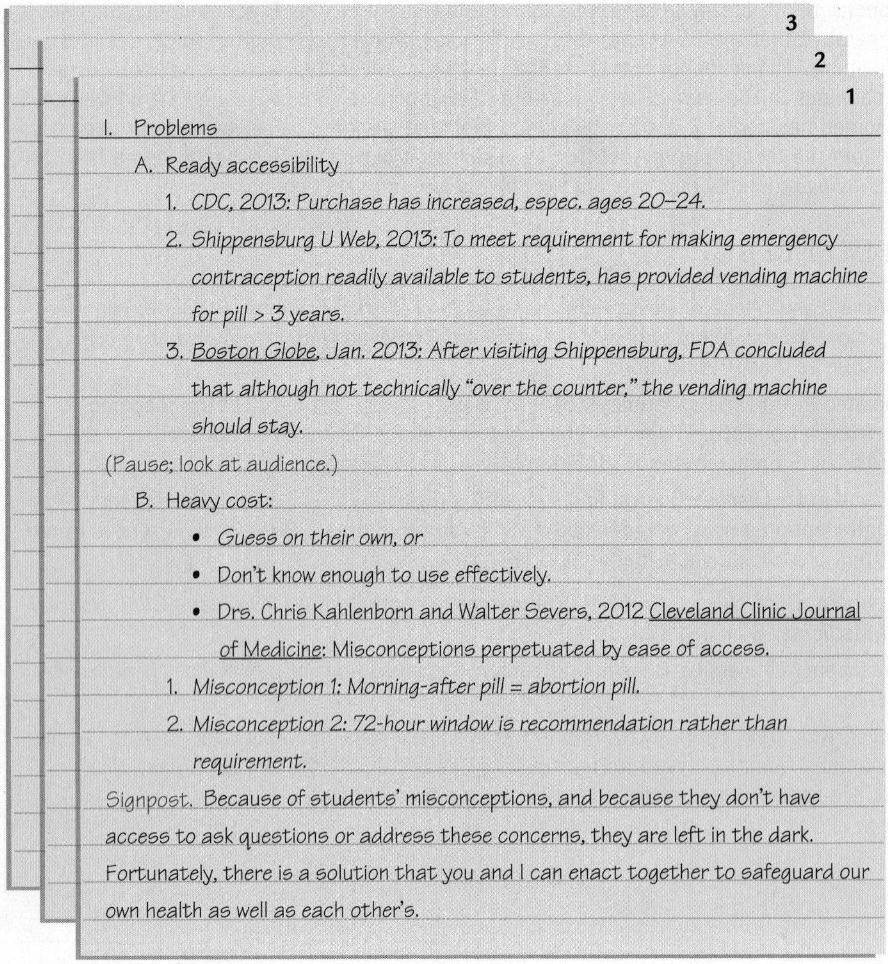

```
                                                              3
                                                           2
                                                        1

   I.  Problems
       A. Ready accessibility
          1. CDC, 2013: Purchase has increased, espec. ages 20–24.
          2. Shippensburg U Web, 2013: To meet requirement for making emergency
             contraception readily available to students, has provided vending machine
             for pill > 3 years.
          3. Boston Globe, Jan. 2013: After visiting Shippensburg, FDA concluded
             that although not technically "over the counter," the vending machine
             should stay.
       (Pause; look at audience.)
       B. Heavy cost:
          • Guess on their own, or
          • Don't know enough to use effectively.
          • Drs. Chris Kahlenborn and Walter Severs, 2012 Cleveland Clinic Journal
             of Medicine: Misconceptions perpetuated by ease of access.
          1. Misconception 1: Morning-after pill = abortion pill.
          2. Misconception 2: 72-hour window is recommendation rather than
             requirement.
   Signpost. Because of students' misconceptions, and because they don't have
   access to ask questions or address these concerns, they are left in the dark.
   Fortunately, there is a solution that you and I can enact together to safeguard our
   own health as well as each other's.
```

Include Your Central Idea, But Not Your Purpose Statement Be sure to include your central idea. But as you will not actually say your purpose statement during your presentation, do not put it on your speaking notes.

Include Supporting Material and Signposts Write out in full any statistics and direct quotations and their sources. Write your key signposts—your initial preview, for example—to ensure that you will not have to grope awkwardly as you move from one idea to another.

Include Delivery Cues Writing in your speaking note cards such cues as "Louder," "Pause," or "Walk two steps left" will remind you to communicate the nonverbal messages you have planned. Write your delivery cues in a different color or font so that you don't confuse them with your verbal content. President Gerald Ford once accidentally read the delivery cue "Look into the right camera" during a speech. Clearly differentiating delivery cues from speech content will help prevent such mistakes.

RECAP

TWO TYPES OF SPEECH OUTLINES

Purpose

Preparation Outline	Allows speaker to examine speech for completeness, unity, coherence, and overall effectiveness. May serve as first rehearsal outline.
Speaking Notes	Include supporting material, signposts, and delivery cues.

STUDY GUIDE — REVIEW, APPLY, AND ASSESS

ORGANIZING YOUR MAIN IDEAS

8.1 List and describe five patterns for organizing the main ideas of a speech.

Organizing the main ideas of your speech in a logical way will help audience members follow, understand, and remember these ideas. For North American audiences, the five most common patterns of organization include topical, chronological, spatial, cause and effect, and problem-solution. These patterns are sometimes combined. Other organizational patterns may be favored in different cultures. The principles of primacy, recency, and complexity can also help you decide which main idea to discuss first, next, and last.

Key Terms

Thinking Critically

Identify the organizational pattern most likely applied to the main ideas for each of the following speeches. If the pattern is topical, do you think the speaker also considered primacy, recency, or complexity? If so, identify which one.

1. PURPOSE STATEMENT: At the end of my speech, the audience will be able to explain three theories about what happened to the dinosaurs.

CENTRAL IDEA: There are at least three distinct theories about what happened to the dinosaurs.

MAIN IDEAS:
   I. A large asteroid hit Earth.
   II. A gradual climate shift occurred.
   III. The level of oxygen in the atmosphere gradually changed.

2. PURPOSE STATEMENT: At the end of my speech, the audience will be able to describe the layout and features of the new university multipurpose sports center.

CENTRAL IDEA: The new university multipurpose sports center will serve the activity needs of the students.

MAIN IDEAS:
   I. The south wing will house an Olympic-size pool.
   II. The center of the building will be a large coliseum.
   III. The north wing will include handball and indoor tennis facilities, as well as rooms for weight lifting and aerobic workouts.

Assessing Your Audience-Centered Speaking Skill

If your topic is controversial and you know or suspect that your audience will be skeptical of or hostile to your ideas, where should you place your most important and/or convincing idea for maximum effectiveness? Explain your answer.

INTEGRATING INTEGRATING YOUR SUPPORTING MATERIAL

8.2 Explain how to integrate supporting material into a speech.

With your main ideas organized, your next task is to integrate your supporting material into a speech. You can organize the supporting material for each main idea according to one of the five common patterns, or according to such strategies as primacy, recency, specificity, complexity, or soft-to-hard evidence.

Key Terms

Thinking Ethically

The principles of primacy and recency are referred to several times in this chapter. If a statistic offers overwhelming evidence of the severity of a given problem, is it ethical for a speaker to save that statistic for last, or should the speaker reveal immediately to the audience how severe the problem is? In other words, is there an ethical distinction between primacy and recency? Discuss your answer.

Thinking Critically

Take notes while listening to either a live or recorded speech. Then organize your notes in standard outline form to reflect the speaker's organization of both main ideas and support material. Try to determine the speaker's organizational strategy, the reasons for it, and its effectiveness.

ORGANIZING YOUR SPEECH FOR THE EARS OF OTHERS: SIGNPOSTING

8.3   Use verbal and nonverbal signposts to organize a speech for the ears of others.

Various types of signposts can help you communicate your organization to your audience. Signposts include verbal and nonverbal transitions, previews, and summaries.

Key Terms

Signposts 164
Preview 164
Initial preview. 164
Internal preview 164
Transition 165
Verbal transition 165
Nonverbal transition 166
Summary 166
Final summary 166
Internal summary 167

Assessing Your Audience-Centered Speaking Skill

Identify and explain three strategies for helping your audience remember the main ideas of your speech.

OUTLINING YOUR SPEECH

8.4   Develop a preparation outline and speaking notes for a speech.

A preparation outline includes your carefully organized main ideas, subpoints, and supporting material; it may also include your specific purpose, introduction, blueprint, internal previews and summaries, transitions, and conclusion. Write each of these elements in complete sentences and standard outline form. Use the preparation outline to begin rehearsing your speech and to help you revise it, if necessary.

After you have rehearsed several times from your preparation outline, you are ready to prepare speaking notes. Although less detailed than a preparation outline, speaking notes usually include supporting material, signposts, and delivery cues.

Key Terms

preparation outline 168
speaking notes 168
mapping 168
standard outline form 169

Thinking Ethically

Can a speaker legitimately claim that a speech is extemporaneous if he or she has constructed a detailed preparation outline? Explain your answer.

Thinking Critically

Geoff plans to deliver his speech using hastily scrawled notes on a sheet of paper torn from his notebook. What advice would you offer him for preparing better speaking notes?

Assessing Your Audience-Centered Speaking Skill

Different instructors have different expectations for outline content and format. Be sure to understand and follow your own instructor's guidelines.

Explore at MyCommunicationLab
Speaker's Workshop: Organizing Your Ideas

9

INTRODUCING AND CONCLUDING YOUR SPEECH

OBJECTIVES

After studying this chapter you should be able to do the following:

9.1
Explain the functions of a speech introduction.

9.2
List and discuss methods for introducing a speech.

9.3
Explain the functions of a speech conclusion.

9.4
List and discuss methods for concluding a speech.

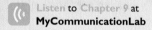

Listen to Chapter 9 at **MyCommunicationLab**

Morris Louis (1912-1962), *Alpha Phi*, 1961. Photo: Tate, London/Art Resource, NY

The average man thinks about what he has said; the above average man about what he is going to say.

—Anonymous

Like all teachers, public-speaking instructors have pet peeves when it comes to their students' work. Of the pet peeves identified by public-speaking teachers in one study, more than 25 percent relate to introductions and conclusions. They include the following:

- Beginning a speech with "OK, ah . . ."
- Apologizing or making excuses at the beginning of the speech for not being prepared
- Beginning a speech with "Hello, my speech is on . . ."
- Saying "In conclusion"
- Ending a speech with "Thank you"
- Ending a speech with "Are there any questions?"[1]

Not every public-speaking instructor considers all of the above to be pet peeves or even tactics to be avoided. But the fact that they appear on this list suggests that you will probably want to consider alternatives. After all, your introduction and conclusion provide your listeners with important first and final impressions of both you and your speech.

Like many speakers, you may think the first task in preparing a speech is to start drafting your introduction. In fact, the introduction is more often the last part of the speech you develop. A key purpose of your introduction is to provide an overview of your message. How can you do that until you know what the message is going to be?

Organizing the body of your speech should precede the crafting of both the introduction and the conclusion. In Chapter 8, we discussed strategies for organizing the body of your speech; using previews, transitions, and summaries to signpost your speech for your audience; and developing a presentation outline and speaking notes. In this chapter we will complete our discussion of speech organization by discussing introductions and conclusions.

> ### CONFIDENTLY CONNECTING WITH YOUR AUDIENCE
>
> #### Be Familiar with Your Introduction and Conclusion
>
> You may feel the most nervous just as you begin your speech. But if you have a well-prepared and well-rehearsed introduction, you'll be able to start with confidence. Rehearse your opening sentences enough times that you can present them while maintaining direct eye contact with your listeners. Being familiar with your conclusion can give you a safe harbor to head for as you end your message. A thoughtfully planned and well-rehearsed introduction and conclusion can help you start and end your speech with poise and assurance.

Purposes of Introductions

9.1 Explain the functions of a speech introduction.

 **Watch** at **MyCommunicationLab**
Video: "Effective Introductions"

Within a few seconds of meeting a person, you form a first impression that is often quite lasting. So, too, do you form a first impression of a speaker and his or her message within the opening seconds of a speech. The introduction may convince you to listen carefully because this is a credible speaker presenting a well-prepared speech, or it may send the message that the speaker is ill-prepared and the message not worth your time. In a ten-minute speech, the introduction will probably last no more than a minute and a half. To say that the introduction needs to be well planned is an understatement, considering how important and yet how brief this portion of any speech is.

As a speaker, your task is to ensure that your introduction convinces your audience to listen to you. As summarized and illustrated in Table 9.1 on page 180, a good introduction must perform five important functions:

- Get the audience's attention.
- Give the audience a reason to listen.

TABLE 9.1 PURPOSES OF YOUR INTRODUCTION

PURPOSE	METHOD
Get the audience's attention.	Use an illustration, a startling fact or statistic, a quotation, humor, a question, a reference to a historical event or to a recent event, a personal reference, a reference to the occasion, or a reference to a preceding speech.
Give the audience a reason to listen.	Tell your listeners how the topic directly affects them.
Introduce the subject.	Present your central idea to your audience.
Establish your credibility.	Offer your credentials. Tell your listeners about your commitment to your topic.
Preview your main ideas.	Tell your audience what you are going to tell them.

- Introduce the subject.
- Establish your credibility.
- Preview your main ideas.

Let's examine each of these five functions in detail.

Get the Audience's Attention

A key purpose of the introduction is to gain favorable attention for your speech. Because listeners form their first impressions of the speech quickly, if the introduction does not capture their attention and cast the speech in a favorable light, the rest of the speech may be wasted on them. The speaker who walks to the podium and drones, "Today I am going to talk to you about . . ." has probably lost most of the audience in those first few boring words. Specific ways to gain the attention of audiences will be discussed later in this chapter.

Watch at **MyCommunicationLab**
Video: "Attention Getting Devices"

We emphasize *favorable* attention for a very good reason. It is possible to gain an audience's attention but in so doing to alienate them or disgust them so that they become irritated instead of interested in what you have to say. For example, a student began a pro-life speech with a graphic description of the abortion process. She caught her audience's attention but made them so uncomfortable that they could hardly concentrate on the rest of her speech.

Another student gave a speech on the importance of donating blood. Without a word, he began by appearing to savagely slash his wrists in front of his stunned audience. As blood spurted, audience members screamed, and one fainted. The blood was real blood, but it wasn't his. The speaker worked at a blood bank, and he was using the bank's blood. He had placed a device under each arm that allowed him to pump out the blood as if from his wrists. He certainly captured his audience's attention! But they never heard his message. The shock and disgust of seeing such a display made that impossible; he did not gain favorable attention.

The moral of our two tales: By all means, be creative in your speech introductions. But also use common sense in deciding how best to gain the favorable attention of your audience. Alienating them is even worse than boring them.

Give the Audience a Reason to Listen

Even after you have captured your listeners' attention, you have to give them some reason to want to listen to the rest of your speech. An unmotivated listener quickly tunes out. You can help establish listening motivation by showing the members of your audience how the topic affects them directly.

In Chapter 7 we presented seven criteria for determining the effectiveness of your supporting material. One of those criteria for determining the effectiveness of your supporting material is *proximity*, the degree to which the information affects your listeners directly. Just as proximity is important to supporting materials, it is also important to speech introductions. "This concerns me" is a powerful reason to listen. Notice how Lauren involved her listeners firsthand with abhorrent labor conditions in Florida tomato fields:

> [If] you've eaten a tomato from a fast-food restaurant, grocery store, or food services business in the last year, you've eaten a tomato picked by the hand of a slave. [She shows two tomatoes to audience.] Can you tell which one? Now I know I'm taking a chance here offering tomatoes to an audience at the beginning of a speech. But the difference between these two is the difference between a fair market and slavery.[2]

Sheena also used proximity to motivate her audience to empathize with people who suffer from exposure to toxic mold:

> Headaches, fatigue, dizziness, and memory impairment seem like ailments that each person in this room has had at one point, right? You stay up late cramming for an exam. The next day, you are fatigued, dizzy, and cannot remember the answers.[3]

It does not matter so much *how* or *when* you demonstrate proximity. But it is essential that, like Lauren and Sheena, you *do* at some point establish that your topic is of vital personal concern to your listeners.

Introduce the Subject

Perhaps the most obvious purpose of an introduction is to introduce the subject of a speech. Within a few seconds after you begin your speech, the audience should have a pretty good idea of what you are going to talk about. Do not get so carried away with jokes or illustrations that you forget this basic purpose. Few things will frustrate your audience more than having to wait until halfway through your speech to figure out what you are talking about! The best way to ensure that your introduction does indeed introduce the subject of your speech is to include a statement of your central idea in the introduction. For example, in introducing his speech on the needs of the aged, this speaker immediately established his subject and central idea:

> If you take away just one thing from what I have to say, I hope you'll come to understand in the next few minutes that the exploding population of seniors demands a conscious, considered, and collaborative response to plan for the health, financial, and social implications of an older population.[4]

Establish Your Credibility

A credible speaker is one whom the audience judges to be a believable authority and a competent speaker. A credible speaker is also someone audience members believe they can trust. As you begin your speech, you should be mindful of your listeners' attitudes toward you. Ask yourself, "Why should they listen to me? What is my background with respect to the topic? Am I personally committed to the issues I am going to speak about?"

Watch at **MyCommunicationLab**
Video: "Generating Credibility"

CONSIDER THE AUDIENCE

Nineteenth-century abolitionist Frederick Douglass was renowned as a great orator. According to biographer Charles W. Chesnutt, Douglass's audiences recognized him as

> a man whose . . . past history gave him the highest right to describe and denounce the iniquities of slavery and contend for the rights of a race.[5]

Likewise, when the Pope travels abroad, people travel great distances and stand for hours in extreme heat or cold to celebrate Mass with him. But most of us cannot take our own credibility for granted when we speak. If you can establish your credibility early in a speech, it will help motivate your audience to listen.

One way to build credibility in the introduction is to be well prepared and to appear confident. Speaking fluently while maintaining eye contact does much to convey a sense of confidence. If you seem to have confidence in yourself, your audience will have confidence in you.

A second way to establish credibility is to tell the audience of your personal experience with your topic. Instead of thinking you boastful, most audience members will listen to you with respect. Twitter CEO Dick Costolo opened his 2013 University of Michigan commencement speech by photographing the graduates, then telling them as he tweeted the photo,

> I'm a professional, so this will only take a second.[6]

Preview Your Main Ideas

Watch at **MyCommunicationLab**
Video: "Transcranial Magnetic Stimulation"

A final purpose of the introduction is to preview the main ideas of your speech. As you saw in Chapter 8, an initial preview statement usually comes near the end of the introduction, included in or immediately following a statement of the central idea. This preview statement allows your listeners to anticipate the main ideas of your speech, which in turn helps ensure that they will remember those ideas after the speech.

As we also noted in Chapter 8, an initial preview statement is an organizational strategy called a *signpost*. Just as signs posted along a highway tell you what is coming up, a signpost in your speech tells the listeners what to expect by enumerating

Dick Costolo, president of Twitter, effectively reinforced his credibility by tweeting a photo of the graduates during the introduction to his graduation address at the University of Michigan.

Photo: Todd McInturf/*The Detroit News*/AP Images

the ideas or points that you plan to present. If, for example, you were giving a speech about racial profiling, you might say,

> To end these crimes against color, we must first paint an accurate picture of the problem, then explore the causes, and finally establish solutions that will erase the practice of racial profiling.[7]

Identifying your main ideas helps organize the message and enhances listeners' learning.

The introduction to your speech, then, should get your audience's attention, give the audience a reason to listen, introduce the subject, establish your credibility, and preview your main ideas. All this—and brevity too—may seem impossible to achieve. But it isn't!

Effective Introductions

9.2   List and discuss methods for introducing a speech.

With a little practice, you will be able to write satisfactory central ideas and preview statements. It may be more difficult to gain your audience's attention and give them a reason to listen to you. Fortunately, there are several effective methods for developing speech introductions. Not every method is appropriate for every speech, but chances are that you can discover among these alternatives at least one type of introduction to fit the topic and purpose of your speech, whatever they might be.

We will discuss ten ways of introducing a speech:

- Illustrations or anecdotes
- Startling facts or statistics
- Quotations
- Humor
- Questions
- References to historical events
- References to recent events
- Personal references
- References to the occasion
- References to preceding speeches

Illustrations or Anecdotes

Not surprisingly, because it is the most inherently interesting type of supporting material, an illustration or **anecdote** can provide the basis for an effective speech introduction. In fact, if you have an especially compelling illustration that you had planned to use in the body of the speech, you might do well to use it in your introduction instead. A relevant and interesting anecdote will introduce your subject and almost invariably gain an audience's attention. Student speaker Matt opened his speech on the dangers associated with the chemical BPA with this extended illustration:

> Three years ago Algeta McDonald's life was taken by breast cancer. She was an absolutely amazing Italian-American woman, who was completely stubborn, but she always brought out the best in anyone she was around. Here was a woman who always ate proper foods and was conscientious of her health in general, every day of her life.
>
> Ask anyone who knew her well what their favorite memory of Algeta was, and I can almost guarantee it's of her carrying around a bright red Nalgene water bottle. This way, she could get her 64 daily ounces of water with certainty. Unfortunately, this happy memory of how she always had her water bottle might change with some information that has come to light recently.[8]

anecdote
An illustration or story

Matt's story effectively captured the attention of his audience and introduced the subject of his speech.

Startling Facts or Statistics

Watch at **MyCommunicationLab**
Video: "Interstate Commerce Clause"

A second method of introducing a speech is to use a startling fact or statistic. Startling an audience with the extent of a situation or problem invariably catches listeners' attention, motivates them to listen further, and helps them remember afterward what you had to say. Will's audience of prospective law students must have been startled to attention by the statistics in his introduction:

> 98 percent of the 2012 graduates of the Thomas Jefferson School of Law in San Diego, California, graduated with an average of $168,800 in student debt.[9]

Quotations

Watch at **MyCommunicationLab**
Video: "Investing in Our Future"

Using an appropriate quotation to introduce a speech is a common practice. Often another writer or speaker has expressed an opinion on your topic that is more authoritative, comprehensive, or memorable than what you can say. Terrika opened her speech on the importance of community with a quotation from poet Johari Kungufu:

> Sisters, Men
> What are we doin?
> What about the babies, our children?
> When we was real we never had orphans or children in joints.
> Come spirits
> drive out the nonsense from our minds and the crap from our dreams
> make us remember what we need, that children are the next life.
> bring us back to the real
> bring us back to the real

> "The Real." Johari Kungufu, in her poem, specifically alludes to a time in African history when children were not confused about who they were.[10]

A different kind of quotation, this one from an expert, was chosen by another speaker to introduce the topic of the disappearance of childhood in America:

> "As a distinctive childhood culture wastes away, we watch with fascination and dismay." This insight of Neil Postman, author of *Disappearance of Childhood*, raised a poignant point. Childhood in America is vanishing.[11]

Because the expert was not widely recognized, the speaker included a brief statement of his qualifications. This authority "said it in a nutshell"—he expressed in concise language the central idea of the speech.

Although a quote can effectively introduce a speech, do not fall into the lazy habit of turning to a collection of quotations every time you need an introduction. There are so many other interesting, and sometimes better, ways to introduce a speech that quotes should be used only if they are extremely interesting, compelling, or very much to the point.

Like the methods of organization discussed in Chapter 8, the methods of introduction are not mutually exclusive. Very often, two or three are effectively combined in a single introduction. For example, Thad combined a quotation and an illustration for this effective introduction to a speech on the funeral industry:

> "Dying is a very dull, dreary affair. And my advice to you is to have nothing whatsoever to do with it." These lingering words by British playwright Somerset

Maugham were meant to draw a laugh. Yet the ironic truth to the statement has come to epitomize the grief of many, including Jan Berman of Martha's Vineyard. In a recent interview with National Public Radio, we learn that Ms. Berman desired to have a home funeral for her mother. She possessed a burial permit and was legally within her rights. But when a local funeral director found out, he lied to her, telling her that what she was doing was illegal.[12]

Humor

Humor, handled well, can be a wonderful attention-getter. It can help relax your audience and win their goodwill for the rest of the speech. University of Texas Professor of Journalism Marvin Olasky told this humorous story to open a speech on disaster response:

> Let me begin with a Texas story about how officials do offer help. It starts with a mom on a farm looking out the window. She sees the family cow munching on grass and her daughter talking with a strange man. The mom furiously yells out the window, "Didn't I tell you not to talk to strangers? You come in this house right now." The girl offers a protest: "But mama, this man says he's a United States senator." The wise mother replies, "In that case, come in this house right now, and bring the cow in with you."
> Let's talk about responses to disaster.[13]

Another speaker used humor to express appreciation for being invited to speak to a group by beginning his speech with this story:

> Three corporate executives were trying to define the word *fame*.
> One said, "Fame is getting invited to the White House to see the President."
> The second one said, "Fame is being invited to the White House and while you are visiting, the phone rings and he doesn't answer it."
> The third executive said, "You're both wrong. Fame is being invited to the White House to visit with the President when his Hot Line rings. He answers it, listens a minute, and then says, 'Here, it's for you!'"
> Being asked to speak today is like being in the White House and the call's for me.[14]

Humor can be an effective way to catch your audience's attention in your introduction. Remember, however, to use humor appropriate to the occasion and the audience.
Photo: Masterfile

Humor need not always be the slapstick comedy of the Three Stooges. It does not even have to be a joke. It may take more subtle forms, such as irony or incredulity. When General Douglas MacArthur, an honor graduate of the U.S. Military Academy at West Point, returned to West Point in 1962, he delivered his now-famous "Farewell to the Cadets." He opened that speech with this humorous illustration:

> As I was leaving the hotel this morning, a doorman asked me, "Where are you bound for, General?" And when I replied, "West Point," he remarked, "Beautiful place. Have you ever been there before?"[15]

MacArthur's brief illustration caught the audience's attention and made them laugh—in short, it was an effective way to open the speech.

If your audience is linguistically diverse or composed primarily of listeners whose first language is not English, you may want to choose an introduction strategy other than humor. Because much humor is created by verbal plays on words, people who do not speak English as their native language may not perceive the humor in an anecdote or quip that you intended to be funny. And humor rarely translates well, as is evident from the following anecdote:

> . . . an Australian news anchor who was interviewing the Dalai Lama with the aid of an interpreter opened the exchange with a joke: "The Dalai Lama walks into a pizza shop and says, 'Can you make me one with everything?'" His Holiness's baffled stare, viewed by nearly two million people on YouTube, presents a lesson in the risks of translating humor.[16]

Just as certain audiences may preclude your use of a humorous introduction, so may certain subjects—for example, Sudden Infant Death Syndrome and rape. Used with discretion, however, humor can provide a lively, interesting, and appropriate introduction for many speeches.

Questions

Watch at **MyCommunicationLab**
Video: "Learn CPR"

Remember the pet peeves listed at the beginning of this chapter? Another pet peeve for some is beginning a speech with a question ("How many of you . . . ?"). The problem is not so much the strategy itself but the lack of mindfulness in the "How many of you?" phrasing.

A thoughtful **rhetorical question**, on the other hand, can prompt your listeners' mental participation in your introduction, getting their attention and giving them a reason to listen. President and CEO of Coca-Cola, Muhtar Kent, began a speech to investors and financial analysts by asking,

> Are we ready for tomorrow, today?[17]

And Richard opened his speech on teenage suicide with this simple question:

> Have you ever been alone in the dark?[18]

rhetorical question
A question intended to provoke thought rather than elicit an answer

To turn questions into an effective introduction, the speaker must do more than just think of good questions to ask. He or she must also deliver the questions effectively. Effective delivery includes pausing briefly after each question so that audience members have time to try to formulate a mental answer. After all, the main advantage of questions as an introductory technique is to hook the audience by getting them to engage in a mental dialogue with you. You may look down at your notes while you ask the question, but effective delivery requires looking back up to reestablish eye contact with listeners. As we discuss in Chapter 11, eye contact signals that the communication channel is open. Establishing eye contact with your audience following a question gives them additional motivation to think of an answer.

Although it does not happen frequently, an audience member may blurt out a vocal response to a question intended to be rhetorical. If you plan to open a speech with a rhetorical question, be aware of this possibility, and plan appropriate reactions. If the topic is light, a Jay Leno–style return quip may win over the audience and turn the interruption into an asset. If the topic is more serious or the interruption is inappropriate or contrary to what you expected, you might reply with something like "Perhaps most of the rest of you were thinking . . .," or you might answer the question yourself.

Questions are commonly combined with another method of introduction. For example, University of Akron president Luis Proenza opened a speech on new strategies for success in higher education with a question followed by a startling statistic:

> What if the airplane had advanced as far and as fast as the computer? Today's jumbo jet would carry one hundred thousand passengers, and it would fly them to the moon and back for $12.50 at 23,400 miles per hour.[19]

Either by themselves or in tandem with another method of introduction, questions can provide effective openings for speeches. Like quotations, however, questions can also be crutches for speakers who have not taken the time to explore other options. Unless you can think of a truly engaging question, work to develop one of the other introduction strategies.

References to Historical Events

What American is not familiar with the opening line of Lincoln's classic Gettysburg Address: "Four score and seven years ago, our fathers brought forth on this continent a new nation, conceived in liberty, and dedicated to the proposition that all men are created equal"? Lincoln's famous opening sentence refers to the historical context of his speech. You, too, may find a way to begin a speech by making a reference to a historic event.

Every day is the anniversary of something. Perhaps you could begin a speech by drawing a relationship between a historic event that happened on this day and your speech objective. Executive speechwriter Cynthia Starks illustrated this strategy in a speech delivered on February 16:

> On this date—Feb. 16, 1923—archeologist Howard Carter entered the burial chamber of King Tutankhamen. There he found a solid gold coffin, Tut's intact mummy, and priceless treasures.
>
> On Feb. 16, 1959, Fidel Castro took over the Cuban government 45 days after overthrowing Fulvencia Battista.
>
> And America's first 9-1-1 emergency phone system went live in Haleyville, Alabama, on Feb. 16, 1968.
>
> Today, I won't be revealing priceless treasures. I promise not to overthrow anyone, or generate any 9-1-1 calls. But I do hope to reveal a few speechwriting secrets, provide a little revolutionary thinking and a sense of urgency about the speeches you ought to be giving.[20]

How do you discover anniversaries of historic events? You could consult "This Day in History" online or download it as an app for your tablet or smartphone.

References to Recent Events

If your topic is timely, a reference to a recent event can be a good way to begin your speech. An opening taken from a recent news story can take the form of an illustration, a startling statistic, or even a quotation, gaining the additional advantages discussed under each of those methods of introduction. Moreover, referring to a recent event increases your credibility by showing that you are knowledgeable about current affairs.

"Recent" does not necessarily mean a story that broke just last week or even last month. An event that occurred within the past year or so can be considered recent. Even a particularly significant event that is slightly older can qualify. The key, says one speaker,

> is to avoid being your grandfather. No more stories about walking up hill both ways to school with a musket on your back and seventeen Redcoats chasing you. Be in the now, and connect with your audience.[21]

Personal References

A reference to yourself can take several forms. You might express appreciation or pleasure at having been asked to speak, as did this speaker:

> I am delighted to participate in this engaging meeting at my graduate alma mater.[22]

Or you might share a personal experience, as did this speaker:

> Like some of you in the audience, I've held many jobs before finding my true calling, from washing cars to waiting tables and taking care of animals. . . .[23]

Although personal references take a variety of forms, what they do best, in all circumstances, is to establish a bond between you and your audience.

References to the Occasion

References to the occasion are often made at weddings, birthday parties, dedication ceremonies, and other such events. For example, New Jersey Governor Chris Christie opened his 2013 "state of the state" address this way:

> Since George Washington delivered the first State of the Union in New York on this day in 1790, it has been the tradition of executive leaders to report on the condition of the nation and state at the beginning of the legislative year. So it is my honor and pleasure to give you this report on the state of our state.[24]

The reference to the occasion can also be combined with other methods of introduction, such as an illustration or a rhetorical question.

References to Preceding Speeches

If your speech is one of several being presented on the same occasion, such as in a speech class, at a symposium, or as part of a lecture series, you will usually not know until shortly before your own speech what other speakers will say. Few experiences will make your stomach sink faster than hearing a speaker just ahead of you speak on your topic. Worse still, that speaker may even use some of the same supporting materials you had planned to use.

When this situation occurs, you must decide on the spot whether referring to one of those previous speeches will be better than using the introduction you originally prepared. It may be wise to refer to a preceding speech when another speaker has spoken on a topic so related to your own that you can draw an analogy. In a sense, your introduction then becomes a transition from that earlier speech to yours. Here is an example of an introduction delivered by a fast-thinking student speaker under such circumstances:

> When Juli talked to us about her experiences as a lifeguard, she stressed that the job was not as glamorous as many of us imagine. Today I want to tell you about another job that appears to be more glamorous than it is—a job that I have held for two years. I am a bartender at the Rathskeller.[25]

As you plan your introduction, remember that any combination of the methods just discussed is possible. With a little practice, you will become confident at choosing from several good possibilities as you prepare your introduction.

Purposes of Conclusions

 9.3 Explain the functions of a speech conclusion.

Your introduction creates an important first impression; your conclusion leaves an equally important final impression. Long after you finish speaking, your audience is likely to remember the effect, if not the content, of your closing remarks.

Unfortunately, many speakers pay less attention to their conclusions than to any other part of their speeches. They believe that if they can get through the first 90 percent of a speech, they can think of some way to conclude it. Perhaps you have had the experience of listening to a speaker who failed to plan a conclusion. Awkward final seconds of stumbling for words may be followed by hesitant applause from an audience that is not even sure the speech is over. It is hardly the best way to leave people who came to listen to you.

An effective conclusion will serve two purposes: It will summarize the speech and provide closure.

Summarize the Speech

A conclusion is a speaker's last chance to review his or her central idea and main ideas for the audience.

 **Watch** at **MyCommunicationLab** **Video:** "Using Recapping/Summary"

Reemphasize the Central Idea in a Memorable Way The conclusions of many famous speeches rephrase the central idea in a memorable way. When on July 4, 1939, New York Yankees legend Lou Gehrig addressed his fans in an emotional farewell to a baseball career cut short by a diagnosis of ALS (amyotrophic lateral sclerosis), he concluded with the memorable line,

> I may have had a tough break, but I have an awful lot to live for.[26]

Speechwriting instructor and former speechwriter Robert Lehrman identifies a more recent memorable conclusion, that of Barack Obama's 2008 presidential victory speech:

> that long closing story about Ann Nixon Cooper, the 106-year-old woman whose life encapsulated the history of the 20th century ("a man touched down on the moon . . . she touched her finger to a screen and cast her vote . . .").[27]

Lehrman notes, "When I teach that speech, students stop texting and start crying."

But memorable endings are not the exclusive property of famous speakers. With practice, most people can prepare similarly effective conclusions. Chapter 10 offers ideas for using language to make your statements more memorable. As a preliminary

The Watch at MyCommunicationLab Video: "Effective Conclusions"

example of the memorable use of language, here is how Noelle concluded her speech on phony academic institutions on the Internet:

> What we have learned from all this is that we, and only we, have the power to stop [fraudulent learning institutions]. So we don't get www.conned.[28]

This speaker's clever play on "dot.com" helped her audience remember her topic and central idea.

The end of your speech is your last chance to impress the central idea on your audience. Do it in such a way that they cannot help but remember it.

Restate the Main Ideas In addition to reemphasizing the central idea of the speech, the conclusion is also likely to restate the main ideas. Note how John effectively summarized the main ideas of his speech on emissions tampering, casting the summary as an expression of his fears about the problem and the actions that could ease those fears:

> I'm frightened. Frightened that nothing I could say would encourage the 25 percent of emissions-tampering Americans to change their ways and correct the factors that cause their autos to pollute disproportionately. Frightened that the American public will not respond to a crucial issue unless the harms are both immediate and observable. Frightened that the EPA will once again prove very sympathetic to industry. Three simple steps will alleviate my fear: inspection, reduction in lead content, and, most importantly, awareness.[29]

Most speakers summarize their main ideas in the first part of the conclusion or as part of the transition between the body of the speech and its conclusion.

Provide Closure

Probably the most obvious purpose of a conclusion is to bring **closure**—to cue the audience that the speech is coming to an end by making it "sound finished."

Use Verbal or Nonverbal Cues to Signal the End of the Speech You can attain closure both verbally and nonverbally. Verbal techniques include using such transitional words and phrases as "finally," "for my last point," and perhaps even "in conclusion."

You may remember that "in conclusion" appears on that list of instructors' pet peeves at the beginning of the chapter. Like opening your speech by asking a rhetorical question, signaling your closing by saying "in conclusion" is not inherently wrong. It is a pet peeve of some instructors because of the carelessness with which student speakers often use it. Such a cue gives listeners unspoken permission to tune out. (Notice what students do when their professor signals the end of class: Books and notebooks slam shut, pens are stowed away, and the class generally stops listening.) A concluding transition needs to be followed quickly by the final statement of the speech.

You can also signal closure with nonverbal cues. You may want to pause between the body of your speech and its conclusion, slow your speaking rate, move out from behind a podium to make a final impassioned plea to your audience, or signal with falling vocal inflection that you are making your final statement.

Motivate the Audience to Respond Another way to provide closure to your speech is to motivate your audience to respond in some way. If your speech is informative, you may want your audience to take some sort of appropriate action—write a letter, buy a product, make a telephone call, or get involved in a cause. In fact, an *action* step is essential to the persuasive organizational strategy called the motivated sequence, which we discuss in Chapter 15.

closure
The quality of a conclusion that makes a speech "sound finished"

At the close of her speech on negligent landlords, Melanie included a simple audience response as part of her action step:

> By a show of hands, how many people in this room rely on rental housing? Look around. It's a problem that affects us all, if not directly, then through a majority of our friends. . . .[30]

Another speaker ended a speech to an audience of travel agents by recommending these specific action steps:

- Continuously develop and improve your professional and business skills.
- Embrace and utilize the new technologies. You are either riding on the new technology highway, or you are standing in the dust, left behind.
- Continuously build and strengthen your top industry organizations locally and nationally so their brands, endorsement, and influence can work powerfully on your behalf.
- Develop a passion for this business and inspire the same in your employees and co-workers.[31]

In both of the preceding examples, the speakers draw on the principle of proximity, discussed in this chapter, to motivate their audiences. When audience members feel that they are or could be personally involved or affected, they are more likely to respond to your message.

Effective Conclusions

Effective conclusions may employ illustrations, quotations, personal references, or any of the other methods of introduction we have discussed. In addition, there are at least two other distinct ways of concluding a speech: with references to the introduction and with inspirational appeals or challenges.

Methods Also Used for Introductions

Any of the methods of introduction discussed earlier can also help you conclude your speech. Quotations, for example, are frequently used in conclusions, as in this commencement address by U2 lead singer Bono:

> Remember what John Adams said about Ben Franklin: "He does not hesitate at our boldest measures but rather seems to think us too irresolute."
>
> Well, this is the time for bold measures. This is the country, and you are the generation.[32]

References to the Introduction

In our discussion of closure, we mentioned referring to the introduction as a way to end a speech. Finishing a story, answering a rhetorical question, or reminding the audience of the startling fact or statistic you presented in the introduction are excellent ways to provide closure. Like bookends at either side of a group of books on your desk, a related introduction and conclusion provide unified support for the ideas in between.

9.4 List and discuss methods for concluding a speech.

 Watch at **MyCommunicationLab Video:** "Conclusions"

 Read at **MyCommunicationLab Learning From Great Speakers:** Patrick Henry

TECHNIQUES FOR EFFECTIVE CONCLUSIONS

- Use any of the techniques for an effective introduction.
- Refer to the introduction of your speech.
- Issue an inspirational appeal or a challenge.

Earlier in this chapter, you read the extended illustration Matt used to open his speech on the dangers associated with BPA. He concluded the speech by referring to that introduction:

What would Algeta have said to me if I were to tell her that her healthy lifestyle would be the reason that she would die one day? Well, she was my grandmother. I knew her very well, and she was completely stubborn, so she would have called me crazy . . . but today I'm going to let you decide what her answer should have been.[33]

Matt's conclusion alludes to his introduction to make his speech memorable, to motivate his audience to respond, and to provide closure.

Inspirational Appeals or Challenges

Another way to end your speech is to issue an inspirational appeal or challenge to your listeners, rousing them to an emotional pitch at the conclusion of the speech. The conclusion becomes the climax. Speechwriter and communication consultant James W. Robinson explains why such conclusions can work well:

It's almost as if, for a few brief moments [the audience] escape from the stressful demands of our high-pressure world and welcome your gifts: insightful vision, persuasive rhetoric, a touch of philosophy, a little emotion, and yes, even a hint of corniness.[34]

NBC news anchor Brian Williams' concluded his commencement address to graduates of Elon College in a memorable way, with an emotional appeal that included throwing a baseball to his son, who was one of the graduates.
Photo: H. SCOTT HOFFMANN/News & Record

One famous example of a concluding inspiration appeal comes from Martin Luther King Jr.'s "Dream" speech, for which you can read the entire transcript in Appendix B. That King's conclusion was both inspiring and memorable has been affirmed by the growing fame of his closing passage through the years since he delivered the speech.

In his 2013 commencement speech to the graduates of Elon University, which included his son Doug, NBC anchor Brian Williams talked about his recent visit to tornado-devastated Moore, Oklahoma. Williams told the graduates that he had met there with a father whose 9-year-old son had been killed by the tornado. As he concluded his speech, Williams noted that the Oklahoma father would give anything he had simply to be able to toss a baseball back and forth with his lost son. Williams then produced a baseball from under his ceremonial robes and tossed it to his own son, proposing that the two have a game of catch when they returned home after the ceremony. Conscious of his entire audience, Williams ended the speech after this powerful symbolic gesture by affirming to listeners that tragedies, as well as joyful events such as graduations, can serve as reminders to us all to be mindful of the importance of how and with whom we choose to spend our time.[35]

King's and Williams's inspiring conclusions reemphasized their central ideas in a memorable way, provided closure to their speeches, and inspired their listeners.

STUDY GUIDE   REVIEW, APPLY, AND ASSESS

PURPOSES OF INTRODUCTIONS

9.1   Explain the functions of a speech introduction.

It is important to begin and end your speech in a way that is memorable and that also provides the repetition audiences need. A good introduction gets the audience's attention, gives the audience a reason to listen, introduces your subject, establishes your credibility, and previews your main ideas.

Introducing your subject and previewing the body of your speech can be accomplished by including your central idea and initial preview statement in the introduction.

Assessing Your Audience-Centered Speaking Skill

How could you motivate your classroom audience to listen to you on each of the following topics?

- Cholesterol
- Elvis Presley
- The history of greeting cards
- Ozone depletion
- Distracted driving

EFFECTIVE INTRODUCTIONS

9.2   List and discuss methods for introducing a speech.

You can gain favorable attention and provide a motivation for listening by using any of the following, alone or in combination: illustrations, startling facts or statistics, quotations, humor, questions, references to historical events, references to recent events, personal references, references to the occasion, or references to preceding speeches, as appropriate.

Key Terms

Thinking Ethically

Marty and Shanna, who are in the same section of a public-speaking class, are discussing their upcoming speeches. Marty has discovered an illustration that she thinks will make an effective introduction. When she tells Shanna about it, Shanna is genuinely enthusiastic. In fact, she thinks it would make a great introduction for her own speech, which is on a different topic. When the students are given schedules for their speeches, Shanna realizes that she will speak before Marty. She badly wants to use the introductory illustration that Marty has discovered. Can she ethically do so, if she cites in her speech the original source of the illustration?

Thinking Critically

Nakai is planning to give his informative speech on Native American music, displaying and demonstrating the use of such instruments as the flute, the Taos drum, and the Yaqui rain stick. How might Nakai best introduce his speech?

PURPOSES OF CONCLUSIONS

9.3   Explain the functions of a speech conclusion.

Your speech's conclusion leaves the final impression of you in your listeners' minds. The two main purposes of the conclusion are to summarize your speech and to provide closure. Your summary should rephrase your central idea in a way that your audience will remember, and it should repeat your main ideas to fix them in the minds of your listeners. Verbal and nonverbal clues that the speech is ending will help to provide your audience with closure. You can also use the conclusion as an opportunity to suggest an action to your audience to motivate your audience to respond in some way to your message.

Key Term

EFFECTIVE CONCLUSIONS

9.4   List and discuss methods for concluding a speech.

Conclusions may take any one of the forms used for introductions. In addition, you can refer to the introduction or make inspirational appeals or challenges.

Thinking Critically

Knowing that you have recently visited the Vietnam Veterans Memorial in Washington, D.C., your American history professor asks you to make a brief presentation to the class about the Wall: its history; its symbolic meaning; and its impact on the families, comrades, and friends of those memorialized there. Write both an introduction and a conclusion for this speech.

✳ Explore at **MyCommunicationLab**
Speaker's Workshop: Developing the
Introduction and Conclusion to Your Speech

Listen to Chapter 10 at **MyCommunicationLab**

Ivan Albertovich Puni (1894–1956), *Flight of Forms* (1919). Photo: The Museum of Modern Art/Licensed by SCALA/Art Resource, NY

A speech is poetry: cadence, rhythm, imagery, sweep! A speech reminds us that words, like children, have the power to make dance the dullest beanbag of a heart.

—Peggy Noonan

I n Figure 10.1 are photos of protest signs that were never intended to be funny.[1] They illustrate that using language accurately, clearly, and effectively can be a challenge, even to those engaging in the impassioned exercise of free speech.

For public speakers, like protestors, it is important to communicate messages both clearly and accurately. At the same time, it is also important to present those messages in such a way that your audience will listen to, remember, and perhaps act on what you have to say.

In this chapter we will focus on the power of language. We will suggest ways to communicate your messages to others accurately and effectively. We will also discuss how the choice of words   word structures can help give your messages distinctive style.

FIGURE 10.1 Sometimes our word choices are unintentionally amusing.

Photo: Natalie Fobes/CORBIS

Photo: Ed Lefkowicz/Demotix/Demotix/Corbis

Photo: Mark Rightmire/ZUMA Press/Corbis

10.1 Describe three differences between oral and written language styles.

Differentiating Oral and Written Language Styles

Your instructor has probably told you not to write your speech out word for word. The professor has said this because there are at least three major differences between oral and written language styles.

- **Oral Style Is More Personal Than Written Style** When speaking, you can look your listeners in the eye and talk to them directly. That personal contact affects your speech and your verbal style. As a speaker, you are likely to use more pronouns (*I, you*) than you would in writing. You are also more likely to address specific audience members by name.

- **Oral Style Is Less Formal Than Written Style** Memorized speeches usually sound as if they were written because the words and phrases are longer, more complex, and more formal than those used by most speakers. Oral style, on the other hand, is characterized by "looser construction, repetition, rephrasing, and comment clauses ('you know'). . . ."[2]

  However, there are great variations within both oral and written styles. One speech may be quite personal and informal, whereas another may have characteristics more often associated with written style. The personality of the speaker or writer, the subject of the discourse, the audience, and the occasion all affect the style of the language used.

- **Oral Style Is More Repetitive Than Written Style** When you don't understand something you are reading in a book or an article, you can stop and reread a passage, look up unfamiliar words in the dictionary, or ask someone for help. When you're listening to a speech, those opportunities usually aren't available. For this reason, an oral style is and should be more repetitive.

  When you study how to organize a speech, you learn to preview main ideas in your introduction, develop your ideas in the body of the speech, and summarize these same ideas in the conclusion. You build in repetition to make sure that your listener will grasp your message. Even during the process of developing an idea, it is sometimes necessary to state it first, restate it in a different way, provide an example, and, finally, summarize it.

RECAP

ORAL VERSUS WRITTEN STYLE

Written style	Less personal, with no immediate interaction between writer and reader
	More formal
	Less repetitive
Oral style	More personal, facilitating interaction between speaker and audience
	Less formal
	More repetitive

10.2 List and explain three ways to use words effectively.

Explore at MyCommunicationLab
Activity: "Language"

Using Words Effectively

Although your speech will be more personal, less formal, and more repetitive than would a paper you might write on the same topic, you will still want to ensure that your message is clear, accurate, and memorable. Your spoken words should be specific, concrete, simple, and correct.

Explore at MyCommunicationLab
Activity: "Power of Words"

Use Specific, Concrete Words

If you were to describe your pet snake to an audience, you would need to do more than say it is a serpent. Instead, you would want to use the most specific term possible, describing your snake as a ball python or, if you were speaking to an audience of scientists, perhaps as a *Python regius*. A specific word or term such as *ball python* refers to an individual member of a class of more general things, such as *serpent* or *snake*.

Specific words are often concrete words, which appeal to one of our five senses, whereas general words are often abstract words, which refer to ideas or qualities. A linguistic theory known as *general semantics* holds that the more concrete your words are, the clearer your communication will be. Semanticists use a continuum called a **ladder of abstraction** to model how something can be described in either concrete or abstract language. Figure 10.2 shows an example of a ladder of abstraction: The words are most abstract at the top of the ladder and become more concrete as you move down the ladder.

Specific, concrete nouns create memorable images, as in this speech delivered by a Wake Forest University student:

> Sometimes when I sleep, I can still hear the voices of my life—night crickets, lions' mating calls, my father's advice, my friend's laughter; I can still hear the voices of Africa.[3]

Specific, concrete verbs can be especially effective. The late Representative Barbara Jordan of Texas, whose language skills one speechwriter describes as "legendary," recognized the power of concrete verbs.[4] For example, the first draft of a passage in her 1992 Democratic National Convention keynote stated:

> The American dream is not dead. It is injured, it is sick, but it is not dead.

Jordan revised the line to read:

> The American dream is not dead. It is gasping for breath, but it is not dead.

The concrete verb phrase "gasping for breath" brings alive the image Jordan intended to create.

When searching for a specific, concrete word, you may want to consult a thesaurus. But in searching for an alternative word, do not feel that you have to choose the most obscure or unusual term to vary your description. Simple language will often evoke the most vivid image for your listeners.

Use Simple Words

The best language is often the simplest. Your words should be immediately understandable to your listeners. Don't try to impress them with jargon and pompous language. Instead, as linguist Paul Roberts advises,

> Decide what you want to say and say it as vigorously as possible . . . and in plain words.[5]

In his classic essay "Politics and the English Language," George Orwell lists rules for clear writing, including this prescription for simplicity:

> Never use a long word where a short one will do. If it is possible to cut a word out, always cut it out. Never use a foreign phrase, a scientific word, or a jargon word if you can think of an everyday English equivalent.[6]

Make audio or video recordings of your practice sessions. As you review the recording, listen for chances to express yourself with simpler and fewer words. Used wisely, simple words communicate with great power and precision.

Use Words Correctly

> I was listening to the car radio one day when a woman reading the news referred to someone as a suede-o-intellectual. I pondered through three traffic lights until I realized she wasn't talking about shoes, but a pseudointellectual.[7]

FIGURE 10.2 A "ladder of abstraction" is used by semanticists to show how a concept, idea, or thing can be described in either concrete or abstract terms.

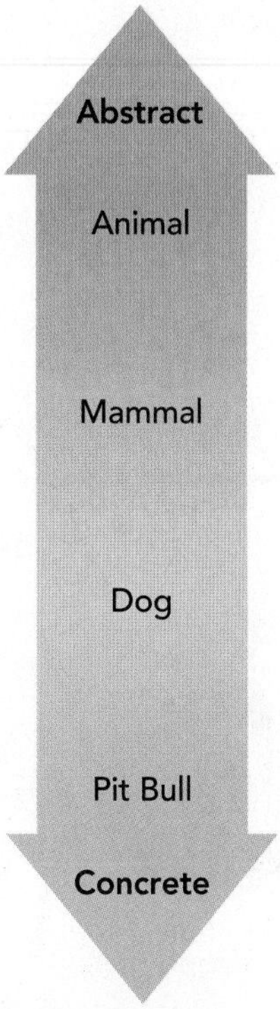

Abstract

Animal

Mammal

Dog

Pit Bull

Concrete

Copyrighted by Pearson Education, Upper Saddle River, NJ

ladder of abstraction
Continuum model of abstract and concrete words for a concept, idea, or thing

Explore at **MyCommunicationLab**
Activity: "Verbal Communication"

A public speech is not the place to demonstrate your lack of familiarity with English vocabulary and grammar. In fact, your effectiveness with your audience depends in part on your ability to use the English language correctly. If you are unsure of the way to apply a grammatical rule, seek assistance from a good English usage handbook. If you are unsure of a word's pronunciation or meaning, use a dictionary. Major online dictionaries provide recordings of the correct pronunciation of words.

Language operates on two levels, and perhaps the greatest challenge to using words correctly is remaining aware of connotations as well as denotations.

Denotation   The **denotation** of a word is its literal meaning, the definition you find in a dictionary. For example, the denotation of the word *notorious* is "famous."

Connotation   The **connotation** of a word is not usually found in a dictionary, but it consists of the meaning we associate with the word, based on our experiences. *Notorious* connotes fame for some dire deed. *Notorious* and *famous* are not really interchangeable. It is just as important to consider the connotations of the words you use as it is to consider the denotations.

Sometimes connotations are personal. For example, the word *table* is defined denotatively as a piece of furniture consisting of a smooth, flat slab affixed on legs. But when you think of the word *table*, you may think of the old oak *table* your grandparents used to have; *table* may evoke for you an image of playing checkers with your grandmother. This is a personal connotation of the word, a unique meaning based on your own experiences. Personal meanings are difficult to predict, but as a public speaker you should be aware of the possibility of triggering audience members' personal connotations. This awareness is particularly important when you are discussing highly emotional or controversial topics.

And finally, if your audience includes people whose first language is not English, to whom the nuances of connotation may not be readily apparent, it may be necessary to explain your intentions in more detail rather than rely on word associations.

Use Words Concisely

Concise does not necessarily mean "short"; rather, it means "succinct" or "to the point." Research suggests that people who use fewer words are perceived by listeners as more powerful or credible, a perception that may be especially helpful to persuasive speakers.[8] In other words, your goal should be to use only as many words as are necessary to convey your message. Consider the following suggestions for using language concisely.

Eliminate Words and Phrases That Add No Meaning to Your Message   Concise language helps your audience follow your organization and can enhance your credibility. Here are phrases you can always eliminate from a speech:

"In my opinion" (just state the opinion)

"And all that" (meaningless)

"When all is said and done" (just say it)

"As a matter of fact" (just state the fact)

"Before I begin, I'd like to say" (you've already begun—just say it)

Phrases such as these are known as clichés. A **cliché** is an overused expression that has become meaningless and perhaps even irritating; using a cliché can make listeners "start tuning out and completely miss the message."[9] One recent list of annoying clichés includes "at the end of the day," "user-friendly," "with all due respect," and "Your call is important to us."[10] Substitute specific, concrete words for clichés.

denotation
The literal meaning of a word

connotation
The meaning listeners associate with a word, based on their experience

concise
Succinct or to the point

cliché
An overused expression

Avoid Narrating Your Speaking Technique There's no need to say, "Here's an interesting story that I think you will like." Just tell the story. Instead of saying, "I'd like to now offer several facts about this matter," just state the facts. Yes, it's useful to provide signposts and internal summaries throughout your message—redundancy is needed in oral messages—but be careful not to provide a cluttering narration about the techniques you're using.

Avoid a Long Phrase When a Short One Will Do

Instead of saying . . .	Say . . .
So, for that reason	So
But at the same time	But
In today's society	Today
Due to the fact	Because
In the course of	During
In the final analysis	Finally

> **RECAP**
>
> ## USING WORDS EFFECTIVELY
>
> To hold your audience's attention, keep your language specific and concrete.
>
> To keep your language simple, avoid a long word when a short one will do.
>
> To use your language correctly, consider connotative as well as denotative meanings.
>
> To speak clearly, be as concise as possible.

Adapting Your Language Style to Diverse Listeners

10.3 Discuss how to adapt your language style to diverse listeners.

To communicate successfully with the diverse group of listeners who comprise your audience, make sure your language is understandable, appropriate, and unbiased.

Use Language That Your Audience Can Understand

Even if you and all your public-speaking classmates speak English, you probably speak many varieties of the language. Perhaps some of your classmates speak in an **ethnic vernacular**, such as "Spanglish," an informal combination of English and Spanish often heard near the United States–Mexico border; Cajun, with its influx of French words, frequently spoken in Louisiana; or African American Vernacular English (AAVE). Some of you may reflect where you grew up by your use of **regionalisms**, words or phrases specific to one part of the country but rarely used in quite the same way in other places. Others of you may frequently use **jargon**, the specialized language of your profession or hobby.

When you give a speech to those who share your ethnic, regional, or professional background, you can communicate successfully with them using these specialized varieties of English. However, when you give a speech to an audience as diverse as the members of your public-speaking class, where do you find a linguistic common ground?

The answer is to use Standard American English. **Standard American English** (SAE) is the language taught by schools and used in the media, business, and the government in the United States. "Standard" does not imply that Standard American English is inherently right and all other forms are wrong, only that it conforms to a standard that most speakers of American English can readily understand—even though they may represent a variety of ethnic, regional, and professional backgrounds.

ethnic vernacular
A variety of English that includes words and phrases used by a specific ethnic group

regionalisms
Words or phrases used uniquely by speakers in one part of a country

jargon
The specialized language of a profession

Standard American English
The English taught by schools and used in the media, business, and government in the United States

To keep your public-speaking class, or any audience, from becoming bored or confused, use language that all listeners can understand. Make words simple, correct, and concise, and try to craft memorable word structures.

Photo: Monkey Business Images/Shutterstock

Use Respectful Language

Shortly after the September 11, 2001, terrorist attacks, U.S. Vice President Dick Cheney made remarks in which he referred to Pakistanis as "Paks." Although he was speaking admiringly of the Pakistani people, he was chided for his use of the term. The variation *Paki* is considered a slur, and *Pak* is only slightly less offensive. Columnist William Safire remarked that

> Cheney probably picked up *Paks* in his Pentagon days, but innocent intent is an excuse only once; now he is sensitized, as are we all.[11]

A speaker whose language defames any group—people of particular ethnic, racial, and religious backgrounds or sexual orientations; women; people with disabilities—or whose language might be otherwise considered offensive or risqué is not only speaking unethically but also running a great risk of antagonizing audience members. In fact, one study suggests that derogatory language used to describe people with disabilities adversely affects an audience's perceptions of the speaker's persuasiveness, competence, trustworthiness, and sociability.[12]

Use Unbiased Language

Even speakers who would never dream of using overtly offensive language may find it difficult to avoid language that more subtly stereotypes or discriminates. Sexist language falls largely into this second category.

Not many years ago, a singular masculine pronoun (*he, him, his*) was the accepted way to refer to a person of unspecified sex:

> Everyone should bring *his* book to class tomorrow.

This usage is now considered sexist and unacceptable. Instead, you may include both a masculine and a feminine pronoun:

> Everyone should bring *his* or *her* book to class tomorrow.

Or you may reword the sentence so that it is plural and thus gender neutral:

☀ Explore at **MyCommunicationLab**
Activity: "Sexist Language"

All students should bring *their* books to class tomorrow.

Also now considered sexist is the use of a masculine noun to refer generically to all people. Although the word *man* is the primary offender, you should also monitor your use of such masculine nouns as *waiter, chairman, fireman,* and *congressman.* Instead, choose such gender-neutral alternatives as *server, chair, firefighter,* and *member of Congress.*

In addition to avoiding masculine nouns and pronouns to refer to all people, avoid sexist language that patronizes or stereotypes people:

Sexist	**Unbiased**
President Barack Obama and Michelle enrolled daughters Malia and Sasha in The Sidwell Friends School in Washington, D.C.	President and Mrs. Obama enrolled daughters Malia and Sasha in The Sidwell Friends School in Washington, D.C. *or* Barack and Michelle Obama enrolled daughters Malia and Sasha in The Sidwell Friends School in Washington, D.C.
The policeman is an underpaid professional who risks his life daily.	Police are underpaid professionals who risk their lives daily.
The male nurse took good care of his patients. (*Note:* The phrase "male nurse" implies that nursing is a typically female profession. The pronoun *his* clarifies the sex of the nurse.)	The nurse took good care of his patients.

It is not always easy to avoid biased language. Even with good intentions and deliberate forethought, you can find yourself at times caught in a bind. For example, suppose that Dr. Pierce is a young black female M.D. If you don't mention her age, race, and gender when you refer to her, you may reinforce your listeners' stereotypical image of a physician as middle-aged, white, and male. But if you *do* mention these factors, you may be suspected of implying that Dr. Pierce's achievement is unusual. There is no easy answer to this dilemma or others like it. You will have to consider your audience, purpose, and the occasion in deciding how best to identify Dr. Pierce.

As women and members of racial, ethnic, and other minorities have become increasingly visible in such professions as medicine, law, engineering, and politics, the public has grown to expect unbiased, inclusive language from news commentators, teachers, textbooks, and magazines—and from public speakers. Language that does not reflect these changes will disrupt your ability to communicate your message to your audience, which may well include members of the minority group to which you are referring.

CONSIDER THE AUDIENCE

RECAP

ADAPTING YOUR LANGUAGE STYLE TO DIVERSE LISTENERS

To communicate successfully with diverse listeners, use language your audience can understand.

To avoid offending your audience, use appropriate language.

To communicate sensitivity to diverse subgroups, use unbiased language.

10.4   List and explain three types of memorable word structures.

Watch at **MyCommunicationLab** Video: "Franklin D. Roosevelt's First Inaugural Address"

Crafting Memorable Word Structures

The president of the United States is scheduled to make an important speech in your hometown. You attend the speech and find his 30-minute presentation both interesting and informative. In the evening, you turn on the news to see how the networks cover his address. All three major networks excerpt the same ten-second portion of his speech. Why? What makes certain portions of a speech quotable or memorable? Former presidential speechwriter Peggy Noonan has said:

> Great speeches have always had great soundbites. . . . They sum up a point, or make a point in language that is pithy or profound.[13]

In other words, memorable speeches are stylistically distinctive. They create arresting images. And they have what a marketing-communication specialist has termed "ear appeal":

> "Ear appeal" phrases can be like the haunting songs of a musical that the members of the audience find themselves humming on the way home. Even if people want to forget them, they can't.[14]

Earlier in this chapter, we discussed the importance of using words that are concrete, unbiased, vivid, simple, and correct. In this section, we turn our attention to groups of words—phrases and sentences—that create drama, figurative images, and cadences. The memorable word structures summarized in Table 10.1 below can help you craft a speech that has both "eye and ear appeal."[15]

TABLE 10.1   CRAFTING MEMORABLE WORD STRUCTURES

WORD STRUCTURES WITH FIGURATIVE IMAGERY	
Metaphor	Makes an implied comparison.
Simile	Compares by using the word *like* or *as*.
Personification	Attributes human qualities to inanimate things or ideas.
WORD STRUCTURES WITH DRAMA	
Short sentence	Emphasizes an important idea by stating it in a few well-chosen words.
Omission	Boils an idea down to its essence by leaving out understood words.
Inversion	Reverses the expected order of words and phrases.
Suspension	Places a key word at the end of a phrase or sentence.
WORD STRUCTURES WITH CADENCE	
Repetition	Repeats a key word or phrase several times for emphasis.
Parallelism	Uses the same grammatical pattern.
Antithesis	Uses parallel structures but opposing meanings in two parts of a sentence.
Alliteration	Uses the same consonant sound twice or more in a phrase.

Creating Figurative Images

One way to make your message memorable is to use figures of speech to create arresting images. A **figure of speech** deviates from the ordinary, expected meanings of words, to make a description or comparison unique, vivid, and memorable. Common figures of speech include metaphors, similes, and personification.

Metaphors and Similes A **metaphor** is an implied comparison of two things that are similar in some vital way. Writer and actor Erik Stolhanske used his own prosthetic leg as a metaphor for any mental or physical obstacles his audience members might face:

> . . . everyone has a "wooden leg" of some kind. I'm living proof that once you realize that your "wooden leg," whatever it may be, is really just in your head, that's when you can stay true to yourself, pursue your dreams with foolish perseverance, and truly achieve success in life—whatever that may mean to you.[16]

Whereas a metaphor is an implied comparison, a **simile** is a more direct comparison that includes the word *like* or *as*. United Parcel Service CEO Scott Davis advised an audience to ignore "naysayers," whose negative message he compared to that of the main character in the children's story "Chicken Little":

> [Naysayers] scurry around like the Henny Pennys of the world, loudly proclaiming to anyone who will listen: "The sky is falling!" "Don't do it!" "It can't be done!"[17]

Speakers often turn to metaphor and simile in times that are especially momentous or overwhelming—times when, as one speaker has said, "the ordinary diction of our lives finds itself unequal to a challenge."[18] In the hours and days after the September 11, 2001, terrorist attacks on the United States, various speakers used such metaphorical phrases as "one more circle of Dante's hell"; "nuclear winter"; and "the crater of a volcano" to describe the site of the destroyed World Trade Center buildings in New York.[19] Such language is sometimes referred to as **crisis rhetoric**.

Personification The attribution of human qualities to inanimate things or ideas is called **personification**. Franklin Roosevelt personified nature as a generous living provider in this line from his first inaugural address:

> Nature still offers her bounty and human efforts have multiplied it. Plenty is at our doorstep.[20]

Creating Drama

Another way to make phrases and sentences memorable is to use the potential of such structures to create drama in your speech—to keep the audience in suspense or to catch them slightly off guard by saying something in a way that differs from the way they expected you to say it.

Short Sentences We have already talked about the value of using short, simple words. Short, simple sentences can have much the same power. Columnist George F. Will points out that the most eloquent sentence in Lincoln's memorable second inaugural address is just four words long:[21]

> And the war came.

Other strategies for achieving drama in your speech include three stylistic devices: omission, inversion, and suspension.

 **Watch** at **MyCommunicationLab Video:** "My Twenty-First Birthday Party"

figure of speech
Language that deviates from the ordinary, expected meaning of words to make a description or comparison unique, vivid, and memorable

metaphor
An implied comparison between two things or concepts

simile
A comparison between two things that uses the word *like* or *as*

crisis rhetoric
Language used by speakers during momentous or overwhelming times

personification
The attribution of human qualities to inanimate things or ideas

President John F. Kennedy's inaugural address included several outstanding examples of memorable word structures. What you can you learn from Kennedy's words to use in your own speeches?

Photo: George Silk/Time Life Pictures/Getty Images

Omission Leaving out a word or phrase that the audience expects to hear is called **omission**. When telegrams were a more common means of communication, senders tried to use as few words as possible because they were charged by the word, and the more they could leave out, the cheaper the telegram was.

To use omission effectively, the words you leave out must be understood by your listeners or readers. For example, a captain of a World War II Navy destroyer used omission to inform headquarters of his successful efforts at sighting and sinking an enemy submarine. Because his audience already understood which vessel he was chasing, the captain was able to spare all details when he cabled back to headquarters:

Sighted sub—sank same.

Using as few words as possible, he communicated his message in a memorable way.

About 2,000 years earlier, another military commander informed his superiors in Rome of his conquest of Gaul with the economical message:

I came, I saw, I conquered.

That commander was Julius Caesar.

Inversion Reversing the normal word order of a phrase or sentence is called **inversion**. John F. Kennedy used inversion when he changed the usual subject-verb-object sentence pattern to object-subject-verb in this brief statement from his inaugural speech:

This much we pledge. . . .[22]

And at a prayer vigil for those killed in the 2012 school shooting in Newtown, Connecticut, Barack Obama inverted the word order of his pledge to the grieving families and community:

. . . whatever measure of comfort we can provide, we will provide.[23]

Suspension Placing a key word or phrase at the end of a sentence rather than at the beginning is known as **suspension**. When you read a mystery novel, you are held in

Watch at MyCommunicationLab
Video: "John F. Kennedy's Inaugural Address"

omission
Leaving out a word or phrase the listener expects to hear

inversion
Reversing the normal word order of a phrase or sentence

suspension
Withholding a key word or phrase until the end of a sentence

suspense until you reach the end and learn "who done it." The stylistic technique of verbal suspension does something similar. Like inversion, suspension changes the expected word order or sentence pattern, in this case to give a key word or phrase the emphasis afforded by placement at the end of a sentence.

Advertisers use the technique of suspension frequently. For example, the Coca-Cola Company used suspension as the cornerstone of one of its most memorable advertising campaigns. Rather than saying "Coke goes better with everything," the copywriter decided to stylize the message by making *Coke* the last word in the sentence. The slogan became "Things go better with Coke." The stylized version was more memorable because it used language in an unexpected way.

Creating Cadence

British Prime Minister and gifted orator Winston Churchill used a "psalm form" for his speech manuscripts, typing them so that they looked like blank verse poetry on the page.[24] The **cadence**, or rhythm, of his speeches was evident from their appearance.

Like Churchill, you can create cadence by using such stylistic devices as repetition, parallelism, antithesis, and alliteration.

Repetition Using a key word or phrase more than once gives rhythm and power to your message and makes it memorable. Perhaps the best-known modern example of **repetition** in a speech is Martin Luther King Jr.'s ringing declaration that became the title of his famous August 28 1963 speech at the Lincoln Memorial in Washington, D.C.

Parallelism Whereas *repetition* refers to using identical words, **parallelism** refers to using identical grammatical patterns. In a 2013 speech to Israeli students in Jerusalem, Barack Obama used parallelism to emphasize similarities between Americans and Israelis:

> We are enriched by faith. We are governed not simply by men and women, but by laws. We are fueled by entrepreneurship and innovation. And we are defined by a democratic discourse. . . .[25]

The four sentences that begin "We are enriched," "We are governed," "We are fueled," and "we are defined" follow the parallel grammatical pattern of *pronoun (we) + verb phrase.*

Antithesis The word *antithesis* means "opposition." In language style, a sentence that uses **antithesis** has two parts with parallel structures but contrasting meanings.

Speakers have long realized the dramatic potential of antithesis. In his first inaugural address, Franklin Roosevelt declared:

> Our true destiny is not to be ministered unto but to minister to ourselves and to our fellow men.[26]

When William Faulkner accepted the Nobel Prize for literature in 1950, he spoke the now famous antithetical phrase,

> I believe that man will not merely endure: he will prevail.[27]

And when journalist David Brooks addressed the 2013 graduating class of Sewanee: The University of the South, he advised,

> Don't think about what you want from life, think about what life wants from you.[28]

cadence
The rhythm of language

repetition
Use of a key word or phrase more than once for emphasis

parallelism
Use of the same grammatical pattern for two or more phrases, clauses, or sentences

antithesis
Opposition, such as that used in parallel two-part sentences in which the second part contrasts in meaning with the first

TABLE 10.2 ANALYZING A MEMORABLE WORD STRUCTURE:
"Ask not what your country can do for you; ask what you can do for your country."
(John F. Kennedy)

STYLISTIC TECHNIQUE	EXAMPLE	DISCUSSION
Techniques That Create Rhythm		
Omission	"Ask not . . ."	The subject, *you*, is not stated.
Inversion	"Ask not . . ."	In casual everyday conversation, we would say, "do not ask" rather than "ask not." The inversion makes the opening powerful and attention-getting.
Suspension	". . . ask what you can do for your country."	The key message, "ask what you can do for your country," is suspended, or delayed, until the end of the sentence. If the sentence structure had been reversed, the impact would not have been as dramatic.
Techniques That Create Drama		
Repetition	"Ask not what <u>your</u> country can do for <u>you</u>; ask what <u>you</u> can do for <u>your</u> country."	A form of the word *you* occurs four times in a sentence of 17 words, reflecting Kennedy's audience-centeredness.
Parallelism	"Ask not <u>what your country can do for you</u>; ask <u>what you can do for your country</u>."	The two clauses use the same grammatical pattern (*what + subject + verb phrase + prepositional phrase*)
Antithesis	" Ask not . . .; ask. . . ."	The two clauses separated by the semicolon have contrasting meanings.
Alliteration	"Ask . . . can . . . can . . . country."	The alliterative *k* sound is repeated four times, at more or less even intervals in the sentence.

An antithetical statement is a good way to end a speech. The cadence it creates will make your final statement memorable.

Alliteration The repetition of a consonant sound (usually an initial consonant) several times in a phrase, clause, or sentence is called **alliteration**. Alliteration adds cadence to a thought. Consider these examples:

Alliterative Phrase	Speaker	Occasion
discipline and direction	Franklin Roosevelt	first inaugural address[29]
virility, valour, and civic virtue	Winston Churchill	speech to U.S. Congress[30]
Seneca Falls, and Selma, and Stonewall	Barack Obama	second inaugural address[31]

Used sparingly, alliteration can add cadence to your rhetoric.

Analyzing an Example of Memorable Word Structure

alliteration

The repetition of a consonant sound (usually the first consonant) several times in a phrase, clause, or sentence

We'd like to illustrate all the techniques for creating drama and cadence with one final example.[32] If you asked almost anyone for the most quoted line from John F. Kennedy's speeches, that quote would probably be this one from his inaugural address:

Ask not what your country can do for you; ask what you can do for your country.[33]

Besides expressing a noble thought, this line is quotable because it uses so many stylistic techniques, including, as shown in Table 10.2, some of the techniques discussed earlier in this chapter.

Although Kennedy's line does not include figurative images, the speech from which it comes does contain memorable figurative language, most notably the metaphors "chains of poverty," "beachhead of cooperation," and "jungle of suspicion."

Kennedy used figurative imagery, drama, and cadence to give his inaugural address "eye and ear appeal" and make it memorable—not just to those who heard it initially but also to those of us who hear, read, and study it more than 50 years later.

Using Memorable Word Structures Effectively

Having explored ways to add style and interest to the language of your speech, we must now consider how best to put those techniques into practice.

 Read at **MyCommunicationLab**
Learning From Great Speakers:
John F. Kennedy

Use Distinctive Stylistic Devices Sparingly Although we have affirmed the value of style, do not overdo it. Including too much highly stylized language can put the focus on your language rather than on your content.

Use Stylistic Devices at Strategic Points in Your Speech Save your use of stylistic devices for times during your speech when you want your audience to remember your key ideas or when you wish to capture their attention. Some kitchen mixers have a "burst of power" switch to help churn through difficult mixing chores with extra force. Think of the stylistic devices we have reviewed as opportunities to provide a burst of power to your ideas. Use them in your opening sentences, statements of key ideas, and conclusion.

Use Stylistic Devices to Economize When sentences become too long or complex, see if you can recast them with antithesis or suspension. Also remember the possibility of omission.

STUDY GUIDE — REVIEW, APPLY, AND ASSESS

DIFFERENTIATING ORAL AND WRITTEN LANGUAGE STYLES

10.1 Describe three differences between oral and written language styles.

Oral language is more personal and less formal than written style. Speakers must also provide their audiences with more repetition than writers need to use.

Assessing Your Audience-Centered Speaking Skill

Some colleges and universities offer a hybrid communication course that provides instruction and practice in both writing and speaking.

If enrolled in such a course and given the assignment to use the same topic, central idea, main idea, and supporting material to develop both a 750-word paper and a 3- to 5-minute speech, how should the paper and the speech differ?

USING WORDS EFFECTIVELY

10.2 List and explain three ways to use words effectively.

Effective speakers use specific, concrete words to evoke clear mental images in their listeners. They also choose simple, respectful, unbiased words. As a speaker, be sure to use words correctly and to keep in mind the connotations of words, as well as their dictionary definitions. And, finally, eliminate unnecessary words and phrases.

Key Terms

Ladder of abstraction 197
Denotation 198
Connotation 198
Concise 198
Cliché. 198

Thinking Ethically

A high school principal asked a student graduation speaker to avoid using the word *rape* in her graduation speech. The student, who had been raped as a 14-year-old sophomore, argued that she wanted to use the concrete word to help her emphasize to her classmates that they could overcome even the most devastating experiences in life. The principal countered that he was suggesting ways to make the language of the speech more appropriate to the occasion and the audience.[34]

What is your opinion on this issue? What would you advise the speaker to do?

Assessing Your Audience-Centered Speaking Skill

A friend asks for advice on making the word choice in her speech as effective as possible. Offer her at least three suggestions, based on this chapter, for using words effectively.

ADAPTING YOUR LANGUAGE STYLE TO DIVERSE LISTENERS

10.3 Discuss how to adapt your language style to diverse listeners.

Use language your listeners can understand. Use appropriate language to avoid offending your audience. Use unbiased language to communicate in a sensitive way to members of subgroups in your audience.

Key Terms

Ethnic vernacular. 199
Regionalism 199
Jargon. 199
Standard American English 199

Assessing Your Audience-Centered Speaking Skill

A letter to an advice columnist suggested that the term *maiden name*, used to refer to the surname a married woman had when single, is offensive to married women who do not change their surnames to those of their husbands.[35]

Do you agree that the term *maiden name* is sexist? Why or why not? How might this question affect you as a public speaker?

CRAFTING MEMORABLE WORD STRUCTURES

10.4 List and explain three types of memorable word structures.

You can create arresting images through such figures of speech as metaphors, similes, and personification. You can create drama by using short sentences for important ideas, strategically omitting words, and structuring sentences with key words at the end to create suspense. Use repetition, alliteration, parallelism, and antithesis to create memorable rhythm or cadence.

Key Terms

Thinking Critically

The following are memorable metaphors from historical speeches:[36]

- I have but one lamp by which my feet are guided, and that is the lamp of experience.
- an iron curtain
- snake pit of racial hatred
- Speak softly and carry a big stick.

First, explain what each metaphor means. Then express the same idea in ordinary language. Explain what each speaker gained or lost by using a metaphor.

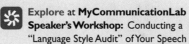

Explore at MyCommunicationLab
Speaker's Workshop: Conducting a
"Language Style Audit" of Your Speech

11 DELIVERING YOUR SPEECH

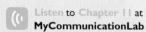

Listen to Chapter 11 at **MyCommunicationLab**

Unknown artist, Genuino speaking to Neapolitan crowd, scene from revolt in Naples fomented by Masaniello, 1620-47 Neapolitan revolutionary.
Photo: Gianni Dagli Orti/The Art Archive at Art Resource, NY

Speak the speech, I pray you, as I pronounced
it to you, trippingly on the tongue.

—William Shakespeare

Wﾠhat's more important: what you say or how you say it? Delivery has long been considered an important part of public speaking. But is the delivery of your speech more important than the content of your message? For centuries, since ancient Greece, famous speakers and speech teachers, such as Aristotle and, later, the Roman rhetorician Quintilian, have argued in favor of the primacy of either the content of the speech or its delivery.[1]

Today, whether you are speaking in front of a live audience or presenting a talk via Skype or other online, mediated method, communication teachers believe that both content and delivery contribute to speaking effectiveness. One survey suggested that "developing effective delivery" is a primary goal of most speech teachers.[2] Considerable research supports the claim that delivery plays an important role in influencing how audiences react to a speaker and his or her message. It is your audience who will determine whether you are successful. Delivery counts.

The Power of Speech Delivery

11.1 Identify three reasons delivery is important to a public speaker.

The way you hold your notes, your gestures and stance, and your impatient adjustment of your glasses all contribute to the overall effect of your speech. **Nonverbal communication** is communication other than through written or spoken language that creates meaning for someone. Nonverbal factors such as your eye contact, posture, vocal quality, and facial expression play a major role in the communication process. As much as 65 percent of the social meaning of messages is based on nonverbal expression.[3] Why does your delivery hold such power to affect how your audience will receive your message? One reason is that listeners expect a good speaker to provide good delivery. Your unspoken message is also how you express your feelings and emotions to an audience. And, ultimately, an audience believes what it *sees* more than what you *say*.

Listeners Expect Effective Delivery

In a public-speaking situation, nonverbal elements have an important influence on the audience's perceptions about a speaker's effectiveness. Communication researcher Judee Burgoon and her colleagues have developed a theory called **nonverbal expectancy theory**. The essence of the theory is this: People have certain expectations as to how you should communicate.[4] If you don't behave as people think you should, your listeners will feel that you have violated their expectations. The theory predicts that if a listener expects you to have effective delivery, and your delivery is poor, you will lose credibility. There is evidence that although many speakers do not deliver speeches effectively, audiences nevertheless expect a good speech to be well delivered.

Different audiences prefer different styles of delivery; there is no ideal style of delivery or set of prescribed gestures that is appropriate for all audiences. As we have also emphasized, audience members with different cultural backgrounds will hold different assumptions about how a speech should be presented.

More than one hundred years ago, speakers were taught to deliver orations using a more formal style of speaking than most people prefer today. In newsreels of speakers during the early part of the twentieth century, their gestures and movements look stilted and unnatural because they were taught to use dramatic, planned gestures. If you are speaking to an audience of a thousand people, using a microphone to reach the back of the auditorium, your listeners may expect a more formal delivery style. But your public-speaking class members would probably find it odd if you spoke to

nonverbal communication
Communication other than written or spoken language that creates meaning

nonverbal expectancy theory
A communication theory that suggests that if listeners' expectations about how communication should be expressed are violated, listeners will feel less favorable toward the communicator of the message

Audience members may respond to a speaker's nonverbal behavior even more strongly than they do to the verbal message. A good speaker uses facial expression and body language to connect with the audience emotionally.

Photo: SuperStock

emotional contagion theory
A theory suggesting that people tend to "catch" the emotions of others

them using a formal oratorical style that resembled the way a politician would have addressed a political rally in 1910.

For most North American listeners today, effective delivery has been described as "platform conversation." It includes having good eye contact with your listeners and using appropriate gestures, just as you do in conversations with your friends. Effective delivery also means your voice has a natural, conversational tone, varied inflection (rather than a droning monotone), and an intensity that communicates that you're interested in your message and your listeners.

Listeners Make Emotional Connections with You through Delivery

Nonverbal behavior is particularly important in communicating feelings, emotions, attitudes, likes, and dislikes to an audience. One researcher found that we communicate as little as 7 percent of the emotional impact of a message by the words we use.[5] About 38 percent hinges on such qualities of voice as inflection, intensity, or loudness, and 55 percent hinges on our facial expressions. Generalizing from these findings, we may say that we communicate approximately 93 percent of emotional meaning nonverbally. Although some scholars question whether these percentages apply to all communication settings, the research does suggest that your delivery provides important information about your feelings and emotions.[6] One study found that when a speaker's delivery was effective, the audience felt greater pleasure and had a more positive emotional response than when the same speaker had poor delivery.[7]

Another reason to pay attention to how you communicate emotions when delivering a speech is that emotions are contagious. **Emotional contagion theory** suggests that people tend to "catch" the emotions of others.[8] If you want your listeners to feel a certain emotion, then it's important for you to express that emotion yourself. Have you ever noticed that when you watch a movie in a crowded movie theater where others are laughing, you're more likely to laugh too? Producers of TV situation comedies use a laugh track or record the laughter of a live audience to enhance the emotional reactions of home viewers; these producers know that emotions are contagious.

Listeners Believe What They See

"I'm very glad to speak with you tonight," drones the speaker in a monotone, eyes glued to his notes. His audience probably does not believe him. When our nonverbal delivery contradicts what we say, people generally believe the nonverbal message. In this case, the speaker is communicating that he's *not* glad to be talking to this audience.

We usually believe nonverbal messages because they are more difficult to fake. Although we can monitor certain parts of our nonverbal behavior, it is difficult to control all of it consciously. Research suggests that a person trying to deceive someone may speak with a higher vocal pitch, at a slower rate, and with more pronunciation mistakes than normal.[9] Blushing, sweating, and changed breathing patterns also often belie our stated meaning. As the saying goes, "What you do speaks so loud, I can't hear what you say."

Methods of Delivery

11.2 Identify and describe four methods of delivery.

The style of delivery you choose will influence your nonverbal behaviors. There are four basic methods of delivery from which a speaker can choose: manuscript speaking, memorized speaking, impromptu speaking, and extemporaneous speaking. They are summarized in Table 11.1 below. Let's consider each in some detail.

Explore at MyCommunicationLab
Activity: "Methods of Delivery"

Manuscript Speaking

You have a speech to present and are afraid you will forget what you have prepared to say. So you write your speech and then read it to your audience.

Watch at MyCommunicationLab
Video: "Types of Speech Delivery"

Speech teachers frown on this approach, particularly for public-speaking students. Reading is usually a poor way to deliver a speech. Although it may provide some insurance against forgetting the speech, **manuscript speaking** is rarely done well enough to be interesting. You have probably attended a lecture that was read and wondered, "Why doesn't he just make a copy of the speech for everyone in the audience rather than reading it to us?"

However, some speeches should be read. One advantage of reading from a manuscript is that you can choose your words very carefully when dealing with a sensitive and critical issue. The president of the United States, for example, often finds it useful to have his remarks carefully scripted.

manuscript speaking
Reading a speech from a written text

TABLE 11.1   METHODS OF DELIVERY

METHOD	DESCRIPTION	DISADVANTAGES	ADVANTAGES
Manuscript speaking	Reading your speech from a prepared text	• Your speech is likely to sound as if it is being read. • It takes considerable skill and practice to make the message sound interesting.	• You can craft the message carefully, which is especially important if it is being presented to the media. • The language can be beautifully refined, polished, and stylized.
Memorized speaking	Giving a speech from memory without using notes	• You may forget your speech. • You may sound overrehearsed and mechanical.	• You can have direct eye contact with the audience. • You can move around freely or use gestures while speaking, since you don't need notes.
Impromptu speaking	Delivering a speech without preparing in advance	• It is challenging to organize your speech well and deliver it smoothly. • Lack of advance preparation and research makes it more difficult to cite evidence and supporting material for the message.	• You can easily adapt to how your audience is reacting to you and your message during the speech. • The audience sees and hears an authentic speech that is spontaneously delivered without notes.
Extemporaneous speaking	Knowing the major ideas, which have been outlined, but not memorizing the exact wording	• It takes time to prepare an extemporaneous speech. • It takes skill to deliver the speech well.	• Your speech is well organized and well researched. • Your speech sounds spontaneous, yet appropriately polished.

When possible, during times of crisis, statements to the press by government, education, or business leaders should be carefully crafted rather than tossed off casually. Although there are times when it is impossible to have a manuscript speech at hand, an inaccurate or misspoken statement in a crisis could have serious consequences.

On those occasions when you do need to use a manuscript, here are several tips to help you deliver your message effectively:[10]

- Indicate in writing on your manuscript where to pause or emphasize certain words. Use a slash mark (/) or some other symbol to remind you to pause in strategic places.

- Type your speech in short, easy-to-scan phrases on the upper two-thirds of the paper so that you do not have to look too far down the page.

- As with any performance, practice with your manuscript before you speak.

- If you're afraid you'll lose your place, unobtrusively use your index finger to keep your place in the manuscript.

- Make eye contact; don't look over listeners' heads.

- Try to take in an entire sentence at a time from your manuscript, so that you can maintain eye contact with your audience throughout each sentence and especially at the end of a sentence.

- Use your normal, natural speed of delivery; do not read the manuscript too quickly.

- Speak with a natural, varied vocal variation so that you don't sound like you're reading.

- Mark the manuscript to help you sound more natural. For example, underline or highlight words or phrases you want to emphasize.

- Use appropriate and natural gestures and movement to add further nonverbal interest and emphasis to your message.

Memorized Speaking

"All right," you think, "since reading a speech is hard to pull off, I'll write my speech out word for word and then memorize it." You're pretty sure that no one will be able to tell because you won't be using notes. **Memorized speaking** also has the advantage of allowing you to have maximum eye contact with the audience. But the key differences between speaking and writing are evident in a memorized speech, just as they can be heard in a manuscript speech. Most memorized speeches *sound* stiff, stilted, and overrehearsed. You also run the risk of forgetting parts of your speech and awkwardly searching for words in front of your audience. And you won't be able to make on-the-spot adaptations to your listeners if your speech is memorized. For these reasons, speech teachers do not encourage their students to memorize speeches for class presentation.

If you are accepting an award, introducing a speaker, making announcements, or delivering other brief remarks, however, a memorized delivery style is sometimes acceptable. But as with manuscript speaking, you must take care to make your presentation sound lively and interesting.

Impromptu Speaking

memorized speaking
Delivering a speech word for word from memory without using notes

impromptu speaking
Delivering a speech without advance preparation

You have undoubtedly already delivered many impromptu presentations. Your response to a question posed by a teacher in class and your unrehearsed rebuttal to a comment made by a colleague during a meeting are examples of impromptu presentations. The impromptu method is often described as "thinking on your feet" or "speaking off the cuff." The advantage of **impromptu speaking** is that you can speak informally, maintaining direct eye contact with the audience. But unless a speaker is extremely talented or has learned and practiced the techniques of impromptu speaking, the speech itself will be unimpressive. An impromptu speech usually lacks logical organization and thorough research. There are times, of course, when you may be called on to speak without advance warning or to improvise when something goes awry in your efforts to deliver your planned message. This was the case when President Bill Clinton was delivering his first State of the Union address in 1993 and the teleprompter scrolled the wrong text of his speech for seven minutes. What did he do as millions of people watched on television? He kept going. Drawing on his years of speaking experience, he continued to speak; no one watching knew about the error until afterward.

If you know you will be giving a speech, prepare and rehearse it. Don't just make mental notes or assume that you will find the words when you need them. It was Mark Twain who said, "A good impromptu speech takes about three weeks to prepare."

Civil rights activist the Reverend Jesse Jackson is known for his skill as an impromptu speaker. It's been reported that he got a *D* in his preaching class because he refused to write his sermons out word for word as his professor requested. He was able to deliver impromptu orations that skillfully and powerfully moved listeners to respond to his message. Once, knowing he was to speak after one of Jackson's charismatically delivered speeches, Martin Luther King Jr. allegedly developed a sudden case of laryngitis.[11] The Reverend Jackson certainly has speaking talent, but he also uses principles and skills that you can use to enhance your impromptu speaking ability. When you are called on to deliver an improvised or impromptu speech, the following guidelines can help ease you through it.

- **Consider your audience.** Just as you have learned to do in other speaking situations, when you are called on for impromptu remarks, think first of your audience. Who are the members of your audience? What are their common characteristics and interests? What do they know about your topic? What do they expect you to say? What is the occasion of your speech? A quick mental review of these questions will help ensure that even impromptu remarks are audience-centered.

- **Be brief.** When you are asked to deliver an off-the-cuff speech, your audience knows the circumstances and will not expect or even want a lengthy discourse. One to three minutes is a realistic time frame for most impromptu situations. Some spur-of-the-moment remarks, such as press statements, may be even shorter.

- **Organize!** Even off-the-cuff remarks should not falter or ramble. Effective impromptu speakers still organize their ideas into an introduction, body, and conclusion. Consider organizing your points using a simple organizational strategy such as chronological order or a topical pattern. A variation on the chronological pattern is the past, present, future model of addressing an issue. This pattern is well known to students who compete in impromptu speaking contests. The speaker organizes the impromptu speech by discussing (1) what has happened in the past, (2) what is happening now, and (3) what may happen in the future.

- **Speak honestly, but with reserve, from personal experience and knowledge.** Because there is no opportunity to conduct any kind of research before delivering an impromptu speech, you will have to speak from your own experience and knowledge. Remember, audiences almost always respond favorably to personal illustrations, so use any appropriate and relevant ones that come to mind. Of course, the more knowledge you have about the subject to be discussed, the easier it will be to speak about it off the cuff. But do not make up information or provide facts or figures you're not certain about. An honest "I don't know" or a very brief statement is more appropriate.

- **Be cautious.** No matter how much knowledge you have, if your subject is at all sensitive or your information is classified, be careful when discussing it during your impromptu speech. If asked about a controversial topic, give

Re-create the Speech Environment When You Rehearse

As you rehearse your speech, don't just sit at your desk and mentally review your message. Instead, stand up and imagine that you are in the very room in which you will deliver your speech while you rehearse your speech out loud. Or, if it is possible, rehearse your speech in the room in which you will present your speech. Just by imagining the exact room and audience you will have when presenting your speech, you are helping to manage your anxiety. When you do give your speech, you will have less anxiety because you've had experience imagining or presenting your speech in the environment in which you will speak.

extemporaneous speaking
Speaking from a written or memorized speech outline without having memorized the exact wording of the speech

an honest but noncommittal answer. You can always elaborate later, but you can never take back something rash you have already said. It is better to be cautious than sorry!

Extemporaneous Speaking

If you are not reading from a manuscript, reciting from memory, or speaking impromptu, what's left? **Extemporaneous speaking** is the approach most communication teachers recommend for most situations. When delivering a speech extemporaneously, you speak from a written or memorized general outline, but you do not have the exact wording in front of you or in memory. You have rehearsed the speech so that you know key ideas and their organization, but not to the degree that the speech sounds memorized. An extemporaneous style is conversational; it gives your audience the impression that the speech is being created as they listen to it, and to some extent it is. Martin Luther King Jr. was an expert in speaking extemporaneously; he typically did not use a manuscript when he spoke. He had notes, but he often drew on the energy of his audience as well as his own natural speaking talents to make his oratory come alive.[12] Dr. King told an interviewer that while delivering his stirring "Dream" speech in 1963, he decided only after he had begun speaking to add the most famous portion of the speech, based on an idea he had used many times before.[13] He made a good decision to improvise. According to a study by the National Endowment for the Humanities, high school seniors were more likely to know the source of Dr. King's famous speech (97 percent) than that of the Gettysburg Address or the Declaration of Independence.[14] You can use the same extemporaneous techniques he used to draw on your audience's energy and make your speech a living message rather than a canned presentation.

Seeing something happening now provides added interest and excitement. An extemporaneous speech sounds live rather than as though it was prepared yesterday or weeks ago. The extemporaneous method reflects the advantages of a well-organized speech delivered in an interesting and vivid manner.

How do you develop an extemporaneous delivery style? Here are tips for what to do at three stages in your rehearsal:

- **Early rehearsal:** When you first rehearse your speech, use as many notes as you need to help you remember your ideas, but each time you rehearse, rely less and less on your notes.

- **Later rehearsal:** When you find yourself starting to use exactly the same words each time you rehearse, you're memorizing your speech; either stop rehearsing or consider other ways of expressing your ideas.

- **Final rehearsal:** Revise your speaking notes so that you need only brief notes or notes for only lengthy quotations.

11.3 Identify and illustrate the characteristics of effective delivery.

 **Explore** at **MyCommunicationLab Activity:** "Physical Delivery"

Characteristics of Effective Delivery

After learning about the four methods of delivery, you now know that for most speaking situations, you should strive for a conversational style. But you may still have a number of specific questions about enhancing the effectiveness of your delivery. Typical concerns include "What do I do with my hands?" "Is it all right to move around while I speak?" "How can I make my voice sound interesting?" Although these concerns may seem daunting, being confident about your ability to present a well-prepared and well-rehearsed speech is the best antidote to jitters about delivery. Practice and a focus on communicating your message to your audience are vital for effective communication and great for your confidence.

To help answer specific questions about presenting a speech, we consider seven categories of nonverbal behavior that affect delivery. Specifically, we will help you improve your eye contact, use appropriate gestures, move meaningfully, maintain an appropriate posture, use facial expressions to communicate emotion, use your voice both to be understood and to maintain interest, and ensure that your personal appearance is appropriate. The ancient Roman orator Cicero, author of *De Oratore*, called these behaviors the "language of the body."[15]

Watch at **MyCommunicationLab**
Video: "Tips for Effective Speech Delivery"

Eye Contact

Of all the aspects of delivery discussed in this chapter, the most important one in a public-speaking situation for North Americans is eye contact. Eye contact with your audience opens communication, keeps your audience interested, and makes you more believable. Each of these functions contributes to the success of your delivery. Eye contact also provides you with feedback about how your speech is coming across.

Benefits of Eye Contact Making eye contact with your listeners clearly shows that you are ready to talk to them. Most people start a conversation by looking at the person they are going to talk to. The same process occurs in public speaking.

Once you've started talking, continued eye contact lets you know how your audience is responding to your speech. You don't need to look at your listeners continuously. As the need arises, you should certainly look at your notes, but you should also look at your listeners frequently, just to see what they're doing.

Most listeners will think you are capable and trustworthy if you look them in the eye. Several studies document a relationship between eye contact and increased speaker credibility.[16] Speakers who make eye contact for less than 50 percent of the length of their presentations are considered unfriendly, uninformed, inexperienced, and even dishonest by their listeners. Eye contact may also make your speech more effective. Another study showed that those audience members who had more than 50 percent eye contact with their speaker performed better in postspeech tests than did those who had less than 50 percent eye contact.[17]

However, not all people from all cultures prefer the same amount of direct eye contact when listening to someone talk. In interpersonal contexts, people from Asian cultures, for example, expect less direct eye contact when communicating with others than do North Americans.

How to Use Eye Contact Effectively Most audiences in the United States prefer that you establish eye contact with them even before you begin your speech with your attention-catching introduction. When it's time to speak, calmly walk to the lectern or to the front of the audience, pause briefly, and look at your audience before you say anything. Eye contact nonverbally sends the message, "I am interested in you; tune me in; I have something I want to share with you."

Here are other tips for effectively establishing eye contact with your audience:

- Have your opening sentence well enough in mind so that you can deliver it without looking at your notes or away from your listeners.
- Establish eye contact with the entire audience, not just with those in the front row or with only one or two people.
- Look to the back as well as the front, and from one side of your audience to the other. But you need not rhythmically move your head back and forth like a lighthouse beacon; it's best not to establish a predictable pattern for your eye contact.

When you deliver your speech to listeners in a different location using videoconferencing technology, look into the camera lens to help listeners feel you are making eye contact with them.

Photo: Ryan McVay/Photodisc/Thinkstock

- Look at individuals, establishing person-to-person contact with them—not so long that it will make a listener feel uncomfortable, but long enough to establish the feeling that you are talking directly to that individual.
- Don't look over your listeners' heads; establish eye-to-eye contact.
- If your speech is being video recorded and there is an audience present, look at your audience rather than only at the camera lens. But if no audience is present, then deliver your speech while looking into the camera lens.

Gestures

The next time you have a conversation with someone, notice how both of you use your hands and bodies to communicate. Important points are emphasized with gestures. You also gesture to indicate places, to enumerate items, and to describe objects. Gestures have the same functions for public speakers. Yet many people who gesture easily and appropriately in the course of everyday conversation aren't sure what to do with their hands when they find themselves in front of an audience.

Adapt Gestures to Audience Members' Cultural Expectations There is evidence that gestures vary from culture to culture. When he was mayor of New York City during the 1930s and 1940s, Fiorello La Guardia, fluent in Yiddish and Italian as well as in English, would speak the language appropriate for each audience. One researcher studied newsreels of the mayor and discovered that with the sound turned off, viewers could still identify the language the mayor was speaking. How? When speaking English, he used minimal gestures. When speaking Italian, he used broad, sweeping gestures. And when speaking Yiddish, he used short and choppy hand movements.

Cultural expectations can help you make decisions about your approach to using gestures. Listeners from Japan and China, for example, prefer a quieter, less flamboyant use of gestures. One Web site that offers tips for people conducting business in India suggests "When you wish to point, use your chin or your full hand, but never just a single finger, as this gesture is used only with inferiors. The chin is not used to signal to superiors. The best way to point is with the full hand."[18] When one of your authors spoke in England, several listeners noted the use of "typical overly expressive American gestures and movement." British listeners seem to prefer that the speaker

CONSIDER THE AUDIENCE

stay behind a lectern and use relatively few gestures. Other Europeans agree they can spot an American speaker because Americans are typically more animated in their use of gestures, movement, and facial expressions than are most European speakers.

Use Natural Gestures Public-speaking teachers often observe several unusual, inappropriate, and unnatural gestures among their students. One common problem is keeping your hands behind your back in a "parade rest" pose. We are not suggesting that you never put your hands behind your back, only that standing at parade rest during an entire speech looks awkward and unnatural and may distract your audience.

Another common position is standing with one hand on the hip in a "broken wing" pose. Worse than the "broken wing" is both hands resting on the hips in a "double broken wing." The speaker looks as though he or she might burst into a rendition of "I'm a Little Teapot." Again, we are not suggesting that you should never place your hands on your hips, only that to hold that one pose throughout a speech looks unnatural and will keep you from using other gestures.

Few poses are more awkward-looking than when a speaker clutches one arm, as if grazed by a bullet. The audience half expects the speaker to call out reassuringly, "Don't worry, Ma; it's only a flesh wound." Similarly, keeping your hands in your pockets can make you look as if you were afraid to let go of your change or your keys.

Some students clasp their hands and let them drop in front of them in a distracting "fig leaf clutch." Gestures can distract your audience in various other ways as well. Grasping the lectern until your knuckles turn white or just letting your hands flop around without purpose or control does little to help you communicate your message.

Functions of Gestures If you don't know what to do with your hands, think about the message you want to communicate. As in ordinary conversation, your hands should simply help emphasize or reinforce your verbal message. Specifically, your gestures can lend strength to or detract from what you have to say by (1) repeating, (2) contradicting, (3) substituting, (4) complementing, (5) emphasizing, and (6) regulating.

- **Repeating.** Gestures can help you repeat your verbal message. For example, you can say, "I have three major points to talk about today," while holding up three fingers. Or you can describe an object as 12 inches long while holding your hands about a foot apart. Repeating what you say through nonverbal means can reinforce your message.

- **Contradicting.** Because your audience will believe what you communicate nonverbally sooner than what you communicate verbally, monitor your gestures to make sure that they are not contradicting what you say. It is difficult to convey an image of control and confidence while using flailing gestures and awkward poses.

- **Substituting.** Not only can your behavior reinforce or contradict what you say, but your gestures can also substitute for your message. Without uttering a word, you can hold up the palm of your hand to calm a noisy crowd. Flashing two fingers to form a V for "victory" or raising a clenched fist are common examples of gestures that substitute for a verbal message.

- **Complementing.** Gestures can also add meaning to your verbal message. A politician who declines to comment on a reporter's question while holding up her hands to augment her verbal refusal is relying on the gesture to complement or provide further meaning to her verbal message.

- **Emphasizing.** You can give emphasis to what you say by using an appropriate gesture. A shaking fist or a slicing gesture with one or both hands helps emphasize a message. So does pounding your fist into the palm of your hand. Other gestures can be less dramatic yet still lend emphasis to what you say. You should try to allow your gestures to arise from the content of your speech and your emotions.

The best gestures are natural, definite, and consistent with your message. Gestures can substitute for words, complement or emphasize them, or regulate the exchange between you and the audience. Which purpose is this speaker's gesture serving?

Photo: photo 5000/Fotolia

• **Regulating.** Gestures can also regulate the exchange between you and your audience. If you want the audience to respond to a question, you can extend both palms to invite a response. During a question-and-answer session, your gestures can signal when you want to talk and when you want to invite others to do so.

How to Use Gestures Effectively One hundred years ago, elocutionists taught their students how to gesture to communicate specific emotions or messages. Today teachers of speech have a different approach. Rather than prescribe gestures for specific situations, they feel it is more useful to offer suitable criteria (standards) by which to judge effective gestures, regardless of what is being said. Here are guidelines to consider when working on your delivery.

• **Stay natural.** Gestures should be *relaxed*, not tense or rigid. Your gestures should flow with your message. Avoid sawing or slashing through the air with your hands unless you are trying to emphasize a particularly dramatic point.

• **Be definite.** Gestures should appear *definite* rather than as accidental brief jerks of your hands or arms. If you want to gesture, go ahead and gesture. Avoid minor hand movements that will be masked by the lectern.

• **Use gestures that are consistent with your message.** Gestures should be *appropriate* for the verbal content of your speech. If you are excited, gesture more vigorously. But remember that rehearsed gestures that do not arise naturally from what you are trying to say are likely to appear awkward and stilted.

• **Vary your gestures.** Strive for *variety* and versatility in your use of gesture. Try not to use just one hand or one all-purpose gesture. Gestures can be used for a variety of purposes, such as enumerating, pointing, describing, and symbolizing an idea or concept (such as clasping your hands together to suggest agreement or coming together).

• **Don't overdo it.** Gestures should be *unobtrusive*; your audience should focus not on the beauty or appropriateness of your gestures but on your message. Your purpose is to communicate a message to your audience, not to perform for your listeners. Your delivery should not receive more attention than your message.

• **Coordinate gestures with what you say.** Gestures should be *well timed* to coincide with your verbal message. When you announce that you have three major points, your gesture of enumeration should occur simultaneously with your utterance of the word *three*. It would be poor timing to announce that you have three points, pause for a second or two, and then hold up three fingers.

• **Make your gestures appropriate to your audience and situation.** Gestures must be adapted to the audience. In more formal speaking situations, particularly when speaking to a large audience, bolder, more sweeping, and more dramatic gestures are appropriate. A small audience in a less formal setting calls for less formal gestures. When presenting your speech via video, such as a videoconference or Skype presentation, it's especially important not to use overly dramatic gestures. The camera lens is generally only a few feet away from you, which tends to amplify the intensity of your gestures and movement for the audience viewing you on a TV or computer screen.

You also need to keep one important principle in mind: Use gestures that work best for you. Don't try to be someone you are not. President Barack Obama's style may work for him, but you are not Barack Obama. Your gestures should fit your own personality. It may be better to use no gestures—to just put your hands comfortably at your side—than to use awkward, distracting gestures or to try to counterfeit someone else's gestures. Your nonverbal delivery should flow from *your* message.

Movement

Should you walk around during your speech, or should you stay in one place? If there is a lectern, should you stand behind it, or would it be acceptable to stand in front of it or to the side? Is it all right to sit down while you speak? Can you move among the audience, as several popular daytime television hosts like to do? You may well find yourself pondering one or more of these questions while preparing for your speeches. The following discussion may help you answer them.

Move Purposefully You may want to move purposefully about while delivering your speech, but take care that your movement does not detract from your message. If the audience focuses on your movement rather than on what you are saying, it would be better to stand still. An absence of movement is better than distracting movement. In short, your movement should be consistent with the verbal content of your message. It should make sense rather than appear as aimless wandering.

Robert Frost said, "Good fences make good neighbors." Professional speech coach Brent Filson says, however, "For my money, good fences make lousy speeches."[19] He recommends, as do we, that you eliminate physical barriers between you and the audience. For more formal occasions, you will be expected to remain standing behind a lectern to deliver your message. But even on those occasions, it can be appropriate to move from behind the lectern to make a point, signal a change in mood, or turn to another idea.

Establish Immediacy Your movement and other nonverbal cues can help you establish immediacy with your listeners. Psychologist Albert Mehrabian defines **immediacy** as "the degree of physical or psychological closeness between people."[20] **Immediacy behaviors** are those that literally or psychologically make your audience feel closer to you; because they create this perception of closeness, immediacy behaviors enhance the quality of the relationship between you and your audience.[21] Immediacy behaviors include the following:

- Standing or moving closer to your listeners
- Coming out from behind a lectern
- Using appropriate levels of eye contact
- Smiling while talking and, more specifically, smiling at individual audience members
- Using appropriate gestures
- Having an appropriately relaxed posture
- Moving purposefully

More than three decades of research on the immediacy cues used by teachers in North American classrooms clearly establish that teachers who are more immediate enhance student learning, increase student motivation to learn, and have higher teacher evaluations.[22] It seems logical to suggest that public speakers who increase immediacy will have similarly positive results. One cautionary note: Listeners—not the speaker—determine the appropriate amount of immediacy. Be vigilantly audience-centered as you seek the appropriate level of immediacy between you and your listeners.

In addition to fostering immediacy, movement can signal the beginning of a new idea or major point in your speech. As you make a transition statement or change from a serious subject to a more humorous one, movement can be a good way to signal that your approach to the speaking situation is changing.

immediacy
The degree of perceived physical or psychological closeness between people

immediacy behaviors
Behaviors such as making eye contact, making appropriate gestures, and adjusting physical distance that enhance the quality of the relationship between speaker and listeners

How to Move Effectively Your use of movement during your speech should make sense to your listeners. Avoid random pacing and overly dramatic gestures. Temper our advice about proximity and other delivery variables by adapting to the cultural expectations of your audience. Consider these final summary tips about moving effectively:

- Make sure your movement is purposeful and is not aimless meandering.
- Your movement should make sense to your listeners.
- Develop immediacy with your audience by appropriately removing barriers between you and your audience.

Posture

Although there have been few formal studies of posture in relation to public speaking, there is evidence that the way you carry your body communicates significant information. One study even suggests that your stance can reflect on your credibility as a speaker.[23] Slouching over the lectern, for example, does not project an image of vitality and interest in your audience.

Functions of Posture Whereas your face and voice play the major role in communicating a specific emotion, your posture communicates the *intensity* of that emotion. If you are happy, your face and voice reflect your happiness; your posture communicates the intensity of your joy.[24]

Since the days of the elocutionists, few speech teachers or public-speaking texts have advocated specific postures for public speakers. Today we believe that the specific stance you adopt should come about naturally, as a result of what you have to say, the environment, and the formality or informality of the occasion. For example, during a very informal presentation, it may be perfectly appropriate as well as comfortable and natural to sit on the edge of a desk. Most speech teachers, however, do not encourage students to sit while delivering classroom speeches. In general, avoid slouching your shoulders, shifting from foot to foot, or drooping your head. Your posture should not call attention to itself. Instead, it should reflect your interest in the speaking event and your attention to the task at hand.

How to Have Good Posture To help you stand tall when delivering a speech, here are two tips to keep in mind. First, stand up straight while pulling your shoulder blades back just a bit. Second, imagine that your head is being held up by a string so that you have direct eye contact with your listeners while standing tall. You don't need to stay frozen in this position. But when you find yourself starting to slump or slouch, pulling your shoulders back and tugging on the imaginary string will give your posture an immediate positive boost.

Facial Expression

Media experts today doubt that Abraham Lincoln would have survived as a politician in our appearance-conscious age of telegenic politicians. His facial expression, according to those who saw him, seemed wooden and unvaried.

Functions of Facial Expressions Your face plays a key role in expressing your thoughts and especially your emotions and attitudes.[25] Your audience sees your face before they hear what you are going to say. Thus, you have an opportunity to set the emotional tone for your message before you start speaking. We are not advocating that you adopt a phony smile that looks insincere and plastered on your face, but a pleasant facial expression helps establish a positive emotional climate. Your facial expression should naturally vary to be consistent with your message. Present somber news with a more serious expression. To communicate interest in your listeners, keep your expression alert and friendly.

According to cross-cultural studies by social psychologist Paul Ekman, nearly all people around the world agree on the general meanings of facial expressions for six primary emotions: happiness, anger, surprise, sadness, disgust, and fear.[26] Humans are physically capable of producing thousands of different facial expressions, but our faces most often express one of these six primary emotions or a blend of expressions rather than a single emotion. Even a culturally diverse audience will usually be able to read your emotional expressions clearly.

How to Use Effective Facial Expressions When you rehearse your speech, consider standing in front of a mirror—or, better yet, record video of yourself practicing your speech. Are you allowing your face to help communicate the emotional tone of your thoughts? Consider these tips for monitoring your facial expression:

- As you rehearse, be mindful of the emotion that you wish your audience members to feel. Monitor your expression so that it communicates the emotion you intend.

- Pay special attention to your facial expression when you begin your speech. Unless you are presenting sad or bad news, have a naturally pleasant, positive facial expressing to signal your interest in communicating with your listeners.

- When presenting a speech that will be seen only on video, take care not to overly exaggerate your facial expression. Close-ups can amplify the intensity of your emotional expressions.

Vocal Delivery

Have you ever listened to a radio announcer and imagined what he or she looked like, only later to see a photograph of the announcer that drastically altered your image? Vocal clues play an important part in creating the impression we have of a speaker. Based on vocal clues alone, you make inferences about a person's age, status, occupation, ethnic origin, income, and a variety of other matters. As a public speaker, your voice is one of your most important delivery tools for conveying your ideas to your audience. Your credibility as a speaker and your ability to communicate your ideas clearly to your listeners will in large part depend on your vocal delivery.

Vocal delivery includes pitch, speech rate, volume, pronunciation, articulation, pauses, and general variation of the voice. A speaker has at least two key vocal obligations to an audience: Speak to be understood, and speak with vocal variety to maintain interest.

Speak to Be Understood To be understood, you need to consider four aspects of vocal delivery: volume, articulation, dialect, and pronunciation.

Volume. The fundamental purpose of your vocal delivery is to speak loudly enough that your audience can hear you. The **volume** of your speech is determined by the amount of air you project through your larynx, or voice box. More air equals more volume of sound. In fact, the way you breathe has more impact on the sound of your voice than almost anything else. To the ancient orators, a person's breath was the source of spiritual power. To breathe is to be filled with a positive, powerful source of energy.

In order to breathe properly, you need to understand how to use your breathing muscles. Your diaphragm, a muscle that lies between your lungs and your abdomen, helps control sound volume by increasing airflow from your lungs through your voice box. If you put your hands on the hollow in the center of your rib cage and say "Ho-ho-ho," you will feel your muscles contracting and the air being forced out

volume
The softness or loudness of a speaker's voice

of your lungs. Breathing from your diaphragm—that is, consciously expanding and contracting your abdomen as you breathe in and out, rather than merely expanding your chest as air flows into your lungs—can increase the volume of sound as well as enhance the quality of your voice.

Articulation. The process of producing speech sounds clearly and distinctly is **articulation**. In addition to speaking loudly enough, you need to say your words clearly, so that your audience can understand them. Without distinct enunciation, or articulation of the sounds that make up words, your listeners may not understand you or may fault you for simply not knowing how to speak clearly and fluently. Here are some commonly misarticulated words.[27]

Dint instead of *didn't*	*Soun* instead of *sound*
Lemme instead of *let me*	*Wanna* instead of *want to*
Mornin instead of *morning*	*Wep* instead of *wept*
Seeya instead of *see you*	*Whadayado* instead of *what do you do*

Many errors in articulation result from simple laziness. It takes effort to articulate speech sounds clearly. Sometimes we are in a hurry to express our ideas, but more often we simply get into the habit of mumbling, slurring, and abbreviating. Such speech flaws may not keep your audience from understanding you, but poor enunciation does reflect on your credibility as a speaker.

The best way to improve your articulation of sounds is first to identify those words or phrases that you have a tendency to slur or chop. Once you have identified them, practice saying the words correctly. Make sure you can hear the difference between the improper and proper pronunciations. A speech teacher can help you check your articulation.

Dialect. Most newscasters in North America use what is called standard American pronunciation and do not typically have a strong dialect. A **dialect** is a consistent style of pronouncing words that is common to an ethnic group or a geographic region such as the South, New England, or the upper Midwest. In the southern part of the United States, people prolong some vowel sounds when they speak. And in the northern Midwest, the word *about* sometimes sounds a bit like "aboat." In the previous century, it took a bit of adjustment for many Americans to get used to President John Kennedy's Bostonian pronunciation of Cuba as "Cuber" and Harvard as "Hahvahd." Lyndon Johnson's Texas twang was a sharp contrast to Kennedy's New England sound. More recently, George W. Bush's Texas lilt also contrasted with the slight southern drawl of his predecessor, Bill Clinton. Although President Obama has less of an identifiable dialect than either Clinton or Bush, he sometimes clips the ends of his words.

Is a dialect detrimental to effective communication with an audience? Although a speaker's dialect may pigeonhole that person as being from a certain part of the country, it won't necessarily affect the audience's comprehension of the information unless the dialect is so pronounced that the listeners can't understand the speaker's words. Research does suggest, however, that listeners tend to prefer a dialect similar to their own.[28] We don't recommend that you eliminate your own mild dialect; but if your word pronunciation is significantly distracting to your listeners, you might consider modifying it.

The four elements of a dialect include intonation pattern, vowel production, consonant production, and speaking rate.

- *Use Proper Intonation* A typical North American intonation pattern is predominantly a rising and falling pattern. The pattern looks something like this:

"Good ^morn^ing. How ^are^ you?"

articulation
The production of clear and distinct speech sounds

dialect
A consistent style of pronouncing words that is common to an ethnic group or geographic region

Intonation patterns of other languages, such as Hindi, may remain on almost the exact same pitch level; North American ears find the monotone pitch distracting.

- *Pronounce Vowels Clearly* Many people who speak English as a second language often clip, or shorten, vowel sounds, which can make comprehension more challenging. Stretching or elongating vowels within words can be a useful skill for such speakers to develop. If this is a vocal skill you need to cultivate, consider recording your speech and then comparing it with the standard American pronunciation you hear on TV or radio.

- *Pronounce Consonants Appropriately* Consonant production varies depending on what language you are speaking. It is sometimes difficult to produce clear consonants that are not overdone. Consonants that are so soft as to be almost unheard may produce a long blur of unintelligible sound rather than a crisply articulated sound.

- *Use an Appropriate Speaking Rate* People whose first language is not English sometimes speak too fast, in the hope this will create the impression that they are very familiar with English. Slowing the rate just a bit often enhances comprehension for native English speakers listening to someone less familiar with English pronunciation. A rate that is too fast also contributes to problems with clipped vowels, soft or absent consonants, and an intonation pattern that is on one pitch level rather than comfortably varied.

Pronunciation. Whereas articulation relates to the clarity of sounds, **pronunciation** concerns the degree to which sounds conform to those assigned to words in standard English. Mispronouncing words can detract from a speaker's credibility.[29] If you are uncertain about how to pronounce a word, look it up in an online dictionary. Most popular dictionaries provide recordings of the correct pronunciations of words. Often, however, we are not aware that we are not using standard pronunciation unless someone points it out.

Some speakers reverse speech sounds, saying "aks" instead of "ask," for example. Some allow an *r* sound to intrude into some words, saying "warsh" instead of "wash," or leave out sounds in the middle of a word by saying "actchally" instead of "actually" or "Febuary" instead of "February." Some speakers also accent syllables in nonstandard ways; they say "po´lice" instead of "po lice´" or "um´brella" rather than "um brel´la."

If English is not your native language, you may have to spend extra time working on your pronunciation and articulation. Here are two useful tips to help you. First, make an effort to prolong vowel sounds. Speeeeak tooooo prooooolooooong eeeeeeach voooooowel sooooooound yooooooooou maaaaaaaake. Second, to reduce choppy-sounding word pronunciation, blend the end of one word into the beginning of the next. Make your speech flow from one word to the next, instead of separating it into individual chunks of sound.[30]

Speak with Variety To speak with variety is to vary your pitch, rate of speech, and pauses. It is primarily through the quality of our voices, as well as our facial expressions, that we communicate emotions, whether we are happy, sad, bored, or excited. If your vocal clues suggest that you are bored with your topic, your audience will probably be bored also. Appropriate variation in vocal pitch and rate as well as appropriate use of pauses can add zest to your speech and help maintain audience attention.

Pitch. Vocal **pitch** is how high or low your voice sounds. You can sing because you can change the pitch of your voice to produce a melody. Lack of variation in pitch has been consistently identified as one of the most distracting characteristics of ineffective speakers: A monotone is boring.

Everyone has a habitual pitch. This is the range of your voice during normal conversation. Some people have a habitually high pitch, others have a low pitch. The

pronunciation
The use of sounds to form words clearly and accurately

pitch
How high or low the voice sounds

pitch of your voice is determined by how fast the folds in your vocal cords vibrate. The faster the vibration, the higher the pitch.

Your voice has **inflection** when you raise or lower the pitch as you pronounce words or sounds. The best public speakers appropriately vary their inflection. We're not suggesting that you need to imitate a top-forty radio disk jockey when you speak. But variation in your vocal inflection and overall pitch helps you communicate the subtlety of your ideas.

In some cultures, vocal inflection plays a major role in helping people interpret the meaning of words. For example, Thai, Vietnamese, and Mandarin Chinese languages purposely use such inflections as monotone, low, falling, high, and rising.[31] If you are a native speaker of a language in which pitch influences meaning, be mindful that listeners do not expect as much change in pitch in many Western languages, although all languages rely on inflection to provide nuances of meaning.

Record your speech as you rehearse and evaluate your use of pitch and inflection. If you are not satisfied with your inflection, consider practicing your speech with exaggerated variations in vocal pitch. Although you would not deliver your speech this way, it may help you explore the expressive options available to you.

Rate. How fast do you talk? Most speakers average between 120 and 180 words per minute. There is no "best" speaking rate. The skill of great speakers does not depend on a standard rate of speech. Daniel Webster purportedly spoke at about 90 words per minute, Franklin Roosevelt at 110, John F. Kennedy at a quick-paced 180. Martin Luther King Jr. started his "Dream" speech at 92 words a minute and was speaking at 145 words per minute during his conclusion.[32] The best rate depends on two factors: your speaking style and the content of your message.

A common fault of many beginning speakers is to deliver a speech too quickly. One symptom of speech anxiety is that you tend to rush through your speech to get it over with. Feedback from others can help you determine whether your rate is too rapid. Recording your message and listening critically to your speaking rate can also help you assess whether you are speaking at the proper speed. Fewer speakers have the problem of speaking too slowly, but a turtle-paced speech will almost certainly make it more difficult for your audience to maintain interest. Remember, your listeners can grasp information much faster than you can speak it.

Pauses. It was Mark Twain who said, "The right word may be effective, but no word was ever as effective as a rightly timed pause." An appropriate pause can often do more to accent your message than any other vocal characteristic. President Kennedy's famous line, "Ask not what your country can do for you; ask what you can do for your country," was effective not only because of its language but also because it was delivered with a pause dividing the two thoughts. Try delivering that line without the pause; it just doesn't have the same power.

Effective use of pauses, also known as *effective timing,* can greatly enhance the impact of your message. Whether you are trying to tell a joke, a serious tale, or a dramatic story, your use of a pause can determine the effectiveness of your anecdote. Jon Stewart, Stephen Colbert, Seth Meyers, David Letterman, Jimmy Fallon, and Ellen Degeneres are masters at timing a punch line.

Beware, however, of the vocalized pause. Many beginning public speakers are uncomfortable with silence and so, rather than pausing where it seems natural and normal, they vocalize sounds such as "umm," "er," "you know," and "ah." We think you will agree that "Ask not, ah, what your, er, country can do, ah, for you; ask, you know, what you, umm, can do, er, for your, uh, country" just doesn't have the same impact as the unadorned original statement.

One research study counted how frequently certain people use "uhs."[33] Science professors in this study said "uh" about 1.4 times a minute; humanities professors timed in at 4.8 times a minute—almost 3.5 times as often. Another psychologist counted the "ums" per minute of well-known speakers. *Wheel of Fortune* host Pat

inflection
The variation in the pitch of the voice

Sajak won the count with almost 10 "ums" per minute; and, although he sometimes pokes fun at well-known politicians who use vocalized pauses, David Letterman was a close second with 8.1. Former president Bill Clinton had only 0.79 vocalized pause per minute. As a public speaker, you don't want to be the winner of this contest by having the most "uhs" and "ums" when you speak. Vocalized pauses will annoy your audience and detract from your credibility; eliminate them.

Silence can be an effective tool in emphasizing a particular word or sentence. A well-timed pause coupled with eye contact can powerfully accent your thought. Asking a rhetorical question of your audience such as "How many of you would like to improve your communication skills?" will be more effective if you pause after asking the question rather than rushing into the next thought. Silence is a way of saying to your audience, "Think about this for a moment." Concert pianist Arthur Schnabel said this about silence and music: "The notes I handle no better than many pianists. But the pauses between the notes, ah, that is where the art resides."[34] In speech, too, an effective use of a pause can add artful emphasis and interest.

Using a Microphone "Testing. Testing. One . . . two . . . three. Is this on?" These are not effective opening remarks. Yet countless public speakers have found themselves trying to begin a speech, only to be upstaged by an uncooperative public address system. No matter how polished your gestures or well-intoned your vocal cues, if you are inaudible or you use a microphone awkwardly, your speech will not have the desired effect.

There are three kinds of microphones, only one of which demands much technique.

- The **lavaliere microphone** is the clip-on type often used by newspeople and interviewees. Worn on the front of a shirt, jacket, or dress, it requires no particular care other than not to thump it or to accidentally knock it off.

- The **boom microphone** is used by makers of movies and TV shows. It hangs over the heads of the speakers and is remote-controlled, so the speaker need not be particularly concerned with it.

- The third kind of microphone, and the most common, is the **stationary microphone**. This is the type that is most often attached to a lectern, sitting on a desk, or standing on the floor. Generally, the stationary microphones used today are multidirectional. You do not have to remain frozen in front of a stationary mike while delivering your speech.

When using a stationary microphone consider these suggestions.

- First, check to make sure that your microphone is indeed multidirectional and can pick up your voice even if you aren't speaking directly into it.

- Second, microphones amplify sloppy habits of pronunciation and enunciation. Therefore, you need to speak clearly and crisply when using a mike. Be especially careful when articulating such "explosive" sounding consonants as *B* and *P*; they can be overamplified by the microphone and produce a slight popping sound. Similarly, a microphone can intensify the sibilance of the *S* sound at the beginning or ending of words (such as in *hiss*, *sometime*, or *silence*). You may have to articulate these sounds with slightly less intensity to avoid creating overamplified, distracting noises.

lavaliere microphone
A microphone that can be clipped to an article of clothing or worn on a cord around your neck

boom microphone
A microphone that is suspended from a bar and moved to follow the speaker; often used in movies and TV

stationary microphone
A microphone attached to a lectern, sitting on a desk, or standing on the floor

Many stationary microphones, like this one, are multidirectional, allowing speakers to move as they talk. When you use any microphone, be careful to avoid explosive word pronunciations or annoying microphone noises.

Photo: Alexey Klementiev/Fotolia

Watch at **MyCommunicationLab**
Video: "Whatever Happened to Sisqo?"

 Watch at **MyCommunicationLab**
Video: "Donald"

 Explore at **MyCommunicationLab**
Activity: "Professional Appearance"

- Third, if you must test a microphone, count or ask the audience whether they can hear you. Blowing on a microphone produces an irritating noise! Do not tap, pound, or shuffle anything near the microphone. These noises, too, will be heard by the audience loudly and clearly. If you are using note cards, quietly slide them aside as you progress through your speech.

- Finally, continue to speak at your normal volume. Some speakers speak more quietly when they have a microphone in front of them, becoming inaudible.

Under ideal circumstances, you will be able to practice beforehand with the same type of microphone you will use when you speak. If you have the chance, figure out where to stand for the best sound quality and how sensitive the mike is to extraneous noise. Practice will accustom you to any voice distortion or echo that might occur so that these sound qualities do not surprise you during your speech.

Personal Appearance

Most people have expectations about the way a speaker should look. One of your audience analysis tasks is to identify what those audience expectations are. This can be trickier than it might at first seem. Appropriate wardrobe varies depending on climate, custom, culture, and audience expectations. In addition, wardrobe styles can quickly become outdated.

Your appearance sets the tone for your talk. For example, most CEOs who speak to their stockholders at the annual stockholders meeting typically wear a suit and tie—but not the late Steve Jobs, head of Apple. To communicate his casual and contemporary approach to business, he often wore jeans and a sweater. The current CEO of Apple, Tim Cook, also adopts a casual look to communicate a comfortable leadership style as does Bill Gates, founder of Microsoft.

There is considerable evidence that your personal appearance affects how your audience responds to you and your message, particularly during the opening moments of your presentation. If you violate their expectations about appearance, you will be less successful in achieving your purpose. One study found, for example, that men who have a nose ring are less likely to be hired during a job interview.[35] Yet this research conclusion is based on a specific situation and time; years from now, a nose ring may have no impact, either positive or negative, on a person's credibility. Our point: It's the audience and the cultural expectations of audience members that determine whether a speaker's personal appearance is appropriate or not, not some fashion guru or magazine editor.

11.4 Use strategies for adapting your delivery when speaking to diverse audiences.

Audience Diversity and Delivery

Most of the suggestions we have offered in this chapter assume that your listeners will be expecting a typical North American approach to delivery. However, many of these assumptions are based on research responses from U.S. college students, who are predominantly white and in their late teens or early twenties, so our suggestions are not applicable to every audience. As we have stressed throughout the book, you need to adapt your presentation to the expectations of your listeners, especially those from different cultural backgrounds. Consider the following suggestions to help you develop strategies for adapting both your verbal and your nonverbal messages for a culturally diverse audience.

- **Avoid an ethnocentric mind-set.** As you learned in Chapter 5, *ethnocentrism* is the assumption that your own cultural approaches are superior to those of other cultures. When considering how to adapt your delivery style to your audience, try to view different approaches and preferences not as right or wrong but merely as different from your own.

- **Consider using a less dramatic style for predominantly high-context listeners.** As you recall from Chapter 5, a high-context culture places considerable emphasis on unspoken messages. Therefore, for a high-context audience, you need not be overly expressive. For example, for many people from Asian countries, a delivery style that included passionate gestures, overly dramatic facial expressions, and frequent movements might seem overdone. A more subtle, less demonstrative approach would create less "noise" and be more effective.

- **Consult with other speakers who have presented to your audience.** Talk with people you may know who are familiar with the cultural expectations of the audience you will address. Ask specific questions. For example, when speaking in Poland, one of the authors expected the speech to start promptly at 11:00 A.M., as announced in the program and on posters. By 11:10 it was clear the speech would not begin on time. In Poland, it turns out, all students know about the "academic quarter." This means that most lectures and speeches begin at least 15 minutes—a quarter hour—after the announced starting time. If the author had asked another professor about the audience's expectations, he would have known this custom in advance. As you observe or talk with speakers who have addressed your target audience, ask these questions:

    What are audience expectations about where I should stand while speaking?

    Do listeners like direct eye contact?

    When will the audience expect me to start and end my talk?

    Will listeners find movement and gestures distracting or welcome?

- **Monitor your level of immediacy with your audience.** As we noted earlier, speaker immediacy involves how close you are to your listeners, the amount of eye contact you display, and whether you speak from behind or in front of a lectern. North Americans seem to prefer immediacy behaviors from speakers. Some cultures may expect less immediacy; the key is not to violate what listeners expect.[36] For example, we've been told that Japanese audiences don't expect speakers to move from behind a lectern and stand very close to listeners. Even in small seminars, Japanese speakers and teachers typically stay behind the lectern.

- **Monitor the intensity of your expression of emotion.** Not all cultures interpret and express emotions the same way. People from the Middle East and the Mediterranean are typically more expressive and animated in their conversation than are Northern Europeans.[37] People from a high-context culture—a culture in which nonverbal messages are exceptionally important (such as Japanese or Chinese)—place greater emphasis on your delivery of a message than do people from a low-context culture (such as North Americans).[38] Remember, however, that even though you may be speaking to an audience from a low-context culture—a culture that places a high value on verbal messages—you do not have license to ignore how you deliver a message. Delivery is always important.

DON'T GET LOST IN TRANSLATION

When you are invited to address listeners who speak a language different from your own and your message is being translated, consider the following tips to ensure that your message will be understood:

- Learn enough of the language to provide at least an opening greeting in the language of your listeners: "Good morning" (*Buenos dias*) or "Good evening" (*Buenos noches*).
- Speak more slowly than normal, to give your translator time to listen and repeat your message.
- Cut your content in half, because your translator will be repeating what you say in the language of your audience. So, if you'd planned on speaking for 20 minutes, you should prepare a presentation of 10 minutes.
- Use short, simple sentences. Pause frequently to give your translator time to translate your message.
- If possible, give your translator an outline of your message.
- Avoid slang, jargon, and figures of speech such as "pony up," "elephant in the room," "piggyback," "clear as a bell," and "thick as thieves."
- Use jokes and humor with caution: Jokes often do not translate well.
- Consider using PowerPoint slides; the slides can help your translator. If possible, have your PowerPoint slides translated into the language of your audience.
- If your audience shows nonverbal clues that something you (or your translator) said is unclear, ask the audience if your message is clear.

Source: "Don't Get Lost in Translation," *Herald,* Vol. 157, 4 (April 2010), p. 32. Reprinted with permission of Community of Christ.

- **Know the code.** Communication occurs when both speaker and listener share the same code system—both verbal and nonverbal. Your words can be translated, and while we offer some tips for working with a translator, learning the nonverbal code of your audience is important, too. One of your authors embarrassed himself with a Caribbean audience because he used a circled thumb and finger gesture to signal "okay" to compliment a student. Later he discovered that for some listeners this was an obscene gesture—like extending a middle finger to a North American audience. Even subtle nonverbal messages communicate feelings, attitudes, and cues about the nature of the relationship between you and your audience, so it is important to avoid gestures or expressions that would offend your listeners.

Although we cannot provide a comprehensive description of each cultural expectation you may face in every educational and professional setting, we can remind you to keep cultural expectations in mind when you rehearse and deliver a speech. We are not suggesting that you abandon your own cultural expectations about speech delivery. Rather, we urge you to become sensitive and responsive to cultural differences. There is no universal dictionary of nonverbal meaning, so spend some time asking people who are from the same culture as your prospective audience about what gestures and expressions your audience will appreciate.

RECAP

AUDIENCE DIVERSITY AND DELIVERY

- Avoid ethnocentrism; don't assume your listeners have a background and culture similar to yours.
- Use more subtle nonverbals for high-context listeners.
- Match immediacy behaviors and expression of emotion to culture.
- Learn nonverbal gesture codes and expectations to avoid distracting your listeners with inappropriate gestures.
- Seek advice from speakers experienced with the audience.

Rehearsing Your Speech: Some Final Tips

11.5   Describe the steps to follow when you rehearse your speech.

Read at **MyCommunicationLab Learning From Great Speakers:** Marcus Tullius Cicero

Just knowing some of the characteristics of effective speech delivery will not make you a better speaker unless you can put those principles into practice. Effective public speaking is a skill that takes practice. Practicing takes the form of rehearsing. As indicated in Figure 11.1, rehearsing your speech helps you prepare to deliver your speech to an audience.

Do you want to make a good grade on your next speech? Research suggests that one of the best predictors of the effectiveness of a speech is the amount of time you spend preparing and rehearsing it; instructors gave higher grades to students who spent more time rehearsing their speeches and lower grades to students who spent less time preparing and rehearsing.[39] The following suggestions can help you make the most of your rehearsal time.

- **Finish drafting your speech outline at least two days before your speech performance.** The more time you have to work on putting it all together, the better.

- **Before you prepare the speaking notes you will use in front of your audience, rehearse your speech aloud.** This will help you determine where you will need notes to prompt yourself.

- **Time your speech.** Revise your speech as necessary to keep it within the time limits set by your instructor or whoever invited you to speak.

- **Prepare your speaking notes.** Use whatever system works best for you. Some speakers use pictorial symbols to remind themselves of a story or an idea. Others use complete sentences or just words and phrases in an outline pattern to prompt them. Many teachers advocate using note cards for speaking notes. Some speakers use an iPad or other electronic display. If you do use electronic notes, it is wise to have a hard copy backup in case you experience technology problems.

- **Rehearse your speech standing up.** This will help you get a feel for your use of gestures as well as your vocal delivery. Do not try to memorize your speech or plan specific gestures. As you rehearse, you may want to modify your speaking notes to reflect appropriate changes.

- **If you can, present your speech to someone else so that you can practice establishing eye contact.** Seek feedback from your captive audience about both your delivery and your speech content.

- **If possible, make an audio or video recording of your speech during the rehearsal stage.** Most smartphones, computers, and tablets have a built-in camera and microphone. When listening to or viewing the recording, observe your vocal and physical mannerisms and make necessary changes. Many speakers still find it useful to practice before a mirror so that they can observe their body language—it's low-tech, but it works.

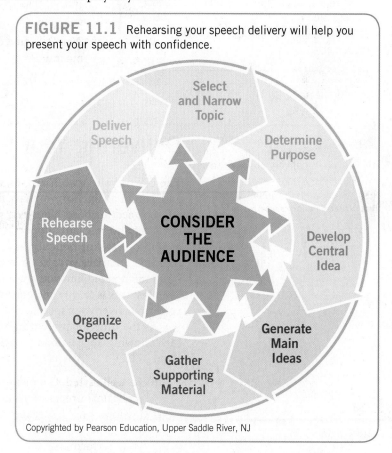

FIGURE 11.1 Rehearsing your speech delivery will help you present your speech with confidence.

Select and Narrow Topic · Determine Purpose · Develop Central Idea · Generate Main Ideas · Gather Supporting Material · Organize Speech · Rehearse Speech · Deliver Speech · **CONSIDER THE AUDIENCE**

DEVELOPING YOUR SPEECH STEP BY STEP

REHEARSE YOUR SPEECH

CONSIDER THE AUDIENCE

Brianne begins to rehearse her speech. From the beginning, she stands and speaks aloud, practicing gestures and movement that seem appropriate to her message.

At first, Brianne uses her preparation outline (pp. 172–173) as speaking notes. These early rehearsals go pretty well, but the speech is running a little short. Brianne knows that she tends to speak fairly rapidly, so she decides to plan more pauses throughout the speech, at points strategically chosen to allow her listeners to absorb an important idea. When she prepares her speaking notes, Brianne writes the delivery cue "Pause" at those points on her note cards.

RECAP

REHEARSING YOUR SPEECH

- Spend more time preparing and rehearsing, to earn a higher grade.
- Finish your outline two days before you speak.
- Rehearse aloud and time your speech before making speaking notes.
- Make rehearsals as much like the real speech as possible.
- Seek feedback, and self-critique video of your rehearsal.

- **Rehearse using all your presentation aids.** As we discuss in the next chapter, don't wait until the last minute to plan, prepare, and rehearse with flipcharts, slides, computer graphics, handouts, or other aids that you will need to manipulate as you speak.

- **Your final rehearsals should re-create, as much as possible, the speaking situation you will face.** If you will be speaking in a large classroom, find a large classroom in which to rehearse your speech. If your audience will be seated informally in a semicircle, then this should be the context in which you rehearse your speech. The more realistic the rehearsal, the more confidence you will gain.

- **Practice good delivery skills while rehearsing.** Remember this maxim: Practice *makes* perfect if practice *is* perfect.

11.6 List four suggestions for enhancing the final delivery of your speech.

Watch at **MyCommunicationLab**
Video: "Performance Anxiety"

Delivering Your Speech

The day of your speech arrives, and you are ready. Using information about your audience as an anchor, you have developed a speech on an interesting topic and with a fine-tuned purpose. Your central idea is clearly identified. You have gathered interesting and relevant supporting material and organized it well. Your speech has an appropriate introduction, a logically arranged body, and a clear conclusion that nicely summarizes your key theme. You have rehearsed your speech several times; it is not memorized, but you are comfortable with the way you express the major ideas. Your last task is calmly and confidently to communicate with your audience. You are ready to deliver your speech.

As the time for presenting your speech to your audience approaches, consider the following suggestions to help you prepare for a successful performance (see Figure 11.2).

- **Be well rested.** Get plenty of sleep before your speech. Last-minute, late-night final preparations can take the edge off your performance. Many professional public speakers also advocate that you watch what you eat before you speak; a heavy meal or too much caffeine can have a negative effect on your performance.

- **Review the suggestions in Chapter 1 for becoming a confident speaker.** It is normal to have prespeech jitters. But if you have developed a well-organized, audience-centered message on a topic of genuine interest to you, you've done all the right things to make your speech a success. Remember some of the other tips for developing confidence: Re-create the speech environment when you rehearse. Use deep breathing techniques to help you relax. Make sure you are especially familiar with your introduction and conclusion. Act calm to feel calm.

- **Arrive early for your speaking engagement.** If the room is in an unfamiliar location, give yourself plenty of time to find it. Budget your time so you do not spend your moments before you speak hurriedly looking for a parking place or frantically trying to attend to last-minute details.

- **Prepare the room and equipment.** You may want to rearrange the furniture or make other changes in the speaking environment. If you are using audiovisual equipment, check to see that it is working properly and set up your support material carefully. Project a PowerPoint slide or two to make sure the image is clear.

- **Visualize success.** Picture yourself delivering your speech in an effective way. Also, remind yourself of the effort you have spent preparing for your speech. A final mental rehearsal can boost your confidence and help ensure success.

Even though we have identified many time-tested methods for enhancing your speech delivery, keep in mind that speech delivery is an art rather than a science. The manner of your delivery should reflect your personality and individual style.

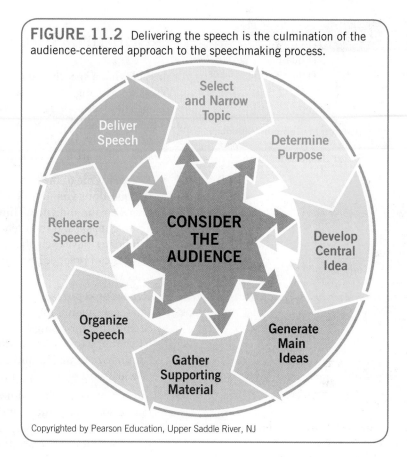

FIGURE 11.2 Delivering the speech is the culmination of the audience-centered approach to the speechmaking process.

Copyrighted by Pearson Education, Upper Saddle River, NJ

RECAP

DELIVERING YOUR SPEECH

- Get a good night's rest.
- Eat carefully.
- Arrive early.
- Visualize success.
- Reinforce your confidence with tips from Chapter 1.

DEVELOPING YOUR SPEECH STEP BY STEP

DELIVER YOUR SPEECH

The long-awaited day of Brianne's speech has come. She slept well last night and ate a light breakfast before coming to class.

Waiting her turn to speak, Brianne breathes deeply and visualizes herself delivering her speech calmly and confidently. When her name is called, she walks to the front of the room and establishes eye contact with her audience before she begins to speak.

During her speech, Brianne focuses on adapting her message to her listeners. She looks at individual members of her audience, uses purposeful and well-timed gestures, and speaks loudly and clearly.

Even before she hears the applause, Brianne knows that her speech has been a success.

11.7 Explain and use strategies for responding to questions from your audience at the end of your speech.

Watch at **MyCommunicationLab**
Video: "The Process of Developing a Speech: Questions and Answers"

Responding to Questions

It's possible that a speech you deliver will be followed by a question-and-answer (Q & A) session. During a Q & A session, your delivery method changes to impromptu speaking. These sessions can be especially challenging because, although you may not know the questions in advance, you will be expected to deliver your answers thoughtfully and smoothly. In addition to the suggestions for impromptu speaking we offered earlier, here are additional tips to make the Q & A period less challenging.[40]

- **Prepare.** One of the best ways to prepare for a Q & A session is to anticipate the questions you may be asked. How do you anticipate questions? You analyze your audience. Think of possible questions those particular listeners might ask, and then rehearse your answers. Prior to presidential debates, candidates have their staff members pepper them with questions so the candidates can practice responding. Perhaps your friends can ask you questions after you've rehearsed your speech for them.

- **Repeat or rephrase the question.** Repeating a question helps in four ways. First, your paraphrase makes sure that everyone can hear the question. Second, paraphrasing ensures that you understand the question before you go charging off with your answer. Third, by paraphrasing, you can succinctly summarize rambling questions. And, finally, repeating the question gives you just a bit of time to think about your answer.

- **Stay on message.** Sometimes listeners may ask questions unrelated to your talk. If so, you'll want to find a way to gently guide your questioner back to the message you have prepared. Keep bringing the audience back to your central idea. Your answers, rather than the questions, are important. We're not suggesting that you dodge questions; you should address the question asked, but then re-emphasize the key points you have made. Some seasoned speakers suggest that you save a bit of your speech to deliver during the Q & A session. It's called giving a "double-barreled" talk.[41] You present your speech, and then, during the Q & A period, you give a second, much briefer speech.

- **Respond to the entire audience, not just the person who asked the question.** Although you can start your response by having eye contact with the person who asked you a question, make sure that you stay audience-centered. Look at all audience members and keep in mind that your response should be relevant to them. If the questioner wants specific information that is of interest only to that person, you could speak with the questioner individually after your speech.

Preparation can help you manage a question-and-answer session smoothly to bring a successful end to the delivery of your speech.

Photo: Stockbyte/Getty Images

- **Ask yourself the first question.** One way to prime the audience for the Q & A session is to ask yourself a challenging question first. For example, you might say, "As we move into Q & A, a number of you may be wondering...." State the question and answer it. Doing this also gives you a comfortable way to make a transition between the speech and the Q & A period. Asking yourself a tough question tells the audience that you're open for serious questions, and it snaps them to attention as well.

- **Listen nonjudgmentally.** Use the effective listening skills that we discussed in Chapter 4. Keep your eyes focused on the person asking the question, lean forward slightly, and give your full attention to the questioner. Audience members expect speakers to be polite and attentive. If you think the question is stupid, don't say so. Just listen and respond courteously. Audience members can judge for themselves whether a question is appropriate or not. Don't wince, grimace, or scowl at the questioner. You'll gain more credibility by keeping your cool than by losing your composure.

- **Neutralize hostile questions.** Every hostile question gives you an opportunity to score points with your listeners. You'll have your listeners' attention; use that attention to your advantage. The following strategies can help.

Restate the question. If the question was a lengthy attack, focus on the essence of the issue. If the question is "Your ideas are just wrong! I'm angry that you have no clue as to how to proceed. Your proposal has been a disaster in the past. Why are you still trying to make it work?" a paraphrase could be "You're asking me why I'm still trying to implement a program that hasn't been successful. From your perspective, the program has failed."

Acknowledge emotions. For example, you could say, "I can understand why you are angry. I share your anger and frustration. It's because of my frustration that I want to give my proposal more time to work."

Don't make the issue personal. Even when a hostile questioner has made you the villain, don't attack the person who asked the question. Keep the conversation focused on issues, not on personalities.

Get to the heart of the issue. Respond directly to a hostile question. Consider restating the evidence you presented in your speech. Or provide new insights to support your position.

- **When you don't know, admit it.** If you've been asked a question to which you don't know the answer, just say so. You can promise to find out more information and then get back to the person later. (If you make such a promise, follow through on it. Ask for the person's business card or email address at the end of the Q & A session.)

- **Be brief.** Even if you've anticipated questions and have a "double-barreled" talk, make it short and to the point.

- **Use organizational signposts.** Quickly organize your responses. If you have two responses to a question, let your listeners know it. Then use a verbal signpost (a statement that clues your audience in to how you're organizing your message) by saying, "I have two responses. First . . ." When you get to your second point, say, "My second point is. . . ." These signposts will both help you stay organized and impress your listeners with your clarity.

- **Indicate when the Q & A period is concluding.** Tell your audience, "I have time for two more questions." Let them know that the Q & A session will soon conclude. Even if you have someone helping you moderate the discussion, you should remain in charge of concluding the session.

RECAP

RESPONDING TO QUESTIONS

- Prepare; ask the first question yourself.
- Listen nonjudgmentally; repeat or rephrase questions.
- Respond to the whole audience.
- Bring off-topic questions back to your message.
- Acknowledge emotions, keep to the issue, and avoid personal responses to hostile questions.
- Admit it when you don't know the answer.
- Keep answers brief and organized.
- Warn audience when Q & A is ending.

STUDY GUIDE

REVIEW, APPLY, AND ASSESS

THE POWER OF SPEECH DELIVERY

11.1   Identify three reasons delivery is important to a public speaker.

Nonverbal communication conveys the majority of the meaning of your speech and nearly all of your emotions to an audience. Nonverbal expectancy theory suggests that your credibility as a speaker depends on meeting your audience's expectations about nonverbal communication. Audiences will believe what they see in your nonverbal communication more readily than what they hear in your words.

Key Terms

Nonverbal communication. 211
Nonverbal expectancy theory . . . 211
Emotional contagion theory. 212

Thinking Ethically

What can listeners do to be less distracted by the delivery and emotional elements of a speaker's message and to focus more on the substance or content of the message?

Assessing Your Audience-Centered Speaking Skill

Based on emotional contagion theory, described on page 212, how you can tell if your audience is "catching" the emotional message you intend to communicate? What specific nonverbal cues should you be looking for to see if your audience is responding to your message as you had planned?

METHODS OF DELIVERY

11.2   Identify and describe four methods of delivery.

Of the four methods of delivery—manuscript, memorized, impromptu, and extemporaneous—the extemporaneous method is the most desirable in most situations. Speak from an outline without memorizing the exact words.

Key Terms

Manuscript speaking. 213
Memorized speaking. 214
Impromptu speaking. 214
Extemporaneous speaking 216

Thinking Critically

Roger was so nervous about his first speech that he practiced it again and again. He could have given the speech in his sleep. He had some great examples, and his instructor had praised his outline. But as he gave his speech, he saw his classmates tuning out. What might he have done wrong, and how could he have rescued his speech?

Assessing Your Audience-Centered Speaking Skill

How can you determine when you have rehearsed long enough so that you can extemporaneously deliver your key ideas to your listeners, but not so long that you are giving a memorized presentation?

CHARACTERISTICS OF EFFECTIVE DELIVERY

11.3   Identify and illustrate the characteristics of effective delivery.

Eye contact is the single most important delivery variable. Make eye contact with the whole audience before and throughout your speech. Your gestures and movements should appear natural and relaxed, definite, consistent with your message, varied, unobtrusive, and coordinated with what you say, as well as appropriate to your audience and situation. Adapt gestures to the cultural diversity of your audience. Use your posture, facial expressions, and vocal cues—including pitch, rate of speaking, and use of pauses—to communicate your emotions. Be sure to speak loudly enough and to articulate clearly. If English is not your native language, you may have to spend extra time working on your pronunciation and articulation.

Key Terms

Immediacy 221
Immediacy behaviors 221
Volume 223
Articulation 224
Dialect 224
Pronunciation. 225
Pitch. 225
Inflection. 226
Lavaliere microphone 227
Boom microphone. 227
Stationary microphone 227

Thinking Ethically

Most politicians at the state or national level hire image consultants to help them project the most positive impression of their skills and abilities. Is it ethical to use such consultants, especially when their sole objective is to manipulate constituents into thinking the speaker is more credible than he or she really is?

Thinking Critically

Monique is self-conscious about her hand gestures, and she often just puts her hands behind her back. What advice would you give Monique to help her use gestures more effectively?

Assessing Your Audience-Centered Speaking Skill

Check your pronunciation. Ask a friend, family member, or classmate to let you know if you are pronouncing all the words in your speech correctly. If you are uncertain how to say a word you want to use, visit an online dictionary to listen to a recording of the pronunciation.

AUDIENCE DIVERSITY AND DELIVERY

11.4   Use strategies for adapting your delivery when speaking to diverse audiences.

Consult with other speakers familiar with your audience to help you avoid ethnocentrism. Consider using a more subtle delivery style with high-context audiences, and match immediacy and emotional expression to the cultural expectations of the majority of listeners. Learn variations in meanings of nonverbal gestures across cultures to avoid giving offense.

Thinking Critically

You are planning to speak to a local group of businesspeople who all share a culture different from your own. What questions might you ask of the person who invited you to speak, in order to help you adapt to your audience?

Assessing Your Audience-Centered Speaking Skill

What can you do to ensure that your speech does not evidence an ethnocentric mind-set when delivering a speech to listeners from a culture different from your own?

REHEARSING YOUR SPEECH: SOME FINAL TIPS

11.5   Describe the steps to follow when you rehearse your speech.

Allow at least two days after finishing your speech outline to practice your speech delivery and develop your speaking notes. As much as possible, re-create the speech environment when you rehearse. Rehearse your speech while keeping your audience in mind; imagine that your audience is in front of you as you practice presenting your message.

Thinking Critically

Jason just never seems to be quite ready on the day he is supposed to give his speech. He has always thought a great deal about his speech and prepared a few notes but usually has not done much else. What specific advice would you give Jason to help him prepare and rehearse his speech to ensure success?

Assessing Your Audience-Centered Speaking Skill

Review the tips for rehearsing your speech presented on page 231. Rate yourself on a scale of 1–5 (1 = poor; 5 = excellent) on each of the suggestions for enhancing your speech rehearsal strategies. Use your self-ratings to develop a plan to improve your rehearsals.

DELIVERING YOUR SPEECH

11.6   List four suggestions for enhancing the final delivery of your speech.

Get a good night's rest before a speech. Visualize your success and reinforce your confidence using the suggestions from Chapter 1 of this book. Arrive early so that you have time to prepare the environment and are not stressed by running late.

Thinking Critically

Aspen felt quite nervous as she gave her speech, and her instructor later commented that she had spoken so fast that some of her words were hard to understand. Review the strategies for managing speech apprehension in Chapter 1 and the delivery advice in this chapter to recommend specific steps Aspen can take to reduce her nervousness as well as slow her speech rate for her next presentation.

Assessing Your Audience-Centered Speaking Skill

It's one thing to read about speech delivery, but it's quite another to see and hear speakers deliver a message. Use what you've learned in this chapter to evaluate the delivery strengths and weaknesses of the speeches at the following sites.

- History Channel Archive of Speeches: Each day a famous speech is highlighted. There is also an archive you can browse to listen to or watch famous speeches: http://www.history.com/speeches.

- MSU Vincent Voice Library: This site will permit you to hear recordings of the voices of U.S. presidents and other historical figures: http://vvl.lib.msu.edu/.

RESPONDING TO QUESTIONS

 11.7 Explain and use strategies for responding to questions from your audience at the end of your speech.

Prepare for Q & A and be ready to ask the first question yourself. Listen nonjudgmentally and repeat or rephrase questions. Respond briefly and to the whole audience. Use strategies described in this chapter to neutralize hostile questions and bring off-topic questions back to your message. Admit it when you don't know an answer. Use organizational signposts to clarify answers and to signal the end of Q & A.

Thinking Critically

Muriel, who has been a church organist for 35 years, is planning to speak to her music club about techniques of playing the pipe organ. What are some questions Muriel might be asked during the Q & A period?

Explore at **MyCommunicationLab**
Speaker's Workshop: Improving Your Speech Delivery

12 USING PRESENTATION AIDS

Hieronymus Bosch (c. 1450–1516), *The Conjurer,* 1475–1480. Musée Municipal, Saint-Germain-en-Laye, France. Photo: Scala/White Images/Art Resource, N.Y.

OBJECTIVES

After studying this chapter you should be able to do the following:

12.1
Discuss five ways in which presentation aids help communicate ideas to an audience.

12.2
Describe the types of presentation aids and identify tips for using them effectively.

12.3
Identify guidelines for developing effective presentation aids.

12.4
Identify guidelines for effectively using presentation aids.

(((Listen to Chapter 12 at **MyCommunicationLab**

The soul never thinks without a picture.

—Aristotle

Perhaps it has happened to you. A professor flashes one PowerPoint™ slide after another while droning on about British history or some other topic. As you sit there, bored out of your socks, you think, "Why doesn't she just hand out the PowerPoint slides or simply put them online and let us go? I don't need her to read her notes to me." Following such a mind-numbing experience, you can understand the phrase "Death by PowerPoint."

PowerPoint and the multitude of other presentation aids that speakers may use—especially visual aids—are powerful tools: They can help communicate your ideas with greater clarity and impact than can words alone. But they can also overwhelm your speech or be so redundant that your audience tunes you out. This chapter will help you avoid being a PowerPoint "executioner" and ensure that your presentation aids add life to your speech rather than kill your message.

A **presentation aid** is any object that reinforces your point visually or aurally so that your audience can better understand it. Charts, photographs, posters, drawings, graphs, PowerPoint slides, movies, and videos are the types of presentation aids that we will discuss. Some of them, such as movies and videos, call on sound as well as sight to help you make your point.

When you are first required to give a speech using presentation aids, you may wonder, "How can I use presentation aids in an informative or persuasive speech? Those kinds of speeches don't lend themselves to visual images." As it happens, almost any speech can benefit from presentation aids. A speech for which you are expected to use presentation aids is not as different from other types of speeches as you might at first think. Your general objective is still to inform, persuade, or entertain. The key difference is that you will use supporting material that can be seen, rather than only heard, by an audience.

In this chapter, we look at presentation aids as an important communication tool, and we examine several kinds. Toward the end of the chapter, we suggest guidelines for using presentation aids in your speeches.

12.1 Discuss five ways in which presentation aids help communicate ideas to an audience.

presentation aid
Anything tangible (drawings, charts, graphs, video images, photographs, sounds) that helps communicate an idea to an audience

The Value of Presentation Aids

Contemporary audiences are quite different from those of more than a century ago, when Thomas Edison invented the kinetoscope, a precursor of the movie camera. Edison said, "When we started out it took the average audience a long time to assimilate each image. They weren't trained to visualize more than one thought at a time."[1] Times have changed. The predominance of visual images—on TV, in movies, on the Internet, and on our phones and mobile devices—attests to how central images are in the communication of information to modern audiences. Today's listeners expect visual support. Presentation aids help your audience *understand* and *remember* your message, and they help you communicate the *organization* of ideas, gain and maintain *attention*, and illustrate a *sequence* of events or procedures.[2]

Presentation Aids Enhance Understanding

Of your five senses, you learn more from sight than from all the others combined. In fact, it has been estimated that more than 80 percent of all information comes to you through sight.[3] To many people, seeing is believing. We are a visually oriented society. For example, most of us learn the news by seeing it presented on TV or the Internet. Because your audience is accustomed to visual reinforcement, it is wise to consider how you can increase their understanding of your speech by using presentation aids.

Presentation Aids Enhance Memory

Your audience will not only have an improved understanding of your speech, but they will also better remember what you say as a result of visual reinforcement.[4] There is evidence that high-tech presentation aids enhance learning.[5] Researchers estimate that you remember 10 percent of what you read, 20 percent of what you hear, 30 percent of what you see, and 50 percent of what you simultaneously hear and see. For example, in your speech about the languages spoken in Africa, your audience is more likely to remember words in Arabic, Swahili, and Hausa if you display the words visually rather than just speak them.

Presentation Aids Help Listeners Organize Ideas

Most listeners need help understanding the structure of a speech. Even if you clearly lay out your major points, use effective internal summaries, and make clear transition statements, your listeners will welcome additional help. Briefly listing major ideas on a PowerPoint slide, a chart, or a poster can add clarity to your talk and help your audience grasp your main ideas. Visually presenting your major ideas during your introduction, for example, can help your audience follow them as you bring them into the body of your speech. And you can display key ideas during your conclusion to help summarize your message succinctly.

Presentation Aids Help You Gain and Maintain Attention

Keshia began her speech about poverty in the United States by showing a photo of the face of an undernourished child. She immediately had the attention of her audience. Chuck introduced his presentation on photography with the flash of his camera. He certainly alerted his audience at that point. Midway through her speech about the lyrics in rap music, Tomoko not only spoke the words but also displayed a giant poster of the song lyrics so that her audience could read the words and sing along. Presentation

Presentation aids can help you capture the attention of your audience. They can help your audience understand the organization of your talk and remember the information you present.

Photo: Creativa

aids not only grab the attention of your listeners but also hold their interest when words alone might not.

Presentation Aids Help Illustrate a Sequence of Events or Procedures

If your purpose is to inform an audience about a process—how to do something or how something functions—you can do this best through actual demonstrations or with a series of visuals. Whether your objective is instructing people on how to make a soufflé or how to build a greenhouse, demonstrating the step-by-step procedures helps your audience understand them.[6] If you wish to explain how hydroelectric power is generated, a series of diagrams can help your listeners understand and visualize the process.

When demonstrating how to make something, such as your prize-winning cinnamon rolls, you can prepare each step of the process ahead of time and show your audience each example as you describe the relevant step; for example, you might have the dough already mixed and ready to demonstrate how you sprinkle on the cinnamon. A climax to your speech could be to unveil a finished pan of rolls still warm from the oven. If time does not permit you to demonstrate how to prepare your rolls, you could have on hand a series of diagrams and photographs to illustrate each step of the procedure.

Contemporary communicators understand the power of visual rhetoric in informing and persuading others. **Visual rhetoric** is the use of images as an integrated element in the total communication effort a speaker makes to achieve his or her speaking goal.[7] To be a visual rhetorician is to assume the role of an audience member and consider not only what a listener hears but also what a listener sees. Today's sophisticated listeners expect a visually satisfying message to help them make sense of what you are saying.

 Read at **MyCommunicationLab**
Learning From Great Speakers:
Ronald Reagan

RECAP

THE VALUE OF PRESENTATION AIDS

They help your audience
- understand your message.
- remember your message.
- see the organization of your message.
- maintain attention.
- understand a sequence of events or procedures.

12.2 Describe the types of presentation aids and identify tips for using them effectively.

 Watch at **MyCommunicationLab**
Video: "The Process of Developing a Speech: Using Presentation Aids"

 Watch at **MyCommunicationLab**
Video: "The Art of Board Breaking"

visual rhetoric
The use of images as an integrated element in the total communication effort a speaker makes to achieve the speaking goal

Types of Presentation Aids

The first question many students ask when they learn they are required to use presentation aids is "What type of presentation aid should I use?" You can choose from three classes of presentation aids: three-dimensional, two-dimensional, and audiovisual.

Three-Dimensional Presentation Aids

Objects You have played the trombone since you were in fifth grade, so you decide to give an informative speech about the history and function of this instrument. Your trombone is the obvious presentation aid that you would show to your audience as you describe how it works. You might even play a few measures to demonstrate its sound and your talent. Or perhaps you are an art major and you have just finished a watercolor painting. Why not bring your picture to class to illustrate your talk about watercolor techniques?

Objects add interest because they are tangible. They can be touched, smelled, heard, and even tasted, as well as seen. Objects are real, and audiences like the real thing.

When you use an object to illustrate an idea, make sure that you can handle the object with ease. If an object is too large, it can be unwieldy and difficult to show to your audience. Tiny objects can only be seen close up. It will be impossible for your listeners to see the detail on your antique thimble, the intricate needlework on your cross-stitch sampler, or the attention to detail in your miniature log cabin. Other objects can be dangerous to handle. One speaker, who attempted a demonstration of how to string an archery bow, made his audience extremely uncomfortable when his almost-strung bow flew over their heads. He certainly got their attention, but he lost his credibility.

Models If it is not possible to bring along the object you would like to show your audience, consider showing them a **model** of it. You cannot bring a World War II fighter plane to class, so buy or build a scale model instead. To illustrate her lecture about human anatomy, one student brought a plastic model of a skeleton; an actual human skeleton would have been difficult to get and carry to class. Similarly, colleges and universities typically do not allow firearms on campus. A drawing that shows the features of a gun is a much safer presentation aid than a real gun or even a toy gun. If you need to show the movable parts of a gun, perhaps a papier-mâché, plastic, or wood model would serve. Make sure, however, that any model you use is large enough to be seen by all members of your audience. When Brad brought his collection of miniature hand-carved guitars to illustrate his talk on rock music, his tiny visuals didn't add to the message; they detracted from it.

Three-dimensional models can help you to explain an object, process, or procedure to your audience in situations where it is impractical or impossible to use the actual object.

Photo: Cultura Limited/SuperStock

People At least since Ronald Reagan, U.S. presidents have used people as visual aids during their State of the Union addresses, relating a poignant story and then asking the protagonist of the story, seated in the balcony, to stand and be recognized. One speechwriter noted that presidents have learned to use this strategy to especially good effect, finding it "a way of coming down from the stage, as it were, and mingling with the crowd."[8]

In classroom speeches, too, people can serve as presentation aids. Amelia, a choreographer for the Ballet Folklorico Mexicano, wanted to illustrate an intricate Latin folk dance, so she arranged to have one of the troupe's dancers attend her speech to demonstrate the dance.

Using people to illustrate your message can be tricky, however. It is usually unwise to ask for spur-of-the-moment help from volunteers while you are delivering your speech. Instead, choose a trusted friend or colleague before your presentation so that you can fully inform him or her about what needs to be done. Rehearse your speech using your living presentation aid.

Also, it is distracting to have your support person stand beside you doing nothing. If you don't need the person to demonstrate something during your opening remarks, wait and introduce the person to your audience when needed.

Finally, do not allow your assistants to run away with the show. For example, don't let your dance student perform the *pas de bourré* longer than necessary to illustrate your technique. Nor should you permit your models to prance about provocatively while displaying your dress designs. And don't allow your buddy to throw you when you demonstrate the wrestling hold that made you the district wrestling champ. Remember, your presentation aids are always subordinate to your speech. You must remain in control.

You can also serve as your own presentation aid to demonstrate or illustrate major points. If you are talking about tennis, you might use your racquet to illustrate your superb backhand or to show the proper way to hold it. If you are a nurse or an emergency room technician giving a talk about medical procedures, by all means wear your uniform to establish your credibility.

Two-Dimensional Presentation Aids

The most common presentation aids are two-dimensional: drawings, photographs, maps, graphs, charts, flipcharts, and chalkboards. A few presenters continue to use

model
A small object that represents a larger object

👁 **Watch** at **MyCommunicationLab**
Video: "Drinking and Driving"

👁 **Watch** at **MyCommunicationLab**
Video: "Sweat"

overhead transparencies. Although two-dimensional aids are the most common, you'll more than likely incorporate them into PowerPoint or other slides to illustrate your message. As we discuss two-dimensional visual aids, we'll offer general suggestions both for using them in the old-fashioned way and for incorporating them into presentation software. A little later in the chapter we'll focus exclusively on how to use computer-generated graphics.

Drawings Drawings are popular and often-used presentation aids because they are easy and inexpensive to make. Drawings can be tailored to your specific needs. To illustrate the functions of the human brain, for example, one student traced an outline of the brain and labeled it to indicate where brain functions are located. Another student wanted to show the different sizes and shapes of tree leaves in the area, so she drew enlarged pictures of the leaves, using appropriate shades of green.

You don't have to be a master artist to develop effective drawings. As a rule, large and simple line drawings are more effective for stage presentations than are detailed images. If you have absolutely no faith in your artistic skill, you can probably find a friend or relative who can help you prepare a useful drawing, or you may be able to use computer software to generate simple line drawings.

Photographs Photographs can be used to show objects or places that cannot be illustrated with drawings or that an audience cannot view directly. The problem with printed photos, however, is that they are usually too small to be seen clearly from a distance. If your listeners occupy only two or three rows, it might be possible to hold a photograph close enough for them to see a key feature of the picture or to display a photo on a computer tablet such as an iPad. Passing a photograph among your listeners is not a good idea either; it creates competition for your audience's attention.

The only way to be sure that a photograph will be effective as a presentation aid for a large audience is to enlarge it, either as a big print or through electronic projection. If you're using nondigital images, you can scan them and have them enlarged. Or, if you're using presentation software such as PowerPoint, you can import your photos into PowerPoint slides to make them large enough for everyone to see.

Twenty years ago, in the era BP (Before PowerPoint), public speakers who wanted to illustrate a talk with photos used 36-millimeter slides projected with a slide projector. Today slides are rarely used because computer-projected images are much easier to work with.

Maps Most maps are designed to be read from a distance of no more than two feet. As with photographs, the details on most maps won't be visible to your audience. You could use a large map, however, to show general features of an area. Or you could use a magnified version of your map. Certain copiers can enlarge images as much as 200 percent. It is possible, using a color copier, to enlarge a standard map of Europe enough for listeners in the last row to see the general features of the continent. Using a dark marker, one speaker highlighted the borders on a map of Europe to indicate the countries she had visited the previous summer (see Figure 12.1). She used a red marker to show the path of her journey. You can also search online for "public domain" maps that you can download without violating copyright laws.

Graphs A **graph** is a pictorial representation of statistical data in an easy-to-understand format. Most graphs used in speeches are prepared using either Excel or Word and then displayed as computer-generated slides.

Why use a graph? Seeing relationships among numbers is better than just hearing statistics. Statistics are abstract summaries of many examples. Most listeners find that graphs help make the data more concrete and easier to understand. Yet research also suggests that in addition to presenting information in a graph, it's important to talk about the information presented.[9] Graphs are particularly effective for showing overall trends and relationships among data. By watching news programs, hearing

graph
A pictorial representation of statistical data

FIGURE 12.1 A map can be an effective visual aid, especially when the speaker personalizes it by highlighting relevant information—such as the route followed in a journey from Edinburgh to Warsaw.

Copyrighted by Pearson Education, Upper Saddle River, NJ

reports, and seeing presentations, you have undoubtedly seen the four most common types of graphs: bar graphs, pie graphs, line graphs, and picture graphs.

- **Bar Graphs.** A **bar graph** consists of flat areas—bars—of various lengths to represent information. The bar graph in Figure 12.2 clearly shows the growth rates of wireless subscribers. It would be more difficult to illustrate your point with words and numbers alone. A graph helps your listeners quickly see comparisons.

bar graph
A graph in which bars of various lengths represent information

FIGURE 12.2 Bar graphs can help make statistical information clearly and immediately visible to your audience.

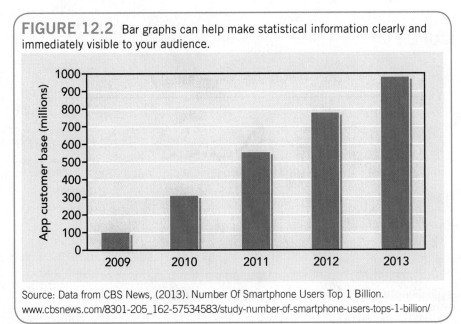

Source: Data from CBS News, (2013). Number Of Smartphone Users Top 1 Billion. www.cbsnews.com/8301-205_162-57534583/study-number-of-smartphone-users-tops-1-billion/

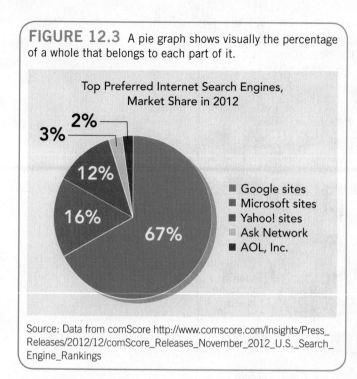

FIGURE 12.3 A pie graph shows visually the percentage of a whole that belongs to each part of it.

Top Preferred Internet Search Engines, Market Share in 2012

- Google sites
- Microsoft sites
- Yahoo! sites
- Ask Network
- AOL, Inc.

Source: Data from comScore http://www.comscore.com/Insights/Press_Releases/2012/12/comScore_Releases_November_2012_U.S._Search_Engine_Rankings

- **Pie Graphs.** A **pie graph** shows the individual shares of a whole. The pie graph in Figure 12.3 shows the top Internet search providers. Pie graphs are especially useful in helping your listeners to see quickly how data are distributed in a given category or area.

- **Line Graphs.** A **line graph** shows relationships between two or more variables. Like bar graphs, line graphs organize statistical data to show overall trends (Figure 12.4). A line graph can cover a greater span of time or numbers than a bar graph without looking cluttered or confusing. As with other types of presentation aids, a simple line graph communicates better than a cluttered one.

- **Picture Graphs.** In place of either a line or a bar, you can use pictures, or symbols, to supplement the data you are summarizing (Figure 12.5). A **picture graph** looks somewhat less formal and less intimidating than other kinds of graphs. One of the advantages of picture graphs is that they use few words or labels, which makes them easier for your audience to read. There are online sources that can help you create your own picture graphs.

pie graph

A circular graph divided into wedges that show each part's percentage of the whole

line graph

A graph that uses lines or curves to show relationships between two or more variables

picture graph

A graph that uses images or pictures to symbolize data

chart

A display that summarizes information by using words, numbers, or images

Charts A **chart** summarizes and presents a great deal of information in a small amount of space (Figure 12.6). Charts have several advantages: They are easy to use, reuse, and enlarge. They can be displayed in a variety of ways, on a flipchart, a poster, or a computer-developed slide. As with all other presentation aids, charts must be simple. Do not try to put too much information on one chart.

The key to developing effective charts is to prepare the lettering of the words and phrases you use very carefully. If the chart contains too much information, audience members may feel it is too complicated to understand, and ignore it. If your chart looks at all cramped or crowded, divide the information into several charts and display each as needed. Do not handwrite the chart; given the availability of computers, a hand-lettered chart may seem unprofessional. We suggest using computer software to prepare large charts or graphs. Make sure your letters are large enough to

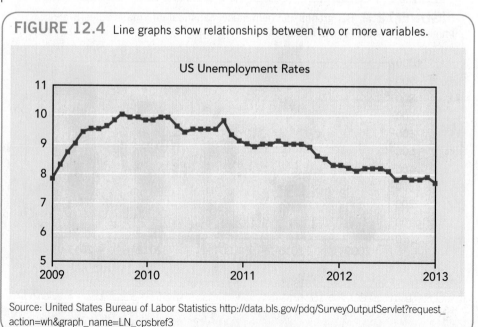

FIGURE 12.4 Line graphs show relationships between two or more variables.

US Unemployment Rates

Source: United States Bureau of Labor Statistics http://data.bls.gov/pdq/SurveyOutputServlet?request_action=wh&graph_name=LN_cpsbref3

be seen clearly in the back row. Use simple words or phrases, and eliminate unnecessary words.

Flipcharts A flipchart consists of a large pad of paper resting on an easel. Flipcharts are sometimes used in business presentations and training sessions, although the prevalence of computer graphics software has reduced their use in corporate presentations. You can either prepare your visual aids before your speech or draw on the paper while speaking. Flipcharts are easy to use. During your presentation, you need only flip the page to reveal your next visual. Flipcharts are best used when you have brief information to display or when you want to summarize comments from audience members during a presentation.

Most experienced flipchart users recommend that you use lined paper to keep your words and drawings neat and well organized. Another suggestion is to pencil in speaking notes on the chart that only you can see. Brief notes on a flipchart are less cumbersome to use than notes on cards or a clipboard.

FIGURE 12.5 Adding visual symbols, such as those in this picture graph, can help your audience maintain interest and understand complex information.

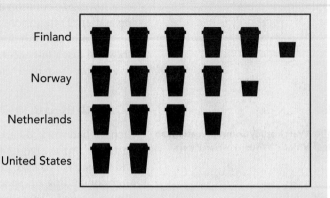

Average Daily Coffee Cups Consumed Per Person Per Day

Finland

Norway

Netherlands

United States

Source: The eLearning Coach. "How to Make Numbers Interesting." (2013) http://theelearningcoach.com/media/graphics/make-numbers-interesting/. Used with permission by Connie Malamed.

Chalkboards and Whiteboards A fixture in classrooms for centuries, chalkboards are often used to offer visual support for spoken words. Whiteboards are replacing chalkboards in both education and business settings; these more contemporary boards serve the same function as chalkboards, but instead of writing on a black or green slate with a piece of chalk, the speaker writes on a whiteboard with a marker. Chalkboards and whiteboards have several advantages: They are inexpensive, simple to use, and low-tech, so you don't need to worry about extension cords or special training. They lend themselves to a variety of content; it's easy to sketch a simple graph, diagram, or map, or to jot a few words on the board.

FIGURE 12.6 Charts summarize and present a great deal of information in a small amount of space.

Team	W	L	Percent	GB	Streak
Toronto	84	59	.583	—	Won 2
Baltimore	78	64	.549	$5\frac{1}{2}$	Lost 2
Milwaukee	77	65	.542	$6\frac{1}{2}$	Won 2
New York	69	74	.483	15	Lost 1

Although you can find a chalkboard or whiteboard in most classrooms and boardrooms, many public-speaking teachers discourage overuse of them. Why? When you write on the board, you have your back to your audience; you do not have eye contact! Some speakers try to avoid that problem by writing on the board before their speech starts. But then listeners often look at the visual rather than listening to the introductory remarks. Moreover, chalkboards and whiteboards are probably the least novel presentation aids, so they are not particularly effective at getting or holding audience attention.

Use a board only for brief phrases or for very simple line diagrams that can be drawn in just a few seconds. It is usually better to prepare a chart, graph, or drawing on a poster or an overhead transparency than to use a chalkboard or whiteboard.

Computer-Generated Presentation Aids

Watch at **MyCommunicationLab**
Video: "Writing Position Papers"

Richard had worked hard on his presentation to the finance committee. He had prepared an impressive-looking poster, distributed a handout of his key conclusions, and rehearsed his speech so that he had a well-polished delivery. But as he sat down after concluding his speech, certain he had dazzled his listeners, a colleague poked him and asked, "Why didn't you use PowerPoint or Prezi slides?"

Basic Principles of Using Computer-Generated Presentation Aids Most audiences, especially those in the corporate world, expect a speaker to use computer-generated presentation aids. The most popular presentation software, PowerPoint, helps you create and present images, photos, words, charts, and graphs.

Prezi is another increasingly popular presentation software program that is cloud-based—the information is accessed on an Internet "cloud" rather than on your own computer. Prezi has many features similar to PowerPoint, but it also has features that let you zoom in and out to help you focus your audience's attention (although overuse of this feature can be nauseously distracting). Prezi also has a feature that lets you look at all of your slides at once, giving you more control to select images to adapt to your audience. So rather than predetermining the precise order of your slides, you can more readily adapt your presentation to your audience while you are speaking.

Keynote, another popular presentation software, was developed for Apple™ computers and devices, although it can be transferred for use in PC computers. Like other graphics programs, it permits users to easily maintain consistency in fonts and colors. Some people especially like its sleek, contemporary appearance.

Although PowerPoint, Prezi, and Keynote can be overused and, like any presentation aid, can distract from your message if used improperly, they nonetheless open up professional-looking possibilities for illustrating your speech.

One of the biggest problems with using computer-generated images is that a speaker may be tempted to shovel large amounts of information at listeners without regard for the listeners' attention span. Research supports our now-familiar admonition that the audience should be foremost in your mind as you develop visual images to support your verbal message.[10]

Since most students learn to use presentation software in school, you will no doubt be familiar with the basic elements of developing a computer-generated image. And because you've undoubtedly seen many computer-generated presentations, you also know that you can incorporate video clips as well as digital photo images on a slide. But, as with any presentation aid, the images or clips that you choose to display must help develop your central idea; otherwise, they will distract your audience from it.

You don't have to be a professional artist to develop attractive images. That's the key advantage of using computer-generated graphics—virtually anyone can use them to craft professional-looking images. In addition to learning the mechanics of the software program, keep the following tips in mind when using computer-generated images.[11] These tips are also summarized in Table 12.1.

TABLE 12.1	**DEVELOP EFFECTIVE COMPUTER-GENERATED VISUALS**
Make text simple	• Use no more than seven lines of text on a single slide • Use bullets • Use parallel structure when writing text
Make visuals unified	• Use a common visual image on each slide • Use a common font • Use a similar background or style for each slide
Choose fonts carefully	• Use serif fonts to increase ease of reading • Use script and sans serif fonts sparingly • Use decorative fonts only for dramatic impact
Choose colors carefully	• Use red and orange to communicate warmth • Use green and blue to communicate calm coolness • Be cautious about using red and green together • Use a light background with darker text to catch attention
Create your visuals well in advance of your presentation	• Use your time to integrate your verbal message with your visual message • Seek advice and assistance from others to help polish your visuals • Practice using your visuals when you rehearse your speech

Copyrighted by Pearson Education, Upper Saddle River, NJ

Tips for Using Computer-Generated Presentation Aids

Watch at **MyCommunicationLab**
Video: "How to Use PowerPoint"

Keep Sights and Sounds Simple In most aspects of communication, simple is better. Even though you *can* use fancy fonts and add as many images as you like to your visual, we have a suggestion for you: Don't. Keep in mind what we've stressed throughout this chapter: Presentation aids *support* your message; they are not your message. Or, as CEO John W. Roe wisely expressed, "Visual aids should be made to steer, not to row."[12]

What are some techniques for keeping your visual message simple? One key concern is to limit the number of words on each slide. Consider these principles:

- Use no more than seven lines of text on any single visual.
- Use bullet points to designate individual items or thoughts.
- Use parallel structure in bulleted lists (for example, begin each bulleted phrase with the same word, as we do in this list).
- Use the heading of each slide to summarize the essential point of the visual; if listeners read only the headings of your visuals, they should still be able to follow the key points of the story you're telling.[13]

Although we've suggested that you could use as many as seven lines of text on a slide, contemporary research suggests that using fewer words and an appropriate image is the best use of computer graphics. Use presentational aids to present images rather than merely repeat the words you say.

Most graphics software lets you add sound effects to highlight your message. But the sound of a racecar zooming across the computer screen or a typewriter clacking as letters pop in place can detract from your speech. Cute sounds will lose their novelty after the first slide or two and can become irritating. We suggest that *you* be the soundtrack, not your computer.

Control Computer Images When using computer-generated slides, there may be times when you want to speak to your audience and not refer to a slide or image. Use a blank slide, or use the remote control of the projector to temporarily project no image.

Repeat Visual Elements to Unify Your Presentation Use a common visual element, such as a bullet or other symbol, at the beginning of each word or phrase on a list. Use common color schemes and spacing to give your visuals coherence. Also avoid mixing different fonts. You get a professional, polished look when you use the same visual style for each of your images.

The most significant advantage of computer graphics is the ease with which they allow you to display attractive visual images. Both color and black-and-white images are available as **clip art**. Clip art consists of pictures and other images that are either in printed form or stored in a computer file. You can incorporate these images into your visuals. Clip art (as shown in Figure 12.7) can give your visuals and graphics a professional touch even if you did not excel in art class. But when using clip art, try to avoid images that your listeners may have seen before; look for fresh, contemporary visuals.

Choose a Typeface with Care You'll be able to choose from among dozens of typefaces and **fonts**. But make an informed choice rather than use a typeface just because it strikes your fancy. Graphic designers divide typefaces into four types: serif, sans serif, script, and decorative. You'll see each of these illustrated in Figure 12.8. Serif fonts, like the one you are reading now, are easier to read for longer passages because the little lines at the tops and bottoms of the letters (called *serifs*) help guide the eye from one letter to the next. Sans serif fonts (*sans* means "without") do not have the extra lines. Script fonts are designed to look like handwriting; although interesting and dramatic, script fonts should be used sparingly because they are harder to read. And you should use decorative fonts only when you want to communicate a special tone or mood. Regardless of which font style or typeface you use, don't use more than one or two typefaces on a single visual; if you do use two, designers suggest they should be from different font categories.

Make Informed Decisions about Using Color Color communicates. Red and orange are warm colors that communicate excitement and interest (which is why most

clip art
Images or pictures stored in a computer file or in printed form that can be used in a presentation aid

fonts
Particular styles of typefaces

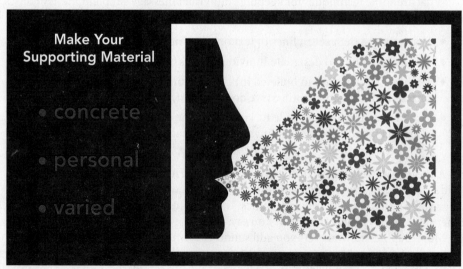

FIGURE 12.7 Copyright-free clip art is readily available at many Web sites. It can give a professional look to your visuals and memorably reinforce your verbal messages.

Source: Shannon Kingston. Copyrighted by Pearson Education, Upper Saddle River, NJ
Photo: Donald Sawvel/Shutterstock

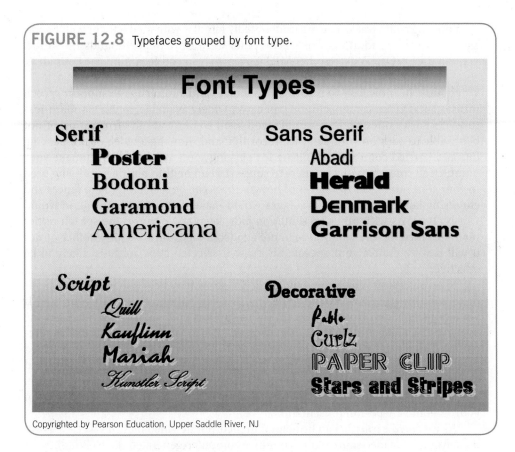

FIGURE 12.8 Typefaces grouped by font type.

fast-food restaurant chains use red, yellow, and orange in their color schemes; they want to make you hungry and catch your attention). Cooler colors such as green and blue have a more calming effect on viewers. Warm colors tend to come forward and jump out at the viewer, whereas cooler colors recede into the background. What are the implications of the power of color to communicate? Consider using warm colors for positive messages (for example, "Profits are up") and cooler colors for more negative messages ("We're losing money").

Designers caution against using certain color combinations. For example, if some audience members are color-blind, they won't be able to distinguish between red and green. And you don't want to get carried away with using color. To unify your presentation, use the same background color on all visuals and no more than two colors for words. A light background with darker-colored words can have a pleasing effect and is easy to see.

Allow Plenty of Time to Prepare Your Presentation Aids Prepare your presentation aids well in advance of your speaking date so that you can make them as attractive and polished-looking as possible. Avoid late-night, last-minute constructions. A sloppy, amateurish presentation aid will convey the impression that you are not a credible speaker, even if you have spent many hours preparing the speech itself. If you haven't used computer-generated graphics before, don't expect to whip out the software manual and produce professional-looking images the night before your presentation. Focus your final hours on rehearsing, not on learning a computer program.

Audiovisual Aids

Audiovisual aids combine sound and images to communicate ideas. With audiovisual aids you combine the power of visual rhetoric with

CONFIDENTLY CONNECTING WITH YOUR AUDIENCE

Practice with Your Presentation Aids to Boost Your Confidence

One source of communication apprehension is uncertainty. By rehearsing with your presentation aids, you reduce uncertainty about your presentation. Whether you are using PowerPoint slides or some other technology, be sure you have practiced using the equipment you will use when you present your message. By reducing the chance for errors and technical miscues, you will also be increasing your confidence in your ability to use your presentation aids without a hitch.

a supporting audio track. You are undoubtedly familiar with media that combine images and sound. In addition to using computer software to import sounds and music, you can use DVDs, iPods, or other MP3 players to help you communicate your ideas.

Video Aids It's now easy to record video images and audio clips to support speech ideas; digital video cameras are inexpensive, widely available, and a standard feature of smartphones. If, for example, you want to illustrate the frustration of not being able to park on your campus, recording and showing a video of full parking lots and harried commuters hunting for parking spots would help you make your point. Or to convince your listeners to support a ban on thin plastic bags being used in your community, show images of how the bags can be seen clinging to fences and cluttering landfills. Such video images would make your point better than would words alone. As with other presentation aids, keep the focus on the speech rather than the video. Before you decide to use a video image, think about whether or not it will really enhance your speech. Short, well-selected clips are most likely to be effective.

Showing a short clip from a movie or TV show may help you make your point or provide an attention-catching opening or a memorable closing to your talk. If you are using video from movies or TV to support your talk, you'll likely get the images from YouTube, other Internet sources, such as Hulu, or commercially prerecorded digital video disks (DVDs). Movies and TV shows, however, are not designed to be supporting material for a speech. Usually they are conceived as self-contained packages, and unless you show only short excerpts, they can overwhelm your speech. Longer videos can exceed your listeners' attention spans and may detract from your live-and-in-person presentation.

As we noted earlier, it can be helpful to incorporate video files (if you can obtain them from your video source) into your own computer-generated slides. Building the video into a slide can give you more control over precisely what clip you are showing as well as the visual context and timing when you play it. You could, for example, show printed lyrics at the same time you show a musician performing.

You can use a variety of devices and technologies to store your videos and play them back during your speech:

- **DVD player.** You may wish to play part of a prerecorded movie or TV show from a DVD. DVD players have several advantages over the older last-century technology of videotape players. Not only does a DVD have excellent picture quality, but also it can be started and stopped with precision.

- **Computers and other electronic devices.** You can store and play your own videos or clips from other sources on your smartphone, tablet computer such as an iPad, or your iPod or other MP3 player. Unless the audience is very small, all of these options, as well as a DVD player, will require you to hook your device to a monitor or a projection system. A 32-inch screen is generally visible to an audience of 25 or 30 people. For a larger audience, you will need either several TVs or monitors or a large-projection TV system. Make sure monitors are available and compatible with your device, or bring your own.

- **The Internet.** If the room in which you are delivering your speech has WiFi or direct Internet access, you could skip storing your video and instead play the video directly from YouTube or another Internet source. You could also retrieve your video or audio material from the "cloud"—computer storage in a remote location. Having a backup of your material on a cloud can enhance the security and ensure that your material will be there when you need it. Playing video directly from the Internet or from cloud storage does, however, carry the risk of losing an Internet connection prior to or during your speech. It will also involve having the technology to access the Internet—either your own equipment or whatever is available in the room.

When using any of these technologies, you'll want to practice using your video and make sure all the equipment you need is available. Unless you're using a wireless system, for example, you might need a cable to connect your storage device to a monitor. We also recommend that, before you give your speech, you do a technical run-through, ensuring that your video image will be ready when you want it.

Audio Aids Audio can be used to complement visual displays. As with video, you can either create your own audio content or use prerecorded sources. You also have a number of options for storage and playback. You might play a few measures of Bach's *Toccata and Fugue in D Minor* from your iPod—or even live, on a portable electronic keyboard—to illustrate a point.

Used sparingly, sound can effectively establish a mood or support your points. While showing PowerPoint slides of her recent Caribbean vacation, one student used a recording of soft steel drum music as an introductory background for her talk. Another student played excerpts of taped interviews with frustrated students who had difficulty figuring out the most recent changes in how to apply for financial aid.

As with video, be sure to rehearse with and master any technology involved with audio aids, and don't let your soundtrack overwhelm or distract from your own words.

Guidelines for Developing Presentation Aids   12.3

Identify guidelines for developing effective presentation aids.

A speech should be more than just what a speaker says, with a few PowerPoint slides or other visual aids added as an afterthought. Spend time carefully developing your visual rhetoric as well as your words. The following commonsense and research-based strategies can help you prepare effective presentation aids for your speeches.

Make Them Easy to See

Without a doubt, the most violated principle of using presentation aids in public speaking is "Make it big!" Countless speeches have been accompanied by a chart or graph with writing too small to read, a computer-generated image not large enough to be legible, or a graph on a flipchart that simply can't be deciphered from the back row. If the only principle you carry away from this chapter is to make your presentation aid large enough to be seen by all in your audience, you will have gained more skill than a majority of speakers who use presentation aids in speeches. *Write big!*

Keep Them Simple

Simple presentation aids usually communicate best. Some students think that the visuals accompanying a speech must be as complicated as a Broadway production, complete with lights and costumes. Resist trying to make your visuals complicated. Text should be limited to key words or phrases. Simple images are better than overly detailed graphics. Don't cram too much information on one chart or computer slide. If you have a lot of information, it is better to use two or three simple charts or slides than to attempt to put all your words on one visual.

This speaker's presentation aids are not big enough for people in the back of the room to see. Write big!

Photo: Arto/Fotolia

Here's an outline of an informative speech that uses simple visual aids (which could be displayed on charts or as computer-generated graphics) to clearly communicate the ideas the speaker wishes to convey.[14]

TOPIC:	Standard editorial symbols
GENERAL PURPOSE:	To inform
SPECIFIC PURPOSE:	At the end of my speech, the audience should be able to use and interpret ten standard symbols for editorial changes in hard-copy written material.

I. The following seven editorial symbols are commonly used to change written text.

A. Use the "pigtail" symbol to delete a letter, a word, or a phrase.

B. Use a caret (it looks like a housetop) to insert a space, a letter, new text, or punctuation.

C. Use what look like two sideways parentheses to remove unwanted space.

D. Use this squiggle line to transpose letters, words, or phrases.

E. Draw three lines under letters to capitalize them.

F. Draw a slash through letters to change them to lowercase.

G. Write the word *stet* to undo previous editing marks.

II. Three editorial symbols are used to rearrange the format of text.

A. Use brackets to add or remove indents or to correct the alignment of text.

B. Use backward bracket marks around text that you want centered on the page.

C. Use a symbol that looks like a backward *p* to mark the beginning of a new paragraph.

After the speech, the speaker could give each audience member a one-page handout summarizing these editorial markings.

Select the Right Presentation Aid

Because there are so many choices, you may wonder, "How do I decide which presentation aid to use?" Here are some suggestions.

- **Consider your audience.** Factors such as audience size dictate the size of the visual you select. If you have a large audience, do not choose a presentation aid unless everyone will be able to see it clearly. The age, interests, and attitudes of your audience also affect your selection of audiovisual support.

- **Think of your speech objective.** Don't select a presentation aid until you have decided on the purpose of your speech.

- **Take into account your own skills and experience.** Use only equipment with which you are comfortable or have had practical experience.

- **Know the room in which you will speak.** If the room has large windows with no shades and no way to dim the lights, do not consider using visuals that require a darkened or semi-darkened room.

Do Not Use Dangerous or Illegal Presentation Aids

Earlier we described a speech in which the speaker accidentally caused an archery bow to fly over the heads of his startled audience. Not only did he lose credibility because he was unable to string the bow successfully, but he also endangered his audience by turning his presentation aid into a flying missile. Dangerous or illegal presentation aids may either shock your audience or physically endanger them. Such aids will also detract from your message. They are never worth the risk of a ruined speech or an injured audience member. If your speech seems to call for a dangerous or illegal object or substance, substitute a picture, a chart, or some other representational device.

RECAP

GUIDELINES FOR DEVELOPING PRESENTATION AIDS

- Make them big.
- Keep them simple.
- Match them to your audience, objectives, skills, and setting.
- Keep them safe and legal.

Guidelines for Using Presentation Aids

12.4 Identify guidelines for effectively using presentation aids.

Explore at **MyCommunicationLab**
Activity: "Presentational Aids"

Now that we have offered strategies for developing effective presentation aids, here are tips for using them for maximum audience impact.

Rehearse with Your Presentation Aids

Jane nervously approached her speech teacher ten minutes before class. She wondered whether class could start immediately because her presentation aid was melting. She had planned to explain how to get various stains out of clothing, and her first demonstration would show how to remove chewing gum. But she had forgotten the gum, so she had to ask for a volunteer from the audience to spit out his gum so she could use it in her demonstration. The ice she had brought to rub on the sticky gum had by this time melted. All she could do was dribble lukewarm water on the gummed-up cloth in an unsuccessful effort to demonstrate her cleaning method. It didn't work. To make matters worse, when she tried to set her poster in the chalkboard tray, it kept falling to the floor. She ended up embarrassed and on the edge of tears. It was obvious that she had not rehearsed with her presentation aids.

Your appearance before your audience should not be the first time you deliver your speech while holding up your chart, turning on the video monitor, operating the remote control to show your slides, clicking on the YouTube video, or using the flipchart. Practice with your presentation aids until you are at ease with them.

Make Eye Contact with Your Audience, Not with Your Presentation Aids

You may be tempted to talk to your presentation aid rather than to your audience. Your focus, however, should remain on your audience. You will need to glance at your visual to make sure that it isn't upside down and that it is the proper one. But do not face it while giving your talk. Keep looking your audience in the eye.

Explain Your Presentation Aids Some speakers believe that they need not explain a presentation aid; they think it's enough just to show it to their audience. Resist this approach. When you exhibit your chart showing the overall decline in the stock market, tell your audience what point you are trying to make. Visual support performs the same function as verbal support: It helps you communicate an idea. Make sure that your audience knows what that idea is. Don't just unceremoniously announce, "Here are the recent statistics on birth rates in the United States" and hold up your visual without further explanation. Tell the audience how to interpret the data. Always set your visuals in a context.

Do Not Pass Objects among Members of Your Audience You realize that your marble collection will be too small to see, so you decide to pass some of your most stunning marbles around while you talk. Bad idea. While you are excitedly describing some of your cat's-eye marbles, you have provided a distraction for your audience. People will be more interested in seeing and touching the marbles than in hearing you talk about them.

What can you do when your object is too small to see without passing it around? If no other speaker follows your speech, you can invite audience members to come up and see your object when your speech is over. If your audience is only two or three rows deep, you can even hold up the object and move in close to the audience to show it while you maintain control. Or you can use your phone to take photos of the object, embed the photos in presentation software, and project the images at a size even a large audience can see.

Use Animals with Caution Most actors are unwilling to work with animals—and for good reason. At best, they may steal the show. And most often they are unpredictable. You may *think* you have the smartest, best-trained dog in the world, but you really do not know how your dog will react to a strange environment and an unfamiliar audience. The risk of having an animal detract from your speech may be too great to make planning a speech around one worthwhile.

A zealous student at a midwestern university a few years ago decided to give a speech on cattle. What better presentation aid, he thought, than a cow? He brought the cow to campus and led her up several flights of stairs to his classroom. The speech in fact went well. But the student had neglected to consider one significant problem: Cows will go upstairs but not down them. (The cow had to be hoisted out a window.)

Another student had a handsome, well-trained German shepherd guard dog. The class was enjoying his speech and his demonstrations of the dog's prowess until the professor from the next classroom poked his head in the door to ask for some chalk. The dog lunged, snarling and with teeth bared, at the unsuspecting professor. Fortunately, he missed—but the speech was concluded prematurely. These and other examples emphasize our point: Use animals with care, if at all.

Animals are neither predictable nor dependable as presentation aids.

Photo: Jason Moore/ZUMA Press/NewsCom

Use Handouts Effectively

Many public-speaking instructors believe that you should not distribute handouts during a speech. Handing out papers in the middle of your presentation will only distract your audience. However, many audiences in businesses and other types of organizations expect a summary of your key ideas in written form or a printout of your PowerPoint or Prezi slides. If you do find it necessary to use written material to reinforce your presentation, keep the following suggestions in mind.

- **Don't distribute your handout during the presentation unless your listeners must refer to the material while you're talking about it.** Do not distribute handouts that have only a marginal relevance to your verbal message. They will defeat your purpose.

- **Control listeners' attention.** If you do distribute a handout and you see that your listeners are giving the written material more attention than they are giving you, tell them where in the handout you want them to focus. For example, you could say, "I see that many of you are interested in the second and third pages of the report. I'll discuss those items in just a few moments. I'd like to talk now about a few examples before we get to page 2."

- **After distributing your handouts, tell audience members to keep the material face down until you're ready to talk about the material.** This will help listeners not to be tempted to peek at your handout instead of keeping their focus on you and your message.

- **Clearly number the pages on your handout material.** This will make it easy for you to direct audience members to specific pages in your handouts.

- **Consider preparing images of each page to project on a computer-prepared slide to make sure your listeners know what page of your handout you want them to focus on.** You'll be able to display the specific page you're talking about. Even if the words are too small for audience members to read, they will be able to see what page you're on if they miss your announcement. With a PowerPoint or Prezi slide, you can also quickly point to the paragraph or chart on the page you want them to focus on. It's not a good idea, however, to economize by *only* displaying detailed material and not providing handouts. The print will be too small to be seen clearly.

- **If your listeners do not need the information during your presentation, tell them that you will distribute a summary of the key ideas at the end of your talk.** Your handout could include a copy of all computer-generated slides or it might summarize the specific action you want your audience to take, as well as distill the key information you have discussed.

Time the Use of Visuals to Control Your Audience's Attention

A skillful speaker knows when to show a supporting visual and when to put it away. It's not wise to begin your speech with all your charts, graphs, and nonrelevant slides in full view unless you are going to refer to them in your opening remarks. Time the display of your visuals to coincide with your discussion of the information contained in them.

Jessica was proud of the huge replica of the human mouth that she had constructed to illustrate her talk on the proper way to brush one's teeth. It stood over two feet tall and was painted pink and white. It was a true work of art. As she began her speech, she set her mouth model in full view of the audience. She opened her speech with a brief history of dentistry in America. But her listeners never heard a word; they were fascinated by the model. Jessica would have done better to cover her presentation with a cloth and then dramatically reveal it when she wanted to illustrate proper tooth brushing.

Here are a few more suggestions for timing your presentation aids:

- **If possible, use a remote control to advance computer-generated images** so you do not have to stay anchored near the computer to advance each slide.

- **Mute or otherwise remove from the audience's view computer images** when you are making a point or telling a story not related to a visual image or word summary. You don't want an image or bulleted list of words unrelated to your message to compete for your listeners' attention. Removing them from view returns the audience's focus to you.

- **Consider asking someone to help you hold your presentation aid or turn the pages of your flipchart.** Make sure you rehearse with your assistant beforehand so that all goes smoothly during your presentation.

Use Technology Effectively

You may be tempted to use some of the newer technologies we have described because of their novelty rather than their value in helping you communicate your message. Some novice speakers will overuse presentation aids simply because they can quickly produce eye-catching visuals. Resist this temptation.

Don't assume that the hardware and software you need will be available in the room where you are speaking. Be sure to ask what kinds of technology exist.

Even if you have asked and you are appropriately prepared based on the information you were given, have a backup plan. You may want to bring your own laptop or a backup flash drive or other device for storing your slides. Another strategy is to email your computer slides to yourself, or back up the files to a cloud storage site, so that you can retrieve them if you need them as a backup.

In spite of the potential problems that using technology may present, innovations such as YouTube and computer images are destined to play a growing role in public speaking. In this technology- and image-dependent culture, listeners expect technology to support a message. Nonetheless, when using technology, keep the basic principles we've offered in mind: Make it big, integrate the words and images into your talk, and properly time your visuals to coincide with your message content. And don't forget to rehearse using the same technology you will use during your talk.

Remember Murphy's Law

According to Murphy's Law, if something can go wrong, it will. When you use presentation aids, you increase the chances that problems or snags will develop when you present your speech. The chart may fall off the easel, you may not find the chalk, the computer in the room may not be compatible with your software. We are not saying that you should be a pessimist but that you should have backup supplies and an alternative plan in case your original plans go awry.

If something doesn't go as you planned, do your best to keep your speech on track. If the chart falls, pick it up and keep talking; don't offer lengthy apologies. If you can't find the chalk, ask a friend to go on a chalk hunt in another room. No computer-generated slides as you had planned? Have all key pieces of information in your notes rather than relying on the computer slides to be your speech notes. A thorough rehearsal, a double-check on your equipment, backup images, and such extra supplies as extension cords and masking tape can help repeal Murphy's Law.

RECAP

GUIDELINES FOR USING PRESENTATION AIDS

- Prepare carefully and practice with aids.
- Maintain eye contact with audience.
- Talk about the information or image on the aid.
- Don't pass around objects.
- Be careful with animals.
- Use handouts and technology effectively.
- Control audience's attention.
- Remember Murphy's Law.

STUDY GUIDE
REVIEW, APPLY AND ASSESS

THE VALUE OF PRESENTATION AIDS

12.1 Discuss five ways in which presentation aids help communicate ideas to an audience.

Presentation aids are tools that help you communicate your ideas more dramatically than words alone can. They help improve listeners' understanding and recollection of your ideas. They can also help you communicate the organization of your ideas, gain and maintain the audience's attention, and illustrate a sequence of events or procedures.

Key Terms

Presentation aid 240
Visual rhetoric 242

Thinking Critically

Identify several public speaking situations that would lend themselves well to using presentation aids. What are some situations in which using presentation aids would not be beneficial?

Assessing Your Audience-Centered Speaking Skill

Mayor Bryan is going to address the board of directors of a large microchip firm, hoping to lure them to his community. He plans to use handouts, several charts, and a short video clip. What advice would you give the mayor to make sure his presentation is effective?

TYPES OF PRESENTATION AIDS

12.2 Describe the types of presentation aids and identify tips for using them effectively.

Three-dimensional presentation aids include objects, models, and people. Two-dimensional presentation aids include drawings, photographs, slides, maps, graphs, charts, flipcharts, and chalkboards. Software graphics and presentation packages can be used to produce many presentation aids inexpensively and efficiently. Audiovisual aids include video clips and audio clips or performances that help communicate ideas to your listeners.

Key Terms

Model 243
Graph 244
Bar graph 245
Pie graph 246
Line graph 246
Picture graph 246
Chart 246

Thinking Critically

Nikki plans to give a talk to the Rotary Club in an effort to encourage the club members to support a local bond issue for a new library. She wants to make sure they understand how cramped and inadequate the current library is. What type of visual support could she use to make her point?

Professor Chou uses only the chalkboard to illustrate her anthropology lectures and then only occasionally writes a word or two. What other types of visual or auditory aids could Professor Chou use in teaching?

Assessing Your Audience-Centered Speaking Skill

Based on the discussion on pages identify three- and two-dimensional types of visual aids and identify advantages and disadvantages of using each type.

GUIDELINES FOR DEVELOPING PRESENTATION AIDS

12.3 Identify guidelines for developing effective presentation aids.

When you prepare your presentation aids, make sure your visuals are large enough to be seen clearly by all of your listeners. Adapt your presentation aids to your audience, the speaking environment, and the objectives of your speech. Prepare your visuals well in advance, and make sure they are not illegal or dangerous to use.

Thinking Ethically

Ceally wants to educate his college classmates about the widespread use of profanity in contemporary music. He would like to play sound clips of some of the most offensive lyrics to illustrate his point. Would you advise Ceally to play these songs, even though doing so might offend members of the audience?

Assessing Your Audience-Centered Speaking Skill

Identify four criteria for effectively developing presentation aids for a speech.

GUIDELINES FOR USING PRESENTATION AIDS

12.4   Identify guidelines for effectively using presentation aids.

As you present your speech, remember to look at your audience, not at your presentation aid; talk about your visual, don't just show it; avoid passing objects among your audience; use handouts to reinforce the main points in your speech; time your visuals carefully; and be sure to have backup supplies and a contingency plan.

Thinking Ethically

Derrick is planning to give a speech about emergency first aid. His brother is a paramedic and a licensed nurse. Is it ethical for Derrick to wear his brother's paramedic uniform without telling his listeners that the outfit belongs to his brother?

Assessing Your Audience-Centered Speaking Skill

Use the following checklist to help you assess your use of presentation aids:

- Do I look at my listeners rather than at my presentation aids while speaking?
- Do I explain my presentation aids rather than just show them?
- If I use handouts, do I carefully time when I distribute the handouts?
- Do I focus my audience's attention on my presentation aid and then have them focus on what I am saying when appropriate?
- Can I skillfully operate any computers, video, audio, or other hardware or software that I plan to use during my presentation?

Explore at MyCommunicationLab
Speaker's Workshop: A Checklist for
Using Effective Presentation Aids

13 SPEAKING TO INFORM

Teacher teaching his students the Universe. "Livre des Proprietes des choses." Miniature. Chateau de Chantilly. France. Photo: Album/Art Resource, NY

Not only is there an art in knowing a thing, but also a certain art in teaching it.

—Cicero

A s you participate in your company's management training class, the group facilitator turns to you and asks you to summarize your team's discussion about the importance of leadership.

Your sociology professor requires each student to give an oral report describing the latest findings from the U.S. census.

At the conclusion of your weekly staff meeting via Skype, your boss asks you to deliver a brief oral report summarizing the new product you and your team are developing.

In each of these situations, your task is to give information to someone. Conveying information to others is a useful skill in most walks of life. You may find that informing others will be an important part of your job, your volunteer work, or your activities with social groups. Whether you are having a spontaneous conversation or delivering a rehearsed speech, your speaking purpose is often to inform or teach someone something you know. One survey of both speech teachers and students who had taken a speech course found that the single most important skill taught in a public-speaking class is how to give an informative speech.[1]

A **speech to inform** shares information with others to enhance their knowledge or understanding of the information, concepts, and ideas you present. When you inform someone, you assume the role of a teacher by defining, illustrating, or elaborating on a topic. You're not trying to persuade listeners to change their behavior. You are giving them information that is useful or interesting.

When you inform, you're typically attempting to achieve three goals:

- *You speak to enhance understanding.* Understanding occurs when a listener accurately interprets the intended meaning of a message.
- *You speak to maintain interest.* You may have carefully selected words, examples, and illustrations to help your listeners understand, but if your listeners become bored and do not focus on your message, you won't achieve your informative-speaking goal.
- *You speak to be remembered.* In Chapter 4, we noted that one day after hearing a presentation, most listeners remember only about half of what they were told. Two days after the presentation, they recall only about 25 percent. Your job as an informative speaker is to improve on those statistics.

In this chapter, we will suggest ways to build on your experience and enhance your skill in informing others. We will identify different types of informative speeches and provide suggestions for achieving your informative-speaking goals: enhancing understanding, maintaining interest, and improving listener recall. Finally, we'll review the audience-centered model of public speaking to help you plan and present your informative message.

speech to inform
A speech that teaches others new information, ideas, concepts, principles, or processes in order to enhance their knowledge or understanding about something

---

13.1   Describe five different types of informative speeches.

Types of Informative Speeches

Informative speeches can be classified according to the subject areas they cover. In many informative presentations you will deliver, your topic will be provided for you, or the nature of the specific speaking opportunity will dictate what you talk about. If, for example, you're updating your boss about a project your work team has been developing, you need not wrack your brain for a speech topic. The topic for your speech is prescribed for you. But if you have an invitation (or assignment) to give an informative speech and the topic choice is up to you, you may need help selecting a topic and developing your purpose. Understanding the different types of informative speeches can give you ideas about how to select a speech topic.

Classifying the types of informative speeches you give can also help you decide how to organize your message. As you will see in Table 13.1 and in the following discussion, the demands of your topic and purpose often dictate a structure for your speech. As you look at these suggestions about structure, however, remember that good organization is only one factor that determines your audience's ability to process your message. After discussing types of informative speeches, we will offer specific techniques to help your audience understand, maintain interest in, and remember your message.

Explore at **MyCommunicationLab** Profile: "Informative Speeches"

Speeches about Objects

A speech about an object might be about anything tangible—anything you can see or touch. You may or may not show the actual object to your audience while you are

TABLE 13.1 TYPES OF INFORMATIVE SPEECHES

SUBJECT	PURPOSE	TYPICAL ORGANIZATIONAL PATTERN	SAMPLE TOPICS
Objects	Present information about tangible things	Topical Spatial Chronological	The Rosetta Stone Museums The Mars Rover Religious icons
Procedures	Review how something works or describe a process	Chronological Topical Complexity	How to . . . 　Use a smartphone app to help you lose weight 　Operate a nuclear-power plant 　Buy a quality used car 　Trap lobsters
People	Describe famous people or personal acquaintances	Chronological Topical	Sojourner Truth Nelson Mandela J. R. R. Tolkien Your grandmother Your favorite teacher
Events	Describe an event that either has happened or will happen	Chronological Topical Spatial	May Day in Oxford, England Inauguration Day Cinco de Mayo
Ideas	Present abstract information or discuss principles, concepts, theories, or issues	Topical Complexity	Communism Immigration Buddhism Reincarnation

talking about it. (Chapter 12 suggests ways to use objects as presentation aids to illustrate your ideas.) Almost any kind of object could form the basis of an interesting speech:

Something from your own collection (baskets, comic books, antiques, baseball cards)

Sports cars

Cellos

Smartphones

Digital video cameras

WWII Memorial

Toys

Antique Fiestaware

English Staffordshire dogs

The time limit for your speech will determine the amount of detail you can share with your listeners. Even in a 30- to 45-minute presentation, you cannot talk about every aspect of any of the preceding objects. So you will need to focus on a specific purpose. Here's a sample outline for a speech about an object:

TOPIC:	Dead Sea Scrolls
GENERAL PURPOSE:	To inform
SPECIFIC PURPOSE:	At the end of my speech, my audience should be able to describe how the Dead Sea Scrolls were found, why they are important to society, and the key content of the ancient manuscripts.

Informative speeches can be classified according to their topic. The type of speech you are giving can help you decide how to organize it. What might be the main ideas in this speaker's talk?

Photo: Marmaduke St. John/Alamy

I. The Dead Sea Scrolls were found by accident.

    A. The scrolls were found in caves near the Dead Sea.

    B. The scrolls were first discovered by a shepherd in 1947.

    C. In the late 1940s and early 1950s, archaeologists and Bedouins found ten caves that contained the Dead Sea Scrolls.

II. The Dead Sea Scrolls are important to society.

    A. The Dead Sea Scrolls are the oldest known manuscripts of any books of the Bible.

    B. The Dead Sea Scrolls give us a look at Jewish life in Palestine over 2,000 years ago.

III. The content of the Dead Sea Scrolls gives us a glimpse of the past.

    A. The Dead Sea Scrolls include all the books of the Old Testament except the book of Esther.

    B. The Dead Sea Scrolls include fragments of the Septuagint, the earliest Greek translation of the Old Testament.

    C. The Dead Sea Scrolls include a collection of hymns sung by the inhabitants of the Qumran Valley.

Speeches about objects may be organized topically, chronologically, or spatially. The speech about the Dead Sea Scrolls is organized topically. It could, however, be revised and organized chronologically: The first major idea could be Jewish life in Palestine 2,000 years ago. The second point could describe how the scrolls were found in the 1940s and 1950s. The final major idea could be the construction in the 1960s of the museum in Jerusalem that houses the famous scrolls. Or the speech could even be organized spatially, describing the physical layout of the caves in which the scrolls were found.

Speeches about Procedures

A speech about a procedure explains how something works (for example, the human circulatory system) or describes a process that produces a particular outcome (such as how grapes become wine). At the close of such a speech, your audience should be able to describe, understand, or perform the procedure you have described. Here are examples of procedures that could be the topics of effective informative presentations:

Watch at **MyCommunicationLab**
Video: "Baking a Cake"

How state laws are made

How the U.S. patent system works

How an e-book reader works

How to refinish furniture

How to write a resume

How to plant an organic garden

How to select a graduate school

Notice that all these examples start with the word *how*. A speech about a procedure usually focuses on how a process is completed or how something can be accomplished. Speeches about procedures are often presented in workshops or other training situations in which people learn skills.

Anita, describing how to develop a new training curriculum in teamwork skills, used an organizational strategy that grouped some of her steps together like this:

I. Conduct a needs assessment of your department.

    A. Identify the method of assessing department needs.

        1. Consider using questionnaires.

    2. Consider using interviews.

    3. Consider using focus groups.

  B. Implement the needs assessment.

II. Identify the topics that should be presented in the training.

  A. Specify topics that all members of the department need.

  B. Specify topics that only some members of the department need.

III. Write training objectives.

  A. Write objectives that are measurable.

  B. Write objectives that are specific.

  C. Write objectives that are attainable.

IV. Develop lesson plans for the training.

  A. Identify the training methods you will use.

  B. Identify the materials you will need.

Anita's audience will remember the four general steps much more easily than if each aspect of the curriculum-development process were presented as a separate step.

Many speeches about procedures include visual aids (see Chapter 12). Whether you are teaching people how to hang wallpaper or how to give a speech, showing them how to do something is almost always more effective than just telling them how to do it.

Speeches about People

A biographical speech could be about someone famous or about someone you know personally. Most of us enjoy hearing about the lives of real people, famous or not, living or dead, who had some special quality. The key to presenting an effective biographical speech is to be selective: Don't try to cover every detail of your subject's life. Relate the key elements in the person's career, personality, or other significant life features so that you are building to a particular point rather than just reciting facts about an individual. Perhaps your grandfather was known for his generosity, for example. Mention notable examples of his philanthropy. If you are talking about a well-known personality, pick information or a period that is not widely known, such as the person's childhood or private hobby.

One speaker gave a memorable speech about his neighbor:

> To enter Hazel's house is to enter a combination greenhouse and zoo. Plants are everywhere; it looks and feels like a tropical jungle. Her home is always warm and humid. Her dog Peppy, her cat Bones, a bird named Elmer, and a fish called Frank can be seen through the philodendron, ferns, and pansies. While Hazel loves her plants and animals, she loves people even more. Her finest hours are spent serving coffee and homemade chocolate pie to her friends and neighbors, playing Uno with family until late in the evening, and just visiting about the good old days. Hazel is one of a kind.

Note how the speech captures Hazel's personality and charm. Speeches about people should give your listeners the feeling that the person is a unique, authentic individual.

One way to talk about a person's life is in chronological order—birth, school, career, marriage, achievements, death. However, when you want to present a specific theme, such as "Winston Churchill, master of English prose," you may decide to organize key experiences topically. First you would discuss Churchill's achievements as a brilliant orator whose words defied Germany in 1940, and then you would trace the origins of his skill to his work as a cub reporter in South Africa during the Boer War of 1899–1902.

Speeches about Events

Where were you on September 11, 2001? Even though you may have been in elementary or pre-school, chances are that you clearly remember where you were and what you were doing on that and other similarly fateful days. Major events punctuate our lives and mark the passage of time.

A major event can form the basis of a fascinating informative speech. You can choose to talk about either an event that you have witnessed or one you have researched. Your goal is to describe the event in concrete, tangible terms and to bring the experience to life for your audience. Were you living in New Jersey when Hurricane Sandy struck? Have you witnessed the inauguration of a president, governor, or senator? Have you experienced the ravages of a flood or earthquake? Or you may want to re-create an event that your parents or grandparents lived through. What was it like to first learn of the death of President Kennedy on November 22, 1963?

You may have heard a recording of the famous radio broadcast of the explosion and crash of the dirigible *Hindenburg* that occurred on May 6, 1937. The announcer's ability to describe both the scene and the incredible emotion of the moment has made that broadcast a classic even today, 80 years after it occurred. As that broadcaster was able to do, your purpose as an informative speaker describing an event is to make that event come alive for your listeners and to help them visualize the scene.

Most speeches built around an event follow a chronological arrangement. But a speech about an event might also describe the complex issues or causes behind the event and thus be organized topically. For example, if you were to talk about the Civil War, you might choose to focus on the three causes of the war:

  I. Political

  II. Economic

  III. Social

Although these main points are topical, specific subpoints may be organized chronologically. However you choose to organize your speech about an event, your audience should be enthralled by your vivid description.

Speeches about Ideas

Speeches about ideas are usually more abstract than other types of speeches. The following principles, concepts, and theories might be topics of idea speeches:

Principles of communication

Freedom of speech

Evolution

Theories of aging

Islam

Communal living

Positive psychology

Most speeches about ideas are organized topically (by logical subdivisions of the central idea) or according to complexity (from simple ideas to more complex ones). The following example illustrates how one student organized an idea topic into an informative speech:

TOPIC:	Freudian Psychology
GENERAL PURPOSE:	To inform
SPECIFIC PURPOSE:	At the end of my speech, the audience should be able to explain Sigmund Freud's concepts of id, ego, and superego.

I. The id is a fundamental element of our personality that is present at birth.

   A. The id seeks pleasure and avoids pain by serving as a source of our needs and desires.

   B. The id is where our basic instincts for survival reside.

   C. The id seeks to meet our biological needs including food and sex.

II. The ego helps us adapt to reality.

   A. The ego mediates between the needs of the id and the reality of what is happening around us.

   B. Our ego regulates our judgment, tolerance, control, and planning for the future.

   C. The ego uses defense mechanisms to help us manage the tension created by the id.

III. The superego is influenced by what we have been taught by our parents, including the cultural norms of society.

   A. The superego helps balance tensions between the id and the ego.

   B. The superego serves as our conscience.

   C. The superego is where our sense of right and wrong resides.

13.2 Effectively and appropriately use four strategies to enhance audience understanding.

Strategies to Enhance Audience Understanding

*Watch at **MyCommunicationLab** Video: "Hurricane Mitigation"*

The skill of teaching and enhancing understanding is obviously important to teachers, but it's also important to virtually any profession. Whether you're a college professor, chief executive officer of a *Fortune* 500 company, or a parent raising a family, you will be called on to teach and explain. The Internet gives us access to a wealth of information, but having access to information is not the same thing as understanding the information. At the heart of creating understanding is the ability to relate the information to listeners. Just because an idea, term, or concept has been around for centuries doesn't mean that it is easy to understand or that audience members understand the relevance of the information to their own lives. How do you enhance someone's knowledge or understanding? We can suggest several powerful strategies.

Speak with Clarity

*Watch at **MyCommunicationLab** Video: "Fife and Drum Corps"*

To speak with clarity is to express ideas so that the listener understands the intended message accurately. Speaking clearly is an obvious goal of an informative speaker. What is not so obvious is *how* to speak clearly. As a speaker you may think you're being clear, but only the listener can tell you whether he or she has received your message. One interesting study made the point that because the information is clear to you, you'll likely think it's also clear to your listener.[2] People were asked to tap the rhythm of well-known songs such as "Happy Birthday to You" or "The Star Spangled Banner" so that another person could guess the song just by hearing the rhythm. About half of the people who tapped the song thought that the listener would easily figure out which song was being tapped. However, less than 2 percent of the listeners could identify the song. (Try it—see if you can beat the 2 percent average.) The point: When you know something, you're likely to think it's clear to someone else. Whether it's how to drive a car or how to care for an aardvark, if you are already familiar with a topic, you're likely to think your task of communicating an idea to someone is easier than it is. Give careful thought to how you will help listeners understand your message. The most effective speakers (those whose message is both understood and appropriately acted on) build in success by consciously developing and presenting ideas with their listeners in mind rather than flinging information at listeners and hoping some of it sticks.

Communication researcher Joseph Chesebro has summarized several research-based strategies you can use to enhance message clarity.[3]

- Preview your main ideas in your introduction.
- Tell your listeners how what you present relates to a previous point.
- Frequently summarize key ideas.
- Provide a visual outline to help listeners follow your ideas.
- Provide a handout prior to your talk with the major points outlined; leave space so that listeners can jot down key ideas.
- Once you announce your topic and outline, stay on message.

Use Principles and Techniques of Adult Learning

Most public-speaking audiences you face will consist of adults. Perhaps you've heard of **pedagogy**, the art and science of teaching children to learn. The word *pedagogy* is based on the Greek words *paid*, which means "child," and *agogus*, which means "guide." Thus, pedagogy is the art and science of teaching children. Adult learning is called **andragogy**.[4] *Andr* is the Greek word that means "adult." Andragogy is the art and science of teaching adults. Researchers and scholars have found andragogical approaches that are best for adults. (If you're a college student over the age of 18, you are an adult learner.) What are andragogical, or adult-learning, principles? Here are the most important ones.[5]

- **Provide information that is applicable to audience members' needs and interests.** Most people who work in business have an in-basket on their desk to receive letters that must be read and work that must be done. Each of us also has a kind of mental in-basket, an agenda for what we want or need to accomplish. If you present adult listeners with information that they can apply immediately to their "in-basket," they are more likely to focus on and understand your message.

pedagogy
The art and science of teaching children

andragogy
The art and science of teaching adults

Which of the andragogical principles presented in this chapter is this instructional speaker following?
Photo: WavebreakMediaMicro/Fotolia

- **Actively involve listeners in the learning process.** Rather than have your listeners sit passively as you speak, ask questions for them to think about or, in some cases, to respond to on the spot.

- **Connect listeners' life experiences with the new information they learn.** Adult listeners are more likely to understand your message when you help them connect new information with their past experiences. The primary way to do this is to know the kinds of experiences that your listeners have had, and then to refer to those experiences as you present your ideas.

- **Make new information relevant to listeners' needs and their busy lives.** Most adults are busy—probably, if pressed, most will say they are too busy for their own good. So when speaking to an adult audience, realize that any information or ideas you share will more likely be heard and understood if you relate what you say to their chock-full-of-activity lives. People working, going to school, raising families, and being involved in their communities need to be shown how the ideas you share are relevant to them.

- **Help listeners solve their problems.** Most people have problems and are looking for solutions to them. People will be more likely to pay attention to information that helps them better understand and solve their problems.

Clarify Unfamiliar Ideas or Complex Processes

If you want to tell your listeners about a complex process, you will need more than definitions to explain what you mean. Research suggests that you can demystify a complex process if you first provide a simple overview of the process with an analogy, a vivid description, or a word picture.[6]

Use Analogies If a speaker said, "The Milky Way galaxy is big," you'd have a vague idea that the cluster of stars and space material making up the Milky Way is large. But if the speaker said, "If the Milky Way galaxy were as big as the continent of North America, our solar system would fit inside a coffee cup," you'd have a better idea of just how big the Milky Way is and, by comparison, how small our solar system is.[7] As we discussed in Chapter 7, an analogy is a comparison of two things. It's an especially useful technique for describing complex processes because it can help someone understand something difficult to grasp (the size of the Milky Way) by comparing it to something already understood (the size of a coffee cup).[8]

By helping your listeners compare something new to something they already know or can visualize, you help to make your message clear. Here's an example of this idea based on what professor of business Chip Heath and communication consultant Dan Heath call the principle of "using what's there—using the information you have (what's there) and relating it to something more familiar."[9] Try this short exercise. Take 15 seconds to memorize the letters below; then close the book and write the letters exactly as they appear here.

J FKFB INAT OUP SNA SAI RS

Most people, say these experts, remember about half of the letters. Now, look below to see the same letters organized differently. The letters haven't changed, but we have regrouped them into acronyms that may make more sense to you. We are more likely to make sense out of something that we already have a mental category for. An analogy works in the same way.

JFK FBI NATO UPS NASA IRS

Use a Vivid, Descriptive Word Picture When you *describe,* you provide more detail than you do when you define something. One way to describe a situation or event is with a word picture. A **word picture** is a lively description that helps your listeners form a mental image by appealing to their senses of sight, taste, smell, sound, and touch.

To create an effective word picture, begin by forming your own clear mental image of the person, place, object, or process before you try to describe it. See it with your "mind's eye."

- What would a listener see if he or she were looking at it?
- What would listeners hear?
- If they could touch the object or do the process, how would it feel to them?
- If your listeners could smell or taste it, what would that be like?

To describe these sensations, choose the most specific and vivid words possible. Onomatopoeic words—words that sound like the sounds they name—such as *buzz, snort, hum, crackle,* or *hiss,* are powerful. So are similes and other comparisons. "The rock was rough as sandpaper" and "the pebble was as smooth as a baby's skin" appeal to both the visual and the tactile senses.

Be sure to describe the emotions that a listener might feel if he or she were to experience the situation you relate. Ultimately, your goal is to use just the right words to evoke an emotional response from the listener. If you experienced the situation, describe your own emotions. Use specific adjectives rather than general terms such as *happy* or *sad.* One speaker, talking about receiving her first speech assignment, described her reaction with these words:

> My heart stopped. Panic began to rise up inside. Me? . . . For the next five days I lived in dreaded anticipation of the forthcoming event.[10]

Note how effectively her choice of such words and phrases as "my heart stopped," "panic," and "dreaded anticipation" describe her terror at the prospect of making a speech—much more so than if she had said simply, "I was scared."

The more vividly and accurately you can describe emotion, the more intimately involved in your description the audience will become.

Appeal to a Variety of Learning Styles

Would you rather hear a lecture, read the lecture, or see pictures about what the speaker is saying? Your choice reflects your preferred learning style. Not everyone has a single preferred style, but many people do. Four common styles are auditory, visual print, visual, and kinesthetic.

- **Auditory learners.** If you'd rather listen to a recorded audio book than read a book, you may be an auditory learner, a person who learns best by hearing.
- **Visual print learners.** If you learn best by seeing words in print, then you are a visual print learner. Most likely you would much rather read material than hear it presented orally.
- **Visual learners.** Barraged daily with images from TV and the Internet, many people have grown to depend on more than words alone to help them remember ideas and information. They are visual learners, who learn best with words and images.
- **Kinesthetic learners.** Kinesthetic learners learn best by moving while learning. They would rather try something than hear it, watch it, or read about it. These learners like active learning methods such as writing while listening or, better yet, participating in group activities.

word picture
A vivid description that appeals to the senses

ENHANCING AUDIENCE UNDERSTANDING

- Keep your message clear.
- Apply adult-learning principles.
  - Provide information that is applicable to listeners' lives.
  - Actively involve listeners in the learning process.
  - Connect listeners' experiences with new information.
  - Make information relevant to listeners.
  - Help listeners solve problems.
- Clarify the unfamiliar or complex:
  - Use analogies.
  - Use vivid descriptions.
  - Use word pictures.
- Plan for many different learning styles.

As you develop your speech and your supporting materials, consider how you can appeal to a variety of learning styles at the same time. Since you'll be giving a speech, your auditory learners will like that. Visual learners like and expect an informative talk to be illustrated with PowerPoint™ images. They will appreciate seeing pictures or having statistics summarized using bar or line graphs or pie charts. Kinesthetic learners will appreciate movement, even small movements such as raising their hands in response to questions. Visual print learners will appreciate handouts, which you could distribute after your talk.

13.3   Effectively and appropriately use three strategies to maintain audience interest.

Watch at **MyCommunicationLab**
Video: "Brain Research of the Sexes"

Strategies to Maintain Audience Interest

No matter how carefully crafted your definitions, how skillfully delivered your description, or how visually reinforcing your presentation aid, if your listeners aren't paying attention, you won't achieve your goal of informing them. Strategies for gaining and holding interest are vital in achieving your speaking goal.

In discussing how to develop attention-catching introductions in Chapter 9, we itemized specific techniques for gaining your listeners' attention. The following strategies build on those techniques.

Motivate Your Audience to Listen to You

Most audiences will probably not be waiting breathlessly for you to talk to them. You will need to motivate them to listen to you.

Some situations have built-in motivations for listeners. A teacher can say, "There will be a test covering my lecture tomorrow. It will count toward 50 percent of your semester grade." Such methods may not make the teacher popular, but they will certainly motivate the class to listen. Similarly, a boss might say, "Your ability to use these sales principles will determine whether you keep your job." Your boss's statement will probably motivate you to learn the company's sales principles. However, because you will rarely have the power to motivate your listeners with such strong-arm tactics, you will need to find more creative ways to get your audience to listen to you.

Never assume that your listeners will be interested in what you have to say. Pique their interest with a rhetorical question. Tell them a story. Tell them how the information you present will be of value to them. As the British writer G. K. Chesterton once said, "There is no such thing as an uninteresting topic; there are only uninterested people."[11]

Tell a Story

Good stories with interesting characters and riveting plots have fascinated listeners for millennia; the words "once upon a time" are usually sure-fire attention-getters. A good story is inherently interesting. Stories are also a way of connecting your message to people from a variety of cultural backgrounds.[12]

One author suggests that, of all the stories ever told since the beginning of time, in all cultures, there are only seven basic plots: overcoming the monster, rags to riches, the quest, voyage and return, comedy, tragedy, and rebirth. Think of a favorite story and see if you can fit it into one of these categories. Another theory boils the history of stories down even further. It suggests that there is really only one basic plot: All stories are about overcoming obstacles to find "home." This view does not suggest that all characters literally find their way home; rather, all stories are about striving to find a place, literal or metaphorical, that represents "home" in some way.[13]

In addition to the plot, the characteristics of a well-told tale are simple yet powerful. Here we elaborate on some of the ideas about storytelling we introduced in Chapter 7. A good story includes conflict, incorporates action, creates suspense, and may also include humor.

- **A good story includes conflict.** Stories that pit one side against another foster attention, as do descriptions of opposing ideas and forces in government, religion, or personal relationships. The Greeks learned long ago that the essential ingredient for a good play, be it comedy or tragedy, is conflict. Conflict is often the obstacle that keeps the people in a story from finding "home."

- **A good story incorporates action.** An audience is more likely to listen to an action-packed message than to one that listlessly lingers on an idea. Good stories have a beginning that sets the stage, a heart that moves to a conclusion, and then an ending that ties up all the loose ends. The key to interest is a plot that moves along.

- **A good story creates suspense.** TV dramas and soap operas long ago proved that the way to ensure high ratings is to tell a story with the outcome in doubt. Suspense is created when the characters in the story may do one of several things. Keeping people on the edge of their seats because they don't know what will happen next is another element in good storytelling.

- **A good story may incorporate humor.** A fisherman went into a sporting-goods store. The salesperson offered the man a wonderful lure for trout: It had beautiful colors, eight hooks, and looked just like a rare Buckner bug. Finally, the fisherman asked the salesperson, "Do fish really like this thing?" "I don't know," admitted the salesperson, "I don't sell to fish."

We could have simply said, "It's important to be audience-centered." But using a bit of humor makes the point while holding the listener's attention.

Not all stories have to be funny. Stories may be sad or dramatic without humor. But adding humor at an appropriate time usually helps maintain interest and attention.

Present Information That Relates to Your Listeners

Throughout this book we have encouraged you to develop an audience-centered approach to public speaking. Being an audience-centered informative speaker means being aware of information that your audience can use. If, for example, you are going to teach your audience about recycling, be sure to talk about specific recycling efforts on your campus or in your own community. Adapt your message to the people who will be in your audience.

Use the Unexpected

On a flight from Dallas, Texas, to San Diego, California, flight attendant Karen Wood made this announcement:

Humorous stories are one way to get and hold listeners' attention. When listeners are interested in your speech, they are more likely to learn the information you want to share with them. What other strategies could the speaker use to keep this audience interested?

Photo: Hill Street Studios/Blend Images/Getty Images

SAMPLE INFORMATIVE SPEECH

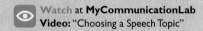

Watch at **MyCommunicationLab**
Video: "Choosing a Speech Topic"

CHOOSING A SPEECH TOPIC

by Roger Fringer[14]

Today I'd like to talk to you about [pause] tables. Tables are wood . . . usually . . . and they are. . . . How often do we sit in a class and feel the intelligence draining out of us? In a speech class, we are given the opportunity to add to that feeling or to add to the intelligence. Selecting a meaningful speech topic will make our speeches interesting, important, as well as being informative. As students, we've all been in the situation of being more anxious than necessary because we are talking about an unfamiliar or uninteresting speech topic. In our public speaking class, we spend a number of hours giving speeches and listening to them. If we have four days of speeches, at what—seven speech topics [per day]—that equals 28 hours spent listening to speeches. Let's not forget that we are paying to listen to those speeches. If our tuition is say, $15,000 a year, that's $875 that we have spent listening to those 28 hours of speeches. We work hard for our tuition, so we should spend it wisely. Spending it wisely means we don't waste our time. We don't waste our own time on preparing and giving the speeches, and we don't waste our classmates' time who have to listen to our speeches. The solution is simple if we take choosing our topic seriously.

I recommend that we choose topics following *The Three I's* to guide us. The first *I* is to make speeches *interesting*. By doing so, we can alleviate the boredom that so often permeates the public speaking classroom. If the topic is interesting to us, we will present it in a manner that shows our interest. We will also keep our audience's attention when we know, as students, they can be thinking about a million other things. Choosing

Roger cleverly captures attention by purposefully starting with an unimaginative topic and using halting delivery that makes listeners wonder, "What's this really about?"

Roger establishes a common bond with his listeners by relating to them as fellow students confronted with the same problem: how to select a topic for a speech.

Rather than just say we waste time and money listening to speeches, Roger uses statistics specifically adapted to his audience; this is a good example of being audience-centered.

He clearly previews his major ideas and links them together by using words that all begin with *I*.

If I could have your attention for a few moments, we sure would love to point out these safety features. If you haven't been in an automobile since 1965, the proper way to fasten your seat belt is to slide the flat end into the buckle. To unfasten, lift up on the buckle and it will release.

As the song goes, there might be fifty ways to leave your lover, but there are only six ways to leave this aircraft: two forward exit doors, two over-wing removable window exits, and two aft exit doors. The location of each exit is clearly marked with signs overhead, as well as red and white disco lights along the floor of the aisle. Made ya look![15]

This clever flight attendant took a predictable announcement and added a few surprises and novel interpretations to make a boring but important message interesting. With just a little thought about how to make your message less predictable, you can add zest and interest to your talks. Listeners will focus on the unexpected. The sample informative speech on this page and the next includes a surprise in the introduction.

Advertisers spend a lot of time trying to get your attention: A young couple is traveling in their car, having a normal, natural conversation and then BAM! CRUNCH!—someone who has run a red light slams into their car. The announcer intones, "Life comes at you fast." You look at the crumpled car and are stunned at how quickly an everyday experience changes in an instant. Like an effective ad, a good speaker knows how to surprise an audience with the same impact as this visual commercial—except that a speaker uses words and stories to metaphorically grab a listener by the shoulders and force him or her to focus on the message.

RECAP

KEEPING THE AUDIENCE INTERESTED

- Tell them why they should want to listen.
- Tell them a good story.
    Describe conflict.
    Describe action.
    Create suspense.
    Use humor when appropriate.
- Tell them how the story affects them.
- Tell them something that surprises them.

an interesting topic will also alleviate some of the angst, anxiety we feel while giving the speech topic.

The second *I* is to make the speech *important*. The speech should not only be interesting but important to us. It should be relevant to our lives now or in the future.

The third *I* is to make the speech *informative*. Let's not waste our tuition money by not learning anything new in those 28 hours of class time. This is our opportunity to learn from each other's experiences and expertise.

Now, just picture yourself putting these ideas into practice. Imagine sitting in a classroom, listening to your classmates talk about issues or ideas that are important to them. They are so excited that you can't help but be excited about the topic with them. You're learning from their life experiences, experiences that you would not have had the opportunity to learn about if it had not been for their speech. Then imagine being able to talk about the experiences and knowledge that are important to you. Sometimes you only have seven minutes to express what is most important to you. Besides that, it's to a captive audience that has no choice but to listen to you. There are few times in our lives when we can have an impact on someone else's life, and we have only a short amount of time to do it. But in our public speaking class, we can have that chance. Let's all think about how we use our time and energy in our public speaking class. I don't want to waste my time or have any unnecessary stress over [pause] tables. I would like all of us to use our opportunities wisely by choosing topics that are interesting, important, and informative.

Here he uses a signpost by clearly noting he's moved to his second point.

Again, he uses a verbal signpost to indicate that this is his third point.

Although Roger's primary purpose is to inform, he uses a hypothetical example to tell the audience how the information he has given them will help them solve a problem: how to find a good speech topic.

Roger provides closure to his message by making a reference to the example he used in his introduction.

Besides surprising your listeners, you might maintain their attention by creating mystery or suspense. Stories are a great way to add drama and interest to a talk—especially a story that moves audience members to try to solve a riddle or a problem. One technique for creating a "mini mystery" is to ask a rhetorical question. You don't necessarily expect an audible answer from audience members, but you do want them to have a mental response. Here's an example: "Would you know what to do if you were stranded, out of gas, at night, without your cell phone?" By getting listeners to ponder your question, you've gotten them actively engaged in your message rather than passively processing your words.[16]

Strategies to Enhance Audience Recall

13.4 Effectively and appropriately use four strategies to enhance audience recall of information presented in an informative speech.

Think of the best teacher you ever had. He or she was probably a good lecturer with a special talent for being not only clear and interesting but also memorable. The very fact that you can remember your teacher is a testament to his or her talent. Like teachers, some speakers are better than others at presenting information in a memorable way. In this section, we review strategies that will help your audiences remember you and your message.

Build In Redundancy

It is seldom necessary for writers to repeat themselves. If readers don't quite understand a passage, they can go back and read it again. When you speak, however, audience

Watch at **MyCommunicationLab**
Video: "What Is Stumbleupon.com?"

members generally cannot stop you if a point in your speech is unclear or if their minds wander. It is helpful to repeat key points.

How do you make your message redundant without insulting your listeners' intelligence? We've already mentioned several techniques in this book. Permit us some redundancy here to make our point.

- Provide a clear preview in the introduction at the beginning of your talk.

- Include an explicit summary of your main points in your conclusion.

- Sprinkle in one or more internal summaries of your key ideas. An internal summary is simply a short review of what you have just presented. Internal summaries make good transitions between major ideas.

- Use numeric signposts (numbering key ideas by saying, "My first point is . . . , My second point is . . . , And now here's my third point . . .") as another way of making sure your audience can identify and remember key points.

- Use a reinforcing visual aid that displays your key ideas.

- If you really want to ensure that listeners come away from your speech with essential information, consider preparing a handout or an outline of key ideas. (But as we noted in the last chapter, when using a handout, make sure the audience remains focused on you, not on your handout.)

Make Your Key Ideas Short and Simple

When we say make your messages short and simple, we don't mean you should give 30-second speeches (although we're sure some speakers and listeners would prefer half-minute speeches to longer, more drawn-out versions). Rather, we mean that when you can distill your key ideas down to a few brief and simple phrases, your audience will be more likely to remember what you say.[17]

Organization signposts accompanied by appropriate gestures add redundancy to your speech, which helps listeners remember the information you present.

Photo: Imabase/Fotolia

Can you remember more than seven things? One classic research study concluded that people can hold only about seven pieces of information (such as the numbers in a seven-digit phone number) in their short-term memory.[18] If you want your listeners to remember your message, don't bombard them with a lengthy list. With the advent of PowerPoint, some speakers may be tempted to spray listeners with a shower of bulleted information. Resist this temptation.

An important speech-preparation technique that we've suggested is to crystallize the central idea of your message into a one-sentence summary of your speech. To help your audience remember your central idea statement, make it short enough to fit on a car bumper sticker. For example, rather than say "The specific words people use and the way people express themselves are influenced by culture and other socioeconomic forces," say "Language shapes our culture and culture shapes our language." The message is not only shorter, but also it uses the technique of antithesis (opposition expressed with a parallel sentence structure) that we discussed in Chapter 10. Perhaps you've heard the same advice expressed as the KISS principle: *Keep It Simple, Sweetheart.* Make your message simple enough for anyone to grasp quickly. Here's the idea phrased as a bumper sticker: Make it short and simple.

Pace Your Information Flow

Organize your speech so that you present an even flow of information, rather than bunch up many significant details around one point. If you present too much new information too quickly, you may overwhelm your audience. Their ability to understand may falter.[19]

You should be especially sensitive to the flow of information if your topic is new or unfamiliar to your listeners. Make sure that your audience has time to process any new information you present. Use supporting materials both to help clarify new information and to slow down the pace of your presentation.

Again, do not try to see how much detail and content you can cram into a speech. Your job is to present information so that the audience can grasp it, not to show off how much you know.

> **RECAP**
>
> ## ENHANCING AUDIENCE RECALL
>
> - Say it again: Build in redundancy.
> - Say it short and simple.
> - Say it at a steady pace.
> - "Say" it with pictures, visuals, and nonverbals.

Reinforce Key Ideas

This last point is one of the most powerful techniques of all: Reinforce key ideas verbally or nonverbally to make your ideas memorable.

Reinforce Ideas Verbally You can reinforce an idea verbally by using such phrases as "This is the most important point" and "Be sure to remember this next point; it's the most compelling one." Suppose you have four suggestions for helping your listeners avoid a serious sunburn, and your last suggestion is the most important. How can you make sure your audience knows that? Just tell them. "Of all the suggestions I've given you, this last tip is the most important one. The higher the SPF level on your sunscreen, the better." Be careful not to overuse this technique. If you claim that every other point is a key point, soon your audience will no longer believe you.

Reinforce Key Ideas Nonverbally How can you draw attention to key ideas nonverbally? Just the way you deliver an idea can give it special emphasis. Gestures serve the purpose of accenting or emphasizing key phrases, as italics do in written messages.

A well-placed pause can provide emphasis and reinforcement to set off a point. Pausing just before or just after making an important point will focus attention on your thought. Raising or lowering your voice can also reinforce a key idea.

Movement can help emphasize major ideas. Moving from behind the lectern to tell a personal anecdote can signal that something special and more intimate is about to be said. As we discussed in Chapter 11, your movement and gestures should be meaningful and natural, rather than seeming arbitrary or forced. Your need to emphasize an idea can provide the motivation for making a meaningful movement.

**Explore at MyCommunicationLab
Activity:** "Build a Speech: Informative Speech"

Developing an Audience-Centered Informative Speech

 13.5   Develop an audience-centered informative speech.

In this chapter, we've described types of informative speeches and offered numerous principles to follow in helping your listeners understand, maintain interest in, and remember your message. But when faced with an informative speaking opportunity, you may still wonder how to go about preparing an informative speech. Our advice: Use the audience-centered speaking model, shown in Figure 13.1 on page 278, to guide you step-by-step through the process.

**Watch at MyCommunicationLab
Video:** "Informative Presentations"

Consider Your Audience

As with any type of speech, an informative talk requires that you consider three general questions of audience analysis: To whom are you speaking? What are their interests, attitudes, beliefs, and values? What do they expect from you? When your general purpose is to inform, you should focus on specific aspects of these three

FIGURE 13.1 You can follow the steps of the audience-centered model of public speaking to craft a successful informative speech.

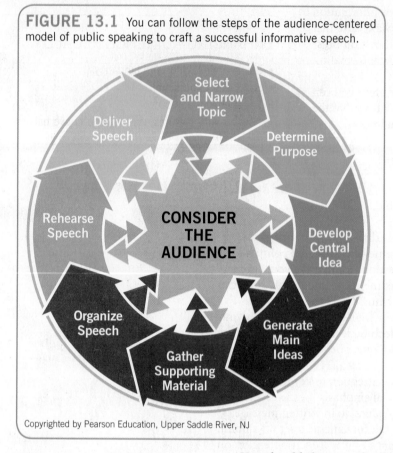

Copyrighted by Pearson Education, Upper Saddle River, NJ

 Read at MyCommunicationLab
Learning From Great Speakers:
Oprah Winfrey

general questions. Part of considering who your audience is will include figuring out, as best you can, their preferred learning styles. Determining listeners' interests, attitudes, beliefs, and values can help you balance your use of strategies to enhance understanding and recall with your need for strategies to maintain interest. You won't need to work as hard to maintain the interest of an audience who is already highly interested in your topic, for example. Careful consideration of the audience's expectations can also help you maintain their interest, perhaps by surprising them with something they do not expect.

Select and Narrow Your Informational Topic

As you select and narrow your topic for an informative presentation, it's especially important to keep your audience in mind. During the early stages of preparing your message, ask yourself, and answer, the question "What do they already know about my topic?" If you misjudge what an audience already knows about your topic, that misjudgment may hamper your development of an effective and precise specific-purpose statement.

You should also consider the question "How interested are they in my topic?" If your audience is both knowledgeable about and interested in your topic, you can provide greater detail and build on the information they already have. If they are likely to be uninterested or uninformed, then you'll need to establish, early in your message, a clear and engaging reason they should tune you in.

Determine Your Informative Purpose

You already know that your general purpose is to inform. You also need to develop a specific behavioral purpose. That is, you need to identify what you'd like the audience to be able to *do* when your finish your speech. "Wait a minute," you might think. "Shouldn't an informative speech be about what the audience should *learn* rather than *do*?" Yes, your purpose is focused on what you want the audience to learn, but we suggest you phrase your learning goal in terms of behavior. Say what you want your audience to *explain, describe, identify, list,* or otherwise *do* to demonstrate their learning.

Here's an example of an imprecise specific-purpose sentence: *At the end of my speech, the audience should know some background about C. S. Lewis's* The Chronicles of Narnia. The word *know* isn't very specific, nor is the phrase *some background.* Precisely what do you want your listeners to know? How can they demonstrate that knowledge? Here's a more precise and effective specific informative-purpose statement: *At the end of my speech, the audience should be able to state three reasons C. S. Lewis wrote* The Chronicles of Narnia.

Why is being precise useful to you? A precise specific-purpose sentence will guide you as you develop your central idea and main ideas, and it is especially important when you organize your message. Merely indicating that you want your audience to know or appreciate some general information provides an unclear road map for getting your audience where you want them to go. If you don't know where you're headed, they won't either. Using specific verbs like *state, restate, summarize, describe, enumerate,* and *list,* and avoiding fuzzy words like *know* and *appreciate,* will focus your thoughts and your message. Think of your specific-purpose sentence as a test question that you're writing for your audience. A test question that asks what you *know* about why C. S. Lewis wrote *The Chronicles of Narnia* is less specific than a question that asks you to *identify three reasons* why the stories were written. You may never actually ask your audience your "test question," but by thinking of your specific purpose as a test question, you'll have a clearer goal in mind, one that will also help you in other areas of preparing your message.

Develop Your Central Idea

With a clear and precise specific-purpose sentence, you'll be better prepared to identify your central idea—a one-sentence summary of your message. Rather than a fuzzy central idea sentence such as "C. S. Lewis wrote the Narnia stories for many reasons," your more specific central idea might be, "Three reasons Lewis wrote the Narnia stories are to connect the 'pictures' he visualized in his head, to write an engaging story for children, and to make a larger point about Christianity." Your central idea sentence is your speech in brief. Someone who heard only your central idea would understand the essence of your message.

Generate Your Main Ideas

If you've developed a specific-purpose sentence and have a well-crafted central idea sentence, it should be easy to generate your main ideas. In our C. S. Lewis example, we identified in our central idea three reasons Lewis wrote the stories. Those three reasons will become the main ideas of the speech. The type of informative talk you are planning will influence your central and main ideas. A speech about an object may lend itself to certain main ideas such as history, features, and uses of the object, whereas a speech about a person might be more likely to have main ideas related to the person's accomplishments or relationship to you, the speaker.

Gather Your Supporting Materials

As you read and research, you look for examples, illustrations, stories, statistics, and other materials that help you achieve your specific purpose. The type of informative speech you plan to make will often suggest ideas for supporting materials. Biographical details and stories will most likely support a speech about a person. Stories, examples, or statistics may help you teach your audience about an event or idea. Remember that supporting materials include presentation aids. As we noted earlier in this chapter, visual aids often make "how-to" speeches about procedures more effective. Speeches about objects also often benefit from visual aids, especially if you are able to show the actual object. As you gather supporting material, continue to think about your audience, who will ultimately judge whether your supporting material is interesting and helpful.

Organize Your Speech

In developing a specific purpose and identifying main ideas, you've already been working on the organization of your message. As you keep your audience in mind, you now determine what the best sequence of your main points should be. Your topic and purpose can also help guide you. As we discussed earlier in the chapter, different types of informative speeches lend themselves to different organizational patterns.

CONFIDENTLY CONNECTING WITH YOUR AUDIENCE

Focus on Your Information Rather Than on Your Fear

You nurture your fear when you focus on your anxiety. Consciously keep your mind off your fear and focused on the message you will present. When you feel your anxiety level rising, do something related to improving your speech rather than let your anxiety get the best of you. Consider reviewing your introduction, taking another look at your main points, or glancing at your conclusion one more time. By changing your focus from your fear to preparing your talk, you are changing the stimulus that may be triggering additional anxiety.

Rehearse Your Presentation

With your well-prepared notes in hand, you're ready to rehearse your speech. As we suggested in Chapter 11, you'll want to rehearse your speech aloud while standing. By recreating the experience of actually delivering your speech, not only are you polishing your delivery, but also you will better manage any apprehension you may have. For informative speeches, it is especially helpful to rehearse in front of other people, especially people who are similar to your listeners, if possible. Seek their feedback about whether you are effectively teaching them about your topic. You may even wish to ask your sample audience the test question you developed as your specific-purpose statement, to determine whether your speech is meeting your learning objectives.

RECAP

AUDIENCE-CENTERED INFORMATIVE SPEAKING

- Select topic—Consider who the audience is and their interests.
- Narrow topic—Find out what the audience already knows.
- Determine purpose—State specific audience actions that will show learning.
- Formulate central and main ideas—Make them clear and simple.
- Gather supporting material—Decide what will help audience maintain interest and learn.
- Organize—Match topic with audience needs.
- Rehearse—Get sample audience feedback.
- Deliver—Adapt to ensure audience comprehension.

Deliver Your Speech

Finally, you're ready to deliver your speech to your audience. With good eye contact, a clear voice, and effective gestures, you command your audience's attention with your well-rehearsed speech. As we discussed in Chapter 11, effective speakers continually look for ways to adapt and modify their message as they speak. Such adaptation is especially important in informative speaking. As you speak, watch your audience closely for signs—such as puzzled facial expressions—that indicate they do not understand something. Be alert, too, for signs of wandering attention, such as fidgeting or lack of eye contact. Be prepared to adapt your message, using the strategies discussed earlier in this chapter for enhancing listeners' understanding and maintaining their attention.

STUDY GUIDE REVIEW, APPLY, AND ASSESS

TYPES OF INFORMATIVE SPEECHES

13.1 Describe five different types of informative speeches.

To inform is to teach someone something you know. Informative speeches have three goals—to enhance understanding, to maintain interest, and to be remembered. To achieve these goals, you can deliver several different types of informative speeches. Speeches about objects discuss tangible things. Speeches about procedures explain a process or describe how something works. Speeches about people can be about either the famous or the little known. Speeches about events describe major occurrences or personal experiences. Speeches about ideas discuss often-abstract principles, concepts, or theories.

Key Term

Speech to inform 262

Thinking Ethically

You are a chemistry major considering whether you should give an informative speech to your public-speaking class about how pipe bombs are made. Is this an appropriate topic for your audience?

Assessing Your Audience-Centered Speaking Skill

Hillary Webster, M.D., will be addressing a medical convention of other physicians to discuss the weight-loss technique she has recently used successfully with her patients. What advice would you give to help her present an effective talk?

STRATEGIES TO ENHANCE AUDIENCE UNDERSTANDING

13.2 Effectively and appropriately use four strategies to enhance audience understanding.

To enhance your listeners' understanding of a message: (1) define ideas clearly, (2) use principles and techniques of adult learning, (3) clarify unfamiliar ideas or complex processes, (4) use descriptions effectively, and (5) combine spoken words, visuals, and kinesthetic opportunities to appeal to listeners with a variety of learning styles.

Key Terms

Pedagogy 269
Andragogy 269
Word picture 271

Thinking Ethically

In order to give your 5-minute speech about nuclear energy, you must greatly simplify what is a very complex process. How can you avoid misrepresenting your topic? Should you let your audience know that you are oversimplifying the process?

Thinking Critically

You have been asked to speak to a kindergarten class about your chosen profession. Identify approaches to this task that would help make your message clear, interesting, and memorable to your audience.

Assessing Your Audience-Centered Speaking Skill

Imagine that you are going to teach a group of adult learners how to prepare an informative speech. How could you incorporate principles of adult learning presented on page 269 to ensure that you addressed their needs?

STRATEGIES TO MAINTAIN AUDIENCE INTEREST

13.3 Effectively and appropriately use three strategies to maintain audience interest.

To gain and maintain interest in your informative talk, follow three important principles. First, motivate your audience to listen to you. Second, tell a story; a well-told story almost always works to keep listeners focused on you and your message. Third, present information that relates to your listeners' interests; in essence, be audience-centered. Finally, use the unexpected to surprise your audience.

Thinking Ethically

Before giving a speech to your class in which you share a story that includes personal information about one of your friends, should you ask permission from your friend?

STRATEGIES TO ENHANCE AUDIENCE RECALL

13.4 Effectively and appropriately use four strategies to enhance audience recall of information presented in an informative speech.

Help your listeners remember what you tell them by being redundant. Be sure to keep your main ideas short and simple. Pacing the flow of your information helps listeners recall your ideas. Reinforcing important points verbally and nonverbally can also help your audience members remember them.

Assessing Your Audience-Centered Speaking Skill

What strategies does your public-speaking teacher use in class to enhance listener recall?

DEVELOPING AN AUDIENCE-CENTERED INFORMATIVE SPEECH

13.5 Develop an audience-centered informative speech.

You can apply principles of informative speaking to adapt the audience-centered model of speaking. Choose and narrow your topic by determining what the audience already knows. Use action words in your specific-purpose statement. The needs of your audience and topic will help you organize your speech and gather supporting materials. Seek audience feedback on your teaching effectiveness as you rehearse, and adapt your delivery, if needed, to ensure that the audience understands your message.

Thinking Critically

Brendan is planning on sharing his experiences with his fraternity brothers about his recent study abroad trip to Oxford, England. What are specific aspects of Brendan's audience that he should keep in mind as he prepares and presents his message?

Assessing Your Audience-Centered Speaking Skill

Redundancy can be especially helpful when you and the audience have language differences. Which of the specific strategies discussed in this chapter for making your message more redundant would increase understanding of an audience whose primary language is different from yours?

 **Explore** at **MyCommunicationLab**
Speaker's Workshop: Developing a Vivid Word Picture

14 UNDERSTANDING PRINCIPLES OF PERSUASIVE SPEAKING

Ronald D. Ginther (1907–1969), *Familiar Scene on the Skid Road*, c. 1935. Watercolor and ink on board. Washington State Historical Society, Tacoma, Washington. Photo: Washington State Historical Society / Art Resource, NY.

OBJECTIVES

After studying this chapter you should be able to do the following:

14.1
Describe the goals of persuasive messages.

14.2
Explain classic and contemporary theories of how persuasion occurs.

14.3
Describe four ways to motivate listeners to respond to a persuasive message.

14.4
Prepare and present an audience-centered persuasive speech.

 Listen to Chapter 14 at **MyCommunicationLab**

. . . the power of speech, to stir men's blood.

—William Shakespeare

283

I t happens to you hundreds of times each day. It appears as commercials on TV, tweets, Internet ads, and Facebook requests from friends; as advertisements in magazines and on billboards; and as fund-raising messages from politicians and charities. It also occurs when you are asked to give money to a worthy cause or to donate blood. "It" is persuasion. Because persuasion is such an ever-present part of your life, it is important for you to understand how it works. What are the principles of an activity that can shape your attitudes and behavior? What do crafters of Internet pop-up ads, salespeople, and politicians know about how to influence your thinking and behavior that you don't know?

In this chapter, we discuss how persuasion works. Such information can sharpen your persuasive skills and can also help you become a more informed receiver of persuasive messages. We will define persuasion and discuss the psychological principles underlying efforts to persuade others. We will also discuss tips for choosing a persuasive speech topic and developing arguments for your speeches. In Chapter 15, we will examine specific strategies for crafting a persuasive speech.

In Chapter 13, we discussed strategies for informative speaking—the oral presentation of new information to listeners so that they will understand and remember what is communicated. The purposes of informing and persuading are closely related. Why inform an audience? Why give new information to others? We often provide information to give listeners new insights that may affect their attitudes and behavior. Information alone has the potential to convince others, but when information is coupled with strategies to persuade, the chances of success increase.

In a persuasive speech, the speaker asks the audience to make a choice, rather than just informing them of the options. As a persuasive speaker, you will do more than teach; you will ask your listeners to respond to the information you share. If you want your listeners to respond to your persuasive appeal, you will need to think carefully about the way you structure your message to achieve your specific purpose. Audience analysis is crucial to achieving your goal. To advocate a particular view or position successfully, you must understand your listeners' attitudes, beliefs, values, and behavior.

| 14.1 | Describe the goals of persuasive messages. |

The Goals of Persuasion

Persuasion is the process of changing or reinforcing attitudes, beliefs, values, or behavior. Note that when trying to persuade someone, you may not necessarily try to change someone's point of view or behavior but, instead, aim to *reinforce* it. Your listeners may already like, believe, or value something, or *sometimes* do what you'd like them to do; you are trying to strengthen their current perspective. Suppose, for example, that your persuasive purpose is to get people to use their recycling trash bins. The audience may already think that recycling is a good thing and may even use their recycling bins at least some of the time. Your speaking goal is to reinforce their behavior so that they use the recycling bins every time.

Because the goal of persuasion is to change or reinforce attitudes, beliefs, values, or behavior, it's important to clarify how these elements differ. Having a clear idea of precisely which of these elements you want to change or reinforce can help you develop your persuasive strategy.

persuasion
The process of changing or reinforcing a listener's attitudes, beliefs, values, or behavior

Changing or Reinforcing Audience Attitudes

Our attitudes represent our likes and dislikes. Stated more precisely, an **attitude** is a learned predisposition to respond favorably or unfavorably toward something.[1] In a persuasive speech, you might try to persuade your listeners to favor or oppose a new shopping mall, to like bats because of their ability to eat insects, or to dislike an increase in the sales tax.

Changing or Reinforcing Audience Beliefs

A persuasive speech could also attempt to change or reinforce a belief. A **belief** is something you understand to be true or false. If you believe in something, you are convinced that it exists or is true. You have structured your sense of what is real and what is unreal to account for the existence of whatever you believe. If you believe in God, you have structured your sense of what is real and unreal to recognize the existence of God.

We hold some beliefs based on faith—we haven't directly experienced something, but we believe anyway. However, most beliefs are typically based on evidence, including past experiences. If you believe the sun will rise in the east again tomorrow, or that nuclear power is safe, you base these beliefs either on what you've directly experienced or on the experience of someone you find trustworthy. Beliefs are also changed by evidence. As a speaker, you might have a difficult time, for example, trying to change an audience's belief that the world is flat; you would need to show that existing evidence supports a different conclusion. Usually it takes a great deal of evidence to change a belief and alter the way your audience structures reality.

attitude
A learned predisposition to respond favorably or unfavorably toward something; likes and dislikes

belief
A way we structure reality to accept something as true or false

value
An enduring concept of good and bad, right and wrong

Changing or Reinforcing Audience Values

A persuasive speech could also seek to change or reinforce a value. A **value** is an enduring concept of right or wrong, good or bad. If you value something, you classify it as good or desirable, and you tend to think of its opposite or its absence as bad or wrong. If you do not value something, you are indifferent to it. Values form the basis of your life goals and the motivating force behind your behavior. Most Americans value honesty, trustworthiness, freedom, loyalty, marriage, family, and money. Understanding what your listeners value can help you refine your analysis of them and adapt the content of your speech to those values.

Most of us acquired our values when we were very young and have held onto them into adulthood. Our values, therefore, are generally deeply ingrained. It is not impossible to change the values of your listeners, but it is much more difficult than trying to change a belief or an attitude. Political and religious points of view, which are usually based on long-held values, are especially difficult to modify.

As Figure 14.1 shows, values are the most deeply ingrained of the three predispositions; they change least frequently. That's why values are at the core of the model. Beliefs change, but not as much as attitudes. Trying to change an audience's attitudes (likes and dislikes) is easier than attempting to change their values. Today we may approve of the president of the United States; tomorrow we may disapprove of him because of an action he has taken. We may still *believe* that the country is financially stable because of the president's programs, and we may still *value* a democratic form of government, but our *attitude* toward the president has changed because of this policy decision.

We suggest that you think carefully about your purpose for making a persuasive speech. Know with certainty whether your objective is to

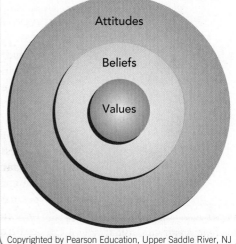

FIGURE 14.1 Your chances of successfully persuading your audience are affected by whether you choose to target listeners' attitudes, beliefs, or values. Attitudes form the outer ring of this model because they are easier to change than beliefs or core values. Beliefs can be changed, but not as easily as attitudes. Values are at the core of the model because they are the most deeply ingrained and change the least frequently.

DEFINING PERSUASION

Persuasion attempts to change or reinforce the following:

- Attitudes: Likes and dislikes
- Beliefs: Perceptions of what is true or false
- Values: What you hold as right and wrong, good or bad
- Behavior: What we do or don't do

change or to reinforce an attitude, a belief, or a value. Then decide what you have to do to achieve your objective.

Changing or Reinforcing Audience Behaviors

Persuasive messages often attempt to do more than change or reinforce attitudes, beliefs, or values—they may attempt to change or strengthen behaviors. Getting listeners to eat more fruits and vegetables and to exercise more are typical goals of the persuasive messages that we hear. It seems logical that knowing someone's attitudes, beliefs, and values will let us predict precisely how that person will behave. But we are complicated creatures, and human behavior is not always neatly predictable. Sometimes our attitudes, beliefs, and values may not appear to be consistent with how we act. For example, you may know that if you're on a low-carb diet, you should avoid that second helping of Dad's homemade chocolate cake, but you cut off a slice and gobble it up anyway.

14.2 Explain classic and contemporary theories of how persuasion occurs.

Explore at MyCommunicationLab
Activity: "Persuasion"

How Persuasion Works

Now that you know what persuasion is and how attitudes, beliefs, and values influence your behavior, you may still have questions about how persuasion actually works. Knowing how and why listeners change their minds and their behavior can help you construct more effective persuasive messages.

Besides enabling you to persuade others, understanding how persuasion works can help you analyze why *you* are sometimes persuaded to think or behave in certain ways. Being conscious of why you respond to specific persuasive messages can help you be a better, more discriminating listener to persuasive pitches.

Many theories and considerable research describe how persuasion works. We'll discuss two approaches here: first, a classical approach identified by Aristotle and, second, a more contemporary theory that builds on the classical approach.

Aristotle's Traditional Approach: Using Ethos, Logos, and Pathos to Persuade

Aristotle, a Greek philosopher and rhetorician who lived and wrote in the fourth century BCE, is the source of many ideas about communication in general and persuasion in particular. As we noted in Chapter 4, he defined *rhetoric* as the process of discovering in any particular case the available means of persuasion. When the goal is to persuade, the communicator selects symbols (words and nonverbal messages, including images and music) to change attitudes, beliefs, values, or behavior. Aristotle identified three general methods (or, using his language, "available means") to persuade: ethos, logos, and pathos.[2]

Ethos   To use **ethos** to persuade, an effective communicator must be credible. Aristotle believed that in order to be credible, a public speaker should be ethical, possess good character, have common sense, and be concerned for the well-being of the audience. The more credible and ethical a speaker is perceived to be, the greater the chances are that a listener will believe in, trust, and positively respond to the persuasive message of the speaker. So one of the means or methods of persuasion is for the communicator to present information that can be trusted and to be believable and trustworthy himself or herself. When a friend wants to convince you to let him borrow your car, he may say, "Trust me. I promise not to do anything wacky with your car.

ethos

The term Aristotle used to refer to a speaker's credibility

I'm a responsible guy." He's appealing to his credibility as an ethical, trusted friend. We'll discuss specific strategies to enhance your credibility and your persuasiveness in the next chapter.

Logos Another means of persuading others is to use **logos**. The word *logos* literally means "the word." Aristotle used this term to refer to the rational, logical arguments that a speaker uses to persuade someone. A skilled persuader not only reaches a logical conclusion but also supports the message with evidence and reasoning. The friend who wants to borrow your car may use a logical, rational argument supported with evidence to get your car keys. He may say, "I borrowed your car last week and I returned it without a scratch. I also borrowed it the week before that and there were no problems—and I filled the tank with gas. So if you loan me your car today, I'll return it just like I did in the past." Your friend is appealing to your rational side by using evidence to support his conclusion that your car will be returned in good shape. In Chapter 15 we'll provide strategies for developing logical, rational arguments and supporting those arguments with solid evidence.

Pathos Aristotle used the term **pathos** to refer to the use of appeals to emotion. We sometimes hold attitudes, beliefs, and values that are not logical but that simply make us feel positive. Likewise, we sometimes do things or buy things to make ourselves feel happy, powerful, or energized. The friend who wants to borrow your wheels may also use pathos—an emotional appeal—to get you to turn over your car keys. He may say, "Look, without transportation I can't get to my doctor's appointment. I'm feeling sick. I need your help. Friends help friends, and I could use a good friend right now." Your buddy is tugging on your emotional heartstrings to motivate you to loan him your car. He's hoping to convince you to behave in a way that makes you feel positive about yourself.

What are effective ways to appeal to listeners' emotions? Use emotion-arousing stories and concrete examples, as well as pictures and music. In the next chapter we'll identify more ethical strategies to appeal to emotions when persuading others.

All three traditional means of persuasion—ethos (ethical credibility), logos (logic), and pathos (emotion)—are ways of motivating a listener to think or behave in certain ways. **Motivation** is the underlying internal force that drives people to achieve their goals. Our motives explain why we do things.[3] Several factors motivate people to respond to persuasive messages: The need to restore balance to their lives and avoid stress, the need to avoid pain, and the desire to increase pleasure have been documented as motives that influence attitudes, beliefs, values, and behavior.

Both Aristotle's traditional approach and the elaboration likelihood model suggest that appeals to emotion can help persuade listeners. Thus, a speaker might accompany a talk promoting the adoption of pets from the local animal shelter with photos of adorable animals to arouse listeners' emotions and propel them to bring home a puppy or kitten.

Photo: MoustacheGirl/Fotolia

ELM's Contemporary Approach: Using a Direct or Indirect Path to Persuade

A newer, research-based framework for understanding how persuasion works is called the **elaboration likelihood model (ELM) of persuasion**.[4] This theory with a long name is actually a simple idea that offers an explanation of how people are persuaded to do something or think about something. Rather than prescribe how to craft a persuasive message from the standpoint of the speaker, as Aristotle does,

logos
Literally, "the word"; the term Aristotle used to refer to logic—the formal system of using rules to reach a conclusion

pathos
The term used by Aristotle to refer to appeals to human emotion

motivation
The internal force that drives people to achieve their goals

elaboration likelihood model (ELM) of persuasion
The theory that people can be persuaded by logic, evidence, and reasoning, or through a more peripheral route that may depend on the credibility of the speaker, the sheer number of arguments presented, or emotional appeals

ELM theory describes how audience members *interpret* persuasive messages. It's an audience-centered theory of how people make sense of persuasive communication.

To **elaborate** means that you *think* about the information, ideas, and issues related to the content of the message you hear. When you elaborate on a message, you are critically evaluating what you hear by paying special attention to the arguments and the evidence the speaker is using. The likelihood of whether or not you elaborate (hence, the term *elaboration likelihood model*) on a message varies from person to person and depends on the topic of the message.

The theory suggests that there are two ways you can be persuaded: (1) the **direct persuasion route** that you follow when you elaborate, consciously think about, or critically evaluate a message, and (2) the **indirect persuasion route**, in which you don't elaborate and are instead influenced by the more peripheral factors of the message and the messenger—you are less aware of why you are persuaded to respond positively or negatively to a message.

The Direct Persuasion Route When you elaborate, you consider what Aristotle would call the underlying logos, or logic, of the message. You carefully and systematically think about the facts, reasoning, arguments, and evidence presented to you, and then you make a thoughtful decision as to whether to believe or do what the persuader wants. For example, you buy a good data package for your smartphone because you are convinced you will benefit from constant access to the Internet; you've read the literature and have made a logical, rational decision. There may be times, however, when you think you are making a decision based on logic, but instead you are being persuaded by less obvious strategies via an indirect path.

The Indirect Persuasion Route If you don't elaborate (that is, if you don't use critical thinking skills while listening), you simply develop an overall impression of what the speaker says and how the speaker says it. The indirect route is a more intuitive than rational process. You can be persuaded by such indirect factors as catchy music used in an advertisement or your positive reaction to the attractive and articulate salesperson who wants to sell you a product. It's not an evaluation of the logic or content of the advertisement or the salesperson's reasoning or evidence that persuades you; it's the overall feeling you have about the product or the salesperson that triggers your purchase. When hearing a speech, you may be persuaded by the appearance of the speaker (he looks nice; I trust him); by the sheer number of research studies in support of the speaker's proposal (there are so many reasons to accept this speaker's proposal; she's convinced me); or by the speaker's use of an emotionally charged story (I can't let that little girl starve; I'll donate 50 cents to save her).

These two theories, Aristotle's theory and ELM theory, both suggest that persuasion is a complex process. Not all of us are persuaded in the same way. Aristotle's theory emphasizes what the *speaker* should do to influence an audience. If the speaker discovers the proper application of a credible and ethical message (ethos), logic (logos), and emotion (pathos), then persuasion is likely to occur. ELM theory describes the different ways *listeners* process the messages they hear. Listeners can be persuaded when they directly elaborate (or actively think about what they hear) and logically ponder how evidence and reasoning make sense. Or, if they do not elaborate, listeners may be persuaded indirectly, based on peripheral factors that don't require as much thought to process, such as the personal appearance of the speaker or the speaker's delivery.

Both theories work together to explain how you can persuade others and how others persuade you. Because you may not know whether your listeners are directly or indirectly influenced by your message (whether they are elaborating or not), you will want to use a balance of ethos, logos, and pathos as you think about how to persuade your listeners. However, it's your *audience,* not you, that will

elaborate
From the standpoint of the elaboration likelihood model (ELM) of persuasion, to think about information, ideas, and issues related to the content of a message

direct persuasion route
Persuasion that occurs when audience members critically examine evidence and arguments

indirect persuasion route
Persuasion that occurs as a result of factors peripheral to a speaker's logic and argument, such as the speaker's charisma or emotional appeals

---

RECAP

MODELS OF PERSUASION

Aristotle's Classical Approach
- Ethos: The credibility of the speaker
- Logos: The logic used to reach a conclusion
- Pathos: The appeal to emotion

Elaboration Likelihood Model
- Direct route—with elaboration; considering the facts, evidence, and logic of the message
- Indirect route—without elaboration; relying on an intuitive feeling in response to peripheral aspects of the message

ultimately make sense out of what they hear. So, in addition to the carefully constructed logic and well-reasoned arguments that you present, you need to be attuned to the indirect factors that can influence your listeners, such as your delivery, your appearance, and a general impression of how prepared you seem to be.

These two theories also help explain how *you* are influenced by others. You are influenced by the ethical appeal, logical arguments, and emotions of a speaker. In addition, ELM theory suggests you may be directly affected by the logic and arguments of a speaker. You may also be influenced, even when you're not aware of it, by such peripheral or indirect elements of the message as the speaker's appearance and delivery. Remaining aware of how you are being persuaded can make you a more effective and critical listener to the multitude of persuasive messages that come your way each day.

How to Motivate Listeners

14.3 Describe four ways to motivate listeners to respond to a persuasive message.

It's late at night and you're watching your favorite talk show. The program is interrupted by a commercial extolling the virtues of a well-known brand of ice cream. Suddenly you remember that you have some of the advertised flavor, Royal Rocky Road. You apparently hadn't realized how hungry you were for ice cream until the ad reminded you of the lip-smacking goodness of the cold, creamy, smooth treat. Before you know it, you are at the freezer, helping yourself to a couple of scoops of ice cream.

If the makers of that commercial knew how persuasive it had been, they would be overjoyed. At the heart of the persuasion process is the audience-centered process of motivating listeners to respond to a message. The ad changed your behavior because the message was tailor-made for you.

Persuasion works when listeners are motivated to respond. What principles explain why you were motivated to go to the freezer at midnight for a carton of ice cream? An audience is more likely to be persuaded when you help members solve their problems or meet their needs. They can also be motivated when you convince them good things will happen to them if they follow your advice or bad things will occur if they don't. We next discuss several ways to motivate listeners; these approaches are summarized in Table 14.1 on page 290.

Use Cognitive Dissonance

Dissonance theory is based on the principle that people strive to solve problems and manage stress and tension in a way that is consistent with their attitudes, beliefs, and values.[5] According to the theory, when you are presented with information inconsistent with your current attitudes, beliefs, values, or behavior, you become aware that you have a problem; you experience a kind of discomfort called **cognitive dissonance**. The word *cognitive* has to do with our thoughts. *Dissonance* means "lack of harmony or agreement." When you think of a dissonant chord in music, you probably think of a collection of unpleasant sounds not in tune with the melody or other chords. Most people seek to avoid problems or feelings of dissonance. Cognitive dissonance, then, means that you are experiencing a way of thinking that is inconsistent and uncomfortable. If, for example, you smoke cigarettes and a speaker reminds you that smoking is unhealthy, this reminder creates dissonance. You can restore balance and solve the problem either by no longer smoking or by rejecting the message that smoking is harmful.

Creating dissonance with a persuasive speech can be an effective way to change attitudes and behavior. The first tactic in such a speech is to identify an existing problem or need. For example, Evie believes that we should only eat organic fruits

Watch at **MyCommunicationLab**
Video: "Bill Gates Criticizes America's High Schools"

cognitive dissonance
The sense of mental discomfort that prompts a person to change when new information conflicts with previously organized thought patterns

TABLE 14.1   HOW TO MOTIVATE LISTENERS TO RESPOND TO YOUR PERSUASIVE MESSAGE

Use Cognitive Dissonance	Telling listeners about existing problems or information that is inconsistent with their currently held beliefs or known information creates psychological discomfort.	Do you value your family's security? Then you're probably worried to learn that many of us would not be able to support our families if we were injured and couldn't work. You can restore your peace of mind by buying our disability insurance policy.
Use Listeners' Needs	People are motivated by unmet needs. The most basic needs are physiological, followed by safety needs, social needs, self-esteem needs, and finally, self-actualization needs.	You could be the envy of people you know if you purchase this sleek new sports car. You will be perceived as a person of high status in your community.
Use Positive Motivation	People will be more likely to change their thinking or pursue a particular course of action if they are convinced that good things will happen to them if they support what the speaker advocates.	You should take a course in public speaking because it will increase your prospects of getting a good job. Effective communication skills are the most sought-after skills in today's workplace.
Use Negative Motivation	People seek to avoid pain and discomfort. They will be motivated to support what a speaker advocates if they are convinced that bad things will happen to them unless they do.	If there is a hurricane, tornado, earthquake, or other natural disaster, the electrical power may be out and you may not be able to fill your car with gas. Without the basics of food and water, you could die. You need to be prepared for a worst-case scenario by having an emergency stockpile of water, food, and gas for your car.

and vegetables. If we don't eat organic foods, we increase the risk of getting cancer because we are consuming chemicals that have been linked to cancer. Evie is seeking to create dissonance by suggesting that we could more readily develop cancer unless we eat organic farm products. The way to reduce our dissonance (and the threat of cancer) is to eat more healthful organic fruits and vegetables—precisely what Evie is advocating. Of course, a speaker can't just assert that something will create a problem. The ethical speaker uses evidence such as facts, statistics, or expert testimony to document the claims. With the strategy of creating dissonance by documenting the harm and then suggesting a way to minimize or eliminate the harm, the speaker is seeking to change listener behavior.

Political candidates use a similar strategy. A mayoral candidate usually tries first to make his or her audience aware of problems in the community and then blames the current mayor for most of the problems. Once dissonance has been created, the candidate then suggests that the problems would be solved, or at least managed better, if he or she were elected mayor. Using the principles of dissonance theory, the mayoral candidate first upsets the audience and then restores their balance and feeling of comfort by offering a solution to the city's problems: his or her selection as mayor.

In using dissonance theory to persuade, speakers have an ethical responsibility not to rely on false claims to create dissonance. Claiming that a problem exists when it does not or creating dissonance about a problem that is unlikely to happen is unethical. When listening to a persuasive message, pay particular attention to the evidence that a speaker uses to convince you that a problem really does exist.

How Listeners Cope with Dissonance Effective persuasion requires more than simply creating dissonance and then suggesting a solution. When your listeners confront dissonant information, various options are available to them besides following your

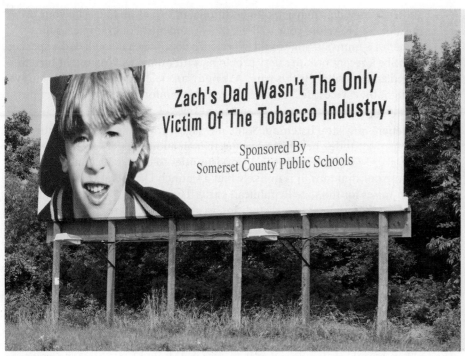

Zach's Dad Wasn't The Only Victim Of The Tobacco Industry.

Sponsored By
Somerset County Public Schools

Effective public-service messages often use cognitive dissonance to change people's behaviors. This technique is also often effective for public speakers.

Photo: Sonda Dawes/The Image Works

suggestions. You need to be aware of the other ways your audience might react before you can reduce their cognitive dissonance.[6]

CONSIDER
THE
AUDIENCE

- **Listeners may discredit the source.** Instead of believing everything you say, your listeners could choose to discredit you. Suppose you drive a Japanese-made car and you hear a speaker whose father owns a Chevrolet dealership advocate that all Americans should drive cars made in the United States. You could agree with him, or you could decide that the speaker is biased because of his father's occupation. Instead of selling your Japanese-made car and buying an American-made car, you could doubt the speaker's credibility and ignore the suggestion to buy American automobiles. As a persuasive speaker, you need to ensure that your audience will perceive you as competent and trustworthy so that they will accept your message.

- **Listeners may reinterpret the message.** A second way your listeners might overcome cognitive dissonance and restore balance is to hear what they want to hear. They may choose to focus on the parts of your message that are consistent with what they already believe and ignore the unfamiliar or controversial parts. If you tell a customer looking at a new kind of computer software that it takes ten steps to get into the word-processing program but that the program is easy to use, the customer might focus on those first ten steps and decide that the software would be too hard to use. Your job as an effective speaker is to make your message as clear as possible so that your audience will not reinterpret it. In this case, your task is to emphasize that the software is easy to use. Choose your words carefully; use simple, vivid examples to keep listeners focused on what's most important.

- **Listeners may seek new information.** Another way that listeners cope with cognitive dissonance is to seek more information on the subject. Your

---

RECAP

COPING WITH COGNITIVE DISSONANCE

When your message gives listeners conflicting thoughts, they might:

- try to discredit you; you need to be competent and trustworthy.
- reinterpret your message; you need to be sure it's clear.
- seek other information; you need to make your information convincing.
- stop listening; you need to make your message interesting.
- be persuaded.

audience members may look for additional information to negate your position and to refute your well-created arguments. For example, as the owner of a minivan, you would experience dissonance if you heard a speaker describe a recent rash of safety problems with minivans. You might turn to a friend and whisper, "Is this true? Are minivans really dangerous? I've always thought they were safe." You would want new information to validate your ownership of a minivan.

- **Listeners may stop listening.** Some messages are so much at odds with listeners' attitudes, beliefs, and values that an audience may decide to stop listening. Most of us do not seek opportunities to hear or read messages that oppose our opinions. It is unlikely that a staunch Democrat would attend a fund-raiser for the state Republican party. The principle of selective exposure suggests that we tend to pay attention to messages that are consistent with our points of view and to avoid those that are not. When we do find ourselves trapped in a situation in which we must hear a message that doesn't support our beliefs, we tend to stop listening. Being aware of the existing attitudes, beliefs, and values of your audience can help you ensure that they won't tune you out.

- **Listeners may change their attitudes, beliefs, values, or behavior.** A fifth way an audience may respond to dissonant information is to do as the speaker wants them to do. As we have noted, if listeners change their attitudes, they will reduce the dissonance that they experience. You listen to a life-insurance salesperson tell you that when you die, your family will have no financial support. This creates dissonance; you prefer to think of your family as happy and secure. So you take out a $250,000 policy to protect your family. This action restores your sense of balance. The salesperson has persuaded you successfully. The goals of advertising copywriters, salespeople, and political candidates are similar: They want you to experience dissonance so that you will change your attitudes, beliefs, values, or behavior.

Use Listeners' Needs

Watch at **MyCommunicationLab**
Video: "Living Wills"

Need is one of the best motivators. The person who is looking at a new car because he or she needs one is more likely to buy than the person who is just thinking about how nice it would be to drive the latest model. The more you understand what your listeners need, the greater the chances are that you can gain and hold their attention and ultimately get them to do what you want. The classic theory that outlines basic human needs was developed by Abraham Maslow.[7] Maslow suggested that there is a hierarchy of needs that motivates everyone's behavior. Figure 14.2 illustrates Maslow's five levels of needs with the most basic at the bottom. Maslow suggested that we need to meet the basic physiological needs (for food, water, and air) before we can be motivated to respond to higher-level needs. Although the hierarchical nature of Maslow's needs has not been consistently supported by research (we can be motivated by several needs at the same time), Maslow's hierarchy provides a useful checklist of potential listener motivations. When attempting to persuade an audience, a speaker tries to stimulate these needs in order to change or reinforce attitudes, beliefs, values, or behavior. Let's examine each of these needs.

Physiological Needs The most basic needs for all humans are physiological: We all need air, water, and food. According to Maslow's theory, unless those needs are met, it will be difficult to motivate a listener to satisfy other needs. If your listeners are hot, tired, and thirsty, it will be more difficult to persuade them to vote for your candidate, buy your insurance policy, or sign your petition in support of local pet-leash laws. Be sensitive to the basic physiological needs of your audience so that your appeals to higher-level needs will be heard.

Safety Needs Listeners are concerned about their safety. We all have a need to feel safe, secure, and protected, and we need to be able to predict that our own and our loved ones' needs for safety will be met. The classic presentation from insurance salespeople includes appeals to our need for safety and security. Many insurance sales efforts include photos of wrecked cars, anecdotes of people who were in ill health and could not pay their bills, or tales of the head of a household who passed away, leaving the basic needs of a family unmet. Appeals to use safety belts, stop smoking, start exercising, and use condoms all play to our need for safety and security.

In a speech titled "Emissions Tampering: Get the Lead Out," John appealed to his listeners' need for safety and security when he began with these observations:

A major American producer is currently dumping over 8,000 tons of lead into our air each year, which in turn adversely affects human health. The producers of this waste are tampering with pollution control devices in order to cut costs. This tampering escalates the amount of noxious gases you and I inhale by 300 to 800 percent. That producer is the American motorist.[8]

FIGURE 14.2 According to Maslow, our needs are ordered in a hierarchy, so that we must satisfy the needs at the base of the pyramid before we are motivated to address higher-level needs. For example, if listeners couldn't afford to meet their basic, physiological needs for food, it would be difficult to sell them a life insurance policy to address their safety needs.

Source: Based on Maslow, Abraham (1954). *Motivation and Personality.* New York: HarperCollins.

Social Needs We all need to feel loved and valued. We need contact with others and reassurance that they care about us. According to Maslow, these social needs translate into our need for a sense of belonging to a group (fraternity, religious organization, friendships). Powerful persuasive appeals are based on our need for social contact. We are encouraged to buy a product or support a particular issue because others are buying the product or supporting the issue. The message is that to be liked and respected by others, we must buy the same things they do or support the same causes they support.

Self-Esteem Needs The need for self-esteem reflects our desire to think well of ourselves. Civil rights activist Jesse Jackson is known for appealing often to the self-worth of his listeners by inviting them to chant "I am somebody." This is a direct appeal to his listeners' need for self-esteem. Advertisers also appeal to that need when they encourage us to believe that we will be noticed by others or stand out in the crowd if we purchase their product. Commercials promoting luxury cars usually invite you to picture yourself in the driver's seat with a beautiful companion beside you while you receive looks of envy from those you pass on the road.

Self-Actualization Needs At the top of Maslow's hierarchy is the need for **self-actualization**. This is the need to fully realize one's highest potential. For many years, the U.S. Army used the slogan "Be all that you can be" to tap into the need for self-actualization. Calls to be the best and the brightest are appeals to self-actualization. According to Maslow's assumption that our needs are organized into a hierarchy, needs at the other four levels must be satisfied before we can be motivated to satisfy the highest-level need.

self-actualization need
The need to achieve one's highest potential

Use Positive Motivation

A Depression-era politician claimed that a vote for him would result in a return to prosperity: "A chicken in every pot" was his positive motivational appeal. Positive motivational appeals are statements suggesting that good things will happen if the speaker's advice is heeded. A key to using positive motivational appeals effectively is to know what your listeners value. Knowing what audience members view as desirable, good, and virtuous can help you select the benefits of your persuasive proposal that best appeal to them.

Emphasize Positive Values What do most people value? A comfortable, prosperous life; stimulating, exciting activity; a sense of accomplishment; world, community, and personal peace; and happiness are some of the many things people value. How can you use those values in a persuasive speech? When identifying reasons for your audience to think, feel, or behave as you want them to, review those common values to determine what benefits would accrue to your listeners. If, for example, you want your listeners to enroll in a sign-language course, what would the benefits be to the audience? You could stress the sense of accomplishment, contribution to society, or increased opportunities for friendship that would develop if they learned this skill. A speech advocating that recording companies print the lyrics of all songs on the label of the recording could appeal to family values.

Emphasize Benefits, Not Just Features A **benefit** is a good result or something that creates a positive feeling for the listener. A **feature** is simply a characteristic of whatever it is that you're talking about. A benefit creates a positive emotional sizzle that appeals to the heart. A feature elicits a rational, cognitive reaction—it appeals to the head. Heart usually trumps head when persuading others.

Most salespeople know that it is not enough just to identify, in general terms, the features of their product. They must translate those features into an obvious benefit that enhances the customer's quality of life. It is not enough for the real-estate salesperson to say, "This floor is the new no-wax vinyl." It is more effective to add, "And this means that you will never have to get down on your hands and knees to scrub another floor." When using positive motivational appeals, be sure your listeners know how the benefits of your proposal can improve their quality of life or the lives of their loved ones.

Use Negative Motivation

"If you don't stop that, I'm going to tell Mom!" Whether he or she realizes it or not, the sibling who threatens to tell Mom is using a persuasive technique called *fear appeal*. One of the oldest methods of trying to change someone's attitude or behavior, the use of a threat is also one of the most effective. In essence, the appeal to fear takes the form of an "if–then" statement: If you don't do *X*, then awful things will happen to you. A persuader builds an argument on the assertion that a need will not be met unless the desired behavior or attitude change occurs. The principal reason that appeals to fear continue to be made in persuasive messages is that they work. Various research studies support the following principles for using fear appeals.[9]

- **A strong threat to a loved one tends to be more successful than a fear appeal directed at the audience members themselves.** A speaker using this principle might say, "Unless you see that your children wear safety belts, they could easily be injured or killed in an auto accident."

- **The more competent, trustworthy, or respected the speaker, the greater the likelihood that an appeal to fear will be successful.** A speaker with less credibility will be more successful with moderate threats. The U.S. Surgeon General will be more successful in convincing people to get a flu shot than you will.

benefit
A good result or something that creates a positive emotional response in the listener

feature
A characteristic of something you are describing

- **Fear appeals are more successful if you can convince your listeners that the threat is real and will probably occur unless they take the action you are advocating.** For example, you could dramatically announce, "Last year, thousands of smokers developed lung cancer and died. Unless you stop smoking, there is a high probability that you could develop lung cancer, too."

- **In general, increasing the intensity of a fear appeal increases the chances that the fear appeal will be effective.** This is especially true if the listener can take action (the action the persuader is suggesting) to reduce the threat.[10] In the past, some researchers and public-speaking textbooks reported that when a speaker creates an excessive amount of fear and anxiety in listeners, the listeners may find the appeal so strong and annoying that they stop listening. More comprehensive research, however, has concluded that there is a direct link between the intensity or strength of the fear appeal and the likelihood that audience members will be persuaded. Fear appeals work. Strong fear appeals seem to work even better than mild ones, assuming there is evidence to back up the threat made by a credible speaker. The speaker who uses fear appeals has an ethical responsibility to be truthful and not exaggerate when trying to arouse listeners' fear.

- **Fear appeals are more successful when you can convince your listeners that they have the power to make a change that will reduce the fear-causing threat.** As a speaker, your goal is not only to arouse their fear, but also to empower them to act. When providing a solution to the fear-inducing problem, make sure you tell your listeners what they can do to reduce the threat.[11] If, for example, you tell your listeners that unless they lose weight, they will die prematurely, they may want to shed pounds but think it's just too hard to do. You'll be a more effective persuader if you couple your fear-arousing message (lose weight or die early) with a strategy to make weight loss achievable (here's a diet plan that you can follow; it is simple and it works). The audience-centered principle again applies. You may think the solution is evident, but will your listeners think the same thing? View the solution from your listeners' point of view.

Powerful fear appeals that offer listeners a way to reduce the threat are likely to be effective. However, fear appeals must be ethical and truthful. This advertisement raised controversy and lost credibility when media reports revealed that the photo had been altered to make the model's leg appear amputated. In fact, the man in the photo has two healthy legs.[12]

Photo: Polaris/Newscom

The effectiveness of the fear appeal is based on the theories of cognitive dissonance and Maslow's hierarchy of needs. The fear aroused creates dissonance, which can be reduced by following the recommendation of the persuader. Appeals to fear are also based on targeting an unmet need. Fear appeals depend on a convincing insistence that a need will go unmet unless a particular action or attitude change occurs.

Cognitive dissonance, needs, and appeals to the emotions, both positive and negative, can all persuade listeners to change their attitudes, beliefs, values, and behavior. Realize, however, that persuasion is not as simple as these approaches may lead you to believe. There is no precise formula for motivating and convincing an audience; attitude change occurs differently in each individual. Persuasion is an art that draws on science. Cultivating a sensitivity to listeners' emotions and needs and ethically using public-speaking strategies you have learned will help make your persuasive messages effective.

CONSIDER THE AUDIENCE

RECAP

USING FEAR APPEALS EFFECTIVELY

Fear appeals are more effective when
- the fear appeal is directed toward loved ones
- you have high credibility
- the threat is perceived as real and may actually happen
- the fear appeal is strongly supported by evidence
- the fear appeal empowers listeners to act

14.4 Prepare and present an audience-centered persuasive speech.

How to Develop Your Audience-Centered Persuasive Speech

Although you now understand what persuasion is and how it works, you may still be concerned about how to go about preparing your persuasive speech. The process of developing a persuasive speech follows the same audience-centered path you would take to develop any speech, as illustrated by our now-familiar model of the speechmaking process in Figure 14.3. You consider your audience at every step when attempting to persuade listeners.

Consider the Audience

Although being audience-centered is important in every speaking situation, it is vital when your objective is to persuade. It would be a challenge to persuade someone without knowing something about his or her interests, attitudes, beliefs, values, and behaviors.

Remember that while you're speaking, audience members have a variety of thoughts running through their heads. Your job as a persuader is to develop a message that anticipates, as best you can, what your audience may be thinking and feeling when they listen to you. You may want to review the elements of audience analysis and adaptation that we presented in Chapter 5 to help you think more concretely about who your listeners are and why they should listen to you. Audience analysis can also help you anticipate and plan to overcome objections your audience may have to your persuasive message.

Consider Audience Diversity Researchers have discovered no universal, cross-cultural approach to persuasion that is effective in every culture. Persuasion works differently for different cultural groups. North Americans, for example, tend to place considerable importance on direct observations and verifiable facts. Our court system places great stock in eyewitness testimony. People in some Chinese cultures, however, consider such evidence unreliable because they believe that what people observe is always influenced by personal motives. In some African cultures, personal testimony is also often suspect; it is reasoned that if you speak up to defend someone, you must have an ulterior motive and, therefore, your observation is discounted.[13] Although your audience may not include listeners from Africa or China, given the growing diversity of Americans, it is increasingly likely that it may. Or you may have listeners from other cultures with still different perspectives. Our point: Don't design a persuasive message using strategies that would be effective only for those with your cultural background. An effective audience-centered communicator is especially sensitive to cultural differences between himself or herself and the audience, while at the same time being cautious not to make stereotypical assumptions about an audience based only on cultural factors.

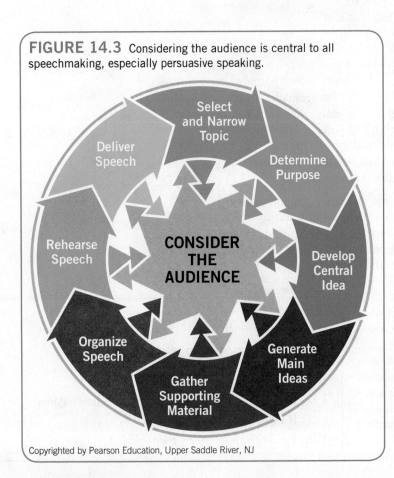

FIGURE 14.3 Considering the audience is central to all speechmaking, especially persuasive speaking.

CONSIDER THE AUDIENCE

Select and Narrow Topic

Determine Purpose

Develop Central Idea

Generate Main Ideas

Gather Supporting Material

Organize Speech

Rehearse Speech

Deliver Speech

Remember Your Ethical Responsibilities as a Persuader As you think about your audience and how to adapt your message to them, we remind you of your ethical responsibilities when persuading others. Fabricating evidence or trying to frighten your listeners with bogus information is unethical. Creating dissonance in the minds of your listeners based on information that you know to be untrue is also unethical. You also have an ethical obligation to tell readers the source of your information. Adapting to your listeners does not mean that you tell people only what they want to hear. It means developing an ethical message to which your audience will listen thoughtfully.

Select and Narrow Your Persuasive Topic

Deciding on a persuasive speech topic sometimes stumps beginning speakers. But rather than pick the first idea that pops into your mind, select a topic that is important to you. What are you passionate about? What issues stir your heart and mind? You'll present a better speech if you've selected a topic you can speak about with sincere conviction. In addition to your interests, always reflect on your audience's passions and convictions. The ideal topic speaks to a need, concern, or issue of the audience as well as to your own interests and zeal. The Internet, Facebook, and You-Tube can help you identify topics that your audience may feel passionately about.

Controversial issues make excellent sources for persuasive topics. A controversial issue is a question about which people disagree: Should the university increase tuition so that faculty members can have a salary increase? Should university students be allowed to take concealed handguns to campus? Should the government gather vast amounts of phone and Internet data in seeking to combat terrorism? In choosing a controversial topic, you need to be audience-centered to know the local, state, national, or international issues that interest your listeners. In addition, the best persuasive speech topics focus on important rather than frivolous issues.

Pay attention to the media and the Internet to stay current on the important issues of the day. Read an online newspaper or magazine, follow news sources on Twitter, or subscribe to a newspaper to keep in touch with issues and topics of interest. Another interesting source of controversial issues is talk radio programs. Both national and local radio call-in programs may give you ideas that are appropriate for a persuasive speech. Even when you already have a clear idea of your speech topic, keeping up with the media and the Internet can give you additional ideas to help narrow your topic or find interesting and appropriate supporting material.

Determine Your Persuasive Purpose

When you want to persuade others, you don't always have to strive for dramatic changes in their attitudes, beliefs, values, and behavior. People rarely make major life changes after hearing just one persuasive message. Your speaking goal may be only to move listeners a bit closer to your ultimate persuasive objective.

Social judgment theory suggests that when listeners are confronted with a persuasive message, their responses fall into one of three categories: (1) a latitude of acceptance, in which they generally agree with the speaker; (2) a latitude of rejection, in which they disagree with the speaker; or (3) a latitude of noncommitment, in which they are not yet committed either to agree or to disagree—they are not sure how to respond.[14]

It is important to know which latitude your listeners are in before you begin so that you can choose a realistic persuasive goal. If most of your listeners are in the latitude of rejection, it will be difficult to move them to the latitude of acceptance in a single 10-minute speech. As shown in Figure 14.4 on page 298, perhaps the best you can do is make them less certain about rejecting your idea by moving them to the latitude of noncommitment. Sometimes, just getting audience members to listen and not reject a new idea may be all you can hope to accomplish in one speech.

social judgment theory
A theory that categorizes listener responses to a persuasive message according to the latitude of acceptance, the latitude of rejection, or the latitude of noncommitment

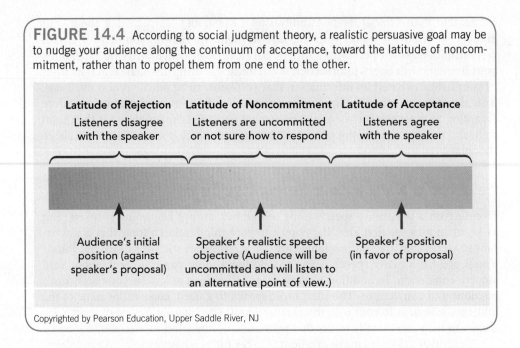

FIGURE 14.4 According to social judgment theory, a realistic persuasive goal may be to nudge your audience along the continuum of acceptance, toward the latitude of noncommitment, rather than to propel them from one end to the other.

Latitude of Rejection	Latitude of Noncommitment	Latitude of Acceptance
Listeners disagree with the speaker	Listeners are uncommitted or not sure how to respond	Listeners agree with the speaker
Audience's initial position (against speaker's proposal)	Speaker's realistic speech objective (Audience will be uncommitted and will listen to an alternative point of view.)	Speaker's position (in favor of proposal)

Copyrighted by Pearson Education, Upper Saddle River, NJ

Develop Your Central Idea and Main Ideas

Watch at **MyCommunicationLab**
Video: "Starbucks"

The overall structure of your speech flows from your central idea and the main ideas that support your central idea. Your central idea, as you recall, is a one-sentence summary of your speech. When persuading others, most speakers find it useful to state their central idea in the form of a proposition. A **proposition** is a statement with which you want your audience to agree. In the following list, note how each proposition is actually the central idea of the speech:

All students should be required to take a foreign language.

Organic gardening is better for the environment than gardening with chemicals.

The United States should not provide economic aid to other countries.

The three categories of propositions are propositions of fact, propositions of value, and propositions of policy. These three types of propositions are summarized in Table 14.2. Determining which category your persuasive proposition fits into not only can help you clarify your central idea, but can also give you an idea of how to select specific persuasive strategies that will help you achieve your specific purpose. Let's examine each type of proposition in more detail.

Proposition of Fact   A **proposition of fact** focuses on whether something is true or false or on whether it did or did not happen. Some propositions of fact are undebatable: Barack Obama received more popular votes than did Mitt Romney in the 2012 presidential election. The Baltimore Ravens won the 2013 Super Bowl. Texas is bigger than Poland. Each of these statements is a proposition of fact that can be verified simply by consulting an appropriate source. For that reason, they do not make good topics for persuasive speeches.

Other propositions of fact will take time and skill—perhaps an entire persuasive speech—to prove. Here are examples of debatable propositions of fact that would make good topics:

When women joined the military, the quality of the military improved.

Adults who were abused as children by their parents are more likely to abuse their own children.

proposition
A statement that summarizes the ideas with which a speaker wants an audience to agree

proposition of fact
A proposition that focuses on whether something is true or false or whether it did or did not happen

TABLE 14.2   PERSUASIVE PROPOSITIONS: DEVELOPING YOUR CENTRAL IDEA

TYPE	DEFINITION	EXAMPLES
Proposition of fact	A statement that focuses on whether something is true or false. Debatable propositions of fact can be good topics for persuasive speeches.	Undebatable: The state legislature has raised tuition 10 percent during the last three years. Debatable: There are more terrorist attacks in the world today than at any previous time in human history.
Proposition of value	A statement that either asserts that something is better than something else or presumes what is right and wrong or good and bad.	The electoral college is a better way to elect presidents than a direct popular vote would be. It is better to keep your financial records on a personal computer than to make calculations by hand.
Proposition of policy	A statement that advocates a change in policy or procedures.	Our community should adopt a curfew for all citizens under eighteen. All handguns should be abolished.

Copyrighted by Pearson Education, Upper Saddle River, NJ

U.S. foreign policy has decreased the probability that the United States will experience more terrorist attacks.

Global climate change is not occurring in our atmosphere.

To prove each of these propositions, a speaker would need to offer specific supporting evidence. To persuade listeners to agree with a proposition of fact, the speaker must focus on changing or reinforcing their beliefs. Most persuasive speeches that focus on propositions of fact begin by identifying one or more reasons why the proposition is true.

The following persuasive speech outline on the topic of low-carb diets is based on a proposition of fact:

TOPIC:	Low-carbohydrate diets
GENERAL PURPOSE:	To persuade
PROPOSITION:	Low-carbohydrate diets are safe and effective.
SPECIFIC PURPOSE:	At the end of my speech, audience members will agree that low-carb diets are safe and effective.
MAIN IDEAS:	I. Carbohydrates are a significant part of our diets.

       A. Many people eat a significant amount of fast food that is laden with carbohydrates.

       B. Lunches provided by the cafeterias in elementary schools include significant amounts of carbohydrates.

       C. Many people eat a significant amount of highly processed, carb-rich foods.

    II. Carbohydrates are making people fat and unhealthy.

       A. A diet rich in carbohydrates leads to obesity.

       B. A diet rich in carbohydrates leads to Type II diabetes.

III. Low-carb diets are a safe and effective way to lose weight and maintain your health.

    A. The safety of such low-carb diets as the South Beach diet or the Paleo Diet is documented by research.

    B. The effectiveness of such low-carb diets is documented by research.

Proposition of Value A **proposition of value** is a statement that calls for the listener to judge the worth or importance of something. Values, as you recall, are enduring concepts of good or bad, right or wrong. Value propositions are statements that something is either good or bad or that one thing or course of action is better than another. Consider these examples:

> It is wrong to turn away immigrants who want to come to the United States.
>
> Communication is a better major than history.
>
> A private-school education is more valuable than a public-school education.
>
> It is better for teachers to carry concealed weapons than to be defenseless against violent school intruders.

Each of these propositions either directly states or implies that something is better than something else. Value propositions often directly compare two things and suggest that one option is better than another.

Manny designed his speech to convince an audience that reggae music is better than rock music.

TOPIC:	Reggae music
GENERAL PURPOSE:	To persuade
PROPOSITION:	Reggae music is better than rock music for three reasons.
SPECIFIC PURPOSE:	After listening to my speech, the audience should listen to reggae music more often than they listen to rock music.
MAIN IDEAS:	I. Reggae music communicates a message of equality for all people.
	II. Reggae music and its rhythms evoke a positive, uplifting mood.
	III. Reggae music draws on a variety of cultural and ethnic traditions.

Proposition of Policy The third type of proposition, a **proposition of policy**, advocates a specific action—changing a policy, procedure, or behavior. Note how all the following propositions of policy include the word *should*; this is a tip-off that the speaker is advocating a change in policy or procedure.

> The Gifted and Talented Program in our school district should have a full-time coordinator.
>
> Our community should set aside one day each month as "Community Cleanup Day."
>
> Wealthy senior citizens should pay for more of their medical costs than poor senior citizens.

In a speech based on a proposition of policy, Paul aimed to convince his audience that academic tenure for college professors should be abolished. He organized his

proposition of value
A proposition that calls for the listener to judge the worth or importance of something

proposition of policy
A proposition that advocates a change in a policy, procedure, or behavior

speech topically, identifying reasons academic tenure is no longer a sound policy for most colleges and universities. To support his proposition of policy, he used several propositions of fact. Note, too, that Paul's specific purpose involved specific action on the part of his audience.

TOPIC:	Academic tenure
GENERAL PURPOSE:	To persuade
PROPOSITION:	Our college, along with other colleges and universities, should abolish academic tenure.
SPECIFIC PURPOSE:	After listening to my speech, audience members should sign a petition calling for the abolition of academic tenure.
MAIN IDEAS:	I. Academic tenure is outdated.
	II. Academic tenure is abused.
	III. Academic tenure contributes to ineffective education.

Here's another outline for a persuasive speech based on a proposition of policy. Again, note how the main ideas are propositions of fact used to support the proposition of policy.

TOPIC:	Computer education
GENERAL PURPOSE:	To persuade
PROPOSITION:	Every person in our society should know how to use a personal computer.
SPECIFIC PURPOSE:	After listening to my speech, all audience members who have not had a computer course should sign up for one.
MAIN IDEAS:	I. Most people who own a personal computer do not know how to use most of its features.
	II. Computer skills will help you with your academic studies.
	III. Computer skills will help you get a good job, regardless of your major or profession.

Gather Supporting Material

When gathering supporting material for your persuasive message, you look for the available means of persuasion to support the main ideas that you have developed to achieve your specific purpose. Recall from earlier in this chapter that Aristotle proposed three primary ways, or available means, of persuading listeners: (1) being a credible and ethical speaker, which includes using credible and ethical supporting material; (2) using effective logic and reasoning to support your main ideas; and (3) using appropriate emotional support. Because the supporting material you develop and use is vital to the effectiveness of your persuasive goal, we devote a major portion of the next chapter to these three means of persuasion.

 Read at **MyCommunicationLab**
Learning From Great Speakers:
Elizabeth Cady Stanton

Organize Your Persuasive Speech

After identifying and gathering ethical, logical, and appropriate emotional support for your message, you'll make final decisions about how to organize your message. As with any speech, you'll have an introduction that should get the audience's attention, give the audience a reason to listen to your message, introduce the subject,

CONFIDENTLY CONNECTING WITH YOUR AUDIENCE

Breathe to Relax

When you feel your body start to tense, take a deep, relaxing breath to help quiet your fears. It's normal to experience a quickened heartbeat and a change in your breathing patterns as physiological responses to increased anxiety. To signal to your brain that *you* are in charge, consciously take several slow breaths. As you breathe, make your breaths unobtrusive; no one need know that you are using a deep-breathing technique to manage your fear. Whether you are at your seat in your classroom getting ready to be the next speaker or sitting on a platform in front of an audience, a few slow, calming breaths will help you relax and calm your spirit.

RECAP

AUDIENCE-CENTERED PERSUASIVE SPEAKING

- Consider audience attitudes, beliefs, values, and behaviors.
- Consider audience diversity.
- Controversial issues make good persuasive topics.
- Use social judgment theory to determine purpose.
- State your central idea as a proposition of fact, value, or policy.
- Find supporting materials that reinforce your credibility, logic, and emotional appeals.
- Use a clear organizational pattern.
- Get feedback as you rehearse.
- Deliver your speech with appropriate emotion.

establish your credibility, and preview your main ideas. The body of your speech should have clearly identified major points with appropriate transitions, signposts, and internal summaries to make sure your key ideas are understandable to your listeners. And finally, you'll have a conclusion that summarizes the essence of your message and provides closure to your speech. When your goal is to persuade, it is especially important to consider your audience and your specific purpose as you consider how you will begin your message, organize your ideas, and conclude your talk. We'll discuss specific approaches and tips for organizing a persuasive speech in the next chapter.

Rehearse and Deliver Your Speech

To bring your ideas to life, the last two elements of the speechmaking process are to rehearse your message out loud and then, finally, to present your talk to your audience. When your goal is to persuade, you may want to make a special effort to rehearse your speech in front of another person or to run some of your ideas past others to check the overall clarity and structure of your message. It is through your delivery that you communicate your passion and enthusiasm for your ideas, so it would be worthwhile to review the suggestions and prescriptions we offered in Chapter 11 for how to ensure that your speech is well delivered.

Although you may have a well-crafted message, without ample emotional energy, your speech may not achieve its purpose. Your eye contact, gestures, movement, posture, facial expression, vocal delivery, and personal appearance are the means by which you'll reinforce your credibility and logic, as well as make an authentic emotional connection with your listeners.

Recall, too, that the elaboration likelihood model predicts that your delivery can, in itself, be persuasive to some of your listeners. No matter how well-reasoned your message, at least some of your listeners are likely to fail to elaborate, or critically consider it. These listeners may instead be persuaded by an indirect route, one based on the emotional connection you make with them in the course of delivering your speech.

STUDY GUIDE
REVIEW, APPLY, AND ASSESS

THE GOALS OF PERSUASION

14.1 Describe the goals of persuasive messages.

Persuasion is the process of changing or reinforcing attitudes, beliefs, values, or behavior. Attitudes are learned predispositions to respond favorably or unfavorably toward something. A belief is a person's understanding of what is true and what is false. A value is a conception of right and wrong.

Key Terms

Thinking Ethically

Zeta plans to give a persuasive speech to convince her classmates that term limits should be imposed for senators and members of Congress—even though she is personally against term limits. Is it ethical to develop a persuasive message that supports an attitude or belief with which you personally disagree?

Assessing Your Audience-Centered Speaking Skill

As you listen to persuasive speeches in your speech class, determine whether the speaker is attempting to change or reinforce an attitude, belief, value, or behavior or more than one of these outcomes.

HOW PERSUASION WORKS

14.2 Explain classic and contemporary theories of how persuasion occurs.

Various theories explain how persuasion works. You can incorporate this theoretical knowledge into your speech preparation in order to deliver a persuasive message. Aristotle suggested using ethos, logos, and pathos as methods to persuade others. The elaboration likelihood model suggests that listeners either follow a direct route to persuasion, in which they elaborate (think about) the issues and evidence, or they can be persuaded via an indirect route when they don't elaborate.

Key Terms

Thinking Critically

If you were attempting to sell a new computer system to the administration of your school, what persuasive principles would you draw on to develop your message?

Assessing Your Audience-Centered Speaking Skill

As you prepare your next persuasive speech, describe how both Aristotle's classic theory of persuasion and the more contemporary ELM theory of persuasion explain why your listeners would be persuaded by your message.

HOW TO MOTIVATE LISTENERS

14.3 Describe four ways to motivate listeners to respond to a persuasive message.

One way to motivate listeners is to cause cognitive dissonance, which evokes the human tendency to strive for balance or consistency in our thoughts. When a persuasive message invites us to change our attitudes, beliefs, values, or behavior, we respond by trying to maintain intellectual balance, or cognitive consistency.

A second approach to motivation is to satisfy listeners' needs. Abraham Maslow identified a five-level hierarchy of needs, including physiological, safety, social, self-esteem, and self-actualization needs.

Third, positive motivational appeals can help you develop a persuasive message by encouraging listeners to respond favorably to your message.

A fourth approach to persuasion is the use of negative motivational appeals. Fear can motivate us to respond favorably to a persuasive suggestion. To avoid pain or discomfort, we may follow the recommendation of a persuasive speaker.

Key Terms

Thinking Ethically

Tom plans to begin his speech on driver safety using a graphic photo of traffic-accident victims who were maimed or killed because they did not use safety belts. Would such a graphic use of fear appeals be ethical?

Thinking Critically

Your local chamber of commerce has asked for your advice in developing a speakers' bureau that would address public-safety issues in your community. What suggestions would you offer to the speakers about how to motivate citizens to behave in ways that would protect them from gang violence, traffic, and severe weather?

Assessing Your Audience-Centered Speaking Skill

Listen to a speech by a member of Congress. Access the *Congressional Record*, which tells what Congress does every day, at www.gpoaccess.gov/crecord/index.html. As you listen or read speeches by U.S. senators and representatives, identify the specific methods they use to attempt to motivate listeners to support a particular idea or conclusion.

HOW TO DEVELOP YOUR AUDIENCE-CENTERED PERSUASIVE SPEECH

14.4   Prepare and present an audience-centered persuasive speech.

Speakers can prepare a persuasive speech by applying broad principles of persuasion to the same processes they use to prepare and present any other kind of speech. A key first concern is to consider the audience at each step of the process. The next concern is to choose an appropriate topic. When crafting your central idea for your persuasive speech, develop a proposition of fact, value, or policy that is reasonable based on your audience's background and expectations. Principles of persuasion can also guide you as you gather supporting materials, organize, rehearse, and deliver your speech.

Key Terms

Assessing Your Audience-Centered Speaking Skill

An important aspect of being audience-centered is to consider audience member diversity. Based on the discussion in your text, identify ways you have ethically attempted to adapt to your audience by keeping the diversity of your audience in mind.

Explore at MyCommunicationLab
Speaker's Workshop:
Developing a Persuasive Speech

15 USING PERSUASIVE STRATEGIES

Felix Joseph Barrias (1822–1907), *Camille Desmoulins (1760–1794) Harangueing the Patriots in the Gardens of the Palais Royal*. Musée Municipal, Chalons-sur-Marne, France. Photo: Scala/White Images/Art Resource, N.Y.

OBJECTIVES

After studying this chapter you should be able to do the following:

15.1
Identify and use strategies to improve your initial, derived, and terminal credibility.

15.2
Use principles of effective logic and evidence to develop a persuasive message.

15.3
Employ effective techniques of using emotional appeal in a persuasive speech.

15.4
Adapt your persuasive message to receptive, neutral, and unreceptive audiences.

15.5
Identify and use strategies for effectively organizing a persuasive speech.

((•)) Listen to Chapter 15 at **MyCommunicationLab**

Speech is power: speech is to persuade, to convert, to compel.

—Ralph Waldo Emerson

"P ersuasion," said rhetoric scholar Donald C. Bryant, "is the process of adjusting ideas to people and people to ideas."[1] To be an audience-centered persuasive speaker is to use ethical and effective strategies to adjust your message so that listeners will thoughtfully respond to your presentation. But precisely what are the strategies that can enhance your credibility, help you develop logical arguments, and use emotional appeals to speak to the hearts of your listeners? In the last chapter, we noted that Aristotle defined rhetoric as the process of discovering the available means of persuasion. In this chapter, we provide more detailed strategies to help you prepare your persuasive speech. Specifically, we will suggest how to gain credibility, develop well-reasoned arguments, and move your audience with emotion. We will also discuss how to adapt your specific message to your audience, and we will end with suggestions for organizing your persuasive message.

15.1 Identify and use strategies to improve your initial, derived, and terminal credibility.

 **Watch** at **MyCommunicationLab** **Video:** "Experience Diversity"

Enhancing Your Credibility

Recall that in Chapter 9, we discussed the importance of *credibility*. Credibility is the audience's perception of a speaker's competence, trustworthiness, and dynamism. As a public speaker, especially one who wishes to persuade an audience, you hope that your listeners will have a favorable attitude toward you. There is a direct relationship between credibility and speech effectiveness: The more credible you are perceived as being by your listeners, the more effective you will be as a persuasive communicator.

As we noted in Chapter 14, Aristotle used the term *ethos* to refer to a speaker's credibility. He thought that to be credible, a public speaker should be ethical, possess good character, have common sense, and be concerned for the well-being of the audience. Quintilian, a Roman teacher of public speaking, also believed that an effective public speaker should be a person of good character. Quintilian's advice was that a speaker should be "a good person speaking well." The importance to a speaker of a positive public image has been recognized for centuries. But don't get the idea that credibility is something that a speaker inherently possesses or lacks. Credibility is based on the listeners' mind-set regarding the speaker. Your listeners, not you, determine whether you have credibility or lack it.

Elements of Your Credibility

Credibility is not just a single factor or single view of you on the part of your audience. Aristotle's speculations as to the factors that influence a speaker's credibility have been generally supported by modern experimental studies. To be credible, you should be perceived as competent, trustworthy, and dynamic.

Competence To be a **competent** speaker is to be considered informed, skilled, or knowledgeable about one's subject.

When you give a speech, you will be more persuasive if you convince your listeners that you are knowledgeable about your topic. If, for example, you say it would be a good idea for everyone to have a medical checkup each year, your listeners might mentally ask, "Why? What are your qualifications to make such a proposal?" But if you support your conclusion with medical statistics showing how having a physical exam each year leads to a dramatically prolonged life, you enhance the credibility of your suggestion. Thus, one way to enhance your competence is to cite credible evidence to support your point.

competent
Being informed, skilled, or knowledgeable about one's subject

Your dynamism, or energy level, is one of the factors that contributes to your credibility as a persuasive speaker.
Photo: Martin Barraud/Stone/Getty Images

Trustworthiness A second major factor that influences your audience's response to you is **trustworthiness**. You trust people whom you believe to be honest; you can also predict what they will do or say in the future.

Earning an audience's trust is not something that you can do simply by saying "Trust me." You earn trust by demonstrating that you have had experience dealing with the issues you talk about. Your listeners would be more likely to trust your advice about how to tour Europe on $50 a day if you had been there than they would if you took your information from a travel guide. Your trustworthiness may be suspect if you advocate something that will result in a direct benefit to you. That's why salespersons and politicians are often stereotyped as being untrustworthy; if you do what they say, they will clearly benefit from a sales commission if you buy a product, or gain power and position if you give your vote.

Dynamism A third factor in credibility is the speaker's **dynamism**, or energy. Dynamism is often projected through delivery. **Charisma** is a form of dynamism. A charismatic person possesses charm, talent, magnetism, and other qualities that make the person attractive and energetic. Many people considered presidents Franklin Roosevelt and Ronald Reagan charismatic speakers.

Phases of Your Credibility

Your credibility in the minds of your listeners evolves over time. Speakers typically establish their credibility in three phases: (1) initial credibility, (2) derived credibility, and (3) terminal credibility.

Initial Credibility The first phase is called **initial credibility**. This is the impression of your credibility that your listeners have even before you speak. Giving careful thought to your appearance and establishing eye contact before you begin your talk will enhance both your confidence and your credibility. It is also wise to prepare a brief description of your credentials and accomplishments so that the person who introduces you can use it in his or her introductory remarks. Even if you are not asked for a statement beforehand, be prepared with one.

Derived Credibility The second phase in the evolution of your credibility is called **derived credibility**. This is the perception the audience develops about you after they

 Watch at **MyCommunicationLab**
Video: "School of the Americas"

trustworthiness
An aspect of a speaker's credibility that reflects whether the speaker is perceived as being believable and honest

dynamism
An aspect of a speaker's credibility that reflects whether the speaker is perceived as energetic

charisma
Characteristic of a talented, charming, attractive speaker

initial credibility
The impression of a speaker's credibility that listeners have before the speaker starts a speech

derived credibility
The perception of a speaker's credibility that is formed during a speech

meet you and as they see you present yourself and your message. Most of this book presents principles and skills that help establish your derived credibility as a speaker. Several specific research-supported skills for enhancing your credibility as you speak include establishing common ground with your audience, supporting your key arguments with evidence, and presenting a well-organized and well-delivered message.

- *Establish common ground with your audience.* You establish common ground by indicating in your opening remarks that you share the values and concerns of your audience. To begin to persuade an audience that she understands why budget cuts upset parents, a politician might speak of her own children.

- *Support your key arguments with evidence.* Having evidence to support your persuasive conclusions strengthens your credibility.[2]

- *Present a well-organized message.* A well-organized message also enhances your credibility as a competent and rational advocate.[3] Regardless of the organizational pattern you use, it is crucial to ensure that your message is logically structured and uses appropriate internal summaries, signposts, and enumeration of key ideas.

- *Deliver your message well.* For most North Americans, regular eye contact, varied vocal inflection, and appropriate attire have positive influences on your ability to persuade listeners to respond to your message.[4] Why does delivery affect how persuasive you are? Researchers suggest that when your listeners expect you to be a good speaker and you aren't, they are less likely to do what you ask them to do.[5] So don't violate their expectations by presenting a poorly delivered speech.

Effective delivery also helps gain and maintain listener attention and affects whether listeners will like you.[6] If you can arouse listeners' attention, and if they like you, you'll be more persuasive than if you don't gain their attention and they don't like you. Do speakers who use humor enhance their credibility? There is some evidence that although using humor may contribute to making listeners like you, humor does not have a major impact on ultimately persuading listeners to support your message.[7]

Terminal Credibility The last phase of credibility, called **terminal credibility**, or final credibility, is the perception of your credibility your listeners have when you finish your speech. The lasting impression you make on your audience is influenced by how you were first perceived (initial credibility) and what you did as you presented your message (derived credibility). It is also influenced by your behavior as, and immediately after, you conclude your speech. For example, maintain eye contact with your audience as you deliver your speech conclusion. Also, don't start leaving the lectern or speaking area until you have finished your closing sentence. Even if there is no planned question-and-answer period following your speech, be ready to respond to questions from interested listeners.

terminal credibility
The final impression listeners have of a speaker's credibility after a speech concludes

RECAP

HOW TO ENHANCE YOUR CREDIBILITY

Initial Credibility:
   Carefully consider your appearance.
   Establish eye contact before speaking.
   Provide a summary of your credentials related to your topic.

Derived Credibility:
   Establish common ground.
   Support arguments with evidence.
   Organize your speech well.
   Deliver your speech well.

Terminal Credibility:
   End with eye contact.
   Be prepared for questions.

15.2 Use principles of effective logic and evidence to develop a persuasive message.

Using Logic and Evidence to Persuade

"We need to cut taxes to improve the economy," claimed the politician on a Sunday-morning talk show. "The stock market has lost 300 points this month. People aren't buying things. A tax cut will put money in their pockets and give the economy a boost." In an effort to persuade reluctant members of her political party to support a tax cut, this politician was using a logical argument supported with evidence that stock prices were dropping. As we noted in Chapter 4 when we discussed how to be a critical listener, logic is a formal system of rules for making inferences. Because wise audience members will be listening, persuasive speakers need to give careful attention to the way they use logic to reach a conclusion. Aristotle called logic *logos*, which means "the word." Using words as well as statistical information to develop logical arguments can make your persuasive efforts more convincing. It can also clarify your own thinking and help make your points clear to your listeners. Logic is central to all persuasive speeches. In Chapter 4, we introduced a discussion of logic and evidence to help you become a critical listener or consumer of messages. Here we'll amplify that discussion to help you use logical arguments and evidence to persuade others.

Aristotle said that any persuasive speech has two parts: First, you state your case. Second, you prove your case. In essence, he was saying that you must present evidence and then use appropriate reasoning to lead your listeners to the conclusion you advocate. Proof consists of the evidence you offer, plus the conclusion you draw from it. Evidence is made up of the facts, examples, statistics, and expert opinions that you use to support the points you wish to make. Reasoning is the process you follow to draw a conclusion from the evidence. The Sunday-morning talk-show politician reached the conclusion that a tax cut was necessary from the evidence that stock prices had tumbled and people weren't buying things. Let's consider the two key elements of proof in greater detail. Specifically, we will look more closely at types of reasoning and ways of testing the quality of evidence.

Understanding Types of Reasoning

Developing well-reasoned arguments for persuasive messages has been important since antiquity. If your arguments are structured in a rational way, you will have a greater chance of persuading your listeners. There are three major ways to structure an argument to reach a logical conclusion: inductively (including reasoning by analogy and reasoning by sign), deductively, and causally. These three structures are summarized in Table 15.1 below. Let's examine each in detail.

Explore at MyCommunicationLab
Activity: "Build a Speech: Persuasive Speech"

TABLE 15.1 COMPARING TYPES OF REASONING

	INDUCTIVE REASONING	DEDUCTIVE REASONING	CAUSAL REASONING
Reasoning begins with . . .	Specific examples	A general statement	Something known
Reasoning ends with . . .	A general conclusion	A specific conclusion	A speculation about something unknown occurring, based on what is known
Conclusion of reasoning is that something is . . .	Probable or improbable	True or false	Likely or not likely
Goal of reasoning is . . .	To reach a general conclusion or discover something new	To reach a specific conclusion by applying what is known	To link something known with something unknown
Example	When tougher drug laws went into effect in Kansas City and St. Louis, drug traffic was reduced. Each city in the United States should therefore institute tougher drug laws because there will be a decrease in drug use.	Instituting tough drug laws in medium-sized communities results in diminished drug-related crime. San Marcos, Texas, is a medium-sized community. San Marcos should institute tough drug laws in order to reduce drug-related crimes.	Since the 70-mile-per-hour speed limit was reinstated, traffic deaths have increased. The increased highway speed has caused an increase in highway deaths.

Inductive Reasoning Reasoning that arrives at a general conclusion from specific instances or examples is known as **inductive reasoning**. Using this classical approach, you reach a general conclusion based on specific examples, facts, statistics, and opinions. You may not know for certain that the specific instances prove that the conclusion is true, but you decide that, in all *probability*, the specific instances support the general conclusion. According to contemporary logicians, you reason inductively when you claim that an outcome is probably true because of specific evidence.

For example, if you were giving a speech attempting to convince your audience that foreign cars are unreliable, you might use inductive reasoning to make your point. You could announce that you recently bought a foreign car that gave you trouble. Your cousin also bought a foreign car that kept stalling on the freeway. Finally, your English professor told you her foreign car has broken down several times in the past few weeks. Based on these specific examples, you ask your audience to agree with your general conclusion: Foreign cars are unreliable.

Testing the Validity of Inductive Reasoning As a persuasive speaker, your job is to construct a sound argument. That means basing your generalization on evidence. When you listen to a persuasive message, notice how the speaker tries to support his or her conclusion. To judge the validity of a **generalization** arrived at inductively, ask the following questions.

- **Are there enough specific instances to support the conclusion?** Are three examples of problems with foreign cars enough to prove your point that foreign cars are generally unreliable? Of the several million foreign cars manufactured, three cars, especially if they are of different makes, are not a large sample. If those examples were supported by additional statistical evidence that more than 50 percent of foreign-car owners complained of serious engine malfunctions, the evidence would be more convincing.

- **Are the specific instances typical?** Are the three examples you cite representative of all foreign cars manufactured? How do you know? What are the data on the performance of foreign cars? Also, are you, your cousin, and your professor typical of most car owners? The three of you may be careless about routine maintenance of your autos.

- **Are the instances recent?** If the foreign cars you are using as examples of poor reliability are more than three years old, you cannot reasonably conclude that today's foreign cars are unreliable products. Age alone may explain the poor performance of your sample.

The logic in this example of problematic foreign cars, therefore, is not particularly sound. The speaker would need considerably more evidence to prove his or her point.

Reasoning by Analogy Reasoning by analogy is a special type of inductive reasoning. An *analogy* is a comparison. This form of inductive reasoning compares one thing, person, or process with another to predict how something will perform and respond. In previous chapters we've suggested that using an analogy is an effective way to clarify ideas and enhance message interest. When you observe that two things have a number of characteristics in common and that a certain fact about one is likely to be true of the other, you have drawn an analogy, reasoning from one example to reach a conclusion about the other. If you try to convince an audience that because laws against using a cell phone while driving in a school zone have cut down on injuries to children in Florida and Missouri, those laws should therefore should be instituted in Kansas, you are reasoning by analogy. You would also be reasoning by analogy if you claimed that because capital punishment reduced crime in Brazil, it should be used

inductive reasoning
Reasoning that uses specific instances or examples to reach a general, probable conclusion

generalization
An all-encompassing statement

in the United States as well. But as with reasoning by generalization, there are questions that you should ask to check the validity of your conclusions.

- **Do the ways in which the two things are alike outweigh the ways they are different?** Can you compare the crime statistics of Brazil to those of the United States and claim to make a valid comparison? Are the data collected in the same way in both countries? Could other factors besides the cell phone laws in Texas and Louisiana account for the lower automobile accident death rate? Maybe differences in speed limits in school zones in those states can account for the difference.

- **Is the assertion true?** Is it really true that capital punishment has deterred crime in Brazil? You will need to give reasons the comparison you are making is valid and evidence that will prove your conclusion is true.

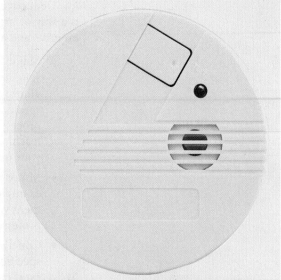

When a smoke alarm goes off, reasoning by sign suggests that something is on fire. What examples of reasoning by sign might you use in a speech?

Photo: sasel77/Fotolia

Reasoning by Sign **Reasoning by sign**, another special type of inductive reasoning, occurs when two things are so closely related that the existence of one thing means that the other thing will happen. For example, white smoke billowing from the chimney of the Sistine Chapel in Rome's Vatican Square is a sign that there is a new pope. A clap of thunder and dark, swirling clouds are signs of rain. One specific sign, or the presence of multiple signs, leads you to a conclusion that something else has happened or will happen.

One student group observed that many students on campus were wearing T-shirts promoting other college and university sports teams rather than the teams on their home campus. They viewed the T-shirts of other teams as a sign of student apathy, deflated school spirit, and disinterest in campus sports. To fix the problem the group wanted to ban students from wearing shirts promoting a team other than the local campus team.

When you use or hear reasoning by sign, consider these questions:

- **Is there a strong, predictive relationship between the sign and the asserted conclusion?** If white smoke always precedes the announcement of a new pope, then there is a strong relationship in which the sign (white smoke) predicts the conclusion (there is a new pope). Does the shirt someone wears (a sign) always predict a lack of school spirit?

- **Is there another explanation for the relationship between the sign and the asserted conclusion?** Simply because students wear shirts promoting another team, does that mean students really don't care about the home team? Perhaps the students just couldn't afford to buy new shirts.

- **Are there multiple signs?** Hearing only thunder may not mean it will rain, but hearing thunder, seeing lightning and dark clouds, and feeling a sudden shift in the wind increase the accuracy of your conclusion that it will rain. If the non-home-team-T-shirt-wearing students also didn't attend the pre-game pep rally or many didn't show up for campus sports events, those would be additional signs of student apathy.

reasoning by sign
Using the existence of one or more events to reach a specific conclusion that another event has occurred or will occur

deductive reasoning
Reasoning that moves from a general statement of principle to a specific, certain conclusion

Deductive Reasoning According to a centuries-old perspective, reasoning from a general statement or principle to reach a specific conclusion is called **deductive reasoning**. This is just the opposite of inductive reasoning. Contemporary logic specialists add that when the conclusion is *certain* rather than probable, you are reasoning deductively. The certainty of your conclusion is based on the validity or truth in the general statement that forms the basis of your argument.

Deductive reasoning can be structured in the form of a syllogism. A **syllogism** is a way of organizing an argument into three elements: a major premise, a minor premise, and a conclusion.

- Major Premise: To reach a conclusion deductively, you start with a general statement that serves as the **major premise**. In a speech attempting to convince your audience that the communication professor teaching your public-speaking class is a top-notch teacher, you might use a deductive reasoning process. Your major premise is "All communication professors have excellent teaching skills." The certainty of your conclusion hinges on the soundness of your major premise.

- Minor Premise: The **minor premise** is a more specific statement about an example that is linked to the major premise. The minor premise in the argument you are advancing is "John Smith, our teacher, is a communication professor."

- Conclusion: The **conclusion** is based on the major premise and the more specific minor premise. The conclusion to our syllogism is "John Smith has excellent teaching skills."

In reasoning deductively, you need to ensure that both the major premise and the minor premise are true and can be supported with evidence. The persuasive power of deductive reasoning derives from the fact that the conclusion cannot be questioned *if* the premises are accepted as true.

Here's another example you might hear in a speech. Ann was trying to convince the city council to refuse a building permit to Mega-Low-Mart, a large chain discount store that wants to move into her town. She believes the new store would threaten her downtown clothing boutique. Here's the deductive structure of the argument she advanced:

Major premise:	Every time a large discount store moves into a small community, the merchants in the downtown area lose business and the town loses tax revenue from downtown merchants.
Minor premise:	Mega-Low-Mart is a large discount store that wants to build a store in our town.
Conclusion:	If Mega-Low-Mart is permitted to open a store in our town, the merchants in the downtown area will lose business and the city will lose tax revenue.

The strength of Ann's argument rests on the validity of her major premise. Her argument is sound if she can prove that the presence of large chain discount stores does, in fact, result in a loss of business and tax revenue for merchants in nearby towns. (Also note Ann's efforts to be audience-centered; addressing the city council, she argues that not only will she lose money, but the city will lose tax revenue as well—something in which city council members are deeply interested.) In constructing arguments for your persuasive messages, assess the soundness of the major premise on which you build your argument. Likewise, when listening to a persuasive pitch from someone using a deductive argument, critically evaluate the accuracy of the major premise.

To test the truth of an argument organized deductively, consider the following questions.

- **Is the major premise (general statement) true?** In our example about communication professors, is it really true that *all* communication professors have excellent teaching skills? What evidence do you have to support this statement? The power of deductive reasoning hinges in part on whether your generalization is true.

- **Is the minor premise (the particular statement) also true?** If your minor premise is false, your syllogism can collapse right there. In our example, it is

syllogism
A three-part argument that consists of a major premise, a minor premise, and a conclusion

major premise
A general statement that is the first element of a syllogism

minor premise
A specific statement about an example that is linked to the major premise; the second element of a syllogism

conclusion
The logical outcome of a deductive argument, which stems from the major premise and the minor premise

easy enough to verify that John Smith is a communication professor. But not all minor premises can be verified as easily. For example, it would be difficult to prove the minor premise in this example:

> Major premise: All gods are immortal.
>
> Minor premise: Zeus is a god.
>
> Conclusion: Therefore, Zeus is immortal.

We can accept the major premise as true because immortality is part of the definition of *god*. But proving that Zeus is a god would be very difficult. In this case, the truth of the conclusion hinges on the truth of the minor premise.

Although we have identified inductive and deductive reasoning as separate types of reasoning, they are related in that the general premise in deductive argument is often reached by noting several examples that support the general premise.[8] Identifying whether you are using inductive or deductive reasoning can help you better analyze and assess your arguments.

Causal Reasoning A third type of reasoning is called **causal reasoning**. When you reason by cause, you relate two or more events in such a way as to conclude that one or more of the events caused the others. For example, you might argue that having unprotected sex causes the spread of sexually transmitted diseases. When reasoning from sign, you suggest that two or more things are related. When reasoning from cause, you suggest that one thing actually caused the other thing to occur.

There are two ways to structure a causal argument. First, you can reason from cause to effect, moving from a known fact to a predicted result. You know, for example, that interest rates have increased in the past week. Therefore, you might argue that *because* the rates are increasing, the Dow Jones Industrial Average will decrease. In this case, you move from something that has occurred (rising interest rates) to something that has not yet occurred (decrease in the Dow). Weather forecasters use the same method of reasoning when they predict the weather. They base a conclusion about tomorrow's weather on what they know about today's meteorological conditions.

A second way to frame a causal argument is to reason backward, from known effect to unknown cause. You know, for example, that a major earthquake has occurred (known effect). To explain this event, you propose that the cause of the earthquake was a shift in a fault line (unknown cause). You cannot be sure of the cause, but you are certain of the effect. A candidate for president of the United States may claim that the cause of current high unemployment (known effect) is mismanagement by the present administration (unknown cause). The candidate then constructs an argument to prove that his assertion is accurate. To prove his case, he needs to have evidence that the present administration mismanaged the economy. The key to developing strong causal arguments is in the use of evidence to link something known with something unknown. An understanding of the appropriate use of evidence can enhance inductive, deductive, and causal reasoning.

Adapting Reasoning for a Culturally Diverse Audience Effective strategies for achieving your persuasive objective will vary depending on the background and cultural expectations of your listeners. If a good portion of your audience has a cultural background different from your own, it's wise not to assume that they will have the same assumptions about what is logical and reasonable that you have.

Most of the logical, rational methods of reasoning discussed in this chapter evolved from classical Greek and Roman traditions of argument. Rhetoricians from the United States typically use a straightforward, factual-inductive method of supporting ideas and reaching conclusions.[9] They identify facts and link them to support a specific proposition or conclusion. For example, in a speech to prove that the government spends more money than it receives, a speaker could cite year-by-year

causal reasoning
Reasoning in which the relationship between two or more events leads you to conclude that one or more of the events caused the others

statistics on income and expenditures to document the point. North Americans also like debates involving a direct clash of ideas and opinions. Our low-context culture encourages people to be more direct and forthright in dealing with issues and disagreement than do high-context cultures.

Not all cultures assume a direct, linear, methodical approach to supporting ideas and proving a point.[10] People from high-context cultures, for example, may expect that participants will establish a personal relationship before debating issues. Some cultures use a deductive pattern of reasoning rather than an inductive pattern. They begin with a general premise and then link it to a specific situation when they attempt to persuade listeners. During several recent trips to Russia, your authors noticed that to argue that communism was ineffective, many Russians started with a general assumption: Communism didn't work. Then they used this assumption to explain specific current problems in areas such as transportation and education.

Middle Eastern cultures usually do not use standard inductive or deductive structures. They are more likely to use narrative methods to persuade an audience. They tell stories that evoke feelings and emotions and use extended analogies, examples, and illustrations, allowing their listeners to draw their own conclusions by inductive association.[11]

Although this text stresses the kind of inductive reasoning that will be persuasive to most North Americans, you may need to use alternative strategies if your audience is from another cultural tradition.

Supporting Your Reasoning with Evidence

Watch at **MyCommunicationLab**
Video: "Protecting Forests with Indigenous Communities"

You cannot persuade by simply stating a conclusion without proving it with evidence. Evidence in persuasive speeches consists of facts, examples, statistics, and expert opinions. In Chapter 7, we discussed using these types of supporting material in speeches. When attempting to persuade listeners, it is essential to make sure that your evidence logically supports the inductive, deductive, or causal reasoning you are using to reach your conclusion.

Facts   When using facts to support your conclusion, make sure each fact is really a fact. A **fact** is something that has been directly observed to be true or can be proved to be true. The shape of the earth, the number of women university presidents, the winner of the 2014 Super Bowl have all been directly observed or counted. Without direct observation or measurement, we can only make an inference. An **inference** is a conclusion based on available evidence or partial information. It's a fact that sales of foreign-made cars are increasing in the United States; it's an inference that foreign-made cars are the highest-quality cars.

Examples   **Examples** are illustrations that are used to dramatize or clarify a fact. For example, one speaker, in an effort to document the increased violence in children's television programs, told her audience, "Last Saturday morning as I watched cartoons with my daughter, I was shocked by the countless times we saw examples of beatings and even the death of the cartoon characters in one half-hour program." The conclusion she wanted her audience to reach: Put an end to senseless violence in children's television programs.

Only valid, true examples can be used to help prove a point. A hypothetical example, one that is fabricated to illustrate a point, should not be used to reach a conclusion. It should be used only to clarify. David encouraged his listeners to join him in an effort to clean up the San Marcos River. He wanted to motivate his audience to help by asking them to "imagine bringing your children to the river ten years from now. You see the river bottom littered with cans and bottles." His example, while effective in helping the audience to visualize what might happen in the future, does not prove that the river ecosystem will deteriorate. It only illustrates what might happen if action isn't taken.

fact
Something that has been directly observed to be true or can be proven to be true by verifiable evidence

inference
A conclusion based on available evidence or partial information

examples
Illustrations used to dramatize or clarify a fact

Opinions *Opinions* can serve as evidence if they are expressed by an expert, someone who can add credibility to your conclusion. The best opinions to use in support of a persuasive argument are those expressed by someone known to be unbiased, fair, and accurate. If the U.S. Surgeon General has expressed an opinion regarding drug testing, his or her opinion would be helpful evidence. Even so, opinions are usually most persuasive when they are combined with other evidence, such as facts or statistics, that supports the expert's position.

Statistics A *statistic* is a number used to summarize several facts or samples. In an award-winning speech, Jeffrey Jamison used statistics effectively to document the serious problem of alkali batteries polluting the environment. He cited evidence from the *New York Times* documenting that "—each year we are adding 150 tons of mercury, 130 tons of lead, and 170 tons of cadmium to the environment."[12] Without these statistics, Jeffrey's claim that alkali batteries are detrimental to the environment would not have been as potent. Again, you may want to review the discussion on the appropriate use of statistics in Chapter 7.

Does the type of evidence you use make a difference in whether your listeners will support your ideas? One research study found that examples and illustrations go a long way in helping to persuade listeners.[13] Additional research documents the clear power of statistical evidence to persuade.[14] And yet another research study concluded that using *both* statistics and specific examples is especially effective in persuading listeners.[15] Poignant examples may touch listeners' hearts, but statistical evidence appeals to their intellect.

Evidence should support your reasoning. If you are using an inductive reasoning strategy (reasoning from specific examples to a general conclusion), you need to make sure you have enough facts, examples, statistics, and credible opinions to support your conclusion. If you reason deductively (from a generalization to a specific conclusion), you need evidence to document the truth of your initial generalization. When developing an argument using causal reasoning, evidence is also vital as you attempt to establish that one or more events caused something to happen.

The cultures of your audience members should influence the types of reasoning, evidence, message structure, and appeals to emotion that you include, as well as the way you deliver your persuasive message.

Photo: Rob/Fotolia

Using Evidence Effectively

We've identified what evidence is and why it's important to use evidence to support your conclusions. But what are the strategies for using evidence effectively? Here are a few suggestions.[16]

Use Credible Evidence   Your listeners are more likely to respond to your arguments when they believe the evidence you use is credible—from a trustworthy, knowledgeable, and unbiased source. Remember, it's the listener, not you, who determines whether evidence is credible.

One type of evidence that is especially powerful is reluctant testimony. **Reluctant testimony** is a statement by someone who has reversed his or her position on a given issue, or is a statement made that is not in the speaker's best interest. For example, at one point the owner of a large construction company, who wanted the contract to build a new dam, was in favor of building the new dam to create a water reservoir. But after further thought, he changed his mind and now is against building the dam. The reluctant testimony of that construction company owner would bolster your argument that the dam is a financial boondoggle. Reluctant testimony is especially effective when presented to a skeptical audience; it demonstrates how another person has changed his or her mind and implicitly suggests that listeners should do the same.[17]

Use New Evidence   By "new" we don't just mean recent, although contemporary evidence to support your point is often perceived to be more credible than out-of-date evidence. But besides seeking up-to-date evidence, try to find evidence that the listener hasn't heard before—evidence that's new to the listener. You don't want your listener to think, "Oh, I've heard all of that before." Audience members are more likely to keep focusing on your message when they are learning something new.

Use Specific Evidence   "Many people will be hurt if we don't do something now to stop global warming," said Julia. How many people will be hurt? What precisely will happen? Julia would make her point more effectively if she offered specific evidence that, for example, identified how many homes would be lost as a result of rising ocean levels rather than speaking of "many people" or "a lot of people."

Use Evidence to Tell a Story   Facts, examples, statistics, and opinions may be credible, new, and specific—yet your evidence will be even more powerful if it fits together to tell a story to make your point. Besides listing the problems that will occur because of global warming, Julia could personalize the evidence by telling a story about how the rising ocean levels will hurt individual families. Using evidence to support a story adds emotional power to your message and makes your evidence seem less abstract.[18]

Use Evidence Appropriate to a Diverse Audience   Because we believe that messages should be audience-centered rather than source-centered, we suggest that you consider your listeners to determine the kind of evidence that will be the most convincing to them. Not all audiences expect a speech to sound like an attorney's summation of a legal case. In fact, some lawyers decide, after "reading" the jury, that the best way to conclude their case is to tell a story rather than to present a litany of the facts and evidence.

According to intercultural communication scholars Myron Lustig and Jolene Koester, "There are no universally accepted standards about what constitutes evidence."[19] They suggest that for some Muslim and Christian audiences, parables or stories are a dramatically effective way to make a point. A story is told and a principle is derived from the lesson of the story. For most North Americans and Europeans, a superior form of evidence is an observed fact. A study by two communication scholars reported that both African Americans and Hispanic Americans found statistical evidence more persuasive than stories alone.[20] Statistics, said the respondents, are more believable and verifiable; stories can more easily be modified. In some African

reluctant testimony

A statement by someone who has reversed his or her position on a given issue

cultures, eyewitness testimony is often not perceived as credible; it's believed that if you speak up to report what you saw, you may have a particular slant on the event and, therefore, what you have to say may not be believable.[21] What may be convincing evidence to you may not be such an obvious piece of evidence for others. If you are uncertain whether your listeners will perceive your evidence as valid and reliable, you could test your evidence on a small group of people who will be in your audience before you address the entire group.

Avoiding Faulty Reasoning

We have emphasized the importance of developing sound, logical arguments supported with appropriate evidence. You have an ethical responsibility to use your skill to construct arguments that are well supported with logical reasoning and sound evidence. Not all people who try to persuade you will use sound arguments to get you to vote for them, buy their product, or donate money to their cause. Many persuaders use inappropriate techniques called fallacies. A **fallacy** is false reasoning that occurs when someone attempts to persuade without adequate evidence or with arguments that are irrelevant or inappropriate. You will be both a better and more ethical speaker and a better listener if you are aware of the following fallacies.

Causal Fallacy The Latin term for the causal fallacy is *post hoc, ergo propter hoc*, which translates as "after this, therefore, because of this." A **causal fallacy** is a statement that makes a faulty causal connection. Simply because one event follows another does not mean that the two are related. If you declared that your school's football team won this time because you sang your school song before the game, you would be guilty of a causal fallacy. There are undoubtedly other factors that explain why your team won, such as good preparation or facing a weaker opposing team. For something to be a cause, it has to have the power to bring about a result. "That howling storm last night knocked down the tree in our backyard" is a logical causal explanation.

Here are more examples of causal fallacies:

The increased earthquake and hurricane activity is caused by the increase in violence and war in our society.

As long as you wear this lucky rabbit's foot, you will never have an automobile accident.

In each instance, there is not enough evidence to support the cause-and-effect conclusion.

Bandwagon Fallacy Someone who argues that "everybody thinks it's a good idea, so you should too" is using the **bandwagon fallacy**. Simply because "everyone" is "jumping on the bandwagon," or supporting a particular point of view, does not make the point of view correct. Sometimes speakers use the bandwagon fallacy in more subtle ways in their efforts to persuade:

Everybody knows that talk radio is our primary link to a free and democratic society.

Most people agree that we spend too much time worrying about the future of Medicare.

Beware of sweeping statements that include you and others without offering any evidence that the speaker has solicited opinions.

Either/Or Fallacy Someone who argues that there are only two approaches to a problem is trying to oversimplify the issue by using the **either/or fallacy**. "It's either vote for higher property taxes or close the library," asserts Daryl at a public hearing on tax

> **RECAP**
>
> ## EFFECTIVE EVIDENCE
>
> You can use four types of evidence:
> - Facts
> - Examples
> - Opinions from experts
> - Statistics
>
> The most effective evidence is:
> - Credible
> - New
> - Specific
> - Part of a story
> - Appropriate to your audience

fallacy
False reasoning that occurs when someone attempts to persuade without adequate evidence or with arguments that are irrelevant or inappropriate

causal fallacy
A faulty cause-and-effect connection between two things or events

bandwagon fallacy
Reasoning that suggests that because everyone else believes something or is doing something, then it must be valid or correct

either/or fallacy
The oversimplification of an issue into a choice between only two outcomes or possibilities

increases. Such a statement ignores all other possible solutions to a complex problem. When you hear someone simplifying the available options by saying it's either this or that, you should be on guard for the either/or fallacy. Rarely is any issue as simple as a choice between only two alternatives. The following are examples of inappropriate either/or reasoning:

> Either television violence is reduced, or we will have an increase in child and spouse abuse.

> Either more people start volunteering their time to work for their community, or your taxes will increase.

Hasty Generalization A person who reaches a conclusion from too little evidence or nonexistent evidence is making a **hasty generalization**. For example, that one person became ill after eating the meat loaf in the cafeteria does not mean that everyone eating in the cafeteria will develop food poisoning. Here are additional hasty generalizations:

> It's clear that our schools can't educate children well—my niece went to school for six years and she still can't read at her grade level.

> The city does a terrible job of taking care of the elderly—my grandmother lives in a city-owned nursing home, and the floors there are always filthy.

Ad Hominem Also known as attacking the person, an **ad hominem** (Latin for "to the man") approach involves attacking characteristics of the person who is proposing an idea rather than attacking the idea itself. A statement such as "We know Janice's idea won't work because she has never had a good idea" does not really deal with the idea, which may be valid. Don't dismiss an idea solely because you have been turned against the person who presented it. Here are examples of ad hominem attacks:

> She was educated in a foreign country and could not possibly have good ideas for improving education in our community.

> Tony is an awful musician and is not sensitive enough to chair the parking committee.

Red Herring The **red herring** fallacy is used when someone attacks an issue by using irrelevant facts or arguments as distractions. This fallacy gets its name from an old trick of dragging a red herring across a trail to divert the dogs that may be following. Speakers use a red herring when they want to distract an audience from the real issues. For example, a politician who has been accused of taking bribes calls a press conference. During the press conference, he talks about the evils of child pornography rather than addressing the charge against him. He is using the red herring technique to divert attention from the real issue—did he or did he not take the bribe? Consider another red herring argument from a speech against gun control: The real problem is not eliminating handguns; the real problem is that pawnshops that sell guns are controlled by the Mafia.

Appeal to Misplaced Authority When ads use baseball catchers to endorse automobiles and TV heroes to sell political candidates or an airline or a hotel, we are faced with the fallacious **appeal to misplaced authority**. Although we have great respect for these people in their own fields, they are no more expert than we are in the areas they are promoting. As both a public speaker and a listener, you must recognize what is valid expert testimony and what is not. For example, a physicist who speaks on the laws of nature or the structure of matter could reasonably be accepted as an expert. But when the physicist speaks on politics, his or her opinion is not that of an ex-

hasty generalization
A conclusion reached without adequate evidence

ad hominem
An attack on irrelevant personal characteristics of the person who is proposing an idea, rather than on the idea itself

red herring
Irrelevant facts or information used to distract someone from the issue under discussion

appeal to misplaced authority
Use of the testimony of an expert in a given field to endorse an idea or product for which the expert does not have the appropriate credentials or expertise

pert and may be no more significant than your own. The following examples are appeals to misplaced authority:

> Former Congressman Smith endorses the new art museum, so every business should get behind it, too.

> Katie Couric thinks this cookie recipe is the best, so you will like it too.

Non Sequitur   When you argue that a new parking garage should not be built on campus because the grass has not been mowed on the football field for three weeks, you are guilty of a **non sequitur** (Latin for "it does not follow"). Grass growing on the football field has nothing to do with the parking problem. Your conclusion simply does not follow from your statement. The following are examples of non sequitur conclusions:

> We should not give students condoms because TV has such a pervasive influence on our youth today.

> You should endorse me for Congress because I have three children.

> We need more parking on our campus because we are the national football champions.

Using Emotion to Persuade

15.3   Employ effective techniques of using emotional appeal in a persuasive speech.

Effective speakers know how to use emotion to make their point. Note these three emotionally evocative moments in classic speeches:[22]

- In his inaugural address, delivered with perfect timing, President John F. Kennedy inspiringly intoned, "And so, my fellow Americans, ask not what your country can do for you—ask what you can do for your country. My fellow citizens of the world, ask not what America will do for you, but what together we can do for the freedom of man."

- After being dismissed from his command duties by President Harry Truman, a still popular General Douglas MacArthur ended his poignant farewell speech to Congress by saying, "Old soldiers never die; they just fade away. And like the old soldier of that ballad, I now close my military career and just fade away."

- When encouraging the British people to be valiant during World War II, Prime Minister Winston Churchill resolutely declared, "We shall go on to the end, we shall fight in France, we shall fight on the seas and oceans, we shall fight with growing confidence and growing strength in the air, we shall defend our island, whatever the cost may be, we shall fight on the beaches, we shall fight on the landing grounds, we shall fight in the fields and the streets, we shall fight on the hills; we shall never surrender."

Great moments in memorable speeches occur when both the minds and hearts are engaged.

Understanding how messages evoke emotions can help you develop appropriate emotional appeals. **Emotional response theory** suggests that emotional responses can be classified along three dimensions—pleasure, arousal, and dominance.[23] First, you respond with varying degrees of *pleasure* or *displeasure*. Pleasurable stimuli

Explore at **MyCommunicationLab**
Activity: "Annotated Outline: Helen Keller International"

Read at **MyCommunicationLab**
Learning From Great Speakers:
Franklin Delano Roosevelt

non sequitur
Latin for "it does not follow"; an idea or conclusion that does not logically relate to or follow from the previous idea or conclusion

emotional response theory
Human emotional responses can be classified as eliciting feelings of pleasure, arousal, or dominance

Arousing your listeners' emotions is often helpful in persuading them to agree with your message.
Photo: Anton Gvozdikov/Fotolia

consist of such things as images of smiling, healthy babies or daydreams about winning millions in a sweepstakes. Stimuli causing displeasure may be TV news stories of child abuse or dreadful images of terrorism.

A second dimension of emotional responses exists on a continuum of *arousal–nonarousal*. You become aroused emotionally, for example, by seeing a snake in your driveway, or you may be lulled into a state of nonarousal by a boring lecture.

The third dimension of emotional responses is one's feeling of *dominance* or *powerlessness* when confronted with some stimulus. When thinking about the destructive force of nuclear weapons or the omnipotence of God, you may feel insignificant and powerless. Or perhaps you feel a sense of power when you imagine yourself conducting a symphony or winning an election.

These three dimensions—pleasure, arousal, and dominance—are believed to form the bases of all emotional responses. Theory predicts that if listeners feel pleasure and are also aroused by something, such as a political candidate or a product, they will tend to form a favorable view of the candidate or product. A listener's feeling of being dominant has to do with being in control and having permission to behave as he or she wishes. A listener who feels dominant is more likely to respond to the message.

As a public speaker trying to sway your listeners to your viewpoint, your job is to ethically use emotional appeals to achieve your goal. If you wanted to persuade your listeners that capital punishment should be banned, you would try to arouse feelings of displeasure and turn them against capital punishment. Advertisers selling soft drinks typically strive to arouse feelings of pleasure in those who think of their product. Smiling people, upbeat music, and good times are usually part of the formula for selling soda pop.

Tips for Using Emotion to Persuade

Although emotional response theory may help you understand how emotions work, as a public speaker your key concern is "How can I ethically use emotional appeals to achieve my persuasive purpose?" Let's consider several methods.

Use Concrete Examples That Help Your Listeners Visualize What You Describe This speaker used a vivid description of the devastation caused by a tornado in Saragosa,

Texas, to evoke strong emotions and persuade listeners to take proper precautions when a storm warning is sounded.

> The town is no more. No homes in the western Texas town remain standing. The church where twenty-one people perished looks like a heap of twisted metal and mortar. A child's doll can be seen in the street. The owner, four-year-old Maria, will no longer play with her favorite toy; she was killed along with five of her play-mates when the twister roared through the elementary school.

Use Emotion-Arousing Words Words and phrases can trigger emotional responses in your listeners. *Mother, flag, freedom,* and *slavery* are among a large number of emotionally loaded words. Patriotic slogans such as "Remember Pearl Harbor" and "Remember 9/11" can also produce strong emotional responses.[24]

Use Nonverbal Behavior to Communicate Your Emotional Response The great Roman orator Cicero believed that if you want your listeners to experience a certain emotion, you should first model that emotion for them. If you want an audience to feel anger at a particular law or event, you must display anger and indignation in your voice, movement, and gesture. As we have noted, delivery plays the key role in communicating your emotional responses. When you want your audience to become excited about and interested in your message, you must communicate that excitement and interest through your delivery.

Keep in mind that listeners' cultures influence how receptive they are to a message and to a speaker's presentation style. Some Latin American listeners, for example, expect speakers to express more emotion and passion when speaking than North American listeners are accustomed to. The best way to assess the preferred speaking style of an audience that is not familiar to you is to observe other successful speakers addressing the audience you will face. Or talk with audience members before you speak to identify expectations and communication-style preferences.

Use Visual Images to Evoke Emotions In addition to nonverbal expressions, pictures or images of emotion-arousing scenes can amplify your speech. An image of a lonely homeowner looking out over his waterlogged house following a ravaging flood in Houston, Texas, can communicate his sense of despair. A picture of children in war-torn Macedonia can communicate the devastating effects of violence with greater impact than mere words alone. In contrast, a photo of a refugee mother and child reunited after an enforced separation can communicate the true meaning of joy. You can use similar images as visual aids to evoke your audience's emotions, both positive and negative. Remember, however, that when you use visual images, you have the same ethical responsibilities as you have when you use verbal forms of support: Make sure your image is from a credible source and that it has not been altered or taken out of context.

Use Appropriate Metaphors and Similes A metaphor is an implied comparison between two things. The person who says, "Our lives are quilts upon which we stitch the patterns of our character. If you don't pay attention to the ethical dimension of the decisions you make, you will be more likely to make a hideous pattern in your life quilt," is using a metaphor. A simile makes a direct comparison between two things using the word *like* or *as*. Here's an example: "Not visiting your academic counselor regularly is like being a gambler in a high-stakes poker game; you're taking a big chance that you're taking the right courses." Several research studies have found that speakers who use appropriate and interesting metaphors and similes are more persuasive than those who don't use such stylistic devices.[25] Using metaphors and similes can create a fresh, emotional perspective on a persuasive point; they can both enhance your credibility and develop an emotional image in a way that non-metaphorical language cannot.[26]

Use Appropriate Fear Appeals The threat that harm will come to your listeners unless they follow your advice is an appeal to fear. As discussed in Chapter 14, listeners can be motivated to change their behavior if appeals to fear are used appropriately. Research suggests that high fear arousal ("You will be killed in an auto accident unless you wear a safety belt") is more effective than moderate or low appeals, if you are a highly credible speaker.[27]

Consider Using Appeals to Several Emotions Appealing to the fears and anxieties of your listeners is one of the most common types of emotional appeals used to persuade, but you could also elicit several other emotions to help achieve your persuasive goal.

- **Hope.** Listeners could be motivated to respond to the prospect of a brighter tomorrow. When Franklin Roosevelt said, "The only thing we have to fear is fear itself," he was invoking hope for the future, as was Barack Obama in his upbeat 2008 campaign phrase, "Yes, we can!"

- **Pride.** When a politician says, "It's time to restore our nation's legacy as a beacon of freedom for all people," she is appealing to national pride. To appeal to pride is to invoke feelings of pleasure and satisfaction based on accomplishing something important. A persuasive appeal to achieve a goal based on pride in oneself or one's country, state, or community can be very powerful.

- **Courage.** Challenging your audience to take a bold stand or to step away from the crowd can emotionally charge your listeners to take action. Referring to courageous men and women as role models can help motivate your listeners to take similar actions. Patrick Henry's famous "Give me liberty, or give me death!" speech appealed to his audience to take a courageous stand on the issues before them.

- **Reverence.** The appeal to the sacred and the revered can be an effective way to motivate. Sacred traditions, revered institutions, and cherished and celebrated individuals can inspire your audience to change or reinforce attitudes, beliefs, values, or behavior. The late Mother Teresa, holy writings, and the school your listeners attended are examples of people, things, and institutions that your listeners may perceive as sacred. As an audience-centered speaker, however, you need to remember that what may be sacred to one individual or audience may not be sacred to another.

CONSIDER THE AUDIENCE

Tap Audience Members' Beliefs in Shared Myths Often people talk about a myth as something that is factually untrue. The Easter Bunny, the Tooth Fairy, and Santa Claus are often labeled myths. But in a rhetorical sense, a **myth** is a belief held in common by a group of people and based on their values, cultural heritage, and faith. A myth may be factual—or it may be based on a partial truth that a group of people believes to be true. Myths are the "big" stories that give meaning and coherence to a group of people or a culture. The myth of the Old West is that the pioneers of yesteryear were strong, adventurous people who sacrificed their lives in search of a better tomorrow. Similarly, our parents, grandparents, and great-grandparents belonged to "the greatest generation" because they overcame a devastating economic depression and were triumphant in two world wars. The myth of the 1950s was that U.S. families were prosperous and lived like Ward and June Cleaver and their sons, Wally and "The Beaver," in the TV program *Leave It to Beaver*. Religious myths are beliefs shared by a group of faithful disciples. So a myth is not necessarily false—it is a belief that a group of people share, one that provides emotional support for the way they view the world.

As a public speaker, you can draw on the myths you and your audience members share to provide emotional and motivational support for your message. Referring to a shared myth is a way to identify with your listeners and help them see how your ideas support their ideas; it can help you develop a common bond with audience members.

myth
A shared belief based on the underlying values, cultural heritage, and faith of a group of people

In trying to convince his listeners to vote, Jason argued, "We can't let down those who fought for our freedom. We must vote to honor those who died for the privilege of voting that we enjoy today." He was drawing on the powerful myth that people have died for our freedoms. To gain parent support for a new high school, Cynthia said, "Our grandparents and great-grandparents lived through the Great Depression and the world wars of the past century so that we can send our children to the best public schools in the world. Vote for the new high school." She was appealing to the myth that the previous generation sacrificed, which gave us a responsibility to sacrifice for our children. Again we emphasize that *myth* does not mean "false" or "made up." People *did* die for our freedom, and our grandparents and great-grandparents *did* live through the Depression and two world wars; a myth is powerful because the audience knows that those events occurred. Myth is the powerful underlying story that evokes an emotional response to a message.

Politicians use myth when they show pictures of themselves surrounded by their families. The underlying myth is "I cherish what you cherish—to live in a country that supports and nurtures the family values we hold dear." Appealing directly or indirectly to the commonly held myths of an audience is a powerful way to evoke emotional support for your message. But as with any form of support, especially emotional support, you have an ethical responsibility to use this strategy wisely and not to exploit your listeners.

Using Emotional Appeals: Ethical Issues

Regardless of which emotions you use to motivate your audience, you have an obligation to be ethical and forthright. Making false claims, misusing evidence to arouse emotions, or relying only on emotions without offering evidence to support a conclusion violates ethical standards of effective public speaking.

A **demagogue** is a speaker who attempts to gain power or control over others by using impassioned emotional pleas and appealing to listeners' prejudices. The word *demagogue* comes from the Greek word *demagogos*, meaning "popular leader." Speakers who become popular by substituting emotion and fallacies in place of well-supported reasoning are guilty of demagoguery. As we discussed in Chapter 3, during the early 1950s, anti-Communist Wisconsin Senator Joseph McCarthy's unethical use of fear appeals backed by little evidence undermined his credibility and earned him a reputation as a demagogue. You have an ethical responsibility not to misuse emotional appeals when persuading others.

Credibility, reasoning, and emotional appeals are the chief means of persuading an audience. Your use of these persuasive strategies depends on the composition of your audience. As we have observed several times before, an early task in the public-speaking process is to analyze your audience. This is particularly important in persuasion. Audience members are not just sitting there waiting to respond to every suggestion a speaker makes.

> **RECAP**
>
> ## TIPS FOR USING EMOTION TO PERSUADE
>
> - Use concrete examples.
> - Use emotion-arousing words.
> - Use visual images.
> - Use appropriate metaphors and similes.
> - Use appropriate fear appeals.
> - Appeal to a variety of emotions.
> - Communicate emotions nonverbally.
> - Tap into shared myths.

Strategies for Adapting Ideas to People and People to Ideas

15.4 Adapt your persuasive message to receptive, neutral, and unreceptive audiences.

We opened this chapter with Donald C. Bryant's pithy definition of persuasion as "the process of adjusting ideas to people and people to ideas."[28] His description of the rhetorical process gets at the heart of what an effective persuader does—he or she ethically adapts the message and the delivery to create agreement.

demagogue
A speaker who gains control over others by using unethical emotional pleas and appeals to listeners' prejudices

Watch at **MyCommunicationLab**
Video: "Second-Hand Smoke"

Audience members may hold differing views of you and your subject. Your task is to find out whether there is a prevailing viewpoint held by a majority of your listeners. If they are generally friendly toward you and your ideas, you need to design your speech differently from the way you would if your listeners were neutral, apathetic, or hostile. Research studies as well as seasoned public speakers can offer useful suggestions for adapting your approach to your audience. We will discuss three general responses your audience may have to you: receptive, neutral, and unreceptive.

Persuading the Receptive Audience

It is always a pleasure to face an audience that already supports you and your message. In speaking to a receptive group, you can explore your ideas in greater depth than otherwise. Here are suggestions that may help you make the most of that kind of speaking opportunity.

Identify with Your Audience To establish common ground with her audience of fellow students, Rita told them, "Just like most of you, I struggle to pay my way through college. That's why I support expanding the campus work-study program." Like Rita, if you are a college student speaking to other college students with similar backgrounds and pressures, point to your similar backgrounds and struggles. Emphasize the similarities between you and your audience. What other common interests do you have? The introductory portion of your speech is a good place to mention those common interests.

Clearly State Your Speaking Objective When speaking to a group of her campaign workers, mayoral candidate Maria Hernandez stated early in her speech, "My reason for coming here today is to ask each of you to volunteer three hours a week to help me become the next mayor of our city." We have stressed several times how important it is to provide an overview of your major point or purpose. This is particularly so when speaking to a group that will support your point of view.[29]

Tell Your Audience Exactly What You Want Them to Do Besides telling your listeners what your speaking objective is, you can also tell them how you expect them to respond to your message. Be explicit in directing your listeners' behavior.

Ask Listeners for an Immediate Show of Support Asking for an immediate show of support helps to cement the positive response you have developed during your speech. For example, Christian evangelists usually speak to favorable audiences. Evangelist Billy Graham, who spoke to more people in live public-speaking situations than anyone else in the twentieth century, always asked those who supported his Christian message to come forward at the end of his sermon.

Use Emotional Appeals Effectively You are more likely to move a favorable audience to action with strong emotional appeals while also reminding them of the evidence that supports your conclusion. When the audience already supports your position, you need not spend a great deal of time on lengthy, detailed explanations or factual information. You can usually assume that your listeners already know much of that material.

Make It Easy for Your Listeners to Act It is a good idea not only to tell your listeners precisely what you want them to do and ask for an immediate response but also to make sure that what you're asking them to do is clear and easy. If you're asking them to write or email someone, hand out postcards already addressed to the recipient or distribute an email address printed on a card for handy reference. If you want listeners to call someone, make sure each person has the phone number—it's even better if you can give a toll-free number.

Persuading the Neutral Audience

Think how many lectures you go to with an attitude of indifference. Probably quite a few. Many audiences will fall somewhere between wildly enthusiastic and unreceptive; they will simply be neutral or indifferent. They may be neutral because they don't know much about your topic or because they haven't made up their minds whether to support your point of view. They may also be indifferent because they don't see how the topic or issue affects them. Regardless of the reason for your listeners' indifference, your challenge is to interest them in your message. Let's look at some approaches to gaining their attention and keeping their interest.

Capture Your Listeners' Attention Early in Your Speech "Bill Farmer died last year, but he's about to fulfill his lifelong dream of going into space."[30] In a speech about the high cost of funerals, Karmen's provocative opening statement effectively captures the attention of her listeners.

Refer to Beliefs That Many Listeners Share When speaking to a neutral audience, identify common concerns and values that you plan to address. Martin Luther King's "Dream" speech (Appendix B) includes references to his listeners' common beliefs.

Relate Your Topic Not Only to Your Listeners but Also to Their Families, Friends, and Loved Ones You can capture the interest of your listeners by appealing to the needs of people they care about. Parents will be interested in ideas and policies that affect their children. People are generally interested in matters that may affect their friends, neighbors, and others with whom they identify, such as members of their own religion or economic or social class.

Be Realistic about What You Can Accomplish Don't overestimate the response you may receive from a neutral audience. People who start with an attitude of indifference are probably not going to become as enthusiastic as you are after hearing just one speech. Persuasion does not occur all at once or on a first hearing of arguments.

Persuading the Unreceptive Audience

One of the biggest challenges in public speaking is to persuade audience members who are against you or your message. If they are hostile toward you personally, your job is to seek ways to enhance your credibility and persuade them to listen to you. If they are unreceptive to your point of view, there are several approaches that you can use to encourage them to listen to you.

Don't Announce Immediately That You Plan to Change Their Minds Paul wondered why his opening sales pitch ("Good morning. I plan to convince you to purchase this fine set of knives at a cost to you of only $250") was not greeted enthusiastically. If you immediately and bluntly tell your listeners that you plan to change their opinions, it can make them defensive. It is usually better to take a more subtle approach when announcing your persuasive intent.[31]

Begin Your Speech by Noting Areas of Agreement before You Discuss Areas of Disagreement In addressing the school board, one community member began his persuasive effort to convince board members they should not raise taxes by stating, "I think each of us here can agree with one common goal: We want the best education for our children." Once you help your audience understand that there are issues on which you agree (even if only that the topic you will discuss is controversial), your listeners may be more attentive when you explain your position.

Don't Expect a Major Shift in Attitude from a Hostile Audience Set a realistic limit on what you can achieve. Remember our discussion of social judgment theory in

Chapter 14, which suggested that listeners fall into three latitudes of reaction to persuasive messages: acceptance, noncommitment, or rejection. You may not be able to move hostile listeners out of the latitude of rejection of your message. A more realistic goal might be to have your listeners hear you out and at least consider some of your points.

Acknowledge the Opposing Points of View That Members of Your Audience May Hold Summarize the reasons individuals may oppose your point of view. Doing this communicates that you at least understand the issues.[32] Your listeners will be more likely to listen to you if they know that you understand their viewpoint. Of course, after you acknowledge the opposing point of view, you will need to cite evidence and use arguments to refute the opposition and support your conclusion. Early in his speech to a neighborhood group about the possibility of building a new airport near their homes, City Manager Anderson acknowledged, "I am aware that a new airport brings unwanted changes to a neighborhood. Noise and increased traffic are not the type of challenges you want near your homes." He went on to identify the actions the city would take to minimize the problems a new airport would cause.

Establish Your Credibility Being thought credible is always an important goal of a public speaker, and it is especially important when talking to an unreceptive audience. Let your audience know about the experience, interest, knowledge, and skill that give you special insight into the issues at hand.

Consider Making Understanding Rather Than Advocacy Your Goal Sometimes your audience disagrees with you because its members just don't understand your point. Or they may harbor a misconception about you and your message. For example, if your listeners think that AIDS is transferred though kissing or other casual contact rather than through unprotected sexual contact, you'll first have to acknowledge their beliefs and then construct a sound argument to show how inaccurate their assumptions are. To change such a misconception and enhance accurate understanding, experienced speakers use a four-part strategy.[33]

1. **Summarize the common misconceptions about the issue or idea you are discussing.** "Many people think that AIDS can be transmitted through casual contact such as kissing or that it can easily be transmitted by your dentist or physician."

2. **State why these misconceptions may seem reasonable.** Tell your listeners why it is logical for them to hold that view, or identify "facts" they may have heard that would lead them to their current conclusion. "Since AIDS is such a highly contagious disease, it may seem reasonable to think it can be transmitted through such casual contact."

3. **Dismiss the misconceptions and provide evidence to support your point.** Here you need sound and credible data to be persuasive. "In fact, countless medical studies have shown that it is virtually impossible to be infected with the AIDS virus unless you have unprotected sexual contact or use unsterilized hypodermic needles that have also been used by someone who has AIDS." In this instance, you would probably cite specific results from two or three studies to lend credibility to your claim.

4. **State the accurate information that you want your audience to remember.** Reinforce the conclusion you want your listeners to draw from the information you presented with a clear summary statement, such as "According to recent research, the most common factor contributing to the spread of AIDS is unprotected sex. This is true for individuals of both sexes and all sexual orientations."

Strategies for Organizing Persuasive Messages

Is there one best way to organize a persuasive speech? The answer is no. Specific approaches to organizing speeches depend on audience, message, and desired objective. But how you organize your speech does have a major effect on your listeners' response to your message.

Research suggests some general principles to keep in mind when preparing your persuasive message.[34]

- **If you feel that your audience may be hostile to your point of view, advance your strongest arguments first.** If you save your best argument for last, your audience may have already stopped listening.

- **Do not bury key arguments and evidence in the middle of your message.** Your listeners are more likely to remember information presented first and last.[35] In speaking to his fraternity about the dangers of drunk driving, Frank wisely began his speech with his most powerful evidence: The leading cause of death among college-age males is alcohol-related automobile accidents. He got their attention with his sobering fact.

- **If you want your listeners to take some action, it is best to tell them what you want them to do at the end of your speech.** If you call for action in the middle of your speech, it won't have the power it would have in your conclusion. You should also tailor your calls to action to the cultural preferences of your audience. In some high-context cultures, such as in Japan and China, you can imply what you'd like your listeners to do rather than spell out the precise action explicitly. In a low-context culture such as the United States, listeners may generally expect you to state more directly the action you'd like them to take.

- **When you think your listeners are well informed and are familiar with the disadvantages of your proposal, it is usually better to present both sides of an issue, rather than just the advantages of the position you advocate.** If you don't acknowledge arguments your listeners have heard, they will probably think about them anyway.

- **Make reference to the counterarguments and then refute them with evidence and logic.** It may be wise to compare your proposal with an alternative proposal, perhaps one offered by someone else. By comparing and contrasting your solution with another recommendation, you can show how your proposal is better.[36]

- **Adapt organization to the culture of your audience.** Most North Americans tend to like a well-organized message with a clear, explicit link between the evidence used and the conclusion drawn. North Americans are also comfortable with a structure that focuses on a problem and then offers a solution or a message in which causes are identified and the effects are specified. Audiences in the Middle East, however, would expect less formal structure and greater use of a narrative style of message development. The audience either infers the point or the speaker may conclude by making the point clear. Being indirect or implicit may sometimes be the best persuasive strategy.

We discussed ways of organizing speeches in Chapter 8, but there are special ways to organize persuasive speeches. Here we present four organizational patterns: problem–solution, refutation, cause and effect, and the motivated sequence. These four patterns are summarized in Table 15.2 on page 328.

TABLE 15.2 ORGANIZATIONAL PATTERNS FOR PERSUASIVE MESSAGES

PATTERN	DEFINITION	EXAMPLE
Problem–solution	Present the problem; then present the solution.	I. The national debt is too high. II. We need to raise taxes to lower the debt.
Refutation	Anticipate your listeners' key objections to your proposal and then address them.	I. Even though you may think we pay too much tax, we are really undertaxed. II. Even though you may think the national debt will not go down, tax revenue will lower the deficit.
Cause and effect	First present the cause of the problem; then note how the problem affects the listeners. Or identify a known effect; then document what causes the effect.	I. The high national debt is caused by too little tax revenue and too much government spending. II. The high national debt will increase both inflation and unemployment.
Motivated sequence	A five-step pattern of organizing a speech; its steps are attention, need, satisfaction, visualization, and action.	I. *Attention:* Imagine a pile of $1,000 bills 67 miles high. That's our national debt. II. *Need:* The increasing national debt will cause hardships for our children and grandchildren. III. *Satisfaction:* We need higher taxes to reduce our debt. IV. *Visualization:* Imagine our country in the year 2050; it could have low inflation and full employment or be stuck with a debt ten times our debt today. V. *Action:* If you want to lower the debt by increasing tax revenue, sign this petition that I will send to our representatives.

Problem–Solution

Watch at **MyCommunicationLab**
Video: "Untreated Depression"

Watch at **MyCommunicationLab**
Video: "Mandatory Minimums"

The most basic organizational pattern for a persuasive speech is to make the audience aware of a problem and then present a solution that clearly solves it. Almost any problem can be phrased in terms of something you want more of or less of. The problem–solution pattern works best when a clearly evident problem can be documented and a solution can be proposed to deal with the well-documented problem.

When you are speaking to an apathetic audience or when listeners are not aware that a problem exists, a problem–solution pattern works nicely. Your challenge will be to provide ample evidence to document that your perception of the problem is accurate. The Sample Persuasive Speech on pages 330–331 shows how Texas State University student Colter Ray met this challenge. You'll also need to convince your listeners that the solution you advocate is the most appropriate one to resolve the problem.

Many political candidates use a problem–solution approach. *Problem:* The government wastes your tax dollars. *Solution:* Vote for me and I'll see to it that government waste is eliminated. *Problem:* We need more and better jobs. *Solution:* Vote for me and I'll institute a program to put people back to work.

Note in the following outline of Jason's speech, "The Dangers of Electromagnetic Fields," how he plans to first document a clear problem and then recommend strategies for managing the problem.

PROBLEM: Power lines and power stations around the country emit radiation and are now being shown to increase the risk of cancer.

I. Childhood leukemia rates are higher in children who live near large power lines.
II. The International Cancer Research Institute in Lyon, France, published a report linking electromagnetic fields and childhood cancer.

SOLUTION: Steps can be taken to minimize our risk of health hazards caused by electromagnetic energy.

I. The federal government should establish enforceable safety standards for exposure to electromagnetic energy.
II. Contact your local power company to make sure its lines are operated safely.
III. Stop using electric blankets.
IV. Use protective screens for computer-display terminals.

The problem–solution arrangement of ideas applies what you learned about cognitive dissonance in Chapter 14. Identify and document a concern that calls for change, and then suggest specific behaviors that can restore cognitive balance.

Refutation

Another way to persuade an audience to support your point of view is to prove that the arguments against your position are false—that is, to refute them. To use refutation as a strategy for persuasion, you first identify objections to your position that your listeners might raise and then refute or overcome those objections with arguments and evidence.

Suppose, for example, you plan to speak to a group of real-estate developers to advocate a new zoning ordinance that would reduce the number of building permits granted in your community. Your listeners will undoubtedly have concerns about how the ordinance will affect their ability to build homes and make money. You could organize your presentation to this group using those two obvious concerns as major issues to refute. Your major points could be as follows:

I. The new zoning ordinance will not cause an overall decrease in the number of new homes built in our community.
II. The new zoning ordinance will have a positive effect on the profits of local real-estate developers.

You would be most likely to use refutation as your organizational strategy when your position was being attacked. Or, if you know what your listeners' chief objections are to your persuasive proposal, you could organize your speech around the arguments your listeners hold.

Research suggests that in most cases it is better to present both sides of an issue rather than just the advantages of the position you advocate. Even if you don't acknowledge arguments your listeners have heard, they will probably think about them anyway.

In her speech to promote organ donation, Tasha used the refutation strategy by identifying several myths that, if believed, would keep people from becoming organ donors.[*] She first identified each myth, or false belief, and then explained why the myth is, in fact, a myth.

I. Myth number 1: *If doctors know I'm an organ donor, they won't work as hard to save me.*
Refutation: Doctors pledge, as part of their Hippocratic oath, that saving your life is paramount. Furthermore, a patient must be declared brain dead before his or her organs may be taken.

[*] Tasha Carlson, "License to Save." From *Winning Orations 2009*, Mankato, MN: Interstate Oratorical Association, 2009. Reprinted with permission.

SAMPLE PERSUASIVE SPEECH

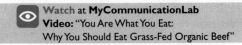
YOU ARE WHAT YOU EAT: WHY YOU SHOULD EAT GRASS-FED ORGANIC BEEF

Colter Ray, Texas State University

Have you ever really thought where your food comes from? And I'm not talking about just the supermarket, but I'm talking about where it came from before the supermarket. For a society that we live in that's so obsessed with fast food and dieting, health, prescriptions, *The Biggest Loser,* and racing for the cure, it's sort of dumbfounding that so many people don't even question where their food is coming from.

> Colter catches his audience's attention with a rhetorical question. He wants his listeners to be more mindful of what they eat and where their food comes from.

I myself started looking into this a while ago and ended up making the decision to switch from the normal ground beef, which is grain-fed ground beef, to organic grass-fed ground beef, and in the two years since I made the switch, I've become much healthier, much more energetic, and overall, just feel better about myself.

> He helps to establish his credibility by noting his personal experience with the topic.

In general I believe that grass-fed ground beef is the better choice when it comes to that or grain-fed, which is what most people buy. So, today we'll look at the unhealthy by-products found in grain-fed ground beef, as well as the unhealthy process by which that beef is made, and then we'll talk a little bit about grass-fed as a possible solution.

> Here, Colter previews his major idea and provides a general overview of his main points. By stating his purpose in his introduction, he is assuming that his audience will be generally favorable toward his goal or at least not hostile to his key purpose.

To begin, let's talk about the unhealthy by-products you might find in a normal tube of ground beef that you would buy from the supermarket. According to Gerald Zirnstein, a former scientist with the U.S. Department of Agriculture, 70 percent of our ground beef that we would buy contains what he calls "pink slime." And this is really just beef trimmings that have been put together and sprayed down with ammonia gas to kill off bacteria. And this pink slime was originally only allowed in dog food and then over time it became allowed to be used in melted-down form in cooking oil. And then finally it was allowed to be used in our ground beef as filler. And so how did this happen? How did we come to adding this pink slime to our ground beef? Well what ended up happening was that Joann Smith, who used to work for the USDA as an undersecretary, ended up saying that it was OK to add this, even though all the USDA scientists were not even willing to go as far as naming this pink slime to be meat. They wanted it to be listed as a separate ingredient, but she said, "No, it's OK," and ignored what they said. And what ends up happening? Well, Joann Smith retires from the USDA and goes and sits on the board of directors for a company called Beef Products Inc., where she makes a cool 1.2 million dollars a year in that position. Now, what's important to know is that Beef Products Inc. is the largest producer of pink slime that is used as this filler meat. So there's a bit of a connection here. Hopefully, you see that, too, that someone that allows pink slime to be added to all our meat, then Beef Products Inc., is the largest supplier of it, their profits rise greatly, and the person who made the decision on the government side of things goes on to become a board member to make over a million dollars a year from that very company.

> In this portion of his speech, Colter states the problem and documents the significance of the problem using statistics and expert testimony.

So now that we've talked about some by-products that you would find in your ground beef, let's talk about the unhealthy process used to make ground beef. So, cows eat grass, and they've done this for centuries, maybe even millions of years. And, so why is it that we are feeding them grain instead? It's because, in order to produce enough meat as quickly as possible, we wanted to fatten up these cows. And so the large producers of ground beef decided that, hey, if we feed them grain, then they'll get fatter quicker, then we can slaughter them and get more meat per cow. But according to the Union of Concerned Scientists, a grain diet for cows leads to more health problems.

> Colter provides a fluent transition to his next point by briefly recapping his ideas and then telling his listeners what he will talk about next.

II. Myth number 2: *If I donate my organs, my family will be charged for the surgical costs.*
Refutation: If you donate your organs, there will be no charge to your family.

III. Myth number 3: *I can't have an open casket funeral if I'm an organ donor.*
Refutation: The donor's body is clothed for burial, so there are no visible signs of donation.

Follow me on this. With more health problems for the cows, they treat the cows by giving them more antibiotics, and after they give them more antibiotics, that means more antibiotics are making their way from the cow onto our plate once we eat the meat. Now, say we start getting sick and we usually take antibiotics to fight off an infection as well; if we've already received those antibiotics from our meat that we're eating, they are going to be less effective once we need those antibiotics to fight off, you know, the sickness that we have and that we're fighting against.

So, the *grain*, on top of that, is a pretty subjective term as well. As I was doing this research, I found out a few interesting things that count as grain. The grain that is fed to our cows, which we turn around and eat, includes feathers, hair, and bone marrow that has been melted down from other animals, as well as swine waste, or as laymen say, pig poop, and also the carcasses of dead, dying, diseased, and disabled animals such as deer and elk.

It gets even better. On top of that, have you ever thought about what happens if, at a farm, maybe a rodent or a roach or a bird, were to get into some of the food and spoil the food? Maybe they ate some of it, maybe they pooped in it. What happens to that food? Does it get thrown out? No, it gets melted down and gets sprayed and heat-treated, so that it kills off the bacteria. And then this is also given to the cows, which then ends up on our plate as well. So, in the long run, we're really just one extra step away from eating rodent and roach feces. It's pretty incredible when you think about the fact that most people haven't thought about what is making it to our plates.

Now that I've worked up your appetite, I want to talk a little bit about grass-fed beef, as well as a possible solution to, hopefully, what you're not going to eat anymore, which would be the grain-fed beef. So, according to the *Journal of Nutrition*, grass-fed beef contains no pink slime, and it also contains less fat and less cholesterol than grain-fed beef. And this is actually not just a recent study; this was a study that was done over the span of 30 years. They found consistently that grass-fed beef had better, or excuse me, lower fat and lower cholesterol, and no random filler meat as well. So on top of that, the same study also says that there is more vitamin A and vitamin E, as well as more antioxidants in grass-fed beef, as well. And there's also a better ratio of Omega-3 and Omega-6 fatty acids in grass-fed beef, which is actually very important for brain health. So a lot of people also like to dismiss grass-fed beef as, "Oh, it's only something that, you know, the hippies would do," or "I'm not all into the organic thing." Well, let me just offer this little fun fact. President Ronald Reagan, the poster child for modern conservatism, demanded that he only had organic beef while he was serving as president of the United States. So, even Ronald Reagan was on board with organic grass-fed beef.

So, today we've talked about the unhealthy by-products that make their way into grain-fed beef, which is pink slime, and the story behind how it even got there in the first place. We have also talked about the unhealthy process by which grain-fed cows are raised, including the antibiotics they are given and what the actual grain consists of when it's not really grain. It's really more of grain and animal carcass. And we've also offered a simple solution, which is to go to the grocery store and at least try to buy organic grass-fed beef.

At least try it once. And so, that's all I ask today, is not to make a life-changing decision to never again eat the ground beef that comes in tubes, but to go out and, at least one time, try grass-fed organic ground beef.

In this section Colter uses the facts, statistics, and expert testimony to draw his key conclusion. He also uses alliteration to express his information in a memorable way.

Colter uses effective description and explanation to further amplify the significance of the problem he is trying to avoid.

Colter contrasts the negative aspects of the problem by noting more positive results by comparison. He wants you to see the advantage of his proposed solution: Eat beef from grass-fed cattle.

As he moves into his conclusion, he summarizes his key arguments.

He ends with a specific call to action, encouraging his listeners to take a small step toward addressing the problem he described.

IV. Myth number 4: *I can't donate my organs because I am too old.*

Refutation: There is no specific age cut-off for organ donation. The final decision is based on overall organ health, not age.

Tasha could have used the refutation strategy to organize her entire speech, or the refutation technique could be used as a portion of a larger organizational strategy such as problem–solution.

If your persuasive presentation using a refutation strategy will be followed by a question-and-answer forum, you should be prepared to answer questions. Credible evidence, facts, and data will be more effective than emotional arguments alone when you want to persuade an audience that you know is not in favor of your persuasive objective. In your postspeech session, you can use your refutation skills to maintain a favorable audience response to your message in the face of criticism or attacks on the soundness of your logic.

Cause and Effect

Watch at **MyCommunicationLab**
Video: "Childhood Obesity"

Like the problem–solution pattern to which it is closely related, the cause-and-effect approach was introduced in Chapter 8 as a useful organizational strategy. One way to use the cause-and-effect method is to begin with an effect, or problem, and then identify the causes of the problem in an effort to convince your listeners that the problem is significant. A speech on the growing problem of gangs might focus on poverty, drugs, and a financially crippled school system.

You could also organize a message by noting the problem and then spelling out the effects of the problem. If you identify the problem as too many unsupervised teenagers roaming your community's streets after 11 P.M., you could organize a speech noting the effects this problem is having on your fellow citizens.

The goal of using cause-and-effect organization for a persuasive speech is to convince your listeners that one event caused another. For example, you may try to reason that students in your state have low standardized test scores because they had poor teachers. Of course, you must prove that no other factors are responsible for the low test scores. It may not be the teachers who caused the low test scores; perhaps it was the lack of parent involvement or one of a number of other factors.

The challenge in using a cause-and-effect organizational strategy is to *prove* that one event *caused* something else to occur. Simply because two events occurred at the same time or in close succession does not prove that there is a cause-and-effect relationship. Earlier we noted the causal fallacy ("after this, therefore, because of this" or *post hoc, ergo propter hoc*). As an example of the challenge in documenting a cause-and-effect relationship, suppose a study that found that many people who spend several hours daily on the Internet are also psychologically depressed. This finding does not necessarily *prove* that Internet use causes depression—other factors could cause the depression. Perhaps people who are depressed are more likely to use the Internet because they find comfort and security in using technology.

Here's how a persuasive speech could be organized using a cause-and-effect strategy:

I. There is high uncertainty about whether interest rates will increase or decrease. *(cause)*

II. Money markets are unstable in Asia, Eastern Europe, and Latin America. *(cause)*

III. There has been a rise in unemployment. *(cause)*

IV. In the late 1920s in the United States, these three conditions were followed by a stock-market crash. They will likely cause another crash today. To avoid losing a lot of money, you should decrease the amount of money you have invested in stocks. *(effect)*

The Motivated Sequence

Watch at **MyCommunicationLab**
Video: "Mandatory Minimums"

The motivated sequence is a five-step organizational plan that has proved successful for several decades. Developed by Alan Monroe, this simple yet effective strategy for organizing speeches incorporates principles that have been confirmed by research and practical experience.[37] Based on the problem–solution pattern, it also uses the cognitive dissonance approach, which we discussed in Chapter 14: First, disturb your

Problem–solution organization and the motivated sequence both involve making your audience aware of a problem. What should you do if you suspect your listeners are unreceptive to your proposed solution?

Photo: Scott Griessel/Fotolia

listeners; then point them toward the specific change you want them to adopt. The five steps are attention, need, satisfaction, visualization, and action.

1. Attention. Your first goal is to get your listeners' attention. In Chapter 9 we discussed specific attention-catching methods of beginning a speech. Remember the particular benefits of using a personal or hypothetical example, a startling statement, an unusual statistic, a rhetorical question, or a well-worded analogy. The attention step is, in essence, the introduction to your speech.

Heather caught listeners' attention at the start of her award-winning speech "End the Use of Child Soldiers"[†] with this riveting introduction:

> When 12-year-old Ishmael Beah left his village in Sierra Leone to perform in a talent show in a town just a few miles away, he had no idea that in a matter of only a few days he would lose everything—his family, his friends, and even his childhood. He returned to find that a rebel army had killed his entire family, and decimated his town.

2. Need. Having gotten the attention of your audience, you need to establish why your topic, problem, or issue should concern your listeners. Arouse dissonance. Tell your audience why the current program, politician, or whatever you're attempting to change is not working. Convince them there is a need for a change. You must also convince your listeners that this need for change affects them directly. During the need step, you should develop logical arguments backed by ample evidence to support your position.

To document the significance of the problem of children being used as soldiers and the need to do something to address the problem, Heather provided specific evidence:

> . . . at any one time, 300,000 children under the age of 18 are forced to fight in military conflicts. As Peter Warren Singer, director of the 21st Century Defense Initiative at the Brookings Institute, states, child warfare is not only a human rights travesty, but also a great threat to global and national security.

[†]Heather Zupanic, "End the Use of Child Soldiers." Speech excerpts on pages 333 through 335 are from *Winning Orations 2009*, Mankato, MN: Interstate Oratorical Association, 2009. Reprinted with permission.

She personalized the problem for her audience this way: "Clearly, this crisis is having an enormous impact on the children themselves, on their nation states, and finally on our own country."

3. Satisfaction. After you present the problem or need for concern, briefly identify how your plan will satisfy the need. What is your solution to the problem? At this point in the speech, you need not go into great detail. Present enough information so that your listeners have a general understanding of how the problem may be solved.

Heather suggested that a solution to the problem of children serving as soldiers included using the United Nations to take legal action to enforce existing treaties and to bring this issue to the attention of government leaders throughout the world. At this point in her speech, she kept her solution—to involve government leaders—general. She waited until the end of her speech to provide specific action that audience members could take to implement her solution. Heather also reinforced the urgency of the need for the audience to act by stating, "Clearly, the time has come to take a stand against the atrocities that child soldiers face."

4. Visualization. Now you need to give your audience a sense of what it would be like if your solution were or were not adopted. You could take a *positive-visualization* approach: Paint a picture with words to communicate how wonderful the future will be if your solution is adopted. You could take a *negative-visualization* approach: Tell your listeners how awful things will be if your solution is not adopted. If they think things are bad now, just wait: Things will get worse.

Heather wanted her listeners to visualize the significant negative results likely to occur if the problem of child soldiers went unsolved. She began with a general statement of what would happen to children if no action were taken.

> The first consequence of child warfare is that these children are left with serious emotional and psychological scarring due to the violence and abuse they must endure.

She further painted her negative picture by using a specific emotional example in which she described additional consequences.

> Ten-year-old Jacques from the Congo described how the Mayi-Mayi militia would often starve him and beat him severely. He says, "I would see others die in front of me. I was hungry very often and I was scared."

Heather also pointed out that if the problem is not addressed soon, it will grow, and more children will be negatively affected.

Heather used only a negative-visualization approach. She could, however, have made her visualization step even stronger by combining negative and positive visualization. A combined positive and a negative visualization tells how problem will be solved if your solution is adopted and describes how the world will be a much worse place if your solution is not adopted. Heather might, for example, have added a description that helped her listeners visualize the virtues of taking action, by describing poignant scenes of children being reunited with their families. Using both a positive and a negative visualization approach demonstrates how the solution you present in the satisfaction step directly addresses the problem you described in the need step of your motivated sequence.

Martin Luther King Jr. drew on visualization as a rhetorical strategy in his moving "Dream" speech (Appendix B, page 364). Note on pages 365–366 how King powerfully and poetically painted a picture with words that continue to provide hope and inspiration today.

5. Action. This last step forms the basis of your conclusion. You tell your audience the specific action they can take to implement your solution. Identify exactly what you want your listeners to do. Give them simple, clear, easy-to-follow steps to achieve your goal. For example, you could give them a phone number to call for more information, provide an address so that they can write a letter of support, hand them a petition to sign at the end of your speech, or tell them for whom to vote.

Heather offered specific actions her listeners could take to address the problem of children serving as soldiers: "The first step we can take is to petition the members of the United Nations to enforce the treaties they have signed, and we can do this by joining the Red Hand Campaign." She made her action step simple and easy when she further explained to her audience:

> You can join this campaign by simply signing your name to a pre-written letter and tracing your hand on a red piece of construction paper after this [speech]. I will then cut and paste your handprint to your letter and forward them on to the UN.

The best action step spells out precisely the action your audience should take. Here, Heather tells her listeners what to do and what will happen next.

You can modify the motivated sequence to suit the needs of your topic and your audience. If, for example, you are speaking to a receptive audience, you do not have to spend a great deal of time on the need step. They already agree that the need is serious. They may, however, want to learn about specific actions that they can take to implement a solution to the problem. Therefore, you would be wise to emphasize the satisfaction and action steps.

Conversely, if you are speaking to a hostile audience, you should spend considerable time on the need step. Convince your audience that the problem is significant and that they should be concerned about the problem. You would probably not propose a lengthy, detailed action.

If your audience is neutral or indifferent, spend time getting their attention and inviting their interest in the problem. The attention and need steps should be emphasized.

The motivated sequence is a guide, not an absolute formula. Use it and the other suggestions about speech organization to help you achieve your specific objective. Be audience-centered; adapt your message to your listeners.

ENHANCING YOUR CREDIBILITY

15.1 Identify and use strategies to improve your initial, derived, and terminal credibility.

Credibility is a listener's view of a speaker. The three factors contributing to credibility are competence, trustworthiness, and dynamism. Initial credibility is your listeners' idea of your credibility before you start speaking. Derived credibility is the perception they form while you speak. Terminal credibility is the perception that remains after you've finished speaking. Specific strategies can enhance all three types of credibility.

Key Terms

Thinking Ethically

Catherine's father has been an editor for a popular Web site. Consequently, she knows a lot about Internet journalism. Is it ethical for Catherine to be introduced as an expert Internet journalist even though she has never been formally trained as a journalist and has held no professional positions as a journalist?

Assessing Your Audience-Centered Speaking Skill

Imagine that you are delivering your final speech of the semester in your public-speaking class. What specific strategies can you implement to enhance your initial, derived, and final credibility as a public speaker in the minds of your classmates?

USING LOGIC AND EVIDENCE TO PERSUADE

15.2 Use principles of effective logic and evidence to develop a persuasive message.

The effectiveness of logical arguments hinges on the proof you employ. Proof consists of evidence plus the reasoning that you use to draw conclusions from the evidence. Three types of reasoning are inductive reasoning, which moves from specific instances or examples to reach a general, probable conclusion; deductive reasoning, which moves from a general statement to reach a specific, more certain conclusion; and causal reasoning, which relates two or more events so as to be able to conclude that one or more of the events caused the others. Two popular types of inductive reasoning include reasoning by analogy and reasoning by sign. You can use four types of evidence: facts, examples, opinions, and statistics. Avoid using fallacious arguments.

Key Terms

Thinking Critically

Josh is speaking to his neighborhood homeowners' association, attempting to persuade his neighbors that a crimewatch program should be organized. What logical arguments and evidence would help him ethically achieve his persuasive objective?

Thinking Ethically

While surfing the Internet, Tony found just the statistics he needs for his persuasive speech. Yet he does not know the original source of the statistics—just the Internet address. Is that sufficient documentation for the statistics?

Assessing Your Audience-Centered Speaking Skill

The following Web sites amplify our discussion of reasoning fallacies to help you assess the arguments in persuasive messages you encounter. Consult these sites to assess your mastery of reasoning fallacies:

- www.nizkor.org/features/fallacies/
- www.unc.edu/depts/wcweb/handouts/fallacies.html
- www.fallacyfiles.org/

USING EMOTION TO PERSUADE

15.3 Employ effective techniques of using emotional appeal in a persuasive speech.

Emotional response theory has identified three dimensions of emotional response to a message: pleasure–displeasure, arousal–nonarousal, and dominance–powerlessness. Specific suggestions for appealing to audience emotions include using examples; emotion-arousing words; nonverbal behavior; selected appeals to fear; and appeals to such emotions as hope, pride, courage, and the revered.

Key Terms

Emotional response theory	319
Myth	322
Demagogue	323

Thinking Ethically

Karl believes strongly that the tragedy of the Holocaust could occur again. He plans to show exceptionally graphic photographs of Holocaust victims during his speech to his public-speaking class. Is it ethical to show graphic, emotion-arousing photos to a captive audience?

Assessing Your Audience-Centered Speaking Skill

You plan to convince your audience that they should donate to a drought-relief organization to help farmers cope with the effects that climate change has had on agriculture in your state. What emotional appeals would be both ethical and effective to support your position?

STRATEGIES FOR ADAPTING IDEAS TO PEOPLE AND PEOPLE TO IDEAS

15.4 Adapt your persuasive message to receptive, neutral, and unreceptive audiences.

Consider the following strategies to adapt ideas to people and people to ideas:

- *To persuade the receptive audience*: Identify with the audience. State your speaking objective. Tell the audience members what you want them to do. Ask for an immediate show of support. Use emotional appeals effectively. Make it easy for your listeners to act.

- *To persuade the neutral audience*: Capture your listeners' attention early in your speech by referring to beliefs that many listeners share. Relate your topic not only to your listeners but also to their families, friends, and loved ones. Be realistic in what you expect to accomplish.

- *For an unreceptive audience*: Don't immediately announce that you plan to change your listeners' minds. Begin your speech by noting areas of agreement before you discuss areas of disagreement. Establish your credibility early in your message. Acknowledge the opposing points of view that members of your audience may hold. Consider making understanding rather than advocacy your goal. Advance your strongest argument first. Don't expect a major shift in attitude from a hostile audience.

Thinking Ethically

Martika wants to convince her classmates, a captive audience, that they should join her in a 24-hour sit-in at the university president's office to protest the recent increase in tuition and fees. The president has made it clear that any attempt to occupy his office after normal office hours will result in arrests. Is it appropriate for Martika to use a classroom speech to encourage her classmates to participate in the sit-in?

Assessing Your Audience-Centered Speaking Skill

You are speaking to your public-speaking class to seek their help to clean up the beautiful San Marvelous River that runs through your community. Since most of the students in your class do not live in your community, they are not particularly interested in this topic, although some of your listeners are interested in environmental issues. What kind of audience are you facing, and what persuasive speaking strategies would be helpful in achieving your speaking goal?

STRATEGIES FOR ORGANIZING PERSUASIVE MESSAGES

15.5 Identify and use strategies for effectively organizing a persuasive speech.

Four patterns for organizing a persuasive speech are problem–solution, refutation, cause and effect, and the motivated sequence. The five steps of the motivated sequence are attention, need, satisfaction, visualization, and action. Adapt the motivated sequence to your specific audience and persuasive objective.

Thinking Critically

You are planning to persuade your audience to support a local ordinance that restricts noise after 10:00 P.M. in your community. Using the motivated sequence, identify ways to catch their attention, establish a need, identify a solution, visualize the benefits of this proposal, and present a specific action step they could join you in taking to help the ordinance pass.

Thinking Critically

Janice is pondering options for organizing her persuasive speech, which has the following purpose: "The audience should support the establishment of a wellness program for our company." Using this purpose, draft the main ideas for a speech organized according to each of the following organizational patterns: problem–solution, refutation, cause and effect, and motivated sequence.

Assessing Your Audience-Centered Speaking Skill

Analyze the "Dream" speech by Martin Luther King that appears in Appendix B to identify Dr. King's strategies for establishing credibility and his use of logic and emotion to achieve his persuasive goals. What elements of the motivated sequence do you see in the speech?

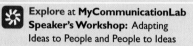

Explore at MyCommunicationLab
Speaker's Workshop: Adapting Ideas to People and People to Ideas

Dan Wiegand. *Iron Curtain*, 2011 National Churchill Museum, Fullerton, Missouri. Photo: David Ulmer/National Churchill Museum

OBJECTIVES

After studying this chapter you should be able to do the following:

16.1

Identify and explain the requirements for two types of speaking situations likely to arise in the workplace.

16.2

List and describe nine types of ceremonial speeches.

16.3

List and explain strategies for creating humor in a speech.

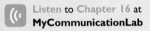
Listen to Chapter 16 at **MyCommunicationLab**

It's like singing "The Star-Spangled Banner" at the World Series. Nobody came to hear you. But it's not an official event unless you do it.

—Barney Frank

There is money in public speaking. Many of the politicians, athletes, and celebrities who speak professionally earn six- or even seven-figure fees for a single talk.

- Former president George W. Bush has charged about $150,000 per speech since leaving the presidency.[1]
- Former vice president and Nobel Peace Prize winner Al Gore has made as much as $156,000 for a speech on global climate change.[2]
- Former British prime minister Tony Blair made almost $616,000—more than $10,000 a minute—for two 30-minute speeches.[3]
- Business, real estate, and entertainment mogul Donald Trump was paid $1.5 million per lecture for 17 seminar appearances.[4]
- And former president Bill Clinton made nearly $40 million in speaking fees in the first years after he left the White House.[5]

But the record speaking fee may still be the $2 million for two 20-minute speeches given by former president Ronald Reagan to a Japanese company in 1989.[6]

Although most of us will never be rewarded so lavishly for our public-speaking efforts, it is likely that at some time we will be asked to make a business or professional presentation or to speak on some occasion that calls for celebration, commemoration, inspiration, or entertainment. Special occasions are important enough and frequent enough to merit study, regardless of the likelihood of their resulting in wealth or fame for the speaker.

In this chapter, we discuss the various types of speeches that may be called for on special occasions, and we examine the specific and unique audience expectations for each one. First, we will discuss two speaking situations that are likely to occur in the workplace. Then we will turn our attention to several types of ceremonial speeches and the humorous after-dinner speech.

16.1 Identify and explain the requirements for two types of speaking situations likely to arise in the workplace.

Public Speaking in the Workplace

In many careers and professions, public speaking is a daily part of the job. Workplace audiences may range from a group of three managers to a huge auditorium filled with company employees. Presentations may take the form of routine meeting management, reports to company executives, training seminars within the company, or public-relations speeches to people outside the company. The occasions and opportunities are many, and chances are good that you will be asked or expected to do some on-the-job public speaking in the course of your career.

Group Presentations

After a group has reached a decision, solved a problem, or uncovered new information, group members often present their findings to others. The audience-centered principles of preparing an effective speech apply to group members who are designing a group oral presentation just as they do to individual speakers.

As our familiar model in Figure 16.1 suggests, the central and most important step is to analyze the audience who will listen to the presentation. Who are these listeners? What are their interests and backgrounds? And what do they need to know? One business consultant suggests,

> Tune your audience in to radio station WIIFM— What's In It For Me. Tell your listeners where the benefits are for them, and they'll listen to everything you have to say.[7]

As you do when developing an individual speech, make sure you have a clear purpose and a central idea divided into logical main ideas. This is a group effort, so you need to make sure *each* group member can articulate the purpose, the central idea, main ideas, key supporting material, and the overall outline for the presentation.

Selecting a Presentation Format Unless a format for your group presentation has been specified, your group will need to determine how to deliver the presentation. Three primary formats for sharing reports and recommendations with an audience are the symposium presentation, the forum presentation, and the panel discussion.

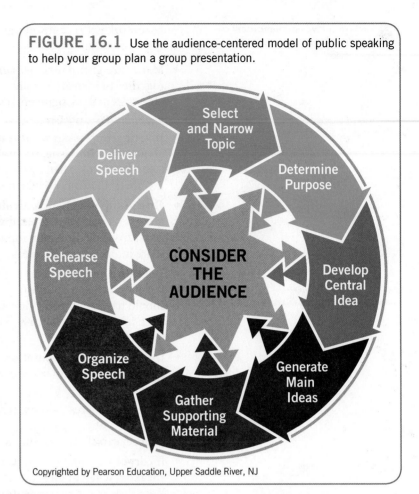

FIGURE 16.1 Use the audience-centered model of public speaking to help your group plan a group presentation.

- A **symposium** is a public discussion during which the members of a group share responsibility for presenting information to an audience. Usually a moderator and the group members are seated in front of the audience, and each group member is prepared to deliver a brief report. Each speaker should know what the others will present so the same ground is not covered twice. At the end of the speeches, the moderator may summarize the key points. The audience can then participate in a question-and-answer session or a forum presentation.

- In a **forum** presentation, audience members direct questions and comments to a group, and group members respond with short impromptu speeches. In ancient Rome, the *forum* was a marketplace where citizens went to shop and discuss the hot issues of the day. It later became a public meeting place where political speeches were often delivered.

  A forum often follows a more structured presentation, such as a symposium or a prepared speech by one group member. Forum presentations work best when all group members know the issues and are prepared to respond unhesitatingly to questioners.

- A **panel discussion** is an informative group presentation. Individuals on the panel may use notes on key facts or statistics, but they do not present formal speeches. Usually a panel discussion is organized and led by an appointed chairperson or moderator.

  An effective moderator gets all the panelists to participate, summarizes their statements, and serves as a gatekeeper to make sure that no member of the panel dominates the discussion. Panel discussions are often followed by a question-and-answer period, or forum.

Planning a Group Presentation Working in groups requires a coordinated team effort. If you are used to developing reports and speeches on your own, it may be a

symposium
A public discussion in which a series of short speeches is presented to an audience

forum
A question-and-answer session that usually follows a public discussion or symposium

panel discussion
A group discussion designed to inform an audience about issues or a problem or to make recommendations

Explore at **MyCommunicationLab**
Activity: "Build a Speech: Business
Presentation"

challenge to work with others on a group assignment. Consider these suggestions for enhancing teamwork:

- **Make sure group members understand the task or assignment, and work together to identify a topic.** Take a few moments to verbalize the goals and objectives of the assignment. Don't immediately plunge in and try to start dividing up the work just so you can hurry off to your next class or responsibility.

- **If your group assignment is to solve a problem or to inform the audience about a specific issue, try brainstorming to develop a topic or question** (see Chapter 6). Then assess your audience's interests as well as group members' interests and talents to help you choose among your ideas.

- **Give group members individual assignments.** After you decide on your group's presentation topic, divide up the tasks involved in investigating the issues. Also devise a plan for keeping in touch with one another frequently to share information and ideas.

- **Develop a group outline.** After group members have researched key issues, begin drafting an outline of your group presentation. Your presentation should have an introduction and a conclusion that reflect your group's work as an integrated problem-solving team. Decide who will present which portions of your outline.

- **Decide on your presentation format.** Determine whether you will use a symposium, a forum, a panel presentation, or some combination of these formats.

- **Rehearse the presentation.** Just as you would for an individual speech, rehearse the presentation. If you are using visual aids, be sure to incorporate them in your rehearsal. Also be sure to time your presentation when you rehearse.

- **Incorporate principles and skills of effective audience-centered public speaking when giving the group presentation.** Adapt to your listeners. Your delivery and comments should be well organized and fluent. Your visual aids should enhance your presentation by being clear and attractive.

Making a Group Presentation By now it should be clear that the skills needed to give a group presentation mirror those we've presented throughout the book. But because

The skills you learn in public-speaking class can help you when you are part of a workplace group presentation.

Photo: Bob Daemmrich/PhotoEdit, Inc

a group presentation creates the additional challenge of coordinating your communication efforts with other group or team members, keep the following tips in mind as you offer your conclusions or recommendations.

- **Clarify your purpose.** Just as with an individual speech, it is important for listeners to know what your group's speaking goal is and to understand why you are presenting the information to them; it is also important for each group member to be reminded of the overarching goal of the presentation. It would be useful if the first speaker could ensure that the audience has a good understanding of the group's purpose. If your group is responding to a specific discussion question, it may be useful to write the question or purpose of the presentation on a chalkboard, whiteboard, flipchart, or PowerPoint™ slide.

- **Use presentation aids effectively.** You can use presentation aids not only to clarify your purpose, but also to summarize key findings and recommendations. Visual aids can serve the important function of unifying your group presentation. If your group is using PowerPoint visuals, consider having each group member use the same template and font style to add to the coordinated look and feel of your presentation.

- **Choose someone to serve as coordinator or moderator.** Groups need a balance between structure and interaction. Without adequate structure, conversation can bounce from person to person and the presentation will lack a clear focus. A moderator can help provide needed structure to a group presentation by introducing both the topic and the group members. A moderator can also help keep track of time and ensure that no one either dominates the discussion or speaks too little.

- **Be ready to answer questions.** Communication, as we've emphasized, is more than just giving people information; it also includes responding to feedback and questions from listeners. Group presentations often include a question-and-answer session (forum) following the presentation. Besides being informed about your topic, it's a wise idea to have thoroughly read any written report the group has distributed.

In Chapter 11, we presented strategies for responding to questions, including tips for responding to hostile questions. If someone asks a question that has just been asked and answered, or asks an irrelevant or poorly worded question, don't criticize the questioner. Be polite, tactful, and gracious. Rather than self-righteously saying, "That's a dumb question" or "Someone just asked that," calmly provide an answer and move on. If you don't understand a question, ask for more clarification. Also, don't let a questioner start making a speech. If it looks as if a questioner is using the question-and-answer period to give an oration, gently ask, "And what is your question?" or "How can we help you?" This approach should elicit a question that you can then address and return the communication process back to the control of the group.

Public-Relations Speeches

People who work for professional associations, blood banks, utility companies, government agencies, universities, churches, or charitable institutions, as well as those employed by commercial enterprises, are often called on to speak to an audience about what their organization does or about a special project the organization has taken on. These speeches are **public-relations speeches**. They are designed to inform the public and improve relations with them—either in general, or because a particular program or situation has raised questions.

> **RECAP**
>
> ## TIPS FOR SUCCESSFUL GROUP PRESENTATIONS
>
> Work as a group to
> - Understand the task.
> - Brainstorm problem solutions.
> - Choose a presentation format.
> - Outline and rehearse the presentation.
> - Make the presentation and answer questions.
>
> Work as an individual to
> - Complete your assignment.
> - Contribute to meetings and rehearsals.
> - Participate in the presentation.

 Watch at **MyCommunicationLab** Video: "Group Project"

 Watch at **MyCommunicationLab** Video: "Intercultural Communication in Italy"

public-relations speeches
Speeches designed to inform the public, to strengthen alliances with them, and in some cases to recommend policy

A public-relations speaker begins by discussing the need or problem that has prompted the speech. Then he or she goes on to explain how the company or organization is working to meet the need or solve the problem—or why it believes there is no problem.

It is important in public-relations speaking to anticipate criticism. The speaker may acknowledge and counter potential problems or objections, especially when past presenters have encountered opposition to the policy or program. The speaker should emphasize the positive aspects of the policy or program and take care not to become defensive. He or she wants to leave the impression that the company or organization has carefully worked through the potential pitfalls and drawbacks. It should be noted that not all public-relations speeches make policy recommendations. Many simply summarize information for those who need to know.

For example, local developer Jack Brooks is well aware that many of those present at the city council meeting are opposed to his developing an area of land within the popular Smythson Creek greenbelt. Rather than ignore their objections, he deliberately and carefully addresses them:

> Many of you here tonight played in the Smythson Creek greenbelt as children. It was there that you learned to swim and that you hiked with your friends. I, too, share memories of those experiences.
>
> I want to assure you that my proposed development will actually help to preserve the greenbelt. We will dedicate in perpetuity an acre of unspoiled greenbelt for each acre we develop. Further, we will actively seek to preserve that unspoiled land by hiring an environmental specialist to oversee its protection.
>
> As things stand now, we risk losing the entire greenbelt to pollution and unmanaged use. I can promise a desirable residential development, plus the preservation of at least half the natural environment.

16.2 — List and describe nine types of ceremonial speeches.

Ceremonial Speaking

Kairos is the Greek term rhetoricians use to describe the circumstances surrounding, or the occasion for, a speech. If the occasion is one that brings people together to celebrate, thank, or praise someone, or to mourn, a speech given on that occasion is known as a **ceremonial,** or **epideictic, speech.** We will explore nine types of ceremonial speeches: introductions, toasts, award presentations, nominations, acceptances, keynote addresses, commencement addresses, commemorative addresses and tributes, and eulogies.

Introductions

Most of us have heard poor introductions. A nervous speaker making a **speech of introduction** stands up and mispronounces the main speaker's name. Or the introducer speaks for five or ten minutes before yielding to the main speaker.

An introductory speech is much like an informative speech. The speaker delivers the introduction to provide information to the audience about the main speaker.

The ultimate purpose of an introduction, however, is to arouse interest in the speaker and his or her topic. In fact, when you are asked to introduce a featured speaker or an honored guest, your purposes are similar to those of a good speech introduction: You need to get the attention of the audience, build the speaker's credibility, and introduce the speaker's general subject. You also need to make the speaker feel welcome, while revealing some of the speaker's personal qualities so that the audience can feel they know the speaker more intimately. There are two cardinal rules for giving introductory speeches:

kairos
The circumstances surrounding the speech or the occasion for a speech

ceremonial (epideictic) speech
A speech delivered on a special occasion for celebration, thanksgiving, praise, or mourning

speech of introduction
A speech that provides information about another speaker

Be Brief The audience has come to hear the main speaker or honor the guest, not to listen to you.

Be Accurate Nothing so disturbs a speaker as having to begin by correcting the introducer. If you are going to introduce someone at a meeting or dinner, ask that person to supply you with biographical data beforehand. If someone else provides you with the speaker's background, make sure the information is accurate. Be certain that you know how to pronounce the speaker's name and any other names or terms you will need to use.

The following short speech of introduction adheres to the two criteria: It's brief, and it's accurate.

> This evening, friends, we have the opportunity to hear one of the most innovative mayors in the history of our community. Mary Norris's experience in running her own real-estate business gave her an opportunity to pilot a new approach to attracting new businesses to our community, even before she was elected mayor in last year's landslide victory. She was recently recognized as the most successful mayor in our state by the Good Government League. Not only is she a skilled manager and spokesperson for our city, but she is also a warm and caring person. I am pleased to introduce my friend Mary Norris.

Finally, keep the needs of your audience in mind at all times. If the person you are introducing truly needs no introduction to the group, do not give one! Just welcome the speaker and step aside. (Note that the president of the United States is always introduced simply: "Ladies and gentlemen, the president of the United States.")

Toasts

Most people are asked at one time or another to provide a **toast** for some momentous occasion—a wedding, a celebration of the birth of a baby, a reunion of friends, a successful business venture. A toast is a brief salute to such an occasion, usually accompanied by a round of drinks and immediately followed by the raising or clinking together of glasses or goblets. The custom is said to have taken its name from the old custom of tossing a bit of bread or a crouton into a beverage for flavoring.[9] "Drinking the toast" was somewhat like enjoying a dunked doughnut.

The modern toast is usually quite short—only a few sentences at most. Some toasts are very personal, as, for example, one given by a wedding guest who is a close friend of both the bride and the groom:

> I would like to say a few words about this couple. You see, I knew Rachel and Ben before they were a couple—when they were friends. I first met Rachel when we were freshmen in high school. Her sarcastic sense of humor has kept me laughing ever since.[10]

In contrast, a toast made by someone who does not know the primary celebrants so well may be more generic. Here is an example of such a generic wedding toast:

> When the roaring flames of your love have burned down to embers, may you find that you've married your best friend.[11]

If you are asked to make an impromptu toast, let your audience and the occasion dictate what you say. Sincerity is more important than wit. At a dinner your authors attended in Moscow a few years ago, all the guests were asked to stand at some point during the meal and offer a toast. Although this Russian custom took

Watch at **MyCommunicationLab** **Video:** "A Wedding Toast"

toast
A brief salute to a momentous occasion

us by surprise, one of our friends gave a heartfelt and well-received toast that went something like this:

> We have spent the past week enjoying both the natural beauty and the man-made marvels of your country. We have visited the exquisite palaces of the czars and stood in amazement before some of the world's great art treasures. But we have also discovered that the most important national resource of Russia is the warmth of her people. Here's to new and lasting friendships.

Our Russian hosts were most appreciative. The rest of us were impressed. Mary's toast was a resounding success because she spoke sincerely about her audience and the occasion.

Award Presentations

Presenting an award is somewhat like introducing a speaker or a guest: Remember that the audience did not come to hear you, but to see and hear the winner of the award. Nevertheless, making an **award presentation**, a speech that accompanies the conferring of an award, is an important responsibility. An award presentation has several distinct components.

Refer to the Occasion of the Presentation First, when presenting an award, you should refer to the occasion of the presentation. Awards are often given to mark the anniversary of a special event, the completion of a long-range task, the accomplishments of a lifetime, or high achievement in some field.

Explain the History and Significance of the Award Next, you should talk about the history and significance of the award. This section of the speech may be fairly long if the audience knows little about the award; it will be brief if the audience is already familiar with the history and purpose of the award. Whatever the award, a discussion of its significance will add to its meaning for the person who receives it.

Name the Award Recipient Finally, you will name the person to whom the award has been given. The longest part of this segment of the speech is a glowing description of the achievements that elicited the award. If the name of the person receiving the award has already been made public, you may refer to him or her by name throughout your description. If you are going to announce the individual's name for the first time, you will probably want to recite the achievements first and leave the person's name for last. Even though some members of the audience may recognize the recipient from your description, you should still save the drama of the actual announcement until the last moment.

Nominations

A **nomination speech** is similar to an award presentation. It too involves noting the occasion and describing the purpose and significance of, in this case, the office to be filled. The person making the nomination should explain clearly why the nominee's skills, talents, and past achievements serve as qualifications for the position. And the actual nomination should come at the end of the speech.

When Senate minority leader Everett Dirksen nominated Barry Goldwater as the Republican presidential candidate in

---

Explore at MyCommunicationLab Activity: "Build a Speech: Special Occasion Speech"

CONSIDER THE AUDIENCE

award presentation
A speech that accompanies the conferring of an award

nomination speech
A speech that officially names someone as a candidate for an office or a position

Both award presenters and speakers accepting awards should speak about the award and what it means to the audience as well as to the winner.

Photo: Inspirestock Inc./Alamy

1964, he emphasized those personal qualities that he thought would appeal to the audience:

> Whether in commerce or finance, in business or industry, in private or public service, there is such a thing as Competence. . . . Barry Goldwater has demonstrated it over and over in his every activity. As Chief of Staff of his state National Guard, he brought about its desegregation shortly after World War II and long before Civil Rights became a burning issue. He brought integration to his own retail enterprises. For his own employees he established the five-day week and a health and life insurance plan. All this was done without fanfare or the marching of bands.[12]

And Dirksen ended his speech with the nomination itself:

> I nominate my friend and colleague Barry Goldwater of Arizona to be the Republican candidate for President of the United States.

Acceptances

Anyone who receives an award or a nomination usually responds with a brief **acceptance speech**. Acceptance speeches may have something of a bad name because of the lengthy, emotional, rambling, and generally boring speeches delivered annually on prime-time TV by the winners of the film industry's Oscars. The late humorist Erma Bombeck once wryly noted,

> People exchange wedding vows in under thirty seconds. . . . You only get thirty seconds to come up with the final "Jeopardy" answer. My kids can demolish a pizza in thirty seconds.
> So how long does it take to say, "Thank you?"[13]

The same audience who may resent a long oration will readily appreciate a brief, heartfelt expression of thanks. In fact, brief acceptance speeches can be quite insightful, even inspiring, and they can leave the audience feeling no doubt that the right person won the award. Two months before he died in 1979, actor John Wayne accepted an honorary Oscar with these touching words:

> Thank you, ladies and gentlemen. Your applause is just about the only medicine a fella would ever need. I'm mighty pleased I can amble here tonight. Oscar and I have something in common. Oscar first came on the Hollywood scene in 1928. So did I. We're both a little weatherbeaten, but we're still here and plan to be around a whole lot longer.[14]

If you ever have to give an acceptance speech, it may be an impromptu speech because you may not know that you have won until the award is presented. A fairly simple formula should help you compose a good acceptance speech on the spur of the moment.

Say Thank You First, you should thank the person making the presentation and the organization that he or she represents. It is also gracious to thank a few people who have contributed greatly to your success—but resist thanking everyone you have ever known, down to the family dog.

Comment on What the Award Means to You Next, you should comment on the meaning or significance of the award to you. You may also wish to reflect on the larger significance of the award to the people and the ideals it honors, as did Barack Obama in his acceptance of the Nobel Peace Prize in 2009:

Watch at **MyCommunicationLab** Video: "2007 Clarion Award, Kevin Spacey"

Watch at **MyCommunicationLab** Video: "Critique: 'Presenting a Dance Award' and 'Accepting a Dance Award'"

acceptance speech
A speech of thanks for an award, nomination, or other honor

I receive this honor with deep gratitude and great humility. It is an award that speaks to our highest aspirations—that for all the cruelty and hardship of our world, we are not mere prisoners of fate. Our actions matter, and can bend history in the direction of justice.[15]

Discuss How the Award Is Relevant to Your Audience Finally, try to find some meaning the award may have for your audience—people who respect your accomplishments and who may themselves aspire to similar achievements. In what has become one of the most often quoted acceptance speeches ever made, novelist William Faulkner dedicated his 1950 Nobel Prize for Literature to

the young men and women already dedicated to the same anguish and travail, among whom is already that one who will some day stand here where I am standing.[16]

Keynote Addresses

A **keynote address** is usually presented at or near the beginning of a meeting or conference. The keynote emphasizes the importance of the topic or the purpose of the meeting, motivates the audience to learn more or work harder, and sets the theme and tone for other speakers and events.

The hardest task of the keynote speaker is arousing audience interest. Legendary musician Bruce Springsteen met this challenge when he delivered his keynote speech at the 2012 SXSW music festival in Austin, Texas.

One way a keynote speaker can interest and inspire is to incorporate examples and illustrations to which the audience can relate. The late Texas congresswoman Barbara Jordan delivered keynote addresses at two Democratic National Conventions, one in 1976 and the other in 1992. Note how she used specific examples in this excerpt from the 1992 address:

keynote address
A speech that sets the theme and tone for a meeting or conference

The American dream . . . is slipping away from too many. It is slipping away from too many black and brown mothers and their children; from the homeless of every color and sex; from the immigrants living in communities without water and sewer systems. The American dream is slipping away from the workers whose jobs are no longer there because we are better at building war equipment that sits in warehouses than we are at building decent housing.[17]

Bruce Springsteen opened his keynote address the 2012 SXSW music festival by wryly pointing out the difficulty in getting an audience's attention for a keynote speech, "How important can this speech be if we're giving it at noon? It can't be that important. Every decent musician in town is asleep. . . ."[18] Springsteen apparently met the challenge of the occasion as his speech was later credited with holding the audience "spellbound."[19]
Photo: Jack Plunkett/AP Images

Commencement Addresses

Cartoonist Garry Trudeau has said that the **commencement address** was invented

Watch at **MyCommunicationLab**
Video: "Commencement Address"

> largely in the belief that outgoing college students should never be released into the world until they have been properly sedated.[20]

Unfortunately, most commencement speeches of the past probably deserved Trudeau's assessment. Commencement speakers often seemed oblivious to their audience on an occasion that demands and deserves audience-centeredness. In contrast, however, more recent commencement speeches have been described as

> much more personal, infused with self-deprecating humor, raunchy asides and references to the speaker's own humble or distant origins.[21]

An audience-centered commencement address must fulfill two important functions.

Praise the Graduates First, the commencement speaker should praise the graduating class. Because the audience includes the families and friends of the graduates, the commencement speaker can gain their goodwill (as well as that of the graduates themselves) by pointing out the significance of the graduates' accomplishments. New York Mayor Michael Bloomberg congratulated the 2013 graduating class of Stanford University with this tribute:

> There's no question that the Class of 2013 is . . . "The greatest class in the history of Stanford!"[22]

Focus on the Future Second, the audience-centered commencement speaker should turn graduates toward the future. A commencement address is not the proper forum in which to bemoan the world's inevitable destruction or the certain gloomy economic future of today's graduates. Rather, commencement speakers should suggest bright new goals and try to inspire the graduates to reach for them, as oceanographer Sylvia Earle did with these words:

> You can hold the world in your hands on your desktop, your laptop. You can Google-earth. You can dive into the ocean in ways that no one who preceded this time could do it. You, literally, hold the world in your hands.[23]

Commencement speakers who want to be audience-centered can pick up additional tips from former Hewlett Packard CEO Carly S. Fiorina, who consulted by email with the graduating class of the Massachusetts Institute of Technology before her commencement address to them. She discovered that students wanted a speech based on life experience, not theory, and advice on how to make the decisions they needed to make in life. And, Fiorina adds, "On one point there was complete unanimity: Please don't run over your time."[24]

Commemorative Addresses

A **commemorative address**, a speech delivered during ceremonies held to celebrate some past event, is likely to include a tribute to the person or persons involved. For example, a speech given on the Fourth of July both commemorates the signing of the Declaration of Independence and pays tribute to those who signed it. Your town's sesquicentennial celebrates both the founding and the founders of the town. And if you were asked to speak at the reception for your grandparents' fiftieth wedding anniversary, you would probably relate the stories they've told you

commencement address
A speech delivered at a graduation or commencement ceremony

commemorative address
A speech delivered during ceremonies held in memory of some past event and/or the person or persons involved

Watch at **MyCommunicationLab**
Video: "Tribute to Steve Prefontaine"

of their wedding day and then go on to praise their accomplishments during their fifty years together.

A commemorative speaker is, in part, an informative speaker. He or she needs to present some facts about the event and/or the people being celebrated. Then the speaker builds on those facts, urging the audience to let past accomplishments inspire them to achieve new goals.

Speaking at Pointe du Hoc, France, during ceremonies in June 1994 to commemorate the fifty-year anniversary of D-Day, President Bill Clinton paid tribute to the assembled veterans:

> We are the children of your sacrifice. We are the sons and daughters you saved from tyranny's reach. We grew up behind the shield of the strong alliances you forged in blood upon these beaches, on the shores of the Pacific and in the skies above us. We flourished in the nation you came home to build. The most difficult days of your lives bought us fifty years of freedom.[25]

His tribute completed, Clinton added this challenge:

> Let us carry on the work you began here. You completed your mission here, but the mission of freedom goes on; the battle continues.

Eulogies

Watch at **MyCommunicationLab**
Video: "Eulogy for Charlie Brown"

A **eulogy**—a speech of tribute delivered when someone has died—can be one of the most significant and memorable and also one of the most challenging forms of commemorative address. As the editor of a recent collection of eulogies notes,

> A good eulogy can be . . . a bridge between the living and the dead, between us and them, memory and eternity. The more specific and real the remembrances spoken, the stronger the bridge.[26]

When you deliver a eulogy, you should mention—indeed, linger on—the unique achievements of the person to whom you are paying tribute and, of course, express a sense of loss. The mother of a child killed in the 2012 Newtown, Connecticut, school shooting, opened her eulogy for her little boy on this heart-wrenching note of grief:

> The sky is crying, and the flags are at half-mast. It is a sad, sad day.[27]

But it is also proper in a eulogy to include personal and even humorous recollections of the person who has died. In his eulogy for his beloved Aunt Betty, John T. Masterson, Jr., related this humorous story:

> Whereas other relatives sent books, clothing, or sensible toys for Christmas and birthdays, Aunt Betty tended toward the offbeat. . . . There was the year she (or the mail order house) got the order number wrong and sent me reflective driveway markers for Christmas. The thing about Aunt Betty was that if you received a gift like that, you didn't recognize it as a mistake; instead, my family and I sat around the Christmas tree trying to figure out the joke![28]

Finally, turn to the living, and encourage them to transcend their sorrow and sense of loss and feel instead gratitude that the dead person was once alive among them.

eulogy
A speech of tribute delivered when someone has died

RECAP

TYPES OF CEREMONIAL SPEECHES

- Introductions
- Toasts
- Award presentations
- Nominations
- Acceptances
- Keynote addresses
- Commencement addresses
- Commemorative addresses and tributes
- Eulogies

After-Dinner Speaking: Using Humor Effectively

16.3   List and explain strategies for creating humor in a speech.

> If you are a human being or even a reasonably alert shrub, chances are that sooner or later a club or organization will ask you to give a speech. The United States is infested with clubs and organizations, constantly engaging in a variety of worthwhile group activities such as (1) eating lunch; (2) eating dinner; (3) eating breakfast; and of course (4) holding banquets. The result is that there is a constant demand for post-meal speakers, because otherwise all you'd hear would be the sounds of digestion.[29]

Watch at **MyCommunicationLab**
Video: "After Dinner Speech"

Read at **MyCommunicationLab**
Learning From Great Speakers:
Dave Barry

With typically irreverent wit, columnist Dave Barry thus begins his observations of the activity known as after-dinner speaking. Certainly he is right about one thing: the popularity of mealtime meetings and banquets with business and professional organizations and service clubs. And such a meeting inevitably requires a humorous **after-dinner speech**.

Interestingly, not only is the after-dinner speech not always after *dinner* (as Barry points out, the meal is just as likely to be breakfast or lunch), but it is also not always *after* anything. The after-dinner speech may be delivered before the meal or even between courses.

Former First Lady Barbara Bush preferred to schedule speeches first and dinner later during state dinners. In another variation, Librarian of Congress James Billington, at a dinner in honor of philosopher Alexis de Tocqueville, served up one speech between each course, "so that one had to earn the next course by listening to the speech preceding it."[30] Regardless of the variation, the after-dinner speech is something of an institution, one with which a public speaker should be prepared to cope.

After-dinner speeches may present information or persuade, but their primary purpose is to entertain—arguably the most inherently audience-centered of the three general purposes for speaking discussed in Chapter 6. We summarize several strategies for entertaining audiences with humor in Table 16.1 and discuss them in detail next.

Humorous Topics

Because humor is listener-centered, the central question for the after-dinner speaker seeking a topic must be this: What do audiences find funny?

after-dinner speech
A humorous presentation, usually delivered in conjunction with a mealtime meeting or banquet

---

TABLE 16.1   STRATEGIES FOR ACHIEVING HUMOR IN AFTER-DINNER SPEECHES

Humorous Topics	Inherently funny subjects or humorous treatments of more serious subjects
Humorous Stories	Funny anecdotes
Humorous Verbal Strategies	
Play on words	An intentional error such as puns, spoonerisms, and malapropisms
Hyperbole	Exaggeration
Understatement	Downplaying a fact or event
Verbal irony	Saying just the opposite of what one means
Wit	An unexpected turn at the end of a fact or incident
Humorous Nonverbal Strategies	Physical or vocal elements such as posture, gesture, pauses, and intonation

The Comedy Gym in Austin, Texas, a school for aspiring stand-up comedians, advocates that speakers start with "themselves, their lives, what makes them laugh."[31] Audiences almost always enjoy hearing a speaker poke fun at himself or herself. Comedy writer John Macks points out that self-deprecating humor is "an instant way to establish a rapport with an audience."[32]

Even serious subjects can lend themselves to humorous presentations. One speechwriter notes that humor can help a speaker achieve rapport with the audience and can help the audience remember the speaker's message:

> If you can find a way to make a point with humor, you've improved the odds of making your message stick. For example, say you're expecting a tax increase, and you want to let your audience know. You might say, "Well, Congress has finally decided how to divide up the pie; trouble is, *we're* the pie."[33]

Increased taxes, not an inherently humorous topic, can still be treated humorously. So can other serious topics. Earlier in this chapter we discussed the use of humor in eulogies. Gun control, the U.S. health care industry, and capitalism—subjects tackled by Michael Moore in the documentary films *Bowling for Columbine, Sicko*, and *Capitalism: A Love Story*—are serious topics made more palatable to listeners by the use of humor. For example, in *Sicko*,

> a scrolling text of the pre-existing medical conditions that insurance companies use to reject prospective applicants is set to the *Star Wars* theme against an outer-space backdrop.[34]

Although Moore's medium is film rather than speech, the same principle applies: Many serious subjects can be treated with humor.

Are any subjects *in*appropriate for an after-dinner speech? A few years ago, comedian Robin Williams appeared on a late-night television talk show to discuss a film in which Williams played a Protestant minister. Spinning off from that character, Williams launched into a comic treatment of pedophilia among Catholic priests that provoked outrage from Catholic organizations.

While Williams's comic routines often push the boundaries of propriety and taste, audience-centered public speakers should exercise greater restraint. Because it is the audience that "gives attempts at humor their success or failure,"[35] topics that might create a great deal of emotional noise (such as grief or anger) for particular audiences would not be good topics for humorous speeches to those groups. A humorous treatment of childhood cancer would most likely only distress an audience of parents who had lost children to that disease.

Humorous Stories

Humorous stories should be simple. Complicated stories and jokes are rarely perceived by audiences as funny. Jay Leno claims that

> Jokes work best when they're easy to understand."[36]

Co-writers Michael Blastland and David Spiegelhalter agree, adding,

> If nothing happens in a story, it is not usually a story, it's a joke.[37]

Successful after-dinner speakers also need a broad repertoire of jokes, humorous anecdotes, and one-liners; one says that she gathers approximately 25 to 30 in preparation for writing a speech.[38] She explains,

The purpose of most after-dinner speeches is to entertain the audience. What humorous strategies can this speaker use?

Photo: pojoslaw/Fotolia

This will be reduced to the best and most appropriate 6 or 7, but one needs as much material as possible to begin with.

Finally, it is important to know your anecdotes very well. Nothing deflates a humorous story more than getting halfway through one and saying, "Oh, and I forgot to tell you. . . ." Rehearse your jokes. Only if you know the material can you hope to deliver it with the intonation and timing that will make it funny.

Humorous Verbal Strategies

A funny story or a one-liner may rely on any of the following verbal strategies for humorous effect.

Pun   Most of us are familiar with the **pun**, which relies on double meanings to create humor. For example, an old joke in which an exasperated speaker tries to explain the meaning of "hide" by shouting, "Hide! Hide! A cow's outside!" provokes the response, "I'm not afraid of cows." The joke relies on two meanings of the word *hide*: to conceal oneself and the skin (*outside*) of an animal.

Spoonerism   Another play on words is the **spoonerism**, named for William Spooner, a professor at Oxford University in the 1930s who frequently used it (inadvertently, in his case). A spoonerism occurs when someone switches the initial sounds of words in a single phrase: "sublic peaking" instead of "public speaking," for example. In one joke that relies on a spoonerism, the Chatanooga Choo-choo becomes the "cat who chewed the new shoes." Many parodies and satires employ spoonerisms to avoid charges of libel or copyright infringement; a spoonerism might be employed to name a boy wizard "Perry Hotter."

Malapropism   Named for the unfortunate character Mrs. Malaprop in Richard Brinsley Sheridan's eighteenth-century play *The School for Scandal*, a **malapropism** is the mistaken use of a word that sounds much like the intended word: "destruction" for "instruction," for example.

Hyperbole   Exaggeration, or **hyperbole**, is often funny. In an after-dinner speech on "The Alphabet and Simplified Spelling," Mark Twain claimed,

> Simplified spelling brought about sun-spots, the San Francisco earthquake, and the recent business depression, which we would never have had if spelling had been left all alone.[39]

Of course, spelling could not have caused such catastrophes, so by using hyperbole, Twain makes his point in a humorous way.

Understatement   The opposite of hyperbole, **understatement** involves downplaying a fact or event. Microsoft founder and Harvard dropout Bill Gates downplayed his meteoric success by telling a graduating class at one Ivy League university,

> I did the best of everyone who failed.[40]

Verbal Irony   A speaker who employs **verbal irony** says just the opposite of what he or she really means. Student Chris O'Keefe opens his speech on reading Shakespeare with this statement:

> At a certain point in my life, I came to the realization that I wanted to spend my life's effort to become a great playwright.[41]

pun
The use of double meanings to create humor

spoonerism
A phrase in which the initial sounds of words are switched

malapropism
The mistaken use of a word that sounds much like the intended word

hyperbole
Exaggeration

understatement
Downplaying a fact or event

verbal irony
Saying the opposite of what one means

Chris reveals the verbal irony of the statement when he continues,

> It has been about an hour and a half now and the feeling is still going strong.

Wit One of the most frequently used verbal strategies for achieving humor is the use of **wit**: relating an incident that takes an unexpected turn at the end. Research suggests that witty humor may enhance a speaker's credibility.[42] Accepting the 2007 Oscar for Best Actress, Helen Mirren paid tribute to the monarch she had portrayed on screen in *The Queen*,

> For 50 years and more, Elizabeth Windsor has maintained her dignity, her sense of duty and her hairstyle.[43]

The wit occurs in the final phrase "her hairstyle," which catches off-guard the audience anticipating another majestic attribute.

Humorous Nonverbal Strategies

After-dinner speakers often create humor through such nonverbal cues as posture, gesture, and voice. Well-timed pauses are especially crucial delivery cues for after-dinner speakers to master. One experienced after-dinner speaker advocates

> a slight pause before the punch line, then pause while the audience is laughing."[44]

It is true that some people seem to be "naturally" funny. If you are not one of them—if, for example, you struggle to get a laugh from even the funniest joke—you may still be able to use the strategies outlined above to prepare and deliver an after-dinner speech that is lighthearted and clever, if not uproariously funny. Such a speech can still be a success.

wit
Relating an incident that takes an unexpected turn at the end

STUDY GUIDE

REVIEW, APPLY, AND ASSESS

PUBLIC SPEAKING IN THE WORKPLACE

16.1 Identify and explain the requirements for two types of speaking situations likely to arise in the workplace.

Public-speaking skills are used frequently in the workplace when making group presentations or representing your company or profession before the public. Group presentation formats include symposium, forum, and panel discussion events. Group members should work individually and with the group to plan and make group presentations. Public-relations speeches inform the public and improve an organization's relationships with its public.

Key Terms

Assessing Your Audience-Centered Speaking Skill

A friend asks your advice about how to prepare for her first presentation to her colleagues in a new job. Explain how she can apply to her workplace speaking task some of the principles and skills you have learned in this book.

CEREMONIAL SPEAKING

16.2 List and describe nine types of ceremonial speeches.

Chances are that at some time you will be called on to speak at an occasion that calls for celebration, commemoration, inspiration, or entertainment. These special-occasion speeches require you to apply your speaking skills to unique situations. This chapter offers advice for making these ceremonial speeches, including introductions, toasts, award presentations, nominations, acceptances, keynote addresses, commencement addresses, commemorative addresses and tributes, and eulogies.

Key Terms

Thinking Ethically

Several Web sites offer eulogy writing services or prewritten generic eulogies, such as a eulogy "for a grandmother," for around $30 to $40. If you were asked to deliver a eulogy, would it be ethical to buy such a speech?

Assessing Your Audience-Centered Speaking Skill

You have been asked to introduce at your school a Pulitzer Prize–winning poet who will be reading from her work. What will you do to ensure that you follow the two cardinal rules of introductory speeches?

AFTER-DINNER SPEAKING: USING HUMOR EFFECTIVELY

16.3 List and explain strategies for creating humor in a speech.

After-dinner speaking is an established institution in which speakers entertain through the use of humorous topics and stories, humorous verbal strategies, and humorous nonverbal strategies.

Key Terms

Explore at **MyCommunicationLab**
Speaker's Workshop: Introducing a Speaker

SPEAKING IN SMALL GROUPS

Groups are an integral part of our lives. Work groups, family groups, therapy groups, committees, and class-project groups are just a few of the groups in which we may participate at one time or another. Chances are that you have had considerable experience in communicating in small groups.

Why learn about group communication in a public-speaking class? Aristotle identified the link between public speaking and group discussion over two thousand years ago when he wrote "Rhetoric is the counterpart of dialectic." He meant that our efforts to persuade are closely linked to our group efforts to search for truth.

In Aristotle's time, people gathered to discuss and decide public issues in a democratic manner. Today we still turn to a committee, jury, or task force to get facts and make recommendations. We still "search for truth" in groups. And, as in ancient Athens, once we believe we have found the truth, we present the message to others in speeches and lectures.

In this appendix, you will learn essential communication principles and skills to help you work as a productive member of a small group. Specifically, you will discover what small group communication is, learn ways to improve group problem solving, enhance your leadership skills, and become an effective group participant or group leader.[1]

What is **small group communication**? It is interaction among three to a dozen people who share a common purpose, feel a sense of belonging to the group, and influence one another. Communication in groups larger than 12 people usually resembles public speaking more than small group communication.

A **team** is a special kind of group. It is a coordinated small group of people organized to work together with clearly defined roles and responsibilities, explicitly stated rules for operation, and well-defined goals.[2] All teams are groups, but not all groups are teams. A team, as our definition suggests, coordinates its efforts through a clearly defined structure of who does what. Think of a sports team in which members play by rules, have assigned roles, and have a clear objective—to win the game. Work teams too have well-defined procedures for accomplishing tasks. Teams are formed for a variety of reasons, such as to sell products, elect a political candidate, or build an international space station.

Working in groups and teams has several advantages compared to working on projects alone. Groups typically make better-quality decisions than do individuals for several reasons:[3]

- Groups usually have more information available.
- Groups are often more creative; the very presence of others can spark innovation.
- When you work in groups, you're more likely to remember what you discussed because you were actively involved in processing information.
- Group participation usually results in group members being more satisfied with their results than if someone had just told them what to do.

Although we've characterized working in groups as a positive experience, you also know that working in groups can be challenging, mainly for these reasons:[4]

- Group members may use excessive pressure to get others to conform to their point of view.

small group communication

Interaction among three to twelve people who share a common purpose, feel a sense of belonging to the group, and influence one another

team

A coordinated small group of people organized to work together with clearly defined roles and responsibilities, explicit rules, and well-defined goals

- One person may dominate the discussion.
- Some group members may rely too much on others and may not do their part.
- Group work is more time-consuming (many people consider this the biggest disadvantage).

The goal of this appendix is to help decrease the disadvantages and increase the advantages of working with others.

Solving Problems in Groups and Teams

A central purpose of many groups and teams is to solve problems. Problem solving is a process of finding ways of overcoming obstacles to achieve a desired goal: How can we raise money for the new library? What should be done to improve the local economy? How can we make higher education affordable for everyone in our state? Each of these questions implies that there is an obstacle (lack of money) blocking the achievement of a desired goal (new library, stronger local economy, affordable education).

Imagine that you have been asked to suggest ways to make a college education more affordable. The problem: The high cost of higher education keeps many people from attending college. How would you begin to organize a group to solve this problem? In 1910, John Dewey, philosopher and educator, identified a method of problem solving that he called **reflective thinking**.[5] His multistep method has been adapted by many groups as a way to organize the process of solving problems. Here are the steps Dewey recommended:

1. Identify and define the problem.
2. Analyze the problem.
3. Generate possible solutions.
4. Select the best solution.
5. Test and implement the solution.

Although not every problem-solving discussion has to follow these steps, reflective thinking does provide a helpful blueprint that can relieve some of the uncertainty that exists when groups try to solve problems.

1. **Identify and Define the Problem** Groups work best when they define their problem clearly and early in their problem-solving process. To reach a clear definition, the group should consider the following questions:

   - What is the specific problem that concerns us?
   - What terms, concepts, or ideas do we need to understand in order to solve the problem?
   - Who is harmed by the problem?
   - When do the harmful effects occur?

   Policy questions can help define a problem and also identify the course of action that should be taken to solve it. As you recall from Chapter 14, policy questions often begin with a phrase such as "What should be done about" or "What could be done to improve." Here are examples:

   - What should be done to improve security at U.S. airports?
   - What should be done to increase employment in our state?
   - What steps could be taken to improve the U.S. trade balance with other countries?

reflective thinking

A method of structuring a problem-solving discussion that involves (1) identifying and defining the problem, (2) analyzing the problem, (3) generating possible solutions, (4) selecting the best solution, and (5) testing and implementing the solution

If your group were investigating the high cost of pursuing a college education, for example, after defining such key terms as "higher education" and "college" and gathering statistics about the magnitude of the problem, you could phrase your policy question this way: "What could be done to reduce the high cost of attending college?"

2. **Analyze the Problem** Ray Kroc, founder of McDonald's, said, "Nothing is particularly hard if you divide it into small jobs." Once the group understands the problem and has a well-worded question, the next step is to analyze the problem. **Analysis** is a process of examining the causes, effects, symptoms, history, and other background information that will help a group reach a solution. Analysis breaks a large problem into smaller parts. When analyzing a problem, a group should consider the following questions:

- What is the history of the problem?
- How extensive is the problem?
- What are the causes, effects, and symptoms of the problem?
- Can the problem be subdivided for further definition and analysis?
- What methods do we already have for solving the problem, and what are their limitations?
- What obstacles might keep us from reaching a solution?

To analyze the problem of the high cost of attending college, your discussion group will have to conduct research into the history of the problem and existing methods of solving it (see Chapter 7).

Included in the process of analyzing the problem is identifying criteria. **Criteria** are standards for identifying an acceptable solution. They help you recognize a good solution when you discover one; criteria also help the group stay focused on its goal. Typical criteria for an acceptable solution specify that the solution should be implemented on schedule, should be agreed to by all group members, should be achieved within a given budget, and should remove the obstacles causing the problem.

3. **Generate Possible Solutions** When your discussion group has identified, defined, and analyzed the problem, you will be ready to generate possible solutions using group brainstorming. Guidelines for effective group brainstorming are similar to those presented in Chapter 6 for brainstorming speech topics.

- **Set aside judgment and criticism.** Criticism and faultfinding stifle creativity. If group members find withholding judgment difficult, you can have the individual members write suggestions on paper first and then share the ideas with the group or use an electronic brainstorming app that allows participants to share ideas anonymously.
- **Think of as many possible solutions to the problem as you can.** All ideas are acceptable, even wild and crazy ones. Piggyback off one another's ideas. All members must come up with at least one idea.
- **Have a member of the group record all the ideas that are mentioned.** Use a flipchart or chalkboard for in-person brainstorming, or an app or collaboration tool for electronic brainstorming, so that all group members can see and respond to the ideas.
- **After a set time has elapsed, evaluate the ideas, using criteria the group has established.** Approach the solutions positively. Do not be quick to dismiss an idea, but do voice any concerns or questions you might have. The group can brainstorm again later if it needs more creative ideas.

As we've noted, some groups find it useful to use technology to help them generate options and solutions.[6] In addition to apps and collaborative tools, a simple method is for group members to brainstorm solutions to a problem individually

analysis
Examination of the causes, effects, and history of a problem in order to understand it better

criteria
Standards for identifying an acceptable solution to a problem

and then email their list of ideas to each other. Or the group's leader could collect all of the ideas, eliminate duplicate suggestions, and then share them with the group. Research suggests that groups can generate more ideas if group members first generate ideas individually and then collaborate.[7]

4. **Select the Best Solution** Next, the group needs to select the solution that best meets the criteria and solves the problem. At this point, the group may need to modify its criteria or even its definition of the problem.

Research suggests that after narrowing the list of possible solutions, the most effective groups carefully consider the pros and the cons of each proposed solution.[8] Groups that don't do this often make poor decisions because they haven't carefully evaluated the implications of their solution; they haven't looked before they leaped.

To help in evaluating the solution, consider the following questions:

- Which of the suggested solutions deals best with the obstacles?
- Does the suggestion solve the problem in both the short term and the long term?
- What are the advantages and disadvantages of the suggested solution?
- Does the solution meet the established criteria?
- Should the group revise its criteria?
- What is required to implement the solution?
- When can the group implement the solution?
- What result will indicate success?

If the group is to reach agreement on a solution, some group members will need to abandon their attachment to their individual ideas for the overall good of the group. Experts who have studied how to achieve **consensus**—support for the final decision by all members—suggest that summarizing frequently and keeping the group oriented toward its goal are helpful. Emphasizing where group members agree, clarifying misunderstandings, writing down known facts for all members to see, and keeping the discussion focused on issues rather than on emotions are also strategies that facilitate group consensus.[9]

5. **Test and Implement the Solution** The group's work is not finished when it has identified a solution. The important questions "How can we put the solution into practice?" and "How can we evaluate the quality of the solution?" have yet to be addressed. The group may want to develop a step-by-step plan that describes the process for implementing the solution, a time frame for implementation, and a list of individuals who will be responsible for carrying out specific tasks.

> **RECAP**
>
> ### STEPS IN PROBLEM SOLVING
>
> 1. Identify and clearly define the problem.
> 2. Analyze the problem and identify criteria.
> 3. Generate possible solutions.
> 4. Select the best solution.
> 5. Test and implement the solution.

Participating in Small Groups

To be an effective group participant, you have to understand how to manage the problem-solving process. But knowing the steps is not enough; you also need to prepare for meetings, evaluate evidence, effectively summarize the group's progress, listen courteously, and be sensitive to conflict.

Come Prepared for Group Discussions

To contribute to group meetings, you need to be informed about the issues. Prepare for group discussions by researching the issues. If the issue before your group is

consensus
The support and commitment of all group members to the decision of the group

removing old asbestos from school buildings, for example, research the most recent scientific findings about various methods of removal. Chapter 7 described how to gather information for your speeches using the Internet and library resources. Use those same research techniques to prepare for group deliberations as well. Bring your research notes to the group; don't just rely on your memory or your personal opinion to carry you through the discussion. Without research, you will not be able to analyze the problem adequately.

Do Not Suggest Solutions before Analyzing the Problem

Research suggests that you should analyze a problem thoroughly before trying to zero in on a solution.[10] Resist the temptation to settle quickly on one solution until your group has systematically examined the causes, effects, history, and symptoms of a problem.

Evaluate Evidence

One study found that a key difference between groups that make successful decisions and those that don't is group members' ability to examine and evaluate evidence.[11] Ineffective groups are more likely to reach decisions quickly without considering the validity of evidence (or sometimes without any evidence at all). Such groups usually reach flawed conclusions.

Help Summarize the Group's Progress

Because it is easy for groups to get off the subject, group members frequently need to summarize what has been achieved and point the group toward the goal or task at hand. One research study suggests that periodic overviews of the discussion's progress can help the group stay on target.[12] Ask questions about the discussion process rather than about the topic under consideration: "Where are we now?" "Could someone summarize what we have accomplished?" and "Aren't we getting off the subject?"

Listen and Respond Courteously to Others

Chapter 4's suggestions for improving listening skills are useful when you work in groups, but understanding what others say is not enough. You also need to respect their points of view. Even when you disagree with someone's ideas, keep your emotions in check and respond courteously. Being closed-minded and defensive usually breeds group conflict.

Help Manage Conflict

In the course of exchanging ideas and opinions about controversial issues, disagreements are bound to occur.[13] You can help prevent conflicts from derailing the problem-solving process by doing the following:

- Keep the discussion focused on issues, not on personalities.
- Rely on facts rather than on personal opinions for evidence.
- Seek ways to compromise; don't assume that there must be a winner and a loser.
- Try to clarify misunderstandings in meaning.
- Be descriptive rather than evaluative and judgmental.
- Keep emotions in check.

If you can apply these basic principles, you can help make your group an effective problem-solving team.

Leading Small Groups

Rudyard Kipling wrote, "For the strength of the pack is the wolf, and the strength of the wolf is the pack." Group members typically need a leader to help the group collaborate effectively and efficiently, and a leader needs followers in order to lead. In essence, **leadership** is the process of influencing others through communication. Some see a leader as one individual empowered to delegate work and direct the group. In reality, however, group leadership is often shared.

Leadership Responsibilities

Leaders are needed to help accomplish tasks and to maintain a healthy social climate for the group. Table A.1 lists specific roles for both *task* leaders and *maintenance* leaders. Rarely does one person perform all these leadership responsibilities, even if a leader is formally appointed or elected. Most often a number of individual group

leadership
The process of influencing others through communication

TABLE A.1   LEADERSHIP ROLES IN GROUPS AND TEAMS

	LEADERSHIP ROLE	DESCRIPTION
Task Leaders	Agenda setter	Helps establish the group's agenda
Help get tasks accomplished	Secretary	Takes notes during meetings and distributes handouts before and during the meeting
	Initiator	Proposes new ideas or approaches to group problem solving
	Information seeker	Asks for facts or other information that helps the group deal with the issues and may also ask for clarification of ideas or obscure facts
	Opinion seeker	Asks for clarification of the values and opinions expressed by group members
	Information giver	Provides facts, examples, statistics, and other evidence that helps the group achieve its task
	Opinion giver	Offers opinions about the ideas under discussion
	Elaborator	Provides examples to show how ideas or suggestions would work
	Evaluator	Makes an effort to judge the evidence and the conclusion the group reaches
	Energizer	Tries to spur the group to further action and productivity
Group Maintenance Leaders	Encourager	Offers praise, understanding, and acceptance of others' ideas
Help maintain a healthy social climate	Harmonizer	Mediates disagreements that occur between group members
	Compromiser	Attempts to resolve conflicts by trying to find an acceptable middle ground between disagreeing group members
	Gatekeeper	Encourages the participation of less talkative group members and tries to limit lengthy contributions of other group members

Source: Based on Kenneth D. Benne and Paul Sheats, "Functional Roles of Group Members," *Journal of Social Issues* 4 (Spring 1948): 41–49.

members each will assume some specific leadership task, based on their personalities, skills, sensitivity, and the group's needs. If you determine that the group needs a clearer focus on the task or that maintenance roles are needed, be ready to influence the group appropriately to help get the job done in a positive, productive way. Leaders of large or formal groups may use parliamentary procedure to bring structure to meetings, for example. If you find yourself in such a leadership situation, Web sites such as Robert's Rules of Order (www.robertsrules.com) can help you implement parliamentary procedure.

Leadership Styles

Leaders can be described by the types of behavior, or leadership styles, that they exhibit as they influence the group to help achieve its goal. When you are called on to lead, do you give orders and expect others to follow you? Or do you ask the group to vote on the course of action to follow? Or maybe you don't try to influence the group at all; perhaps you prefer to hang back and let the group work out its own problems.

These strategies describe three general leadership styles: *authoritarian*, *democratic*, and *laissez-faire*.[14] Authoritarian leaders assume positions of superiority, giving orders and assuming control of the group's activity. Although authoritarian leaders can usually organize group activities with a high degree of efficiency and virtually eliminate uncertainty about who should do what, most problem-solving groups prefer democratic leaders.

Having more faith in their groups than do authoritarian leaders, democratic leaders involve group members in the decision-making process rather than dictate what should be done. Democratic leaders focus more on guiding discussion than on issuing commands.

Laissez-faire leaders allow group members complete freedom in all aspects of the decision-making process. They do little to help the group achieve its goal. This style of leadership (or nonleadership) often leaves a group frustrated because the group then lacks guidance and has to struggle with organizing the work. Table A.2 compares the three styles.

TABLE A.2   LEADERSHIP STYLE

	AUTHORITARIAN LEADERS	DEMOCRATIC LEADERS	LAISSEZ-FAIRE LEADERS
Group Policy Formation	All policies are determined by the leader.	All policies are a matter of group discussion and decision; leader assigns and encourages group discussion and decision making.	Complete non-participation by leader in policy decisions.
Group Activity Development	Group techniques and activities are dictated by the leader, one at a time; future steps are largely unknown to group members.	Discussion yields broad perspectives and general steps to the group goal; when technical advice is needed, leader suggests alternative procedures.	Leader supplies needed materials, making it clear that he or she can supply information when asked, but takes no other part in the discussion.
Source of Work Assignments	Leader dictates specific work tasks and teams; leader tends to remain aloof from active group participation except when directing activities.	Members are free to work with anyone; group decides on division of tasks.	Complete freedom for individuals or group to choose assignments; minimal leader participation.
Praise/Criticism	Leader tends to be personal in praise or criticism of each member.	Leader is objective and fact-oriented in praise and criticism, trying to be a regular group member in spirit without doing too much of the work.	Leader offers infrequent spontaneous comments on member activities and makes no attempt to appraise or control the course of events.

What is the most effective leadership style? Research suggests that no single style is effective in every group situation. Sometimes a group needs a strong authoritarian leader to make decisions quickly so that the group can achieve its goal. Although most groups prefer a democratic leadership style, leaders sometimes need to assert their authority to get the job done. The best leadership style depends on the nature of the group task, the power of the leader, and the relationship between the leader and his or her followers.

One contemporary approach to leadership is transformational leadership. Transformational leadership is not so much a particular style of leadership as it is a quality or characteristic of relating to others.[15] **Transformational leadership** is the process of influencing others by building a shared vision of the future, inspiring others to achieve, developing high-quality individual relationships with others, and helping people see how what they do is related to a larger framework or system. To be a transformational leader is not just to perform specific tasks or skills but also to have a philosophy of helping others see the big picture and inspiring them to make the vision of the future a reality.[16] Transformational leaders are good communicators who support and encourage rather than demean or demand.

RECAP

LEADERS OF SMALL GROUPS

1. Contribute to tasks and maintenance.
2. Adapt their leadership style to group needs.
3. Work toward transformational leadership.

transformational leadership

The process of influencing others by building a shared vision of the future, inspiring others to achieve, developing high-quality individual relationships with others, and helping people see how what they do is related to a larger framework or system

I Have a Dream[1]

by Martin Luther King Jr., Washington, D.C., August 28, 1963

I am happy to join with you today in what will go down in history as the greatest demonstration for freedom in the history of our nation.

Five score years ago, a great American, in whose symbolic shadow we stand today, signed the Emancipation Proclamation. This momentous decree came as a great beacon light of hope to millions of Negro slaves, who had been seared in the flames of withering injustice. It came as a joyous daybreak to end the long night of their captivity.

But one hundred years later, the Negro is still not free. One hundred years later, the life of the Negro is still sadly crippled by the manacles of segregation and the chains of discrimination. One hundred years later, the Negro lives on a lonely island of poverty in the midst of a vast ocean of material prosperity. One hundred years later, the Negro is still languished in the corners of American society and finds himself an exile in his own land. And so we've come here today to dramatize a shameful condition.

In a sense we've come to our nation's Capitol to cash a check. When the architects of our republic wrote the magnificent words of the Constitution and the Declaration of Independence, they were signing a promissory note to which every American was to fall heir. This note was a promise that all men—yes, black men as well as white men—would be guaranteed the inalienable rights of life, liberty, and the pursuit of happiness. It is obvious today that America has defaulted on this promissory note insofar as her citizens of color are concerned. Instead of honoring this sacred obligation, America has given the Negro people a bad check—a check which has come back marked "insufficient funds."

But we refuse to believe that the bank of justice is bankrupt. We refuse to believe that there are insufficient funds in the great vaults of opportunity of this nation. And so we've come to cash this check—a check that will give us upon demand the riches of freedom and the security of justice.

We have also come to this hallowed spot to remind America of the fierce urgency of now. This is no time to engage in the luxury of cooling off or to take the tranquilizing drug of gradualism. Now is the time to make the real promises of democracy. Now is the time to rise from the dark and desolate valley of segregation to the sunlit path of racial justice. Now is the time to lift our nation from the quicksands of racial injustice to the solid rock of brotherhood. Now is the time to make justice a reality for all of God's children.

NOTE: You can watch and listen to this speech online. Search for either the speech title or speaker to find video and audio recordings.

It would be fatal for the nation to overlook the urgency of the moment. This sweltering summer of the Negro's legitimate discontent will not pass until there is an invigorating autumn of freedom and equality. Nineteen sixty-three is not an end, but a beginning. Those who hope that the Negro needed to blow off steam and will now be content will have a rude awakening if the nation returns to business as usual. There will be neither rest nor tranquility in America until the Negro is granted his citizenship rights. The whirlwinds of revolt will continue to shake the foundations of our nation until the bright day of justice emerges.

But there is something that I must say to my people, who stand on the warm threshold which leads into the palace of justice. In the process of gaining our rightful place, we must not be guilty of wrongful deeds. Let us not seek to satisfy our thirst for freedom by drinking from the cup of bitterness and hatred. We must forever conduct our struggle on the high plane of dignity and discipline. We must not allow our creative protest to degenerate into physical violence. Again and again we must rise to the majestic heights of meeting physical force with soul force. The marvelous new militance which has engulfed the Negro community must not lead us to a distrust of all white people. For many of our white brothers, as evidenced by their presence here today, have come to realize that their destiny is tied up with our destiny. They have come to realize that their freedom is inextricably bound to our freedom. We cannot walk alone.

As we walk, we must make the pledge that we shall always march ahead. We cannot turn back. There are those who are asking the devotees of civil rights, "When will you be satisfied?"

We can never be satisfied as long as the Negro is the victim of the unspeakable horrors of police brutality. We can never be satisfied as long as our bodies, heavy with the fatigue of travel, cannot gain lodging in the motels of the highways and hotels of the cities. We cannot be satisfied as long as the Negro's basic mobility is from a smaller ghetto to a larger one. We can never be satisfied as long as our children are stripped of their selfhood and robbed of their dignity by signs stating "For Whites Only." We cannot be satisfied as long as a Negro in Mississippi cannot vote and a Negro in New York believes he has nothing for which to vote. No, no, we are not satisfied, and we will not be satisfied until justice rolls down like waters, and righteousness like a mighty stream.

I am not unmindful that some of you have come here out of great trials and tribulations. Some of you have come fresh from narrow jail cells. Some of you have come from areas where your quest for freedom left you battered by the storms of persecution and staggered by the winds of police brutality. You have been the veterans of creative suffering. Continue to work with the faith that unearned suffering is redemptive. Go back to Mississippi, go back to Alabama, go back to South Carolina, go back to Georgia, go back to Louisiana, go back to the slums and ghettos of our Northern cities, knowing that somehow this situation can and will be changed. Let us not wallow in the valley of despair.

I say to you today, my friends, so even though we face the difficulties of today and tomorrow, I still have a dream. It is a dream deeply rooted in the American dream.

I have a dream that one day this nation will rise up and live out the true meaning of its creed, "We hold these truths to be self-evident, that all men are created equal."

I have a dream that one day on the red hills of Georgia the sons of former slaves and the sons of former slaveowners will be able to sit down together at the table of brotherhood.

I have a dream that one day even the state of Mississippi, a state sweltering with the heat of injustice, sweltering with the heat of oppression, will be transformed into an oasis of freedom and justice.

I have a dream that my four little children will one day live in a nation where they will not be judged by the color of their skin but by the content of their character. I have a dream today.

I have a dream that one day, down in Alabama, with its vicious racists, with its governor having his lips dripping with the words of interposition and nullification, one day right there in Alabama little black boys and black girls will be able to join hands with little white boys and white girls as sisters and brothers. I have a dream today.

I have a dream that one day every valley shall be exalted, every hill and mountain shall be made low, the rough places will be made plain and the crooked places will be made straight, and the glory of the Lord shall be revealed, and all flesh shall see it together.

This is our hope. This is the faith that I go back to the South with. With this faith we will be able to hew out of the mountain of despair a stone of hope. With this faith we will be able to transform the jangling discords of our nation into a beautiful symphony of brotherhood. With this faith we will be able to work together, to pray together, to struggle together, to go to jail together, to stand up for freedom together knowing that we will be free one day.

This will be the day—this will be the day when all of God's children will be able to sing with new meaning:

"My country, 'tis of thee, sweet land of
    liberty, of thee I sing.
Land where my fathers died, land of the
    pilgrims' pride,
From every mountainside, let
    freedom ring!"

And if America is to be a great nation, this must become true.

So let freedom ring from the prodigious hilltops of New Hampshire.

Let freedom ring from the mighty mountains of New York.

Let freedom ring from the heightening
Alleghenies of Pennsylvania!

Let freedom ring from the snowcapped Rockies of Colorado!

Let freedom ring from the curvaceous slopes of California!

But not only that: Let freedom ring from Stone Mountain of Georgia!

Let freedom ring from Lookout Mountain of Tennessee!

Let freedom ring from every hill and molehill of Mississippi.

From every mountainside, let freedom ring.

And when this happens, when we allow freedom to ring—when we let it ring from every village and every hamlet, from every state and every city—we will be able to speed up that day when all of God's children, black men and white men, Jews and Gentiles, Protestants and Catholics, will be able to join hands and sing, in the words of the old Negro spiritual:

"Free at last! Free at last! Thank God almighty, we are free at last!"

Second Inaugural Address[2]

by Barack Obama, January 21, 2013

Watch at **MyCommunicationLab:** "Second Inaugural Address"

Vice President Biden, Mr. Chief Justice, Members of the United States Congress, distinguished guests, and fellow citizens:

Each time we gather to inaugurate a President we bear witness to the enduring strength of our Constitution. We affirm the promise of our democracy. We recall that what binds this Nation together is not the colors of our skin or the tenets of our faith or the origins of our names. What makes us exceptional—what makes us American—is our allegiance to an idea articulated in a declaration made more than two centuries ago:

> We hold these truths to be self-evident, that all men are created equal; that they are endowed by their Creator with certain unalienable rights; that among these are life, liberty, and the pursuit of happiness.

Today we continue a never-ending journey to bridge the meaning of those words with the realities of our time. For history tells us that while these truths may be self-evident, they've never been self-executing; that while freedom is a gift from God, it must be secured by His people here on Earth. The patriots of 1776 did not fight to replace the tyranny of a king with the privileges of a few or the rule of a mob. They gave to us a republic, a government of and by and for the people, entrusting each generation to keep safe our founding creed.

And for more than 200 years, we have.

Through blood drawn by lash and blood drawn by sword, we learned that no union founded on the principles of liberty and equality could survive half-slave and half-free. We made ourselves anew, and vowed to move forward together.

Together, we determined that a modern economy requires railroads and highways to speed travel and commerce, schools and colleges to train our workers.

Together, we discovered that a free market only thrives when there are rules to ensure competition and fair play.

Together, we resolved that a great nation must care for the vulnerable and protect its people from life's worst hazards and misfortune.

Through it all, we have never relinquished our skepticism of central authority nor have we succumbed to the fiction that all society's ills can be cured through government alone. Our celebration of initiative and enterprise, our insistence on hard work and personal responsibility, these are constants in our character.

But we have always understood that when times change, so must we; that fidelity to our founding principles requires new responses to new challenges; that preserving our individual freedoms ultimately requires collective action. For the American people can no more meet the demands of today's world by acting alone than American soldiers could have met the forces of fascism or communism with muskets and militias. No single person can train all the math and science teachers we'll need to equip our children for the future, or build the roads and networks and research labs that will bring new jobs and businesses to our shores. Now more than ever, we must do these things together, as one nation and one people.

This generation of Americans has been tested by crises that steeled our resolve and proved our resilience. A decade of war is now ending. An economic recovery has begun. America's possibilities are limitless, for we possess all the qualities that this world without boundaries demands: youth and drive; diversity and openness; an endless capacity for risk and a gift for reinvention. My fellow Americans, we are made for this moment and we will seize it—so long as we seize it together.

For we, the people, understand that our country cannot succeed when a shrinking few do very well and a growing many barely make it. We believe that America's prosperity must rest upon the broad shoulders of a rising middle class. We know that America thrives when every person can find independence and pride in their work; when the wages of honest labor liberate families from the brink of hardship. We are true to our creed when a little girl born into the bleakest poverty knows that she has the same chance to succeed as anybody else, because she is an American; she is free and she is equal, not just in the eyes of God, but also in our own.

We understand that outworn programs are inadequate to the needs of our time. So we must harness new ideas and technology to remake our government, revamp our tax code, reform our schools, and empower our citizens with the skills they need to work harder, learn more, reach higher. But while the means will change, our purpose endures: a nation that rewards the effort and determination of every single American. That is what this moment requires. That is what will give real meaning to our creed.

We, the people, still believe that every citizen deserves a basic measure of security and dignity. We must make the hard choices to reduce the cost of health care and the size of our deficit. But we reject the belief that America must choose between caring for the generation that built this country and investing in the generation that will build its future. For we remember the lessons of our past, when twilight years were spent in poverty and parents of a child with a disability had nowhere to turn.

We do not believe that in this country freedom is reserved for the lucky, or happiness for the few. We recognize that no matter how responsibly we live our lives, any one of us at any time may face a job loss or a sudden illness or a home swept away in a terrible storm. The commitments we make to each other through Medicare and Medicaid and Social Security, these things do not sap our initiative, they strengthen us. They do not make us a nation of takers; they free us to take the risks that make this country great.

We, the people, still believe that our obligations as Americans are not just to ourselves, but to all posterity. We will respond to the threat of climate change, knowing that the failure to do so would betray our children and future generations. Some may still deny the overwhelming judgment of science, but none can avoid the devastating impact of raging fires and crippling drought and more powerful storms.

The path towards sustainable energy sources will be long and sometimes difficult. But America cannot resist this transition, we must lead it. We cannot cede to other nations the technology that will power new jobs and new industries, we must claim its promise. That's how we will maintain our economic vitality and our national treasure—our forests and waterways, our croplands and snow-capped peaks. That is how we will preserve our planet, commanded to our care by God. That's what will lend meaning to the creed our fathers once declared.

We, the people, still believe that enduring security and lasting peace do not require perpetual war. Our brave men and women in uniform, tempered by the flames of battle, are unmatched in skill and courage. Our citizens, seared by the memory of those we have lost, know too well the price that is paid for liberty. The knowledge of their sacrifice will keep us forever vigilant against those who would do us harm. But we are also heirs to those who won the peace and not just the war; who turned sworn enemies into the surest of friends—and we must carry those lessons into this time as well.

We will defend our people and uphold our values through strength of arms and rule of law. We will show the courage to try and resolve our differences with other nations peacefully—not because we are naive about the dangers we face, but because engagement can more durably lift suspicion and fear.

America will remain the anchor of strong alliances in every corner of the globe. And we will renew those institutions that extend our capacity to manage crisis abroad, for no one has a greater stake in a peaceful world than its most powerful nation. We will support democracy from Asia to Africa, from the Americas to the Middle East, because our interests and our conscience compel us to act on behalf of those who long for freedom. And we must be a source of hope to the poor, the sick, the marginalized, the victims of prejudice—not out of mere charity, but because peace in our time requires the constant advance of those principles that our common creed describes: tolerance and opportunity, human dignity and justice.

We, the people, declare today that the most evident of truths—that all of us are created equal—is the star that guides us still; just as it guided our forebears through Seneca Falls and Selma and Stonewall; just as it guided all those men and women, sung and unsung, who left footprints along this great Mall, to hear a preacher say that we cannot walk alone; to hear a King proclaim that our individual freedom is inextricably bound to the freedom of every soul on Earth.

It is now our generation's task to carry on what those pioneers began. For our journey is not complete until our wives, our mothers and daughters can earn a living equal to their efforts. Our journey is not complete until our gay brothers and sisters are treated like anyone else under the law—for if we are truly created equal, then surely the love we commit to one another must be equal as well. Our journey is not complete until no citizen is forced to wait for hours to exercise the right to vote. Our journey is not complete until we find a better way to welcome the striving, hopeful immigrants who still see America as a land of opportunity—until bright young students and engineers are enlisted in our workforce rather than expelled from our country. Our journey is not complete until all our children, from the streets of Detroit to the hills of Appalachia, to the quiet lanes of Newtown, know that they are cared for and cherished and always safe from harm.

That is our generation's task—to make these words, these rights, these values of life and liberty and the pursuit of happiness real for every American. Being true to our founding documents does not require us to agree on every contour of life. It does not mean we all define liberty in exactly the same way or follow the same precise path to happiness. Progress does not compel us to settle centuries-long debates about the role of government for all time, but it does require us to act in our time.

For now decisions are upon us and we cannot afford delay. We cannot mistake absolutism for principle or substitute spectacle for politics or treat name-calling as reasoned debate. We must act, knowing that our work will be imperfect. We must act, we must act knowing that today's victories will be only partial and that it will be up to those who stand here in 4 years and 40 years and 400 years hence to advance the timeless spirit once conferred to us in a spare Philadelphia hall.

My fellow Americans, the oath I have sworn before you today, like the one recited by others who serve in this Capitol, was an oath to God and country, not party or faction. And we must faithfully execute that pledge during the duration of our service. But the words I spoke today are not so different from the oath that is taken each time a soldier signs up for duty or an immigrant realizes her dream. My oath is not so different from the pledge we all make to the flag that waves above and that fills our hearts with pride.

They are the words of citizens and they represent our greatest hope. You and I, as citizens, have the power to set this country's course. You and I, as citizens, have the obligation to shape the debates of our time—not only with the votes we cast, but with the voices we lift in defense of our most ancient values and enduring ideals.

Let us, each of us, now embrace with solemn duty and awesome joy what is our lasting birthright. With common effort and common purpose, with passion and dedication, let us answer the call of history and carry into an uncertain future that precious light of freedom.

Thank you. God bless you, and may He forever bless these United States of America.

Message. Messenger. Audience.[3]

by Daniel Rose, October 15, 2012

Watch at **MyCommunicationLab:** "Message. Messenger. Audience."

Friends, Romans, countrymen, lend me your ears. I come to bury Caesar, not to praise him. The evil that men do lives after them. The good is oft interred with their bones. So let it be with Caesar.

That's how Shakespeare opens one of history's greatest speeches. What a beginning!

And gentlemen in England now a-bed shall think themselves accursed they were not here, and hold their manhoods cheap whilst any speaks that fought with us upon Saint Crispin's day.

That's how he ends another of the world's most memorable orations.

I know not what course others may take, but as for me, give me liberty or give me death.

Patrick Henry's ending is part of our national heritage.

That is how great speeches are constructed. A strong beginning, a convincing middle and a rousing end, delivered with conviction by a speaker with authority, whose goal is to convince an audience open to persuasion. At the moment, this seems a lost art. The speeches at this year's Republican and Democratic National Conventions—with the exception of Bill Clinton's rousing performance and a few others—reflect what has happened to public speaking in America. Angry polemic, gracelessly expressed, delivered to already-converted partisans, is standard fare. A nation moved by Lincoln at Gettysburg and by FDR's fireside chats, by Jack Kennedy's asking what we can do for our country and by Lyndon Johnson's proclaiming that "we shall overcome" deserves better.

Effective public speaking is not rocket science. Twenty-five hundred years ago Aristotle observed that credibility (ethos), logic (logos) and emotion (pathos) underlay all good speeches, and that vivid images and appropriate use of figures of speech would reach the hearts and minds of a targeted audience. Few of us are called upon, like Winston Churchill in 1940, to revive the self-confidence of a nation, or like Joan of Arc, to encourage one's compatriots as she was being burned at the stake. We may be father of the bride or maid of honor, eulogist at a funeral, commencement speaker or recipient of an honor; the basic rules remain the same.

Suiting the talk to the occasion is common sense ("decorum" the ancients called it), but many a best man does not realize that the bawdy joke well-received at a bachelor party is in poor taste at the wedding; or as Mitt Romney discovered, the "47 percent" comment that went over well with "true believers" was a disaster before a broader audience.

Good "delivery"—what Demosthenes called the first, second and third requirements for a great speech—has become rare in American life. Nine out of ten of us mumble to the front row rather than boom out to the back row. Many nervously speak quickly before an audience rather than use the slower pace that experts recommend. Good speakers use judicious pauses for emphasis and dramatic impact, raising or lowering the voice as indicated.

Some techniques used by experts can be dangerous for amateurs. In the Carter–Reagan presidential debate, for example, when Carter passionately leveled his fiercest attack, Reagan chuckled, threw his head back and said, "There you go again!" The audience exploded with laughter, and the election was over. An amateur should not try this. Debates, essays and speeches are different art forms. The Mitt Romney who bored his public with his convention acceptance speech energized them at the first presidential debate, while the reverse was the case with President Obama. Ronald Reagan and Bill Clinton excelled at both forms, while neither could write a decent essay.

When, in the spring of 1963, our friend Bayard Rustin invited my wife and me to have dinner with him and Martin Luther King, Jr., we had just been deeply moved by reading MLK's extraordinary *Letter From Birmingham Jail*, one of the most powerful and eloquent missives of all time. Denied stationery in his cell, King poured out his thoughts on toilet paper and in the margins of newspapers, while Birmingham Police Chief Bull Connor (a name out of Restoration comedy) turned fire hoses and police dogs on non-violent protesters. King's letter was a reply to eight white clergymen who called his actions "unwise and untimely." King's evocation of St. Paul and of Socrates, Aquinas and Martin Buber—his citing Shadrach, Meshach and Abednego's refusal to obey the laws of Nebuchadnezzar—and his portrayal of the terror and despair of black children throughout the South, should be required reading in every American school.

When we gave our contribution to help plan the Washington protest for later that summer, I hid my fear that bringing together vast numbers of Civil Rights activists and red-necked southern police could result in a counterproductive riot. The Reverend was certain that the event's tone would be spiritual. And his "I Have a Dream" speech became one of our nation's greatest orations. "I Have a Dream" has been called the most important and influential speech of the 20th century. Addressing a transfixed audience, standing resolutely, his back to the Lincoln Memorial, King began his speech with, "Five score years ago, a great American, in whose symbolic shadow we stand today, signed the Emancipation Proclamation." What a man, what a setting, what an opening!

After evoking the Declaration of Independence and the Constitution as "promissory notes," he declared that America had defaulted, the check had come back marked "insufficient funds"; and he proclaimed (like Amos in the Old Testament) that he would not be satisfied until, "justice rolls down like waters and righteousness like a mighty stream." He went on to describe his dream ("deeply rooted in the American Dream"), echoing the powerful resonance of the Biblical Isaiah. He cited "My Country 'tis of Thee" and finished with the old Negro spiritual refrain "Free at last! Free at last! Thank God Almighty, we are free at last!" And the nation responded by supporting Lyndon Johnson's Civil Rights legislation.

In the classical world, Aeschines warned the Athenian Assembly of threats from Philip II of Macedon, and everyone commented on how eloquently Aeschines spoke. Demosthenes then rose to give his *Philippic,* and the Assembly shouted, "Let us march against Philip!"

Studying memorable speeches can be helpful, and educational as well. The greatest secular speech of all time, Pericles' *Funeral Oration,* as reported by Thucydides 2,600 years ago, conveys ideas we would do well to ponder today. Think of our Millionaires' Congress: Pericles says, "Advancement in public life falls to reputation for capacity, class considerations not being allowed to interfere with merit; nor does poverty bar the way. If a man is able to serve the state, he is not hindered by the obscurity of his condition." Consider the mega yachts of our hedge funders on the political right, as Pericles notes, "We cultivate refinement without extravagance and knowledge without effeminacy; wealth we employ more for use than for show." How many on our political left could dispute his point that, "The real disgrace of poverty is not in owning to the fact but in declining the struggle against it."

Lou Gehrig's "Farewell to Baseball," at which I cried as a young boy, expressed a modesty, a gratitude for the good things life had given him, that is unthinkable from our gladiators of today.

Studying failures—or lost opportunities—may be even more helpful to mistake-prone amateurs. Studying great "saves" can be instructive, too. Richard Nixon's emotional "Checkers" speech, for example, effectively ended talk of the embarrassing "Nixon Scandal Fund." Mitt Romney's self-confident, authoritative manner in the first Presidential debate of 2012, his eye-contact with the audience and his smiling gazes at his adversary, did much in the audience's view to overcome the weakness of his argument.

The failure of Obama's advisors and "handlers" to prepare him adequately for the first debate will be notable in political history. David Axelrod, Obama's chief advisor, noted after the debate, "The president showed up with the intent of answering questions and having a discussion. Romney showed up to deliver a performance, and he delivered a very good performance." As Reagan's speechwriter Peggy Noonan said years ago, "A speech is part theater and part political declaration," and Axelrod should have listened. When Axelrod was asked why Obama did not address Romney's "47 percent" gaffe, he replied, "The president obviously didn't see the appropriate opportunity." The appropriate opportunity? O's opening statement could have been, "Governor Romney is concerned about some of us; I am concerned about all Americans, including the 47 percent."

O's talk petered out. My suggestion for an ending would have been: "We have started the recovery from the disaster we inherited; with your support we will finish it." Michelle Obama's convention speech was widely praised, and the audience came away feeling that this good woman loved her husband. Necessary but not sufficient! I would have added to her remarks: "The man I live with may look calm, but he spends sleepless nights over our casualties in Iraq and Afghanistan, and agonizes over students who can't find jobs and unemployed workers whose insurance is running out."

Martin Luther King, Jr. wrote his own sermons and speeches. John F. Kennedy's were written by Ted Sorensen, Ronald Reagan's were by Peggy Noonan, Barack

Obama's by Jon Favreau. Franklin Roosevelt corrected his own talks, but the first drafts were written by skilled writers like Sam Rosenman, Robert Sherwood, Archibald Macleish, and others. If you get help for a major talk, or have someone prepare a draft, you are in good company. But writing your own material can not only be fun, but also educational. E.M. Forster's comment, "How do I know what I think until I hear what I say?" states it clearly.

Plunge in and write your own; but remember Aristotle's ethos, logos and pathos; Cicero's decorum; Demosthenes' delivery; and the one attribute of all great speeches—say something worth saying!

Elvis[4]

by Angelitta Armijo, Texas State University

Watch at **MyCommunicationLab:** "Elvis"

Can you imagine being a singer with 150 different albums and singles that have been certified gold, platinum, or multiplatinum? Neither can I. But according to *Elvis.com*, that's the reality for Elvis Presley.

Although Elvis is no longer with us, his influence on the rock industry remains prevalent today. After all, he paved the way for groups such as the Beatles and Led Zeppelin. I personally have been an Elvis fan for as long as I can remember. I grew up on him, and I own many of his albums on CD, cassette, and vinyl. I also own every movie that he's ever starred in, including some of his TV specials, which I'll talk about later.

Elvis Presley was an American kid who grew up on the wrong side of the tracks and later became the King of Rock-n-Roll. To better understand Elvis, you need to know about his early days of life before he was famous, his early career, and his shift in career focus, which was prevalent until the end of his life.

Let's begin with Elvis's humble beginnings. Elvis was born into a poor family, but he kept his eyes on his dreams and his love of music. Elvis Aaron Presley was born January 8, 1935, in Tupelo, Mississippi, to Gladys and Vernon Presley. Actually, Elvis was born as a twin, but his brother, Jesse Garon, died at birth, leaving Elvis to be raised as an only child, according to the A&E Network. Also according to A&E Network, Elvis was very dedicated to his family and especially to his mother, whom he loved very much. His family encouraged him to be active in church, and it was in church that he discovered his love of singing and music. When he was ten years old, he received his first guitar, and throughout his childhood and young adult life, he was involved in many talent shows.

According to Elvis.com, the family moved to Memphis in 1948 to seek financial security and job security. Soon after graduating high school in 1953 in Memphis, Elvis became a truck driver. It was during his truck-driving years that Elvis recorded a few songs at Sun Records for his mother for her birthday. It was at Sun Records where his career began, because Sam Phillips asked him to record more songs, in hopes of finding a star.

So now that you know about Elvis's beginnings, we can discuss his rise to fame and early successes. Elvis's career began at Sun Records and grew as his fans wanted to see him on stage, on TV, and on the silver screen. According to *Rolling Stone*, one of the recordings requested by Sam Phillips, "That's Alright Mama," became Elvis's first single in 1954. This single, and many of Elvis's other singles, showed the influence of blues music, which he discovered in Memphis. By 1955, Elvis was signed to RCA, a premier record label. In 1956, his first album was released, titled *Elvis Presley*. According to Elvis.com, this record was #1 on the *Billboard* Pop Charts for 10 weeks and was also Elvis's first gold album, selling over a million copies.

Throughout the rest of the '50s, Elvis appeared on many variety shows such as the *Ed Sullivan Show* and starred in his first movie, *Love Me Tender*. In 1960, after two years in the army, Elvis taped a special *Welcome Home Elvis* edition of Frank Sinatra's TV show. He received $125,000 for appearing on the show—which, according to Elvis.com, was a record sum of money for an appearance at that time. According to IMDb, Elvis released 27 films throughout the '60s. This was obviously his career focus at that time. He also put out many soundtracks for these movies; some of them include *GI Blues*, *Blue Hawaii*, and *Viva Las Vegas*.

After covering Elvis's early life and career, we can now discuss his career change. The obvious shift from movies to music came with Elvis's 1968 *Comeback Tour Special*, initially entitled *Elvis*. Elvis used the 1968 *Comeback Special* to be taken more seriously, and he ended the special on a personal note, by closing with the song *If I Can Dream*. This song was in response to the tragedies that had occurred in the 1960s, such as the assassination of JFK, Martin Luther King Jr., and Bobby Kennedy, all men whom Elvis respected. This was a sign he was ready to be taken more seriously. His movies changed as well; he finished up his acting career with a few movies that were less cheesy and had more serious plots.

In 1973, Elvis made history. His *Aloha from Hawaii Special* was broadcast via satellite to 40 countries and viewed by 1 to 1.5 billion people, according to Elvis.com. Also according to Elvis.com, 51 percent of Americans viewed the *Aloha from Hawaii Special*. That means it was seen in more American households than the walk on the moon was! Elvis continued to sell out shows and venues such as Madison Square Garden and Las Vegas until his career ended in 1977 with his death.

You can see that Elvis's life is something for the history books. He came from humble beginnings and catapulted himself into a thriving career to become the King of Rock-n-Roll. Now you know about his life before fame, his early fame and rise to stardom, and a career shift that he focused on. Now—as Elvis would say—"Thank you, thank you very much."

ENDNOTES

CHAPTER 1

1. Louis Nizer, *Reflections Without Mirrors*, quoted in Jack Valenti, *Speak Up with Confidence: How to Prepare, Learn, and Deliver Effective Speeches* (New York: Morrow, 1982) 34.
2. Judy C. Pearson, Jeffrey T. Child, and David H. Kahl, Jr., "Preparation Meeting Opportunity: How Do College Students Prepare for Public Speeches?" *Communication Quarterly* 54.3 (Aug. 2006): 351.
3. Pearson, Child, and Kahl, "Preparation Meeting Opportunity," 355.
4. James C. Humes, *The Sir Winston Method: Five Secrets of Speaking the Language of Leadership* (New York: Morrow, 1991) 13–14.
5. Charles Schwab, as quoted in Brent Filson, *Executive Speeches: Tips on How to Write and Deliver Speeches from 51 CEOs* (New York: Wiley, 1994) 45.
6. Value investors portal. "Warren Buffet on Communication Skills." *YouTube.* 6 December 2010. Web. http://www.youtube.com/watch?v=tpgcEYpLzP0 Accessed May 14, 2013.
7. Dee-Ann Durbin, "Study: Plenty of Jobs for Graduates in 2000," *Austin American-Statesman* (5 Dec. 1999): A28.
8. Dan B. Curtis, Jerry L. Winsor, and Ronald D. Stephens, "National Preferences in Business and Communication Education," *Communication Education* 38 (Jan. 1989): 6–14. See also Iain Hay, "Justifying and Applying Oral Presentations in Geographical Education," *Journal of Geography in Higher Education* 18.1 (1994): 44–45.
9. Jerry L. Winsor, Dan B. Curtis, and Ronald D. Stephens, "National Preferences in Business and Communication Education: A Survey Update," *Journal of the Association for Communication Administration* (3 Sept. 1997): 174.
10. University of Wisconsin–River Falls, Career Services, "What Skills and Attributes Employers Seek When Hiring Students." 4 June 2007 <http://www.uwrf.edu/ccs/skills/htm>.
11. Camille Luckenbaugh and Kevin Gray, "Employers Describe Perfect Job Candidate," National Association of Colleges and Employers Survey. 4 June 2007 <http://www.naceweb.org/press/display.asp?year=2003&prid=169>.
12. Randall S. Hansen and Katharine Handsen, "What Do Employers Really Want? Top Skills and Values Employers Seek from Job-Seekers." 4 June 2007 <http://www.quintcareers.com/job_skills_values.html>.
13. L. M. Boyd, syndicated column, *Austin American-Statesman* (8 Aug. 2000): E3.
14. Herman Cohen, *The History of Speech Communication: The Emergence of a Discipline: 1914–1945* (Annandale, VA: Speech Communication Association, 1994) 2.
15. Barack Obama, "Remarks by the President at Sandy Hook Interfaith Prayer Vigil," *The White House Briefing Room.* 16 Dec 2012. Web. 5 July 2013 <http://www.whitehouse.gov/the-press-office/2012/12/16/remarks-president-sandy-hook-interfaith-prayer-vigil>.

16. Survey conducted by R. H. Bruskin and Associates, *Spectra* 9 (Dec. 1973): 4; D. Wallechinsky, Irving Wallace, and Amy Wallace, *The People's Almanac Presents the Book of Lists* (New York: Morrow, 1977).
17. K. K. Dwyer and M. M. Davidson, "Is Public Speaking Really More Feared Than Death?" *Communication Research Reports* 29, 2 (April–June 2012): 99–107.
18. Steven Booth Butterfield, "Instructional Interventions for Reducing Situational Anxiety and Avoidance," *Communication Education* 37 (1988): 214–23; also see Michael Motley, *Overcoming Your Fear of Public Speaking: A Proven Method* (New York: McGraw-Hill, 1995).
19. Joe Ayres and Theodore S. Hopf, "The Long-Term Effect of Visualization in the Classroom: A Brief Research Report," *Communication Education* 39 (1990): 75–78.
20. John Burk, "Communication Apprehension among Masters of Business Administration Students: Investigating a Gap in Communication Education," *Communication Education* 50 (Jan. 2001): 51–58; Lynne Kelly and James A. Keaten, "Treating Communication Anxiety: Implications of the Communibiological Paradigm," *Communication Education* 49 (Jan. 2000): 45–57; Amber N. Finn, Chris R. Sawyer, and Ralph R. Behnke, "Audience-Perceived Anxiety Patterns of Public Speakers," *Communication Education* 51 (Fall 2003): 470–81.
21. Judy C. Pearson, Lori DeWitt, Jeffery T. Child, David H. Kahl, and Vijay Dandamudi, "Facing the Fear: An Analysis of Speech-Anxiety Content in Public-Speaking Textbooks," *Communication Research Reports* 24 (2007): 159–68; G. D. Bodie, "A Racing Heart, Rattling Knees, and Ruminative Thoughts: Defining and Explaining Public Speaking Anxiety," *Communication Education* 59 (2010): 70–105.
22. Kay B. Harris, Chris R. Sawyer, and Ralph R. Behnke, "Predicting Speech State Anxiety from Trait Anxiety, Reactivity, and Situational Influences," *Communication Quarterly* 54 (2006): 213–26; M. J. Beatty, A. D. Heisel, R. J. Lewis, M. E. Pence, A. Reinhart, and Y. Tian, "Communication Apprehension and Resting Alpha Range Asymmetry in the Anterior Cortex," *Communication Education* 60, 4 (2011): 441–60.
23. Amy M. Bippus and John A. Daly, "What Do People Think Causes Stage Fright? Naïve Attributions About the Reasons for Public-Speaking Anxiety," *Communication Education* 48 (1999): 63–72.
24. Yang Lin and Andrew S. Rancer, "Sex Differences in Intercultural Communication Apprehension, Ethnocentrism, and Intercultural Willingness to Communicate," *Psychological Reports* 92 (2003): 195–200.
25. S. Shimotsu and T. P. Mottet, "The Relationships Among Perfectionism, Communication Apprehension, and Temperament," *Communication Research Reports* 26, 3 (2009): 188–97.
26. Bodie, "A Racing Heart, Rattling Knees, and Ruminative Thoughts: Defining, Explaining, and Treating Public Speaking Anxiety."

27. Amber N. Finn, Chris R. Sawyer, and Paul Schrodt, "Examining the Effect of Exposure Therapy on Public Speaking State Anxiety," *Communication Education* 58 (2009): 92–109.

28. Michael J. Beatty, James C. McCroskey, and A. D. Heisel, "Communication Apprehension as Temperamental Expression: A Communibiological Paradigm," *Communication Monographs* 65 (1998): 197–219; Michael J. Beatty and Kristin Marie Valencic, "Context-Based Apprehension Versus Planning Demands: A Communibiological Analysis of Anticipatory Public Speaking Anxiety," *Communication Education* 49 (Jan. 2000): 58–71; Valerie A. MacIntyre, P. D. MacIntyre, and G. Carre, "Heart Rate as a Predictor of Speaking Anxiety," *Communication Research Reports*, 27, 4 (2010): 286–97; Michael J. Beatty, A. D. Heisel, R. J. Lewis, M. E. Pence, A. Reinhart, and Y. Tian, "Communication Apprehension and Resting Alpha Range Asymmetry in the Anterior Cortex," *Communication Education* 60, 4 (2011): 441–60.

29. Kay B. Harris, Chris R. Sawyer, and Ralph R. Behnke, "Predicting Speech State Anxiety from Trait Anxiety, Reactivity, and Situational Influences," *Communication Quarterly* 54 (May 2006): 213–26.

30. Kelly and Keaten, "Treating Communication Anxiety."

31. Maili Porhola, "Orientation Styles in a Public-Speaking Context," paper presented at the National Communication Association convention, Seattle, Washington, Nov. 2000; Ralph R. Behnke and Michael J. Beatty, "A Cognitive-Physiological Model of Speech Anxiety," *Communication Monographs* 48 (1981): 158–63.

32. Shannon C. McCullough, Shelly G. Russell, Ralph R. Behnke, Chris R. Sawyer, and Paul L. Witt, "Anticipatory Public Speaking State Anxiety as a Function of Body Sensations and State of Mind," *Communication Quarterly* 54 (2006): 101–09.

33. Ralph R. Behnke and Chris R. Sawyer, "Public Speaking Anxiety as a Function of Sensitization and Habituation Processes," *Communication Research Reports* 53 (Apr. 2004): 164–73.

34. Paul L. Witt and Ralph R. Behnke, "Anticipatory Speech Anxiety as a Function of Public Speaking Assignment Type," *Communication Education* 55 (2006): 167–77.

35. Maili Porhola, "Arousal Styles During Public Speaking," *Communication Education* 51 (Oct. 2002): 420–38.

36. Kelly and Keaten, "Treating Communication Anxiety."

37. M. J. Beatty, A. D. Heisel, R. J. Lewis, M. E. Pence, A. Reinhart, and Y. Tian, "Communication Apprehension and Resting Alpha Range Asymmetry in the Anterior Cortex," *Communication Education* 60, 4 (2011): 441–60.

38. Leon Fletcher, *How to Design and Deliver Speeches* (New York: Longman, 2001 following) 3.

39. Research suggests that because public-speaking anxiety is complex (both a trait and a state), with multiple and idiosyncratic causes, using a combination of intervention strategies may be best in attempting to manage communication apprehension. See Bodie, "A Racing Heart, Rattling Knees, and Ruminative Thoughts."

40. Desiree C. Duff, Timothy R. Levine, Michael J. Beatty, Jessica Woolbright, and Hee Sun Park, "Testing Public Anxiety Treatments Against a Credible Placebo Control," *Communication Education* 56 (2007): 72–88.

41. Peter D. MacIntyre and J. Renee MacDonald, "Public-Speaking Anxiety: Perceived Competence and Audience Congeniality," *Communication Education* 47 (Oct. 1998): 359–65.

42. Ralph R. Behnke and Chris R. Sawyer, "Public-Speaking Procrastination as a Correlate of Public-Speaking Communication Apprehension and Self-Perceived Public-Speaking Competence," *Communication Research Reports* 16 (1999): 40–47.

43. Quoted by Petula Dovrak, "Channeling the Grief," *Austin American-Statesman* (14 Oct., 2009): A9.

44. Dovrak, "Channeling the Grief."

45. Joe Ayres, Terry Schliesman, and Debbie Ayres Sonandre, "Practice Makes Perfect but Does It Help Reduce Communication Apprehension?" *Communication Research Reports* 15 (Spring 1998): 170–79.

46. Melanie Booth-Butterfield, "Stifle or Stimulate? The Effects of Communication Task Structure on Apprehensive and Non-Apprehensive Students," *Communication Education* 35 (1986): 337–48; Charles R. Berger, "Speechlessness: Causal Attributions, Emotional Features, and Social Consequences," *Journal of Language & Social Psychology* 23 (June 2004): 147–79.

47. Joe Ayres, Tim Hopf, and Elizabeth Peterson, "A Test of Communication-Orientation Motivation (COM) Therapy," *Communication Reports* 13 (Winter 2000): 35–44; Joe Ayres and Tanichya K. Wongprasert, "Measuring the Impact of Visualization on Mental Imagery: Comparing Prepared Versus Original Drawings," *Communication Research Reports* 20 (Winter 2003): 45–53.

48. Joe Ayers and Theodore S. Hopf, "Visualization: A Means of Reducing Speech Anxiety," *Communication Education* 34 (1985): 318–23. Although researchers have found evidence that visualization is helpful, some question whether visualization techniques work better than just gaining experience in public speaking. Critics of systematic desensitization argue that there may be a placebo effect: Just thinking that a treatment will reduce apprehension may contribute to reduced apprehension. See Duff, Levine, Beatty, Woolbright, and Park, "Testing Public Anxiety Treatments Against a Credible Placebo Control."

49. Ayres and Wongprasert, "Measuring the Impact of Visualization on Mental Imagery."

50. Ayres and Wongprasert, "Measuring the Impact of Visualization on Mental Imagery."

51. Joe Ayres and Debbie M. Ayres Sonandre, "Performance Visualization: Does the Nature of the Speech Model Matter?" *Communication Research Reports* 20 (Summer 2003): 260–68.

52. Stephen R. Covey, *The 7 Habits of Highly Successful People* (New York: Simon and Schuster, 1989).

53. Duff, Levine, Beatty, Woolbright, and Park, "Testing Public Anxiety Treatments Against a Credible Placebo Control."

54. Joe Ayres and Brian L. Heuett, "An Examination of the Impact of Performance Visualization," *Communication Research Reports* 16 (1999): 29–39.

55. Penny Addison, Ele Clay, Shuang Xie, Chris R. Sawyer, and Ralph R. Behnke, "Worry as a Function of Public Speaking State Anxiety Type," *Communication Reports* 16 (Summer 2003): 125–31.

56. Chad Edwards and Suzanne Walker, "Using Public Speaking Learning Communities to Reduce Communication Apprehension," *Texas Speech Communication Journal* 32 (2007): 65–71; also see Chia-Fang (Sandy) Hsu, "The Relationship of Trait Anxiety, Audience Nonverbal Feedback, and Attributions to Public Speaking State Anxiety," *Communication Research Reports* 26.3 (August 2009): 237–46.

57. Diane Honour, "Speech Performance Anxiety for Non-Native Speakers," *The Florida Communication Journal* 36 (2007): 57–66.

58. Finn, Sawyer, and Schrodt, "Examining the Effect of Exposure Therapy on Public Speaking State Anxiety."

59. Lisa M. Schroeder, "The Effects of Skills Training on Communication Satisfaction and Communication Anxiety in the Basic Speech Course," *Communication Research Reports* 19 (2002): 380–88; Alain Morin, "History of Exposure to Audiences as a Developmental Antecedent of Public Self-Consciousness," *Current Research in Social Psychology* 5 (Mar. 2000): 33–46.

60. MacIntyre and MacDonald, "Public-Speaking Anxiety"; Peter D. MacIntyre and K. A. Thivierge, "The Effects of Audience Pleasantness, Audience Familiarity, and Speaking Contexts on Public-Speaking Anxiety and Willingness to Speak," *Communication Quarterly* 43 (1995): 456–66; Peter D. MacIntyre, K. A. Thivierge, and J. Renee MacDonald, "The Effects of Audience Interest, Responsiveness, and Evaluation on Public-Speaking Anxiety and Related Variables," *Communication Research Reports* 14 (1997): 157–68.

61. MacIntyre and MacDonald, "Public-Speaking Anxiety"; R. B. Rubin, A. M. Rubin, and F. F. Jordan, "Effects of Instruction on Communication Apprehension and Communication Competence," *Communication Education* 46 (1997): 104–14.

62. G. M. Hodis, N. R. Bardhan; and F. A. Hodis, "Patterns of Change in Willingness to Communicate in Public Speaking Contexts: A Latent Growth Modeling Analysis," *Journal of Applied Communication Research* 38, 3 (2010): 248–67.

CHAPTER 2

1. The late Waldo Braden, longtime professor of speech communication at Louisiana State University, presented a memorable speech at the 1982 meeting of the Florida Speech Communication Association in which he emphasized "The audience writes the speech" to indicate the importance and centrality of being an audience-centered speaker.

2. Patricia A. Sullivan, "Signification and African-American Rhetoric: A Case Study of Jesse Jackson's 'Common Ground and Common Sense' Speech," *Communication Quarterly* 41.1 (1993): 1–15.

3. Adetokunbo F. Knowles-Borishade, "Paradigm for Classical African Orature," Christine Kelly et al., eds., *Diversity in Public Communication: A Reader* (Dubuque, IA: Kendall-Hunt, 1994): 100.

4. J. C. Pearson, J. T. Child, and D. H. Kahl, Jr., "Preparation Meeting Opportunity: How Do College Students Prepare for Public Speeches?" *Communication Quarterly*, 54:3 (Aug. 2006): 351–66.

5. Clifford Stoll, as cited in Kevin A. Miller, "Capture: The Essential Survival Skill for Leaders Buckling Under Information Overload," *Leadership* (Spring 1992): 85.

6. Don Hewitt, interview broadcast on *60 Minutes*, 24 Jan. 2010.

7. Greg Winter, "The Chips Are Down: Frito-Lay Cuts Costs with Smaller Servings," *Austin American-Statesman* 2 Jan. 2001: A6.

8. These statistics are from an Allstate Insurance advertisement, *The New York Times* 17 Feb. 2010: A24.

9. We thank Barbara Patton of Texas State University for sharing her speech outline with us.

10. Pearson, Child, and Kahl, "Preparation Meeting Opportunity."

11. Grace Hildenbrand, "Cinderella," Texas State University student speech, 2013.

CHAPTER 3

1. Jason Pontin, "Free Speech in the Era of Its Technological Amplification," *MIT Technology Review* 116.2 (March/April 2013): 62.

2. National Communication Association, "NCA Credo for Communication Ethics," 1999. 27 June 2001.

3. "Obama Counter-Terrorism Speech Interrupted by Heckler," UPI.com. 23 May 2013.

4. Samuel Walker, *Hate Speech* (Lincoln: U of Nebraska P, 1994): 162.

5. "Libel and Slander," *The Ethical Spectacle.* 1 June 1997.

6. "Three Decades Later, Free Speech Vets Return to UC Berkeley," *Sacramento Bee* 3 Dec. 1994: A1.

7. James S. Tyre, "Legal Definition of Obscenity, Pornography." 1 June 1997.

8. "Supreme Court Rules: Cyberspace Will Be Free! ACLU Hails Victory in Internet Censorship Challenge." *American Civil Liberties Union Freedom Network.* 26 June 1997.

9. Sue Anne Pressley, "Oprah Winfrey Wins Case Filed by Cattlemen," *Washington Post* 27 Feb. 1998.

10. Associated Press, "Free-Speech, Other Groups File Briefs Opposing Patriot Act." 4 Nov. 2003.

11. Brian Schweitzer, "Proclamation of Clemency for Montanans Convicted under the Mon-tana Sedition Act in 1918–1919." 3 May 2006. (Thanks to George Moss, Vaughn College, Flushing, NY, for providing the authors with a copy of this document.)

12. Terry Phillips, "Opinion: In Defense of Free Speech and Helen Thomas." MercuryNews.com. 15 June 2010.

13. Bill Carter and Felicity Barringer, "Patriotic Time, Dissent Muted," *The New York Times* 28 Sept. 2001: A1.

14. Walker, *Hate Speech*, 2.

15. Daniel Downs and Gloria Cowan, "Predicting the Importance of Freedom of Speech and the Perceived Harm of Hate Speech," *Journal of Applied Social Psychology* 42.6 (June 2012): 1372.

16. Edwin R. Bayley, *Joe McCarthy and the Press* (Madison: Wisconsin U P, 1981) 29.

17. Chidsey Dickson, "Re: question." Online posting. 27 Oct. 2005. WPA Listserv.

18. "Spurlock Sorry for Speech," *Austin American-Statesman* (29 Mar. 2006): A2.

19. Kathy Fitzpatrick, "U.S. Public Diplomacy," *Vital Speeches of the Day* (April 2004): 412–17.

20. *Publication Manual of the American Psychological Association*, 6th ed. (Washington, DC: American Psychological Association, 2010): 16.

21. Scott Jaschik, "Graduation Shame." Insidehighered.com. 22 Apr. 2010.

22. Eodice, Michele, "Plagiarism, Pedagogy, and Controversy: A Conversation with Rebecca Moore Howard." *Issues in Writing* 13.1 (Fall/Winter 2002).

23. "75 to 98 Percent of College Students Have Cheated," *Education-portal.com* (June 29, 2011).

24. www.non-plagiarized-termpapers.com.

25. Todd Holm, "Public Speaking Students' Perceptions of Cheating," *Communication Research Reports* (Winter 2002): 70.

26. Waldo W. Braden, *Abraham Lincoln, Public Speaker* (Baton Rouge: Louisiana State U P, 1988): 90.

CHAPTER 4

1. Study conducted by Paul Cameron, as cited in Ronald B. Adler and Neil Town, *Looking Out/Looking In: Interpersonal Communications* (New York: Holt, Rinehart and Winston, 1981): 218.

2. L. Boyd, Syndicated column, *Austin American-Statesman* 7 Dec. 1995: E7.

3. John T. Masterson, Steven A. Beebe, and Norman H. Watson, *Invitation to Effective Speech Communication* (Glenview, IL: Scott, Foresman, 1989): 4.

4. B. R. Brunner, "Listening, Communication & Trust: Practitioners' Perspectives of Business/Organizational Relationships," *The International Journal of Listening* 22 (2008): 123–32.

5. Laura Ann Janusik, "Building Listening Theory: The Validation of the Conversational Listening Span," *Communication Studies* 58. 2 (2007): 139–56.

6. Frank E. X. Dance, *Speaking Your Mind: Private Thinking and Public Speaking* (Dubuque, IA: Kendall/Hunt, 1994).

7. Ralph G. Nichols and Leonard A. Stevens, "Six Bad Listening Habits," in *Are You Listening?* (New York: McGraw-Hill, 1957).

8. Albert Mehrabian, *Nonverbal Communication* (Hawthorne, NY: Aldine, 1972).

9. Paul Ekman and Wallace Friesen, "Head and Body Cues in the Judgement of Emotion: A Reformulation," *Perceptual and Motor Skills* 25 (1967): 711–24.

10. K. K. Halone and L. L. Pecchioni, "Relational Listening: A Grounded Theoretical Model," *Communication Reports* 14 (2001): 59–71.

11. Halone and Pecchioni, "Relational Listening."

12. Paul Rankin, "Listening Ability: Its Importance, Measurement and Development," *Chicago Schools Journal* 12 (Jan. 1930): 177–79.

13. R. Emmanuel, J. Adams, K. Baker, E. K. Daufin, C. Ellington, F. Fits, J. Himsel, L. Holladay, and David Okeowo, "How College Students Spend Their Time Communicating," *International Journal of Listening* 22 (2008): 13–28.

14. Nichols and Stevens, "Six Bad Listening Habits."

15. Kitty W. Watson, Larry L. Barker, and James B. Weaver, *The Listener Style Inventory* (New Orleans: LA SPECTRA, 1995).

16. G. D. Bodie, D. L. Worthington, and C. C. Gearhart, "The Listening Styles Profile-Revised (LSP-R): A Scale Revision and Evidence for Validity," *Communication Quarterly* 16 (2013); 72–90; S. L. Sargent and James B. Weaver, "Correlates Between Communication Apprehension and Listening Style Preferences," *Communication Research Reports* 14 (1997): 74–78.

17. See Larry L. Barker and Kitty W. Watson, *Listen Up* (New York: St. Martin's Press, 2000); also see M. Imhof, "Who Are We as We Listen? Individual Listening Profiles in Varying Contexts," *International Journal of Listening* 18 (2004): 36–45.

18. Sargent and Weaver, "Correlates Between Communication Apprehension and Listening Style Preference."

19. D. L. Worthington, "Exploring the Relationship Between Listening Style Preferences and Personality," *International Journal of Listening* 17 (2003): 68–87.

20. M. D. Kirtley and J. M. Honeycutt, "Listening Styles and Their Correspondence with Second Guessing," *Communication Research Reports* 13 (1996): 174–82.

21. Harold Barrett, *Rhetoric and Civility: Human Development, Narcissism, and the Good Audience* (Albany: SUNY, 1991) 154.

22. Chad Edwards and Suzanne Walker, "Using Public Speaking Learning Communities to Reduce Communication Apprehension," *Texas Speech Communication Journal* 32 (2007): 65–71.

23. Patricia Sullivan, "Signification and African-American Rhetoric: A Case Study of Jesse Jackson's 'Common Ground and Common Sense' Speech," *Communication Quarterly* 41.1 (1993): 11.

24. Cited in Marie Hochmuth, ed., *A History and Criticism of American Public Address*, Vol. 3 (New York: Longmans, Green, 1955) 4; and in James R. Andrews, *The Practice of Rhetorical Criticism* (New York: Macmillan, 1983): 3–4.

25. Mike Allen, Sandra Berkowitz, Steve Hunt, and Allan Louden, "A Meta-Analysis of the Impact of Forensics and Communication Education on Critical Thinking," *Communication Education* 48 (Jan. 1999): 18–30.

26. For a comprehensive list of definitions of rhetoric, see Patricia Bizzell and Bruce Herzberg, eds., *The Rhetorical Tradition: Readings from Classical Times to the Present* (Boston: Bedford, 1990).

27. Aristotle, *On Rhetoric*. Translated by George A. Kennedy (New York: Oxford University Press, 1991): 14.

28. Isocrates, *Isocrates*, Vol. II. Translated by George Norlin (Cambridge, MA: Harvard University Press, 1929). Also see "Isocrates," in Bizzell and Herzberg, *The Rhetorical Tradition*.

29. Kenneth Burke, *A Rhetoric of Motives* (Berkeley: University of California Press, 1950). Also see Barry Brummett, *Reading Rhetorical Theory* (Fort Worth, TX: Harcourt College Publishers, 2000): 741.

30. Andrews, *The Practice of Rhetorical Criticism*.

31. Masterson, Beebe, and Watson, *Invitation to Effective Speech Communication*.

32. Robert Rowland, *Analyzing Rhetoric: A Handbook for the Informed Citizen in a New Millennium* (Dubuque, IA: Kendall/Hunt, 2002): 17–28.

CHAPTER 5

1. Robert H. Farrell, ed., *Off the Record: The Private Papers of Harry S Truman* (New York: Harper & Row, 1980): 310.

2. For background information about this quotation see http://answers.google.com/answers/threadview?id=398104

3. N. Howe and W. Strauss, *Millennials Rising: The Next Great Generation* (New York: Vintage, 2000). Also see Hank Karp, Connie Fuller, and Danilo Sirias, *Bridging the Boomer–Xer Gap: Creating Authentic Teams for High Performance at Work* (Palo Alto, CA: Davies-Black, 2002).

4. For an excellent review of gender and persuasibility research see Daniel J. O'Keefe, *Persuasion: Theory and Research* (Newbury Park, CA: Sage, 1990): 176–77. Also see James B. Stiff, *Persuasive Communication* (New York: Guilford Press, 1994): 133–36.

5. O'Keefe, *Persuasion*.

6. O'Keefe, *Persuasion*.

7. Gregory Herek, "Study Offers 'Snapshot' of Sacramento-Area Lesbian, Gay, and Bisexual Community." 23 July 2001 <http://psyweb.ucdavis.edu/rainbow/html/sacramento_study.html>. For an excellent literature review about sexual orientation and communication, see T. P. Mottet, "The Role of Sexual Orientation in Predicting Outcome Value and Anticipated Communication Behaviors," *Communication Quarterly* 48 (2000): 233–39.

8. See R. Lewontin, "The Apportionment of Human Diversity," *Evolutionary Biology* 6 (1973): 381–97; H. A. Yee, H. H. Fairchild, F. Weizmann, and E. G. Wyatt, "Addressing Psychology's Problems with Race," *American Psychologist* 48 (1994): 1132–40; D. Matsumoto and L. Juang, *Culture and Psychology* (Belmont, CA: Wadsworth/Thompson, 2004): 16.

9. The research summarized here is based on pioneering work by Geert Hofstede, *Culture's Consequences: International Differences in Work-Related Values* (Beverly Hills, CA: Sage, 1984). Also see Edward T. Hall, *Beyond Culture* (New York: Doubleday, 1976).

10. Richard Perez-Pena, "U.S. Bachelor Degree Rate Passes Milestone," *The New York Times*, 23 February 12 <http://www.nytimes.com/2012/02/24/education/census-finds-bachelors-degrees-at-record-level.html?_r=0>.

11. M. E. Ryan, "Another Way to Teach Migrant Students," *Los Angeles Times*, March 31, 1991: B20, as cited by M. W. Lustig and J. Koester, *Intercultural Competence: Interpersonal Communication Across Cultures* (Boston: Allyn & Bacon, 2003): 11.

12. G. Chen and W. J. Starosta, "A Review of the Concept of Intercultural Sensitivity," *Human Communication* 1 (1997): 7.

13. Susan Saulny, "Black? White? Asian? More Young Americans Choose All of the Above," *The New York Times*, 30 January 2011: 1, 20–21.

14. *Newsweek*, 12 July 1999, 51.

15. United States Census Bureau. 8 Feb. 2010. <http://www.prb.org/AmeristateTemplate>.

16. United States Census Bureau, <http://www.census.gov/hewsroom/releases/archives/population/cb12-243.html>.

17. David W. Kale, "Ethics in Intercultural Communication," *Intercultural Communication: A Reader*, 6th ed., eds. Larry A. Samovar and Richard E. Porter (Belmont, CA: Wadsworth, 1991): 423; also see discussion in Lustig and Koester, *Intercultural Competence.*

18. Donald E. Brown, "Human Universals and Their Implications," in N. Roughley, ed., *Being Humans: Anthropological Universality and Particularity in Transdisciplinary Perspectives* (New York: Walter de Gruyter, 2000). For an applied discussion of these universals, see Steven Pinker, *The Blank Slate: The Modern Denial of Human Nature* (London: Penguin Books, 2002).

19. Larry A. Samovar and Richard E. Porter, *Communication Between Cultures.* (Stamford, CT: Wadsworth and Thomson Learning, 2006): 29.

20. Brianne Geise, "Access Is Not Enough: Requiring Counsel with University Sale of the Morning-After Pill," Texas State University, 2013.

21. Sweets, "Mark Twain in India," *The Fence Painter: Bulletin of the Mark Twain Boyhood Home Associates* 26 (Winter 1996): 1.

22. For an excellent discussion of how to adapt to specific audience situations, see Jo Sprague and Douglas Stuart, *The Speaker's Handbook* (Belmont, CA: Wadsworth and Thompson, 2005): 345.

23. Devorah Lieberman, *Public Speaking in the Multicultural Environment* (Boston: Allyn & Bacon, 2000). Also see Edward T. Hall, *Silent Language* (Greenwich, CT: Fawcett, 1959); and Edward T. Hall, *The Hidden Dimension* (Garden City, NY: Doubleday, 1966).

CHAPTER 6

1. Mary Carmichael, "Speeches Strike a Similar Tone," *The Boston Globe* 8 June 2012.

2. Carmichael.

3. Roger Fringer, "Choosing a Speech Topic," in Tasha Van Horn, Lori Charron, and Michael Charron, *Allyn & Bacon Video II User's Guide*, 2002.

4. Bruce Gronbeck, from his presidential address delivered at the annual conference of the Speech Communication Association, Nov. 1994.

5. Henry H. Sweets III, "Mark Twain's Lecturing Career Continuation—Part II," *The Fence Painter* (Winter 2000–2001).

6. Alex F. Osborn, *Applied Imagination* (New York: Scribner's, 1962).

7. Monique Russo, "The 'Starving Disease' or Anorexia Nervosa," student speech, University of Miami, 1984.

8. Brian Sosnowchik, "The Cries of American Ailments," *Winning Orations 2000* (Mankato, MN: Interstate Oratorical Association, 2000): 114.

9. Judith Humphrey, "Taking the Stage: How Women Can Achieve a Leadership Presence," *Vital Speeches of the Day* (May 2001): 437.

10. Adapted from Erin Gallagher, "Upholstered Furniture Fires: Sitting in the Uneasy Chair," *Winning Orations 2000* (Mankato, MN: Interstate Oratorical Association, 2000): 99–101.

11. "Shuttle Missions." *Space Shuttle.* Nasa.gov, 29 August 2011.

12. Adapted from Nicole Tremel, "The New Wasteland: Computers," *Winning Orations 2000* (Mankato, MN: Interstate Oratorical Association, 2000): 37–40.

13. Patrick Martin, "The Energy Cure that Kills: Hydraulic Fracturing for Natural Gas," *Winning Orations 2011* (Mankato, MN: Interstate Oratorical Association, 2011): 147.

CHAPTER 7

1. "Types of Web Sites," Xavier University Library, 2010.

2. Elizabeth Kirk, "Practical Steps in Evaluating Internet Resources." 7 May 2001.

3. Ralph R. Behnke and Chris R. Sawyer, "Public-Speaking Procrastination as a Correlate of Public-Speaking Communication Apprehension and Self-Perceived Public-Speaking Competence," *Communication Research Reports* 16 (1999): 40–47; J. C. Pearson, J. T. Child, and D. H. Kahl, Jr., "Preparation Meeting Opportunity: How Do College Students Prepare for Public Speeches?" *Communication Quarterly* 54.3 (Aug. 2006): 351–66.

4. Charles Osgood, "On Civility in the Media," *Vital Speeches of the Day* (September 2011): 316–18.

5. Michael Cunningham, quoted in Dinitia Smith, "In the Age of the Overamplified, a Resurgence for the Humble Lecture," *New York Times* 17 Mar. 2006: B1, B5.

6. Sandra Zimmer, quoted in Vickie K. Sullivan, "Public Speaking: The Secret Weapon in Career Development," *USA Today* 24–25 May 2005: 133.

7. Hillary Rodham Clinton, "Women's Progress Is Human Progress," *Vital Speeches of the Day* (May 2010): 199–203.

8. Kevin Rudd, "The Apology to the Forgotten Australians," *Vital Speeches of the Day* (January 2010): 2–6.

9. Olli-Pekka Kallasvuo, "Connecting the Next Billion: The New Frontier of Upward Mobility," *Vital Speeches of the Day* (March 2010): 130–33.

10. Professor Frazer White, University of Miami.

11. Tunette Powell, "It's Not the Addict, It's the Drug: Redefining America's War on Drugs," *Winning Orations 2012* (Mankato, MN: Interstate Oratorical Association, 2012): 102.

12. Andrew B. Wilson, "How to Craft a Winning Speech," *Vital Speeches of the Day* (September 2005): 685–89.

13. David Cameron, "I'm for a Referendum on British Membership in the EU," *Vital Speeches of the Day* (February 2013): 34–35.

14. Alexandria Wisner, "Lithium Cell Batteries: The Power to Kill," *Winning Orations 2011* (Mankato, MN: Interstate Oratorical Association, 2011): 30.

15. Matthew Cossolotto, "An Urgent Call to Action for Study Abroad Alumni to Help Reduce Our Global Awareness Deficit," *Vital Speeches of the Day* (December 2009): 564–68.

16. Patrick Martin, "The Energy Cure that Kills: Hydraulic Fracturing for Natural Gas," *Winning Orations 2012* (Mankato, MN: Interstate Oratorical Association, 2012): 147.

17. Nicole Platzar, "Rated 'D' for Deficiency: The Sunshine Vitamin," *Winning Orations 2012* (Mankato, MN: Interstate Oratorical Association, 2012): 71.

18. James Stanfill, "Entomophagy: The Other Other White Meat," *Winning Orations 2009* (Mankato, MN: Interstate Oratorical Association, 2009): 24.

19. Throbjørn Jagland, "May Good Government Win in Europe," *Vital Speeches of the Day* (February 2013): 52–54.

20. Indra Nooyi, "Short-Term Demands vs. Long-Term Responsibilities," *Vital Speeches of the Day* (June 2010): 246–50.

21. Ivan Seidenberg, "How the Government Can Promote a Healthy, Competitive Communications Industry," *Vital Speeches of the Day* (1 Dec. 2009): 540–43.

22. "Sorry, You've Got the Wrong Number," *New York Times* 26 May 2001: A17.

23. Michael Blastland and David Spiegelhalter, *The Norm Chronicles: Stories and Numbers about Danger* (London: Profile Books, 2013): 47.

24. Daniel Hinderliter, "Collaborative Consumption," *Winning Orations 2012* (Mankato, MN: Interstate Oratorical Association, 2012): 140.

25. A. Barry Rand, "Rebuilding the Middle Class: A Blueprint for the Future," *Vital Speeches of the Day* (March 2013): 72–76.

26. Andie Malterud, "Dropping the Bomb on Water Fluoridation," *Winning Orations 2012* (Mankato, MN: Interstate Oratorical Association, 2012): 151.

27. Dena Craig, "Clearing the Air about Cigars," *Winning Orations 1998* (Mankato, MN: Interstate Oratorical Association, 1998): 13.

28. Sergio Marchionne, "Navigating the New Automotive Epoch," *Vital Speeches of the Day* (1 Mar. 2010): 134–37.

29. Kevin King, "Blue Zones," prepared for Individual Events/Informative Speaking Competition, The University of Texas, Spring 2013. Reprinted by permission of Kevin King.

30. Michael Kelley, "The New *Catch-22*: Unemployment Discrimination," *Winning Orations 2012* (Mankato, MN: Interstate Oratorical Association, 2012): 57.

CHAPTER 8

1. Joel Ayres, "The Impact of Time, Complexity, and Organization on Self-Reports of Speech Anxiety," *Communication Research Reports* 5.1 (June 1988): 58–63.

2. Information in this example comes from National Institutes of Health, "Stem Cells: A Primer," May 2000.

3. Adapted from John Kuehn, untitled speech, *Winning Orations 1994* (Mankato, MN: Interstate Oratorical Association, 1994): 83–85.

4. Dennis Lloyd, "Instant Expert: A Brief History of iPod," *iLounge* 26 June 2004; "Apple iPod, History of an Icon," *ipod games* 20 June 2007.

5. Beth Survant, "Let There Be Light," *Winning Orations 2011* (Mankato, MN: Interstate Oratorical Association, 2011): 53.

6. Sarah Perez, "YouTube Reaches 4 Billion Views Per Day," techcrunch.com 23 January 2012; Glenn Chapman, "YouTube Serving Up Two Billion Videos Daily," *Google News* 16 May 2010.

7. Philip Shenon, "A Showcase for Indian Artifacts," *New York Times* 29 Aug. 2004: TR 3.

8. Adapted from Vonda Ramey, "Can You Read This?" *Winning Orations 1985* (Mankato, MN: Interstate Oratorical Association, 1985): 32–35.

9. Adapted from Joseph Jones, "The Facts About For-Profit Universities," *Winning Orations 2011* (Mankato, MN: Interstate Oratorical Association, 2011): 74.

10. Cynthia Starks, "How to Write a Speech," *Vital Speeches of the Day* (April 2010).

11. The following information is adapted from Deborah A. Lieberman, *Public Speaking in the Multicultural Environment* (Englewood Cliffs, NJ: Prentice Hall, 1994).

12. Martin Medhurst, "The Text(ure) of the World in Presidential Rhetoric," *Vital Speeches of the Day* (June 2012).

13. John Seffrin, "The Worst Pandemic in the History of the World," *Vital Speeches of the Day* (April 2004).

14. Anastasia Danilyuk, "Alternatives to Imprisonment," *Winning Orations 2011* (Mankato, MN: Interstate Oratorical Association, 2011): 97.

15. Nichole Olson, "Flying the Safer Skies," *Winning Orations 2000* (Mankato, MN: Interstate Oratorical Association, 2000): 122.

16. Adapted from "Student Dies in Beach Sand Pit: Experts Warn of Suffocation Danger," *The Christian Science Monitor* 24 August 2012.

17. Robert Gore, untitled speech, *Winning Orations 2012* (Mankato, MN: Interstate Oratorical Association, 2012): 87.

18. Molly A. Lovell, "Hotel Security: The Hidden Crisis," *Winning Orations 1994* (Mankato, MN: Interstate Oratorical Association, 1994): 18.

19. Neela Latey, "U.S. Customs Procedures: Danger to Americans' Health and Society," *Winning Orations 1986* (Mankato, MN: Interstate Oratorical Association, 1986): 22.

20. Susan Stevens, "Teacher Shortage," *Winning Orations 1986* (Mankato, MN: Interstate Oratorical Association, 1986): 27.

21. Nicole Platzar, "Rated 'D' for Deficiency: The Sunshine Vitamin," *Winning Orations 2012* (Mankato, MN: Interstate Oratorical Association, 2012): 73.

22. Ben Crosby, "The New College Disease," *Winning Orations 2000* (Mankato, MN: Interstate Oratorical Association, 2000): 133.

23. Lori Van Overbeke, "NutraSweet," *Winning Orations 1986* (Mankato, MN: Interstate Oratorical Association, 1986): 58.

24. John O'Brien, quoted in Brent Filson, *Executive Speeches* (New York: Wiley, 1994) 144–45.

25. Charles Parnell, "Speechwriting: The Profession and the Practice," *Vital Speeches of the Day* (15 Jan. 1990): 56.

26. The sample outline in this chapter is adapted from Brianne Geise, "Access Is Not Enough: Requiring Counsel with University Sale of the Morning-After Pill," Texas State University, 2013.

27. Clive Thompson, "PowerPoint Makes You Dumb," *New York Times Magazine* 14 December 2003: 88.

CHAPTER 9

1. K. Phillip Taylor, "Speech Teachers' Pet Peeves: Student Behaviors That Public Instructors Find Annoying, Irritating, and Unwanted in Student Speeches," *Florida Communication Journal* 33.2 (2005): 56.

2. Lauren Holstein, "Slavery in the Sunshine State," *Winning Orations 2012* (Mankato, MN: Interstate Oratorical Association, 2012): 34.

3. Sheena Holliday, "Uninvited Visitor," *Winning Orations 2003* (Mankato, MN: Interstate Oratorical Association, 2003): 84.

4. Edwin Pittock, "America's Crisis in Aging," *Vital Speeches of the Day* (February 2004).

5. Charles W. Chesnutt, *Frederick Douglass*. Electronic edition published by Academic Affairs Library, University of North Carolina at Chapel Hill, 2001.

6. Cadie Thompson, "Twitter CEO Dick Costolo Gives New Grads Advice to Be 'Bold,'" *CNBC* 6 May 2013.

7. Jennifer Sweeney, "Racial Profiling," *Winning Orations 2000* (Mankato, MN: Interstate Oratorical Association, 2000): 1.

8. Matt Miller, "A Situational Speech: Bisphenol A," *Winning Orations 2009* (Mankato: MN: Interstate Oratorical Association, 2009).

9. Statistics from "Which Law School Graduates Have the Most Debt?" *U.S. News and World Report Best Law Schools*, 2013.

10. Terrika Scott, "Curing Crisis with Community," *Winning Orations 1995* (Mankato, MN: Interstate Oratorical Association, 1995): 11.

11. Theresa Clinkenbeard, "The Loss of Childhood," *Winning Orations 1984* (Mankato, MN: Interstate Oratorical Association, 1984): 4.

12. Thad Noyes, "Dishonest Death Care," *Winning Orations 1999* (Mankato, MN: Interstate Oratorical Association, 1999): 73.

13. Marvin Olasky, "Responding to Disaster," *Vital Speeches of the Day* (November 2006): 744.

14. Joe Griffith, *Speaker's Library of Business Stories, Anecdotes, and Humor* (Englewood Cliffs, NJ: Prentice Hall, 1990): 335.

15. Douglas MacArthur, "Farewell to the Cadets," address delivered at West Point, 12 May 1962. Reprinted in Richard L. Johannesen, R. R. Allen, and W. A. Linkugel, eds., *Contemporary American Speeches*, 7th ed. (Dubuque, IA: Kendall/Hunt, 1992): 393.

16. Jascha Hoffman, "Me Translate Funny One Day," *The New York Times Book Review* 21 October 2012: 31.

17. Muhtar Kent, "Are We Ready for Tomorrow, Today?" *Vital Speeches of the Day* (March 2010): 117-21.

18. Richard Propes, "Alone in the Dark," *Winning Orations 1985* (Mankato, MN: Interstate Oratorical Association, 1985): 22.

19. Luis Proenza, "Relevance, Connectivity and Productivity." *Vital Speeches of the Day* (February 2010): 89-92.

20. Cynthia Starks, "How to Write a Speech," *Vital Speeches of the Day* (April 2010): 153-56.

21. Adam Winegarden, "The After-Dinner Speech," in Tasha Van Horn, Lori Charron, and Michael Charron, eds., *Allyn & Bacon Video II User's Guide*, 2002.

22. William G. Durden, "Just Do Science," *Vital Speeches of the Day* (March 2013): 67-71.

23. Chris Miller, "Remember Both the Art and the Business Involved in Collision Repair," *Vital Speeches of the Day* (May 2010): 203-13.

24. Chris Christie, "The Adults Are in Charge," *Vital Speeches of the Day* (March 2013): 82-87.

25. Student speech, University of Miami, 1981.

26. Lou Gehrig, "Farewell Speech," *Lou Gehrig: The Official Web Site* 23 June 2007.

27. Robert Lehrman, "Victory Speeches," *The New York Times* 7 November 2012.

28. Noelle Stephens, "The WWW.CON of Higher Education," *Winning Orations 1999* (Mankato, MN: Interstate Oratorical Association, 1999): 12.

29. John Ryan, "Emissions Tampering: Get the Lead Out," *Winning Orations 1985* (Mankato, MN: Interstate Oratorical Association, 1985): 63.

30. Melanie Loehwing, untitled speech, *Winning Orations 2003* (Mankato, MN: Interstate Oratorical Association, 2003): 23-24.

31. Richard Kelley, "Ready, Aim, Thrive: Strategies for 2007," *Vital Speeches of the Day* (December 2006): 763-67.

32. Bono, "Because We Can, We Must." University of Pennsylvania, *Almanac Between Issues* 19 May 2004.

33. Miller, "A Situational Speech: Bisphenol A."

34. James W. Robinson, "Create a Fireworks Finale," *Executive Speeches* (April 1989): 41-44.

35. Tyler Kingkade, "Brian Williams Elon Commencement Speech Included Heartwarming Message to His Son," *The Huffington Post* 28 May 2013.

CHAPTER 10

1. "10 Hilarious Protest Signs," *Blognoscor* 16 October 2010.

2. David Crystal, "Speaking of Writing and Writing of Speaking," *Longman Dictionaries: Express Yourself with Confidence!* (Pearson Education, 2005).

3. Nemanja Savic, "Hope—in the Voices of Africa," speech delivered at Wake Forest University, 14 May 2006. *Window on Wake Forest.* 15 May 2006.

4. Max Woodfin, "Three among Many Lives Jordan Touched," *Austin American-Statesman* 20 January 1996: A13.

5. Paul Roberts, "How to Say Nothing in Five Hundred Words," in William H. Roberts and Gregoire Turgeson, eds., *About Language* (Boston: Houghton Mifflin, 1986): 28.

6. George Orwell, "Politics and the English Language," in William H. Roberts and Gregoire Turgeson, eds., *About Language* (Boston: Houghton Mifflin, 1986): 282.

7. Erma Bombeck, "Missing Grammar Genes Is, Like, the Problem," *Austin American-Statesman* 3 March 1992.

8. Sik Ng & James J. Bradac, *Power in Language: Verbal Communication and Social Influence. Language and Language Behaviors,* Vol. 3. (1993). http://psycnet.apa.org/psycinfo/1993-98279-000

9. John Lister, quoted in "At the End of the Day, It Annoys." Associated Press. 24 March 2004.

10. Shelley Matheson, "The Most Annoying Clichés Ever," *The Scottish Sun* 8 January 2010.

11. William Safire, "Words at War," *New York Times Magazine* 30 September 2001.

12. John S. Seiter, Jarrod Larsen, and Jacey Skinner, "'Handicapped' or 'Handicapable?': The Effects of Language about Persons with Disabilities on Perceptions of Source Credibility and Persuasiveness," *Communication Reports* 11:1 (1998): 21–31.

13. Peggy Noonan, *What I Saw at the Revolution* (New York: Random House, 1990): 71.

14. Michael M. Klepper, *I'd Rather Die Than Give a Speech* (New York: Carol Publishing Group, 1994): 45.

15. We acknowledge the following source for several examples used in our discussion of language style: William Jordan, "Rhetorical Style," *Oral Communication Handbook* (Warrensburg, MO: Central Missouri State U, 1971–1972): 32–34.

16. Eric Stolhanske, "Advice from a Kid with a Wooden Leg," *Vital Speeches of the Day* (July 2012): 211–16.

17. Scott Davis, "Class Begins Today," *Vital Speeches of the Day* (August 2011): 279–80.

18. Samuel Hazo, "Poetry and Public Speech," *Vital Speeches of the Day* (April 2007): 685–89.

19. Michiko Kakutani, "Struggling to Find Words for a Horror Beyond Words," *New York Times* 13 September 2001: E1.

20. Franklin Roosevelt, inaugural address of 1933 (Washington, DC: National Archives and Records Administration, 1988): 22.

21. George F. Will, "'Let Us . . .'? No, Give It a Rest," *Newsweek* 22 January 2001: 64.

22. John F. Kennedy, inaugural address, 20 Jan. 1961, in Bower Aly and Lucille F. Aly, eds., *Speeches in English* (New York: Random House, 1968): 272.

23. Barack Obama, "Can We Honestly Say We're Doing Enough?" *Vital Speeches of the Day* (February 2013): 34–35.

24. Garrison Keillor, *The Writer's Almanac.* 20 August 2012.

25. Barack Obama, "Look at the World Through Their Eyes," *Vital Speeches of the Day* (May 2013): 138–42.

26. Roosevelt, inaugural address of 1933.

27. William Faulkner, speech in acceptance of the Nobel Prize for Literature, delivered 10 Dec. 1950, in Houston Peterson, ed., *A Treasury of the World's Great Speeches* (New York: Simon & Schuster, 1965): 814–15.

28. David Brooks, baccalaureate address at Sewanee: The University of the South. *Sewanee Today* 11 May 2013.

29. Roosevelt, inaugural address of 1933.

30. Winston Churchill, address to the Congress of the United States, delivered on 26 Dec. 1941, in Bower Aly and Lucille F. Aly, eds., *Speeches in English* (New York: Random House, 1968): 233.

31. Barack Obama, inaugural address of 2013. washingtonpost.com 21 January 2013.

32. Adapted from Jordan, *Oral Communication Handbook,* 34.

33. Kennedy, inaugural address.

34. "Reference to Rape Edited from Graduation Speech," *Kansas City Star* 5 June 1995: B3.

35. "Dear Abby," *San Marcos Daily Record* 5 January 1993: 7.

36. Activity developed by Loren Reid, *Speaking Well* (New York: McGraw-Hill, 1982): 96.

CHAPTER 11

1. For an excellent discussion of the importance of speaker delivery according to both classical and contemporary rhetoricians, see J. Fredal, "The Language of Delivery and the Presentation of Character: Rhetorical Action in Demosthenes' 'Against Meidias,'" *Rhetoric Review* 20 (2001): 251-67.

2. James W. Gibson, John A. Kline, and Charles R. Gruner, "A Reexamination of the First Course in Speech at U.S. Colleges and Universities," *Speech Teacher* 23 (Sept. 1974): 206–14.

3. Ray Birdwhistle, *Kinesics and Context* (Philadelphia: University of Pennsylvania, 1970).

4. Judee K. Burgoon and Beth A. Le Poire, "Nonverbal Cues and Interpersonal Judgments: Participant and Observer Perceptions of Intimacy, Dominance, Composure, and Formality," *Communication Monographs* 66 (1999): 105–24; Beth A. Le Poire and Stephen M. Yoshimura, "The Effects of Expectancies and Actual Communication on Nonverbal Adaptation and Communication Outcomes: A Test of Interaction Adaptation Theory," *Communication Monographs* 66 (1999): 1–30.

5. Albert Mehrabian, *Nonverbal Communication* (Hawthorne, NY: Aldine, 1972).

6. D. Lapakko, "Three Cheers for Language: A Closer Examination of a Widely Cited Study of Nonverbal Communication," *Communication Education* 46 (1997): 63–67.

7. Steven A. Beebe and Thompson Biggers, "The Effect of Speaker Delivery upon Listener Emotional Response," paper presented at the International Communication Association meeting, May 1989.

8. Elaine Hatfield, J. T. Cacioppo, and R. L. Rapson, *Emotional Contagion* (New York: Cambridge University Press, 1994); also see John T. Cacioppo, Gary G. Berntson, Jeff T. Larsen, Kirsten M. Poehlmann, and Tiffany A. Ito, "The Psychophysiology of Emotion," in Michael Lewis and Jeannette M. Haviland-Jones, eds., *Handbook of Emotions*, 2nd ed. (New York: Guilford Press, 2004): 173–91.

9. Paul Ekman, Wallace V. Friesen, and K. R. Schere, "Body Movement and Voice Pitch in Deception Interaction," *Semiotica* 16 (1976): 23–27; Mark Knapp, R. P. Hart, and H. S. Dennis, "An Exploration of Deception as a Communication Construct," *Human Communication Research* 1 (1974): 15–29.

10. Roger Ailes, *You Are the Message* (New York: Doubleday, 1989): 37–38; Gellis Communications, "Top Tips for Preparing and Delivering a Manuscript Speech." 4 Nov. 2011. http://www.gellis.com/blog/top-tips-preparing-and-delivering-manuscript-speech; David W. Richardson, "Delivering a Manuscript Speech." 2013. http://www.richspeaking.com/articles/manuscript_speech.html.

11. David Gates, "Prince of the Podium," *Newsweek* 14 June 1996: 82.

12. *Austin-American Statesman*, 15 Jan. 2007: A11.

13. Eric J. Sundquist, *King's Dream* (New Haven: Yale University Press, 2009): 14.

14. Sundquist, *King's Dream,* 2.

15. Cicero, *De Oratore,* vol. 4, translated by E. W. Sutton (Cambridge: Harvard University Press, 1988).

16. Steven A. Beebe, "Eye Contact: A Nonverbal Determinant of Speaker Credibility," *Speech Teacher* 23 (Jan. 1974): 21–25; Steven A. Beebe, "Effects of Eye Contact, Posture and Vocal Inflection upon Credibility and Comprehension," *Australian Scan Journal of Nonverbal Communication* 7-8 (1979–1980): 57–70; Martin Cobin, "Response to Eye Contact," *Quarterly Journal of Speech* 48 (1963): 415–19.

17. Beebe, "Eye Contact," 21–25.

18. Khera Communications, "Business Tips for India," *More Business*, 2001. 8 June 2004. www.morebusiness.com/running_your_business/management/d930585271.brc? highlightstring=Business+Tips+for+India.

19. Brent Filson, *Executive Speeches: Tips on How to Write and Deliver Speeches from 51 CEOs* (New York: Wiley, 1994).

20. Albert Mehrabian, *Silent Messages* (Belmont, CA: Wadsworth, 1971).

21. For a comprehensive review of immediacy in an instructional context, see Virginia P. Richmond, Derek R. Lange, and James C. McCroskey, "Teacher Immediacy and the Teacher-Student Relationship," in Timothy P. Mottet, Virginia P. Richmond, and James C. McCroskey, *Handbook of Instructional Communication: Rhetorical and Relational Perspectives* (Boston: Allyn & Bacon, 2006): 167–93.

22. See Virginia P. Richmond, Joan Gorham, and James C. McCroskey, "The Relationship Between Selected Immediacy Behaviors and Cognitive Learning," in M. McLaughlin, ed., *Communication Yearbook* 10 (Beverly Hills, CA: Sage, 1987): 574–90; Joan Gorham, "The Relationship Between Verbal Teacher Immediacy Behaviors and Student Learning," *Communication Education* 37 (1988): 40–53; Diane M. Christophel, "The Relationship Among Teacher Immediacy Behaviors, Student Motivation, and Learning," *Communication Education* 39 (1990): 323–40; James C. McCroskey, Virginia P. Richmond, Aino Sallinen, Joan M. Fayer, and Robert A. Barraclough, "A Cross-Cultural and Multi-Behavioral Analysis of the Relationship Between Nonverbal Immediacy and Teacher Evaluation," *Communication Education* 44 (1995): 281–90; Timothy P. Mottet and Steven A. Beebe, "Relationships Between Teacher Nonverbal Immediacy, Student Emotional Response, and Perceived Student Learning," *Communication Research Reports* 19 (Jan. 2002).

23. Michael J. Beatty, "Some Effects of Posture on Speaker Credibility," library paper, University of Central Missouri, 1973.

24. Albert Mehrabian and M. Williams, "Nonverbal Concomitants of Perceived and Intended Persuasiveness," *Journal of Personality and Social Psychology* 13 (1969): 37–58.

25. Paul Ekman, Wallace V. Friesen, and S. S. Tomkins, "Facial Affect Scoring Technique: A First Validity Study," *Semiotica* 3 (1971).

26. Paul Ekman and Wallace Friesen, *Unmasking the Face* (Englewood Cliffs, NJ: Prentice Hall, 1975); D. Keltner and P. Ekman, "Facial Expression of Emotion," in M. Lewis and J. M. Haviland-Jones, eds., *Handbook of Emotions* (New York: Gilford, 2000): 236–49; D. Keltner, P. Ekman, G. S. Gonzaga, and J. Beer, "Facial Expression of Emotion," in R. J. Davidson, K. R. Scherer, and H. H. Goldsmith, eds., *Handbook of Affective Sciences* (New York: Oxford University Press, 2003): 415–32.

27. Adapted from Lester Schilling, *Voice and Diction for the Speech Arts* (San Marcos: Southwest Texas State University, 1979).

28. Mary M. Gill, "Accent and Stereotypes: Their Effect on Perceptions of Teachers and Lecture Comprehension," *Journal of Applied Communication* 22 (1994): 348–61.

29. Kenneth K. Sereno and G. J. Hawkins, "The Effects of Variations in Speakers' Nonfluency upon Audience Ratings of Attitude Toward the Speech Topic and Speakers' Credibility," *Speech Monographs* 34 (1967): 58–74; Gerald R. Miller and M. A. Hewgill, "The Effect of Variations in Nonfluency on Audience Ratings of Source Credibility," *Quarterly Journal of Speech* 50 (1964): 36–44; Mehrabian and Williams, "Nonverbal Concomitants of Perceived and Intended Persuasiveness."

30. These suggestions were made by Jo Sprague and Douglas Stuart, *The Speaker's Handbook* (Fort Worth, TX: Harcourt Brace Jovanovich, 1992): 331, and were based on research by Patricia A. Porter, Margaret Grant, and Mary Draper, *Communicating Effectively in English: Oral Communication for Non-Native Speakers* (Belmont, CA: Wadsworth, 1985).

31. James W. Neuliep, *Intercultural Communication: A Contextual Approach* (Boston: Houghton Mifflin, 2000): 247.

32. Stephen Lucas, *The Art of Public Speaking* (New York: Random House, 1986): 231.

33. Research cited by Leo Fletcher, *How to Design and Deliver Speeches* (New York: Addison Wesley Longman, 2001): 73.

34. "Comment," *The New Yorker* 1 Mar. 1993.

35. John S. Seiter and Andrea Sandry, "Pierced for Success? The Effects of Ear and Nose Piercing on Perceptions of Job Candidates' Credibility, Attractiveness, and Hirability," *Communication Research Reports* 20.4 (2003): 287–98.

36. For an excellent review of the effects of immediacy in the classroom, see Mehrabian, *Silent Messages*; also see James C. McCroskey, Aino Sallinen, Joan M. Fayer, Virginia P. Richmond, and Robert A. Barraclough, "Nonverbal Immediacy and Cognitive Learning: A Cross-Cultural Investigation," *Communication Education* 45 (1996): 200–11.

37. Larry A. Samovar and Richard E. Porter, *Communication Between Cultures* (Stamford, CT: Thomson Learning, 2001): 166.

38. William B. Gudykunst, *Bridging Differences: Effective Intergroup Communication* (Thousand Oaks, CA: Sage, 1998): 12.

39. Kent E. Menzel and Lori J. Carrell, "The Relationship Between Preparation and Performance in Public Speaking," *Communication Education* 43 (1994): 17–26; Tony E. Smith and Ann Bainbridge Frymier, "Get 'Real': Does Practicing Speeches Before an Audience Improve Performance?" *Communication Quarterly* 54.1 (Feb. 2006): 111–25; Judy C. Pearson, Jeffrey T. Child, and David H. Kahl, Jr., "Preparation Meeting Opportunity: How Do College Students Prepare for Public Speeches?" *Communication Quarterly* 54.3 (Aug. 2006): 351–66.

40. Filson, *Executive Speeches*.

41. Filson, *Executive Speeches*.

CHAPTER 12

1. Brent Filson, *Executive Speeches: Tips on How to Write and Deliver Speeches from 51 CEOs* (New York: Wiley, 1994): 212.

2. Emil Bohn and David Jabusch, "The Effect of Four Methods of Instruction on the Use of Visual Aids in Speeches," *Western Journal of Speech Communication* 46 (Summer 1982): 253–65.

3. J. S. Wilentz, *The Senses of Man* (New York: Crowell, 1968).

4. Michael E. Patterson, Donald F. Dansereau, and Dianna Newbern, "Effects of Communication Aids and Strategies on Cooperative Teaching," *Journal of Educational Psychology* 84 (1992): 453–61.

5. Louise Rehling, "Teaching in a High-Tech Conference Room: Academic Adaptations and Workplace Simulations," *Journal of Business and Technical Communication* 19.1 (Jan. 2005): 98–113.

6. Richard E. Mayer and Valerie K. Sims, "For Whom Is a Picture Worth a Thousand Words? Extensions of a Dual-Coding Theory of Multimedia Learning," *Journal of Educational Psychology* 86 (1994): 389–401.

7. Dale Cyphert, "The Problem of PowerPoint: Visual Aid or Visual Rhetoric?" *Business Communication Quarterly* (Mar. 2004): 80–84.

8. Andrew Wilson, "In Defense of Rhetoric," *Toastmaster* 70.2 (Feb. 2004): 8–11.

9. Roxanne Parrott, Kami Sikl, Kelly Dorgan, Celeste Condit, and Tina Harris, "Risk Comprehension and Judgments of Statistical Evidentiary Appeals: When a Picture Is Not Worth a Thousand Words," *Human Communication Research* 31 (July 2005): 423–52.

10. Rebecca B. Worley and Marilyn A. Dyrud, "Presentations and the PowerPoint Problem," *Business Communication Quarterly* 67 (Mar. 2004): 78–80.

11. We acknowledge Dan Cavanaugh's excellent supplement *Preparing Visual Aids for Presentation* (Boston: Allyn & Bacon/Longman, 2001) as a source for many of our tips and suggestions.

12. Filson, *Executive Speeches*.

13. For a good discussion of how to develop and use PowerPoint visuals, see Jerry Weissman, *Presenting to Win: The Art of Telling Your Story* (Upper Saddle River, NJ: Financial Times/Prentice Hall, 2003).

14. We thank Stan Crowley, a student at Texas State University, for his permission to use his speech outline.

CHAPTER 13

1. John R. Johnson and Nancy Szczupakiewicz, "The Public Speaking Course: Is It Preparing Students with Work-Related Public Speaking Skills?" *Communication Education* 36 (Apr. 1987): 131–37.

2. Pamela J. Hinds, "The Curse of Expertise: The Effects of Expertise and Debiasing Methods on Predicting Novice Performance," *Journal of Experimental Psychology: Applied* 5 (1999): 205–21. Research summarized in Chip Heath and Dan Heath, *Made to Stick: Why Some Ideas Survive and Others Die* (New York: Random House, 2007): 19–21.

3. Joseph L. Chesebro, "Effects of Teacher Clarity and Nonverbal Immediacy on Student Learning, Receiver Apprehension, and Affect," *Communication Education* 52 (Apr. 2003): 135–47.

4. Malcolm Knowles, *The Adult Learner: A Neglected Species*, 3rd ed. (Houston: Gulf Publishing, 1990).

5. Steven A. Beebe, Timothy P. Mottet, and K. David Roach, *Training and Development: Communicating for Success* (Boston: Pearson, 2013).

6. Katherine E. Rowan, "A New Pedagogy for Explanatory Public Speaking: Why Arrangement Should Not Substitute for Invention," *Communication Education* 44 (1995): 236–50.

7. Philip Yancy, *Prayer: Does It Make Any Difference?* (Grand Rapids, MI: Zondervan, 2006): 20.

8. Michael A. Boerger and Tracy B. Henley, "The Use of Analogy in Giving Instructions," *Psychological Record* 49 (1999): 193–209.

9. Heath and Heath, *Made to Stick*, 63–64.

10. Marcie Groover, "Learning to Communicate: The Importance of Speech Education in Public Schools," *Winning Orations 1984* (Mankato, MN: Interstate Oratorical Association, 1984): 7.

11. As cited by Eleanor Doan, *The New Speaker's Sourcebook* (Grand Rapids, MI: Zondervan, 1968).

12. C. S. Lewis, "On Stories," *Essays Presented to Charles Williams*, C. S. Lewis, ed. (Oxford: Oxford University Press, 1947); also see Walter R. Fisher, *Communication as Narration: Toward a Philosophy of Reason, Value, and Action* (Columbia: University of South Carolina Press, 1987).

13. Christopher Booker, *The Seven Basic Plots: Why We Tell Stories* (London: Continuum, 2004). The theory that all stories are about "finding home" is from Steven A. Beebe, *C. S. Lewis:*

Chronicles of a Master Communicator (San Marcos, TX: Texas State University, 2013).

14. Roger Fringer, "Choosing a Speech Topic," *Student Speeches Video* (Boston: Allyn & Bacon, 2003).

15. Heath and Heath, *Made to Stick*.

16. See Bruce W. A. Whittlesea and Lisa D. Williams, "The Discrepancy-Attribution Hypothesis II: Expectation, Uncertainty, Surprise, and Feelings of Familiarity," *Journal of Experimental Psychology: Learning, Memory, and Cognition* 2 (2001): 14–33; also see Suzanne Hidi, "Interest and Its Contribution as a Mental Resource for Learning," *Review of Educational Research* 60 (1990): 549–71; Mark Sadoski, Ernest T. Goetz, and Maximo Rodriguez, "Engaging Texts: Effects of Concreteness of Comprehensibility, Interest, and Recall in Four Text Types," *Journal of Educational Psychology* 92 (2000): 85–95.

17. Heath and Heath, *Made to Stick,* 51–52.

18. George Miller, "The Magical Number Seven, Plus or Minus Two," *Psychological Review* 63 (1956): 81–97.

19. D. K. Cruickshank and J. J. Kennedy, "Teacher Clarity," *Teaching & Teacher Education* 2 (1986): 43–67.

CHAPTER 14

1. Martin Fishbein and I. Ajzen, *Belief, Attitude, Intention, and Behavior: An Introduction to Theory and Research* (Reading, MA: Addison-Wesley, 1975).

2. Aristotle, *On Rhetoric*, translated by George A. Kennedy (New York: Oxford University Press, 1991): 14.

3. For a discussion of motivation in social settings, see Douglas T. Kenrick, Steven L. Neuberg, and Robert B. Cialdini, *Social Psychology: Unraveling the Mystery* (Boston: Allyn & Bacon, 2002).

4. For a discussion of the elaboration likelihood model, see R. Petty and D. Wegener, "The Elaboration Likelihood Model: Current Status and Controversies," in S. Chaiken and Y. Trope, eds., *Dual Process Theories in Social Psychology* (New York: Guilford, 1999): 41–72; also see R. Petty and J. T. Cacioppo, *Communication and Persuasion: Central and Peripheral Routes to Attitude Change* (New York: Springer-Verlag, 1986).

5. Leon Festinger, *A Theory of Cognitive Dissonance* (Evanston, IL: Row, Peterson, 1957).

6. For additional discussion, see Wayne C. Minnick, *The Art of Persuasion* (Boston: Houghton Mifflin, 1967).

7. Abraham H. Maslow, "A Theory of Human Motivation," in *Motivation and Personality* (New York: Harper & Row, 1954), chapter 5.

8. John Ryan, "Emissions Tampering: Get the Lead Out," *Winning Orations 1985* (Mankato, MN: Interstate Oratorical Association, 1985): 50.

9. For a discussion of fear appeal research, see Irving L. Janis and Seymour Feshbach, "Effects of Fear-Arousing Communications," *Journal of Abnormal and Social Psychology* 48 (January 1953): 78–92; Frederick A. Powell and Gerald R. Miller, "Social Approval and Disapproval Cues in Anxiety-Arousing Situations," *Speech Monographs* 34 (June 1967): 152–59; Kenneth L. Higbee, "Fifteen Years of Fear Arousal: Research on Threat Appeals, 1953–68," *Psychological Bulletin* 72 (December 1969): 426–44.

10. Paul A. Mongeau, "Another Look at Fear-Arousing Persuasive Appeals," in Mike Allen and Raymond W. Preiss, eds., *Persuasion: Advances Through Meta-Analysis* (Cresskill, NJ: Hampton Press, 1998): 65.

11. K. Witte, "Putting the Fear Back into Fear Appeals: The Extended Parallel Process Model," *Communication Monographs* 59 (1992): 329–47.

12. Patrick McGeehan, "Blame Photoshop, Not Diabetes, for This Amputation," *New York Times,* January 24, 2012 http://www.nytimes.com/2012/01/25/nyregion/in-health-dept-ad-photoshop-not-diabetes-took-leg.html?_r=1&

13. See discussions in Myron W. Lustig and Jolene Koester, *Intercultural Competence: Interpersonal Communication Across Cultures* (Boston: Allyn & Bacon, 2012): 347; Larry A. Samovar and Richard E. Porter, *Communication Between Cultures* (Stamford, CT: Wadsworth and Thomson Learning, 2010): 29.

14. C. W. Sherif, M. Sherif, and R. E. Nebergall, *Attitudes and Attitude Change: The Social Judgment-Involvement Approach* (Philadelphia: Saunders, 1965).

CHAPTER 15

1. Donald C. Bryant, "Rhetoric: Its Functions and Its Scope," *Quarterly Journal of Speech* 39 (December 1953): 26.

2. J. C. Reinard, "The Empirical Study of the Persuasive Effects of Evidence: The Status after Fifty Years of Research," *Human Communication Research* 15 (1988): 3–59.

3. James C. McCroskey and R. S. Rehrley, "The Effects of Disorganization and Nonfluency on Attitude Change and Source Credibility," *Speech Monographs* 36 (1969): 13–21.

4. John F. Kennedy, "Inaugural Address (January 20, 1961)," in Bower Aly and Lucille F. Aly, eds., *Speeches in English* (New York: Random House, 1968): 272.

5. Judee K. Burgoon, T. Birk, and M. Pfau, "Nonverbal Behaviors, Persuasion, and Credibility," *Human Communication Research* 17 (1990): 140–69.

6. Segrin, "The Effects of Nonverbal Behavior on Outcomes of Compliance Gaining Attempts."

7. Robin L. Nabi, Emily Moyer-Guse, and Sahara Byrne, "All Joking Aside: A Serious Investigation into the Persuasive Effect of Funny Social Issue Messages," *Communication Monographs* 74 (March 2007): 29–54.

8. For a discussion of the perceived link between inductive and deductive reasoning, see Evan Heit and Caren M. Rotello, "Relations Between Inductive Reasoning and Deductive Reasoning," *Journal of Experimental Psychology* 36 (2010): 805–12.

9. For an excellent discussion of the influence of culture on public speaking, see Devorah A. Lieberman, *Public Speaking in the Multicultural Environment* (Englewood Cliffs, NJ: Prentice Hall, 1994): 10.

10. Devorah Lieberman and G. Fisher, "International Negotiation," in Larry A. Samovar and Richard E. Porter, eds., *Intercultural Communication: A Reader* (Belmont, CA: Wadsworth, 1991): 193–200.

11. Lieberman and Fisher, "International Negotiation."

12. Jeffrey E. Jamison, "Alkali Batteries: Powering Electronics and Polluting the Environment," *Winning Orations 1991* (Mankato, MN: Interstate Oratorical Association, 1991): 43.

13. H. B. Brosius and A. Bathelt, "The Utility of Exemplars in Persuasive Communications," *Communication Research* 21 (1994): 48–78.

14. Lisa L. Massi-Lindsey and Kimo Ah Yun, "Examining the Persuasive Effect of Statistical Messages: A Test of Mediating Relationships," *Communication Studies* 54 (Fall 2003):

306–21; D. C. Kazoleas, "A Comparison of the Persuasive Effectiveness of Qualitative versus Quantitative Evidence: A Test of Explanatory Hypotheses," *Communication Quarterly* 41 (1993): 40–50; also see M. Allen and R. W. Preiss, "Comparing the Persuasiveness of Narrative and Statistical Evidence Using Meta-Analysis," *Communication Research Reports* (1997): 125–31.

15. Franklin J. Boster, Kenzie A. Cameron, Shelly Campo, Wen-Ying Liu, Janet K. Lillie, Esther M. Baker, and Kimo Ah Yun, "The Persuasive Effects of Statistical Evidence in the Presence of Exemplars," *Communication Studies* 51 (Fall 2000): 296–306; also see E. J. Baesler and Judee K. Burgoon, "The Temporal Effects of Story and Statistical Evidence on Belief Change," *Communication Research* 21 (1994): 582–602.

16. Reinard, "The Empirical Study of the Persuasive Effects of Evidence," 37–38.

17. William L. Benoit and I. A. Kennedy, "On Reluctant Testimony," *Communication Quarterly* 47 (1999): 376–87. Although this study raises questions about whether reluctant testimony is persuasive, reluctant testimony as well as neutral testimony is better than testimony perceived to be obviously biased.

18. E. J. Baesler, "Persuasive Effects of Story and Statistical Evidence," *Argumentation and Advocacy* 33 (1997): 170–75.

19. Myron W. Lustig and Jolene Koester, *Intercultural Competence: Interpersonal Communication Across Cultures* (Boston: Allyn & Bacon, 2009).

20. K. Ah Yun and L. L. Massi, "The Differential Impact of Race on the Effectiveness of Narrative versus Statistical Appeals to Persuade Individuals to Sign an Organ Donor Card," paper presented at the meeting of the Western States Communication Association, Sacramento, CA; cited by Massi-Lindsey and Ah Yun, "Examining the Persuasive Effect of Statistical Messages."

21. Lustig and Koester, *Intercultural Competence,* 241.

22. Jamie Frater, "Top 10 Great Historic Speeches," http://listverse.com/2008/06/01/top-10-great-historic-speeches/ accessed June 14, 2013.

23. Albert Mehrabian and J. A. Russell, *An Approach to Environmental Psychology* (Cambridge: MIT Press, 1974); T. Biggers and B. Pryor, "Attitude Change as a Function of Emotion-Eliciting Qualities," *Personality and Social Psychology Bulletin* 8 (1982): 94–99; Steven A. Beebe and T. Biggers, "Emotion-Eliciting Qualities of Speech Delivery and Their Effect on Credibility and Comprehension," paper presented at the annual meeting of the International Communication Association, New Orleans, May 1989.

24. Donald Dean Morely and Kim B. Walker, "The Role of Importance, Novelty, and Plausibility in Producing Belief Change," *Communication Monographs* 54 (1987): 436–42; also see Chip Heath and Dan Heath, *Made to Stick: Why Some Ideas Survive and Others Die* (New York: Random House, 2007): 63–97.

25. John W. Bowers and Michael M. Osborn, "Attitudinal Effects of Selected Types of Concluding Metaphors in Persuasive Speeches," *Speech Monographs* 33 (1966): 147–55; James C. McCroskey and W. H. Combs, "The Effects of the Use of Analogy on Attitude Change and Source Credibility," *Journal of Communication* 19 (1969): 333–39; N. L. Reinsch, "An Investigation of the Effects of the Metaphor and Simile in Persuasive Discourse," *Speech Monographs* 38 (1971): 142–45.

26. Pradeep Sopory and James Price Dillard, "The Persuasive Effects of Metaphor: A Meta-Analysis," *Human Communication Research* 28 (July 2002): 382–419.

27. See Irving Janis and S. Feshback, "Effects of Fear-Arousing Communication," *Journal of Abnormal and Social Psychology* 48 (1953): 78–92; Fredric A. Powell, "The Effects of Anxiety-Arousing Message When Related to Personal, Familial, and Impersonal Referents," *Speech Monographs* 32 (1965): 102–06.

28. Donald C. Bryant, "Rhetoric: Its Functions and Its Scope," *Quarterly Journal of Speech* 39 (December 1953): 26.

29. William L. Benoit, "Forewarning and Persuasion," in Mike Allen and Raymond W. Preiss, eds., *Persuasion: Advances Through Meta-Analysis* (Cresskill, NJ: Hampton Press, 1998): 139–54.

30. Karmen Kirtley, "Grave Matter: The High Cost of Living," *Winning Orations 1997* (Mankato, MN: Interstate Oratorical Association, 1997).

31. Benoit, "Forewarning and Persuasion."

32. Mike Allen, "Comparing the Persuasive Effectiveness of One- and Two-Sided Messages," in Mike Allen and Raymond W. Preiss, eds., *Persuasion: Advances Through Meta-Analysis* (Cresskill, NJ: Hampton Press, 1998): 87–98.

33. Katherine E. Rowan, "A New Pedagogy for Explanatory Public Speaking: Why Arrangement Should Not Substitute for Invention," *Communication Education* 44 (1995): 236–50.

34. Carl I. Hovland, Arthur A. Lunsdaine, and Fred D. Sheffield, "The Effects of Presenting 'One Side' versus 'Both Sides' in Changing Opinions on a Controversial Subject," in *Experiments on Mass Communication* (Princeton: Princeton University Press, 1949). Also see Arthur Lunsdaine and Irving Janis, "Resistance to 'Counter-Propaganda' Produced by a One-Sided versus a Two-Sided 'Propaganda' Presentation," *Public Opinion Quarterly* (1953): 311–18.

35. N. Miller and Donald T. Campbell, "Recency and Primacy in Persuasion as a Function of the Timing of Speeches and Measurements," *Journal of Abnormal and Social Psychology* 59 (1959): 1–9; Adrian Furnham, "The Robustness of the Recency Effect: Studies Using Legal Evidence," *Journal of General Psychology* 113 (1986): 351–57; R. Rosnow, "Whatever Happened to the 'Law of Primacy'?" *Journal of Communication* 16 (1966): 10–31.

36. Robert B. Ricco, "Analyzing the Roles of Challenge and Defense in Argumentation," *Argumentation and Advocacy* 39 (Summer 2002): 1–22.

37. Douglas Ehninger, Bruce E. Gronbeck, Ray E. McKerrow, and Alan H. Monroe, *Principles and Types of Speech Communication* (Glenview, IL: Scott, Foresman, 1986): 15.

CHAPTER 16

1. Robert Watts and Michael Sheridan, "Blair Is World's Best Paid Speaker," *London Times,* April 5, 2009.

2. Jason Buckland, "Highest-Paid Public Speakers," *Canada msnmoney,* October 20, 2011.

3. "10 Highest-Paid Public Speakers in the World," www.onlineuniversities.com, April 27, 2010.

4. "10 Highest-Paid Public Speakers in the World."

5. "Clinton's Speaking Fees Nearly Total $40 Million," *Huffington Post,* February 23, 2007.

6. Leslie Wayne, "In World Where Talk Doesn't Come Cheap, Former Officials Are Finding Lucrative Careers," *New York Times,* March 10, 2004: A14.

7. Roger E. Flax, "A Manner of Speaking," *Ambassador* (May–June 1991): 37.

8. Peter D. MacIntyre and K. A. Thivierge, "The Effects of Audience Pleasantness, Audience Familiarity, and Speaking Contexts on Public-Speaking Anxiety and Willingness to Speak," *Communication Quarterly* 43 (1995): 456–66.

9. *Slainte! Toasts, Blessings, and Sayings.* March 1998.

10. Sarah Husberg, "A Wedding Toast," in Tasha Van Horn, Lori Charron, and Michael Charron, eds., *Allyn & Bacon Video II User's Guide,* 2002.

11. Jeff Brooks, *Wedding Toasts.* March 1998.

12. Everett M. Dirksen, "Nominating Speech for Barry Goldwater" (July 15, 1964), in James R. Andrews and David Zarefsky, eds., *Contemporary American Voices* (New York: Simon & Schuster, 1965) 815.

13. Erma Bombeck, "Abbreviated Thank-you's Allow Us More Time to Study Danson's Head," *Austin American-Statesman,* June 22, 1993: F3.

14. Cindy Pearlman, "Oscar Speeches: Statues in Their Hands, Feet in Their Mouths," *Austin American-Statesman,* March 24, 1997: E8.

15. Barack Obama, "A Just and Lasting Peace," *Vital Speeches of the Day* (February 1, 2010): 50–53.

16. William Faulkner, acceptance of the Nobel Prize for literature (December 10, 1950), in Houston Peterson, ed., *A Treasury of the World's Great Speeches* (New York: Simon & Schuster, 1965) 815.

17. Barbara Jordan, "Change: From What to What?" *Vital Speeches of the Day* (August 15, 1992): 651.

18. "Exclusive: The Complete Text of Bruce Springsteen's SXSW Keynote Address," *Rolling Stone Music,* March 28, 2012.

19. Gary Graff, "Bruce Springsteen's SXSW Keynote: 'Stay Hard, Stay Hungry,'" billboard.com, March 15, 2012.

20. David Abel, "Commencement Addresses Leave Audiences Lost," *Boston Globe,* June 5, 2000: B4.

21. Richard Pérez-Peña, "In Looser Tone, Speakers Urge Graduates to Take Risks and Be Engaged," *The New York Times,* June 15, 2013.

22. "Mike Bloomberg's Remarks from Stanford University's 122nd Commencement," mikebloomberg.com, June 16, 2013.

23. Sylvia Earle, "The Best Time in History for Whatever You're Going to Do Next," *Vital Speeches of the Day* (August 2012): 254–58.

24. Abel, "Commencement Addresses Leave Audiences Lost," B4.

25. Bill Clinton, speech at Pointe du Hoc, France (June 1994), as quoted in David Shribman, "President, a Child of World War II, Thanks a Generation," *Boston Globe,* June 7, 1994: 1.

26. Cyrus Copeland, "Death, Be Not Ponderous," *New York Times,* October 31, 2004.

27. Veronique Pozner, "Momma Loves You, Little Man," *Vital Speeches of the Day* (February 2013): 36.

28. John T. Masterson, Jr., eulogy for Betty Stalvey, New Braunfels, TX, March 26, 2005.

29. Dave Barry, "Speak! Speak!" *Austin American-Statesman,* June 2, 1991: C4.

30. Sarah Booth Conroy, "State Dinners Offer Speech as First Course," *Austin American-Statesman,* November 10, 1989.

31. Debi Martin, "Laugh Lines," *Austin American-Statesman,* May 20, 1988: D1.

32. Jon Macks, *How to Be Funny* (New York: Simon & Schuster, 2003).

33. Matt Hughes, "Tricks of the Speechwriter's Trade," *Management Review* 79 (November 1990): 56–58.

34. Michael Koresky, "Prognosis: Dire, Michael Moore's 'Sicko'," *indieWIRE,* June 22, 2007.

35. John C. Meyer, "Humor as a Double-Edged Sword: Four Functions of Humor in Communication," *Communication Theory* 10 (August 2000): 311.

36. Joe Queenan, "How to Tell a Joke," *Reader's Digest* (September 2003): 73.

37. Michael Blastland and David Spiegelhalter, *The Norm Chronicles: Stories and Numbers about Danger* (London: Profile Books, 2013) 42.

38. Alison White, "Writing a Humorous Speech," bizinternet.com June 2004.

39. Mark Twain, "The Alphabet and Simplified Spelling," address at the dedication of the New York Engineers' Club, December 9, 1907. *Mark Twain's Speeches; with an Introduction by William Dean Howells* (University of Virginia Library: Electronic Text Center).

40. Bill Gates, 2007 Harvard commencement address, *Harvard University Gazette Online,* June 7, 2007.

41. Chris O'Keefe, untitled speech, in John K. Boaz and James Brey, eds., *1987 Championship Debates and Speeches* (Speech Communication Association and American Forensic Association, 1987) 99.

42. Owen H. Lynch, "Humorous Communication: Finding a Place for Humor in Communication Research," *Communication Theory* 12.4 (November 2002): 423–45.

43. "Mirren 'Too Busy' to Meet Queen," *BBC News,* May 10, 2007.

44. Susan Wallace, "Seriously, How Do I Write a Humorous Speech?" as reported by Mike Dicerbo, *Leadership in Action,* November 1, 2000.

APPENDIX A

1. Group communication principles presented in this chapter are adapted from Steven A. Beebe and John T. Masterson, *Communicating in Small Groups: Principles and Practices,* 11th ed. (Boston: Pearson, 2015).

2. Our definition of team is based on a discussion in Beebe and Masterson, *Communicating in Small Groups*; and in Steven A. Beebe, Susan J. Beebe, and Diana K. Ivy, *Communication Principles for a Lifetime* (Boston: Pearson, 2013): 240–41; J. R. Katzenback and D. K. Smith, *The Wisdom of Teams: Creating the High-Performance Organization* (New York: Harper Business, 1993); M. Schrage, *No More Teams! Mastering the Dynamics of Creative Collaboration* (New York: Currency Doubleday, 1995); D. D. Chrislip and C. E. Larson, *Collaborative Leadership* (San Francisco, CA: Jossey-Bass, 1994); C. Klein, D. DiazGranados, E. Salas, H. Le, C. S. Burke, R. Lyons, and G. F. Goodwin, "Does Team Building Work?" *Small Group Research* 40, no. 2 (2009): 181–222; A. N. Pieterse, D. van Knippenberg, and W. P. van Ginkel, "Diversity in Goal Orientation, Team Reflexivity, and Team Performance," *Organizational Behavior and Human Decision Processes* 114 (2011): 153–64.

3. For discussions of the advantages and disadvantages of working in small groups, see Norman R. F. Maier, "Assets and Liabilities in Group Problem Solving: The Need for an Integrative Function," *Psychological Review* 74 (1967): 239–49; Michael Argyle, *Cooperation: The Basis of Sociability* (London: Routledge, 1991); J. Surowiecki, *The Wisdom of Crowds* (New York: Anchor, 2005); P. R. Laughlin, E. C. Hatch, J. Silver, and L. Boh, "Groups Perform Better Than the Best Individuals on Letters-to-Numbers Problems: Effects on Group Size," *Journal of Personality and Social Psychology* 90 (2006): 644–51. J. S. Mueller, "Why Individuals in Larger Teams Perform Worse," *Organizational Behavior and Human Decision Processes* 117 (2012): 111–24; B. R. Staats, K. L. Milkman, and C. R. Fox, "The Team Scaling Fallacy: Underestimating the Declining Efficiency of Larger Teams," *Organizational Behavior and Human Decision Processes* 118 (2012): 132–42; B. M. Waller, L. Hope, N. Burrowes, and E. R. Morrison, "Twelve (Not So) Angry Men: Managing Conversational Group Size Increases Perceived Contribution by Decision Makers," *Group Processes & Intergroup Relations* 14, no. 6 (2011): 835–43.

4. Maier, "Assets and Liabilities in Group Problem Solving"; Argyle, *Cooperation.*

5. John Dewey, *How We Think* (Boston: Heath, 1910).

6. P. L. McLeod, "Effects of Anonymity and Social Comparison of Rewards on Computer-Mediated Group Brainstorming," *Small Group Research* 42, no. 2 (2011): 475–503; H. Barki, "Small Group Brainstorming and Idea Quality: Is Electronic Brainstorming the Most Effective Approach?" *Small Group Research* 32 (2001): 158–205; B. A. Nijstad, W. Stroebe, and H. F. M. Lodewijkx, "Cognitive Stimulation and Interference in Groups: Exposure Effects in an Idea Generation Task," *Journal of Experimental Social Psychology* 38 (2002): 535–44; E. F. Rietzchel, B. A. Nijstad, and W. Stroebe, "Productivity Is Not Enough: A Comparison of Interactive and Nominal Brainstorming Groups on Idea Generation and Selection," *Journal of Experimental Social Psychology* 42 (2006): 244–51; also see P. B. Paulus, M. T. Dzindolet, H. Coskun, and V. K. Putman, "Social and Cognitive Influences in Group Brainstorming: Predicting Production Gains and Losses," *European Review of Social Psychology* 12 (2002): 299–326.

7. K. L. Dugosh, P. B. Paulus, E. J. Roand, and H. C. Yang, "Cognitive Stimulation in Brainstorming," *Journal of Personality and Social Psychology* 79 (2000): 722–35.

8. R. Y. Hirokawa and A. J. Salazar, "Task-Group Communication and Decision-Making Performance," in L. Frey, ed., *The Handbook of Group Communication Theory and Research* (Thousand Oaks, CA: Sage, 1999): 167–91; D. Gouran and R. Y. Hirokawa, "Functional Theory and Communication in Decision-Making and Problem-Solving Groups: An Expanded View," in R. Y. Hirokawa and M. S. Poole, eds., *Communication and Group Decision Making* (Thousand Oaks, CA: Sage, 1996): 55–80.

9. C. A. VanLear and E. A. Mabry, "Testing Contrasting Interaction Models for Discriminating Between Consensual and Dissentient Decision-Making Groups," *Small Group Research* 30 (1999): 29–58; also see T. J. Saine and D. G. Bock, "A Comparison of the Distributional and Sequential Structures of Interaction in High and Low Consensus Groups," *Central States Speech Journal* 24 (1973): 125–39.

10. Randy Y. Hirokawa and Roger Pace, "A Descriptive Investigation of the Possible Communication-Based Reasons for Effective and Ineffective Group Decision Making," *Communication Monographs* 50 (Dec. 1983): 363–79.

11. Randy Y. Hirokawa, "Group Communication and Problem-Solving Effectiveness: An Investigation of Group Phases," *Human Communication Research* 9 (Summer 1983): 291–305.

12. Dennis S. Gouran, "Variables Related to Consensus in Group Discussion of Question of Policy," *Speech Monographs* 36 (Aug. 1969): 385–91.

13. For a summary of research about conflict management in small groups, see S. M. Farmer and J. Roth, "Conflict-Handling Behavior in Work Groups: Effects of Group Structure, Decision Processes, and Time," *Small Group Research* 29 (1998): 669–713; also see Beebe and Masterson, *Communicating in Small Groups*; J. Sell, M. J. Lovaglia, E. A. Mannix, C. D. Samuelson, and R. K. Wilson, "Investigating Conflict, Power, and Status Within and Among Groups," *Small Group Research* 30 (1999): 44–72; K. J. Behfar, E. A. Mannix, Randall S. Peterson, and W. M. Trochim, "Conflict in Small Groups: The Meaning and Consequences of Process Conflict," *Small Group Research* 42, no. 2 (2011): 127–76; L. L. Greer, H. M. Caruso, and K. A. Jehn, "The Bigger They Are, the Harder They Fall: Linking Team Power, Team Conflict, and Performance," *Organizational Behavior and Human Decision Process* 116 (2011): 116–28.

14. Ralph White and Ronald Lippitt, "Leader Behavior and Member Reaction in Three 'Social Climates,'" in Darwin Cartwright and Alvin Zander, eds., *Group Dynamics*, 3rd ed. (New York: Harper & Row, 1968): 319.

15. Peter M. Senge, "Leading Learning Organizations," in Richard Beckhard et al., eds., *The Leader of the Future* (San Francisco: Jossey-Bass, 1996); Bernard M. Bass and M. J. Avolio, "Transformational Leadership and Organizational Culture," *International Journal of Public Administration* 17 (1994): 541–54; Lynn Little, "Transformational Leadership," *Academic Leadership* 15 (Nov. 1999): 4–5.

16. Francis Y. Yammarino and Alan J. Dubinsky, "Transformational Leadership Theory: Using Levels of Analysis to Determine Boundary Conditions," *Personnel Psychology* 47 (1994): 787–809; L. Little, "Transformational Leadership," *Academic Leadership* 15 (Nov. 1999): 4–9.

APPENDIX B

1. Martin Luther King Jr., "I Have a Dream," reprinted by arrangement with The Heirs to the Estate of Martin Luther King Jr., c/o Writers House, as agent for the proprietor, New York, NY. Copyright 1963. Dr. Martin Luther King Jr., copyright renewed in 1991 Coretta Scott King.

2. Barack Obama, "Inaugural Address," as appeared in *Daily Compilation of Presidential Documents.* January 21, 2013.

3. Daniel Rose, Burstyn Memorial Lecture at Hunter College, New York City, as appeared in *Vital Speeches of the Day* (December 2012): 392–94.

4. Angelitta Armijo, "Elvis," Texas State University student speech, 2013.

CREDITS

CHAPTER 1

Quotation, Mark Twain. Quotation, James C. Humes, *The Sir Winston Method: Five Secrets of Speaking the Language of Leadership* (New York: Morrow, 1991) 13–14. Quotation, Charles Schwab, as quoted in Brent Filson, *Executive Speeches: Tips on How to Write and Deliver Speeches from 51 CEOs* (New York: Wiley, 1994) 45. Quotation, Dee-Ann Durbin, "Study: Plenty of Jobs for Graduates in 2000," *Austin American-Statesman* 5 Dec. 1999: A28. Quotation, Quintillian. Quotation, L. M. Boyd, syndicated column, *Austin American-Statesman* 8 Aug. 2000: E3. Quotation, Franklin D. Roosevelt. Quotation, Ronald Reagan. Quotation, Elie Wiesel, "The Perils of Indifference," April 12, 1999. Quotation, Barack Obama, "Remarks by the President at Sandy Hook Interfaith Prayer Vigil" The White House Briefing Room. 16 Dec 2012. Web. 05 July 2013 http://www.whitehouse.gov/the-press-office/2012/12/16/remarks-president-sandy-hook-interfaith-prayer-vigil. Quotation, George Jessel. Quotation, Jerry Seinfeld. Quotation, Judy Shepard, quoted by Petula Dovrak, "Channeling the Grief," *Austin American-Statesman.* 14 Oct. 2009: A9. Quotation, Stephen R. Covey, *The 7 Habits of Highly Successful People* (New York: Simon and Schuster, 1989).

CHAPTER 2

Quotation, Daniel Webster, U.S. Secretary of State, 1850-1852. Quotation, H.V. Prochnow. *700 Illusrations and Ideas for Speakers.* Baker Publishing Group, Reprint Edition, December 1994, p. 21. Quotation, Marcus Tullius Cicero. *De Officiis.* Translated by Walter Miller. Loeb edn. Cambridge: Harvard University Press, 1913. Quotation, J. C. Pearson, J. T. Child, and D. H. Kahl, Jr., "Preparation Meeting Opportunity: How Do College Students Prepare for Public Speeches?" *Communication Quarterly,* 54:3 (Aug. 2006): 351-66. Quotation, Clifford Stoll, as cited in Kevin A. Miller, "Capture: The Essential Survival Skill for Leaders Buckling Under Information Overload," *Leadership* (Spring 1992): 85. Quotation, Woodrow Wilson. Speech, "Cinderella," reprinted by permission of Grace Hildenbrand.

CHAPTER 3

Quotation, Franklin D. Roosevelt. Quotation, Dick Costolo, quoted by Laura Sydell. *On Its 7th Birthday, Is Twitter Still The 'Free Speech Party'?* NPR, March 21, 2013. Quotation, Jason Pontin, "Free Speech in the Era of Its Technological Amplification," MIT *Technology Review* 116.2 (March/April 2013): 62. Excerpt, used with permission from the National Communication Association, www.natcom.org. Quotation, Barack Obama, quoted in "Obama Counter-Terrorism Speech Interrupted by Heckler," UPI.com. 23 May 2013. Quotation, Samuel Walker, *Hate Speech* (Lincoln: U of Nebraska P, 1994): 162. Quotation, "Libel and Slander," *The Ethical Spectacle.* 1 June 1997. Quotation, Carol Christ, quoted in "Three Decades Later, Free Speech Vets Return to UC Berkeley," *Sacramento Bee* 3 Dec. 1994: A1. Quotation, James S. Tyre, "Legal Definition of Obscenity, Pornography." 1 June 1997.

Quotation, "Supreme Court Rules: Cyberspace Will Be Free! ACLU Hails Victory in Internet Censorship Challenge." American Civil Liberties Union Freedom Network. 26 June 1997. Quotation, Oprah Winfrey, quoted by Sue Anne Pressley, "Oprah Winfrey Wins Case Filed by Cattlemen," *Washington Post* 27 Feb. 1998. Quotation, Associated Press, "Free-Speech, Other Groups File Briefs Opposing Patriot Act." 4 Nov. 2003 Quotation, Brian Schweitzer, "Proclamation of Clemency for Montanans Convicted under the Montana Sedition Act in 1918–1919." 3 May 2006. (Thanks to George Moss, Vaughn College, Flushing, NY, for providing the authors with a copy of this document.) Quotation, Terry Phillips, "Opinion: In Defense of Free Speech and Helen Thomas." *MercuryNews.com.* 15 June 2010. Quotation, Samuel Walker, *Hate Speech* (Lincoln: U of Nebraska P, 1994) 162. Quotation, Edwin R. Bayley, *Joe McCarthy and the Press* (Madison: Wisconsin U P, 1981) 29. Quotation, Morgan Spurlock, quoted in "Spurlock Sorry for Speech," *Austin American-Statesman* 29 Mar. 2006: A2. Quotation, Kathy Fitzpatrick, "U.S. Public Diplomacy," *Vital Speeches of the Day* (April 2004): 412–17. Quotation, *Publication Manual of the American Psychological Association,* 6th ed. (Washington, DC: American Psychological Association, 2010) 16. Quotation, Scott Jaschik, "Graduation Shame." Insidehighered .com. 22 Apr. 2010.

CHAPTER 4

Quotation, Plutarch. Quotation, K. K. Halone and L. L. Pecchioni, "Relational Listening: A Grounded Theoretical Model," *Communication Reports* 14 (2001): 59–71. Quotation, Aristotle. Quotation, Harold Barrett, *Rhetoric and Civility: Human Development, Narcissism, and the Good Audience* (Albany: SUNY, 1991): 154. Quotation, Patricia Sullivan, "Signification and African-American Rhetoric: A Case Study of Jesse Jackson's 'Common Ground and Common Sense' Speech," *Communication Quarterly* 41.1 (1993): 11. Quotations, Isocrates, *Isocrates,* Vol. II. Translated by George Norlin (Cambridge, MA: Harvard University Press, 1929). Also see "Isocrates," in Bizzell and Herzberg, *The Rhetorical Tradition.* Quotations, Kenneth Burke, *A Rhetoric of Motives* (Berkeley: University of California Press, 1950). Also see Barry Brummett, *Reading Rhetorical Theory* (Fort Worth, TX: Harcourt College Publishers, 2000) 741.

CHAPTER 5

Quotation, Aristotle. Quotation, Harry S. Truman, quoted in Robert H. Farrell, ed., *Off the Record: The Private Papers of Harry S Truman* (New York: Harper & Row, 1980): 310. Quotation, Socrates. Quotation, Sweets, "Mark Twain in India," *The Fence Painter: Bulletin of the Mark Twain Boyhood Home Associates* 26 (Winter 1996): 1. Quotation, Donald E. Brown, "Human Universals and Their Implications," in N. Roughley, ed., *Being Humans: Anthropological Universality and Particularity in Transdisciplinary Perspectives* (New York: Walter de Gruyter, 2000). Developing Your Speech Step by Step: "Access Is Not

Enough: Requiring Counsel with University Sale of the Morning-After Pill," speech by Brianne Giese. Reprinted by permission of Brianne Giese.

CHAPTER 6

Quotation, Cicero. Quotation, Mary Carmichael, "Speeches Strike a Similar Tone," *The Boston Globe* 8 June 2012. Quotation, Allyn & Bacon, Student Speeches Video, "Choosing a Speech Topic," by Roger Fringer, © 2003. Reproduced by permission of Pearson Education, Inc. Quotation, Bruce Gronbeck, from his presidential address delivered at the annual conference of the Speech Communication Association, Nov. 1994. Quotation, Monique Russo, "The 'Starving Disease' or Anorexia Nervosa," student speech, University of Miami, 1984. Quotation, Brian Sosnowchik, "The Cries of American Ailments," *Winning Orations 2000* (Mankato, MN: Interstate Oratorical Association, 2000): 114. Quotation, Judith Humphrey, "Taking the Stage: How Women Can Achieve a Leadership Presence," *Vital Speeches of the Day* (May 2001): 437. Quotation, "Shuttle Missions." *Space Shuttle.* Nasa.gov, 29 August 2011. Quotation, adapted from Nicole Tremel, "The New Wasteland: Computers," *Winning Orations 2000* (Mankato, MN: Interstate Oratorical Association, 2000): 37–40. Quotation, Patrick Martin, "The Energy Cure that Kills: Hydraulic Fracturing for Natural Gas," *Winning Orations 2011* (Mankato, MN: Interstate Oratorical Association, 2011): 147. Developing Your Speech Step by Step: "Access Is Not Enough: Requiring Counsel with University Sale of the Morning-After Pill," speech by Brianne Giese. Reprinted by permission of Brianne Giese.

CHAPTER 7

Quotation, Ivan Petrovich Pavlov, Bequest to the Academic Youth of Soviet Russia (1936). Quotation, Charles Osgood, "On Civility in the Media," *Vital Speeches of the Day* (September 2011): 316-18. Quotation, Michael Cunningham, quoted in Dinitia Smith, "In the Age of the Overamplified, a Resurgence for the Humble Lecture," *New York Times* 17 Mar. 2006: B1, B5. Quotation, Sandra Zimmer, quoted in Vickie K. Sullivan, "Public Speaking: The Secret Weapon in Career Development," *USA Today* 24–25 May 2005: 133. Quotation, Hillary Rodham Clinton, "Women's Progress Is Human Progress," *Vital Speeches of the Day* (May 2010): 199–203. Quotation, Kevin Rudd, "The Apology to the Forgotten Australians," *Vital Speeches of the Day* (January 2010): 2–6. Quotation, Olli-Pekka Kallasvuo, "Connecting the Next Billion: The New Frontier of Upward Mobility," *Vital Speeches of the Day* (March 2010): 130–33. Quotation, Professor Frazer White, University of Miami. Quotation, Tunette Powell, "It's Not the Addict, It's the Drug: Redefining America's War on Drugs," *Winning Orations 2012* (Mankato, MN: Interstate Oratorical Association, 2012): 102. Quotation, Andrew B. Wilson, "How to Craft a Winning Speech," *Vital Speeches of the Day* (September 2005): 685–89. Quotation, David Cameron, "I'm for a Referendum on British Membership in the EU," *Vital Speeches of the Day* (February 2013): 34-35. Quotation, Alexandria Wisner, "Lithium Cell Batteries: The Power to Kill," *Winning Orations 2011*. Interstate Oratorical Association, Mankato, MN, Editor Larry Schnoor. Quotation, Matthew Cossolotto, "An Urgent Call to Action for Study Abroad Alumni to Help Reduce Our Global Awareness Deficit," *Vital Speeches of the Day* (December 2009): 564-68. Quotation, Patrick Martin, "The Energy Cure that Kills: Hydraulic Fracturing for Natural Gas," *Winning Orations 2012*. Interstate Oratorical Association, Mankato, MN, Editor Larry Schnoor. Quotation, Nicole Platzar, "Rated 'D' for Deficiency: The Sunshine Vitamin," *Winning Orations 2012*. Inter-

state Oratorical Association, Mankato, MN, Editor Larry Schnoor. Quotation, James Stanfill, "Entomophagy: The Other Other White Meat," *Winning Orations 2009* (Mankato, MN: Interstate Oratorical Association, 2009): 24. Quotation, Throbjørn Jagland, "May Good Government Win in Europe," *Vital Speeches of the Day* (February 2013): 52-54. Quotation, Indra Nooyi, "Short-Term Demands Vs. Long-Term Responsibilities," *Vital Speeches of the Day* (June 2010): 246–50. Quotation, Ivan Seidenberg, "How the Government Can Promote a Healthy, Competitive Communications Industry," *Vital Speeches of the Day* (1 Dec. 2009): 540-43. Quotation, Michael Blastland and David Spiegelhalter, *The Norm Chronicles: Stories and Numbers about Danger* (London: Profile Books, 2013): 47. Quotation, Daniel Hinderliter, "Collaborative Consumption," *Winning Orations 2012*. Interstate Oratorical Association, Mankato, MN, Editor Larry Schnoor. Quotation, A. Barry Rand, "Rebuilding the Middle Class: A Blueprint for the Future," *Vital Speeches of the Day* (March 2013): 72-76. Quotation, Andie Malterud, "Dropping the Bomb on Water Fluoridation," *Winning Orations 2012*. Interstate Oratorical Association, Manakato, MN, Editor Larry Schnoor. Quotation, Dena Craig, "Clearing the Air about Cigars," *Winning Orations 1998* (Mankato, MN: Interstate Oratorical Association, 1998): 13. Quotation, Sergio Marchionne, "Navigating the New Automotive Epoch," *Vital Speeches of the Day* (1 Mar. 2010): 134–37. Quotation, Kevin King, "Blue Zones," prepared for Individual Events/ Informative Speaking Competition, The University of Texas, Spring 2013. Reprinted by permission of Kevin King. Quotation, Michael Kelley, "The New Catch-22: Unemployment Discrimination," *Winning Orations 2012*. Interstate Oratorical Association, Mankato, MN, Editor Larry Schnoor. Developing Your Speech Step by Step: "Access Is Not Enough: Requiring Counsel with University Sale of the Morning-After Pill," speech by Brianne Giese. Reprinted by permission of Brianne Giese.

CHAPTER 8

Quotation, Alfred North Whitehead. Quotation, Dennis Lloyd, "Instant Expert: A Brief History of iPod," *iLounge* 26 June 2004; "Apple iPod, History of an Icon," *ipod games* 20 June 2007. Quotation, Beth Survant, "Let There Be Light," *Winning Orations 2011* (Mankato, MN: Interstate Oratorical Association, 2011): 53. Quotation, Sarah Perez, "YouTube Reaches 4 Billion Views Per Day," *techcrunch .com* 23 January 2012; Glenn Chapman, "YouTube Serving Up Two Billion Videos Daily," *Google News* 16 May 2010. Quotation, Philip Shenon, "A Showcase for Indian Artifacts," *New York Times* 29 Aug. 2004: TR 3. Quotation, Vonda Ramey, "Can You Read This?" *Winning Orations 1985*. Interstate Oratorical Association, Mankato, MN, Editor Larry Schnoor. Quotation, Joseph Jones, "The Facts About For-Profit Universities," *Winning Orations 2011*. Interstate Oratorical Association, Mankato, MN, Editor Larry Schnoor. Stem-Cell speech outline, Information in this example comes from National Institutes of Health, "Stem Cells: A Primer," May 2000. Family health profile speech outline, Adapted from John Kuehn, untitled speech, *Winning Orations 1994* (Mankato, MN: Interstate Oratorical Association, 1994): 83–85. Quotation, Cynthia Starks, "How to Write a Speech," *Vital Speeches of the Day* (April 2010). Reprinted by permission of the author. Quotation, Martin Medhurst, "The Text(ure) of the World in Presidential Rhetoric," *Vital Speeches of the Day* (June 2012). Quotation from John Seffrin, Reprinted by the permission of the American Cancer Society, Inc. All rights reserved. Quotation, Anastasia Danilyuk, "Alternatives to Imprisonment," *Winning Orations 2011*. Interstate Oratorical Association, Mankato, MN, Editor

Larry Schnoor. Quotation, Nichole Olson, "Flying the Safer Skies," *Winning Orations 2000*. Interstate Oratorical Association, Mankato, MN, Editor Larry Schnoor. Quotation, Robert Gore, untitled speech, *Winning Orations 2012*. Interstate Oratorical Association, Mankato, MN, Editor Larry Schnoor. Quotation, Molly A. Lovell, "Hotel Security: The Hidden Crisis," *Winning Orations 1994* (Mankato, MN: Interstate Oratorical Association, 1994): 18. Quotation, Neela Latey, "U.S. Customs Procedures: Danger to Americans' Health and Society," *Winning Orations 1986*. Interstate Oratorical Association, Mankato, MN, Editor Larry Schnoor. Quotation, Susan Stevens, "Teacher Shortage," *Winning Orations 1986*. Interstate Oratorical Association, Mankato, MN, Editor Larry Schnoor. Quotation, Nicole Platzar, "Rated 'D' for Deficiency: The Sunshine Vitamin," *Winning Orations 2012*. Interstate Oratorical Association, Mankato, MN, Editor Larry Schnoor. Quotation, Ben Crosby, "The New College Disease," *Winning Orations 2000* (Mankato, MN: Interstate Oratorical Association, 2000): 133. Quotation, Lori Van Overbeke, "Nutra-Sweet," *Winning Orations 1986* (Mankato, MN: Interstate Oratorical Association, 1986): 58. Quotation, John O'Brien, quoted in Brent Filson, *Executive Speeches* (New York: Wiley, 1994): 144–45. Quotation, Charles Parnell, "Speechwriting: The Profession and the Practice," *Vital Speeches of the Day* (15 Jan. 1990): 56. Developing Your Speech Step by Step: "Access Is Not Enough: Requiring Counsel with University Sale of the Morning-After Pill," speech by Brianne Giese. Reprinted by permission of Brianne Giese.

CHAPTER 9

Opening quotation, Anonymous. Quotation, Lauren Holstein, "Slavery in the Sunshine State," *Winning Orations* 2012. Interstate Oratorical Association, Mankato, MN, Editor Larry Schnoor. Quotation, Sheena Holliday, "Uninvited Visitor," *Winning Orations* 2003 (Mankato, MN: Interstate Oratorical Association, 2003): 84. Quotation, Edwin Pittock, "America's Crisis in Aging," *Vital Speeches of the Day* (February 2004). Quotation, Charles W. Chesnutt, *Frederick Douglass.* Electronic edition published by Academic Affairs Library, University of North Carolina at Chapel Hill, 2001. Quotation, Cadie Thompson, "Twitter CEO Dick Costolo Gives New Grads Advice to Be 'Bold,'" *CNBC* 6 May 2013. Quotation, Jennifer Sweeney, "Racial Profiling," *Winning Orations 2000* (Mankato, MN: Interstate Oratorical Association, 2000): 1. Quotations, Matt Miller, "A Situational Speech: Bisphenol A," *Winning Orations 2009*. Interstate Oratorical Association, Mankato, MN, Editor Larry Schnoor. Quotation, Statistics from "Which Law School Graduates Have the Most Debt?" *U.S. News and World Report Best Law Schools*, 2013. Quotation, Terrika Scott, "Curing Crisis with Community," *Winning Orations 1995*. Interstate Oratorical Association, Mankato, MN, Editor Larry Schnoor. Quotation, Theresa Clinkenbeard, "The Loss of Childhood," *Winning Orations 1984* (Mankato, MN: Interstate Oratorical Association, 1984): 4. Quotation, Thad Noyes, "Dishonest Death Care," *Winning Orations 1999*. Interstate Oratorical Association, Mankato, MN, Editor Larry Schnoor. Quotation, Marvin Olasky, "Responding to Disaster," *Vital Speeches of the Day* (November 2006): 744. Reprinted by permission of Marvin Olasky. Quotation, Joe Griffith, *Speaker's Library of Business Stories, Anecdotes, and Humor* (Englewood Cliffs, NJ: Prentice Hall, 1990): 335. Quotation, Douglas MacArthur, "Farewell to the Cadets," address delivered at West Point, 12 May 1962. Reprinted in Richard L. Johannesen, R. R. Allen, and Wil A. Linkugel, eds., *Contemporary American Speeches*, 7th ed. (Dubuque, IA: Kendall/Hunt, 1992): 393. Quotation, Jascha Hoffman, "Me Translate Funny One Day," *The New York Times Book Review* 21 October 2012: 31. Quotation, Muhtar

Kent, "Are We Ready for Tomorrow, Today?" *Vital Speeches of the Day* (March 2010): 117–21. Quotation, Richard Propes, "Alone in the Dark," *Winning Orations 1985* (Mankato, MN: Interstate Oratorical Association, 1985): 22. Quotation, Luis Proenza, "Relevance, Connectivity and Productivity." *Vital Speeches of the Day* (February 2010): 89–92. Quotation, Cynthia Starks, "How to Write a Speech," *Vital Speeches of the Day* (April 2010): 153-56. Reprinted by permission of the author. Quotation, Adam Winegarden, "The After-Dinner Speech," in Tasha Van Horn, Lori Charron, and Michael Charron, eds., *Allyn & Bacon Video II User's Guide,* 2002. Quotation, William G. Durden, "Just Do Science," *Vital Speeches of the Day* (March 2013): 67-71. Quotation, Chris Miller, "Remember Both the Art and the Business Involved in Collision Repair," *Vital Speeches of the Day* (May 2010): 203-13. Quotation, Chris Christie, "The Adults Are in Charge," *Vital Speeches of the Day* (March 2013) 82-87. Quotation, Student speech, University of Miami, 1981. Quotation, Lou Gehrig, "Farewell Speech," *Lou Gehrig: The Official Web Site* 23 June 2007. Quotation, Robert Lehrman, "Victory Speeches," *The New York Times* 7 November 2012. Quotation, Noelle Stephens, "The WWW.CON of Higher Education," *Winning Orations 1999* (Mankato, MN: Interstate Oratorical Association, 1999): 12. Quotation, John Ryan, "Emissions Tampering: Get the Lead Out," *Winning Orations 1985*. Interstate Oratorical Association, Mankato, MN, Editor Larry Schnoor. Quotation, Melanie Loehwing, untitled speech, *Winning Orations 2003* (Mankato, MN: Interstate Oratorical Association, 2003): 23–24. Quotation, Richard Kelley, "Ready, Aim, Thrive: Strategies for 2007," *Vital Speeches of the Day* (December 2006): 763–67. Quotation, Bono, "Because We Can, We Must," University of Pennsylvania, *Almanac Between Issues* 19 May 2004. Quotation, James W. Robinson, "Create a Fireworks Finale," *Executive Speeches* (April 1989): 41–44. Developing Your Speech Step by Step: "Access Is Not Enough: Requiring Counsel with University Sale of the Morning-After Pill," speech by Brianne Giese. Reprinted by permission of Brianne Giese.

CHAPTER 10

Quotations, Peggy Noonan. *What I Saw at the Revolution: A Political Life in the Reagan Era.* Random House, 2003. Quotation, David Crystal, "Speaking of Writing and Writing of Speaking," *Longman Dictionaries: Express Yourself with Confidence!* (Pearson Education, 2005). Quotation, Nemanja Savic, "Hope in the Voices of Africa," speech delivered at Wake Forest University, 14 May 2006. *Window on Wake Forest.* 15 May 2006. Quotation, Rep. Barbara Jordan, 1992 Democratic National Convention Keynote Address. Quotation, Paul Roberts, "How to Say Nothing in Five Hundred Words," in William H. Roberts and Gregoire Turgeson, eds., *About Language* (Boston: Houghton Mifflin, 1986): 28. Quotation, George Orwell, "Politics and the English Language," in William H. Roberts and Gregoire Turgeson, eds., *About Language* (Boston: Houghton Mifflin, 1986): 282. Quotation, Erma Bombeck, "Missing Grammar Genes Is, Like, the Problem," *Austin American-Statesman* 3 March 1992. Quotation, John Lister, quoted in "At the End of the Day, It Annoys." *Associated Press.* 24 March 2004. Quotation, William Safire, "Words at War," *New York Times Magazine* 30 September 2001. Quotation, Michael M. Klepper, *I'd Rather Die Than Give a Speech* (New York: Carol Publishing Group, 1994): 45. Quotations, We acknowledge the following source for several examples used in our discussion of language style: William Jordan, "Rhetorical Style," *Oral Communication Handbook* (Warrensburg, MO: Central Missouri State U, 1971–1972): 32–34. Quotation, Eric Stolhanske, "Advice from a Kid with a Wooden Leg," *Vital Speeches of the Day* (July

2012): 211-16. Quotation, Scott Davis, "Class Begins Today," *Vital Speeches of the Day* (August 2011): 279-80. Quotations, Franklin D. Roosevelt, inaugural address of 1933 (Washington, DC: National Archives and Records Administration, 1988) 22. Quotation, George F. Will, "'Let Us . . .'? No, Give It a Rest," *Newsweek* 22 January 2001: 64. Quotation, Caesar. Quotation, John F. Kennedy, Inaugural Address, 20 Jan. 1961, in Bower Aly and Lucille F. Aly, eds., *Speeches in English* (New York: Random House, 1968): 272. Quotation, Barack Obama, "Look at the World Through Their Eyes," *Vital Speeches of the Day* (May 2013): 138-42. Quotation, William Faulkner, speech in acceptance of the Nobel Prize for Literature, delivered 10 Dec. 1950, in Houston Peterson, ed., *A Treasury of the World's Great Speeches* (New York: Simon & Schuster, 1965): 814–15. Quotation, David Brooks, baccalaureate address at Sewanee: The University of the South. *Sewanee Today* 11 May 2013. Developing Your Speech Step by Step: "Access Is Not Enough: Requiring Counsel with University Sale of the Morning-After Pill," speech by Brianne Giese. Reprinted by permission of Brianne Giese.

CHAPTER 11

Quotation, William Shakespeare. *Hamlet.* 1601. Quotation, James W. Gibson, John A. Kline, and Charles R. Gruner, "A Reexamination of the First Course in Speech at U.S. Colleges and Universities," *Speech Teacher* 23 (Sept. 1974): 206–14. List of tips for delivering a manuscript speech, Roger Ailes, *You Are the Message* (New York: Doubleday, 1989): 37–38; Gellis Communications. "Top Tips for Preparing and Delivering a Manuscript Speech." November 4, 2011. http://www.gellis.com/blog/top-tips-preparing-and-delivering-manuscript-speech; Richardson, David W. "Delivering a Manuscript Speech." 2013. http://www.richspeaking.com/articles/manuscript_speech.html. Quotation, Cicero, *De Oratore*, vol. 4, translated by E. W. Sutton (Cambridge: Harvard University Press, 1988). Quotation, Khera Communications, "Business Tips for India," *More Business*, 2001. 8 June 2004 www.morebusiness.com/running_your_business/management/d930585271.brc? highlightstring=Business+Tips+for+India Quotations, Brett Filson. *Executive Speeches: Tips on How to Write and Deliver Speeches from 51 CEOs* (New York: Wiley, 1994). Quotation, Albert Mehrabian, *Silent Messages* (Belmont, CA: Wadsworth, 1971). Quotation, Arthur Schnabel, "Comment," *The New Yorker* 1 Mar. 1993. Developing Your Speech Step by Step: "Access Is Not Enough: Requiring Counsel with University Sale of the Morning-After Pill," speech by Brianne Giese. Reprinted by permission of Brianne Giese.

CHAPTER 12

Quotations, Aristotle. *On the Soul* (350 BCE). Quotations, Brett Filson. *Executive Speeches: Tips on How to Write and Deliver Speeches from 51 CEOs* (New York: Wiley, 1994). Quotation, Andrew Wilson, "In Defense of Rhetoric," *Toastmaster* 70.2 (Feb. 2004): 8–11.

CHAPTER 13

Quotation, Cicero. *De Legibus*, II, 19. Quotations, Chip Heath and Dan Heath, *Made to Stick* (Random House, 2007): 63–64. Quotation, Marcie Groover, "Learning to Communicate: The Importance of Speech Education in Public Schools," *Winning Orations 1984* (Mankato, MN: Interstate Oratorical Association, 1984): 7. Quotation, G.K. Chesterton, as cited by Eleanor Doan, *The New Speaker's Sourcebook* (Grand Rapids, MI: Zondervan, 1968). Speech, Allyn & Bacon, Student Speeches Video, "Choosing a Speech Topic," by Roger Fringer, © 2003. Reproduced by permission of Pearson Education, Inc.

CHAPTER 14

Quotation, William Shakespeare. Quotation, John Ryan, "Emissions Tampering: Get the Lead Out," *Winning Orations 1985*. Interstate Oratorical Association, Mankato, MN, Editor Larry Schnoor.

CHAPTER 15

Quotation, Ralph Waldo Emerson. Quotations, Donald C. Bryant, "Rhetoric: Its Functions and Its Scope," *Quarterly Journal of Speech* 39 (Dec. 1953): 26. Quotation, Jeffrey E. Jamison, "Alkali Batteries: Powering Electronics and Polluting the Environment," *Winning Orations 1991* (Mankato, MN: Interstate Oratorical Association, 1991): 43. Quotation, Myron W. Lustig and Jolene Koester, *Intercultural Competence: Interpersonal Communication Across Cultures* (Boston: Allyn & Bacon, 2009). Quotation, Jamie Frater, "Top 10 Great Historic Speeches," http://listverse.com/2008/06/01/top-10-great-historic-speeches/ accessed June 14, 2013. Speech, Colter Ray, "You Are What You Eat: Why You Should Eat Grass Fed Organic Beef," Original speech presented at Texas State University, 2013. Used by permission. Quotation, Tasha Carlson, "License to Save." From *Winning Orations 2009*. Interstate Oratorical Association, 2009, Mankato, MN, Editor Larry Schnoor. Quotations, Heather Zupanic, "End the Use of Child Soldiers." Speech excerpts on pages 363 through 365 from *Winning Orations 2009*. Interstate Oratorical Association, Mankato, MN, Editor Larry Schnoor.

CHAPTER 16

Quotation, Barney Frank. Quotation, Copyrighted by Pearson Education, Upper Saddle River, NJ. Quotation, Sarah Husberg, "A Wedding Toast," in Tasha Van Horn, Lori Charron, and Michael Charron, eds., *Allyn & Bacon Video II User's Guide, 2002.* Quotation, Jeff Brooks, *Wedding Toasts.* March 1998. (http://zinnia.umfacad.maine.edu/~donaghue/toasts07.html Quotation, Everett M. Dirksen, "Nominating Speech for Barry Goldwater" (15 July 1964), in James R. Andrews and David Zarefsky, eds., *Contemporary American Voices* (New York: Simon & Schuster, 1965): 815. Quotation, Erma Bombeck, "Abbreviated Thank-you's Allow Us More Time to Study Danson's Head," *Austin American-Statesman* 22 June 1993: F3. Quotation, Cindy Pearlman, "Oscar Speeches: Statues in Their Hands, Feet in Their Mouths," *Austin American-Statesman* 24 March 1997: E8. Quotation, Barack Obama, "A Just and Lasting Peace," *Vital Speeches of the Day* (1 February 2010): 50–53. Quotation, William Faulkner, acceptance of the Nobel prize for literature (10 December 1950), in Houston Peterson, ed., *A Treasury of the World's Great Speeches* (New York: Simon & Schuster, 1965): 815. Quotation, Barbara Jordan, "Change: From What to What?" *Vital Speeches of the Day* (15 August 1992): 651. Quotation, David Abel, "Commencement Addresses Leave Audiences Lost," *Boston Globe* 5 June 2000: B4. Quotation, Richard Pérez-Peña, "In Looser Tone, Speakers Urge Graduates to Take Risks and Be Engaged," *The New York Times* 15 June 2013. Quotation, "Mike Bloomberg's Remarks from Stanford University's 122nd Commencement," mikebloomberg.com 16 June 2013. Quotation, Sylvia Earle, "The Best Time in History for Whatever You're Going to Do Next." *Vital Speeches of the Day* (August 2012): 254-58. Quotation, David Abel, "Commencement Addresses Leave Audiences Lost," *Boston Globe* 5 June 2000: B4. Quotation, Bill Clinton, speech at Pointe du

Hoc, France (June 1994), as quoted in David Shribman, "President, a Child of World War II, Thanks a Generation," *Boston Globe* 7 June 1994: 1. Quotation, Cyrus Copeland, "Death, Be Not Ponderous," *New York Times* 31 October 2004. Quotation, Veronique Pozner, "Momma Loves You, Little Man," *Vital Speeches of the Day* (February 2013): 36. Quotation, John T. Masterson, Jr., eulogy for Betty Stalvey, New Braunfels, TX, 26 March 2005. Quotation, Dave Barry, "Speak! Speak!" *Austin American-Statesman* 2 June 1991: C4. Quotation, Sarah Booth Conroy, "State Dinners Offer Speech as First Course," *Austin American-Statesman* 10 November 1989. Quotation, Debi Martin, "Laugh Lines," *Austin American-Statesman* 20 May 1988: D1. Quotation, Jon Macks, *How to Be Funny* (New York: Simon & Schuster, 2003). Quotation, Matt Hughes, "Tricks of the Speechwriter's Trade," *Management Review* 79 (November 1990): 56–58. Quotation, Michael Koresky, "Prognosis: Dire, Michael Moore's 'Sicko'," *indiewire* 22 June 2007. Reprinted by permission of SnagFilms, Inc. Quotation, John C. Meyer, "Humor as a Double-Edged Sword: Four Functions of Humor in Communication," *Communication Theory* 10 (August 2000): 311. Quotation, Joe Queenan, "How to Tell a Joke," *Reader's Digest* September 2003: 73. Quotation, Michael Blastland and David Spiegelhalter, *The Norm Chronicles: Stories and Numbers about Danger* (London: Profile Books, 2013): 42. Quotation, Mark Twain, "The Alphabet and Simplified Spelling," address at the dedication of the New York Engineers' Club, 9 December 1907. *Mark Twain's Speeches; with an Introduction by William Dean Howells* (University of Virginia Library: Electronic Text Center). Quotation, Bill Gates, 2007 Harvard commencement address, *Harvard University Gazette Online* 7 June 2007. Quotation, Chris O'Keefe, untitled speech, in John K. Boaz and James Brey, eds., *1987 Championship Debates and Speeches* (Speech Communication Association and American Forensic Association, 1987): 99. Quotation, Helen Mirren, "Mirren 'Too Busy' to Meet Queen," *BBC News* 10 May 2007. Quotation, Susan Wallace, "Seriously, How Do I Write a Humorous Speech?" as reported by Mike Dicerbo, *Leadership in Action* 1 November 2000.

APPENDIX A

Rudyard Kipling, "The Law of the Wolves," in *The Second Jungle Book* 1895.

APPENDIX B

"I Have a Dream," speech by Martin Luther King Jr. Reprinted by arrangement with The Heirs to the Estate of Martin Luther King Jr., c/o Writers House as agent for the proprietor New York, NY. ©1963 Dr. Martin Luther King, Jr. © renewed 1991 Coretta Scott King. "Second Inaugural Address," by Barack Obama. The White House. "Message. Messenger. Audience." lecture by Daniel Rose October 15, 2012. Used by permission. "Elvis," speech by Angelitta Armijo, Texas State University.

INDEX